CIVIL
DISOBEDIENCE

An Encyclopedic History of Dissidence in the United States

Volume Two

Mary Ellen Snodgrass

SHARPE REFERENCE
an imprint of M.E. Sharpe, Inc.

SHARPE REFERENCE

Sharpe Reference is an imprint of **M.E. Sharpe, Inc.**

M.E. Sharpe, Inc.
80 Business Park Drive
Armonk, NY 10504

© 2009 by M.E. Sharpe, Inc.

Library of Congress Cataloging-in-Publication Data

Snodgrass, Mary Ellen.
Civil disobedience: an encyclopedic history of dissidence in the United States / Mary Ellen Snodgrass.
    p. cm.
Includes bibliographical references and index.
ISBN 978-0-7656-8127-0 (hardcover: alk. paper)
1. Civil disobedience—United States—History. I. Title.

JC328.3.S64 2008
303.6'10973—dc22

2008007975

Cover photos provided by the following (clockwise, from top): Chris Kleponis/Stringer/AFP/Getty Images; Michael Rougier/Stringer/Time & Life Pictures/Getty Images; Library of Congress; Don Craves/Time & Life Pictures/Getty Images.

Printed and bound in the United States of America

The paper used in this publication meets the minimum requirements of
American National Standard for Information Sciences
Permanence of Paper for Printed Library Materials,
ANSI Z 39.48.1984.

(c) 10 9 8 7 6 5 4 3 2 1

Publisher: Myron E. Sharpe
Vice President and Director of New Product Development: Donna Sanzone
Vice President and Production Director: Carmen Chetti
Executive Editor and Manager of Reference: Todd Hallman
Executive Development Editor: Jeff Hacker
Project Manager: Jeanne Marie Healy
Program Coordinator: Cathleen Prisco
Editorial Assistant: Alison Morretta
Text Design: Carmen Chetti and Jesse Sanchez
Cover Design: Jesse Sanchez

Contents

Topic Finder

Biographies

Baez, Joan
Berrigan brothers
Braden, Anne, and Carl Braden
Brown, John
Celia
Chávez, César
Coffin, Levi
Coffin, William Sloane, Jr.
Davis, Angela
Day, Dorothy
Doy, John W.
Drayton, Daniel
Fairbank, Calvin, and Delia Ann Webster
Farmer, James
Fonda, Jane
Garner, Margaret
Garrison, William Lloyd
Ginsberg, Allen
Goldman, Emma
Hutchinson, Anne, and Mary Dyer
Jones, Mother
King, Martin Luther, Jr.
Lay, Benjamin
Maule, Thomas
Minkins, Fredric "Shadrach"
O'Hare, Kate Richards
Parks, Rosa
Powell, Adam Clayton, Jr.
Randolph, A. Philip
Richardson, Gloria
Rustin, Bayard
Sheehan, Cindy
Sheen, Martin
Sims, Thomas M.
Standing Bear
Stanley, Rick
Thoreau, Henry David
Tubman, Harriet
Vaughan, Hester
Wilkins, Roy
Woolman, John

Causes, Issues, and Sources of Protest

abolitionism
abortion
apartheid
birth control
bootleg AIDS drugs
busing, school
death penalty
educating slaves
euthanasia
female genital mutilation
First Amendment rights
flag burning
flag saluting
Fugitive Slave Law of 1850
gay and lesbian rights
genocide protest
Guantánamo
Iraq War
Japanese internment
Kaho'Olawe, Hawaii
marijuana
nuclear protest
obscenity and pornography
peace movement
peyote
polygamy
tax resistance
temperance
Vieques, Puerto Rico
Vietnam War
voter registration
woman suffrage

Forms of Protest

bootleg AIDS drugs
civil disobedience
conscientious objectors
draft card burning
educating slaves
fish-ins
flag burning

CIVIL
DISOBEDIENCE

Volume Two

CHRONOLOGY
Historic Acts of Conscience

Chronology
Historic Acts of Conscience

1634	Massachusetts Puritans banish Roger Williams from Salem after he challenges the state church.
1637	William King of Salem, Massachusetts, defies Puritan law by sheltering Quakers from persecution.
March 22, 1638	At an official inquiry, Anne Marbury Hutchinson suffers persecution for disobeying the Puritan theocracy in Boston.
June 1650	Baptists at Swansea, Massachusetts, go on trial for religious nonconformity.
May 31, 1651	At Lynn, Massachusetts, Baptists go to jail for rejecting infant baptism.
1654	Peter Gaunt and Lydia Hampton Gaunt boycott Puritan worship services in Sandwich, Massachusetts.
July 1656	Ann Austin and Mary Fisher endure brutal physical examination for signs of witchcraft and five weeks' imprisonment at Prison Lane for owning books that dispute Puritan beliefs.
winter 1656–1657	A Boston court exiles Nicholas Upsal for slipping food to eight Quakers jailed for heresy.
1657	Religious dissidents Mary Dyer and Anne Burden share dark cells in a Boston jail.
	Mary Clark becomes the first woman scourged in America after she mutinies against Boston Puritans.
1658	Sheriff Coarsey strikes with a saber the shoulder of pacifist Richard Keene, Sr., the first antiwar dissident in the New World to suffer official punishment.
1660	Mary Dyer goes to the gallows for protesting the execution of religious dissenters in Boston.
October 1660	Mary Wright of Oyster Bay, Long Island, incurs jailing for charging Puritans with cruelty.
March 1662	Quaker dissident George Wilson dies in jail at Jamestown, Virginia, after sores putrify under the ox chain that tethers him to an Indian inmate.
winter 1664	At Dover, New Hampshire, constables strip and tie three female Quakers to carts for 10 lashes each at Dover, Boston, Dedham, Hampton, Ipswich, Linn, Newbury, Rowley, Roxbury, Salisbury, and Windham as the procession passes through each town.
early 1666	Deacon John Farnum earns jailing at Boston, excommunication, and exile for lay preaching and for denouncing infant baptism.
May 3, 1669	At Salem, Massachusetts, Thomas Maule receives 10 lashes for opposing the Puritan majority.
1674	The Rogerenes, a Quaker sect in Connecticut, earn arrest, fines, and prison sentences for refusing to pay church taxes and for laboring on Sunday.
July 1682	Congregational forces oust a Baptist minister, William Screven, from York, Maine, for defiance of the theocracy.
1688	At an assembly in Germantown, Pennsylvania, Francis Daniel Pastorius pens the first formal protest of slavery in America.
1689	Pennsylvanians, influenced by the antimilitarism of William Penn, resist forming militias.

December 12, 1695	In Salem, Massachusetts, Thomas Maule endures lashings for religious dissent and for charging clergy with inhuman persecution of women during the Salem witch trials of 1692.
1703	Two Quaker residents of Bristol County, Massachusetts, refuse to bear arms against Indian raiders.
1731	Benjamin Lay stirs Philadelphia Quakers against British oppression, capital punishment, and slavery.
August 1735	John Peter Zenger, publisher of the *New York Weekly Journal,* faces charges of sedition and wins a landmark judgment favoring freedom of speech.
1737	At Oyster Bay, Long Island, the Motts and Underhills aid runaway slaves.
February 1744	A constable drives dissenting Baptists at Saybrook, Connecticut, through the snow to a New London prison.
October 15, 1752	Widow Elizabeth Tracy Backus and her son, Samuel Backus, go to prison at Norwich, Connecticut, for refusing to pay a religious tax.
1755	Daniel Corbet and Mary Brinton Corbet turn Blackbird Hundred at Smyrna, Delaware, into a slave hiding place.
March 1756	The citizens of Nantucket, Massachusetts, work out a compromise with Quakers by assessing an annual military tax on pacifists.
summer 1756	Pacifists in Winchester, Virginia, go to prison for refusing to answer roll call or to bear arms during the French and Indian War.
1760	Members of the Nicholite sect of Quakers in Delaware and Maryland earn jail time for pacifism and abolitionism.
1761	Liberty Men at Hancock, Lincoln, Kennebec, and Somerset counties in Maine fight for property rights against wealthy Boston speculators.
1763	A Quaker groundskeeper at Touro Synagogue in Newport, Rhode Island, shuttles runaway slaves through the building, which Jewish congregants stock with food and clothing.
1765	At Culpeper, Virginia, a posse jails Elijah Craig on rye bread and water for preaching against Anglican teachings.
	At Boston, the first Sons of Liberty cell begins plotting protest of British occupation.
	An all-out class war between patriots and loyalists strikes Mecklenburg County, North Carolina.
	In Philadelphia, John Bubenheim Bayard leads a Sons of Liberty protest of the tea tax.
	Following passage of the Stamp Act, Patrick Henry of Red Hill, Virginia, openly denounces the British bureaucracy and becomes a beacon for the colony's Sons of Liberty.
August 1765	Connecticut Sons of Liberty begin burning stamp agents in effigy and march around the state assembly three times brandishing cudgels.
August 14, 1765	Sons of Liberty in Boston hang in effigy Massachusetts Lieutenant Governor Andrew Oliver, a locally born stamp distributor.
fall 1765	The Norwich, Connecticut, Sons of Liberty lead public raillery and unflattering caricature of stamp agents.
September 1765	Sons of Liberty in Williamsburg, Virginia, protest the stamp agency of Colonel George Mercer before his arrival in North America.
September 2, 1765	At Annapolis, Maryland, the colonial underground dismantles the store of stamp master Zachariah Hood and threatens to kill the Tory merchant.
September 12, 1765	At Portsmouth, New Hampshire, a Sons of Liberty cell hangs the tax collector in effigy and hauls three dummies to the Hay Market to burn at a mock funeral for American Liberty.

September 19, 1765	Durkee's Irregulars, a paramilitary brigade of 500 Sons of Liberty, advance with three trumpeters to Wethersfield, Connecticut, and bully the British stamp agent at a mock court.
October 1765	Sons of Liberty at Wilmington, North Carolina, stop British authorities from offloading documents enforcing the Stamp Act.
October 5, 1765	Philadelphia Sons of Liberty force the resignation of the stamp agent and coerce tea merchants to suspend sales of East India Company stock.
October 19, 1765	Sons of Liberty at Charleston, South Carolina, hoist an effigy of a stamp agent on a 40-foot (12-meter) gibbet.
late October 1765	The torching of a mannequin by Sons of Liberty at Princeton, New Jersey, threatens the House Speaker for his loyalty to the Stamp Act.
October 31, 1765	New York Sons of Liberty assemble at Fort George and demand tax stamps, which they destroy in a bonfire.
November 1765	Samuel Adams forms Boston's first Sons of Liberty shock troops.
	Hugh Waddell leads North Carolina Sons of Liberty in seizing the British war sloop *Diligence* at Brunswick landing.
November 1, 1765	Sons of Liberty raid the federal stamp closet at Fort Johnson on James Island, South Carolina.
	New York Daughters of Liberty weave homespun fabric to replace imported English brocade and broadcloth.
November 5, 1765	Georgia watermen protest the Stamp Act at Savannah harbor.
January 1766	North Carolina Regulators begin burning stamp agents in effigy.
January 9, 1766	Sons of Liberty at Puddledock, New Hampshire, process over Swing Bridge to hoist the first "no stamp" banner in the 13 colonies.
January 13, 1766	Sons of Liberty in Wallingford, Connecticut, propose fining stamp users 20 shillings for adhering to the Stamp Act.
February 1766	Quaker pacifists at Woodbridge, New Jersey, urge nonviolence from the Sons of Liberty.
	Sons of Liberty in Charleston, South Carolina, threaten to destroy a profiteer's schooner.
February 15, 1766	New York City Sons of Liberty burn stamps at a Pennsylvania coffeehouse before agents can relay them to distributors in Maryland.
February 19, 1766	Some 1,000 Sons of Liberty confront North Carolina Governor William Tyron over taxation by the British Crown and force the reopening of the port at Brunswick.
March 4, 1766	Daughters of Liberty meeting at the home of Ephraim Brown in Providence, Rhode Island, vow to court only men who risk life and property for the sake of freedom.
April 1766	At Portsmouth, Virginia, a Sons of Liberty chapter tars, feathers, and dunks a stamp agent.
April 10, 1766	At Bristol, Rhode Island, Daughters of Liberty raise a toast to revolt.
May 1766	New York Liberty Boys incite a brawl in defiance of the Quartering Act of 1765.
May 5, 1766	Hannah Roe Bostwick McDougall heads a Daughters of Liberty protest down Broadway to the New York City jail to demand the release of her husband and other Sons of Liberty.
1767	An uprising of South Carolina smallholders echoes patriot disenchantment with colonial bureaucracy and general lawlessness.
	Elijah Burt and Deborah Colton Burt begin receiving refugee slaves in East Longmeadow, Massachusetts.

1767	Along the York River, the Virginia colonial underground shoots runaway slaves seeking to flag down British ships, gain their freedom, and join the opposition.
May 30, 1767	At Flushing, New York, Quakers denounce as un-Christian the abduction and sale of Africans.
August 31, 1767	Boston Sons of Liberty vow to combat the Townshend Acts, which impose duties on goods imported into the colonies.
1768	In Williamsburg, Virginia, James Childs survives five months in a prison drunk tank, a bomb, sulfur fumes, and poisoned food for challenging the Episcopal theocracy.
	Paul Revere organizes a foot patrol known as the "mechanics," or Liberty Boys, who sabotage British equipment and steal munitions for use by the Boston opposition.
	Benjamin Franklin's newspaper, the *Pennsylvania Gazette,* prints a three-stave poem written by Quaker poet Milcah Martha Moore and issued by 20 Daughters of Liberty opposing the sale of British goods.
February 1768	Samuel Adams issues an intercolonial letter summoning patriots to unite against taxation without representation.
April 27, 1768	North Carolina Sons of Liberty menace a tax clerk at Anson County who collects fees and duties for the British Crown.
August 14, 1768	Boston's Daughters of Liberty cheer from their windows as the Sons sing their anthem around the Liberty Tree.
1769	Authorities at Ashfield, Massachusetts, seize 398 acres (161 hectare) from tax-evading Baptists.
July 26, 1769	Bigots at Middlesex, Virginia, discover that persecution and capricious jailings only increase Baptist fervor and support for the ministry.
August 14, 1769	Boston Sons of Liberty celebrate four years of protest with a group toast at the Liberty Tree.
1770	In Philadelphia, Anthony Benezet opens the School for Black People and Their Descendants.
January 1770	Sons and Daughters of Liberty post a handbill denouncing the sale of British goods and coerce merchants to surrender both profits and stocks of tea from Boston warehouses.
mid-January 1770	At a confrontation with British regulars, the poorly armed Liberty Boys of Boston meet bayonets and sabers with sled runners.
February 1770	At Boston, the nation's first Daughters of Liberty cell reaches a membership of 300.
May 16, 1771	At Hillsborough, North Carolina, an antitax force battles Tories at Alamance Creek and advances the Regulator war against exploitation by landowners.
November 12, 1771	At Falmouth, Maine, a mob captures the deputy customs official and parades him through town.
June 9, 1772	Sons of Liberty in Providence, Rhode Island, protest taxation without representation by looting and burning the royal brig *Gaspee.*
1773	Dissident Baptist pastor John Weatherford of Pittsylvania, Virginia, wards off attackers who try to slice his hands with knives.
December 1773	The underground at Charleston, South Carolina, forbids the landing of 257 chests of East India Company tea at the harbor.
December 16, 1773	Some 150 patriots hurl 35,000 pounds (16,000 kilograms) of tea into the harbor during the Boston Tea Party, the nation's most famous colonial act of civil disobedience.
December 17, 1773	Some 100 Daughters of Liberty follow up on the revolt by mobbing a profiteer who raised prices on coffee to take advantage of the dearth of tea in Boston.

December 17, 1773	At a meeting attended by more than 2,000 people, Sons of Liberty in New York City form a phalanx to oust British tea ships from the city's harbor.
1774	In Canterbury, New Hampshire, Zadock Wright faces land seizure and persecution for his Tory loyalty.
	A Sons of Liberty cell raises a Liberty Pole in Williamsburg, Virginia, and brandishes tar and feathers as a warning to merchants who violate the tea boycott.
January 29, 1774	The Boston Sons of Liberty rope, drag to the gallows, and tar and feather a customs agent, whom they douse with tea poured down his throat through a funnel.
early March 1774	Sons of Liberty dump 28 tea chests from the brig *Fortune* into Boston harbor.
April 23, 1774	New York City Sons of Liberty force the trader ship *Nancy* out of the harbor.
May 19, 1774	Philadelphia Sons of Liberty hold a planning session for a continental congress.
July 1774	A boarding party at Charleston, South Carolina, dumps tea into the confluence of the Ashley and Cooper rivers.
July 4, 1774	At the Windham tavern, Connecticut Sons of Liberty surround the building and threaten to trundle the stamp agent out of town on a cart.
August 21, 1774	Sons of Liberty at Providence, Rhode Island, tar and feather the hardware shop of a Tory merchant.
September 15, 1774	When the sloop *Cynthia* from Newfoundland approaches Keatings Wharf in York, Maine, Sons of Liberty confiscate the cargo and burn the tea.
October 19, 1774	Annapolis, Maryland, Sons of Liberty force a ship owner to ground the brig *Peggy Stewart* and burn it along with 2,320 pounds (1,053 kilograms) of tea.
October 25, 1774	In Edenton, North Carolina, Daughters of Liberty issue a proclamation against British goods.
November 7, 1774	Sons of Liberty in Yorktown, Virginia, toss a tea chest from the brig *Virginia* into the York River.
November 22, 1774	At Brunswick, New Jersey, some 40 Sons of Liberty dress in Indian garb and seize tea from the brig *Grayhound*.
December 14, 1774	Sons of Liberty march through Portsmouth, New Hampshire, to drum and fife and raid Fort William and Mary at Newcastle.
1775	Conscientious objectors in Philadelphia endure public ridicule while tormentors parade them through the city to a drumbeat.
	Mercy Otis Warren celebrates the Boston Tea Party with a boldly satiric drama, *The Group*.
	At Colchester, Connecticut, Daughters of Liberty support an antitax initiative.
	At Fayetteville, North Carolina, Daughters of Liberty make public displays of their antitax fervor.
April 14, 1775	Benjamin Franklin and James Pemberton organize the Society for the Relief of Free Negroes Held in Bondage.
April 21, 1775	Edward Weyman leads the Liberty Boys on a raid of the state house in Charleston, South Carolina; the arms and ammunition they confiscate are stored for patriots' use during the American Revolution.
May 11, 1775	Georgia Sons of Liberty raid the royal powder magazine in Savannah and distribute supplies to fellow rebels in South Carolina.

June 12, 1775	On Machias Bay, Maine, Sons of Liberty seize the British schooner *Margaretta* and christen it the *Machias Liberty* for use as a privateer.
July 20, 1775	The Boston Sons of Liberty rifle the home of a pacifist who refuses to support the patriot militia.
August 1775	Sons of Liberty in Smithfield, Virginia, egg a stamp agent, coat him in pitch and feathers, and ride him out of town.
March 1777	When British General William Howe plots an invasion of Philadelphia, Thomas McClunn leads a revolt of 150 Quaker pacifists against providing the Continental army with money and provisions.
March 15, 1777	To the call for volunteers for the Continental army, Quakers present a united pacifist front.
August 28, 1777	The Committee on Spies targets 11 Philadelphia Quakers as dangers to the state.
September 7, 1777	Quaker pacifists incur exile from Philadelphia at their own expense to Winchester, Virginia.
1780	Freedman Paul Cuffe of Cuttyhunk Island, Massachusetts, declines to pay a tax in defiance of state control of disenfranchised blacks.
July 1780	Shaker leader Ann Lee faces a jail sentence for treason for encouraging others to resist military involvement.
1783	Paul Cuffe, working as a sea captain at Westport, Massachusetts, collaborates with a Pequot in relaying slaves from Atlantic coast harbors to Philadelphia and Wilmington, Delaware.
1786	George Washington applauds Philadelphia Quakers for piloting Virginia runaways to free territory.
September 12, 1786	At Concord, Massachusetts, 250 rebels prevent a courthouse session from beginning until officials address rural grievances.
1790s	Frontiersmen in Litchfield, Maine, led by Baptist elder James Shurtleff, demand the right to free wilderness land as a reward for their service to the Continental army in the 1770s.
July 27, 1791	Dissident farmers meet at Redstone, Pennsylvania, to plan countermeasures to the whiskey tax.
March 29, 1797	Some 200 Maine farmers and laborers advance on the Wiscasset jail to free dissidents.
summer 1801	The abduction of 10-year-old slave Wagelma from Philadelphia concludes with a harbor tussle between the kidnapper and Isaac Tatem Hopper, a Quaker agent of the Underground Railroad.
1807	Thomas Siah Bonneau opens a school and establishes a library in Charleston, South Carolina, in violation of laws against educating black students.
April 1808	Nathan Barlow and Thomas Brackett of Falmouth, Maine, release one of the Liberty Men from a constable at Fairfax.
August 23, 1808	The Reverend John Chavis, a freedman circuit rider in central North Carolina, advertises classes for black students in the *Raleigh Register.*
September 7, 1812	Officers force nine Shaker conscientious objectors to march with the Northwestern Army to Dayton, Ohio.
January 1813	Godefroy Dorfeuille boldly advertises in the *Louisiana Courier* for more pupils for his illegal New Orleans slave school.
1818	Jean Julien Fromantin trains black children at the St. John the Baptist Catholic Church in Savannah, Georgia.
1820s	George C. Mendenhall and brother Richard Mendenhall operate a slave trade school at Jamestown, North Carolina.
	In her teens, Angelina Emily Grimké of Union, South Carolina, holds literacy classes for slaves.

1823	Levi Coffin begins aiding the Underground Railroad in New Garden, North Carolina.
1824	Hicksite Quakers assert the rights of slaves by sheltering the oppressed in Cass County, Michigan.
1826	Sylvia Morris opens a primary school for blacks in Alexandria, Virginia.
1829	At Harveysburg, Ohio, Elizabeth Burgess Harvey and Jesse Harvey establish the East End School to serve both black and Indian children.
1830s	Jane Grey Cannon Swisshelm risks a pro-slavery backlash while teaching black girls in Louisville, Kentucky.
1831	Prudence Crandall creates a civic furor by admitting Sarah Harris, a black child, to her Canterbury, Connecticut, academy.
	Following the flight of Tice Davids, a field hand who broke from slavery in Kentucky to freedom in Ripley, Ohio, his frustrated owner described the departure route as an "underground railroad."
January 1, 1831	William Lloyd Garrison's weekly abolitionist newspaper *The Liberator* champions civil disobedience on behalf of slaves and enlists volunteers to serve the Underground Railroad.
October 1831	William Lloyd Garrison's inflammatory editorials on the Underground Railroad precipitate a reward of $1,500 from the Vigilance Association of South Carolina for the jailing of circulators of *The Liberator*.
1833	The American Anti-Slavery Society in Philadelphia enlists volunteers, couriers, and outriders and organizes a sophisticated detection and spy network.
March 1833	Alphonso M. Sumner admits free and slave children to his school in Nashville, Tennessee.
1835	Slave rescuer David Ruggles starts the New York Committee of Vigilance to monitor the rights and security of blacks.
	A throng of pro-South agitators hauls abolitionist editor William Lloyd Garrison through Boston by a noose about the neck.
November 25, 1835	The Reverend John Rankin of Ripley, Ohio, condones lawbreaking on behalf of the Underground Railroad.
January 1836	In New York City, William Lloyd Garrison and Theodore Dwight Weld teach a two-week training course for new Underground Railroad conductors.
May 9, 1837	At the Anti-Slavery Convention of American Women in New York City, Lydia Maria Francis Child and Lucretia Coffin Mott set a tone of informed lawbreaking.
1838	Chance Shaw and John Rankin rescue Eliza Harris and her two-year-old son Harry after Harris crosses the Ohio River barefoot by leaping on chunks of ice.
August 1839	At Farmington, Connecticut, slave rescuers Solomon Cowles and Polly Gleason Cowles support Joseph Cinqué during his jailing and trial for murder and piracy of the slave vessel *Amistad*.
1840s	James Porter of Charleston, South Carolina, secretly teaches reading to slaves in a room with an escape hatch that enables him to flee police raids.
	In Kentucky, Quaker spy Wright Maudlin conducts escaped slaves from Bourbon County to free territory.
1841	Joshua Reed Giddings earns censure from the U.S. Congress for defending slaves transported from Hampton Roads, Virginia.
1842	Catholic nuns in New Orleans open a school offering orphans and elderly blacks both domestic vocational training and reading and writing instruction.
1843	At Far West, Missouri, Joseph Smith, Jr., introduces polygamy to members of the Mormon faith.
January 16, 1843	Amos Bronson Alcott goes to jail at Sudbury, Massachusetts, for tax resistance.

August 21, 1843	Henry Highland Garnet of Troy, New York, and Gerrit Smith promote any means of sabotaging the sale and transport of slaves and any form of bodily harm to slave owners, kidnappers, bounty hunters, and U.S. marshals.
1844	Quakers in Hamilton County, Indiana, assist the runaway Rhodes family in making a home.
June 23, 1844	For ferrying escaped slaves from Pensacola, Florida, Captain Jonathan Walker is captured and his right palm branded with a double S for "slave stealer."
September 28, 1844	Calvin Fairbank and Delia Ann Webster earn prison sentences after freeing Lewis Hayden, Harriet Bell Hayden, and her son Jo from slavery in Lexington, Kentucky.
1846	Brigham Young leads Mormon pilgrims from Kirtland, Ohio, to Nauvoo, Illinois.
April 25, 1846	After the outbreak of the Mexican-American War, Henry David Thoreau of Concord, Massachusetts, refuses to pay a village poll tax.
July 1846	Myrtilla Miner trains black girls at the Newton Female Institute in Whitesville, Mississippi, until planters remind her that instructing blacks is a criminal offense.
	Henry David Thoreau goes to jail in Concord, Massachusetts, for nonpayment of six years' worth of back taxes.
	Abigail Kelley Foster faces armed posses, riots, mockery, courtroom challenge, and an arrest for disseminating abolitionist literature on the Sabbath.
1847	In Cincinnati, Ohio, Levi Coffin opens a free labor store known in Underground Railroad code as the "dispatcher's office."
	In St. Louis, Missouri, the Reverend John Berry Meachum and wife Mary Meachum defy state law by opening a floating school for former slaves aboard a steamboat on the Mississippi River.
April 15, 1848	Captain Daniel Drayton attempts the largest slave rescue in the history of abolitionism aboard the schooner *Pearl* from the Chesapeake & Delaware Canal in Washington, DC, to New Jersey.
July 9, 1848	Jane Hunt joins other female Underground Railroad agents at Waterloo, New York, in discussing ways of liberating female slaves from sexual slavery.
July 19, 1848	Lucretia Coffin Mott and Elizabeth Cady Stanton begin agitating for suffrage at the Women's Rights Convention at Seneca Falls, New York.
1849	Henry David Thoreau sets the standard for New World nonviolent protest with a succinct anarchist manifesto, *Civil Disobedience*.
December 1850	Harriet Tubman ventures south to Baltimore to retrieve three families by sea from Cambridge, Maryland.
February 12, 1851	Predecessors to the Massasoit Guards aid the jailbreak of runaway slave Fredric "Shadrach" Minkins from a Boston courthouse.
February 21, 1851	William Lloyd Garrison publishes an article in *The Liberator* advocating civil disobedience in defiance of the Fugitive Slave Law of 1850.
April 3, 1851	Underground Railroad agents plot to free Thomas M. Sims from a Boston jail.
September 11, 1851	The first shootout over the Fugitive Slave Law of 1850 begins at the waystation of Underground Railroad agent William Parker in Christiana, Pennsylvania.
October 1, 1851	John Thomas leads the jailbreak liberating freedman William "Jerry" McHenry from the custody of U.S. marshals in Syracuse, New York.
	Henry David Thoreau transports runaway slave Henry Williams from Concord, Massachusetts, to a relay to Canada.
December 1851	Harried Tubman ferries 11 slaves from Maryland to Canada.

1852	Harriet Beecher Stowe publishes a model of civil disobedience, *Uncle Tom's Cabin* (1852), the nation's most inflammatory antislavery publication.
fall 1852	Harriet Tubman leaves Cape May, New Jersey, to guide nine slaves from Maryland.
1853	Jewish agents free a victim of slave hunters from a federal jail in Chicago.
1854	The Massasoit Guards form illegally to circumvent the Fugitive Slave Law of 1850.
March 11, 1854	Sherman Miller Booth leads the jailbreak of Joshua Glover, a slave from Missouri, from a cell in Milwaukee, Wisconsin.
May 26, 1854	Thomas Wentworth Higginson, Theodore Parker, and Wendell Addison Phillips distribute axes and beams to a Boston mob that batters the courthouse door to free Georgia fugitive Anthony Burns.
1855	During the settlement of Kansas Territory, an extralegal Jayhawker militia led by James Montgomery terrorizes pro-slavery insurgents and settlers.
1856	In North Carolina, agitated slaveholders force an end to slave schools and run some teachers out of the state.
January 30, 1856	In Cincinnati, Ohio, Margaret Garner slits her daughter Mary's throat to prevent her recapture by an enslaver.
mid-November 1856	Samuel Green, Jr., of Indian Creek, Maryland, helps Harriet Tubman shield two slaves from a posse.
winter 1856–1857	Harriet Tubman transports her parents by wagon from Maryland to Ontario, Canada.
September 11, 1857	Mormon polygamists stymie Colonel Albert Sidney Johnston's cavalry at Echo Canyon, Utah.
1858	In Boston, suffragist Lucy Stone censures the taxation of disenfranchised women.
September 13, 1858	The rescue of John Price, a runaway slave from Mason County, Kentucky, involves students from Oberlin College in Ohio.
December 20, 1858	John Brown leads a two-day raid in Missouri and transports 11 slaves and a newborn through the snow via Mound City and Holton, Kansas, to Ontario, Canada.
1859	John F. Cook, Jr., receives warning from Washington, DC, officials that his continued teaching of black students will lead to his arrest.
September 23, 1859	Underground Railroad lawbreakers aid Dr. John W. Doy and son Charles Doy in breaking out of jail in Missouri and returning to service of runaway slaves passing through Lawrence, Kansas.
September 28, 1859	Mexican Americans follow Juan Nepomuceno Cortina in an idealistic revolt at Brownsville, Texas, against the exploitation and dispossession of non-English-speaking Tejanos.
October 16, 1859	Insurrectionist John Brown raids the federal armory at Harpers Ferry, Virginia (now West Virginia), with the intent of launching a national slave revolt.
1860s	In Natchez, Mississippi, slave cook Milla Granson organizes midnight classes in a remote slave cabin.
1860	Edwin Purdy incurs 60 lashes and a prison sentence for operating a backyard slave school in Augusta, Georgia.
April 27, 1860	At Auburn, New York, Harriet Tubman seizes runaway Charles Nalle from custody by raising a fire alarm.
October 1860	Lucretia Coffin Mott denounces federal enforcement of slave catching as obedience to an unjust law.
December 1860	Harriet Tubman transports six adults and a baby from Maryland to the North.

1861	Lydia Jackson Emerson and philosopher Ralph Waldo Emerson of Concord, Massachusetts, enlist slave rescuers to extend the frontier network through Kansas.
April 9, 1861	At the outbreak of the U.S. Civil War, Alfred Henry Love of Philadelphia champions nonviolence.
April 29, 1861	The first extralegal black paramilitary regiment of the U.S. Civil War forms in Newport, Rhode Island.
May 1861	In North Carolina, the military forces conscientious objectors to work in the medical corps or in salt mines.
May 4, 1861	Union soldiers stop enforcing the Fugitive Slave Law of 1850.
September 17, 1861	In Hampton, Virginia, locals overlook Mary Smith Kelsey Peake's classes for blacks, which later form the basis of Hampton University.
April 1862	The Confederate draft law alienates Louisiana Cajuns of the southern prairies.
August 19, 1862	Horace Greeley, editor of the *New York Tribune,* targets President Abraham Lincoln with an editorial calling for an end to the flesh trade.
October 27, 1862	At Labadieville, Louisiana, Cajun conscripts worsen Confederate army losses by abandoning weapons and fleeing inland.
1863	Whites threaten Lucy Skipworth for teaching blacks in Hopewell, Alabama.
	Harriet Tubman collaborates with Union General James Montgomery to rescue 700 slaves along the Combahee River in South Carolina.
March 18, 1863	In Salisbury, North Carolina, 50 females armed with axes and hatchets confront food hoarders and profiteers.
April 2, 1863	Mothers of starved children in Richmond, Virginia, systematically sack a commissary.
May 1863	Unarmed Cajun Jayhawkers of Bayou Teche, Louisiana, initiate aggressive civil disobedience to both the Confederate and Union forces.
August 1863	Shaker elders summarize their protest of militarism to President Abraham Lincoln.
September 1863	Women launch a food riot in Mobile, Alabama, and demand "Food or Death."
March 1864	When the Red River campaign requires additional Confederate conscripts in Louisiana, impressment gangs force Cajun Jayhawkers back into uniform.
June 1, 1864	Confederate President Jefferson Davis demands that Cajun Jayhawkers accept amnesty and return to the army or be shot on sight.
June 15, 1864	Four masked highwaymen shoot John Kline of Broadway, Virginia, for protesting the draft of pacifists.
December 24, 1864	In Pulaski, Tennessee, formation of the Ku Klux Klan advances the cause of white supremacists.
1866	As pioneers and U.S. cavalry move west, the Universal Peace Union battles the near genocide of Plains Indians.
February 8, 1868	While Hester Vaughan awaits hanging for infanticide, the Working Women's National Association mobilizes a protest at the Cooper Institute in New York City.
March 6, 1872	Anthony Comstock seizes New York physician Charles Mancher for selling rubber contraceptives.
November 2, 1872	Anthony Comstock arrests Victoria Claflin Woodhull and Tennessee Celeste Claflin for denouncing male sexual hypocrisy in articles published in *Woodhull & Claflin's Weekly.*
November 5, 1872	Susan B. Anthony courts arrest by voting in the presidential election in Rochester, New York.

1874	Mother Jones delivers tirades during the Long Strike, which pits capitalists against coal miners in western Pennsylvania.
	Mormon elder George Reynolds enters the Nebraska State Penitentiary at Lincoln for polygamy.
April 1874	In Cincinnati, Ohio, 43 women go to jail for praying for temperance in front of a saloon.
mid-July 1877	Mother Jones supports militant Baltimore & Ohio rail strikers in Pittsburgh, Pennsylvania, by organizing female agitators.
November 3, 1877	Ezra Hervey Heywood and Robert Green Ingersoll enter custody in New York City for publishing birth control advertisements in *The Word.*
	Dennis Kearney, a rabble-rouser against Chinese laborers in San Francisco, California, goes to jail for disturbing the peace.
1878	Anthony Comstock hounds Ann Trow Lohman to suicide in New York City for performing abortions and distributing abortifacients and contraceptives.
June 1878	Sarah Blakeslee Chase of Brownhelm, Ohio, goes to prison for selling vaginal syringes in New York City.
December 10, 1878	DeRobigne Mortimer Bennett, editor of the weekly *The Truth Seeker,* serves 13 months at hard labor at Albany Penitentiary in New York for defying the Comstock censorship laws.
January 1879	Chief Standing Bear guides 66 Ponca from an Oklahoma reservation toward refuge among the Omaha in Nebraska.
January 16, 1882	Federal authorities clamp down on polygamists for felonious cohabitation with more than one woman.
fall 1884	Federal raids in Arizona, Idaho, and Utah net prominent Mormon polygamists.
May 4, 1886	A riot breaks out in Haymarket Square in Chicago when 2,000 strikers agitate for an eight-hour workday and protest police brutality.
February 23, 1887	Moses Harman of Valley Falls, Kansas, serves time for publishing an article on marital rape in *Lucifer, the Light Bearer.*
January 22, 1890	Mother Jones co-founds the United Mine Workers (UMW) in Columbus, Ohio.
1891	Under death threats, Mother Jones aids striking Dietz miners in Norton, Virginia.
June 1892	Emma Goldman supports a strike in Homestead, Pennsylvania, by the Amalgamated Association of Iron and Steel Workers.
1894	In Kansas, Carry Nation launches militant vigilantism against liquor.
March 25, 1894	To aid the poor and unemployed, Jacob Coxey initiates the nation's first march on Washington, DC.
April 30, 1894	Mother Jones directs one flank of Jacob Coxey's army of the unemployed to the U.S. Capitol.
May 1, 1894	Mother Jones decries the brutality of deputies and state militia against striking employees of the Baltimore & Ohio Railroad in Pittsburgh.
May 11, 1894	The Pullman Strike involves the American Railway Union in a suicidal civil disobedience to management and results in the first federal antilabor injunction.
June 26, 1894	Eugene V. Debs organizes the "Debs Rebellion," the nation's largest strike to date, in Chicago, St. Louis, and Ludlow, Kentucky.
1895	While canvassing for woman suffrage in Salt Lake City, Susan B. Anthony urges Mormon women to seek autonomy outside polygamous marriages.

June 15, 1895	In a speech to carpet dyers and weavers in Philadelphia, Mother Jones legitimizes worker unrest as evidence of an ongoing industrial war against capitalism.
1897	Temperance worker Ada Harriet Miser Kepley of Effingham, Illinois, survives a beating with a rubber hose by the son of a liquor distributor.
summer 1897	German and Polish immigrant strikers at the Lehigh and Wilkes-Barre Coal Company at Hazleton, Pennsylvania, square off against an antilabor sheriff's department.
1898	Protesters trash the Universal Peace Union headquarters at Independence Hall, Philadelphia, for the organization's opposition to the Spanish-American War.
late November 1899	Mother Jones rallies the wives of Erie Company miners in Arnot, Pennsylvania, by singing the doxology.
December 27, 1900	Carry Nation serves jail time in Wichita, Kansas, for destroying a bar at the Hotel Carey.
1901	Wardens apprehend John Blackbird for gill-netting on the Bad River Reservation in Wisconsin.
January 26, 1901	At Topeka and Enterprise, Kansas, Carry Nation fights alcohol and whoring.
February 18, 1901	Mother Jones rallies female silk workers in Scranton, Pennsylvania, and shames their exploiters for demoralizing women.
1902	Mother Jones ridicules tight-pursed mill owners at Manayunk and Port Richmond, Pennsylvania, and proposes that Italian and Polish workers open a soup line for hungry capitalists.
summer 1902	A "Black Maria" hauls temperance worker Carry Nation from Coney Island, New York, to a Brooklyn jail, where a policeman breaks her hand.
June 20, 1902	In Clarksburg, West Virginia, police nab Mother Jones for violating an injunction against assembling disgruntled strikers of the Fairmont Coal Company.
spring 1903	Mother Jones coordinates a children's march championing 75,000 textile and carpet employees in Kensington, Pennsylvania.
November 1903	Emma Goldman establishes New York City's Free Speech League, a First Amendment movement combating anti-alien, anti-anarchist laws.
January 14, 1904	Police seize Carry Nation in Philadelphia for breaking up saloons.
April 1904	In Telluride, Colorado, the president of the Western Federation of Miners faces charges of superimposing the grievances of gold and silver miners on an American flag.
	Mother Jones muscles into a labor dispute in Carbon County, Utah, where a skirmish spills over from a street to the hillside.
late September 1904	Temperance workers enter custody for smashing plate glass at a liquor wholesaler in Hannibal, Missouri.
1906	Police stop Elizabeth Gurley Flynn from blocking traffic on behalf of New York City's hotel workers.
February 20, 1906	Mother Jones campaigns in Bisbee, Arizona, on behalf of striking laborers of the Copper Queen Mining Company.
March 1906	Police in Buffalo, New York, demand that Emma Goldman stop delivering talks in German, Russian, and Yiddish.
1909	Temperance leader Carry Nation wields three hatchets named Faith, Hope, and Charity to destroy the Union Station bar in Washington, DC.

November 1909	Prompted by a walkout of workers at the Triangle Shirtwaist Company in New York City, 20,000 sweatshop seamstresses strike to protest low wages and unsafe working conditions.
November 30, 1909	Elizabeth Gurley Flynn faces conspiracy charges in Spokane, Washington, for union enlistment.
1910	To promote worker solidarity, Mother Jones scrubs beer bottles alongside female washers at breweries in Milwaukee, Wisconsin.
	Christian missionaries in Montana try to stamp out peyote use among the Crow, who import the ritual from the Northern Cheyenne.
January 26, 1910	Carry Nation battles a red light district in Butte, Montana.
January 1912	Elizabeth Gurley Flynn and William Haywood go to jail for organizing the "Bread and Roses" factory strike at the American Woolen Company in Lawrence, Massachusetts.
June 1912	In Greensburg, Pennsylvania, Mother Jones visits miners' wives and children jailed by police for disturbing the peace; she advises the inmates to sing all night.
February 9, 1913	Margaret Sanger publishes a blank column in *The Call*, symbolizing the suppression of reproductive health information by the U.S. Post Office.
February 13, 1913	While organizing the Paint Creek–Cabin Creek colliery strike in Pratt, West Virginia, Mother Jones enters custody for inciting a riot.
February 14, 1913	From a military jail in Charleston, West Virginia, Mother Jones endorses civil disobedience.
February 25, 1913	After members of the Industrial Workers of the World (IWW) go to jail for rallying silk workers in Paterson, New Jersey, journalist Jack Reed antagonizes a police officer to gain access to the cell of organizer William Haywood.
March 3, 1913	A suffrage procession shuts down Washington, DC, the day before Woodrow Wilson's presidential inauguration.
March 1914	Helen Keller protests police suppression of a workers' march in Sacramento, California.
March 15, 1914	The Menominee of Phlox, Wisconsin, resist laws forbidding the ceremonial use of peyote.
March 22, 1914	Mother Jones disobeys the governor's orders by returning to a strike zone in Walsenburg, Colorado.
October 2, 1914	Police in Minot, North Dakota, silence Antoinette Funk for delivering a suffrage address in the streets.
1915	Mother Jones challenges New York City transit workers to demand their rights.
August 6, 1915	Anthony Comstock engineers the arrest of Emma Goldman and Ben Reitman for distributing birth control pamphlets.
November 19, 1915	A firing squad executes union organizer Joe Hill in Salt Lake City, on a trumped-up charge of murder.
October 12, 1916	Margaret Sanger battles police harassment of the nation's first birth control clinic in Brooklyn, New York.
1917	During World War I, more than 600 pacifists choose jail rather than betray their religious ideals.
	Federal agents seize Mennonite pastor and missionary Rhine Wiegner Benner of Job, West Virginia, for treason for opposing the sale of war bonds.
January 10, 1917	Near suffrage headquarters in Washington, DC, Alice Paul mobilizes an all-female strike force of the National Woman's Party.

February 20, 1917	Immigrant women in New York City foment hunger riots against profiteering grocers.
March 4, 1917	Alice Paul masterminds the Grand Picket of the Woodrow Wilson White House.
April 1917	Police in Duluth, Minnesota, arrest union organizer Elizabeth Gurley Flynn on a vagrancy charge and banish her from town.
	Jeannette Rankin, the first female elected to the U.S. Congress, denounces militarism during World War I.
	Upon U.S. entry into World War I, Christian pacifist Ammon Hennacy begins two years of imprisonment in the U.S. Federal Penitentiary in Atlanta, Georgia, for refusing conscription.
July 29, 1917	Federal marshals lodge Kate Richards O'Hare at a Fargo, North Dakota, jail after she canvasses Kansas, Missouri, and Oklahoma on behalf of pacifism.
August 1, 1917	In Butte, Montana, vigilantes kidnap and lynch union organizer Frank Little.
August 3, 1917	Leaders of the Green Corn Rebellion rally 1,000 white, black, Cherokee, Creek, and Muskogee of Sasakwa, Oklahoma, against the U.S. Selective Service and profiteering on World War I.
August 14, 1917	Heckling, gunfire, bludgeoning, and the ripping of banners assail suffragist picketers at the White House.
August 16, 1917	Dorothy Day and Alice Paul incur arrest for picketing the White House on behalf of woman suffrage.
fall 1917	Elmer Liechty enters a cell at Fort Leavenworth, Kansas, until January 1919 for refusing to wear a military uniform and disregarding orders.
September 1917	IWW officials face arrest for sedition for opposing President Woodrow Wilson's decision to involve the United States in World War I.
November 15, 1917	At an Arlington, Virginia, workhouse, guards initiate a "Night of Terror" by beating suffragist inmates.
April 8, 1918	At Fort Hancock, New Jersey, conscientious objector Ernest Gellert dies mysteriously from a rifle bullet.
May 3, 1918	*Star and Stripes* reports that military police capture New Jersey's first conscientious objector; he is sentenced to three months in the brig.
May 8, 1918	Federal authorities silence a Jehovah's Witness for urging soldiers to refuse orders of their superiors.
May 24, 1918	Hutterite brothers at Camp Lewis, Washington, endure jailing in underwear and straitjackets and later starvation in an unlighted, unheated dungeon at Alcatraz Island, California. At Fort Leavenworth, Kansas, two of the brothers die of pneumonia.
June 22, 1918	At Camp Sheridan, Alabama, Carl Haessler begins a 12-year prison sentence at hard labor for refusing to serve as a machine gunner of the Forty-sixth Army Infantry.
July 1918	While imprisoned at Fort Leavenworth, Kansas, conscientious objector Noah Leatherman endures solitary confinement.
July 7, 1918	Sheriff Jasper Duke's hunt for draft evaders in Arkansas sparks the Cleburne County Draft War.
August 1918	At Fort Lewis, Washington, conscientious objectors endure hot and cold water torture and near hanging in a tree until mounted military police rescue them.
winter 1918	A mock hanging at Fort Andrews nearly strangles Jewish conscientious objector Philip Grosser.
November 1918	Conscientious objector Julius Firestone dies at Camp Hancock, Georgia, after guards tar and feather him.
1919	Mother Jones negotiates the release of chained prisoners in Kanawha County, West Virginia.

January 27, 1919	Dunkard (Church of the Brethren) conscientious objector Maurice Hess gains release from Camp Meade at Fort Riley, Kansas, after enduring solitary confinement on bread and water, handcuffing in a standing position, and sleeping on concrete.
September 1919	After passage of an anti-assembly ordinance in Duquesne, Pennsylvania, police jail 40 steel mill laborers for disorderly conduct.
November 11, 1919	American Legion members hang union organizer Wesley Everett and sack the IWW assembly hall.
1920s	Lucy Perkins Carner of York, Pennsylvania, agitates against war taxes.
May 1920	In Mingo County, West Virginia, workers for the Stone Mountain Coal Company demand UMW membership.
1921	Police arrest social reformer and religious lay leader Dorothy Day in a raid on IWW headquarters in Chicago and charge her with prostitution.
July 14, 1921	Italian immigrants Nicola Sacco and Bartolomeo Vanzetti are found guilty of murder by a jury in Massachusetts; supporters begin seven years of unsuccessful protest to spare the men execution.
August 1, 1921	Supporting striking coal miners at Matewan, West Virginia, Mother Jones leads a rally at the state capitol for free speech and the right of assembly.
August 25, 1921	A shootout at Blair Mountain, West Virginia, involves 15,000 miners in defense of workers' rights.
April 1922	Kate Richards O'Hare organizes a children's march on the White House to demand amnesty for imprisoned fathers who joined the Green Corn Rebellion of 1917.
1923	A Crow Indian named Big Sheep co-founds the Native American Church of Montana as a constitutional defiance of laws against peyote use.
	Mother Jones negotiates with Governor Ephraim Franklin Morgan the release of jailed miners in Logan County, West Virginia.
May 13, 1925	The Scopes "Monkey" trial in Dayton, Tennessee, pits defense attorney Clarence Darrow against orator William Jennings Bryan in the trial of John T. Scopes for teaching evolution in a public school.
July 1925	A. Philip Randolph defends black workingmen by organizing the Brotherhood of Sleeping Car Porters, the first African American labor union.
1928	The first arrest of a Jehovah's Witness for selling *Watchtower* tracts without a license carries charges of selling on Sunday and disturbing the peace.
	Mary Coffin Ware Dennett of Worcester, Massachusetts, enters jail for mailing a pamphlet titled "The Sex Side of Life" (1918).
May 27, 1929	Hungarian Jewish linguist and musician Rosika Schwimmer enters exile as a nonreligious conscientious objector.
April 21, 1930	Adam Clayton Powell, Jr., marches 6,000 followers to the front door of New York's city hall to demand more black doctors and improved health care for Harlem residents.
1932	Emma Zepeda Tenayuca risks jailing at age 16 for picketing the Finck Cigar Company in San Antonio, Texas.
	Bonus Marchers, veterans of World War I, demand early payment of a bonus due in 1945 to counter poverty and the effects of the Great Depression.
winter 1932	Tillie Lerner Olsen enters a cell in Kansas City, Kansas, for distributing leaflets and for haranguing meat packers in Omaha and Kansas City to unionize.
1934	Police silence Tillie Olsen and Jack Olsen in San Francisco, California, for fomenting a citywide strike of 100,000 workers to raise wages for longshoremen.

1934	Jesus Pallares leads Mexican immigrants in Gallup, New Mexico, in a riot over hiring and wage bias against nonwhite coal miners at the Gallup American Company.
late November 1934	Security guards halt Roy Wilkins from picketing the office of the U.S. attorney general in Washington, DC, for ignoring the crime of lynching.
October 22, 1935	In Minersville, Pennsylvania, a school principal expels students Lillian Gobitas and her brother, William H. Gobitas, both Jehovah's Witnesses, for refusing to salute the flag.
December 1935	A sheriff's raid on polygamists at Short Creek, Arizona, attempts to dissuade Mormon lawbreakers.
1936	Adam Clayton Powell, Jr., unleashes tirades against lynching and proposes a boycott of the Olympic Games in Berlin to denounce racial discrimination against nonwhite athletes.
September 1936	Some 485,000 U.S. laborers begin a six-month application of sit-down strikes, a nonviolent method that leaves them open to charges of trespass but relatively safe from harm.
November 17, 1936	A sit-down strike achieves success for 1,000 employees at the Bendix Aviation factory in South Bend, Indiana.
	Labor organizer Richard Frankensteen and some 900 employees idle Midland Steel in Detroit, Michigan.
November 28, 1936	Brothers Roy, George, and Walter Reuther lead a pair of sit-down strikes in Detroit at the Kelsey-Hayes Wheel Company.
January 1, 1937	The newly formed United Auto Workers of America begins unionizing General Motors workers at Flint, Michigan.
March 19, 1937	Adam Clayton Powell, Jr., unites the ghetto against white-owned businesses in Harlem, New York.
May 28, 1937	Sampson Tulee, a member of the Yakima tribe, sues Washington State fisheries director B.M. Brennan for limiting access to traditional native netting grounds.
January 31, 1938	In San Antonio, Texas, Emma Zepeda Tenayuca leads a strike of 12,000 Mexican pecan shellers amid police harassment, capricious arrests, and tear gas.
February 12, 1938	Two thousand people form the Greater New York Coordinating Committee on Employment, a political pressure group protesting high rates of black unemployment.
1939	Before the start of the World's Fair in New York City, Adam Clayton Powell, Jr., pickets the Empire State Building to gain 600 more jobs for black workers.
	Richard Bartlett Gregg of Putney, Vermont, advises dissidents on draft evasion, alternative service to a wartime economy, and taxes supporting armed conflict.
September 1939	Two Mormons go on trial in St. George, Utah, for polygamy.
1940	Adam Clayton Powell, Jr., faces the pistols of security guards when he barges into the U.S. House of Representatives to demand an omnibus civil rights bill.
1941	Michael J. Quill and Adam Clayton Powell, Jr., organize a protest march of striking New York City bus employees.
spring 1941	A. Philip Randolph plots a July demonstration of 100,000 marchers in Washington, DC, to denounce the military's Jim Crow policies and traditions.
April 23, 1941	In the first strike by imprisoned conscientious objectors, 16 people earn solitary confinement for refusing to work, eat, or obey orders.
1942	On a bus from Nashville, Tennessee, Bayard Rustin enters police custody for declining to sit in the back.

January 1942	Walter Barnett, a Jehovah's Witness living near Charleston, West Virginia, maintains that saluting the American flag infringes on his beliefs.
February 19, 1942	President Franklin D. Roosevelt issues Executive Order 9066 sanctioning the internment of 3,000 Japanese males, both immigrant and first-generation U.S. citizens.
March 28, 1942	Minoru Yasui of Hood River, Oregon, protests the slandering of his father as a spy and the penning of Japanese males in the North Portland Livestock Pavilion.
April 1942	Conscientious objector Frederick Howard Richards, a Quaker, is sentenced to one year and one day at the Federal Correctional Institution in Danbury, Connecticut, for defying the draft.
May 30, 1942	Fred Korematsu of San Leandro, California, refuses to yield to the unconstitutional seizure of Japanese Americans.
summer 1942	George Yamada of Minatare, Nebraska, counters the denunciation of pacifists and the random jailing and widespread internment of Japanese Americans.
October 20, 1942	Gordon Kiyoshi Hirabayashi of Seattle, Washington, defies curfew and declines to relocate to Camp Tule, California.
November 14, 1942	Guards at Camp Poston, Arizona, arrest two Japanese American evacuees, triggering a mass strike.
December 5, 1942	Japanese American internees revolt over meat and sugar theft from the commissary at the desert camp at Manzanar, California.
1943	A secular humanist, conscientious objector Mathias Kauten pursues a court case recognizing conscience as proof of religious feeling.
April 6, 1943	Gandhian conscientious objector Bronson P. Clark enters the Federal Reformatory at Chillicothe, Ohio, where a chain links his leg irons to those of fellow conscientious objector Charles Butcher.
May 13, 1943	Black conscientious objectors William H. Sutherland, Jr., and Albon Platt Man, Jr., protest segregation at Lewisburg Federal Penitentiary in Pennsylvania.
May 14, 1943	Civil rights advocate James Farmer organizes a sit-in at the Jack Spratt lunch counter in Chicago.
September 13, 1943	Federal agents begin routing all Japanese American dissenters to Camp Tule, California.
March 20, 1944	Pacifist soldiers risk prison by refusing combat training at Fort McClellan, Alabama.
July 21, 1944	James M. Omura foments a draft revolt at Heart Mountain, Wyoming.
September 9, 1944	During the imprisonment of conscientious objector Corbett Bishop at the Federal Correctional Institution in Milan, Michigan, his punishments range from deprivation of clothing and being diapered to beating with blackjacks, chaining to a heavy ball, and nasal force-feeding.
December 10, 1944	Conscientious objectors volunteer for an experimental starvation diet at the University of Minnesota Laboratory of Physiological Hygiene in St. Paul.
April 4, 1945	Lieutenant Daniel "Chappie" James, Jr., a member of the Tuskegee Airmen, rallies soldiers to perch on bar stools at the all-white officers' club in Seymour, Indiana.
late summer 1945	Conscientious objector Manuel Tallis fasts for 12 days to protest segregated mess halls at the Federal Prison Camp in Tucson, Arizona.
December 1945	Two flashlight-wielding raiders seize Nisqually teenager Billy Frank, Jr., for fishing Indian-style at Frank's Landing, Washington.
1947	The House Committee on Un-American Activities, popularly referred to as the House Un-American Activities Committee (HUAC), blackmails 324 witnesses to divulge the names of suspected Communists in the Hollywood film industry.

1947	After formation of the League for Nonviolent Civil Disobedience Against Military Segregation, A. Philip Randolph threatens to advise blacks to dodge military conscription to a racist army.
April 1947	Igal Roodenko of New York City joins black and white freedom fighters in the Journey of Reconciliation, an effort to smash Jim Crow laws and end incarceration on chain gangs.
April 9, 1947	During the two-week Journey of Reconciliation, Bayard Rustin goes to jail in Chapel Hill, North Carolina, and faces 30 days on a chain gang.
October 27, 1947	Dalton Trumbo leads the defiance of the "Hollywood Ten" to the proceedings of the HUAC.
1948	During the Korean War, T. Vail Palmer of Concordville, Pennsylvania, becomes the first conscientious objector to enter prison for failure to register for the draft.
	Horace Champney formalizes a tax rebellion in Cleveland, Ohio.
July 26, 1953	Mohave County peace officers arrest 32 male polygamists in Short Creek, Arizona, and send their 263 children to foster homes.
May 15, 1954	Anne McCarty Braden and Carl Braden of Shively, Kentucky, purchase a house in a white neighborhood on behalf of a black family.
summer 1954	In Charlotte, North Carolina, Reginald Armistice Hawkins precedes protesters to the airport restaurant to demand service for black diners.
June 15, 1955	Dorothy Day, Abraham Johannes Muste, and Grace Paley protest nuclear proliferation and civil defense air-raid drills in New York's City Hall Park.
December 1, 1955	The Reverend Martin Luther King, Jr., and Jo Ann Robinson, head of the Women's Political Council, support black seamstress Rosa Parks for refusing to move to the back of a bus in Montgomery, Alabama; a yearlong boycott of the city's bus system is launched.
1956	Some 5,000 Ku Klux Klansmen form a brotherhood to battle threats to white supremacy in Tuscaloosa, Alabama.
January 30, 1956	An assailant tosses a bomb onto the front porch of the home of the Reverend Martin Luther King, Jr., in Montgomery, Alabama.
1957	The Southern Christian Leadership Conference, founded by the Reverend Martin Luther King, Jr., and the Reverend Ralph Abernathy, validates a variety of methods of protesting injustice.
March 25, 1957	U.S. customs officers prohibit the importation of Allen Ginsberg's poem *Howl* (1956) for obscenity.
August 6, 1957	On the twelfth anniversary of the bombing of Hiroshima, Japan, protesters trespass on the Camp Mercury nuclear testing site at Yucca Flats, Nevada.
April 5, 1958	George Willoughby sails the yacht *Golden Rule* from San Pedro, California, toward the off-limits Eniwetok Proving Grounds in the Marshall Islands to interrupt nuclear bomb tests.
July 19, 1958	In Wichita, Kansas, Ronald Walters, a leader of the National Association for the Advancement of Colored People, chastises a clerk at the F.W. Woolworth lunch counter who refuses to serve blacks seated on the premises.
August 19, 1958	At Katz Drugs in Oklahoma City, Barbara Posey and Clara Luper force integration of lunch service.
September 3, 1958	Police in Montgomery, Alabama, arrest the Reverend Martin Luther King, Jr., for loitering near the recorder's court.
June 20, 1959	Demonstrators lead the "Omaha Action," a march from Lincoln to Omaha, Nebraska, to protest the international arms race.
July 1, 1959	At the Mead Ordnance Plant of Offutt Air Force Base in Nebraska, dissenters trespass on an intercontinental ballistic missile complex of the Strategic Air Command.

July 1, 1959	1,600 Quaker protesters of biological, chemical, and nuclear warfare begin a nine-month round-the-clock sit-in at the gates of Fort Detrick, Maryland.
July 21, 1959	Marjorie Swann and A.J. Muste go to jail for climbing a fence at an intercontinental ballistic missile site outside Omaha, Nebraska.
1960	James Farmer plans lunch counter sit-ins to demonstrate black outrage at segregation from Greensboro, North Carolina, across the South.
	Paul Edward Theroux repudiates obligatory ROTC training at the University of Massachusetts at Amherst.
January 1960	Adam Clayton Powell, Jr., charges New York City police with plotting a 36-hour racist foray in Harlem that nets 105 arrests.
February 1, 1960	Freshmen at North Carolina Agricultural and Technical College in Greensboro, North Carolina, provoke the management of the F.W. Woolworth lunch counter by demanding service.
February 9, 1960	Carl Wesley Matthews launches a copy of the Greensboro sit-in at an S.H. Kress lunch counter in nearby Winston-Salem, North Carolina.
March 15, 1960	A sit-in at Orangeburg, South Carolina, results in 350 arrests.
March 28, 1960	Students court arrest for disturbing the peace in Baton Rouge, Louisiana, during a sit-in at a Kress dime store.
August 9, 1960	Roy Kepler trespasses at the Lawrence Berkeley Laboratory in California to denounce the bombing of Nagasaki, Japan, 15 years earlier.
October 19, 1960	The Reverend Martin Luther King, Jr., begins serving four months at Georgia's Reidsville State Prison for trespass during a sit-in at an Atlanta restaurant.
	In Atlanta, Georgia, Marion Wright Edelman joins Spelman College students in a sit-in that results in her arrest.
1961	Ammon Hennacy of the Catholic Worker movement abets tax resistance in Phoenix, Arizona, and in Salt Lake City.
January 31, 1961	Students from Friendship College in Rock Hill, South Carolina, picket whites-only lunch counters.
February 1961	Ella Baker directs Student Nonviolent Coordinating Committee (SNCC) involvement in Freedom Rides through the South.
	Diane Nash goes to jail in Rock Hill, South Carolina, for protesting segregation in public facilities.
spring 1961	James Lawson, Jr., instructs Freedom Riders on nonviolent techniques and legal rights in the event of arrest.
April 30, 1961	Following the failed U.S. invasion of the Bay of Pigs in Cuba, David T. Dellinger holds a round-the-clock fast and peace vigil in Washington, DC.
May 1961	Police brutalize John R. Lewis in a Montgomery, Alabama, bus terminal, for ordering food at a segregated counter.
May 29, 1961	In Jackson, Mississippi, a judge sentences James Farmer and 26 Freedom Riders to 40 days in jail for integrating waiting areas, water fountains, and restrooms.
summer 1961	At a clash in Montgomery, Alabama, during the Freedom Rides, police nab the Reverend William Sloane Coffin, Jr., the Reverend Ralph David Abernathy, and others for disturbing the peace at a segregated lunch counter at the Trailways bus terminal.
August 1961	After Ku Klux Klansmen assault picketers at the courthouse in Monroe, North Carolina, police bludgeon and jail SNCC leader James Forman for rioting.

August 26, 1961	In McComb, Mississippi, two students face 36 days in jail for disturbing the peace at a Woolworth's lunch counter.
September 1961	In Liberty, Mississippi, onlookers beat Freedom Rider Travis Britt unconscious and murder Herbert Lee.
September 7, 1961	Courthouse registrar John Q. Wood of Tylertown, Mississippi, declines to register blacks and pistol-whips John Hardy of Nashville, Tennessee.
October 1961	Activists Bella Abzug and Dagmar Wilson organize Women Strike for Peace (WSP), a 60-city protest of nuclear weapons, the Berlin Wall crisis, and the House Committee on Un-American Activities.
November 1961	In Albany, Georgia, SNCC youth set up waves of civil disobedience in the whites-only waiting room of the bus terminal.
	Civil rights drives in southwest Georgia precipitate 1,000 arrests.
November 1, 1961	The WSP musters 1,500 women to process through Washington, DC, to the White House to demand a moratorium on nuclear proliferation from President John F. Kennedy.
December 16, 1961	Police collar the Reverend Martin Luther King, Jr., in Albany, Georgia, for obstructing the sidewalk.
April 26, 1962	WSP members lead 3,000 marchers down Fifth Avenue during the Vietnam Peace Parade in New York City.
May 27, 1962	Harold Stallings sails the trimaran *Everyman I* from Sausalito, California, to the South Pacific to protest nuclear testing at Johnston Island.
July 4, 1962	Franklin Zahn and demonstrators aboard the *Everyman II* depart Honolulu to breach the Atomic Energy Commission testing area at Christmas Island.
July 27, 1962	Officers stop the Reverend Martin Luther King, Jr., in Albany, Georgia, from praying at city hall.
August 31, 1962	Fannie Lou Hamer suffers a beating by police in Indianola, Mississippi, after she tries to register to vote.
October 20, 1962	Lenny Bruce's stand-up comedy act at the Troubadour in West Hollywood, California, earns him a year's jail time for obscenity.
February 1963	The SNCC launches a desegregation movement in Selma, Alabama, by registering black citizens to vote.
February 2, 1963	Reies López Tijerina initiates La Alianza Federal de las Mercedes (Federal Alliance of Land Grants) in Albuquerque, New Mexico, to demand civil rights for Mexican Americans.
March 25, 1963	The Reverend Martin Luther King, Jr., leads 3,500 people on the Selma to Montgomery March through Alabama.
April 12, 1963	The Reverend Ralph Abernathy and the Reverend Martin Luther King, Jr., enter jail in Birmingham, Alabama, for demonstrating without a permit.
May 14, 1963	Gloria Richardson spearheads the Cambridge Nonviolent Action Committee to demand desegregation of schools, hospitals, libraries, and businesses in Cambridge, Maryland.
June 3, 1963	A police assault in a jail in Winona, Mississippi, leaves Fannie Lou Hamer semiblinded and permanently handicapped.
August 1963	SNCC members retreat to Greenwood, Mississippi, to recover from torture inflicted at Parchman Farm.
August 8, 1963	Three SNCC activists incur arrest at an evening protest march in Americus, Georgia.
August 28, 1963	Officials in Plaquemine, Louisiana, seize James Farmer for disturbing the peace and lodge him in jail, where Ku Klux Klan members plot to assassinate him.

Bayard Rustin directs the March on Washington for Jobs and Freedom, which draws 250,000 people, the largest protest march to the capital in the nation's history.

September 15, 1963	The Reverend Martin Luther King, Jr., mourns the murder of four young girls at a bombed-out Sunday school in Birmingham, Alabama, and counsels angry blacks to embrace nonviolent resistance.
November 9, 1963	On the Quebec–Washington–Guantánamo Walk for Peace, marchers suffer police brutality in Griffin, Georgia, for distributing leaflets.
March 2, 1964	Actor Marlon Brando courts arraignment for fishing with Indians of Washington State.
March 7, 1964	Berkeley, California, police arrest Mario Savio and Jack Weinberg for a sit-in at the Sheraton Palace Hotel promoting the employment of black domestics.
March 31, 1964	Comedian Lenny Bruce challenges American prudery with on-stage humor at the Café au Go Go in Greenwich Village, New York, where police silence him for uttering sexual slang.
April 21, 1964	At Cook's Landing, Washington, plainclothes agents ram and seize a boat on the Columbia River and knife boat owner Madeline Alexander Weeks for fishing.
April 23, 1964	At Flushing Meadows, New York, James Farmer manages a sit-in blocking the door to the New York City pavilion at the World's Fair to demand school integration and an end to racial bias in hiring.
June 11, 1964	The Reverend Martin Luther King, Jr., and Andrew Young, Jr., risk arrest in St. Augustine, Florida, by trying to order food at the segregated Monson Motel Restaurant.
June 21, 1964	SNCC volunteers James Chaney, Andrew Goodman, and Michael Schwerner are kidnapped, assaulted, and shot to death by racists in Philadelphia, Mississippi.
December 4, 1964	Dagmar Wilson and Donna Allen appeal charges of contempt of Congress for their testimony of double-talk to the HUAC.
February 2, 1965	Police in Selma, Alabama, charge the Reverend Martin Luther King, Jr., for demanding voting rights for blacks.
March 20, 1965	David Henry Mitchell of New Canaan, Connecticut, charges the U.S. government with constitutional, legal, ethical, and political dereliction in the Vietnam War.
March 25, 1965	The Reverend Martin Luther King, Jr., organizes members of the clergy and 3,200 protesters in a peace procession down Highway 80 from Selma to Montgomery, Alabama.
July 7, 1965	Estelle Trebert Griswold of Hartford, Connecticut, wins a battle in the U.S. Supreme Court establishing the right of sexual privacy for married couples.
August 1965	Folksinger and activist Joan Baez pickets the White House in support of an end to the Vietnam War.
September 16, 1965	César Chávez and the United Farm Workers of America (UFW) initiate the Delano grape boycott in California.
October 13, 1965	After some 80 game wardens attack protesters at a fish-in at Frank's Landing, Washington, comedian Dick Gregory and his wife, Lillian Smith, risk jail for net-fishing.
October 15, 1965	David J. Miller of Syracuse, New York, sets an example of public draft card burning and ignores a court order to get another card.
October 26, 1965	About 50 Indians parade to the federal courthouse in Seattle, Washington, to protest unlawful search and seizure.
November 2, 1965	In defiance of the Vietnam War, Alice Herz and Norman R. Morrison immolate themselves outside the Pentagon office of Secretary of Defense Robert McNamara.
November 6, 1965	Lieutenant Henry H. Howe risks arrest by protesting the Vietnam War out of uniform at a demonstration in El Paso, Texas.

November 27, 1965	Some 25,000 war protesters led by Students for a Democratic Society storm Washington, DC.
December 16, 1965	In Des Moines, Iowa, Christopher Eckhardt, John F. Tinker, and Mary Beth Tinker earn suspension from school for wearing black armbands in protest of the Vietnam War.
January 22, 1966	The Reverend Martin Luther King, Jr., and the Reverend Ralph Abernathy radicalize Chicago slum dwellers.
February 6, 1966	Dick Gregory and Lillian Smith go to jail for defending native fishing rights at Frank's Landing, Washington.
March 1966	The UFW marches to Sacramento, California, to voice *la causa* to the state legislature.
June 7, 1966	The Reverend Martin Luther King, Jr., heads the March Against Fear from Memphis, Tennessee, to Jackson, Mississippi.
June 30, 1966	At Fort Hood, Texas, three U.S. Army privates refuse combat assignments in Vietnam.
October 1966	The Alianza Movement seizes Echo Amphitheater Park in New Mexico's Kit Carson National Forest and names the camp the Republic of San Joaquín del Río Chama.
December 25, 1966	Joan Baez pickets on behalf of condemned prisoners at San Quentin State Prison in Santa Monica, California.
1967	A Quaker action group protests the Vietnam War by transporting relief parcels, medical supplies, and Red Cross funds to noncombatants in Hanoi.
April 4, 1967	At Riverside Church in New York City, the Reverend Martin Luther King, Jr. denounces the bombing of North Vietnam.
April 15, 1967	A public rally of 175 draft card burners in New York City's Central Park ushers in mass defiance of the U.S. Selective Service.
June 2, 1967	Howard B. Levy begins a three-year sentence at hard labor at Fort Leavenworth, Kansas, for refusing to train U.S. Special Forces Green Beret medics.
July 1967	While speaking in Cambridge, Maryland, black radical H. Rap Brown survives an attempted assassination.
October 1967	Joan Baez begins the first of two jail terms in Santa Rita Rehabilitation Center for holding a sit-in at a draft center in Oakland, California.
October 16, 1967	In Boston, the Reverend William Sloane Coffin, Jr., explains to a crowd the ethics of civil disobedience through draft resistance and draft card burning during the "Hell No, We Won't Go" movement.
October 21, 1967	In Arlington, Virginia, Catholic priest Daniel Berrigan defames Secretary of State Robert McNamara at a rally of 75,000 war protesters assailing the Pentagon.
October 30, 1967	The Reverend Martin Luther King, Jr. enters jail in Birmingham, Alabama, for contempt of court.
December 5, 1967	Police nab poet Allen Ginsberg and pediatrician Benjamin Spock for conspiracy during an antiwar demonstration at a military induction center in New York City.
1968	Students for a Democratic Society holds a poster campaign against the ROTC program at the University of Wisconsin at Milwaukee to protest the waste of life on battlefields.
January 1968	The Jeanette Rankin Brigade marches on Washington, DC, to demand an end to the Southeast Asian conflict.
late January 1968	Father Daniel Berrigan and college professor Howard Zinn travel to Hanoi to negotiate the liberation of three U.S. pilots imprisoned by the North Vietnamese.

March 1968	The Reverend Martin Luther King, Jr., advances the cause of striking garbage workers in Memphis, Tennessee.
March 8, 1968	Captain Dale H. Noye, a psychology instructor at the U.S. Air Force Academy, receives a one-year sentence for refusing an order to ready pilots for combat.
March 31, 1968	On the steps of the South Boston Courthouse, David Paul O'Brien contests the constitutionality of the law against mutilating or destroying draft cards.
May 17, 1968	Philip and Daniel Berrigan and seven other protesters raid the Catonsville, Maryland, draft board and burn files with homemade napalm.
August 25, 1968	David T. Dellinger and other radicals organize a mass demonstration in Chicago preceding the Democratic National Convention.
October 12, 1968	Lieutenant Susan Schnall receives a six-month sentence at hard labor for an antiwar informational picket conducted around Oakland, California.
October 27, 1968	Philip Berrigan becomes the first American priest to be arrested for civil disobedience after he leads the Baltimore Four on a raid of the Maryland Customs House and soaks 1-A draft files in blood.
March 22, 1969	At the Dow Chemical headquarters in Washington, DC, burglars hang photos of Vietnamese children maimed and scarred by napalm.
April 1969	At Harvard University in Cambridge, Massachusetts, police injure dissenters and arrest them for an anti-ROTC sit-in at University Hall.
June 28, 1969	To ward off police raids of gay bars, radicals incite a riot at the Stonewall Inn, a gathering spot for nonwhite gay men in New York City.
July 4, 1969	The War Resisters League Women Against Daddy Warbucks, a highly visible protest group in Manhattan, flaunts a raid on eight draft boards.
November 14, 1969	Members of the American Indian Movement (AIM) occupy the Alcatraz Island prison in San Francisco, California, to draw attention to Indian privations.
November 15, 1969	A half million pacifists converge on Washington, DC, to denounce the Vietnam War.
1970s	Folksinger Joan Baez challenges the Vietnam War and nuclear proliferation by refusing to pay 60 percent of her federal taxes.
March 8, 1970	AIM members reclaim Fort Lawton near Seattle, Washington.
March 18, 1970	Susan Brownmiller promotes a feminist demonstration at the *Ladies Home Journal* office on Park Avenue in downtown Manhattan.
April 1970	Jane Elizabeth Hodgson, an obstetrician in St. Paul, Minnesota, tests anti-abortion laws by terminating a pregnancy.
	Actress Jane Fonda tours Fort Mead, Maryland, where military police silence her for off-limits antiwar crusading.
	Robin Morgan and Ti-Grace Atkinson occupy Grove Press in April to combat pornography and the glorification of rape.
early May 1970	More than 30 ROTC buildings across the United States are set on fire by antiwar, antidraft activists.
summer 1970	The UFW leads 10,000 California field laborers on a lettuce boycott.
June 1970	The first gay pride parade draws 10,000 marchers to New York City to process from Greenwich Village to Central Park.
June 6, 1970	AIM members reclaim native lands lost to the government in Lassen National Forest, California.

September 1970	AIM members launch a three-month sit-in at Mount Rushmore, South Dakota.
September 9, 1970	Tacoma police club and seize 59 alleged fishers camped on the Puyallup River, Washington.
November 3, 1970	AIM members occupy a Nike missile base outside Davis, Colorado.
November 18, 1970	At Plymouth, Massachusetts, AIM members occupy the *Mayflower II* at Plimoth Plantation.
1971	White supremacists resist court-ordered busing in Pontiac, Michigan, with marches, sick-outs, and sit-ins.
February 1971	Actress and antiwar activist Jane Fonda enlivens a Vietnam Veterans Against the War rally in Valley Forge, Pennsylvania.
February 18, 1971	Puerto Rican dissidents squat at Flamenco Beach on the island of Culebra to protest the U.S. seizure and pollution of Vieques.
May 16, 1971	In Minneapolis, Minnesota, AIM demands possession of the Twin Cities Naval Air Station for development into a cultural and educational center.
June 13, 1971	Daniel Ellsberg discredits the Nixon Administration for its handling of the Vietnam War by leaking the Pentagon Papers to the *New York Times.*
July 4, 1971	Russell Means arranges a peaceful AIM demonstration at Mount Rushmore, South Dakota.
August 14, 1971	AIM members overrun a Coast Guard lifeboat station at McKinley Beach in Milwaukee, Wisconsin, and turn it into a school and halfway house.
September 27, 1971	Clyde Bellecourt and 40 AIM members protest the collection of Indian skeletons at Colorado State University in Denver.
November 5, 1971	Greenpeace sails two vessels to Amchitka, Alaska, to denounce nuclear testing.
March 4, 1972	An AIM protest by Russell Means and Dennis Banks results in the first conviction of a white murderer of an Indian in Nebraska history.
April 23, 1972	At Fort Totten Indian Reservation, North Dakota, 30 AIM members hold a sit-in protesting police brutality.
May 1972	Jane Fonda lauds students at the University of California, Los Angeles, for denouncing the campus ROTC as a training ground for killers.
May 9, 1972	At Meyerhoff Park on the campus of the University of California, Los Angeles, Students for a Democratic Society members charge Chancellor Charles E. Young with warmongering by championing the ROTC program.
July 1972	Jane Fonda visits the North Vietnamese in Hanoi to commiserate with peasants whose dikes crumble under persistent U.S. bombing.
mid-July 1972	Clyde Bellecourt trespasses on an archaeological dig site outside Welch, Minnesota, exposes film to light, confiscates tools, backfills trenches, and burns field notes detailing desecration of Indian tombs.
September 1972	The Reverend William Sloane Coffin, Jr., joins a peaceful mission to Hanoi to bring home three prisoners of war and campaigns for amnesty for draft evaders.
November 3, 1972	AIM heads the Trail of Broken Treaties motorcade from Seattle to Washington, DC, where members hold a five-day sit-in at the Bureau of Indian Affairs.
December 25, 1972	Joan Baez visits prisoners of war in Hanoi, North Vietnam.

February 27, 1973	Russell Means leads AIM in a reclamation of Wounded Knee at the Pine Ridge Reservation in South Dakota.
August 1973	César Chávez and Dorothy Day enter custody along with UFW members in strikes at Delano, California, against lettuce growers in the San Joaquin Valley.
October 2, 1973	Officials charge Kenneth C. Edelin of Washington, DC, with manslaughter for performing an abortion.
1974	Ronald L. Kovic rallies handicapped veterans, survivors of the Vietnam War, in a 17-day fast at the office of U.S. Senator Alan Cranston in Los Angeles, California.
March 8, 1974	Frederick Tribble and Michael Tribble of the Lac Courte Oreilles Ojibwa go to jail for fishing off the Wisconsin reservation.
September 12, 1974	Protests of court-ordered busing in Boston require efforts by 400 city cops on motorcycles and horses and state officers in cruisers to quell disorder.
1975	Robert Randall, founder of the Alliance for Cannabis Therapeutics, goes to jail in Washington, DC, for growing marijuana as a palliative for glaucoma.
February 1975	The UFW boycotts Gallo wines.
August 30, 1975	Charles Kauluwehi Maxwell leads an unauthorized goat-hunting and fish-seining party on Kaho'Olawe, Hawaii.
1976	Joseph D. Quinlan and Julia Duane Quinlan force the removal of their daughter Karen Ann from a ventilator.
January 6, 1976	In defiance of the U.S. military, 10 boatloads of native Hawaiians occupy Kaho'Olawe.
February 2, 1977	George Helm, Francis Ka'uhane, and Charles Warrington warn President Jimmy Carter that dissent will continue on Kaho'Olawe until the military decamps.
March 7, 1977	The drowning deaths of two Hawaiians off Molokini produce the first martyrs to the Kaho'Olawe repatriation.
May 29, 1977	The Animal Liberation Front (ALF) frees two Atlantic bottlenose dolphins from the University of Hawaii marine laboratory in Honolulu.
February 11, 1978	Dennis Banks and Darlene "Kamook" Nichols launch the Longest Walk, an Indian protest that reaches Washington, DC, on July 15.
June 14, 1978	Allen Ginsberg and Peter Orlovsky court arrest by blocking train shipments of plutonium to the Rocky Flats nuclear weapons factory near Boulder, Colorado.
May 19, 1979	At Vieques, Puerto Rico, 150 fishermen from Esperanza set the tone of peaceful group lawbreaking by celebrating Catholic mass on the beach.
May 21, 1979	Gays in San Francisco, California, launch the White Night, a spontaneous rampage against injustice toward a minority sexual orientation.
November 11, 1979	Jailers cloak the severe beating of a dissident at Vieques, Puerto Rico, by faking the man's suicide.
late 1970s	An influx of political refugees from El Salvador and Guatemala evokes sympathy in pacifists, who resurrect the Underground Railroad concept.
April 28, 1980	During a mass protest of nuclear weapons, dissenters converge on Washington, DC, to protest the use of atomic power against smaller nations.
1981	David Sohappy and son David Sohappy, Jr., of Harrah, Washington, are arrested for selling 317 salmon to an undercover federal agent.
	Crosby Wilfredo Orantes-Hernandez survives a pistol-whipping by immigration agents in Culver City, California, and fights illegal interrogation and deportation with a class-action suit against federal agents.

March 21, 1981	Earth First! members fake a 300-foot (90-meter) crack in the Glen Canyon Dam on the Colorado River.
May 4, 1981	James A. Corbett, a Quaker rancher in Tucson, Arizona, directs the first of a stream of Central American refugees to shelter.
October 1981	People for the Ethical Treatment of Animals (PETA) leader Alex Pacheco exposes cruelty to 16 macaques and a rhesus monkey at the Institute for Behavioral Research in Silver Springs, Maryland.
1982	Greenpeace members swim through a sea patrol to protest the impact of ordnance explosion on humpback whales near KahoʻOlawe, Hawaii.
March 24, 1982	John M. Fife, a Presbyterian minister and member of the Sanctuary Movement, establishes rescue missions for Central American refugees at churches along a covert route.
April 16, 1982	Harry Kunihi Mitchell paddles a surfboard to KahoʻOlawe to protest island desecration.
May 26, 1983	In Hillcrest, Virginia, Joseph Grace sets a women's health clinic on fire.
1984	Jim Corti, a clinical nurse at the AIDS Project Los Angeles, smuggles low-cost AIDS remedies across the border from Tijuana, Mexico.
February 1984	Federal agents seize two Brownsville, Texas, refugee transporters, Stacey Lynn Merkt and Sister Diane Muhlenkamp, whom Amnesty International declares prisoners of conscience.
May 28, 1984	An ALF raid at the University of Pennsylvania shames lab psychologists for using a hydraulic hammer to inflict brain injury on baboons.
August 22, 1984	Gregory Lee Johnson's flag burning during an anti–Ronald Reagan, anti–nuclear weapons protest in Dallas, Texas, ignites debate over flag desecration.
November 22, 1984	A sit-in at the South African Embassy in Washington, DC, protests apartheid.
December 25, 1984	Bombers for Jesus destroys three women's health clinics in Pensacola, Florida, that practice abortion.
1985	At the Crystal River State Archaeological Site near Tampa, Florida, AIM director Sheridan Murphy protests the disinterring of five Timucuan graves dating to 500 B.C.E.
	Jim Corti and Martin Delaney initiate importation of exotic AIDS curatives and guerrilla drug trials on unauthorized compounds.
January 1, 1985	Joan Andrews ransacks a Florida women's health clinic in Broward County.
July 2, 1985	Michael D. Bray, a member of the Army of God, conspires to explode a pipe bomb at a women's health clinic in Baltimore.
1986	Cesár Chávez initiates a second California grape boycott in the San Joaquin Valley.
	Stacy Lynn Merkt, a volunteer at Casa Oscar Romero asylum for Mexican refugees in Brownsville, Texas, goes to prison for transporting illegal aliens to McAllen, Texas.
	Father Patrick Bergin and Martin Sheen court arrest in New York City by blocking a door in protest of President Ronald Reagan's commitment to nuclear arms.
1987	Dennis Banks protests grave robbing in Uniontown, Kentucky, where diggers uncover 1,200 native tombs.
	Dr. Jack Kevorkian advertises for candidates for his death hospice near Detroit, Michigan.
April 15, 1987	The AIDS Coalition to Unleash Power (ACT-UP) disrupts business at a New York City post office by waving anti–Ronald Reagan posters.
1988	Women supporting a coal strike in Pittston, Virginia, name their auxiliary the Daughters of Mother Jones.

March 20, 1988	The Reverend William Sloane Coffin, Jr., risks jailing by infiltrating a nuclear test site outside Las Vegas, Nevada.
April 3, 1988	Philip Berrigan goes to prison for boarding the USS *Iowa* in Norfolk, Virginia, to sabotage two Tomahawk cruise missiles.
1989	Colonel Margarethe Cammermeyer fights discharge from the U.S. Army after revealing her lesbianism during an interview required of those seeking top secret clearance for admission to the War College.
April 1989	In Miami, Jim Corti and Martin Delaney begin testing Compound Q on AIDS patients.
September 1989	Peter Staley, a victim of AIDS, dispatches ACT-UP members to the New York Stock Exchange on Wall Street to handcuff themselves at floor level.
October 30, 1989	Shawn D. Eichman of San Dimas, California, burns an American flag at the entrance to the state capitol building in Seattle, Washington, to protest the federal Flag Protection Act.
1990	Robert Mapplethorpe's disturbing, explicit photography generates debate in the U.S. Congress concerning the use of funds from the National Endowment of the Arts for works that citizens deem indecent or obscene.
	Father Roy Bourgeois establishes the School of the Americas (SOA) Watch as a deterrent to the U.S. Army's proliferation of global terrorism.
May 24, 1990	Timber cutters retaliate against protester Judi Bari of Earth First! by exploding a pipe bomb under her car in Oakland, California.
June 4, 1990	In Holly, Michigan, Janet Elaine Adkins hires Dr. Jack Kevorkian to aid her suicide by a lethal intravenous solution in his Volkswagen van.
August 2, 1990	Before the beginning of the Persian Gulf War, Shawn D. Eichman burns an American flag at a military recruiting station in Times Square, New York City.
November 1990	At SOA Watch headquarters, 10 volunteers create a mock "Hall of Fame" to honor Latin American thugs, drug czars, and assassins.
January 22, 1991	ACT-UP member John Weir disrupts broadcasts of the *CBS Evening News* with cries of "Fight AIDS, not Arabs." Simultaneously, Jon Greenberg chains himself to Robert MacNeil's desk during a broadcast of the *MacNeil/Lehrer NewsHour* on PBS to protest inaction on AIDS research.
March 31, 1991	Philip Berrigan disarms the guided missile cruiser USS *Gettysburg* at Bath, Maine.
April 30, 1991	Greenpeace members go to jail for protesting the Keystone Portland Cement Company kiln in Bath, Pennsylvania, where workers fire the boiler with toxic solvents.
October 13, 1991	Martin Sheen and Paul Connett, an analyst for Work on Waste USA, enter custody for leading a trespass at Waste Management, Inc., in New York City.
February 28, 1992	The ALF ends animal vivisection at Michigan State University in East Lansing by setting fire to the laboratory.
summer 1992	Alicia Littletree orchestrates the Albion Uprising, a two-month sit-in for Earth First! to halt clear-cutting of giant redwoods in Mendocino, California.
December 1992	The Florida AIM chapter seizes the Moog Midden/Yat Kitischee indigenous grave complex at Indian Station near Clearwater.
December 1, 1992	Greenpeace members climb the Sears Tower in Chicago and hoist an antinuclear banner to mark the fiftieth anniversary of the first nuclear reactor.
March 10, 1993	Rescue America member Michael Allan Griffen shoots David Gunn, an abortion provider in Pensacola, Florida.

April 1993	Reuben Snake, Jr., a Winnebago elder from Nebraska, vindicates the consumption of native peyote as an eternal source of comfort and strength.
April 17, 1993	Police round up Greenpeace members at an antinuclear camp-in at a missile test site near Beatty, Nevada.
December 7, 1993	Philip Berrigan sabotages equipment on two Strike Eagle fighter-bombers at Seymour Johnson Air Force Base in Goldsboro, North Carolina.
October 18, 1994	In Los Angeles, California, Winona LaDuke chains herself to a truck axle on behalf of old-growth forests harvested for General Telephone & Electronics telephone books.
1996	Juan Romagoza opens La Clinica del Pueblo (The People's Clinic) in Washington, DC, as a refuge of the Sanctuary Movement.
November 19, 1996	At the Cargill grain terminal in Destrehan, Louisiana, Terri Johns calls media attention to genetically engineered soybeans.
January 17, 1997	Dissidents in Washington, DC, denounce the death penalty at a rally marking the twentieth year of its reinstatement.
July 21, 1997	ALF saboteurs shut down Cavel West, Inc., a horse slaughterhouse in Redmond, Oregon.
September 1997	SOA Watch targets the Fort Benning school by defacing the entrance sign with blood-red paint.
December 10, 1997	Julia Butterfly Hill stages a sit-in atop a 200-foot (60-meter) redwood marked for felling in Arcata, California.
1998	Michael Schiavo spotlights the caregiver's dilemma by petitioning a court to allow doctors to stop the abdominal tube feeding of his wife, Theresa Marie Schiavo.
August 30, 1998	George Reding begins an assisted suicide service in Albuquerque, New Mexico, by supplying an overdose of pentobarbital to Donna Brennan.
October 19, 1998	At Lackawanna County Prison in Scranton, Pennsylvania, William Pickard and Jeffrey Garis merit criminal prosecution for obstructing justice and for picketing to influence a judge to end the death penalty.
January 8, 1999	Narcotics officers in Kearny, Arizona, arrest Leonard Mercado, co-founder of the Peyote Foundation, for growing peyote plants in his garden.
April 1999	SOA Watchers march around the Pentagon in Arlington, Virginia, demanding closure of the U.S. facility, alleging it as a training field for rapists, torturers, and assassins.
April 16, 1999	In front of the World Bank in Washington, DC, helmeted police face off against SOA Watchers wearing red bandanas, the common shield of Latino death squads.
April 21, 1999	Ismael Guadalupe-Ortiz and Tito Kayak begin a camp-in at Vieques, Puerto Rico.
May 8, 1999	Rubén Berríos camps illegally at Camp García, Puerto Rico.
June 26, 1999	Six hundred AIM members rally at Whiteclay, Nebraska, in protest of alcohol sales to Indians.
August 9, 1999	Military police silence Martin Sheen for praying for peace in protest of nuclear weapon manufacture at the Los Alamos National Laboratory in New Mexico.
October 30, 1999	At Reedy Mound, Florida, an AIM protest draws media attention to grave plundering by amateur archaeologists.
December 20, 1999	At the Warfield Air National Guard Base in Middle River, Maryland, Philip Berrigan defaces and disarms the gatling guns on A-10 Warthog planes, which fired depleted uranium in Iraq and Yugoslavia.
January 2000	Police collar Pamelyn Ferdin for brandishing an elephant bullhook at an anticircus protest in Woodland Hills, California.

February 21, 2000	Protesters schedule a Peace for Vieques March in Chicago, Los Angeles, New York City, and Philadelphia.
February 29, 2000	One-hundred-fifty dissidents mob the U.S. Supreme Court building in Washington, DC, to save condemned cop killer Mumia Abu-Jamal from execution.
May 21, 2000	Fifty students at Shawnee Mission North High School in Kansas City, Kansas, picket for the cessation of arms training of 160 ROTC cadets.
June 25, 2000	SOA Watch holds a nonviolent demonstration in St. Louis, Missouri, outside the headquarters of Monsanto, maker of herbicides that drug enforcement agents use in Colombia to eradicate the cocaine trade.
July 31, 2000	During the Republican National Convention, in front of Philadelphia City Hall, nine SOA Watchers dramatize the massacre of Latin Americans with uniformed hit men, red spray paint, and pine coffins.
August 6, 2000	Father Carl Kabat trespasses on a nuclear missile silo in Weld County, Colorado.
October 8, 2000	Actor Martin Sheen and Lawrence Turk of Greenpeace incur arrest for trespass at Vandenberg Air Force Base outside Santa Barbara, California, a command post dedicated to space surveillance and lethal satellites.
October 31, 2000	Philadelphia police battle 100 protesters who vilify injustice in Texas, the home state of President George W. Bush, for leading the nation in executions.
November 5, 2000	Puerto Rican militants scale the crown of the Statue of Liberty in New York Harbor in protest of ordnance explosions on Vieques.
November 13, 2000	The Reverend William Sloane Coffin, Jr., abets gay rights strategists in awaiting arrest and handcuffing at the Soulforce vigil, which blocks the entrance to the Shrine of the Immaculate Conception in Washington, DC.
November 21, 2000	Martin Sheen sprinkles fake blood at the School of the Americas at Fort Benning, Georgia.
January 2001	James Warren "Flaming Eagle" Mooney faces Utah deputies, who charge him with drug trafficking and racketeering for growing peyote.
April 30, 2001	At an anticolonial demonstration at the University of Puerto Rico in Rio Piedras, Pedro Colón Almenas incurs a one-year prison sentence at Guaynabo Federal Prison for striking an ROTC officer.
May 1, 2001	On Vieques, militants hide from a SWAT team, Coast Guard cutters, and overhead surveillance by helicopters.
June 2001	Sheridan Murphy protests grave robbing at a Paleo-Indian site at the Little Salt Spring sinkhole in Sarasota County, Florida.
	The American Civil Liberties Union sues the city of Shreveport, Louisiana, for arresting PETA protester Cynthia Lieberman for mocking the Ringling Brothers and Barnum & Bailey Circus.
June 1, 2001	Sailors moor small craft in patrolled zones of Vieques, Puerto Rico.
September 3, 2001	Bomb runs over Vieques inflame five militants to trespass.
December 15, 2001	As a gesture toward Second Amendment rights, Rick Stanley flaunts a revolver during a gun rally at the Denver Civic Center in Colorado.
June 24, 2002	Polygamist Thomas Arthur Green of Joab County, Utah, earns cell time for child rape and bigamy.
September 2002	Rick Stanley carries a sidearm to the Thornton Harvest Fest in Colorado.
September 17, 2002	Santa Cruz, California, city council members hold a marijuana giveaway as a protest of heavy-handed government sweeps of the homes of the sick and dying.

September 23, 2002	U.S. Capitol police seize protestors for handcuffing themselves to the White House fence in defiance of laws restricting the use of marijuana for pain relief.
October 2, 2002	Code Pink: Women for Peace zeroes in on the Iraq War by holding a birthday party for nonviolence advocate Mohandas Gandhi in front of the White House.
2003	Julia Butterfly Hill of Mount Vernon, Missouri, heads a tax revolt by refusing to pay a portion of a lawsuit settlement to the Internal Revenue Service.
January 10, 2003	Double brigades breach the security fence at Camp García, Vieques.
March 21, 2003	Students at Haverford College protest the Iraq War by blocking the doors to the Federal Building at Penn Square in Philadelphia.
May 1, 2003	At Vieques, jubilant islanders wreck equipment and buildings abandoned by the U.S. Navy.
June 26, 2003	Code Pink lambastes the administration of George W. Bush by hoisting a banner-sized pink slip atop the Century Plaza Hotel in Washington, DC, announcing the firing of the president for lying about weapons of mass destruction in Iraq.
August 20, 2003	In Portland, Oregon, Greenpeace orders the arrest of President George W. Bush for jeopardizing the national forest system.
October 20, 2003	Nathaniel Heatwole courts arrest for concealing box cutters, matches, bleach, and modeling clay in plastic bags aboard 737 passenger jets bound from Baltimore to Houston and New Orleans.
winter 2003	During the Iraq War, the Reverend William Sloane Coffin, Jr., abets Cindy Sheehan, mother of a soldier killed in combat, in maligning the prowar policies of President George W. Bush.
April 9, 2004	Father Carl Kabat arms himself with a jackhammer and trespasses on a missile silo at New Raymer, Colorado.
May 11, 2004	Sergeant Kevin Benderman goes to prison at Fort Lewis, Washington, for refusing to serve in the Iraq War.
May 17, 2004	In Miami, Florida, Greenpeace whistle-blowers post an anti–George W. Bush banner on the cargo ship *Jade* to alert the public to the smuggling of 70 tons of mahogany from the Amazon rainforest in Brazil.
June 2004	To publicize genocide at Darfur in western Sudan, demonstrators in Washington, DC, rage at the slaughter of some 30,000 Sudanese over an 18-month period.
June 18, 2004	Cindy Sheehan supports military families challenging President George W. Bush face to face at Fort Lewis, Washington, on the waste of life in the Iraq War.
October 9, 2004	AIM members in Denver, Colorado, block a traditional Sons of Italy parade honoring Christopher Columbus.
January 20, 2005	At the second inaugural of President George W. Bush, Cindy Sheehan lectures an audience on war losses.
August 2005	A satire of meat market packaging in Peoria, Illinois, precedes the arrest of PETA members Eric Deardorff and Melissa Sehgal for disorderly conduct.
August 6, 2005	In a ditch across from the ranch of President George W. Bush in Crawford, Texas, Cindy Sheehan mounts a round-the-clock protest of the Iraq War.
August 31, 2005	War protester Cindy Sheehan organizes the Bring Them Home Now Tour.
September 2005	A security officer at Redwood Middle School in Napa, California, detains Toni Kay Scott for an infraction of the school dress code—knee socks picturing Tigger, a character in A.A. Milne's *Winnie the Pooh*.

September 26, 2005	Cindy Sheehan leads a Code Pink contingent during a demonstration at the White House gate, until city police carry her away.
September 29, 2005	Tariq Khan angers an ROTC member at an enlistment effort in Fairfax, Virginia, by wearing a sign declaring "Recruiters Tell Lies."
November 2005	Christian anarchists with the Catholic Worker movement defy the ROTC by digging graves and burying black coffins beneath tombstones at the University of Missouri at Columbia.
November 18, 2005	At Eugene, Oregon, on "National Stand Down Day," female war resisters from Code Pink declare that "Outraged Women Say No to War."
December 2005	Michelle Y. Cho and Brandi Valladolid earn arrest at city hall in Providence, Rhode Island, for posing nearly naked on behalf of fur-free holidays.
January 2006	U.S. Army First Lieutenant Ehren Watada of Honolulu, Hawaii, becomes the first commissioned officer to decline deployment to an Iraqi combat zone.
	Father David Velásquez of Maywood, California, declares his parish a compassionate hospitality center to Central American refugees.
January 31, 2006	When she dons a T-shirt numbering the dead in the Iraq War at 2,245, on January 31, 2006, Capitol security guards remove Cindy Sheehan from the House gallery during President George W. Bush's State of the Union speech and charge her with unlawful conduct.
March 6, 2006	At the United Nations complex in New York City, police arrest Code Pink leader Medea Benjamin and Cindy Sheehan for protesting the Iraq War.
June 28, 2006	Members of Grandmothers for Peace risk arrest for defiant trespass while volunteering for enlistment at the Philadelphia Armed Forces Center.
July 4, 2006	At a "Troops Home Fast" rally in Washington, mounted police and motorcycle cops arrest a 71-year-old member of Code Pink.
July 12, 2006	Code Pink marches to Capitol Hill in Washington, DC, to demand closure of the U.S. prison in Guantánamo, Cuba, an offshore detention facility that falls outside constitutional demands for civil rights.
late August 2006	Polygamist Warren Steed Jeffs of San Francisco faces charges of child rape and sexual misconduct.
September 19, 2006	For denouncing the inhumane imprisonment and torture of Iraqis, Father Luis Barrios suffers police brutality at the United Nations complex in New York City.
November 3, 2006	At a Times Square recruiting station in New York City, 66 students organize a nonviolent sit-in opposing military exclusion and dishonorable discharges to gays.
	Mark David Ritscher sets himself afire in Chicago in protest of the Iraq War.
November 19, 2006	SOA Watch volunteers hold a die-in at Fort Benning, Georgia.
January 1, 2007	Code Pink members celebrate New Year's Day by mounting a peace vigil at opposite ends of the Golden Gate Bridge in San Francisco.
January 6, 2007	Cindy Sheehan visits Cuba and urges the closure of the U.S. military prison at Guantánamo.
January 10, 2007	A global protest denounces atrocities at the offshore prison in Guantánamo, Cuba.
January 27, 2007	Jane Fonda takes a public stand against President George W. Bush at a peace rally at the U.S. Navy Memorial on the National Mall in Washington, DC.
February 2007	Kathy Kelly protests the Iraq War at the office of U.S. Senator John McCain in Washington, DC.

mid-February 2007	In Gastonia, North Carolina, the re-emergence of former Ku Klux Klan Imperial Wizard Virgil Griffin presages a revolt against the hiring of Latinos.
March 11, 2007	A blockade in Tacoma, Washington, hampers the loading of 300 Stryker armored vehicles for shipping to Iraq.
March 19, 2007	Hundreds walk from the National Cathedral in Washington, DC, to the White House lawn for a candlelight peace vigil protesting the Iraq War.
spring 2007	In Seattle, Washington, Michael Ramos and Roberta Ray begin organizing an outreach of the Sanctuary Movement in the Pacific Northwest.
April 1, 2007	Martin Sheen enters custody for trespassing on a nuclear test site at Mercury, Nevada.
July 23, 2007	Cindy Sheehan holds a sit-in at the Rayburn Building on Capitol Hill after demanding the impeachment of President George W. Bush and Vice President Dick Cheney.

Acts of Conscience and Civil Disobedience

Acts of Conscience and Civil Disobedience

Target of Act/Date	Name, Occupation	Location	Act	Consequence
abandonment				
2/8/1868	Vaughan, Hester, domestic	Philadelphia	infanticide	pardoned
abortion				
1985	Andrews, Joan, activist	Broward County, FL	destroyed property	prison
7/21/2001	Stanfield, Kevin, clergy	Wichita, KS	blocked traffic	arrest
7/21/2001	Thompson, Daniel, clergy	Wichita, KS	blocked traffic	arrest
AIDS neglect				
1/1988	Banzhaf, Marion D., activist	New York City	disrupted office	
1987	Bordowitz, Gregg, filmmaker	New York City	protest	
1985	Brewer, Joe, psychotherapist	San Francisco	bootleg drugs	
1984	Corti, Jim, nurse	Los Angeles	bootleg drugs	
1984	Delaney, Martin, financier	Sausalito, CA	bootleg drugs	
5/1989	Ellis, Paul	Miami, FL	bootleg drugs	
9/1/2005	Hermes, Kris, activist	New York City	assault, incited a riot	arrest, police brutality
5/1989	Huseman, Clark, doctor's assistant	San Francisco	bootleg drugs	
1987	Kramer, Larry, playwright	New York City	protest	
5/1989	Levin, Alan, immunologist	San Francisco	bootleg drugs	
8/26/2004	Lugg, Amanda, educator	New York City	nude protest	
1/1988	Maggenti, Maria, activist	New York City	disrupted office	
5/1989	McGrath, Michael S., doctor	San Francisco	bootleg drugs	
1987	Northrop, Ann, television producer	New York City	protest	
1997	Sawyer, Eric, activist	New York City	march	
1987	Sikorowski, Mark, designer	New York City	protest	
8/26/2004	Smith, Eustacia, activist	New York City	nude protest	
3/24/1987	Staley, Peter, bond trader	New York City	sit-in	
5/1989	Waites, Lawrence, doctor	San Francisco	bootleg drugs	
1/22/1991	Weir, John, writer	New York City	disrupted television broadcast	
1987	Woodard, Ken, art director	New York City	protest	
alcohol sale and consumption				
1897	Kepley, Ada Harriet Miser, lawyer	Effingham, IL	destroyed property	fine, beaten
4/1874	Leavitt, Emily Wilder Sherman	Cincinnati, OH	obstructed a sidewalk	arrest
9/1904	McHenry, Myra Gains Warren, crusader	Hannibal, MO	destroyed property	jail
9/28/1904	McHenry, Myra Gains Warren, crusader	Wichita, KS	destroyed property	jail
9/1904	Muntz, Lydia, crusader	Hannibal, MO	destroyed property	jail
9/28/1904	Muntz, Lydia, crusader	Wichita, KS	destroyed property	jail
12/27/1900	Nation, Carry Amelia Moore, evangelist	Wichita, KS	destroyed property	jail
4/1901	Nation, Carry Amelia Moore, evangelist	Kansas City, KS	obstructed traffic	arrest

Target of Act/Date	Name, Occupation	Location	Act	Consequence
2/5/1901	Nation, Carry Amelia Moore, evangelist	McKane, KS	destroyed property	arrest
7/1901	Nation, Carry Amelia Moore, evangelist	Topeka, KS	destroyed property	jail
6/1902	Nation, Carry Amelia Moore, evangelist	Coney Island, NY	destroyed property	jail, battery
1/14/1904	Nation, Carry Amelia Moore, evangelist	Philadelphia	destroyed property	jail, battery
9/1904	Nation, Carry Amelia Moore, evangelist	Hannibal, MO	destroyed property	jail
9/28/1904	Nation, Carry Amelia Moore, evangelist	Wichita, KS	destroyed property	jail
9/1904	Wilhoite, Lucy, crusader	Hannibal, MO	destroyed property	jail
9/28/1904	Wilhoite, Lucy, crusader	Wichita, KS	destroyed property	jail

alien refugee abuse

Target of Act/Date	Name, Occupation	Location	Act	Consequence
1980s	Aguilar, María del Socorro Pardo de	Tucson, AZ	alien asylum, transport	charged
5/9/2007	Bobo, Kim, activist	Chicago	alien asylum	
3/24/1982	Carr, Nan	Tucson, AZ	alien asylum	
1980s	Clark, Anthony, priest	Tucson, AZ	alien asylum, transport	
5/4/1981	Corbett, James A., rancher	Tucson, AZ	alien asylum, transport	
5/4/1981	Corbett, Patricia Collins, rancher	Tucson, AZ	alien asylum, transport	
2007	Coskey, Laurie, rabbi	San Diego, CA	alien asylum	
4/13/1984	Elder, John A.	Tucson, AZ	alien asylum, transport	
1980s	Elford, Ricardo, priest	Tucson, AZ	alien asylum, transport	
1980s	Espinosa, Mary Kay Dean, teacher	Tucson, AZ	alien asylum, transport	
2007	Estrada, Richard, priest	Los Angeles	alien asylum	
3/24/1982	Fife, John M., clergy	Tucson, AZ	alien asylum, recruiting	
1980s	Fitzpatrick, John Joseph, archbishop	Brownsville, TX	alien asylum	
1980s	Flaherty, Katherine	Tucson, AZ	alien asylum	
1980s	Hutchinson, Peggy, activist	Tucson, AZ	alien asylum, transport	
1982	Kennon, Ken, clergy	Tucson, AZ	alien asylum, transport	
1980s	LeWin, Wendy, activist	Tucson, AZ	alien asylum, transport	
1980s	MacDonald, Nena, activist	Tucson, AZ	alien asylum, transport	
3/24/1982	Mann, Hilda	Tucson, AZ	alien asylum	
2/1984	Merkt, Stacy Lynn	Brownsville, TX	alien asylum	prison
2/1984	Muhlenkamp, Diane, nun	Brownsville, TX	alien asylum	prison
1980s	Nicgorski, Darlene, nun	Tucson, AZ	alien asylum, transport	
1981–1990	Olivares, Luis, priest	Los Angeles	abetted alien asylum	
1980s	Priester, Anna, nun	Tucson, AZ	alien asylum, transport	charged
1980s	Quiñones, Ramón Dagoberto, priest	Tucson, AZ	alien asylum, transport	
4/2007	Ramos, Michael	Seattle	alien asylum	
4/2007	Ray, Roberta	Seattle	alien asylum	
1986	Romagoza, Juan, surgeon	Washington, DC	alien rescue	
5/9/2007	Ruiz, Juan Carlos, priest	New York City	alien rescue	
5/9/2007	Salvatierra, Alexia, clergy	Los Angeles	alien rescue	
5/9/2007	Swilley, Reginald, clergy	San Jose, CA	alien rescue	
1987	Ufford-Chase, Rick, missionary	Tucson, AZ	alien asylum, transport	
1/2006	Velásquez, David, priest	Maywood, CA	alien asylum	
1980s	Waddell, Mary, nun	Tucson, AZ	alien asylum, transport	charged

Target of Act/Date	Name, Occupation	Location	Act	Consequence
1983	Weakland, Rembert, archbishop	Milwaukee, WI	alien asylum, transport	
1980s	Weizenbaum, Joseph, rabbi	Tucson, AZ	alien asylum, transport	
1980s	Willis-Conger, Philip, activist	Tucson, AZ	alien asylum, transport	

alien refugees

Target of Act/Date	Name, Occupation	Location	Act	Consequence
1/1/2005	Gilchrist, Jim, activist	Tombstone, AZ	paramilitary	
1/1/2005	Simcox, Chris, activist	Tombstone, AZ	paramilitary	

animal rights

Target of Act/Date	Name, Occupation	Location	Act	Consequence
1982	Cate, Dexter, teacher	Kaho'Olawe, HI	trespass	
12/2005	Cho, Michelle Y., activist	Providence, RI	public nudity	arrest
1/18/2006	Cho, Michelle Y., activist	Minneapolis, MN	public nudity	arrest
1/20/2006	Cho, Michelle Y., activist	Madison, WI	public nudity	arrest
2/28/1992	Coronado, Rodney Adam, activist	East Lansing, MI	arson, looting	lawsuit
12/2/2004	Coronado, Rodney Adam, activist	Sabino Canyon, AZ	destroyed property	
12/2/2004	Crozier, Matthew, activist	Sabino Canyon, AZ	destroyed property	
8/2005	Deardorff, Eric, activist	Peoria, IL	public nudity	arrest
1/2000	Ferdin, Pamelyn, nurse	Woodland Hills, CA	contraband weapon	jail
1982	Leaman, Denver, agronomist	Kaho'Olawe, HI	trespass	
5/29/1977	LeVasseur, Kenneth W., scientist	Honolulu, HI	freed animals	
6/2001	Lieberman, Cynthia, activist	Shreveport, LA	mockery	arrest
1980	Newkirk, Ingrid, activist	Norfolk, VA	protest	
1980	Pacheco, Alex, student	Norfolk, VA	protest	
10/1981	Pacheco, Alex, student	Silver Spring, MD	spying	death threats
10/24/1997	Samuel, Justin Clayton, activist	Sheboygan, MI	freed animals	
8/2005	Sehgal, Melissa, activist	Peoria, IL	public nudity	arrest
5/29/1977	Sipman, Steve, scientist	Honolulu, HI	freed animals	
12/2005	Valladolid, Brandi, activist	Providence, RI	public nudity	arrest
10/24/1997	Young, Peter Daniel, activist	Sheboygan, MI	freed animals	

anti-abortion laws

Target of Act/Date	Name, Occupation	Location	Act	Consequence
1893	Chase, Sarah Blakeslee, doctor	New York City	lectured, sold birth control devices	prison
10/2/1973	Edelin, Kenneth C., doctor	Boston	manslaughter	tried
1970	Hodgson, Jane, doctor	St. Paul, MN	performed abortion	lost license
7/19/2001	Klein, Joshua	Wichita, KS	battery	arrest
1878	Lohman, Ann Trow, activist	New York City	performed abortion	suicide
7/19/2001	Rose, Karen	Wichita, KS	battery	arrest

apartheid

Target of Act/Date	Name, Occupation	Location	Act	Consequence
11/24/1984	Berry, Mary Frances, politician	Washington, DC	unlawful entry	handcuffed, arrest
11/24/1984	Conyers, John, politician	Washington, DC	unlawful entry	
11/24/1984	Dellums, Ronald Verni, politician	Washington, DC	unlawful entry	

Target of Act/Date	Name, Occupation	Location	Act	Consequence
11/24/1984	Fauntroy, Walter Edward, clergy	Washington, DC	unlawful entry	handcuffed, arrest
11/24/1984	Hayes, Charles Arthur, politician	Washington, DC	unlawful entry	
11/24/1984	Lowery, Joseph Echols, clergy	Washington, DC	unlawful entry	
11/24/1984	Norton, Eleanor Holmes, politician	Washington, DC	unlawful entry	
11/24/1984	Rangel, Charles Bernard, politician	Washington, DC	unlawful entry	
11/24/1984	Robinson, Randall, politician	Washington, DC	unlawful entry	handcuffed, arrest

Asian workers

1877	Kearney, Denis, labor organizer	San Francisco	arson, assault	

biological warfare

1971	Carner, Lucy Perkins, sociologist	Fort Detrick, MD	blocked a gate	
7/1/1959	Scott, Lawrence, activist	Fort Detrick, MD	sit-in	
1971	Scott, Lawrence, activist	Fort Detrick, MD	blocked a gate	
7/1/1959	Scott, Viola Maria Standley, activist	Fort Detrick, MD	sit-in	
7/1/1959	Walker, Charles C., activist	Fort Detrick, MD	sit-in	

black rights

12/24/1864	Crowe, James Rankin, law student	Sheffield, AL	paramilitary	
11/3/1979	Dawson, Edward, activist	Greensboro, NC	paramilitary, spy	
1974	Duke, David Ernest, activist	Lafayette, LA	mail and tax fraud	prison
1920	Effinger, Virgil Hubert, activist	Lima, OH	anti-Semitic leader	
2/2007	Fincher, Edward, activist	Gastonia, NC	paramilitary officer	
12/24/1864	Forrest, Nathan Bedford, general	Chapel Hill, TN	paramilitary leader	
12/24/1864	Gordon, George Washington, general	Pulaski, TN	paramilitary organizer	
2/2007	Griffin, Virgil, activist	Gastonia, NC	anti-Latino leader	
11/3/1979	Hennis, E.H., activist	Greensboro, NC	paramilitary spy	
12/24/1864	Jones, J. Calvin, musician	Pulaski, TN	paramilitary	
12/24/1864	Kennedy, John B., lawyer	Lawrenceburg, TN	paramilitary	
12/24/1864	Lester, John Calhoun, lawyer	Giles, TN	paramilitary	
12/24/1864	McCord, Frank Owen, editor	Moulton, AL	paramilitary	
12/24/1864	Reed, Richard Robert, lawyer	Giles, TN	paramilitary	
1920	Shepard, William Jacob, activist	Bellaire, OH	paramilitary leader	
1915	Simmons, William Joseph	Stone Mountain, GA	paramilitary organizer	

bureaucracy, colonial

1767	Calhoun, Patrick, peace officer	Abbeville, SC	paramilitary	
7/1768	Gibson, Gideon, farmer, builder	Liberty County, SC	paramilitary leader	
5/1769	Gilbert, Jonathan, peace officer	Beaverdam Creek, SC	paramilitary	
1767	Kirkland, Moses, soldier	Abbeville, SC	paramilitary	
5/1769	Musgrove, John, planter	Saluda, SC	paramilitary	

Target of Act/Date	Name, Occupation	Location	Act	Consequence

busing

9/1971	Miles, Robert, farmer, evangelist	Pontiac, MI	firebombing	prison

campaign finance corruption

10/26/1999	Corner, Betsy, activist	Washington, DC	rally, protest banner	arrest
10/26/1999	Crowe, Frances, activist	Washington, DC	rally, protest banner	arrest
10/26/1999	Kehler, Randy, activist	Washington, DC	rally, protest banner	arrest
11/15/1999	Kehler, Randy, activist	Boston	sit-in	

child labor

1894	Jones, Mary "Mother," labor organizer	Birmingham, AL	protest	
1903	Jones, Mary "Mother," labor organizer	Kensington, PA	public march	

Civil War

1861	Barnard, Vincent S., botanist	Kennett Square, PA	refused to serve	scorn
1860s	Benedict, Judson D., clergy	Aurora, NY	refused to serve	prison
1863–1865	Carrière, Hilaire	Bois Mallet, LA	refused to serve	shot
1863–1865	Carrière, Ozémé	Bois Mallet, LA	refused to serve	shot
1863–1865	Carrière, Ursin	Bois Mallet, LA	refused to serve	shot
1863	Conway, Moncure, clergy	Falmouth, VA	refused to serve	exile
1863	Dakin, Peter, farmer	Ferrisburg, VT	refused to serve	stockade, torture
1861–1863	Dobbins, Jesse Virgil, farmer	Yadkin County, NC	refused to serve	fled
1861–1863	Dobbins, William, farmer	Yadkin County, NC	refused to serve	fled
1861–1863	Eads, Harvey L., bishop	South Union, KY	protest	
1861–1863	Guillory, Martin	Bois Mallet, LA	refused to serve	shot
1863	Hockett, Himelius Mendenhall, blacksmith	Guilford, NC	refused to serve	torture
1863	Hockett, Jesse Davis, blacksmith	Guilford, NC	refused to serve	torture
1863	Hockett, William B., blacksmith	Guilford, NC	refused to serve	torture
1863	Laughlin, Seth Wade	Randolph, NC	refused to serve	beaten to death
7/21/1863	Love, Alfred Henry, merchant	Philadelphia	refused to profiteer	lost business
1863	Macomber, Lindley M., nurseryman	Grande Isle, VT	refused to serve	stockade, torture
1863	Macon, Gideon, farmer	Concord, NC	refused to serve	threat of hanging
1863	Macy, Jesse, author	Knightstown, IN	refused to serve	forced service
1860s	Moore, Rachel W., nurse	Philadelphia	protest	threats
1863	Pratt, John Wesley	Tyler, WV	refused to serve	forced service
7/13/1863	Pringle, Cyrus Guernsey, diarist	Charlotte, VT	refused to serve	stockade, torture
1860s	Prouty, Lorenzo D., industrialist	Shirley, MA	refused to serve	
1860s	Prouty, Nathan Converse, farmer	Shirley, MA	refused to serve	guardhouse
1861–1863	Rankin, John N.	South Union, KY	protest	
1863–1865	Saunier, Carmelite Carrière	Bois Mallet, LA	abetted draft evaders	shot
1863	Smedley, Edwin	Philadelphia	refused to serve	forced march
1863	Smedley, William H.	Philadelphia	refused to serve	forced march
1863–1865	Stevens, William Byrd, clerk	Montpelier, VT	refused to serve	

Target of Act/Date	Name, Occupation	Location	Act	Consequence
1863	Swift, Henry D.	South Dedham, MA	refused to serve	stockade, torture
1860s	Taber, Horace S.	Temple, NH	refused to serve	forced service
5/1863	Vallandigham, Clement Laird, congressman	Dayton, OH	refused to serve	prison
1860s	Weld, Charles Stewart	Suffolk, MA	refused to serve	humiliation

colonial emancipation

7/1780	Darrow, David, soldier, missionary	Albany, NY	loyalty to England	jail
7/1780	Hammond, Hezekiah, farmer	Albany, NY	loyalty to England	jail
7/1780	Harlow, Calvin, clergy	Albany, NY	loyalty to England	jail
7/1780	Hocknell, John, landowner	Albany, NY	loyalty to England	jail
7/1780	Lee, Ann, prophet	Albany, NY	loyalty to England	jail, threats
7/1780	Lee, William, blacksmith	Albany, NY	loyalty to England	jail
7/1780	Meachum, Joseph, Jr., clergy	Albany, NY	loyalty to England	jail
7/1780	Partington, Mary, missionary	Albany, NY	loyalty to England	jail
7/1780	Pratt, Joel	Albany, NY	loyalty to England	jail
7/1780	Whittaker, James, disciple	Albany, NY	loyalty to England	jail
1774	Wright, Zadock	Canterbury, NH	loyalty to England	jail

colonial taxation

8/1765	Adams, John, lawyer	Boston	paramilitary organizer	
8/14/1769	Adams, John, lawyer	Boston	paramilitary	
8/1765	Adams, Samuel, lawyer	Boston	paramilitary	
12/16/1773	Adams, Samuel, lawyer	Boston	sabotage	
1765	Adair, Robert	Baltimore	paramilitary	
1765	Aisquith, William	Baltimore	paramilitary	
12/16/1773	Akeley, Francis	Boston	sabotage	
11/21/1772	Alexander, Alexander, teacher	Charleston, SC	paramilitary	
1765	Alexander, Robert	Baltimore	paramilitary	
5/9/1771	Alexander, William, farmer	Rocky River, NC	spying	
1765	Allen, Michael	Baltimore	paramilitary	
6/9/1772	Allen, Paul, merchant	Providence, RI	arson, looted	
1765	Allen, William, ex-mayor	Philadelphia	propagandist	
2/1765	Allicocke, Joseph, provisioner	New York City	paramilitary	
12/16/1755	Armitt, John, cooper	Philadelphia	protest	
11/21/1772	Ash, Cato, carpenter	Charleston, SC	paramilitary	
1765	Ashe, John Baptiste, assemblyman	Wilmington, NC	underground leader	
5/9/1771	Ashmore, James Samuel, farmer	Rocky River, NC	spying	
8/1765	Avery, John, clockmaker	Boston	paramilitary	
7/4/1774	Backus, Ebenezer, merchant	Windham, CT	harassment	
1765	Baker, William	Baltimore	paramilitary	
2/1765	Bancker, Flores, surveyor	New York City	paramilitary	
12/16/1773	Barber, Nathaniel, merchant	Boston	sabotage	
10/25/1774	Barker, Penelope	Edenton, NC	denounced British goods	
11/21/1772	Barlow, J., saddler	Charleston, SC	paramilitary	

Target of Act/Date	Name, Occupation	Location	Act	Consequence
12/16/1773	Barnard, Samuel	Boston	sabotage	
12/16/1755	Bartram, James, carpenter	Philadelphia	sabotage	
12/16/1773	Bass, Henry, merchant	Boston	sabotage	
12/16/1773	Bassett, Joseph	Boston	sabotage	
12/16/1773	Bates, Edward	Boston	sabotage	
1765	Bayard, John Bubenheim, merchant, statesman	Philadelphia	protest	
12/16/1773	Beals, Adam, Jr.	Boston	sabotage	
11/21/1772	Beekman, Bernard, plumber	Charleston, SC	paramilitary	
11/21/1772	Berwick, Simon, Jr., cobbler	Charleston, SC	paramilitary	
7/4/1774	Bissell, Hezekiah, lawyer	Windham, CT	intimidation	
12/16/1773	Bolter, Thomas, builder	Boston	sabotage	
11/21/1772	Bookless, Henry Y., wheelwright	Charleston, SC	paramilitary	
6/9/1772	Bowen, Ephraim, distiller	Providence, RI	arson, looted	
1765	Bowly, Daniel	Baltimore	paramilitary	
1765	Bradford, William, printer	Philadelphia	propagandist	
12/16/1773	Bradlee, Ann Dunlap, housewife	Boston	sabotage	
12/16/1773	Bradlee, David	Boston	sabotage	
12/16/1773	Bradlee, James	Boston	sabotage	
12/16/1773	Bradlee, Josiah	Boston	sabotage	
8/1765	Bradlee, Nathaniel, carpenter	Boston	paramilitary	
12/16/1773	Bradlee, Nathaniel, carpenter	Boston	sabotage	
12/16/1773	Bradlee, Thomas	Boston	sabotage	
12/16/1773	Brewer, James, pumpmaker	Boston	sabotage	
6/9/1772	Briggs, Aaron, slave	Providence, RI	arson, looted	
6/9/1772	Brown, Abial	Providence, RI	arson, looted	
11/21/1772	Brown, James, housewright	Charleston, SC	paramilitary	
6/9/1772	Brown, John	Providence, RI	arson, looted	
12/16/1773	Brown, John	Boston	sabotage	
6/9/1772	Brown, Joseph, merchant	Providence, RI	arson, looted	
12/16/1773	Brown, Seth Ingersoll, carpenter	Boston	sabotage	
6/19/1771	Brown, William	Hillsborough, NC	paramilitary	
12/16/1773	Bruse, Stephen, merchant	Boston	sabotage	
2/1765	Brush, Thomas, landowner	Huntington, NY	paramilitary	
11/4/1765	Bryan, Jonathan, planter	Savannah, GA	paramilitary	
9/12/1769	Bryan, Jonathan, planter	Savannah, GA	boycott	
1765	Buchanan, Archibald	Baltimore	paramilitary	
1765	Buchanan, William	Baltimore	paramilitary	
6/9/1772	Bucklin, Joseph, restaurateur	Providence, RI	arson, looted	
11/4/1765	Bulloch, Archibald	Savannah, GA	backer	
3/19/1766	Burbank, Silas, soldier	Scarborough, ME	rifled a residence	
1765	Burton, Benjamin	York, ME	led protest	
12/16/1773	Burton, Benjamin	Boston	sabotage	
1765	Butler, Zebulon, soldier	Norwich, CT	paramilitary	
1765	Calhoun, James	Baltimore	paramilitary	

Target of Act/Date	Name, Occupation	Location	Act	Consequence
11/21/1772	Calvert, John, clerk	Charleston, SC	paramilitary	
12/16/1773	Campbell, Nicholas, sailor	Boston	sabotage	
11/21/1772	Cannon, Daniel, carpenter	Charleston, SC	paramilitary	
12/16/1773	Carleton, George	Boston	sabotage	
10/19/1774	Carroll, Charles, lawyer	Annapolis, MD	arson	
5/9/1771	Caruthers, Robert, farmer	Rocky River, NC	sabotage	
11/1774	Cary, Archibald	Williamsburg, VA	intimidation	
2/1765	Chambers, Rowland	Oyster Bay, NY	paramilitary	
1765	Chamier, Daniel	Baltimore	paramilitary	
3/1/1766	Chase, Samuel, lawyer	Annapolis, MD	denounced poll tax	
3/8/1766	Chase, Thomas, clergy	Baltimore	paramilitary, orator	
12/16/1773	Chase, Thomas, distiller	Boston	sabotage	
12/16/1773	Child, Nathaniel	Boston	sabotage	
12/16/1773	Clark, Jonathan, merchant	Boston	sabotage	
12/16/1773	Clarke, Benjamin, cooper	Boston	sabotage	
2/22/1770	Clarke, Charity	Marlborough, MA	funeral procession	
1765	Clemm, William	Baltimore	paramilitary	
12/16/1773	Cochran, John	Boston	sabotage	
5/9/1771	Cockerham, Benjamin	Rocky River, NC	sabotage	
2/1765	Colden, Alexander, surveyor	New York City	paramilitary	
11/21/1772	Coleman, Thomas, upholsterer	Charleston, SC	paramilitary	
12/16/1773	Colesworthy, Gilbert	Boston	sabotage	
12/16/1773	Collidge, S.	Boston	sabotage	
12/16/1773	Collier, Gershom (or Gersham)	Boston	sabotage	
12/16/1773	Collson, Adam, leather worker	Boston	sabotage	
12/16/1773	Condy, James Foster, bookseller	Boston	sabotage	
2/1765	Conklin, Cornelius, soldier	Huntington, NY	paramilitary	
12/16/1773	Coolidge, Daniel	Boston	sabotage	
12/16/1773	Coolidge, Joseph	Boston	sabotage	
12/16/1773	Coolidge, Samuel	Boston	sabotage	
12/16/1773	Cooper, Samuel, cooper	Boston	sabotage	
1765	Courtney, Hercules	Baltimore	paramilitary	
1765	Cox, James	Baltimore	paramilitary	
12/16/1773	Cox, William	Boston	sabotage	
12/16/1773	Crafts, Thomas, Jr.	Boston	sabotage	
12/16/1773	Crane, John, carpenter	Boston	sabotage	
1765	Cresap, Thomas, frontiersman	Oldtown, MD	paramilitary organizer	
12/16/1773	Crockett	Boston	sabotage	
3/31/1766	Curle, William Roscoe Wilson	Norfolk, VA	paramilitary organizer	
12/16/1773	Curtis, Obadiah	Boston	sabotage	
8/1765	Cushing, Thomas, politician	Boston	informant	
8/1765	Cutt, Samuel, merchant	Portsmouth, NH	paramilitary	
1765	Cuyler, Jane Latouche	Savannah, GA	paramilitary host	
12/16/1773	Dana, Thomas, Jr.	Boston	sabotage	
8/1765	Davenport, John	Portsmouth, NH	paramilitary	

Target of Act/Date	Name, Occupation	Location	Act	Consequence
5/9/1771	Davis, Robert, farmer	Rocky River, NC	sabotage	
12/16/1773	Davis, Robert, importer	Boston	sabotage	
8/1765	Daws, Tom, brickmason	Boston	paramilitary	
12/16/1773	DeCarteret, John	Boston	sabotage	
12/16/1773	Decker, David	Boston	sabotage	
2/1765	Delancey, James, aristocrat	New York City	paramilitary	
1770	Delancey, James, aristocrat	New York City	paramilitary organizer	
1765	Dever, John	Baltimore	paramilitary	
1768	Dickinson, John, composer	Talbot, MD	paramilitary	
12/16/1773	Dickman, John	Boston	sabotage	
11/21/1772	Dill, Joseph, carpenter	Charleston, SC	paramilitary	
12/16/1773	Dolbeare, Edward, cooper	Boston	sabotage	
12/16/1773	Dolbeare, Samuel	Boston	sabotage	
2/1765	Dow, Volkert P.	Albany, NY	paramilitary	
7/25/1768	Downer, Silas	Providence, RI	demonstration	
6/9/1772	Dunn, Samuel	Providence, RI	arson, looted	
9/19/1765	Durkee, John, soldier	Windham, CT	commander	
12/16/1773	Duton, George	Boston	sabotage	
1765	Duvall, George	Baltimore	paramilitary	
12/16/1773	Dyar, John, Jr.	Boston	sabotage	
1765	Dyer, Eliphalet, lawyer	Norwich, CT	paramilitary recruiter	
6/9/1772	Easterbrooks, Abe	Providence, RI	arson, looted	
6/9/1772	Easterbrooks, Nathaniel	Providence, RI	arson, looted	
12/16/1773	Eaton, Joseph, hatter	Boston	sabotage	
12/16/1773	Eckley, Joseph Eayres, barber	Boston	sabotage	
8/1765	Edes, Benjamin, publisher, printer	Boston	paramilitary	
12/16/1773	Edes, Benjamin, publisher, printer	Boston	sabotage	
4/13/1766	Edes, Thomas, printer	Boston	delivered messages	
11/21/1772	Edwards, William, saddler	Charleston, SC	paramilitary	
11/22/1774	Elmer, Ebenezer	Greenwich, NJ	destroyed tea	
12/16/1773	Etheridge, George	Boston	sabotage	
12/16/1773	Etheridge, William, mason	Boston	sabotage	
12/16/1773	Fenno, Samuel, builder	Boston	sabotage	
11/21/1772	Field, William, carver	Charleston, SC	paramilitary	
11/22/1774	Fithian, Philip Vickers, clergy	Greenwich, NJ	destroyed tea	
11/21/1772	Flagg, George, painter	Charleston, SC	paramilitary	prison
2/1765	Fonda, Jelles Douwe, judge	Albany, NY	paramilitary	
1765	Foote, Abigail, diarist	Colchester, CT	paramilitary supporter	
2/22/1770	Foote, Betsy	Marlborough, MA	funeral procession	
6/12/1775	Foster, Benjamin	Machias, ME	seized a ship	
12/16/1773	Foster, Samuel	Boston	sabotage	
12/16/1773	Fracker, Thomas	Boston	sabotage	
1765	Franciscus, George	Baltimore	paramilitary	
1768	Franklin, Benjamin, publisher	Philadelphia	propaganda	

Target of Act/Date	Name, Occupation	Location	Act	Consequence
12/16/1773	Frothingham, Nathaniel, Jr., coachmaker	Boston	sabotage	
1766	Frye, Eleanor	East Greenwich, RI	paramilitary organizer	
11/21/1772	Fullerton, John, carpenter	Charleston, SC	paramilitary	
12/16/1773	Fulton, John	Boston	sabotage	
12/16/1773	Fulton, Sarah Bradlee	Boston	abetted sabotage	
8/1765	Gadsden, Christopher, merchant	Charleston, SC	paramilitary organizer	
11/1/1765	Gadsden, Christopher, merchant	Charleston, SC	paramilitary organizer	
11/21/1772	Gadsden, Christopher, merchant	Charleston, SC	street patrol leader	prison
8/1765	Gains, George	Portsmouth, NH	paramilitary	
12/16/1773	Gammell, John, carpenter	Boston	sabotage	
12/16/1773	Gay, Eliazar	Boston	sabotage	
12/16/1773	Gerrish, Thomas	Boston	sabotage	
12/16/1773	Gill, John, publisher	Boston	sabotage	
6/9/1772	Godfrey, Caleb, slaver	Providence, RI	arson, looted	
6/9/1772	Godfrey, Samuel, privateer	Providence, RI	arson, looted	
12/16/1773	Gore, Samuel, housepainter	Boston	sabotage	
12/16/1773	Grant, Moses, upholsterer	Boston	sabotage	
12/16/1773	Greene, Nathaniel	Boston	sabotage	
6/9/1772	Greene, Rufus, Jr., shipman	Providence, RI	arson, looted	
12/16/1773	Greenleaf, John	Boston	sabotage	
6/9/1772	Greenwood, John, artist	Providence, RI	arson, looted	
1765	Griest, Isaac	Baltimore	paramilitary	
1765	Griffith, Benjamin	Baltimore	paramilitary	
1768	Griffits, Hannah, poet	Philadelphia	paramilitary	
1765	Griswold, Matthew, lawyer	Lyme, CT	paramilitary organizer	
12/16/1773	Guy, Timothy	Boston	sabotage	
5/9/1771	Hadley, Joshua, soldier	Rocky River, NC	sabotage	
1775	Hadley, Joshua, soldier	Fayetteville, NC	paramilitary organizer	
1765	Hall, Caleb	Baltimore	paramilitary	
11/21/1772	Hall, John, coachmaker	Charleston, SC	paramilitary	
11/21/1772	Hall, William, carpenter	Charleston, SC	paramilitary	
1770	Hamilton, Alexander, student	New York City	spying	
4/22/1774	Hamilton, Alexander, student	New York City	spying, destroyed tea	
6/9/1772	Hammond, Benjamin, caulker	Providence, RI	arson, looted	
12/16/1773	Hammond, Samuel, farmer	Boston	sabotage	
8/1765	Hancock, John, merchant-trader	Boston	paramilitary	
12/16/1773	Hancock, John, merchant	Boston	sabotage	
1765	Harnett, Cornelius, Jr., merchant	Wilmington, NC	paramilitary organizer	
2/19/1766	Harnett, Cornelius, Jr., merchant	Brunswick, NC	burned an effigy, reopened the port	
4/12/1770	Harnett, Cornelius, Jr., merchant	Brunswick, NC	paramilitary leader	
12/16/1773	Harrington, Peter	Boston	sabotage	
6/9/1772	Harris, Joseph	Providence, RI	arson, looted	
1765	Harvey, Benjamin, frontiersman	Norwich, CT	paramilitary	

Target of Act/Date	Name, Occupation	Location	Act	Consequence
12/16/1773	Haskins, William	Boston	sabotage	
11/21/1772	Hawes, Benjamin, painter	Charleston, SC	paramilitary	
12/16/1773	Hendley, William, mason	Boston	sabotage	
8/1765	Hendrickson, Daniel	Freehold, NJ	paramilitary raider	
8/1765	Henry, Patrick, orator, politician	Red Hill, VA	spokesman	
2/1765	Henry, Robert, cloth dealer	Albany, NY	paramilitary	
12/16/1773	Hewes, George R.T., cobbler	Boston	sabotage	
12/16/1773	Hicks, John	Boston	sabotage	
2/1765	Hobart, John Sloss, stockman	Huntington, NY	paramilitary	
12/16/1773	Hobbs, Samuel, tanner	Boston	sabotage	
1765	Hollingsworth, Stephen	Baltimore	paramilitary	
1760–1770s	Holt, John, publisher	New York City	propaganda	
12/16/1773	Hooten, John, oarmaker	Boston	sabotage	
1765	Hopkins, Gerard	Baltimore	paramilitary	
6/9/1772	Hopkins, John B., shipmaster	Providence, RI	arson, looted	
12/16/1773	Horton, Elisha	Boston	sabotage	
12/16/1773	Houghton, Elijah	Boston	sabotage	
11/4/1765	Houstoun, John, lawyer	Savannah, GA	paramilitary organizer	
5/1766	Howard, Richard	Huntington, NY	paramilitary host	
11/21/1772	Howard, Robert, carpenter	Charleston, SC	paramilitary	
12/16/1773	Howard, Samuel, shipwright	Boston	sabotage	
12/16/1773	Howe, Edward Compton, ropemaker	Boston	sabotage	
2/1765	Hughes, Hugh, state quartermaster	New York City	paramilitary	
12/16/1773	Hunnewell, Jonathan, child	Boston	sabotage	
12/16/1773	Hunnewell, Richard, mason	Boston	sabotage	
12/16/1773	Hunnewell, Richard, Jr.	Boston	sabotage	
12/16/1773	Hunstable, Thomas	Boston	sabotage	
12/16/1773	Hunt, Abraham, wine merchant	Boston	sabotage	
10/1765	Hunter, James, orator	Brunswick, NC	paramilitary organizer	
fall 1765	Huntington, Jedediah, soldier	Norwich, CT	paramilitary	
8/1765	Huntington, Samuel, lawyer	Norwich, CT	burned tea	
7/4/1774	Huntington, Simeon	Windham, CT	harassment	
10/1765	Husband, Herman, tractarian	Brunswick, NC	paramilitary organizer	
12/16/1773	Ingersoll, Daniel, builder	Boston	sabotage	
6/9/1772	Jacobs, Justin	Providence, RI	arson, looted	
12/16/1773	Jameson, Charles, child	Boston	sabotage	
12/16/1773	Jameson, Robert	Boston	sabotage	
6/9/1772	Jencks, Joseph	Providence, RI	arson, looted	
8/1765	Johnson, Stephen, clergy	Lyme, CT	paramilitary organizer	
11/21/1772	Johnson, William, ironworker	Charleston, SC	paramilitary	prison
11/4/1765	Jones, Noble Wimberley, politician	Savannah, GA	backer	
11/21/1772	Jones, Robert, saddler	Charleston, SC	paramilitary	
12/16/1773	Joy, Jared	Boston	sabotage	
1765	Keener, Melchior	Baltimore	paramilitary	
1773	Kelley, Moses, sheriff	Goffstown, NH	paramilitary host	

Target of Act/Date	Name, Occupation	Location	Act	Consequence
2/1765	Ketcham, John, cobbler	New York City	paramilitary	
10/31/1765	Ketcham, John, cobbler	New York City	threats	
6/9/1772	Kilton, John Jenckes, privateer	Providence, RI	arson, looted	
10/25/1774	King, Elizabeth	Edenton, NC	paramilitary host	
6/9/1772	Kinnicut, Hezekiah, soldier	Providence, RI	arson, looted	
12/16/1773	Kinnison, David, soldier, farmer	Boston	sabotage	
2/1765	Laight, Edward, importer	New York City	paramilitary	
2/1765	Lamb, John, merchant, tractarian	New York City	paramilitary	
12/14/1774	Langdon, John	Portsmouth, NH	paramilitary raider	
8/1765	Langdon, Samuel, college president	Portsmouth, NH	paramilitary leader	
7/4/1774	Larrabee, Timothy, lawyer	Windham, CT	intimidation	
12/16/1773	Lash, Robert	Boston	sabotage	
7/4/1774	Lathrop, Benjamin, blacksmith	Windham, CT	intimidation	
11/21/1772	Laughton, John, coachmaker	Charleston, SC	paramilitary	
11/21/1772	Laughton, William, tailor	Charleston, SC	paramilitary	
1766	Lawton, Mary Easton	Newport, RI	paramilitary host	
1766	Lawton, Robert	Newport, RI	paramilitary host	
12/16/1773	Learned, Amariah	Boston	sabotage	
11/21/1772	Lebby, Nathaniel, carpenter	Charleston, SC	paramilitary	
9/19/1765	Ledlie, Hugh, merchant	New London, CT	backer	
12/16/1773	Lee, Joseph, merchant	Boston	sabotage	
12/16/1773	Lee, Nathaniel	Boston	sabotage	
9/1765	Lee, Richard Henry, peace officer	Williamsburg, VA	protest	
3/1/1766	Lendrum, Andrew, clergy	Annapolis, MD	paramilitary leader	
1765	Leverly, George	Baltimore	paramilitary	
1765	Levington, Aaron	Baltimore	paramilitary	
12/16/1773	Lincoln, Amos, builder	Boston	sabotage	
1765	Lindenberger, George Ernst	Baltimore	paramilitary	
6/9/1772	Lindsey, Benjamin, sea captain	Newport, RI	sabotage	
8/1765	Livingston, William, lawyer	Elizabethtown, NJ	paramilitary coordinator	
12/16/1773	Locke, John	Boston	sabotage	
11/21/1772	Lockwood, Joshua, clockmaker	Charleston, SC	propaganda	
12/16/1773	Loring, Mathew, leather worker	Boston	sabotage	
12/16/1773	Lovering, Joseph, apprentice	Boston	sabotage	
12/16/1773	Ludden, Joseph	Boston	sabotage	
6/9/1772	Luther, Abner	Providence, RI	arson, looted	
1765	Lux, William	Baltimore	paramilitary	
12/16/1773	Lyon, David	Boston	sabotage	
1765	Lyon, William	Baltimore	paramilitary	
11/4/1765	MacHenry, James	Savannah, GA	paramilitary host	
12/16/1773	Machin, Thomas, laborer	Boston	sabotage	
12/16/1773	Macintosh, Peter	Boston	sabotage	
8/1765	Mackintosh, Ebenezer, cobbler	Boston	rifled a residence	
12/16/1773	Mackintosh, Ebenezer, cobbler	Boston	sabotage	arrest
12/16/1773	MacNeill, Archibald	Boston	sabotage	

Target of Act/Date	Name, Occupation	Location	Act	Consequence
8/1765	Manning, Thomas	Portsmouth, NH	paramilitary	
12/16/1773	Marston, John	Boston	sabotage	
12/16/1773	Martin, John	Boston	sabotage	
12/16/1773	Martin, William P.	Boston	sabotage	
11/21/1772	Matthews, John, cobbler	Charleston, SC	paramilitary	
6/9/1772	Mawney, John, doctor	Providence, RI	arson, looted	
12/16/1773	Maxwell, Thomas	Boston	sabotage	
12/16/1773	May, John	Boston	sabotage	
11/21/1772	Mazyck, Isaac, merchant	Charleston, SC	paramilitary host	
2/1765	McDougall, Alexander, merchant, tractarian	New York City	paramilitary	
1774	McDougall, Alexander, merchant, tractarian	New York City	destroyed tea	
1765	McDougall, Hannah Roe Bostwick	New York City	paramilitary	
1765	McLane, John	Baltimore	paramilitary	
12/16/1773	Mead, John	Boston	sabotage	
12/16/1773	Mellius, Henry	Boston	sabotage	
12/16/1773	Melville, Thomas, clerk	Boston	sabotage	
1774	Mifflin, Thomas, merchant	Philadelphia	paramilitary organizer	
12/16/1773	Miller, Aaron John	Boston	sabotage	
12/16/1773	Mills, John	Boston	sabotage	
1765	Moale, Richard	Baltimore	paramilitary	
12/16/1773	Molineux, William, merchant	Boston	sabotage	
11/21/1772	Moncrief, Richard, carpenter	Charleston, SC	paramilitary	
12/16/1773	Moore, Francis	Boston	sabotage	
1768	Moore, Milcah Martha, poet	Philadelphia	propaganda	
12/16/1773	Moore, Thomas, wharfsman	Boston	sabotage	
11/21/1772	Morris, Mark, painter	Charleston, SC	propaganda	
12/16/1773	Morse, Anthony	Boston	sabotage	
2/1765	Mott, Gershom, merchant	New York City	paramilitary	
12/16/1773	Mountford, Joseph, cooper	Boston	sabotage	
2/1765	Mulligan, Hercules, haberdasher	New York City	paramilitary	
1770	Mulligan, Hercules, haberdasher	New York City	spying	
1/13/1770	Mulligan, Hercules, haberdasher	New York City	brawling	
4/22/1774	Mulligan, Hercules, haberdasher	New York City	destroyed tea	
2/1765	Mulligan, Hugh, banker, importer	New York City	paramilitary	
1770	Mulligan, Hugh, banker, importer	New York City	spying	
11/21/1772	Munclean, Peter, clerk	Charleston, SC	paramilitary	
12/16/1773	Newell, Eliphelet, barkeep	Boston	sabotage	
12/16/1773	Nicholls, Joseph	Boston	sabotage	
3/1/1766	Nicholson, Joseph Hopper	Annapolis, MD	paramilitary leader	
2/1765	Nicoll, Charles, importer	New York City	paramilitary	
11/21/1772	Nightingale, Thomas, saddler, horse breeder	Charleston, SC	paramilitary	
12/16/1773	Nowell, Samuel	Boston	sabotage	

Target of Act/Date	Name, Occupation	Location	Act	Consequence
6/12/1775	O'Brien, Dennis, lumberman	Machias, ME	seized a ship	
6/12/1775	O'Brien, Gideon, lumberman	Machias, ME	seized a ship	
6/12/1775	O'Brien, Jeremiah, lumberman	Machias, ME	seized a ship	
6/12/1775	O'Brien, John, lumberman	Machias, ME	seized a ship	
6/12/1775	O'Brien, Joseph, lumberman	Machias, ME	seized a ship	
6/12/1775	O'Brien, William, lumberman	Machias, ME	seized a ship	
6/9/1772	Olney, Simeon Hunt, barkeep	Providence, RI	arson, looted	
6/9/1772	Ormsbee, Ezra, sailor	Providence, RI	arson, looted	
8/1765	Otis, James, lawyer	Boston	organized paramilitary	
3/1/1766	Paca, William	Annapolis, MD	denunciation	
6/9/1772	Page, Benjamin, shipmaster	Providence, RI	arson, looted	
12/16/1773	Palmer, Joseph Pease	Boston	sabotage	
12/16/1773	Parker, Jonathan, farmer	Boston	sabotage	
1765	Patton, George	Baltimore	paramilitary	
12/16/1773	Payson, Joseph, builder	Boston	sabotage	
6/9/1772	Pearce, Daniel, drummer	Newport, RI	sabotage	
12/16/1773	Pearce, William, barber	Boston	sabotage	
12/16/1773	Peck, Samuel, cooper	Boston	sabotage	
8/1765	Perry, David, cobbler	Killingly, CT	burned tea	
12/16/1773	Peters, John	Boston	sabotage	
12/16/1773	Pitman, Isaac	Boston	sabotage	
12/16/1773	Pitts, Lendall, market clerk	Boston	sabotage	
12/16/1773	Pitts, Samuel	Boston	sabotage	
12/16/1773	Porter, Thomas, merchant	Boston	sabotage	
2/1765	Potter, Gilbert, doctor	Huntington, NY	paramilitary	
6/9/1772	Potter, Simeon, shipman	Providence, RI	arson, looted	
12/16/1773	Prentiss, Henry	Boston	sabotage	
12/16/1773	Prentiss, Nathaniel Surtees	Boston	sabotage	
12/16/1773	Prince, John, clergy	Boston	sabotage	
12/16/1773	Proctor, Edward, importer	Boston	sabotage	
6/19/1771	Pugh, James, gunsmith	Hillsborough, NC	paramilitary	hanged
12/16/1773	Purkitt, Henry, cooper	Boston	sabotage	
1765	Purviance, Samuel, Jr.	Baltimore	paramilitary	
9/19/1765	Putnam, Israel, soldier	Pomfret, CT	paramilitary leader	
12/16/1773	Putnam, Seth	Boston	sabotage	
2/1765	Quackenbos, Walter, lawyer	New York City	paramilitary	
12/16/1773	Quincy, Josiah, II, lawyer	Boston	sabotage	
12/16/1773	Randall, John	Boston	sabotage	
8/1765	Randolph, Peyton, politician	Williamsburg, VA	paramilitary	
12/16/1773	Reed, Joseph	Boston	sabotage	
1774	Reed, Joseph, lawyer	Philadelphia	paramilitary organizer	
8/1765	Revere, Paul, silversmith	Boston	paramilitary	
12/16/1773	Revere, Paul, silversmith	Boston	sabotage	
12/14/1774	Revere, Paul, silversmith	Portsmouth, NH	paramilitary raider	
12/16/1773	Rice, Benjamin	Boston	sabotage	

Target of Act/Date	Name, Occupation	Location	Act	Consequence
10/1773	Rice, Thomas, peace officer	Wiscasset, ME	harbor violence	
12/16/1773	Robins, Jonathan Dorby	Boston	sabotage	
2/1765	Robinson, Thomas, merchant	New York City	paramilitary	
12/16/1773	Roby, Joseph	Boston	sabotage	
11/21/1772	Rogers, Uzziah, wheelwright	Charleston, SC	paramilitary	
2/1765	Roseboom, Myndert, merchant	Albany, NY	paramilitary	
1771	Rowan, Robert, sheriff	Cumberland County, NC	paramilitary leader	
1765	Rusk, David	Baltimore	paramilitary	
12/16/1773	Russell, John, mason	Boston	sabotage	
12/16/1773	Russell, William, teacher	Boston	sabotage	
6/9/1772	Salisbury, Nathan, soldier	Providence, RI	arson, looted	
11/21/1772	Saunders, Peter, saddler	Charleston, SC	paramilitary	
1765	Savery, William	Baltimore	paramilitary	
12/16/1773	Sawtelle, Jonathan	Boston	sabotage	
12/16/1773	Sayward, George	Boston	sabotage	
2/1765	Scott, John Morin, lawyer	New York City	paramilitary	
12/16/1773	Sears, Edmund	Boston	sabotage	
2/1765	Sears, Isaac, merchant	New York City	paramilitary	
11/1/1765	Sears, Isaac, merchant	New York City	paramilitary leader	
6/1767	Sears, Isaac, merchant	New York City	raised a liberty pole	
4/1774	Sears, Isaac, merchant	New York City	closed harbor	
11/1775	Sears, Isaac, merchant	New York City	destroyed a press	jail
12/16/1773	Sessions, Robert, laborer	Boston	sabotage	
12/16/1773	Shed, Joseph, carpenter	Boston	sabotage	
11/21/1772	Sheed, George, plumber, peace officer	Charleston, SC	paramilitary	
6/9/1772	Sheldon, Christopher, merchant	Providence, RI	arson, looted	
6/9/1772	Shepard, Benjamin	Providence, RI	arson, looted	
1765	Shields, David	Baltimore	paramilitary	
1765	Simpson, Benjamin, mason	York, ME	led protest	
12/16/1773	Simpson, Benjamin, mason	Boston	sabotage	
12/16/1773	Slater, Peter, Jr., ropemaker	Boston	sabotage	
12/16/1773	Slope, Samuel	Boston	sabotage	
12/16/1773	Smith, Ephraim	Boston	sabotage	
6/9/1772	Smith, James	Providence, RI	arson, looted	
1765	Smith, John	Baltimore	paramilitary	
8/1765	Smith, Richard, Jr., lawyer	Burlington, NJ	led revolt	
6/9/1772	Smith, Turpin, shipmaster	Providence, RI	arson, looted	
1765	Smith, William	Baltimore	paramilitary	
2/1765	Sneething, Barak	Oyster Bay, NY	paramilitary	
12/16/1773	Snelling, Josiah	Boston	sabotage	
2/1765	Solomon, Haym, linguist	New York City	paramilitary	
1770	Solomon, Haym, linguist	New York City	spying	
12/16/1773	Spear, Thomas	Boston	sabotage	
1765	Spear, William	Baltimore	paramilitary	

Target of Act/Date	Name, Occupation	Location	Act	Consequence
12/16/1773	Sprague, Samuel, mason	Boston	sabotage	
12/16/1773	Spurr, John	Boston	sabotage	
12/16/1773	Starr, James	Boston	sabotage	
12/16/1773	Stearns, Phineas, blacksmith	Boston	sabotage	
1765	Sterrett, James	Baltimore	paramilitary	
1765	Sterrett, John	Baltimore	paramilitary	
12/16/1773	Stevens, Ebenezer, carpenter	Boston	sabotage	
12/16/1773	Stoddard, James	Boston	sabotage	
12/16/1773	Story, Elisha, doctor	Boston	sabotage	
8/1765	Sturges, Jonathan, lawyer	Fairfield, CT	paramilitary organizer	
12/14/1774	Sullivan, John	Portsmouth, NH	paramilitary raider	
6/9/1772	Sutton, Robert	Providence, RI	arson, looted	
12/16/1773	Swan, James, accounting clerk	Boston	sabotage	
6/9/1772	Swan, Thomas	Providence, RI	arson, looted	
11/21/1772	Swarle, Thomas, painter	Charleston, SC	paramilitary	
8/1765	Swift, Henry	Boston	paramilitary	
6/9/1772	Sylvester, Amos	Providence, RI	arson, looted	
11/21/1772	Tebout, Tunis, blacksmith	Charleston, SC	paramilitary	
7/27/1774	Telfair, Edward, politician	Savannah, GA	condemned port bill	
5/11/1775	Telfair, Edward, politician	Savannah, GA	raid	
2/1765	Ten Eyck, Abraham, merchant	Albany, NY	paramilitary treasurer	
8/1765	Thomas, Isaiah, publisher	Boston	paramilitary	
1770	Thomas, Isaiah, publisher	Boston	paramilitary	
1774	Thomson, Charles, teacher	Philadelphia	paramilitary organizer	
6/9/1772	Tillinghest, Joseph, shipmaster	Providence, RI	arson, looted	
9/28/1765	Timothy, Peter, publisher	Charleston, SC	propaganda	
7/1770	Timothy, Peter, publisher	Charleston, SC	propaganda	
7/27/1774	Tondee, Peter, barkeep	Savannah, GA	condemned port bill	
5/11/1775	Tondee, Peter, barkeep	Savannah, GA	raid	
12/16/1773	Tower, Abraham	Boston	sabotage	
2/1765	Townsend, Benjamin	Oyster Bay, NY	paramilitary	
2/1765	Townsend, George, peace officer	Oyster Bay, NY	paramilitary	
11/21/1772	Trezevant, Theodore, tailor	Charleston, SC	paramilitary	
12/16/1773	Trow, Bartholomew, Jr.	Boston	sabotage	
12/16/1773	Truman, John	Boston	sabotage	
8/1765	Trumbull, Jonathan, politician	Lebanon, CT	paramilitary recruiter	
11/21/1772	Trusler, William, butcher	Charleston, SC	paramilitary	
12/16/1773	Tucker, Benjamin, Jr.	Boston	sabotage	
8/1765	Tuckerman, Edward, baker	Boston	paramilitary	
1765	Uhler, Erasmus	Baltimore	paramilitary	
12/16/1773	Urann, Thomas, ship joiner	Boston	sabotage	
2/1765	Van Rensselaer, Jeremiah, surveyor	Albany, NY	paramilitary	
11/21/1772	Verree, Joseph, carpenter	Charleston, SC	propaganda	
11/1765	Waddell, Hugh, soldier	Wilmington, NC	seized a ship	
11/4/1766	Walton, George, lawyer	Savannah, GA	backer	

Target of Act/Date	Name, Occupation	Location	Act	Consequence
1765	Warfield, Charles Alexander	Baltimore	paramilitary	
8/1765	Warren, Joseph, doctor	Boston	paramilitary	
1/1770	Warren, Joseph, doctor	Boston	raid	
12/16/1773	Warren, Joseph, doctor	Boston	sabotage	
8/1765	Warren, Mercy Otis, playwright, upholsterer	Boston	propaganda	
7/4/1774	Warren, Nathaniel	Windham, CT	intimidation	
1765	Watson, James	York, ME	led protest	
12/16/1773	Watson, James, sea captain	Boston	sabotage	
2/1765	Weekes, George	Oyster Bay, NY	paramilitary	
2/1765	Weekes, Michael	Oyster Bay, NY	paramilitary	
1765	Wells, Cyprian	Baltimore	paramilitary	
1765	Wells, George	Baltimore	paramilitary	
12/16/1773	Wells, Henry	Boston	sabotage	
12/16/1773	Wells, Thomas	Boston	sabotage	
11/21/1772	Weyman, Edward, glass grinder	Charleston, SC	paramilitary	
4/21/1775	Weyman, Edward, glass grinder	Charleston, SC	raid	
11/15/1780	Weyman, Edward, glass grinder	Charleston, SC	raid	prison
12/16/1773	Wheeler, Josiah, builder	Boston	sabotage	
6/9/1772	Whipple, Abraham, shipmaster	Providence, RI	arson, looted	
5/9/1771	White, James, Jr.	Rocky River, NC	sabotage	
5/9/1771	White, John, Jr.	Rocky River, NC	sabotage	
12/16/1773	White, Thomas	Boston	sabotage	
5/9/1771	White, William	Rocky River, NC	sabotage	
5/9/1771	White, William, Jr.	Rocky River, NC	sabotage	
12/16/1773	Whitehead, John	Boston	sabotage	
1760s–1770s	Whiting, Daniel, barkeep	Dover, MA	paramilitary host	
2/1765	Wiley, William, merchant	New York City	paramilitary	
11/21/1772	Wilkes, John	Charleston, SC	paramilitary	
2/1765	Willett, Marinus, soldier	New York City	paramilitary	
12/16/1773	Williams, David	Boston	sabotage	
12/16/1773	Williams, Isaac	Boston	sabotage	
12/16/1773	Williams, Jeremiah, blacksmith	Boston	sabotage	
2/1765	Williams, Nathan, lawyer	Huntington, NY	paramilitary	
12/16/1773	Williams, Thomas, apprentice	Boston	sabotage	
12/16/1773	Willis, Charles	Boston	sabotage	
12/16/1773	Willis, Nathaniel, printer	Boston	sabotage	
1765	Willson, William	Baltimore	paramilitary	
2/22/1770	Winslow, Anna	Marlborough, MA	funeral procession	
1765	Winters, Elisha	Baltimore	paramilitary	
8/1765	Winthrop, Hannah Fayerweather Tolman	Cambridge, MA	propaganda	
10/1773	Wood, Abiel, merchant	Wiscasset, ME	harbor violence	
12/16/1773	Wyeth, Joshua, apprentice	Boston	sabotage	
2/1765	Young, Thomas, doctor	Albany, NY	paramilitary	

Target of Act/Date	Name, Occupation	Location	Act	Consequence
8/1765	Young, Thomas, doctor	Boston	paramilitary	
12/16/1773	Young, Thomas, doctor	Boston	sabotage	
11/21/1772	Young, Thomas, mason	Charleston, SC	paramilitary	

Comstock Act

Target of Act/Date	Name, Occupation	Location	Act	Consequence
7/1916	Allison, Van Kleek, student	New York City	birth control information	arrest
5/20/1916	Ashley, Jessie, lawyer	New York City	birth control information	arrest
1874	Bass, Morris, merchant	New York City	sold contraceptives	confiscation
12/10/1878	Bennett, DeRobigne Mortimer, publisher	New York City	birth control treatise	fine, prison at hard labor
6/7/1965	Buxton, Charles Lee, doctor	Hartford, CT	birth control information	jail, fine
10/27/1916	Byrne, Ethel Higgins, nurse	New York City	birth control information	workhouse, force-feeding
6/1878	Chase, Sarah Blakeslee, doctor	New York City	sold contraceptives	charged
11/2/1872	Claflin, Tennessee Celeste, publisher	New York City	obscenity	arrest
1902	Craddock, Ida C., writer	Chicago	birth control information	prison sentence
1928	Dennett, Mary Coffin Ware, activist	Worcester, MA	birth control information	arrest
5/20/1916	Eastman, Ida Rauh, sculptor	New York City	birth control information	arrest
1876	Farr, H. Gustavus, merchant	Indiana	sold contraceptives	arrest
10/20/1916	Goldman, Emma, lecturer	New York City	obscenity	arrest
2/23/1887	Harman, Moses, publisher	Valley Falls, KS	birth control information	jail
5/1/1890	Harman, Moses, publisher	Valley Falls, KS	birth control information	jail, fine
6/1895	Harman, Moses, publisher	Valley Falls, KS	birth control information	prison at hard labor
11/3/1877	Heywood, Angela Fiducia Tilton, feminist	Princeton, MA	mailed pamphlets	
11/3/1877	Heywood, Ezra Hervey, publisher	Boston	mailed pamphlets	prison at hard labor
12/19/1878	Heywood, Ezra Hervey, publisher	New York City	mailed pamphlets	
5/1890	Heywood, Ezra Hervey, publisher	Princeton, MA	mailed pamphlets	prison
11/3/1877	Ingersoll, Robert Green, lawyer	Princeton, MA	birth control information	arraigned
1887	Knoedler, Herman, art dealer	New York City	sold art nudes	jail, fine
2/1928	Konikow, Antoinette Kay Bucholz	Boston	birth control information	jail
1878	Lohman, Ann Trow, activist	New York City	sold contraceptives	charged
1905	MacFadden, Bernarr, fitness expert	New York City	nude photos	confiscation
3/6/1872	Mancher, Charles, doctor	New York City	sold contraceptives	charged
7/1916	Marion, Katharina Schafer, suffragist	New York City	birth control information	arrest
10/27/1916	Mindall, Fania, interpreter	New York City	birth control information	arrest
19113	Ortiz, Philippe, art dealer	New York City	displayed nudes	threat
8/6/1915	Reitman, Ben L., doctor	Portland, OR	birth control information	fine
2/11/1916	Reitman, Ben L., doctor	New York City	birth control leaflets	jail
12/12/1916	Reitman, Ben L., doctor	Cleveland, OH	birth control leaflets	jail
12/15/1916	Reitman, Ben L., doctor	Rochester, NY	birth control leaflets	arrest
2/9/1913	Sanger, Margaret Louise Higgins, nurse, publisher	New York City	birth control information	
8/1914	Sanger, Margaret Louise Higgins, nurse, publisher	New York City	birth control information	arrest, fled

Target of Act/Date	Name, Occupation	Location	Act	Consequence
10/27/1916	Sanger, Margaret Louise Higgins, nurse, publisher	New York City	birth control information	workhouse
11/1921	Sanger, Margaret Louise Higgins, nurse, publisher	New York City	birth control lecture	arrest
9/10/1915	Sanger, William, publisher	New York City	birth control information	arrest, jail
1872	Sickel, Morris, merchant	New York City	made contraceptives	jail, fine
7/1916	Smedley, Agnes, journalist, suffragist	New York City	birth control information	arrest
1878	Soule, Asa Titus, merchant	Rochester, NY	birth control information	fine
5/20/1916	Stokes, Rose Pastor, activist	New York City	birth control information	arrest
1929	Stone, Hannah Mayer, doctor	New York City	birth control information	impounded
11/2/1872	Train, George Francis, lawyer	New York City	obscenity	jail
11/1921	Winsor, Mary, orator	New York City	birth control information	arrest
11/2/1872	Woodhull, Victoria Claflin, publisher	New York City	obscenity	arrest

Cuban invasion

5/1961	Dellinger, David T., activist	Washington, DC	fast, vigil	jail, intimidation
5/1961	Steed, Bob, journalist	Washington, DC	fast, vigil	jail, intimidation

death penalty

12/25/1966	Baez, Joan, folksinger	San Quentin, CA	picket	
1/18/2005	Blair, Steven, teacher	San Quentin, CA	protest	
1/17/1997	Bonowitz, Abraham J., activist	Washington, DC	protest	intimidation
12/1/2005	Bonowitz, Abraham J., activist	Austin, TX	protest	charged
2/4/2004	Carlstadt, Hal, activist	San Quentin, CA	obstructed traffic	arrest
1658	Davis, Nicholas	Barnstable, MA	protest	
1658	Dyer, Mary Barrett, preacher	Boston	protest	
1/18/2005	Farrell, Mike, actor	San Quentin, CA	protest	
10/19/1998	Garis, Jeffrey, clergy	Scranton, PA	obstructed justice	arrest
10/31/2000	Kaufman, Sarah, student	Philadelphia	sit-in	arrest
10/31/2000	Macomber, Amanda, student	Philadelphia	sit-in	arrest
10/19/1998	Pickard, William, clergy	Scranton, PA	obstructed justice	arrest
1658	Robinson, William	Boston	protest	
2/4/2004	Romney, Hugh, activist	San Quentin, CA	obstructed traffic	arrest
2/4/2004	Sawyer, Paul, clergy	San Quentin, CA	obstructed traffic	arrest
1658	Scott, Patience, child	Providence, RI	protest	
1658	Stephenson, Marmaduke	Boston	protest	
10/31/2000	Tankel, Jared, student	Philadelphia	sit-in	arrest
2/4/2004	Vitale, Louis, priest	San Quentin, CA	obstructed traffic	arrest

debt

1787	Austin, Abigail	Berkshire County, MA	jailbreak	
1786–1787	Bardwell, Perez	Williamsburg, MA	paramilitary	
10/19/1794	Black, John	Bedford, PA	paramilitary	
10/19/1794	Bolton, Daniel	Bedford, PA	paramilitary	

Target of Act/Date	Name, Occupation	Location	Act	Consequence
10/19/1794	Bonham, William	Bedford, PA	paramilitary	
10/19/1794	Bradford, David	Bedford, PA	paramilitary	hunted by cavalry
7/1794	Bradford, William	Mingo, PA	mail theft	martial law
10/19/1794	Burnett, John	Bedford, PA	paramilitary	
10/19/1794	Burney, Thomas	Bedford, PA	paramilitary	
5/1932	Butler, Smedley Darlington, soldier	Washington, DC	paramilitary	
7/28/1932	Carlson, Eric, veteran	Washington, DC	paramilitary	killed
10/19/1794	Corbley, John, Baptist clergy	Bedford, PA	paramilitary	
10/19/1794	Crawford, William	Bedford, PA	paramilitary	
10/19/1794	Criswell, John	Bedford, PA	paramilitary	
10/19/1794	Curtis, Marmaduke	Bedford, PA	paramilitary	
10/19/1794	Hamilton, John, sheriff	Bedford, PA	paramilitary	
1791–1794	Holcroft, John, distiller	Bedford, PA	paramilitary leader	
10/19/1794	Husband, Herman, tractarian	Bedford, PA	paramilitary	died in custody
7/28/1932	Hushka, William, veteran	Washington, DC	paramilitary	killed
1894	Jones, Mary "Mother," labor organizer	Gibson, TN	protest	
10/19/1794	Kerr, James	Bedford, PA	paramilitary	
10/19/1794	Lockery, John, miller	Bedford, PA	paramilitary	
10/19/1794	Lucas, George	Bedford, PA	paramilitary	
1794	Marshall, James, soldier	Indiana County, PA	paramilitary	
7/16/1794	McFarlane, James, soldier	Allegheny, PA	paramilitary leader	shot
7/16/1794	Miller, Oliver	Allegheny, PA	paramilitary	shot
7/1794	Mitchell, John	Mingo, PA	mail theft	martial law
10/19/1794	Mounts, Caleb	Bedford, PA	paramilitary	
10/19/1794	Nye, Samuel	Bedford, PA	paramilitary	
10/19/1794	Parry, Joseph	Bedford, PA	paramilitary	
10/19/1794	Philson, Robert, soldier	Bedford, PA	paramilitary	
10/19/1794	Porter, Robert	Bedford, PA	paramilitary	
10/19/1794	Scott, Joseph	Bedford, PA	paramilitary	
10/19/1794	Sedgwick, Thomas, distiller	Bedford, PA	paramilitary	
10/19/1794	Stewart, James	Bedford, PA	paramilitary	
10/19/1794	Vigol, Philip	Bedford, PA	paramilitary	
10/19/1794	Walker, Isaac	Bedford, PA	paramilitary	
5/1932	Waters, Walter Willis, worker	Portland, OR	paramilitary	
1787	Wilcox, Polly Mansfield	Berkshire County, MA	jailbreak	
10/19/1794	Wisegarver, George	Bedford, PA	paramilitary	

draft

6/8/1918	Abbe, Cleveland, Jr., meteorologist	Washington, DC	protest	fired
2/11/1918	Ackerman, Ralph, industrialist	New Ulm, MN	protest	forced to resign
12/11/1917	Adams, Dorothy, teacher	Carson City, NV	protest	fired
6/12/1918	Albrink, Fred, highway inspector	Columbus, OH	protest	suspended
10/21/1967	Baez, Joan, folksinger	Arlington, VA	blocked an entrance	arrest
3/13/1918	Battig, Leon, teacher	Ottumwa, IA	protest	painted yellow

Target of Act/Date	Name, Occupation	Location	Act	Consequence
12/27/1917	Baumann, Charles W., patrolman	Indianapolis, IN	protest	fired
1861	Beecher, Henry Ward, clergy	Brooklyn, NY	supported pacifism	
1/13/1918	Beilfuss, Paul	Philadelphia	protest	nearly lynched
8/2/1917	Benefield, William L., farmer	Sasakwa, OK	conspiracy, vandalism	
3/25/1918	Bergen, Frances	Benton, IL	protest	banished
12/31/1917	Best, Charles W., harnessmaker	Indianapolis, IN	protest	fired
10/30/1917	Bigelow, Herbert Seely, clergy	Newport, KY	protest	kidnapped, lashed
10/30/1917	Binder, Stephen, writer	Brooklyn, NY	protest	confiscation
7/3/1969	Boskey, Jill Ann, activist	New York City	destroyed property	arrest
5/24/1918	Brueger, Mary, teacher	Los Angeles	protest	fired
12/17/1917	Canter, Albert M., teacher	Clayton, NJ	protest	banished
6/17/1918	Carr, C.R., teacher	Olympia, WA	protest	fired
10/1917	Cattell, J. McKeen, teacher	New York City	protest	fired
10/21/1967	Chomsky, Noam, linguist	Arlington, VA	blocked an entrance	arrest
10/16/1967	Coffin, William Sloane, Jr. clergy	New Haven, CT	conspiracy	charged
9/25/1972	Coffin, William Sloane, Jr., clergy	Hanoi, Vietnam	protest	
8/2/1917	Crane, Roy, farmer	Sasakwa, OK	conspiracy, vandalism	prison
12/19/1918	Criseler, George P., teacher	Rochester, MN	protest	fired
7/3/1969	Czarnik, Kathy, activist	New York City	destroyed property	arrest
8/31/1863	Dakin, Peter, farmer	Culpeper, VA	protest	
10/1917	Dana, Henry Wadsworth Longfellow, teacher	New York City	protest	fired
10/21/1967	Davis, Angela, teacher	Arlington, VA	blocked an entrance	arrest
1960	Day, Dorothy, reformer, editor	New York City	protest	jail
1948	Dellinger, David T., activist	New York City	protest	assault
10/21/1967	Deming, Barbara, writer	Arlington, VA	blocked an entrance	arrest
3/13/1918	Dieterle, John, teacher	Ann Arbor, MI	protest	fired
10/21/1967	Dohrn, Bernadine, anarchist	Arlington, VA	blocked an entrance	arrest
12/4/1917	Dutsch, Henry	Hugo, CO	protest	tarred, feathered
11/15/1917	Ellis, J.H., clergy	Newport, AR	protest	assault, jail
1861	Emerson, Ralph Waldo, philosopher	Concord, MA	supported pacifism	
8/1/1863	Evans, Frederick W.	New Lebanon, NY	supported pacifism	
10/16/1967	Ferber, Michael, teacher	New Haven, CT	conspiracy	charged
3/13/1918	Ficken, Richard O., teacher	Ann Arbor, MI	protest	fired
3/13/1918	Florer, Warren W., teacher	Ann Arbor, MI	protest	fired
10/21/1967	Fonda, Jane, actor	Arlington, VA	blocked an entrance	arrest
3/16/1918	Friederich, August	Scotland, SD	protest	banished
8/1/1863	Gates, Benjamin	New Lebanon, NY	supported pacifism	
7/3/1969	Geddes, Maggie, activist	New York City	destroyed property	arrest
8/22/1863	Gerhard, Benjamin	Philadelphia	supported pacifism	
1861	Giddings, Joshua Reed, politician	Jefferson, OH	supported pacifism	
12/1919	Goldman, Emma, orator	New York City	protest	deported
10/16/1967	Goodman, Mitchell, writer	New Haven, CT	conspiracy	charged
1861	Greeley, Horace, editor	New York City	supported pacifism	
7/3/1969	Green, Valentine, activist	New York City	destroyed property	arrest

Target of Act/Date	Name, Occupation	Location	Act	Consequence
1939	Gregg, Richard Bartlett, moralist	Pendle Hill, PA	denounced war	
5/1/1918	Han, George W., student	Berkeley, CA	protest	expelled
4/22/1918	Hang, Christy, publisher	Connellsville, PA	protest	confiscation
4/22/1918	Hang, William, publisher	Connellsville, PA	protest	confiscation
8/2/1917	Harjo, John, farmer	Sasakwa, OK	conspiracy, vandalism	
1917	Herschberger, Guy Franklin	Goshen, IN	protest	
10/26/1918	Hieminz, Frank X., bartender	St. Louis, MO	protest	saloon closed
3/21/1918	Hoffman, Henry	Altus, OK	protest	assault, tarred, feathered
6/19/1918	Hopt, Erwin B., teacher	Lincoln, NE	protest	forced out
8/27/1918	Irvin, Clara M.	Spokane, WA	protest	confiscation
1940s	Johnson, Paul	Texarkana, AR	opposed the draft	prison
8/27/1918	Jordan, David Starr, educator	Baltimore	protest	assault
1/22/1918	Keenan, L.H., lawyer	Elkins, WV	protest	tarred, feathered
2/13/1918	Kennan, Ellen, teacher	Denver	protest	fired
7/3/1969	Kennedy, Pat, activist	New York City	destroyed property	arrest
5/11/1918	Kimmons, I., draftsman	Portland, OR	protest	fired
6/15/1864	Kline, John, missionary	Broadway, VA	protest	shot
3/13/1918	Kostermann, W.W.	Ann Arbor, MI	protest	fired
3/23/1918	Kovalsky, John, clergy	Christopher, IL	protest	tarred, feathered
11/3/1917	Lamonte, Frank S., lawyer	Evansville, IN	protest	disbarred
3/5/1918	Larson, Esther	Omaha, NE	protest	fired
10/21/1967	Lens, Sidney, historian	Arlington, VA	blocked an entrance	arrest
10/21/1967	Levertov, Denise, poet	Arlington, VA	blocked an entrance	arrest
6/26/1918	Levin, Rose, student	San Francisco	protest	denied a diploma
2/14/1918	Liebig, H.C., teacher	Harrisburg, PA	protest	fired
10/21/1967	Lowell, Robert, poet	Arlington, VA	blocked an entrance	arrest
6/19/1918	Lucker, G.W.A., teacher	Lincoln, NE	protest	forced out
11/8/1918	Lunde, Theo H., activist	Chicago	protest	confiscation
3/25/1918	Lundin, Gust, draftee	Duluth, MN	protest	tarred, feathered
10/21/1967	Macdonald, Dwight, author	Arlington, VA	blocked an entrance	arrest
8/31/1863	Macomber, Lindley M., nurseryman	Culpeper, VA	protest	
1918	Magon, Ricardo Flores	Fort Leavenworth, KS	protest	prison
8/10/1917	Martin, M.L., mail carrier	Marion, OH	protest	fired
8/2/1917	Martin, William M., farmer	Sasakwa, OK	conspiracy, vandalism	prison
2/12/1918	Metzen, John L., lawyer	Staunton, IL	protest	assault, tarred
10/15/1965	Miller, David J., student	Syracuse, NY	burned draft card	
12/18/1863	Moore, Benjamin P., Jr.	Bel Air, MD	draft evasion	
1966	Mott, Jeremy, activist	Ridgewood, NJ	burned draft card	
8/2/1917	Munson, H.H. "Rube," miner	Sasakwa, OK	conspiracy, vandalism	prison
1942	Muste, Abraham Johannes, activist		supported draft evasion	
2/13/1918	Nafe, Gertrude, teacher	Denver	protest	fired
8/31/1918	Nelles, Walter, lawyer	New York City	protest	raided
8/31/1918	Oberden, Severino, labor leader	Staunton, IL	protest	assault, tarred

Target of Act/Date	Name, Occupation	Location	Act	Consequence
3/28/1918	Oberlee, Frank	Clarksville, AR	protest	tarred, feathered
3/31/1966	O'Brien, David Paul	Boston	draft card burning	prison
12/10/1917	Oburn, Emmett A.	St. Louis, MO	protest	assault
4/1922	O'Hare, Kate Richards, orator	Washington, DC	protest march	
9/13/1918	Park, Alice, activist	Portland, OR	protest	confiscation
1948	Peck, James	Washington, DC	chained to a fence	
1689	Penn, William, governor	Philadelphia	refused to institute draft	
6/19/1918	Persinger, Edward B., teacher	Lincoln, NE	protest	forced to resign
1861	Phillips, Wendell Addison, orator	Boston	supported pacifism	
8/31/1863	Pringle, Cyrus Guernsey, horticulturist	Culpeper, VA	protest	
1863	Prouty, Lorenzo D., industrialist	Shirley, MA	protest	
1863	Prouty, Nathan Converse, farmer	Shirley, MA	protest	
1947	Randolph, Asa Philip, organizer	Albany, NY	protest	
10/16/1967	Raskin, Marcus, political aide	New Haven, CT	conspiracy	charged
1/22/1918	Rempfer, William C.	Mitchell, SD	protest	deported
3/16/1918	Rempfer, William C.	Scotland, SD	protest	banished
1947	Reynolds, Grant, organizer	Albany, NY	protest	
7/30/1863	Royce, Samuel	Boston	abetted draft evasion	
11/1943	Rustin, Bayard Taylor, activist	Ashland, KY	refused draft	prison
1948	Rustin, Bayard Taylor, activist	New York City	protest	assault
12/17/1917	Ryland, Edwin P., clergy	Hollywood, CA	protest	fired
9/15/1918	Schaper, William August, teacher	Minneapolis, MN	protest	fired
3/31/1918	Schimmel, E.A., teacher	Ashland, WI	protest	tarred, feathered
10/1982	Schmucker, Mark A., student	Goshen, IN	refused to register	fine
5/24/1929	Schwimmer, Rosika, lecturer	Chicago	protest	citizenship revoked
8/23/1917	Sims, W.T., clergy	York, SC	protest	lynched
1860s	Smedley, Edwin	Philadelphia	protest	
1860s	Smedley, William H.	Philadelphia	protest	
8/2/1917	Spence, Homer Carlos, farmer	Sasakwa, OK	conspiracy, vandalism	
10/16/1967	Spock, Benjamin, doctor	New Haven, CT	conspiracy	charged
10/21/1967	Spock, Benjamin, doctor	Arlington, VA	blocked an entrance	arrest
10/21/1967	Spock, Jane Cheney, activist	Arlington, VA	blocked an entrance	arrest
12/18/1917	Starck, W.A., clergy	Audubon, IA	protest	assault, nearly lynched
11/22/1917	Stratemeyer, E.H.	Osakis, MN	protest	tarred, feathered
1861	Sumner, Charles, senator	Boston	supported pacifism	
1862	Swift, Henry D., inventor	South Dedham, MA	protest	
1863	Taber, Horace S.	Temple, NH	protest	
12/18/1917	Tennegkeit, Fred	Audubon, IA	protest	assault, nearly lynched
10/16/1967	Thomas, Norman, socialist	New Haven, CT	conspiracy	charged
5/1863	Vallandigham, Clement Laird, politician	Dayton, OH	incited draft evasion	prison
7/11/1918	Varrelman, F. Alfred, teacher	San Francisco	protest	fired
1/5/1918	Von Hoegen, Maximilian, translator	Hartford, CT	protest	assault
3/9/1918	Walz, William Emanuel, dean of law school	Bangor, ME	protest	fired

Target of Act/Date	Name, Occupation	Location	Act	Consequence
7/1917	Webster, Frank A., mail carrier	St. Paul, MN	protest	fired
3/21/1918	Westbrook, O.F.	Altus, OK	protest	assault, tarred, feathered
11/25/1917	Whipple, Leonidas Rutledge, teacher	Charlottesville, VA	protest	fired
3/20/1918	White, Elmer	Yerington, NV	protest	lashed
3/13/1918	Wiegand, Henry J.	Ann Arbor, MI	protest	fired
5/13/1918	Wusterbarth, Fred W., postmaster	Newark, NJ	protest	citizenship revoked

dress code

12/16/1965	Eckhardt, Christopher, student	Des Moines, IA	wore black armband	suspended
9/2005	Scott, Toni Kay, student	Napa, CA	wore Tigger socks	detained
12/16/1965	Tinker, John F., student	Des Moines, IA	wore black armband	suspended
12/16/1965	Tinker, Mary Beth, student	Des Moines, IA	wore black armband	suspended

euthanasia ban
(* indicates multiple acts on the same date)
(** indicates body left at emergency room)

6/4/1990	Kevorkian, Murad "Jack," pathologist	Holly, MI	lethal IV	injunction
10/23/1991	Kevorkian, Murad "Jack," pathologist	Sodus, MI	lethal IV	
10/23/1991	Kevorkian, Murad "Jack," pathologist	Roseville, MI	lethal gas	
5/15/1992	Kevorkian, Murad "Jack," pathologist	Clawson, MI	lethal gas	
9/26/1992	Kevorkian, Murad "Jack," pathologist	Waterford, MI	lethal gas	
11/23/1992	Kevorkian, Murad "Jack," pathologist	Waterford, MI	lethal gas	
12/15/1992*	Kevorkian, Murad "Jack," pathologist	Auburn Hills, MI	lethal gas	
12/15/1992*	Kevorkian, Murad "Jack," pathologist	Auburn Hills, MI	lethal gas	
1/20/1993	Kevorkian, Murad "Jack," pathologist	Huron, MI	lethal gas	
2/4/1993*	Kevorkian, Murad "Jack," pathologist	Leland, MI	lethal gas	
2/4/1993*	Kevorkian, Murad "Jack," pathologist	Leland, MI	lethal gas	
2/12/1993	Kevorkian, Murad "Jack," pathologist	Southfield, MI	lethal gas	
2/15/1993	Kevorkian, Murad "Jack," pathologist	Roseville, MI	lethal gas	
2/18/1993*	Kevorkian, Murad "Jack," pathologist	Waterford, MI	lethal gas	
2/18/1993*	Kevorkian, Murad "Jack," pathologist	Waterford, MI	lethal gas	
5/16/1993	Kevorkian, Murad "Jack," pathologist	Detroit, MI	lethal gas	
8/4/1993	Kevorkian, Murad "Jack," pathologist	Detroit, MI	lethal gas	
9/9/1993	Kevorkian, Murad "Jack," pathologist	Redford, MI	euthanasia	
10/22/1993	Kevorkian, Murad "Jack," pathologist	Royal Oak, MI	lethal gas	
11/22/1993	Kevorkian, Murad "Jack," pathologist	Royal Oak, MI	lethal gas	
11/26/1994	Kevorkian, Murad "Jack," pathologist	Royal Oak, MI	lethal gas	
5/8/1995	Kevorkian, Murad "Jack," pathologist	Royal Oak, MI	lethal gas	
5/12/1995	Kevorkian, Murad "Jack," pathologist	Pontiac, MI	lethal gas	
6/26/1995	Kevorkian, Murad "Jack," pathologist	Springfield, MI	lethal gas	
11/8/1995*	Kevorkian, Murad "Jack," pathologist	Pontiac, MI	lethal gas	
11/8/1995*	Kevorkian, Murad "Jack," pathologist	Pontiac, MI	lethal gas	
1/29/1996	Kevorkian, Murad "Jack," pathologist	Oakland, MI	lethal gas	

Target of Act/Date	Name, Occupation	Location	Act	Consequence
5/7/1996	Kevorkian, Murad "Jack," pathologist	Farmington Hills, MI	euthanasia	
6/10/1996	Kevorkian, Murad "Jack," pathologist	Pontiac, MI	lethal gas	
6/18/1996	Kevorkian, Murad "Jack," pathologist	Pontiac, MI	lethal gas	
6/21/1996	Kevorkian, Murad "Jack," pathologist	Pontiac, MI	lethal gas	
7/5/1996	Kevorkian, Murad "Jack," pathologist	Royal Oak, MI	lethal injection	
7/9/1996	Kevorkian, Murad "Jack," pathologist	Pontiac, MI	lethal injection	
8/7/1996	Kevorkian, Murad "Jack," pathologist	Pontiac, MI	lethal injection	
8/17/1996	Kevorkian, Murad "Jack," pathologist	Pontiac, MI	lethal injection	
8/20/1996	Kevorkian, Murad "Jack," pathologist	Ionia, MI	euthanasia	
8/22/1996	Kevorkian, Murad "Jack," pathologist	location unknown**	lethal injection	
8/23/1996	Kevorkian, Murad "Jack," pathologist	location unknown**	lethal injection	
9/2/1996	Kevorkian, Murad "Jack," pathologist	location unknown**	lethal injection	
9/7/1996	Kevorkian, Murad "Jack," pathologist	location unknown**	euthanasia	
9/29/1996	Kevorkian, Murad "Jack," pathologist	location unknown**	euthanasia	
10/10/1996	Kevorkian, Murad "Jack," pathologist	location unknown**	euthanasia	
10/17/1996	Kevorkian, Murad "Jack," pathologist	Pontiac, MI	euthanasia	
10/24/1996	Kevorkian, Murad "Jack," pathologist	Pontiac, MI	euthanasia	
2/2/1997*	Kevorkian, Murad "Jack," pathologist	Pontiac, MI	lethal injection	
2/2/1997*	Kevorkian, Murad "Jack," pathologist	Pontiac, MI	lethal injection	
3/7/1997	Kevorkian, Murad "Jack," pathologist	Romulus, MI	euthanasia	
3/19/1997	Kevorkian, Murad "Jack," pathologist	Livonia, MI	euthanasia	
3/23/1997	Kevorkian, Murad "Jack," pathologist	Warren, MI	euthanasia	
4/8/1997	Kevorkian, Murad "Jack," pathologist	Romulus, MI	euthanasia	
5/3/1997	Kevorkian, Murad "Jack," pathologist	Detroit, MI	lethal IV	
6/25/1997	Kevorkian, Murad "Jack," pathologist	Southfield, MI	lethal gas	
7/3/1997	Kevorkian, Murad "Jack," pathologist	Wayne, MI	euthanasia	
7/3/1997	Kevorkian, Murad "Jack," pathologist	Macomb, MI	euthanasia	
8/13/1997	Kevorkian, Murad "Jack," pathologist	Farmington Hills, MI	lethal injection	
8/26/1997	Kevorkian, Murad "Jack," pathologist	Farmington Hills, MI	lethal injection	
8/29/1997	Kevorkian, Murad "Jack," pathologist	Farmington Hills, MI	euthanasia	
9/3/1997	Kevorkian, Murad "Jack," pathologist	Bloomfield, MI	lethal injection	
9/8/1997	Kevorkian, Murad "Jack," pathologist	Romulus, MI	euthanasia	
9/21/1997	Kevorkian, Murad "Jack," pathologist	Bloomfield, MI	euthanasia	
9/29/1997	Kevorkian, Murad "Jack," pathologist	Detroit, MI	euthanasia	
10/3/1997	Kevorkian, Murad "Jack," pathologist	Oakland, MI	euthanasia	
10/8/1997	Kevorkian, Murad "Jack," pathologist	Bloomfield, MI	euthanasia	
10/9/1997	Kevorkian, Murad "Jack," pathologist	Oakland, MI	lethal injection	
10/30/1997	Kevorkian, Murad "Jack," pathologist	Detroit, MI	euthanasia	
11/14/1997	Kevorkian, Murad "Jack," pathologist	Detroit, MI	lethal gas	
11/23/1997	Kevorkian, Murad "Jack," pathologist	Pontiac, MI	euthanasia	
11/23/1997	Kevorkian, Murad "Jack," pathologist	Detroit, MI	euthanasia	
12/3/1997	Kevorkian, Murad "Jack," pathologist	Detroit, MI	euthanasia	
12/11/1997	Kevorkian, Murad "Jack," pathologist	Romulus, MI	lethal injection	
12/16/1997	Kevorkian, Murad "Jack," pathologist	Allen Park, MI	euthanasia	
12/16/1997	Kevorkian, Murad "Jack," pathologist	Pontiac, MI	euthanasia	

Target of Act/Date	Name, Occupation	Location	Act	Consequence
12/27/1997*	Kevorkian, Murad "Jack," pathologist	Pontiac, MI	euthanasia	
12/27/1997*	Kevorkian, Murad "Jack," pathologist	Pontiac, MI	euthanasia	
1/8/1998	Kevorkian, Murad "Jack," pathologist	Pontiac, MI	euthanasia	
1/18/1998	Kevorkian, Murad "Jack," pathologist	Pontiac, MI	lethal injection	
2/3/1998	Kevorkian, Murad "Jack," pathologist	Pontiac, MI	euthanasia	
2/23/1998	Kevorkian, Murad "Jack," pathologist	Royal Oak, MI	euthanasia	
2/26/1998	Kevorkian, Murad "Jack," pathologist	Southfield, MI	lethal injection	
3/5/1998*	Kevorkian, Murad "Jack," pathologist	Pontiac, MI	lethal injection	
3/5/1998*	Kevorkian, Murad "Jack," pathologist	Pontiac, MI	lethal injection	
3/13/1998	Kevorkian, Murad "Jack," pathologist	Detroit, MI	euthanasia	
3/28/1998	Kevorkian, Murad "Jack," pathologist	Southfield, MI	euthanasia	
4/9/1998	Kevorkian, Murad "Jack," pathologist	Huron, MI	lethal injection	
4/13/1998	Kevorkian, Murad "Jack," pathologist	Pontiac, MI	lethal injection	
4/16/1998*	Kevorkian, Murad "Jack," pathologist	Oakland, MI	lethal injection	
4/16/1998*	Kevorkian, Murad "Jack," pathologist	Oakland, MI	lethal injection	
4/24/1998	Kevorkian, Murad "Jack," pathologist	Rochester Hills, MI	cyanide	
5/7/1998	Kevorkian, Murad "Jack," pathologist	Royal Oak, MI	euthanasia	
5/19/1998	Kevorkian, Murad "Jack," pathologist	Royal Oak, MI	euthanasia	
6/7/1998	Kevorkian, Murad "Jack," pathologist	Oakland, MI	assault, resisted arrest	fine
11/22/1998	Kevorkian, Murad "Jack," pathologist	Oakland, MI	lethal injection, murder	prison
6/7/1998	Reding, George, psychiatrist	Oakland, MI	assault, resisted arrest	fine
8/30/1998	Reding, George, psychiatrist	Albuquerque, NM		

evolutionism ban

5/7/1925	Baldwin, Roger Nash, activist	Dayton, TN	abetted teaching of evolutionism	
5/7/1925	Rappelyea, George Washington, mining engineer	Dayton, TN	abetted teaching of evolutionism	
5/7/1925	Scopes, John Thomas, teacher	Dayton, TN	taught evolutionism	fine

exile

1657	Burden, Anne	Boston	ignored banishment	prison in the dark, confiscation
1657	Dyer, Mary Barrett, preacher	Boston	ignored banishment	prison in the dark

farm debt

9/1985	Field, Sally, actor	Washington, DC	protest	
9/1985	Fonda, Jane, actor	Washington, DC	protest	
9/1985	Lange, Jessica, actor	Washington, DC	protest	
9/1985	Spacek, Sissy, actor	Washington, DC	protest	

female genital mutilation ban

3/29/2001	Adem, Khalid	Gwinnett County, GA	maimed his child	prison
1/2004	Bertrang, Todd Cameron	Santa Clarita, CA	conspiracy	arrest
1/2004	Faulkinbury, Robyn	Santa Clarita, CA	conspiracy	arrest

Target of Act/Date	Name, Occupation	Location	Act	Consequence
fishing ban				
1901	Blackbird, John, fisher	Bad River, WI	gill-netted	arrest
3/2/1964	Brando, Marlon, actor	Seattle	fished	arrest
10/7/1965	Bridges, Alvin, fisher	Frank's Landing, WA	fished	seized
10/13/1965	Bridges, Alvin, fisher	Frank's Landing, WA	fish-in	canoe crushed
12/1945	Frank, Billy, Jr., fisher	Frank's Landing, WA	gill-netted	seized
10/7/1965	Frank, Billy, Jr., fisher	Frank's Landing, WA	gill-netted	seized, canoe confiscated
9/9/1970	Frank, Tobin, student	Frank's Landing, WA	fished	seized
3/2/1964	Gregory, Dick, comedian	Seattle	supported SAIA	
10/13/1965	Gregory, Dick, comedian	Frank's Landing, WA	fish-in	arrest
2/6/1966	Gregory, Dick, comedian	Frank's Landing, WA	rally	jail
10/13/1965	Gregory, Lillian Smith	Frank's Landing, WA	fish-in	arrest
2/6/1966	Gregory, Lillian Smith	Frank's Landing, WA	rally	jail
1916	Kennedy, Fayette, fisher	Cattaraugus, NY	spear-fished	arrest
1916	Kennedy, Warren, fisher	Cattaraugus, NY	spear-fished	arrest
10/13/1965	McCloud, Donald, fisher	Frank's Landing, WA	fished illegally	canoe crushed
3/1/1966	McCloud, Edith, fisher	Frank's Landing, WA	obstructed police	canoe crushed
10/13/1965	McCloud, Janet Renecker, fisher	Frank's Landing, WA	resisted arrest	attacked
3/1/1966	McCloud, Janet Renecker, fisher	Frank's Landing, WA	obstructed police	arrest
10/13/1965	McCloud, Jeffrey, student	Frank's Landing, WA	fish-in	canoe crushed
7/1960	McCoy, Joseph, fisher	Skagit River, WA	gill-netted	arrest
10/13/1965	Roberts, Evan, Jr., mediator	Frank's Landing, WA	attended fish-in	raid
10/13/1965	Sanchez, Dorian, student	Frank's Landing, WA	fish-in	canoe crushed
3/2/1964	Satiacum, Bob, activist	Seattle	fished	jail
9/21/1964	Satiacum, Clara	Tacoma, WA	outran police	arrest
9/21/1964	Satiacum, Susan	Tacoma, WA	outran police	arrest
10/13/1965	Satiacum, Susan	Frank's Landing, WA	resisted arrest	arrest
1981	Sohappy, David, fisher	Harrah, WA	sold fish	arrest
1981	Sohappy, David, Jr., fisher	Harrah, WA	sold fish	arrest
1/1961	Starr, James, fisher	Green River, WA	gill-netted	arrest
1/1961	Starr, Louis, Jr., fisher	Green River, WA	gill-netted	arrest
3/8/1974	Tribble, Frederick, fisher	Hayward, WI	spear-fished	arrest
3/8/1974	Tribble, Michael, fisher	Hayward, WI	spear-fished	arrest
5/6/1939	Tulee, Sampson, fisher	Celilo Falls, WA	dip-netted	arrest
1/1961	Wayne, Leonard, fisher	Green River, WA	gill-netted	arrest
4/21/1964	Weeks, Madeline Alexander	Cook's Landing, WA	fished	boat rammed
1916	White, Willis, Jr., fisher	Cattaraugus, NY	spear-fished	arrest
1/1993	Wilbur, Tony, fisher	Wolf River, WI	fished	
10/26/1965	Wright, Elaine	Seattle	protest march	
3/2/1964	Yaryan, John J., priest	Seattle	supported SAIA	
flag burning ban				
10/30/1989	Eichman, Shawn D., activist	Seattle	flag burning	arrest
8/2/1990	Eichman, Shawn D., activist	New York City	flag burning	fine, community service

Target of Act/Date	Name, Occupation	Location	Act	Consequence
8/22/1984	Johnson, Gregory Lee, activist	Dallas, TX	war protest	fine, prison
8/2/1990	Urgo, Joseph R., activist	New York City	flag burning	fine, community service

flag saluting

1942	Barnett, Gathie, student	Charleston, WV	classroom disobedience	expulsion
1942	Barnett, Marie, student	Charleston, WV	classroom disobedience	expulsion
10/23/1935	Gobitas, Lillian, student	Minersville, PA	classroom disobedience	expulsion
10/23/1935	Gobitas, William H., student	Minersville, PA	classroom disobedience	expulsion

food prices

2/20/1917	Harris, Ida, reformer	New York City	hunger riot	
4/2/1863	Jackson, Mary, vendor	Richmond, VA	rioted, looted	charged
4/2/1863	Meredith, Minerva, butcher	Richmond, VA	looted	charged

free press ban

11/17/1734	Alexander, James, lawyer	New York City	libel	disbarment
5/8/1918	Binder, Stephen, writer	Brooklyn, NY	antiwar writings	confiscation of work
11/2/1872	Claflin, Tennessee Celeste, publisher	New York City	obscenity	arrest
4/22/1848	Crooks, Adam, missionary	Columbiana, OH	abolitionist pamphlet	jail
3/25/1957	Ferlinghetti, Lawrence, promoter	San Francisco	sold a banned book	arrest
1911	Gompers, Samuel, union organizer	St. Louis, MO	published a list	limited speech
8/19/1862	Greeley, Horace, editor	New York City	protest	
4/22/1848	McBride, Jesse, missionary	Columbiana, OH	abolitionist pamphlet	jail
3/25/1957	Murao, Shigeyoshi, merchant	San Francisco	sold a banned book	arrest
4/22/1848	Robinson, Marius Racine, editor	Mahoning County, OH	editorial	tarred, feathered
5/8/1918	Rutherford, Joseph Franklin, lawyer	New York	distributed tracts	prison
2/9/1913	Sanger, Margaret Louise Higgins, nurse, publisher	New York City	birth control information	
8/1914	Sanger, Margaret Louise Higgins, nurse, publisher	New York City	birth control information	arrest, fled
10/27/1916	Sanger, Margaret Louise Higgins, nurse, publisher	New York City	birth control information	workhouse
9/10/1915	Sanger, William, publisher	New York City	birth control information	arrest, jail
11/17/1734	Smith, William, lawyer	New York City	libel	disbarment
11/2/1872	Woodhull, Victoria Claflin, publisher	New York City	obscenity	arrest
11/17/1734	Zenger, Peter, publisher	New York City	libel	jail

free speech ban

1/6/1907	Berkman, Alexander, lecturer	New York City	conspiracy	arrest
10/4/1961	Bruce, Lenny, comedian	San Francisco	comic act	arrest
10/20/1962	Bruce, Lenny, comedian	West Hollywood, CA	comic act	arrest
12/4/1962	Bruce, Lenny, comedian	Chicago	comic act	jail

Target of Act/Date	Name, Occupation	Location	Act	Consequence
3/31/1964	Bruce, Lenny, comedian	New York City	comic act	workhouse
4/26/1908	Buwalda, William, soldier	San Francisco	attended a speech	court-martial, prison at hard labor
1/14/1909	Buwalda, William, soldier	San Francisco	unlawful assembly	jail
12/4/1962	Carlin, George, comedian	Chicago	comic act	jail
1972	Carlin, George, comedian	Milwaukee, WI	obscenity	arrest
11/9/1963	Dellinger, David T., activist	Griffin, GA	war protest	
11/19/1963	Dellinger, David T., activist	Macon, GA	war protest	arrest
2/1964	Dellinger, David T., activist	Albany, GA	war protest	arrest
3/1994	Diana, Mike, cartoonist	Largo, FL	obscenity	arrest
1834	Dresser, Amos, student	Cincinnati, OH	abolitionism	expelled, lashed
3/25/1957	Ferlinghetti, Lawrence, promoter	San Francisco	sold a banned book	arrest
11/30/1909	Flynn, Elizabeth Gurley, activist	Spokane, WA	disorderly conduct	arrest
2/25/1913	Flynn, Elizabeth Gurley, activist	Paterson, NJ	abetted a strike	arrest
5/1976	Flynt, Larry, publisher	Dayton, OH	obscenity	arrest
1/24/2002	Frederick, Joseph, student	Juneau, AK	promarijuana banner	suspension
9/7/1908	Edelsohn, Becky, lecturer	New York City	conspiracy	jail
1894	Goldman, Emma, lecturer	Homestead, PA	conspiracy	prison
4/1901	Goldman, Emma, lecturer	Philadelphia	conspiracy	arrest
mid-1902	Goldman, Emma, lecturer	Wilkes-Barre, PA	conspiracy	banned
mid-1902	Goldman, Emma, lecturer	McKeesport, PA	conspiracy	banned
10/30/1906	Goldman, Emma, lecturer	New York City	riot	arrest
11/23/1906	Goldman, Emma, lecturer	New York City	conspiracy	
3/9/1907	Goldman, Emma, lecturer	Columbus, OH	conspiracy	banned
3/16/1907	Goldman, Emma, lecturer	Detroit, MI	conspiracy	banned
3/1908	Goldman, Emma, lecturer	Chicago	conspiracy	fine
4/1908	Goldman, Emma, lecturer	San Francisco	conspiracy	banned
9/7/1908	Goldman, Emma, lecturer	New York City	conspiracy	jail
10/27/1908	Goldman, Emma, lecturer	Indianapolis, IN	conspiracy	banned
11/7/1908	Goldman, Emma, lecturer	Omaha, NE	conspiracy	locked out
12/13/1908	Goldman, Emma, lecturer	Everett, WA	conspiracy	banned
12/13/1908	Goldman, Emma, lecturer	Bellingham, WA	conspiracy	arrest, exile
1/17/1909	Goldman, Emma, lecturer	San Francisco	unlawful assembly	jail
3/14/1909	Goldman, Emma, lecturer	El Paso, TX	conspiracy	banned
5/14/1909	Goldman, Emma, lecturer	New Haven, CT	conspiracy	banned
5/28/1909	Goldman, Emma, lecturer	Brooklyn, NY	conspiracy	banned
6/8/1909	Goldman, Emma, lecturer	East Orange, NJ	conspiracy	banned
8/11/1909	Goldman, Emma, lecturer	New York City	conspiracy	banned
9/3/1909	Goldman, Emma, lecturer	Burlington, VT	conspiracy	banned
9/8/1909	Goldman, Emma, lecturer	Worcester, MA	conspiracy	banned
9/24/1909	Goldman, Emma, lecturer	Philadelphia	conspiracy	banned
1/1910	Goldman, Emma, lecturer	Hannibal, MO	conspiracy	intimidation
2/1910	Goldman, Emma, lecturer	Springfield, IL	conspiracy	intimidation
4/1910	Goldman, Emma, lecturer	Denver	conspiracy	arrest

Target of Act/Date	Name, Occupation	Location	Act	Consequence
11/1910	Goldman, Emma, lecturer	Washington, DC	conspiracy	banned
11/1910	Goldman, Emma, lecturer	Indianapolis, IN	conspiracy	banned
12/1910	Goldman, Emma, lecturer	Baltimore	conspiracy	intimidation
1/17/1911	Goldman, Emma, lecturer	Columbus, OH	conspiracy	banned
3/5/1911	Goldman, Emma, lecturer	Staunton, IL	conspiracy	intimidation
10/13/1911	Goldman, Emma, lecturer	New York City	conspiracy	intimidation
5/29/1912	Goldman, Emma, lecturer	Oakland, CA	conspiracy	banned
5/30/1913	Goldman, Emma, lecturer	San Diego, CA	conspiracy	arrest
8/9/1913	Goldman, Emma, lecturer	Seattle	conspiracy	arrest
12/15/1913	Goldman, Emma, lecturer	Paterson, NJ	conspiracy	banned
1/4/1914	Goldman, Emma, lecturer	Philadelphia	conspiracy	intimidation
3/9/1914	Goldman, Emma, lecturer	Philadelphia	conspiracy	intimidation
8/6/1915	Goldman, Emma, lecturer	Portland, OR	birth control information	fine
2/11/1916	Goldman, Emma, lecturer	New York City	birth control lecture	arrest, prison
5/20/1916	Goldman, Emma, lecturer	New York City	birth control information	arrest
7/9/1917	Goldman, Emma, lecturer	Jefferson City, MO	conspiracy	prison
7/15/1917	Goldman, Emma, lecturer	New York City	conspiracy	office closed
8/1917	Goldman, Emma, lecturer	New York City	conspiracy	confiscation
9/11/1917	Goldman, Emma, lecturer	New York City	conspiracy	banned
10/30/1917	Goldman, Emma, lecturer	New York City	conspiracy	prison
12/14/1917	Goldman, Emma, lecturer	New York City	conspiracy	prison
12/1919	Goldman, Emma, lecturer	New York City	conspiracy	deported
6/7/1965	Griswold, Estelle Trebert, activist	Hartford, CT	birth control information	jail, fine
5/20/1916	Hall, Bolton, hardware dealer	New York City	birth control information	arrest
6/4/1963	Hefner, Hugh, publisher	Chicago	obscenity	arrest
8/28/1968	Hoffman, Abbie, author	Chicago	obscenity	arrest
11/15/1969	Joplin, Janis, singer	Tampa, FL	obscenity	arrest
1972	Lovelace, Linda, actor	Binghamton, NY	obscenity	arrest
11/9/1963	Lyttle, Bradford, activist	Griffin, GA	war protest	
11/19/1963	Lyttle, Bradford, activist	Macon, GA	war protest	arrest
2/1964	Lyttle, Bradford, activist	Albany, GA	war protest	arrest
12/12/1695	Maule, Thomas, tailor	Salem, MA	sold tracts	burned books
1961	Miller, Henry, novelist	New York City	obscenity	arrest
3/25/1957	Murao, Shigeyoshi, merchant	San Francisco	sold a banned book	arrest
2/1964	Muste, Abraham Johannes, activist	Albany, GA	war protest	
1972	Reems, Harry, actor	Binghamton, NY	obscenity	arrest
11/1921	Sanger, Margaret Louise Higgins, nurse, publisher	New York City	birth control lecture	arrest
3/31/1964	Solomon, Howard, club owner	New York City	comic act	workhouse
6/10/1992	Sturman, Reuben, book dealer	Las Vegas, NV	obscenity	arrest
3/1908	Reitman, Ben L., doctor	Bellingham, WA	conspiracy	banned
9/7/1908	Reitman, Ben L., doctor	New York City	conspiracy	arrest
12/14/1908	Reitman, Ben L., doctor	Bellingham, WA	conspiracy	banned
1/17/1909	Reitman, Ben L., doctor	San Francisco	unlawful assembly	jail
4/1910	Reitman, Ben L., doctor	Denver	conspiracy	arrest

Target of Act/Date	Name, Occupation	Location	Act	Consequence
8/9/1913	Reitman, Ben L., doctor	Seattle	conspiracy	arrest
12/3/1964	Savio, Mario, student	Berkeley, CA	protest of campus policy	campus ban, jail
5/24/1929	Schwimmer, Rosika, lecturer	Chicago	protest	
5/22/1839	Wilson, Sherry	Queen Anne's County, MD	abolitionism	prison
1963	Zappa, Frank, guitarist	Los Angeles	obscenity	arrest

French and Indian War

Target of Act/Date	Name, Occupation	Location	Act	Consequence
12/16/1755	Armitt, John, cooper	Philadelphia	aided Indian refugees	
12/16/1755	Bartram, James, carpenter	Philadelphia	aided Indian refugees	
12/16/1755	Benezet, Anthony, tractarian	Philadelphia	aided Indian refugees	
12/16/1755	Brown, Thomas	Philadelphia	aided Indian refugees	
12/16/1755	Brown, William, clergy	Philadelphia	aided Indian refugees	
12/16/1755	Carleton, Thomas	Philadelphia	aided Indian refugees	
12/16/1755	Churchman, John, clergy	Philadelphia	aided Indian refugees	
12/16/1755	Eastburn, Samuel, blacksmith	Philadelphia	aided Indian refugees	
12/16/1755	Ely, Joshua, farmer	Philadelphia	aided Indian refugees	
12/16/1755	Evans, John, clergy	Philadelphia	aided Indian refugees	
12/16/1755	Farrington, Abraham, clergy	Philadelphia	aided Indian refugees	
12/16/1755	Fothergill, Sam, clergy	Philadelphia	aided Indian refugees	
12/16/1755	Horne, William	Philadelphia	aided Indian refugees	
12/16/1755	Jackson, William	Philadelphia	aided Indian refugees	
12/16/1755	Pemberton, John, trader, clergy	Philadelphia	protest	
12/16/1755	Scarborough, John, clergy	Philadelphia	aided Indian refugees	
1756	Standley, William	Loudon County, VA	refused to serve	lashed, prison at hard labor
12/16/1755	Stanton, Daniel, clergy	Philadelphia	aided Indian refugees	
12/16/1755	Trotter, Benjamin, cabinetmaker	Philadelphia	aided Indian refugees	
12/16/1755	White, Joseph, clergy	Philadelphia	aided Indian refugees	
1/12/1755	Woolman, John, tailor, philosopher	Northampton, PA	aided Indian refugees	
12/16/1755	Yarnell, Mordecai, clergy	Philadelphia	aided Indian refugees	
12/16/1755	Zane, Isaac, merchant	Philadelphia	aided Indian refugees	

Fugitive Slave Law of 1850

Target of Act/Date	Name, Occupation	Location	Act	Consequence
1859–1863	Burkle, Jacob, baker, stockman	Memphis, TN	slave transport	
1850s	Chaplin, William Lawrence, orator	the South	spying, conspiracy	
1851	Concklin, Seth	Florence, AL	slave rescue	
4/3/1851	Dana, Richard Henry, Jr., lawyer	Boston	jailbreak	
10/1/1852	Douglass, Frederick, orator	Syracuse, NY	public harangue	
1850s	Emerson, Lydia Jackson	Concord, MA	slave rescue, recruiter	
4/3/1851	Emerson, Ralph Waldo, philosopher	Concord, MA	slave transport, recruiter	
3/1851	French, Rodney, sea captain	New Bedford, MA	halted slave recapture	
10/1/1851	Fuller, James Canning, Jr., druggist	Skaneateles, NY	jailbreak	
4/3/1851	Garrison, William Lloyd, editor	Boston	jailbreak	denounced

Target of Act/Date	Name, Occupation	Location	Act	Consequence
9/1851	Garrison, William Lloyd, editor	Boston	conspiracy, propaganda	
10/1/1851	Gibbs, Leonard Dean, lawyer	Union Village, NY	denunciation	
1850s	Gibson, John	Jefferson City, MO	conducted slaves	died in prison
1853	Greenebaum, Michael G., lawyer	Chicago	protest	
4/3/1851	Grimes, Archibald, clergy	Boston	jailbreak	
2/15/1851	Hayden, Harriet Bell	Boston	harbored escaped slave	
2/15/1851	Hayden, Jo, child	Boston	harbored escaped slave	
2/15/1851	Hayden, Lewis	Boston	jailbreak	tried
10/1/1852	Higgins, Thomas Wentworth, clergy	Syracuse, NY	public harangue	
5/26/1854	Higginson, Thomas Wentworth, clergy	Boston	protest, jailbreak	hurt, indicted
10/1/1851	Hoyt, Hiram, doctor	Syracuse, NY	jailbreak	
4/3/1851	Jackson, Francis, historian	Boston	jailbreak	
8/20/1855	Kelley, J.W.B., postmaster	Atchison, KS	protest	stoned, tarred
10/1/1851	Loguen, Jermaine Wesley, clergy	Syracuse, NY	jailbreak	forced to flee
4/3/1851	Loring, Ellis Gray, lawyer	Boston	jailbreak	
11/1/1851	May, Samuel Joseph, clergy	Syracuse, NY	protest, recruiter	
9/11/1851	Mendenhall, Dinah Hannum	Kennett Square, PA	slave rescue	
10/1/1851	Merrick, Charles	Syracuse, NY	jailbreak	
10/1/1851	Merrick, Montgomery, mason	Syracuse, NY	jailbreak	
10/1/1851	Merrick, Sylvanus	Syracuse, NY	jailbreak	forced to flee
1856	Mitchell, William, soldier	Wamego, KS	protest, skirmishing	
9/1850	Monroe, James, clergy	Oberlin, OH	slave rescue	
9/1851	Mott, Lucretia Coffin, orator	Philadelphia	denunciation	
10/1/1851	Norton, Jo	Washington, DC	jailbreak	forced to flee
9/1850	Parker, Theodore, clergy	Boston	protest	
4/3/1851	Parker, Theodore, clergy	West Fitchburg, MA	protest	
6/1854	Parker, Theodore, clergy	Boston	protest	
9/1850	Peck, Henry Everard, clergy	Oberlin, OH	slave rescue	
5/26/1854	Phillips, Wendell Addison, orator	Boston	protest, jailbreak	
7/4/1856	Phillips, Wendell Addison, orator	Boston	protest	
10/1/1851	Salmon, William Lyman, tanner	Granby, NY	jailbreak	tried
4/3/1851	Sewall, Samuel Edmund, lawyer	Boston	jailbreak	
5/1851	Smith, Gerrit, politician	Syracuse, NY	public harangue	
10/1/1851	Smith, Gerrit, politician	Peterboro, NY	jailbreak	
10/1/1852	Smith, Gerrit, politician	Syracuse, NY	public harangue	
9/13/1858	Swisshelm, Jane Grey Cannon, educator, author	Louisville, KY	protest	
7/1856	Tappan, Samuel Forster, Jr.	Lawrence, KS	gun running	
10/1/1851	Thomas, John, journalist	Syracuse, NY	jailbreak	
4/3/1851	Thoreau, Henry David, philosopher	Concord, MA	protest	
1850s	Torrey, Charles Turner, clergy	Albany, NY	spying, conspiracy	
10/1/1851	Vashon, George Boyer, lawyer	Pittsburgh	jailbreak	
10/1/1851	Ward, Samuel Ringgold, clergy	New York City	jailbreak	
10/1/1851	Wheaton, Charles Augustus, hardware dealer	Syracuse, NY	jailbreak	

Target of Act/Date	Name, Occupation	Location	Act	Consequence
gay persecution				
1989	Cammermeyer, Margarethe, nurse	Seattle	admitted homosexuality	ousted from military
11/3/2006	Ciervo, Clare, student	New York City	sit-in	arrest
1987	Coffin, William Sloane, Jr., clergy	Strafford, VT	demonstration	
11/13/2000	Coffin, William Sloane, Jr., clergy	Washington, DC	blocked an entrance	arrest, handcuffed
5/1/1970	Falstein, Jesse	New York City	sit-in	arrest
1978	Feinstein, Diane, mayor	San Francisco	support	
1978	Fonda, Jane, actor	San Francisco	support	
11/3/2006	Golomb, Julia, student	New York City	sit-in	arrest
5/1/1970	Griffo, Michaela	New York City	sit-in	arrest
11/3/2006	Hamilton, Leslie, student	New York City	sit-in	arrest
11/27/1978	Milk, Harvey, politician	San Francisco	lawmaking	shot
11/27/1978	Moscone, George, mayor	San Francisco	lawmaking	shot
11/3/2006	Peterson, Curt, student	New York City	sit-in	arrest
11/3/2006	Rodriguez, David, student	New York City	sit-in	arrest
11/13/2000	Taft, Fran, activist	Washington, DC	blocked an entrance	arrest, handcuffed
11/3/2006	Whinn, Peter, student	New York City	sit-in	arrest
11/13/2000	White, Mel, clergy	Washington, DC	blocked an entrance	arrest, handcuffed
genetic food engineering				
11/19/1996	Johnson, Teri, activist	Destrehan, LA	demonstration	
genocide				
5/1/2006	Clooney, George, actor	Washington, DC	protest	
7/13/2004	Cohen, Ben, businessman	Washington, DC	blocked an entrance	arrest
7/13/2004	Edgar, Robert W., clergy	Washington, DC	blocked an entrance	arrest
7/13/2004	Fauntroy, Walter Edward, clergy	Washington, DC	blocked an entrance	arrest
7/13/2004	Greenfield, Jerry, businessman	Washington, DC	blocked an entrance	arrest
7/13/2004	Gregory, Dick, comedian	Washington, DC	blocked an entrance	arrest
7/13/2004	Hoeffel, Joseph M., congressman	Washington, DC	blocked an entrance	arrest
4/28/2006	Lantos, Tom, congressman	Washington, DC	protest	arrest
4/28/2006	Lee, Sheila, congresswoman	Washington, DC	protest	arrest
1866	Love, Alfred Henry, merchant	Philadelphia	opposed	lost business
7/13/2004	Madison, Joe, performer	Washington, DC	blocked an entrance	arrest
4/28/2006	McGovern, James P., congressman	Washington, DC	protest	arrest
4/28/2006	Moran, Jim, congressman	Washington, DC	protest	arrest
1966	Mott, Jeremy, activist	Ridgewood, NJ	burned draft card	prison
4/28/2006	Olver, John Walter, congressman	Washington, DC	protest	arrest
7/13/2004	Rangel, Charles Bernard, politician	Washington, DC	blocked an entrance	arrest
5/1/2006	Rusesabagina, Paul, film producer	Washington, DC	protest	
7/13/2004	Rush, Bobby Lee, congressman	Washington, DC	blocked an entrance	arrest
5/16/2006	Watt, Melvin Luther, congressman	Washington, DC	protest	

Target of Act/Date	Name, Occupation	Location	Act	Consequence
Guantánamo prison				
1/11/2007	Iqbal, Asif	Washington, DC	protest	
1/10/2007	Ki-moon, Ban, United Nations secretary-general	Washington, DC	protest	
1/10/2007	Sheehan, Cindy, activist	Washington, DC	protest	
2006	Zewawai, Zohra, activist	Guantánamo, Cuba	protest	
1/10/2007	Zewawai, Zohra, activist	Washington, DC	protest	
gun carry ban				
12/15/2001	Stanley, Richard Eugene, merchant	Denver	carrying contraband weapon	confiscation
9/2002	Stanley, Richard Eugene, merchant	Denver	carrying contraband weapon	confiscation, jail, fine
hazardous waste				
4/30/1991	Eisen, Audrey Louise, activist	Bath, PA	protest	arraigned
4/30/1991	Sellers, John, activist	Bath, PA	protest	arraigned
heresy				
1657	Allen, William	Sandwich, MA	Quaker worship	warning
1663	Ambrose, Alice, preacher	Dover, NH	preached	lashed
1661	Bowne, John	Flushing, NY	Quaker worship, protest	arrest, exile
8/9/1656	Brend, William, preacher	Salem, MA	Quaker worship	jail
1658	Brend, William, preacher	Sandwich, MA	refused an oath	flogged
1658	Brown, Judith	Plymouth, MA	Quaker worship	lashed
1657	Burden, Anne	Boston	preached	jailed in the dark, exile, confiscation
1661	Christopherson, Wenlock	Boston	defied Puritans	exile
1663	Coleman, Anna, preacher	Dover, NH	preached	lashed
8/9/1656	Copeland, John	Salem, MA	Quaker worship	jail
1658	Copeland, John	Salem, MA	defied Puritans	jail
4/15/1658	Copeland, John	Cape Cod, MA	defied Puritans	scourged
1658	Davis, Nicholas	Plymouth, MA	Quaker worship	prison, exile
1657	Dowdney, Richard	Dedham, MA	delivered a message	
1657	Dowdney, Richard	Boston	Quaker worship	lashed, exile, confiscation
1638	Dyer, Mary Barrett, preacher	Boston	defied Puritans	exile
1657	Dyer, Mary Barrett, preacher	Boston	preached	jailed in the dark, exile, confiscation
1658	Dyer, Mary Barrett, preacher	New Haven, CT	defied Puritans	exile
1659	Dyer, Mary Barrett, preacher	Boston	visited Quakers	jail
10/19/1659	Dyer, Mary Barrett, preacher	Boston	defied Puritans	death sentence
6/1/1660	Dyer, Mary Barrett, preacher	Boston	defied Puritans	hanged
1638	Dyer, William, milliner	Boston	defied Puritans	exile
1666	Farnum, John, deacon	Boston	preached	jail, exile
1666	George, John	Boston	defied Puritans	jail

Target of Act/Date	Name, Occupation	Location	Act	Consequence
8/9/1656	Gibbons, Sarah	Boston	Quaker worship	jail
1666	Goold, Thomas	Boston	defied Puritans	jail
1659	Greenfield, Thomas	Boston	refused to testify	jail
10/1660	Harper, Deborah Perry	Plymouth, MA	aided Quakers	prison, exile
10/1660	Harper, Robert	Plymouth, MA	aided Quakers	prison, exile
1658	Harris, Thomas, preacher	Boston	preached	prison, lashed, low rations
3/22/1638	Hawkins, Jane, midwife	Boston	feminist teachings	banished
8/1657	Hodgson, Robert	Long Island, NY	preached	jail, lashed, fine, prison at hard labor
8/9/1656	Holder, Christopher	Salem, MA	Quaker worship	jail
1658	Holder, Christopher	Salem, MA	defied Puritans	throttled, jail
4/15/1658	Holder, Christopher	Cape Cod, MA	defied Puritans	scourged
6/3/1658	Holder, Christopher	Cape Cod, MA	defied Puritans	ear lopped
4/15/1658	Holder, Mary Scott	Cape Cod, MA	defied Puritans	prison
1662	Hooton, Elizabeth, preacher	Boston	visited imprisoned Quakers	abandoned
ca. 1665	Hooton, Elizabeth, preacher	Cambridge, MA	professed Quaker creed	whipped, abandoned
10/6/1659	Howland, Henry, constable	Plymouth, MA	Quaker worship	fine, confiscation
3/22/1638	Hutchinson, Anne Marbury, midwife	Boston	feminist teachings	banished
1658	Leddra, William, preacher	Plymouth, MA	Quaker worship	prison
3/14/1661	Leddra, William, preacher	Boston	Quaker worship	shackled, prison, hanging
1657	Newland, John	Sandwich, MA	Quaker worship	warning
1661	Norton, Humphrey, teacher	Boston	Quaker worship	lashed, jail, starvation
1666	Osborne, Priscilla Brighton	Boston	defied Puritans	ousted
1666	Osborne, Thomas	Boston	defied Puritans	jail
1658	Pearson, Peter	Plymouth, MA	Quaker worship	prison, lashed
8/9/1656	Prince, Mary	Boston	Quaker worship	jail
10/27/1659	Robinson, William, clergy	Boston	preached	confiscation, exile, hanged
1669	Robinson, William, clergy	Salem, MA	aided a heretic	fine, exile
4/15/1658	Scott, Katherine Marbury	Cape Cod, MA	defied Puritans	flogged, prison
4/15/1658	Scott, Patience	Cape Cod, MA	defied Puritans	prison
1658	Shattuck, Samuel	Salem, MA	aided Quakers	jail, flogged, exile
1669	Shattuck, Samuel	Salem, MA	aided a heretic	fine, exile
1657	Smith, Bathsheba	New London, CT	defied Puritans	threat
1658	Southwick, Cassandra Burnell	Salem, MA	defied Puritans	jail, threat
1658	Southwick, Laurence	Salem, MA	defied Puritans	jail, threat
10/27/1659	Stephenson, Marmaduke	Boston	preached	exile, hanging
8/9/1656	Thurston, Thomas	Boston	Quaker worship	jail
1663	Tomkins, Mary, preacher	Dover, NH	preached	lashed
8/1656	Waugh, Dorothy, servant	Boston	proselytized	starvation, jail, exile
8/9/1656	Waugh, Dorothy, servant	Boston	Quaker worship	jail
8/1657	Waugh, Dorothy, servant	New Amsterdam, NY	defied Puritans	jail
8/1656	Weatherhead, Mary	Boston	proselytized	starvation, jail, exile

Target of Act/Date	Name, Occupation	Location	Act	Consequence
8/9/1656	Weatherhead, Mary	Boston	Quaker worship	jail
8/1657	Weatherhead, Mary	New Amsterdam, NY	defied Puritans	jail
11/3/1659	Wharton, Edward	Boston	defied Puritans	scourged, fine
1634	Williams, Roger, clergy	Salem, MA	preached	ousted
1662	Wilson, George, soldier	Jamestown, VA	Quaker worship	shackled, died in jail
10/1660	Wright, Mary	Oyster Bay, NY	defied Puritans	jail

Hispanic displacement

Target of Act/Date	Name, Occupation	Location	Act	Consequence
9/28/1859	Cabrera, Tomás, ranch hand	Brownsville, TX	paramilitary	pistol-whipped
7/13/1859	Cortina, Juan Nepomuceno, soldier	Brownsville, TX	shot at a marshal	
9/28/1859	Cortina, Juan Nepomuceno, soldier	Brownsville, TX	jailbreak	
5/1861	Cortina, Juan Nepomuceno, soldier	Brownsville, TX	rebellion	house arrest
6/5/1967	Tijerina, Reies López, preacher	Echo Park, NM	sought land rights	

homelessness

Target of Act/Date	Name, Occupation	Location	Act	Consequence
1930s	Powell, Adam Clayton, Jr., clergy, politician	Harlem, NY	propaganda	
10/7/1989	Snyder, Mitch, advertiser	Washington, DC	march, trespass	arrest

House Committee on Un-American Activities

Target of Act/Date	Name, Occupation	Location	Act	Consequence
1949	Adler, Larry, musician	Hollywood, CA	contempt of Congress	exile
12/4/1964	Allen, Donna, economist	Washington, DC	contempt of Congress	
1951	Bernstein, Walter, screenwriter	Hollywood, CA	contempt of Congress	blacklist
1950	Bessie, Alvah, novelist, journalist	Hollywood, CA	contempt of Congress	prison, fine, blacklist,
1950	Biberman, Herbert J., director, scenarist	Hollywood, CA	contempt of Congress	prison, fine, exile
1951	Blitzstein, Marc, composer	Hollywood, CA	contempt of Congress	blacklist, exile
1951	Brand, Phoebe, actor	Hollywood, CA	contempt of Congress	blacklist
1950s	Brecht, Bertolt, playwright	Hollywood, CA	contempt of Congress	exile
1950s	Butler, Hugo, screenwriter	Hollywood, CA	contempt of Congress	blacklist
1951	Carnovsky, Morris, actor	Hollywood, CA	contempt of Congress	blacklist
1952	Chaplin, Charles, comedian	Hollywood, CA	contempt of Congress	visa denied
1950s	Cobb, Lee J., actor	Hollywood, CA	contempt of Congress	
1950	Cole, Lester, playwright, director	Hollywood, CA	contempt of Congress	prison, fine, exile
1950s	Comingore, Dorothy	Hollywood, CA	contempt of Congress	smeared
1953	Copland, Aaron, composer	Hollywood, CA	contempt of Congress	blacklist, censored
1950s	Crum, Bartley Cavanaugh	Hollywood, CA	contempt of Congress	smeared
1951	Da Silva, Howard, actor	Hollywood, CA	contempt of Congress	blacklist
1950s	Dassin, Jules, actor	Hollywood, CA	contempt of Congress	smeared
1950	Dmytryk, Edward, editor	Hollywood, CA	contempt of Congress	prison
1948	Durr, Clifford, lawyer	Hollywood, CA	contempt of Congress	blacklist
1950s	Eisler, Hanns, composer	Hollywood, CA	contempt of Congress	blacklist, exile
1950	Fast, Howard, writer	Hollywood, CA	contempt of Congress	blacklist, prison
1951	Foreman, Carl, producer	Hollywood, CA	contempt of Congress	blacklist, exile
1950s	Garfield, John, actor	Hollywood, CA	contempt of Congress	

Target of Act/Date	Name, Occupation	Location	Act	Consequence
1950s	Gordon, Bernard, screenwriter	Hollywood, CA	contempt of Congress	
1952	Gough, Lloyd, actor	Hollywood, CA	contempt of Congress	blacklist
1951	Grant, Lee, actor	Hollywood, CA	contempt of Congress	blacklist
1951	Hammett, Dashiell, writer	Hollywood, CA	contempt of Congress	jail
1952	Hellman, Lillian, playwright	Hollywood, CA	contempt of Congress	blacklist, jail
1950	Hobart, Rose, actor	Hollywood, CA	contempt of Congress	blacklist
1950	Holliday, Judy, actor	Hollywood, CA	contempt of Congress	blacklist
1952	Holliday, Judy, actor	Hollywood, CA	contempt of Congress	smeared
1953	Hughes, Langston, poet	Hollywood, CA	contempt of Congress	smeared
1952	Hunt, Marsha, actor	Hollywood, CA	contempt of Congress	blacklist
1952	Jaffe, Sam, actor	Hollywood, CA	contempt of Congress	blacklist
1947	Kelson, Perl, actor	Hollywood, CA	contempt of Congress	blacklist
1950	Lardner, Ring, Jr., journalist	Hollywood, CA	contempt of Congress	blacklist, prison, fine
1950s	Lawrence, Marc, actor	Hollywood, CA	contempt of Congress	
1950	Lawson, John Howard, screenwriter	Hollywood, CA	contempt of Congress	prison, fine, blacklist, exile
1949	Lee, Canada, actor	Hollywood, CA	contempt of Congress	blacklist
1950	Loeb, Philip, actor	Hollywood, CA	contempt of Congress	blacklist
1950s	Losey, Joseph, director	Hollywood, CA	contempt of Congress	blacklist
1950	Maltz, Albert, playwright	Hollywood, CA	contempt of Congress	blacklist, prison, fine
1950	Meredith, Burgess, actor	Hollywood, CA	contempt of Congress	blacklist
1954	Miller, Arthur, playwright	Hollywood, CA	contempt of Congress	passport cancelled
1950	Morgan, Henry, comedian	Hollywood, CA	contempt of Congress	blacklist
1947	Morley, Karen, actor	Hollywood, CA	contempt of Congress	blacklist
1950	Mostel, Zero, comic actor	Hollywood, CA	contempt of Congress	blacklist
1950s	Ornitz, Samuel, screenwriter	Hollywood, CA	contempt of Congress	prison, fine, blacklist
1953	Palca, Alfred, writer, producer	Hollywood, CA	contempt of Congress	blacklist, censored
1950	Parker, Dorothy, satirist	Hollywood, CA	contempt of Congress	blacklist
1947	Parks, Larry, actor	Hollywood, CA	contempt of Congress	blacklist
1952	Revere, Anne, actor	Hollywood, CA	contempt of Congress	blacklist
1950	Robeson, Paul, actor, singer, writer	Hollywood, CA	contempt of Congress	blacklist, exile
1949	Robinson, Earl Hawley, composer	Hollywood, CA	contempt of Congress	blacklist
1950	Scott, Adrian, screenwriter, producer	Hollywood, CA	contempt of Congress	prison, fine, blacklist
1950	Scott, Hazel, pianist, singer	Hollywood, CA	contempt of Congress	censored
1956	Seeger, Pete, folksinger	Hollywood, CA	contempt of Congress	convicted, blacklist
1953	Shaw, Artie, bandleader	Hollywood, CA	contempt of Congress	
1951	Shaw, Irwin, playwright	Hollywood, CA	contempt of Congress	blacklist, exile
1950	Shirer, William Lawrence, historian	Hollywood, CA	contempt of Congress	blacklist
1950	Sondergaard, Gale, actor	Hollywood, CA	contempt of Congress	exile
1950s	Stander, Lionel Jay, actor	Hollywood, CA	whistling "The Internationale"	libeled
1951	Trumbo, Dalton, screenwriter	Hollywood, CA	contempt of Congress	prison, fine, blacklist
1952	Wanamaker, Sam, actor, director	Hollywood, CA	contempt of Congress	blacklist, exile
1948	Welles, Orson, actor, director	Hollywood, CA	contempt of Congress	blacklist, exile
1948	White, Josh, singer, guitarist	Hollywood, CA	contempt of Congress	blacklist
12/4/1964	Wilson, Dagmar, activist	Washington, DC	contempt of Congress	

Target of Act/Date	Name, Occupation	Location	Act	Consequence
human rights abuse in Sudan				
7/13/2004	Fauntroy, Walter Edward, clergy	Washington, DC	felonious entry	arrest
7/13/2004	Rangel, Charles Bernard, politician	Washington, DC	felonious entry	arrest
7/13/2004	Robinson, Randall	Washington, DC	felonious entry	arrest
illegal assembly				
1654	Gaunt, Lydia Hampton	Sandwich, MA	Quaker worship	fine
1654	Gaunt, Peter	Sandwich, MA	Quaker worship	fine
impressment at sea				
1704	Anthony, Thomas	Portsmouth, RI	refused to serve	confined
1704	Smith, John	Portsmouth, RI	refused to serve	confined
Indian displacement				
11/14/1969	Anderson, Wallace Mad Bear, prophet, medicine man	Alcatraz, CA	trespass	
2/27/1973	Aquash, Anna Mae, activist	Wounded Knee, SD	paramilitary	
11/1975	Aquash, Anna Mae, activist	Oregon	escape from custody	arrest, assassination
2/27/1973	Aquash, Nogeeshik, artist	Wounded Knee, SD	paramilitary	
10/11/2004	Badhand, Yank, elder	Denver	protest	
11/14/1969	Banks, Dennis James, activist	Alcatraz, CA	trespass	
2/27/1973	Bear Runner, Oscar	Wounded Knee, SD	paramilitary	
1/1879	Bear Shield	Omaha, NE	left a reservation	
11/14/1969	Bellecourt, Clyde, activist	Alcatraz, CA	trespass	
1970	Bennett, Ramona, educator	Tacoma, WA	defied officers	arrest, threat
11/14/1969	Bergen, Candace, actor	Alcatraz, CA	trespass	
1879	Big Snake	Baxter Springs, OK	left a reservation	shot
11/14/1969	Brando, Marlon, actor	Alcatraz, CA	trespass	
9/1971	Brightman, Lehman L., historian	Mount Rushmore, SD	paramilitary	
10/11/2004	Dann, Carrie, activist	Denver	protest	
11/14/1969	Drath, Marjorie, artist	Alcatraz, CA	trespass	
11/14/1969	Drath, Phillip, rancher	Alcatraz, CA	trespass	
11/14/1969	Fonda, Jane, actor	Alcatraz, CA	trespass	
3/8/1970	Fonda, Jane, actor	Fort Lawton, WA	protest	
2/27/1973	Hat, Sally, teacher	Wounded Knee, SD	paramilitary	
10/9/2004	Morris, Glenn T., teacher	Denver	protest	
11/14/1969	Oakes, Richard, activist	Alcatraz, CA	trespass	
3/8/1970	Peltier, Leonard, mechanic	Fort Lawton, WA	protest	
1/1879	Prairie Flower	Omaha, NE	left a reservation	
1/1879	Primo, Suzette	Omaha, NE	left a reservation	arrest
11/14/1969	Quinn, Anthony, actor	Alcatraz, CA	trespass	
3/8/1970	Satiacum, Bob, chief	Fort Lawton, WA	protest	
1/1879	Standing Bear, chief	Omaha, NE	left a reservation	arrest

Target of Act/Date	Name, Occupation	Location	Act	Consequence
1/1879	Standing Bear, Fanny	Omaha, NE	left a reservation	arrest
10/11/2004	Tinker, George Edward, theologian	Denver	protest	
11/14/1969	Trudell, John, poet, actor	Alcatraz, CA	trespass	
11/14/1969	Trudell, Lou	Alcatraz, CA	trespass	
3/8/1970	Whitebear, Bernie Reyes, activist	Fort Lawton, WA	protest	

Indian grave robbery

1987	Banks, Dennis James, activist	Uniontown, KY	protest	
10/30/1999	Beaulieu, Ruby, activist	New Port Richey, FL	protest	
1985	Murphy, Sheridan, activist	Tampa, FL	protest	

Indian wars

1703	Macomber, Thomas, doctor	Taunton, MA	draft evasion	prison
1703	Smith, John	Bristol, MA	draft evasion	prison
1743	Woolman, John, tailor, philosopher	Northampton, PA	protested usurpation	

Iraq War

5/14/2006	Adams, Hunter Campbell, doctor	Washington, DC	march	
2005	Asner, Ed, actor	Crawford, TX	protest	
2005	Baez, Joan, folksinger	Crawford, TX	protest	
9/26/2005	Baez, Joan, folksinger	Washington, DC	protest	
2/11/2007	Barrios, Luis, priest	New York City	protest	arrest
2/13/2007	Barrios, Luis, priest	New York City	protest	arrest
2006	Bazzi, Zack, soldier	Fallujah, Iraq	protest film	
3/2003	Benderman, Kevin, soldier	Fort Hood, TX	defied orders	prison
3/6/2006	Benjamin, Medea, author	New York City	protest	arrest
9/26/2005	Bond, Julian, activist	Washington, DC	protest	
6/28/2006	Brix, Michael, activist	Philadelphia	blocked doors	jail, fine
6/28/2006	Brown, Marion, activist	Philadelphia	blocked doors	jail, fine
5/2007	Cantu, Ronn, soldier	Los Angeles		
2004	Coffin, William Sloane, Jr., clergy	Washington, DC	protest	
3/20/2003	Diaz, Jennifer, student	Chicago	vigil, demonstration	
3/21/2003	Eisenberg-Guyot, Nadja, student	Philadelphia	blocked a building	
2005	Ellsberg, Daniel, activist	Crawford, TX	protest	
1/27/2007	Ensler, Eve, dramatist	Washington, DC	protest	
6/2007	Ergo, Mike, soldier	Walnut Creek, CA	e-mail protest	
2006	Fonda, Jane, actor	Crawford, TX	protest	
1/27/2007	Fonda, Jane, actor	Washington, DC	protest	
3/21/2003	Ford, Dana, student	Philadelphia	blocked a building	
6/28/2006	Fultz, Jason, activist	Philadelphia	blocked doors	jail, fine
1/27/2007	Glover, Danny, actor	Washington, DC	protest	
3/21/2003	Hanlon-Smith, Jamie, student	Philadelphia	blocked a building	
6/28/2006	Haw, Cassandra Haino, activist	Philadelphia	blocked doors	jail, fine
6/28/2006	Haw, Christopher, activist	Philadelphia	blocked doors	jail, fine

Target of Act/Date	Name, Occupation	Location	Act	Consequence
9/26/2005	Jackson, Jesse, clergy	Washington, DC	protest	
7/4/2006	Jon-Paul, Chloe, retiree	Washington, DC	rally	arrest
2/2007	Kelly, Kathy, activist	Washington, DC	sit-in	prison
3/21/2003	Liem, Elizabeth, student	Philadelphia	blocked a building	
2005	Lynd, Staughton, history professor	New Haven, CT	sued Pentagon	
6/2007	Magruder, Jabar, soldier	Walnut Creek, CA	anti-enlistment protest	
7/4/2006	Mallard, Geoffrey, disabled veteran	Washington, DC	rally	arrest
7/23/2007	McGovern, Raymond, CIA analyst	Washington, DC	sit-in	arrest, fine
6/28/2006	Metzler, Sylvia, activist	Philadelphia	blocked doors	jail, fine
2006	Moriarty, Mike, soldier	Fallujah, Iraq	protest film	
3/21/2003	Morris, Sarah, student	Philadelphia	blocked a building	
3/21/2003	Noterman, Elsa, student	Philadelphia	blocked a building	
6/2007	O'Neill, Sean, soldier	Walnut Creek, CA	anti-enlistment protest	
1/27/2007	Penn, Sean, actor	Washington, DC	protest	
2006	Pink, Steven, soldier	Fallujah, Iraq	protest film	
3/20/2003	Ritscher, Mark David "Malachi," jazz musician	Chicago	self-immolation	
1/27/2007	Robbins, Tim, actor	Washington, DC	protest	
6/28/2006	Sanchez, Sonia, poet	Philadelphia	trespass	arrest
5/14/2006	Sarandon, Susan, actor	Washington, DC	demonstration	
1/27/2007	Sarandon, Susan, actor	Washington, DC	protest	
9/26/2005	Sharpton, Al, clergy	Washington, DC	protest	
8/6/2005	Sheehan, Cindy, activist	Crawford, TX	vigil	
9/26/2005	Sheehan, Cindy, activist	Washington, DC	tied to a fence	arrest
1/31/2006	Sheehan, Cindy, activist	Washington, DC	wore protest T-shirt	charged
3/6/2006	Sheehan, Cindy, activist	New York City	blocked an entrance	arrest
5/14/2006	Sheehan, Cindy, activist	Washington, DC	demonstration	
7/23/2007	Sheehan, Cindy, activist	Washington, DC	sit-in	arrest, fine
9/10/2007	Sheehan, Cindy, activist	Washington, DC	shouted	arrest
8/28/2005	Sheen, Martin, actor	Crawford, TX	protest	
1/2006	Vadim, Vanessa, activist	Honolulu, HI	refused deployment	demotion
6/22/2006	Watada, Ehren, soldier	Honolulu, HI	refused deployment	charged
1/27/2007	Waters, Maxine, congresswoman	Washington, DC	protest	
6/28/2006	Willoughby, Lillian, activist	Philadelphia	blocked doors	jail, fine
1/27/2007	Woolsey, Lynn, congresswoman	Washington, DC	protest	
7/23/2007	Yearwood, Lennox, Jr., veteran	Washington, DC	sit-in	arrest, fine

jail rules

10/14/1656	Upsal, Nicholas, innkeeper	Boston	fed prisoners	fine, jail

Japanese internment

10/20/1942	Hirabayashi, Gordon Kiyoshi, student	Seattle	defied curfew	
5/30/1942	Korematsu, Fred Toyosaburo, welder	San Leandro, CA	defied curfew	
7/21/1944	Omura, James M., journalist	Heart Mountain, WY	protest	charged

Target of Act/Date	Name, Occupation	Location	Act	Consequence
12/5/1942	Tayama, Fred	Manzanar, CA	revolt	beaten
3/28/1942	Yasui, Minoru, lawyer	Hood River, OR	defied curfew	lost citizenship

Kaho'Olawe, Hawaii destruction

Target of Act/Date	Name, Occupation	Location	Act	Consequence
1/6/1976	Aluli, Kimo, merchant	Kaho'Olawe, HI	trespass	
1/6/1976	Aluli, Noa Emmett, doctor	Kaho'Olawe, HI	trespass	arrest
8/30/1975	DeFries, Emma, priestess	Kaho'Olawe, HI	conspiracy	
8/30/1975	Hanchett, Barbara, activist	Kaho'Olawe, HI	conspiracy	
1/6/1976	Helm, George Jarrett, Jr., musician	Kaho'Olawe, HI	trespass	
2/2/1977	Helm, George Jarrett, Jr., musician	Kaho'Olawe, HI	trespass	
3/7/1977	Helm, George Jarrett, Jr., musician	Kaho'Olawe, HI	trespass	
8/30/1975	Kanakaole, Edith, elder	Kaho'Olawe, HI	conspiracy	
8/30/1975	Kapuni, Lani, activist	Kaho'Olawe, HI	conspiracy	
2/2/1977	Ka'uhane, Francis, activist	Kaho'Olawe, HI	trespass	
1/6/1976	Kealoha, Sam, soldier	Kaho'Olawe, HI	trespass	fine, prison
8/30/1975	Ku, Clara, activist	Kaho'Olawe, HI	trespass	
8/30/1975	Lee, Mary, activist	Kaho'Olawe, HI	conspiracy	
1/6/1976	Lind, Ian, journalist	Kaho'Olawe, HI	trespass	
8/30/1975	Maxwell, Charles Kauluwehi, Sr., storyteller	Kaho'Olawe, HI	trespass	
1/6/1976	Maxwell, Charles Kauluwehi, Sr., storyteller	Kaho'Olawe, HI	trespass	
1995	Maxwell, Charles Kauluwehi, Sr., storyteller	Kaho'Olawe, HI	protest	
1/6/1976	Miles, Ellen, activist	Kaho'Olawe, HI	trespass	
3/7/1977	Mitchell, Billy, activist	Kaho'Olawe, HI	trespass	
4/16/1982	Mitchell, Harry Kunihi, carpenter, healer	Kaho'Olawe, HI	trespass	
1/6/1976	Mitchell, Kimo, park ranger	Kaho'Olawe, HI	trespass	
3/7/1977	Mitchell, Kimo, park ranger	Kaho'Olawe, HI	trespass	
1/6/1976	Morse, Stephen, reformer	Kaho'Olawe, HI	trespass	
1/6/1976	Mowat, Karl, activist	Kaho'Olawe, HI	trespass	fine, prison
1/6/1976	Prejean, Gail Kawaipuna, comedian	Kaho'Olawe, HI	trespass	
1/6/1976	Ritte, Walter, Jr., teacher	Kaho'Olawe, HI	trespass	fine, prison
2/2/1977	Ritte, Walter, Jr., teacher	Kaho'Olawe, HI	trespass	
1990	Saiki, Patricia Fukuda, politician	Kaho'Olawe, HI	protest	
1/6/1976	Sawyer, Richard, activist	Kaho'Olawe, HI	trespass	fine, prison
2/2/1977	Sawyer, Richard, activist	Kaho'Olawe, HI	trespass	
1/6/1976	Villalba, Karla, student	Kaho'Olawe, HI	trespass	
8/20/1975	Wainui, Rose, activist	Kaho'Olawe, HI	conspiracy	
2/2/1977	Warrington, Charles, activist	Kaho'Olawe, HI	trespass	

Korean War

Target of Act/Date	Name, Occupation	Location	Act	Consequence
1950	Harper, Robin	Wallingford, PA	refused to serve	
1950	Norton, Edgar R., music student	Glen Falls, NY	pacifism	

Target of Act/Date	Name, Occupation	Location	Act	Consequence
1948	Palmer, T. Vail, ethicist	Concordville, PA	refused to register	prison
1/1951	Seaver, David	Haverford, PA	refused to register	prison
1/1951	Seaver, Paul	Haverford, PA	refused to register	prison

Kosovo bombing

6/8/1999	Legg, Sam, college director	Washington, DC	protest	arrest

labor exploitation

11/1909	Beard, Mary Ritter, activist	New York City	strike	jail
9/2/1921	Blizzard, Bill, miner	Matewan, WV	strike	arrest
2/25/1913	Boyd, Sumner, activist	Paterson, NJ	mill strike	prison
1/29/1912	Caruso, Joseph, agitator	Lawrence, MA	strike	prison
8/1/1921	Chambers, Ed, police officer	Matewan, WV	abetted unionism	assassinated
5/4/1886	Engel, George, worker	Chicago	strike	hanged
1/29/1912	Ettor, Joseph, activist	Lawrence, MA	murder	charged
11/11/1919	Everett, Wesley, activist	Centralia, WA	union organizing	lynched
11/28/1909	Feligno, Charley, agitator	Spokane, WA	union organizing	prison
5/4/1886	Fielden, Samuel, agitator	Chicago	factory strike	prison
5/4/1886	Fischer, Adolph, compositor	Chicago	promoted unions	hanged
1905	Flynn, Elizabeth Gurley, activist	Schenectady, NY	blocked traffic	arrest
1906	Flynn, Elizabeth Gurley, activist	New York City	street corner speech	arrest
9/28/1908	Flynn, Elizabeth Gurley, activist	Missoula, MT	street speech	arrest
1909	Flynn, Elizabeth Gurley, activist	Philadelphia	demonstration	arrest
11/28/1909	Flynn, Elizabeth Gurley, activist	Spokane, WA	chained to a lamppost	arrest
1911	Flynn, Elizabeth Gurley, activist	Philadelphia	strike speech	arrest
1912	Flynn, Elizabeth Gurley, activist	New York City	hotel strike	arrest
1/1912	Flynn, Elizabeth Gurley, activist	Lawrence, MA	mill strike	jail
2/25/1913	Flynn, Elizabeth Gurley, activist	Paterson, NJ	mill strike	arrest
1914	Flynn, Elizabeth Gurley, activist	Salt Lake City	defense of Joe Hill	arrest
1916	Flynn, Elizabeth Gurley, activist	Spokane, WA	protest	arrest
1916	Flynn, Elizabeth Gurley, activist	Mesaba, MN	strike	arrest
1917	Flynn, Elizabeth Gurley, activist	Chicago	defense of IWW	arrest
4/1917	Flynn, Elizabeth Gurley, activist	Duluth, MN	pacifism	banished
9/10/1897	Futa, John, miner	Lattimer, PA	march	shot
1/29/1912	Giovannitti, Arturo M., activist	Lawrence, MA	strike	prison
8/1/1921	Hatfield, Albert Sidney, police chief	Matewan, WV	abetted unionism	assassinated
1/1912	Haywood, William Dudley, labor organizer	Lawrence, MA	mill strike	jail
1921	Haywood, William Dudley, labor organizer		promoted unions	exile
11/19/1915	Hill, Joe, singer	Salt Lake City	supported unionism	executed
9/10/1897	Jurich, Steve, miner	Lattimer, PA	march	shot
9/2/1921	Keeney, Frank, miner	Matewan, WV	strike	arrest
1913	Keller, Helen Adams, author	New York City	promoted unions	
3/1914	Keller, Helen Adams, author	Sacramento, CA	promoted unions	

Target of Act/Date	Name, Occupation	Location	Act	Consequence
5/4/1886	Lingg, Louis, carpenter	Chicago	factory strike	prison
11/28/1909	Little, Frank, agitator	Spokane, WA	union organizing	prison
8/1/1917	Little, Frank, agitator	Butte, MT	union organizing	lynched
1/29/1912	LoPizzo, Anna	Lawrence, MA	strike	shot
9/2/1921	Mooney, Fred, miner	Matewan, WV	strike	arrest
5/4/1886	Neebe, Oscar William, yeast maker	Chicago	factory strike	prison
1934	Olsen, Jack, warehouse clerk	San Francisco	strike	jail
1932	Olsen, Tillie Lerner, writer	Kansas City, KS	distributed leaflets	jail
1934	Olsen, Tillie Lerner, writer	San Francisco	strike	jail
11/1909	O'Reilly, Leonora, activist	New York City	strike	jail
5/4/1886	Parsons, Albert Richard, editor	Chicago	promoted unions	hanged
5/4/1886	Parsons, Lucy Gonzalez, author	Chicago	factory strike	
7/1925	Randolph, Asa Philip, editor	Chicago	promoted unions	
2/25/1913	Quinlan, Patrick J., activist	Paterson, NJ	mill strike	prison
5/4/1886	Schwab, Michael, bookbinder	Chicago	factory strike	prison
1937	Seidman, Joel, author	Chicago	propaganda	
5/4/1886	Spies, August Vincent Theodore, writer	Chicago	distributed pamphlets	hanged
2/25/1913	Tresca, Carlo, activist	Paterson, NJ	mill strike	

labor organization ban

Target of Act/Date	Name, Occupation	Location	Act	Consequence
12/29/1936	Addes, George, labor organizer	Flint, MI	promoted unions	
1946	Alinsky, Saul David, criminologist	Chicago	promoted unions	prison
1966	Baez, Joan, folksinger	Santa Monica, CA	demonstration	
12/10/1970	Baez, Joan, folksinger	Salinas, CA	abetted picket	
9/2/1921	Blizzard, Bill, miner	Matewan, WV	conspiracy, murder	jail
2/13/1913	Boswell, Charles H., editor	Charleston, WV	promoted solidarity	arrested
2/25/1913	Boyd, Frederick Sumner, activist	Paterson, NJ	strike	jail
9/16/1965	Chávez, César, labor leader	Delano, CA	violated court order	
3/1966	Chávez, César, labor leader	Sacramento, CA	march	
6/1970	Chávez, César, labor leader	Delano, CA	strike, boycott	
12/10/1970	Chávez, César, labor leader	Salinas, CA	picket	jail, death threats
8/1973	Chávez, César, labor leader	Delano, CA	picket, refused to leave cell	jail
2/1975	Chávez, César, labor leader	Delano, CA	boycott	
1986	Chávez, César, labor leader	Delano, CA	boycott, fast	
7/1988	Chávez, César, labor leader	Delano, CA	boycott, fast	
9/1990	Chávez, César, labor leader	Los Angeles	violated a court order	arrest
1/1937	Coburn, William, laborer	Flint, MI	strike	killed
12/29/1936	Dale, Ralph, labor organizer	Flint, MI	promoted unions	
1921	Day, Dorothy, reformer, editor	Chicago	organized	charged with prostitution
8/1973	Day, Dorothy, reformer, editor	Delano, CA	organized	jail
12/29/1936	DeLong, Earl, labor organizer	Flint, MI	promoted unions	shot
12/29/1936	Dollinger, Genora Johnson, labor leader	Flint, MI	promoted unions	
11/11/1919	Everett, Wesley, activist	Centralia, WA	labor organizing	lynched

Target of Act/Date	Name, Occupation	Location	Act	Consequence
11/30/1909	Filigno, Charley, activist	Spokane, WA	conspiracy	prison
9/28/1908	Flynn, Elizabeth Gurley, activist	Missoula, MT	street speech	arrest
1906	Flynn, Helen Gurley, activist	New York City	speech	arrest
9/1919	Foster, William Z., labor organizer	Duquesne, PA	labor assembly	jail
11/17/1936	Frankensteen, Richard, labor leader	Detroit, MI	sit-down strike	
7/1988	Goldberg, Whoopi, actor	Delano, CA	boycott, fast	
1891	Hado, Dud, union organizer	Norton, VA	concealed weapon	fine
6/20/1902	Hagerty, Thomas J., priest	Clarksburg, WV	violated a court injunction	arraigned
12/29/1936	Hapgood, Mary Donovan, labor leader	Flint, MI	promoted unions	
12/29/1936	Hapgood, William Powers, labor leader	Flint, MI	promoted unions	
12/30/1905	Haywood, William Dudley, labor organizer	Denver	murder	tried
12/29/1936	Hendricks, Nellie Besson, labor leader	Flint, MI	promoted unions	
11/19/1915	Hill, Joe, singer	Salt Lake City	murder	firing squad
1988	Huerta, Dolores, labor organizer	San Francisco	picket	clubbed
7/1988	Jackson, Jesse, clergy	Delano, CA	boycott, fast	
12/29/1936	Johnson, Kermit, labor leader	Flint, MI	promoted unions	
7/15/1877	Jones, Mary "Mother," labor organizer	Norton, VA	public harangue	
1/22/1890	Jones, Mary "Mother," labor organizer	Columbus, OH	public harangue	
1891	Jones, Mary "Mother," labor organizer	Norton, VA	public harangue	death threat
6/15/1895	Jones, Mary "Mother," labor organizer	Philadelphia	public harangue	
11/1899	Jones, Mary "Mother," labor organizer	Arnot, PA	public rally, march	
2/18/1901	Jones, Mary "Mother," labor organizer	Scranton, PA	public rally, march	
1902	Jones, Mary "Mother," labor organizer	Manayunk, PA	public harangue	
6/20/1902	Jones, Mary "Mother," labor organizer	Clarksburg, WV	violated injunction	arraigned
4/24/1904	Jones, Mary "Mother," labor organizer	Helper, UT	public harangue	arson, jail
2/20/1906	Jones, Mary "Mother," labor organizer	Bisbee, AZ	public harangue	
1910	Jones, Mary "Mother," labor organizer	Milwaukee, WI	promoted solidarity	
6/1912	Jones, Mary "Mother," labor organizer	Greensburg, PA	promoted solidarity	
2/13/1913	Jones, Mary "Mother," labor organizer	Charleston, WV	promoted solidarity	arrested
1/4/1914	Jones, Mary "Mother," labor organizer	Trinidad, CO	abetted insurrection	deported
1/12/1914	Jones, Mary "Mother," labor organizer	Trinidad, CO	abetted insurrection	deported
3/1/1914	Jones, Mary "Mother," labor organizer	Trinidad, CO	abetted insurrection	deported
3/22/1914	Jones, Mary "Mother," labor organizer	Walsenburg, CO	strike	jail
4/20/1914	Jones, Mary "Mother," labor organizer	Ludlow, CO	fund-raising	arrest
1915	Jones, Mary "Mother," labor organizer	New York City	public harangue	
8/20/1919	Jones, Mary "Mother," labor organizer	Homestead, PA	speech	arrest, fine
9/1919	Jones, Mary "Mother," labor organizer	Duquesne, PA	labor assembly	jail
8/1/1921	Jones, Mary "Mother," labor organizer	Mingo County, WV	conspiracy	
11/3/1877	Kearney, Dennis, labor organizer	San Francisco	public speech	arrest
9/2/1921	Keeney, Frank, miner	Matewan, WV	conspiracy, murder	arrest
4/8/1968	King, Coretta Scott, activist	Memphis, TN	protest	
3/28/1968	King, Martin Luther, Jr., clergy	Memphis, TN	march	shot, tear gas
12/29/1936	Kraus, Henry, labor organizer	Flint, MI	promoted unions	

Target of Act/Date	Name, Occupation	Location	Act	Consequence
12/29/1936	Krause, Charles I., labor leader	Flint, MI	promoted unions	
12/29/1936	Lewis, John Llewellyn, labor leader	Flint, MI	promoted unions	
11/30/1909	Little, Frank, activist	Spokane, WA	conspiracy	prison
8/1/1917	Little, Frank, activist	Butte, MT	labor organization	lynched
9/21/1983	Lopez, Rene	Fresno, CA	voted in a union election	shot
12/29/1936	Martin, Homer, labor organizer	Flint, MI	promoted unions	
9/2/1921	Mooney, Fred, miner	Matewan, WV	conspiracy, murder	arrest
7/1988	Olmos, Edward James, actor	Delano, CA	boycott, fast	
1934	Pallares, Jesus, union organizer	Gallup, NM	promoted unions	deported
12/29/1936	Pitts, Ruth, labor leader	Flint, MI	blocked gates	
2/25/1913	Quinlan, Patrick J., activist	Paterson, NJ	lectured	prison
12/29/1936	Reuther, Fania Sankin, labor leader	Flint, MI	sit-down strike	
11/28/1936	Reuther, Roy, labor leader	Detroit, MI	sit-down strike	
11/28/1936	Reuther, Victor George, labor leader	Detroit, MI	sit-down strike	
11/28/1936	Reuther, Walter Philip, labor leader	Detroit, MI	sit-down strike	
12/29/1936	Roy, Tekla, labor leader	Flint, MI	blocked gates	
7/1988	Sheen, Martin, actor	Delano, CA	boycott, fast	
7/1988	Simon, Carly, folksinger	Delano, CA	boycott, fast	
1932	Tenayuca, Emma Zepeda, labor organizer	San Antonio, TX	picket	jail
1/31/1938	Tenayuca, Emma Zepeda, labor organizer	San Antonio, TX	strike	police brutality, jail, death threat
8/25/1939	Tenayuca, Emma Zepeda, labor organizer	San Antonio, TX	promoted unions	mob violence
12/29/1936	Travis, Bob, labor organizer	Flint, MI	promoted unions	
2/25/1913	Tresca, Carlo, activist	Paterson, NJ	labor organizing	arrest
11/1924	Valdane, Robert, dam builder	Los Angeles	distributed literature	prison, exile
12/29/1936	Van Zandt, Roscoe, labor leader	Flint, MI	promoted unions	
12/29/1936	Walker, Teeter, labor leader	Flint, MI	promoted unions	

land profiteering

Target of Act/Date	Name, Occupation	Location	Act	Consequence
5/1808	Barlow, Nathan, farmer	Albion, ME	jailbreak, assault	prison at hard labor
1/1808	Brackett, Daniel, farmer	Fairfax, ME	paramilitary leader	
1/1808	Brackett, Thomas, farmer	Falmouth, ME	jailbreak	
1790s	Ely, Samuel, clergy, tractarian	Northport, ME	paramilitary leader	
1790s	Shurtleff, James, Baptist elder	Litchfield, ME	paramilitary leader	lynching

loyalty oath

Target of Act/Date	Name, Occupation	Location	Act	Consequence
8/28/1777	Affleck, Isabella	Philadelphia	agitation	
8/28/1777	Affleck, Thomas, cabinetmaker	Philadelphia	treason	prison
8/28/1777	Asheton, Robert, merchant	Philadelphia	treason	prison
8/28/1777	Ashton, Thomas, merchant	Philadelphia	treason	prison
8/28/1777	Ayres, E.	Philadelphia	treason	prison
8/28/1777	Bond, Phineas, doctor	Philadelphia	treason	exile
1658	Brend, William, London	Salem, MA	refused loyalty oath	lashed
8/28/1777	Brown, Elijah, Sr., grain merchant	Philadelphia	treason	parole

Target of Act/Date	Name, Occupation	Location	Act	Consequence
8/28/1777	Brown, Mary Armitt	Philadelphia	agitation	
8/28/1777	Chew, Benjamin	Philadelphia	treason	banished
8/28/1777	Coombe, Thomas, clergy	Philadelphia	treason	exile
8/28/1777	Drinker, Elizabeth	Philadelphia	agitation	
8/28/1777	Drinker, Henry, ironmaster	Philadelphia	treason	prison
7/15/1779	Drinker, Henry, ironmaster	Philadelphia	treason	jail
8/28/1777	Eddy, Charles, ironmonger	Philadelphia	treason	prison
8/28/1777	Emlen, Caleb	Philadelphia	treason	prison
8/28/1777	Emlen, Samuel, Jr.	Philadelphia	treason	prison
8/28/1777	Fisher, Esther	Philadelphia	agitation	
8/28/1777	Fisher, Joshua, textile merchant	Philadelphia	treason	prison
8/28/1777	Fisher, Miers, merchant, lawyer	Philadelphia	treason	prison
8/28/1777	Fisher, Samuel Rowland, merchant	Philadelphia	treason	prison
7/15/1779	Fisher, Samuel Rowland, merchant	Philadelphia	treason	jail
8/28/1777	Fisher, Sarah Logan	Philadelphia	agitation	
8/28/1777	Fisher, Sarah Redwood	Philadelphia	agitation	
8/28/1777	Fisher, Thomas, merchant	Philadelphia	treason	prison
8/28/1777	Fox, Joseph, carpenter	Philadelphia	treason	prison
8/28/1777	Galloway, John	Philadelphia	treason	prison
8/28/1777	Gilpin, Thomas, merchant, farmer	Philadelphia	treason	prison
8/28/1777	Hollingshead, William, silversmith	Philadelphia	treason	prison
8/28/1777	Hunt, John, merchant	Philadelphia	treason	forcible arrest, prison
8/28/1777	Hunt, Rachel	Philadelphia	agitation	
8/28/1777	Imlay, William, politician	Philadelphia	treason	prison
8/28/1777	Jackson, Samuel	Philadelphia	treason	prison
8/28/1777	James, Abel, merchant	Philadelphia	treason	prison
8/28/1777	James, John	Philadelphia	treason	forced to flee
8/28/1777	Jervis, Charles, merchant	Philadelphia	treason	prison
8/28/1777	Jervis, Elizabeth Walton	Philadelphia	agitation	
8/28/1777	Jervis, Rebecca	Philadelphia	agitation	
8/28/1777	Jones, Owen, Jr., merchant	Philadelphia	treason	prison
8/28/1777	Jones, Susanna Evans	Philadelphia	agitation	
8/28/1777	Kuhn, Adam, doctor	Philadelphia	treason	prison
8/28/1777	Lennox, William, Jr.	Philadelphia	treason	prison
8/28/1777	Lenox, David	Philadelphia	treason	prison
8/28/1777	Livezey, Thomas	Philadelphia	treason	prison
1917	McDowell, Mary Stone, teacher	Brooklyn, NY	refused pledge	fired
8/28/1777	Murdoch, Samuel	Philadelphia	treason	prison
8/28/1777	Pemberton, Hannah Zane	Philadelphia	agitation	
8/28/1777	Pemberton, Israel, Jr., merchant	Philadelphia	treason	forcible arrest, prison
8/28/1777	Pemberton, James, merchant	Philadelphia	treason	prison
8/28/1777	Pemberton, John, trader, clergy	Philadelphia	treason	prison
8/28/1777	Pemberton, Mary Stansbury	Philadelphia	agitation	
8/28/1777	Pemberton, Phebe Lewis	Philadelphia	agitation	
8/28/1777	Penn, John, Sr.	Philadelphia	treason	banished

Target of Act/Date	Name, Occupation	Location	Act	Consequence
8/28/1777	Pennington, Edward, businessman	Philadelphia	treason	prison, vandalism
8/28/1777	Pennington, Sarah Shoemaker	Philadelphia	agitation	
8/28/1777	Pike, Thomas, dancemaster, fencing teacher	Philadelphia	treason, violated curfew	house arrest
8/28/1777	Pleasants, Mary Pemberton	Philadelphia	agitation	
8/28/1777	Pleasants, Samuel, merchant	Philadelphia	treason	forcible arrest, prison
8/28/1777	Roberts, George	Philadelphia	treason	prison
8/28/1777	Roberts, Hugh	Philadelphia	treason	prison
8/28/1777	Shoemaker, Samuel, merchant	Philadelphia	treason	prison
8/28/1777	Smith, Elizabeth	Philadelphia	agitation	
8/28/1777	Smith, William, clergy	Philadelphia	treason	exile
8/28/1777	Smith, William Drewit, druggist	Philadelphia	treason	prison
8/28/1777	Starr, James	Philadelphia	treason	stoned
8/28/1777	Stedman, Alexander	Philadelphia	treason	prison
8/28/1777	Stedman, Charles, Jr., investor	Philadelphia	treason	prison
8/28/1777	Warder, Jeremiah, trader	Philadelphia	treason	prison
8/28/1777	Wharton, Rachel Midcalf	Philadelphia	agitation	
8/28/1777	Wharton, Thomas, Sr., merchant	Philadelphia	treason	jail, prison, land confiscated
8/28/1777	Zane, Isaac, ironworker	Philadelphia	treason	stoned

lynching

Target of Act/Date	Name, Occupation	Location	Act	Consequence
11/1934	Dorsey, Emmett, teacher	Washington, DC	paraded illegally	arrest
11/1934	Lovett, Edward P., lawyer	Washington, DC	paraded illegally	arrest
11/1934	Murphy, George B., Jr., editor	Washington, DC	paraded illegally	arrest
1930s	Powell, Adam Clayton, Jr., clergy, politician	Harlem, NY	propaganda	
8/28/1955	Powell, Adam Clayton, Jr., clergy, politician	Washington, DC	rally	
11/1934	Wilkins, Roy, editor	Washington, DC	paraded illegally	arrest

marijuana ban

Target of Act/Date	Name, Occupation	Location	Act	Consequence
8/2002	Epis, Bryan James	Butte County, CA	grew marijuana	prison
9/23/2002	McVay, Doug, activist	Washington, DC	handcuffed to a fence	arrest
1975	Randall, Robert, speechwriter	Washington, DC	marijuana use	arrest
9/23/2002	Thomas, Charles, activist	Washington, DC	handcuffed to a fence	arrest

marriage laws

Target of Act/Date	Name, Occupation	Location	Act	Consequence
1886	Harman, Lillian, publisher	Valley Falls, KS	cohabitation	prison
1886	Walker, Edwin Cox, editor	Valley Falls, KS	cohabitation	prison

Mexican Revolution

Target of Act/Date	Name, Occupation	Location	Act	Consequence
1911	Jones, Mary "Mother," labor organizer	Washington, DC	protest	

Target of Act/Date	Name, Occupation	Location	Act	Consequence
Mexican-American War				
1840s	Thoreau, Henry David, philosopher	Concord, MA	resisted taxes	jail
military aggression				
7/3/1969	Boskey, Jill Ann, activist	New York City	destroyed property	arrest
10/21/1967	Chomsky, Noam, linguist	Arlington, VA	trespass, blocked traffic	arrest
7/3/1969	Czarnik, Kathy, activist	New York City	destroyed property	arrest
10/20/1967	Deming, Barbara, journalist	Arlington, VA	trespass, blocked traffic	arrest
7/3/1969	Green, Valentine, activist	New York City	destroyed property	arrest
7/3/1969	Kennedy, Pat, activist	New York City	destroyed property	arrest
10/21/1967	Lens, Sidney, historian	Arlington, VA	trespass, blocked traffic	arrest
10/21/1967	Levertov, Denise, poet	Arlington, VA	trespass, blocked traffic	arrest
10/21/1967	Lowell, Robert, poet	Arlington, VA	trespass, blocked traffic	arrest
10/21/1967	Macdonald, Dwight, author	Arlington, VA	trespass, blocked traffic	arrest
10/21/1967	Spock, Jane Cheney, activist	Arlington, VA	trespass, blocked traffic	arrest
militia service				
1658	Keene, Richard, Sr., planter	Calvert County, MD	refused to serve	struck with a saber
1704	Matthews, Samuel	Cape May, NJ	refused to serve	fine
1681	Maule, Thomas, tailor	Salem, MA	refused to serve	
Nicaragua, U.S. interference in				
1981	Coffin, William Sloane, Jr., clergy	New Haven, CT	protest, sanctuary	
nonattendance of church				
1676	Rogers, John, Jr.	New London, CT	avoided Puritan service	arrest
1676	Rogers, Mary Jordan	New London, CT	avoided Puritan service	arrest
7/6/1675	Screven, William, clergy	York, ME	avoided Puritan service	charged
nuclear power				
11/1/1961	Abzug, Bella Savitsky, politician	Washington, DC	demonstration	
11/1/1961	Allen, Donna, economist	Washington, DC	march	
5/27/1962	Baez, Joan, folksinger	San Francisco	demonstration	jail
1970s	Baez, Joan, folksinger	Los Altos, CA	tax resistance	
2/12/1997	Baggerly, Steve J., journalist	Bath, ME	sabotage	prison
4/26/1962	Becker, Norma, teacher	New York City	march	
1986	Bergin, Patrick, priest	New York City	blocked a door	
5/17/1968	Berrigan, Daniel, priest	Catonsville, MD	sabotage	prison
11/24/1983	Berrigan, Elizabeth McAlister	Rome, NY	sabotage	jail
9/9/1980	Berrigan, Philip, activist	King of Prussia, PA	sabotage	prison
4/3/1988	Berrigan, Philip, activist	Norfolk, VA	sabotage	prison
3/31/1991	Berrigan, Philip, activist	Bath, ME	sabotage	

Target of Act/Date	Name, Occupation	Location	Act	Consequence
12/7/1993	Berrigan, Philip, activist	Goldsboro, NC	sabotage	jail
2/12/1997	Berrigan, Philip, activist	Bath, ME	sabotage	prison
12/20/1999	Berrigan, Philip, activist	Middle River, MD	sabotage	prison
8/6/1957	Bigelow, Albert S., architect	Yucca Flats, NV	demonstration	
5/1/1958	Bigelow, Albert S., architect	Eniwetok Atoll, Marshall Islands	contempt of court	jail
6/4/1958	Bigelow, Albert S., architect	Eniwetok Atoll, Marshall Islands	contempt of court	jail
3/20/1988	Blake, Robert, actor	Las Vegas, NV	trespass	
4/3/1988	Boertje, Gregory, soldier	Norfolk, VA	sabotage	prison
1948	Carner, Lucy Perkins, sociologist	York, PA	protested	
8/6/1957	Choate, Prentiss	Yucca Flats, NV	demonstration	arrest
1980s	Coffin, William Sloane, Jr. clergy	New York City	protest	
3/20/1988	Coffin, William Sloane, Jr. clergy	Las Vegas, NV	trespass	
2/12/1997	Colville, Mark, journalist	Bath, ME	sabotage	prison
10/31/1991	Connett, Paul, toxicologist	New York City	singing, trespass	arrest
1986	Costner, Pat, chemist	New York City	blocked a door	home burned
2/12/1997	Crane, Susan, activist	Bath, ME	sabotage	prison
12/20/1999	Crane, Susan, activist	Middle River, MD	sabotage	prison
6/15/1955	Day, Dorothy, reformer, editor	New York City	protest	jail
1956	Day, Dorothy, reformer, editor	New York City	protest	jail
1959	Day, Dorothy, reformer, editor	New York City	protest	jail
12/7/1993	Dear, John, priest	Goldsboro, NC	sabotage	jail
4/28/1980	Dellinger, David T., activist	Washington, DC	blocked a heliport	arrest
4/1/2007	Dunn, Carrie, activist	Mercury, NV	trespass	arrest
3/20/1988	Ellsberg, Daniel, activist	Las Vegas, NV	trespass	
5/6/1979	Fonda, Jane, actor	Washington, DC	rally	
12/7/1993	Fredriksson, Lynn, activist	Goldsboro, NC	sabotage	jail
12/7/1993	Friedrich, Bruce, journalist	Goldsboro, NC	sabotage	jail
3/20/1988	Garr, Teri, actor	Las Vegas, NV	trespass	
10/6/2002	Gilbert, Carol, nun	Greeley, CO	sabotage	prison
6/14/1978	Ginsberg, Allen, poet	Boulder, CO	blocked a train	jail
9/9/1980	Hammer, Dean, student	King of Prussia, PA	sabotage	prison
10/6/2002	Hudson, Jackie, nun	Greeley, CO	sabotage	prison
5/1/1958	Huntington, William Reed, sailor	Eniwetok Atoll, Marshall Islands	contempt of court	jail
6/4/1958	Huntington, William Reed, sailor	Eniwetok Atoll, Marshall Islands	contempt of court	jail
9/9/1980	Kabat, Carl, priest	King of Prussia, PA	sabotage	prison
8/6/2000	Kabat, Carl, priest	Weld County, CO	sabotage	arrest
4/9/2004	Kabat, Carl, priest	New Raymer, CO	sabotage	arrest
3/20/1988	Kasem, Casey, radio announcer	Las Vegas, NV	trespass	
2/12/1997	Kelly, Steven, priest	Bath, ME	sabotage	prison
12/20/1999	Kelly, Steven, priest	Middle River, MD	sabotage	prison
3/20/1988	Knight, Shirley, actor	Las Vegas, NV	trespass	

Target of Act/Date	Name, Occupation	Location	Act	Consequence
4/3/1988	Lawrence, Andrew	Norfolk, VA	sabotage	prison
3/31/1991	Lewis, Tom, poet	Bath, ME	sabotage	
2/12/1997	Lewis, Tom, poet	Bath, ME	sabotage	prison
1958	Lyttle, Bradford	Cheyenne, WY	protest	
6/30/1946	Man, Albon Platt, Jr.	Arlington, VA	picket	
9/9/1980	Mass, Elmer, teacher	King of Prussia, PA	sabotage	prison
4/3/1988	McKenna, Margaret, nun	Norfolk, VA	sabotage	prison
4/28/1980	McReynolds, David, activist	Washington, DC	blocked a heliport	arrest
4/17/1993	Mento, Jack, artist	Beatty, NV	camp-in	
5/27/1962	Merton, Thomas, monk	San Francisco	denunciation	
7/6/1959	Meyer, Karl, activist	Omaha, NE	trespass	jail, prison
5/6/1979	Mitchell, Joni, singer	Washington, DC	rally	
9/9/1980	Montgomery, Anne, nun	King of Prussia, PA	sabotage	prison
6/15/1955	Muste, Abraham Johannes, activist	New York City	protest	jail
8/6/1957	Muste, Abraham Johannes, activist	Las Vegas, NV	blocked traffic	jail
6/20/1959	Muste, Abraham Johannes, activist	Omaha, NE	blocked traffic, trespass	jail
7/1/1959	Muste, Abraham Johannes, activist	Omaha, NE	blocked traffic, trespass	jail, fine
7/21/1959	Muste, Abraham Johannes, activist	Omaha, NE	trespass	jail
5/6/1979	Nader, Ralph, politician	Washington, DC	rally	
6/14/1978	Orlovsky, Peter, poet	Boulder, CO	blocked a train	jail
4/28/1980	Paley, Grace, author	Washington, DC	blocked a heliport	arrest
8/6/1957	Peck, James, journalist	Yucca Flats, NV	demonstration	arrest
5/1/1958	Peck, James, journalist	Eniwetok Atoll, Marshall Islands	contempt of court	jail
6/4/1958	Peck, James, journalist	Eniwetok Atoll, Marshall Islands	contempt of court	jail
8/6/1957	Peterson, Gonar, educator	Yucca Flats, NV	demonstration	arrest
8/6/1957	Pickus, Robert, organizer	Yucca Flats, NV	demonstration	arrest
10/6/2002	Platt, Ardeth, nun	Greeley, CO	sabotage	prison
9/9/1980	Rush, Molly, reformer	King of Prussia, PA	sabotage	prison
9/9/1980	Schuchardt, John, lawyer	King of Prussia, PA	sabotage	prison
8/6/1957	Scott, Lawrence	Yucca Flats, NV	demonstration	arrest
7/1/1959	Scott, Lawrence	Fort Detrick, MD	protest	
7/1/1959	Scott, Viola Maria Standley	Fort Detrick, MD	protest	
12/1/1992	Sellers, John, activist	Chicago	trespass	
1986	Sheen, Martin, actor	New York City	blocked a door	
8/1988	Sheen, Martin, actor	Phoenix, AZ		
10/31/1991	Sheen, Martin, actor	New York City	sang, trespass	arrest
8/9/1999	Sheen, Martin, actor	Los Alamos, NM	prayed, trespass	arrest
10/8/2000	Sheen, Martin, actor	Santa Barbara, CA	trespass	arrest
4/1/2007	Sheen, Martin, actor	Mercury, NV	trespass	arrest
5/1/1958	Sherwood, Orion W., seaman	Eniwetok Atoll, Marshall Islands	contempt of court	jail
6/4/1958	Sherwood, Orion W., seaman	Eniwetok Atoll, Marshall Islands	contempt of court	jail

Target of Act/Date	Name, Occupation	Location	Act	Consequence
4/28/1980	Spock, Benjamin, doctor	Washington, DC	blocked a heliport	arrest
5/27/1962	Stallings, Harold, sailor	Sausalito, CA	contempt of court	jail
7/21/1959	Swann, Marjorie, teacher	Omaha, NE	trespass	jail
1989	Tchozewski, Darrell Chet, activist	Rocky Flats, CO	demonstration	
10/8/2000	Turk, Lawrence, nurse	Santa Barbara, CA	trespass	arrest
4/17/1993	Vitale, Louis, priest	Beatty, NV	camp-in	
4/1/2007	Vitale, Louis, priest	Mercury, NV	trespass	arrest
7/1/1959	Walker, Charles C.	Fort Detrick, MD	protest	
12/20/1999	Walz, Elizabeth, teacher	Middle River, MD	sabotage	prison
11/5/1971	Watson, Paul, activist	Amchitka, AK	protest	
1958	Whitney, Norman Jehiel	Cheyenne, WY	protest	
5/1/1958	Willoughby, George	Eniwetok Atoll, Marshall Islands	contempt of court	jail
6/4/1958	Willoughby, George	Eniwetok Atoll, Marshall Islands	contempt of court	jail
8/6/1957	Willoughby, Lillian, activist	Yucca Flats, NV	demonstration	arrest
11/1/1961	Wilson, Dagmar, artist	Washington, DC	demonstration	
4/1/2007	Wright, Ann, soldier	Mercury, NV	trespass	arrest
7/6/1959	Wyman, David S.	Omaha, NE	trespass	jail
7/6/1959	Young, Wilmer Job, teacher	Omaha, NE	trespass	jail
7/4/1962	Zahn, Franklin, engineer	Los Angeles	contempt of court	jail, confiscation

Olympics

1936	Powell, Adam Clayton, Jr., clergy, politician	Harlem, NY	wrote editorials	

park curfew

8/6/1988	Ginsberg, Allen, poet	New York City	protest	assault

Persian Gulf War

3/31/1990	Eichman, Shawn D., activist	New York City	flag burning	arrest
3/31/1990	Urgo, Joseph R., activist	New York City	flag burning	arrest

peyote ban

4/28/1962	Anderson, Leon B.	Needles, CA	peyote worship	arrest
1926	Bethune, Frank, farmer	Reno, MT	peyote worship	
1926	Big Sheep, farmer	Lodge Grass, MT	peyote use	shackled
1923	Bird Above, farmer	Bighorn, MT	peyote worship	arrest
1990	Black, Galen, drug counselor	Douglas County, OR	peyote worship	lost job
1990	Blue Bird, James, healer	Medicine Root, SD	peyote worship	
1993	Cook, Loretta Afraid-of-Bear	Slim Butte, SD	peyote use	
1960s	Crow Dog, Leonard, priest	Rosebud, SD	peyote worship	
1960s	Martinez, Lorenzo, spiritualist	Grand Junction, CO	peyote worship	
1995	Mercado, Leonard, activist	Kearny, AZ	peyote growing	arrest

Target of Act/Date	Name, Occupation	Location	Act	Consequence
1/8/1999	Mercado, Leonard, activist	Kearny, AZ	peyote growing	arrest, prison
1995	Mercado, Raven, activist	Kearny, AZ	peyote growing	arrest
1/2001	Mooney, James, activist	Benjamin, UT	peyote worship	
1/2001	Mooney, Linda, activist	Benjamin, UT	peyote worship	
2/14/1914	Neck, Mitchell, spiritualist	Phlox, WI	receiving peyote	arrest
4/28/1962	Nez, Dan Dee	Needles, CA	peyote worship	arrest
1960s	Old Coyote, Barney, storyteller	Bighorn, MT	peyote worship	
1900s	Parker, Quanah, leader	Fort Sill, OK	peyote worship	
1960s	Prescott, Thomas, priest	Wittenberg, WI	peyote worship	
1900s	Rave, John, spiritualist	Thurston, NE	peyote worship	
1990	Smith, Alfred, drug counselor	Douglas County, OR	peyote worship	lost job
4/1993	Snake, Reuben A., Jr.	Winnebago, NE	peyote use	
1994	Spotted Elk, Abraham, spiritualist	Ethete, WY	peyote worship	
1926	Stewart, Tom, farmer	Grass Lodge, MT	peyote worship	
1993	Strong, Ted	Satus, WA	peyote use	
1900s	Whiteman, John, priest	Apache, OK	peyote worship	
4/28/1962	Woody, John	Needles, CA	peyote worship	arrest

police brutality

Target of Act/Date	Name, Occupation	Location	Act	Consequence
1981	Hernandez, Crosby Wilfredo Orantes, refugee	Culver City, CA	sought asylum	pistol-whipped
3/1914	Keller, Helen Adams, writer	Sacramento, CA	denunciation	
6/1943	Powell, Adam Clayton, Jr., clergy, politician	New York City	propaganda	
1/1960	Powell, Adam Clayton, Jr., clergy, politician	New York City	rally	

polygamy ban

Target of Act/Date	Name, Occupation	Location	Act	Consequence
7/2006	Barlow, Dale Evans	Colorado City, AZ	sex with a minor	prison
7/2006	Barlow, David Romaine	Colorado City, AZ	sex with a minor	prison
7/2006	Barlow, Donald Robert	Colorado City, AZ	sex with a minor	prison
5/12/1945	Barlow, John Yates	Short Creek, AZ	bigamy	prison
7/2006	Barlow, Randolph Joseph	Colorado City, AZ	sex with a minor	prison
7/2006	Barlow, Terry Darger	Colorado City, AZ	sex with a minor	prison
7/2006	Bateman, David Romaine	Colorado City, AZ	sex with a minor	prison
1915	Broadbent, Joseph Leslie, author	Lehi, UT	bigamy	
5/1885	Brown, Francis Almond	Ogden, UT	bigamy	prison, fine
1/19/1885	Cannon, Angus Munn, mayor	St. George, UT	bigamy	prison, fine
9/1885	Cannon, Angus Munn, mayor	St. George, UT	bigamy	prison, fine
1/1886	Cannon, George Quayle, printer	Salt Lake City	bigamy	prison, fine
9/1888	Cannon, George Quayle, printer	Salt Lake City	bigamy	prison, fine
8/1882	Clawson, Lydia Spencer	Salt Lake City	cohabitation	prison, fine
1884	Clawson, Lydia Spencer	Salt Lake City	cohabitation	prison, fine
8/1882	Clawson, Rudger Judd	Salt Lake City	bigamy	prison, fine
1884	Connelly, Annie Gallifant	Salt Lake City	cohabitation	prison, fine

Target of Act/Date	Name, Occupation	Location	Act	Consequence
3/7/1944	Darger, David Brigham, city clerk	Colorado City, AZ	bigamy	prison
3/7/1944	Dockstader, Theral	Colorado City, AZ	bigamy	prison
7/2006	Fischer, Kelly, contractor	Colorado City, AZ	sex with a minor	prison
1899	Grant, Heber Jeddy, apostle	Salt Lake City	bigamy	prison, fine
6/24/2002	Green, Thomas Arthur	Joab County, UT	child rape, bigamy	prison
6/24/2002	Hampton, Brigham Young, memoirist	Salt Lake City	bigamy	
7/2006	Holm, Rodney Hans, policeman	Colorado City, AZ	sex with a minor	prison
1846	Hyde, Orson	Spring City, UT	bigamy	
8/2006	Jeffs, Warren Steed, principal	Las Vegas, NV	abetted rape	prison
9/1939	Jessop, Fred, poultry farmer	St. George, UT	bigamy	prison
9/1939	Jessop, Richard Seth, farmer	St. George, UT	bigamy	prison
7/2006	Jessop, Vergel Bryce	Colorado City, AZ	child abuse	prison
3/7/1944	Jessop, Vergel Yeates	Colorado City, AZ	bigamy	prison
3/1887	John, David	Salt Lake City	bigamy	prison, fine
12/1935	Johnson, Price William	Lees Ferry, AZ	bigamy	prison
5/12/1945	Kelsch, Louis Alma	Salt Lake City	cohabitation	prison
2/1886	Lyman, Francis Marion, soldier	Provo, UT	bigamy	prison, fine
1884	Merrill, Isabella Maria Harris	Salt Lake City	cohabitation	prison, fine
5/1885	Miner, Aurelius, lawyer	Salt Lake City	bigamy	prison, fine
1884	Musser, Amos Milton, clerk	Salt Lake City	bigamy	prison, fine
1902	Musser, Joseph White, publisher	Salt Lake City	bigamy	prison
5/12/1945	Musser, Joseph White, publisher	Salt Lake City	marriage to minors	
5/6/2008	Neison, Wendell Loy	Eldorado, TX	bigamy	
1884	Newsome, Lucy Maria Devereux	Salt Lake City	cohabitation	prison, fine
1862	Ogston, Cyril	Salt Lake City	bigamy	exile
1886	Penrose, Charles William, hymn writer	Salt Lake City	bigamy	exile
1860s	Pratt, Orson, mathematician	Salt Lake City	bigamy	lost wives
1874	Reynolds, George	Lincoln, NE	bigamy	prison
1843	Rigson, Sidney, religious leader	Hiram, OH	bigamy	killed
1889	Roberts, Brigham Henry, author	Salt Lake City	bigamy	prison, ousted from Congress
1884	Roundy, Nellie White	Salt Lake City	cohabitation	prison, fine
1878	Smith, Eliza Roxey Snow	Salt Lake City	cohabitation	
6/27/1844	Smith, Hyrum, religious leader	Carthage, IL	bigamy	assassinated
1843	Smith, Joseph, Jr., religious leader	Hiram, OH	bigamy	tarred, feathered
6/27/1844	Smith, Joseph, Jr., religious leader	Carthage, IL	bigamy	assassinated
1880s	Smith, Joseph Fielding, clerk	Salt Lake City	bigamy	exile
1884	Snell, Eliza Shafer	Salt Lake City	cohabitation	prison, fine
1882	Snow, Erastus, teacher	Salt Lake City	bigamy	exile
11/20/1885	Snow, Lorenzo, teacher	Ogden, UT	bigamy	prison, fine
12/1935	Spencer, Isaac Carling, laborer	Short Creek, AZ	bigamy	prison
1944	Steed, Rulon Timpson	Salt Lake City	bigamy	prison
3/7/1944	Stubbs, Lawrence Ritchie	Colorado City, AZ	bigamy	prison

Target of Act/Date	Name, Occupation	Location	Act	Consequence
1885	Tanner, Joseph Marion, professor	Provo, UT	bigamy	forced to resign from job
1847	Taylor, John, president	Salt Lake City	bigamy	exile
5/12/1945	Timpson, Alma Willard	Salt Lake City	cohabitation	prison
1884	White, Elizabeth Ann Starkey	Salt Lake City	cohabitation	prison, fine
1840s	Woodruff, Wilford, clergy	Salt Lake City	bigamy	forced to flee
1893	Woolley, Lorin Calvin	Salt Lake City	bigamy	
1846	Young, Brigham	Salt Lake City	bigamy	
5/12/1945	Zitting, Charles Frederick	Harrisville, UT	bigamy	prison

pornography

Target of Act/Date	Name, Occupation	Location	Act	Consequence
4/1970	Atkinson, Ti-Grace, author	New York City	intimidation	
4/1970	Morgan, Robin, editor	New York City	intimidation	

prison conditions

Target of Act/Date	Name, Occupation	Location	Act	Consequence
1919	Jones, Mary "Mother," labor organizer	Kanawha County, WV	public harangue	
1923	Jones, Mary "Mother," labor organizer	Logan County, WV	protest	
3/2006	Mahony, Roger, cardinal	Los Angeles	protest	
2/25/1918	Reed, John, journalist	Paterson, NH	protest	jail

prisoners of war

Target of Act/Date	Name, Occupation	Location	Act	Consequence
12/25/1972	Baez, Joan, folksinger	Hanoi, Vietnam	prison visit	
1/1968	Berrigan, Daniel, priest	Hanoi, Vietnam	passport violation	
1/1968	Zinn, Howard, professor	Hanoi, Vietnam	passport violation	

property rights

Target of Act/Date	Name, Occupation	Location	Act	Consequence
4/1808	Barlow, Nathan, farmer	Fairfax, ME	assault	
4/1808	Brackett, Thomas, farmer	Fairfax, ME	assault	

Pullman Palace Car Company

Target of Act/Date	Name, Occupation	Location	Act	Consequence
May–August 1894	Curtis, Jennie, seamstress	Chicago	protest	
May–August 1894	Debs, Eugene Victor, locomotive fireman	Chicago	contempt of court	jail
May–August 1894	Howard, George W., rail conductor	Chicago	contempt of court	jail
May–August 1894	Jones, Mary "Mother," labor organizer	Chicago	propaganda	
May–August 1894	Keliher, Sylvester, railway carman	Chicago	contempt of court	jail
May–August 1894	Rogers, Lewis W., editor	Chicago	contempt of court	jail

quartering of troops

Target of Act/Date	Name, Occupation	Location	Act	Consequence
12/16/1769	McDougall, Alexander, merchant, tractarian	New York City	propaganda	arrest
12/16/1769	McDougall, Hannah Roe Bostwick	New York City	protest	
4/4/1758	Woolman, John, tailor, philosopher	Philadelphia	refused payment	

Target of Act/Date	Name, Occupation	Location	Act	Consequence
racism				
1961	Aaron, Julian	Washington, DC	Freedom Rider	
12/1/1955	Abernathy, Ralph David, clergy	Montgomery, AL	supported bus protest	
12/15/1961	Abernathy, Ralph David, clergy	Albany, GA	supported Freedom Rider	jail
4/12/1963	Abernathy, Ralph David, clergy	Birmingham, AL	contempt of court	jail, fine
3/25/1965	Abernathy, Ralph David, clergy	Selma, AL	march	mob attack
1/22/1966	Abernathy, Ralph David, clergy	Chicago	rally	threats
8/5/1966	Abernathy, Ralph David, clergy	Chicago	rally	stoned
2/1971	Abernathy, Ralph David, clergy	Las Vegas, NV	march	
4/9/1947	Adams, Louis, clergy	Greensboro, NC	integrated a bus	
1/31/1964	Allen, Louis, logger	Liberty, MS	murder witness	shot
3/25/1963	Baez, Joan, folksinger	Selma, AL	march	mob attack
8/28/1963	Baez, Joan, folksinger	Washington, DC	demonstration	
2/2/1965	Baez, Joan, folksinger	Selma, AL	march	
4/9/1947	Baker, Ella, activist	Washington, DC	integrated a bus	
4/15/1960	Baker, Ella, activist	Raleigh, NC	protest	
2/1961	Baker, Ella, activist	Washington, DC	organized Freedom Rides	
4/15/1947	Banks, Dennis, jazz musician	Asheville, NC	integrated a bus	fine
4/23/1947	Banks, Dennis, jazz musician	Culpeper, VA	integrated a bus	arrest
5/20/1961	Barbee, William	Montgomery, AL	Freedom Rider	injured
1/1961	Barry, Marion Shepilov, politician	Rock Hill, SC	Freedom Rider	arrest
3/25/1965	Berrigan, Philip, priest	Selma, AL	march	mob attack, jail
6/1941	Bethune, Mary McLeod, educator	Washington, DC	conspiracy	
2/1961	Bevel, James, sailor	Rock Hill, SC	Freedom Rider	arrest
5/4/1961	Bigelow, Albert	Washington, DC	Freedom Rider	beaten
1961	Blankenheim, Edward, carpenter	Washington, DC	Freedom Rider	
5/14/1963	Booth, Mabel St. Clair, activist	Cambridge, MD	restaurant sit-in	jail
3/1965	Boynton, Amelia, activist	Selma, AL	promoted integration	assault
5/14/1961	Britt, Travis	Jackson, MS	Freedom Rider	jail
9/1961	Britt, Travis	Liberty, MS	Freedom Rider	beaten
4/20/1947	Bromley, Ernest, clergy	Roanoke, VA	integrated a bus	
3/18/1970	Brownmiller, Susan, author	New York City	intimidation	
8/29/1961	Bryant, Curtis Conway, barber	McComb, MS	encouraged a teen to protest	arrest
3/25/1965	Bunche, Ralph, scientist	Selma, AL	march	mob attack
1961	Burks, Catherine	Washington, DC	Freedom Rider	
4/15/1960	Carmichael, Stokely, student	Washington, DC	protest	
1961	Carmichael, Stokely, student	Washington, DC	Freedom Rider	
6/7/1966	Carmichael, Stokely, student	Memphis, TN	march	
1940s	Carner, Lucy Perkins, sociologist	York, PA	sit-ins	
1961	Castle, Jean, student	Washington, DC	Freedom Rider	
11/3/1979	Cauce, César, activist	Greensboro, NC	protest	shot
6/21/1964	Chaney, James, plasterer	Meridian, MS	protest	shot
1961	Chatham, Price	Washington, DC	Freedom Rider	
1944	Chávez, César, labor leader	Delano, CA	sit-in	arrest

Target of Act/Date	Name, Occupation	Location	Act	Consequence
2/1971	Chávez, César, labor leader	Las Vegas, NV	march	
1961	Coffin, William Sloan, Jr., clergy	Washington, DC	Freedom Rider	
1961	Collins, Lucretia, student	Washington, DC	Freedom Rider	
1955	Colvin, Claudette, student	Montgomery, AL	integrated a bus	arrest
1961	Cox, Benjamin Elton, clergy	Washington, DC	Freedom Rider	
10/13/1970	Davis, Angela, teacher	New York City	conspiracy, kidnap, violence	jail
3/1970	Day, Dorothy, reformer, editor	Americus, GA	protested racism	drive-by shooting
1961	Dennis, David, student	Washington, DC	Freedom Rider	
1961	Diederich, Paul, divinity student	Washington, DC	Freedom Rider	
1961	Dolan, John Luther, student	Washington, DC	Freedom Rider	
8/28/1963	Dylan, Bob, singer	Washington, DC	demonstration	
1961	Fankhouser, David Brokaw, student	Washington, DC	Freedom Rider	
4/9/1947	Farmer, James Leonard, clergy	Washington, DC	integrated a bus	
1957	Farmer, James Leonard, clergy	Raleigh, NC	conference	
1961	Farmer, James Leonard, clergy	Washington, DC	Freedom Rider	
5/24/1961	Farmer, James Leonard, clergy	Jackson, MS	Freedom Rider	jail
1962	Farmer, James Leonard, clergy	New York City	picketed	
8/28/1963	Farmer, James Leonard, clergy	Plaquemine, LA	activism	stalked, jail, death threat
9/28/1963	Farmer, James Leonard, clergy	New York City	sit-in	arrest
1964	Farmer, James Leonard, clergy	Mississippi	investigated church arson	
4/13/1947	Felmet, Joseph, activist	Chapel Hill, NC	integrated a bus	arrest
3/18/1970	Firestone, Shulamith, author	New York City	intimidation	
8/2/1961	Forman, James, activist	Monroe, NC	Freedom Rider	police brutality, jail
10/13/1970	Franklin, Aretha, singer	New York City	protest	
4/23/1964	Fruchter, Norman D., editor	New York City	sit-in	arrest
10/13/1970	Giovanni, Nikki, poet	New York City	protest	
6/21/1964	Goodman, Andrew, student	Meridian, MS	protest	shot
1961	Gordon, Albert, teacher	Washington, DC	Freedom Rider	
1961	Green, Stephen, student	Washington, DC	Freedom Rider	
1963	Gregory, Dick, comedian	Chicago	promoted integration	
1962	Grubb, Enez Stafford, activist	Cambridge, MD	protest	
3/18/1970	Hammer, Signe, author	New York City	intimidation	
4/23/1964	Harrington, Edward Michael, author	New York City	sit-in	arrest
8/26/1961	Hayes, Elmer, student	McComb, MS	sit-in	jail
1961	Herrman, Susan, student	Washington, DC	Freedom Rider	
3/25/1965	Heschel, Abraham Joshua, rabbi	Selma, AL	march	mob attack
4/19/1947	Houser, George	Cincinnati, OH	integrated a bus	threat
10/13/1970	Jagger, Mick, singer	New York City	protest	
4/12/1947	Johnson, Andrew, student	Durham, NC	integrated a bus	arrest
4/13/1947	Johnson, Andrew, student	Chapel Hill, NC	integrated a bus	arrest
4/13/1947	Jones, Charles M., clergy	Chapel Hill, NC	abetted integration	death threat, lost job
12/1/1955	King, Martin Luther, Jr., clergy	Montgomery, AL	supported bus protest	
1/26/1956	King, Martin Luther, Jr., clergy	Montgomery, AL	led a procession	arrest
1/30/1956	King, Martin Luther, Jr., clergy	Montgomery, AL	church meeting	home bombed

Target of Act/Date	Name, Occupation	Location	Act	Consequence
1957	King, Martin Luther, Jr., clergy	Raleigh, NC	conference	
1/27/1957	King, Martin Luther, Jr., clergy	Montgomery, AL	protest	unexploded bomb
9/3/1958	King, Martin Luther, Jr., clergy	Montgomery, AL	loitering	police brutality
5/21/1960	King, Martin Luther, Jr., clergy	Montgomery, AL	rally	mob attack
5/21/1961	King, Martin Luther, Jr., clergy	Montgomery, AL	Freedom Rider	threats
12/15/1961	King, Martin Luther, Jr., clergy	Albany, GA	supported Freedom Ride	jail
7/11/1964	King, Martin Luther, Jr., clergy	St. Augustine, FL	protest	
7/18/1964	King, Martin Luther, Jr., clergy	Harlem, NY	demonstration	stoned
3/25/1965	King, Martin Luther, Jr., clergy	Selma, AL	march	mob attack
1/22/1966	King, Martin Luther, Jr., clergy	Chicago	rally	threats
6/7/1966	King, Martin Luther, Jr., clergy	Memphis, TN	march	stoned
8/5/1966	King, Martin Luther, Jr., clergy	Chicago	rally	
4/4/1967	King, Martin Luther, Jr., clergy	New York City	led protest	
3/28/1968	King, Martin Luther, Jr., clergy	Memphis, TN		
1961	Lafayette, Bernard, Jr., student	Washington, DC	Freedom Rider	
1961	Lane, Mark, lawyer	Washington, DC	Freedom Rider	
1961	Lawson, James Morris, clergy	Washington, DC	organized Freedom Rides	job threat, expelled
2/1961	Lee, Bernard Scott, activist	Washington, DC	Freedom Rider	
9/24/1961	Lee, Herbert, farmer	Liberty, MS	sitting in truck	shot
10/13/1970	Lennon, John, singer	New York City	protest	
1961	Leonard, Frederic, student	Washington, DC	Freedom Rider	
1961	Levine, Eugene, teacher	Washington, DC	Freedom Rider	
8/30/1961	Lewis, Isaac	McComb, MS	sit-in	jail
1957	Lewis, John Robert, student	Raleigh, NC	conference	
5/4/1961	Lewis, John Robert, student	Washington, DC	Freedom Rider	beaten
5/20/1961	Lewis, John Robert, student	Montgomery, AL	Freedom Rider	injured
5/24/1961	Lewis, John Robert, student	Montgomery, AL	Freedom Rider	injured
3/18/1963	Lewis, John Robert, student	Washington, DC	protest	
9/1963	Lewis, John Robert, student	Selma, AL	protest	jail
3/1965	Lewis, John Robert, student	Montgomery, AL	march	assault
4/9/1947	Lynn, Conrad J., lawyer	Petersburg, VA	integrated a bus	threats, arrest
5/24/1961	Mahoney, William, student	Sunflower County, MS	Freedom Rider	torture
6/7/1966	McKissick, Floyd, lawyer	Memphis, TN	march	
1961	McNichols, Steve, student	Washington, DC	Freedom Rider	
1961	Moody, John, Jr., student	Washington, DC	Freedom Rider	
4/9/1947	Moorman, Natalie, activist	Washington, D.C	integrated a bus	
3/1970	Morgan, Elizabeth, activist	Americus, GA	racism	drive-by shooting
2/1961	Moses, Robert Parris, activist	Washington, DC	Freedom Rider	
1961	Mulholland, Joan Trumpower, student	Washington, DC	Freedom Rider	
4/9/1947	Murray, Pauli, activist	Washington, DC	integrated a bus	
4/9/1947	Muste, Abraham Johannes, activist	Washington, DC	integrated a bus	
2/1961	Nash, Diane, student	Rock Hill, SC	lunch counter sit-in	jail
11/3/1979	Nathan, Michael Ronald, doctor	Greensboro, NC	protest	shot
1961	Nelson, Frank, student	Washington, DC	Freedom Rider	

Target of Act/Date	Name, Occupation	Location	Act	Consequence
4/22/1947	Nelson, Wallace Floyd, lecturer	Amherst, VA	led protest	threat, arrest
1961	Nixon, Sandra, student	Washington, DC	Freedom Rider	
1961	O'Neal, Helen, student	Washington, DC	Freedom Rider	
1939	Paige, Myles A., judge	Harlem, NY	picketed	
12/1/1955	Parks, Raymond, barber	Montgomery, AL	protest	lost job
1944	Parks, Rosa, seamstress	Montgomery, AL	integrated a bus	ejected
12/1/1955	Parks, Rosa, seamstress	Montgomery, AL	integrated a bus	arrest, lost job
4/12/1947	Peck, James, journalist	Durham, NC	integrated a bus	arrest
4/12/1947	Peck, James, journalist	Chapel Hill, NC	integrated a bus	battery
4/15/1957	Peck, James, journalist	Asheville, NC	integrated a bus	fine
1961	Peck, James, journalist	Washington, DC	Freedom Rider	beaten
1930s	Phillips, Donnellan, activist	Harlem, NY	protest	
10/13/1970	Poindexter, David R., activist	Chicago	aiding a felon	jail
4/21/1930	Powell, Adam Clayton, Jr., clergy, politician	Harlem, NY	protest	
3/25/1931	Powell, Adam Clayton, Jr., clergy, politician	Harlem, NY	protest	
1933	Powell, Adam Clayton, Jr., clergy, politician	Harlem, NY	picketed	
1939	Powell, Adam Clayton, Jr., clergy, politician	Harlem, NY	picketed, boycott	
1940	Powell, Adam Clayton, Jr., clergy, politician	Washington, DC	trespass	arrest
1941	Powell, Adam Clayton, Jr., clergy, politician	New York City	march	
6/1941	Powell, Adam Clayton, Jr., clergy, politician	Washington, DC	conspiracy	
1963	Powell, Adam Clayton, Jr., clergy, politician	Cambridge, MD	defended sit-ins	
1941	Quill, Michael J., union organizer	New York City	march	
6/1941	Randolph, Asa Philip, organizer	Washington, DC	conspiracy	
1943	Randolph, Asa Philip, organizer	Chicago	rally	
1943	Randolph, Asa Philip, organizer	New York City	rally	
1948	Randolph, Asa Philip, organizer	Washington, DC	protest	
1948	Randolph, Asa Philip, organizer	Philadelphia	protest	
1957	Randolph, Asa Philip, organizer	Raleigh, NC	conference	
8/28/1963	Randolph, Asa Philip, organizer	Washington, DC	march	
8/29/1961	Reagan, Cordelle, student	McComb, MS	encouraged a teen to protest	arrest
11/1961	Reagon, Bernice Johnson, musician	Albany, GA	Freedom Rider	jail
5/14/1963	Richardson, Donna, student	Cambridge, MD	restaurant sit-in	reformatory
5/14/1963	Richardson, Gloria, piano teacher, activist	Cambridge, MD	restaurant sit-in	jail
5/17/1963	Richardson, Gloria, piano teacher, activist	Cambridge, MD	plotted a riot	arrest
6/11/1964	Richardson, Gloria, piano teacher, activist	Cambridge, MD	picketed	arrest
12/1955	Robinson, Jo Ann Gibson, activist	Montgomery, AL	protest	

Target of Act/Date	Name, Occupation	Location	Act	Consequence
4/13/1947	Roodenko, Igal	Chapel Hill, NC	integrated a bus	arrest
4/11/1947	Rustin, Bayard Taylor, activist	Petersburg, VA	integrated a bus	
4/12/1947	Rustin, Bayard Taylor, activist	Durham, NC	integrated a bus	arrest
4/13/1947	Rustin, Bayard Taylor, activist	Chapel Hill, NC	integrated a bus	arrest, chain gang
12/1/1955	Rustin, Bayard Taylor, activist	Montgomery, AL	supported bus protest	
8/28/1963	Rustin, Bayard Taylor, activist	Washington, DC	demonstration	
4/23/1964	Rustin, Bayard Taylor, activist	New York City	sit-in	arrest
11/3/1979	Samson, William Evan, activist	Greensboro, NC	protest	shot
10/13/1970	Sanchez, Sonia, poet	New York City	protest	
3/7/1964	Savio, Mario, student	Berkeley, CA	sit-in	arrest
6/21/1964	Schwerner, Michael, reformer	Meridian, MS	protest	shot
1961	Shilman, Kenneth, student	Washington, DC	Freedom Rider	
5/17/1961	Shuttlesworth, Fred Lee, clergy	Washington, DC	Freedom Rider	arrest
5/21/1960	Shuttlesworth, Fred Lee, clergy	Montgomery, AL	rally	stoned, teargassed
5/21/1961	Shuttlesworth, Fred Lee, clergy	Montgomery, AL	Freedom Rider	threats
5/20/1961	Sieganthaler, John, Sr., assistant attorney general	Washington, DC	Freedom Rider	injured
5/24/1961	Singer, Felix	Sunflower County, MS	Freedom Rider	torture
1961	Singleton, Helen, student	Washington, DC	Freedom Rider	
1961	Singleton, Robert, student	Washington, DC	Freedom Rider	
1961	Smith, George Bundy, student	Washington, DC	Freedom Rider	
1961	Smith, Jerome, student	Washington, DC	Freedom Rider	
1955	Smith, Mary Louise, student	Montgomery, AL	integrated a bus	arrest
2/1961	Smith, Ruby Doris	Rock Hill, SC	Freedom Rider	firebombed, jail
11/3/1979	Smith, Sandi Neely, student	Greensboro, NC	protest	shot
2/1971	Spock, Benjamin, doctor	Las Vegas, NV	march	
1961	Steward, Richard, student	Washington, DC	Freedom Rider	
5/24/1961	Sullivan, Terry	Sunflower County, MS	Freedom Rider	torture
2/1971	Sutherland, Donald, actor	Las Vegas, NV	march	
8/30/1961	Talbert, Robert	McComb, MS	sit-in	jail
1961	Teale, Buron Lewis, machinist	Washington, DC	Freedom Rider	
5/4/1961	Thomas, Henry, student	Washington, DC	Freedom Rider	mob threat
8/30/1961	Travis, Brenda, student	McComb, MS	sit-in	
1961	Walker, Wyatt Tee, clergy	Washington, DC	Freedom Rider	
11/3/1979	Waller, James Michael, activist	Greensboro, NC	protest	shot
8/26/1961	Watkins, Hollis, student	McComb, MS	sit-in	jail
3/7/1964	Weinberg, Jack, activist	Berkeley, CA	sit-in	arrest
5/14/1963	White, Reva Dinez, activist	Cambridge, MD	restaurant sit-in	jail
1961	Wilbur, Susan, student	Washington, DC	Freedom Rider	
1957	Wilkins, Roy, organizer	Raleigh, NC	conference	
1960	Wilkins, Roy, activist	Washington, DC	march	
3/15/1965	Wilkins, Roy, activist	Selma, AL	march	
4/19/1957	Worthy, William	Cincinnati, OH	integrated a bus	
3/25/1965	Young, Andrew	Selma, AL	march	mob attack

Target of Act/Date	Name, Occupation	Location	Act	Consequence
1957	Young, Whitney Moore, Jr., activist	Raleigh, NC	conference	
5/20/1961	Zweng, Jim, divinity student	Montgomery, AL	Freedom Rider	beaten

rain forest pillaging

5/17/2004	Anderson, Scott, activist	Miami, FL	boarded a vessel	prison
5/17/2004	Hosta, Hillary, activist	Miami, FL	boarded a vessel	prison
5/17/2004	Paul, Scott, activist	Miami, FL	boarded a vessel	prison

rape

4/1970	Atkinson, Ti-Grace, author	New York City	intimidation	arrest
6/23/1855	Celia, housekeeper	Fulton, MO	manslaughter	executed
4/1970	Morgan, Robin, editor	New York City	intimidation	arrest

religious persecution

1663	Alby, Benjamin	Rehoboth, MA	preached	expelled
10/30/1667	Alby, Benjamin	Rehoboth, MA	preached	expelled
1663	Ambrose, Alice	Dover, NH	preached	stripped, lashed
July 1656	Austin, Ann, preacher	Boston	blasphemy	books burned, prison
1773	Backus, Isaac, clergy	Middleborough, MA	demanded rights	
1774	Backus, Isaac, clergy	Boston	demanded rights	
7/1/1773	Barrow, David, preacher	Portsmouth, VA	preached	torture
1751	Barstow, Jeremiah	Sturbridge, MA	religious unorthodoxy	confiscation, prison
4/14/1685	Beebe, Samuel, Jr.	New London, CT	disrupted worship	lashed
1751	Bloyce, Abraham	Sturbridge, MA	religious unorthodoxy	confiscation
1751	Blunt, John	Sturbridge, MA	religious unorthodoxy	confiscation
7/26/1725	Bolles, John	Groton, CT	broke the Sabbath	prison, fine
7/26/1725	Bolles, Joseph	Groton, CT	broke the Sabbath	prison, fine
7/8/1677	Bowers, Elizabeth	Boston	wore sackcloth and ash	lashed
1661	Bowne, John, preacher	Flushing, NY	worship	banished, fine
7/8/1677	Brewster, Margaret, prophet	Boston	wore sackcloth and ash	lashed
1663	Brown, James	Rehoboth, MA	preached	expelled
7/2/1667	Brown, James	Rehoboth, MA	preached	fine
10/30/1667	Brown, James	Rehoboth, MA	preached	expelled
2/1744	Buckley, Job	Saybrook, CT	religious unorthodoxy	prison
1650	Buell, Mary Post	Swansea, MA	religious unorthodoxy	arrest
6/1650	Buell, William	Swansea, MA	religious unorthodoxy	arrest
3/11/1659	Buffum, Joshua	Salem, MA	blasphemy	
8/1771	Burrus, John, clergy	Culpeper, VA	preached	prison
1663	Butterworth, John	Rehoboth, MA	preached	expelled
10/30/1667	Butterworth, John	Rehoboth, MA	preached	expelled
1663	Carpenter, James	Rehoboth, MA	preached	expelled
10/30/1667	Carpenter, James	Rehoboth, MA	preached	expelled
8/1771	Cheming, Bartholomew, clergy	Culpeper, VA	preached	prison
1765	Childs, James, clergy	Culpeper, VA	preached	harassment, jail

Target of Act/Date	Name, Occupation	Location	Act	Consequence
1661	Christopherson, Wenlock	Boston	blasphemy	exile
1657	Clark, Mary, preacher	Boston	blasphemy	scourged
5/31/1651	Clarke, John, clergy	Lynn, MA	religious nonconformity	jail, fine
1663	Coleman, Anna	Dover, NH	preached	stripped, lashed
1751	Coller, Phineas	Sturbridge, MA	religious unorthodoxy	confiscation
1751	Corey, John	Sturbridge, MA	religious unorthodoxy	prison
1765	Craig, Elijah, preacher	Culpeper, VA	preached	jail on bread and water
1765	Craig, John, preacher	Lexington, VA	religious unorthodoxy	stalking, ridicule
1765	Craig, Lewis, clergy	Culpeper, VA	preached	jail, harassment
8/1771	Craig, Lewis, clergy	Culpeper, VA	preached	prison
5/31/1651	Crandall, John, elder	Lynn, MA	religious nonconformity	jail, fine
5/1850	Crooks, Adam, missionary	Jamestown, NC	distributed literature	jail
7/26/1725	Culver, John	Groton, CT	broke the Sabbath	prison, fine
7/26/1725	Culver, Sarah Hibbard	Groton, CT	broke the Sabbath	prison, fine
7/26/1725	Davis, Andrew	Groton, CT	broke the Sabbath	prison, fine
1653	Doughty, Francis, clergy	Flushing, NY	religious unorthodoxy	exile
1751	Draper, John	Sturbridge, MA	religious unorthodoxy	confiscation, prison
9/28/1653	Dunster, Henry, educator	Cambridge, MA	refused infant baptism	lost job, exile
1659	Dyer, Mary Barrett, preacher	Boston	contempt of court	hanged
7/8/1677	Easton, John, Jr.	Boston	wore sackcloth and ash	lashed
1666	Farnum, John	Boston	religious unorthodoxy	jail
July 1656	Fisher, Mary, preacher	Boston	blasphemy	burned books, prison
1751	Fisk, Henry, deacon	Sturbridge, MA	religious unorthodoxy	confiscation, prison
9/1773	Fletcher, Asaph, clergy	Chelmsford, MA	demanded rights	
1661	Gaunt, Lydia Hampton	Sandwich, MA	housed missionaries	confiscation
1661	Gaunt, Peter	Sandwich, MA	housed missionaries	confiscation
1666	George, John	Boston	religious unorthodoxy	jail
8/1771	Goodrick, James, clergy	Culpeper, VA	preached	prison
1666	Goold, Thomas	Boston	flight from arrest	
3/1668	Goold, Thomas	Boston	religious unorthodoxy	tried
1637	Gorton, Samuel	Boston	blasphemy	prison, exile
1638	Gorton, Samuel	Plymouth, MA	blasphemy	prison, exile
1639	Gorton, Samuel	Newport, RI	blasphemy	pillory, lashed
1643	Gorton, Samuel	Boston	blasphemy	prison at hard labor
7/26/1769	Greenwood, James	Middlesex, VA	religious unorthodoxy	jail
11/11/1656	Hallett, William, sheriff	Flushing, NY	religious unorthodoxy	fired, fine
1659	Harper, Deborah Perry	Boston	claimed a Quaker corpse	prison, exile
1659	Harper, Robert	Boston	claimed a Quaker corpse	prison, exile
1764	Harvey, Samuel	Montague, MA	religious unorthodoxy	confiscation
1765	Harris, Samuel, clergy	Culpeper, VA	preached	jail, harassment
6/1650	Hazel, John	Swansea, MA	religious unorthodoxy	arrest
5/31/1651	Hazel, John	Lynn, MA	religious unorthodoxy	jail, fine, lashed
8/1771	Herndon, Edward, clergy	Culpeper, VA	preached	prison
6/1650	Holmes, Obadiah	Swansea, MA	religious unorthodoxy	arrest
5/31/1651	Holmes, Obadiah	Lynn, MA	religious unorthodoxy	jail, fine, lashed

Target of Act/Date	Name, Occupation	Location	Act	Consequence
1662	Hooton, Elizabeth	Boston	visited Quaker prisoners	abandoned
1657	Howland, Arthur	Plymouth, MA	refused bond	prison
3/2/1658	Howland, Arthur	Plymouth, MA	seditious letter	prison, fine
10/6/1659	Howland, Henry, constable	Plymouth, MA	refused jury duty	
5/1/1660	Howland, Henry, constable	Plymouth, MA	illegal meetings	fine
10/2/1660	Howland, Henry, constable	Plymouth, MA	illegal meetings	fine, confiscation
11/1665	Howland, Henry, constable	Plymouth, MA	harbored Quakers	fine, confiscation
1765	Ireland, James, clergy	Culpeper, VA	preached	jail, attempted assassination
1637	King, William	Salem, MA	sheltered Quakers	exile, confiscation
1663	Kingsley, Eldad	Rehoboth, MA	preached	fine
10/30/1667	Kingsley, Eldad	Rehoboth, MA	preached	expelled
after 1767	Lane, Dutton, clergy	Meherrin, VA	religious unorthodoxy	silenced
1774	Lee, Ann, prophet	Albany, NY	blasphemy	jail
fall 1656	Locke, Robert, sea captain	Boston	contempt of court	jail
6/1650	Mann, Mrs. James	Swansea, MA	religious unorthodoxy	arrest
1765	Marsh, William, clergy	Culpeper, VA	preached	jail, harassment
3/1671	Maule, Thomas, tailor	Salem, MA	broke the Sabbath	lashed
12/12/1695	Maule, Thomas, tailor	Salem, MA	sold tracts	books burned
5/1850	McBride, Jesse, missionary	Jamestown, NC	distributed literature	jail
7/8/1677	Miles, Mary	Boston	wore sackcloth and ash	lashed
7/1/1773	Mintz, Edward, preacher	Portsmouth, VA	preached	torture
1764	Montague, Richard, soldier	North Leverett, MA	religious unorthodoxy	jail, confiscation
1751	Morse, David, elder	Sturbridge, MA	religious unorthodoxy	confiscation
1751	Moulton, Elder	Sturbridge, MA	religious unorthodoxy	prison, exile
1663	Myles, John, clergy	Rehoboth, MA	religious unorthodoxy	exile
7/2/1667	Myles, John, clergy	Rehoboth, MA	preached	fine
10/30/1667	Myles, John, clergy	Rehoboth, MA	preached	expelled
1751	Newell, John, deacon	Sturbridge, MA	religious unorthodoxy	confiscation
1650	Newman, Samuel, scholar	Swansea, MA	religious unorthodoxy	harassed
1661	Norton, Humphrey	Boston	blasphemy	jail
1666	Osborne, Priscilla Brighton	Boston	religious unorthodoxy	excommunicated
1666	Osborne, Thomas	Boston	religious unorthodoxy	jail
1751	Perry, Jonathan	Sturbridge, MA	religious unorthodoxy	confiscation
1751	Perry, Josiah	Sturbridge, MA	religious unorthodoxy	prison
3/11/1659	Phelps, Nicholas	Salem, MA	blasphemy	threat
1751	Pike, John	Sturbridge, MA	religious unorthodoxy	confiscation
8/1771	Pitman, James	Culpeper, VA	religious unorthodoxy	prison
4/14/1685	Prentis, Elizabeth Rogers, child	New London, CT	disrupted worship	
1765	Read, James, clergy	Culpeper, VA	preached	jail, harassment
1762	Rich, Elisha	Royalston, MA	refused to renounce faith	threat
1751	Robbins, Benjamin	Sturbridge, MA	religious unorthodoxy	confiscation
10/27/1659	Robinson, William, preacher	Boston	sacrilege	confiscation, hanged
1676	Rogers, Bathsheba	New London, CT	broke the Sabbath	prison, fine
1676	Rogers, Elizabeth Rowland	New London, CT	broke the Sabbath	prison, fine

Target of Act/Date	Name, Occupation	Location	Act	Consequence
1676	Rogers, James, cooper	New London, CT	broke the Sabbath	prison, fine
4/14/1685	Rogers, James, cooper	New London, CT	disrupted worship	lashed
4/14/1685	Rogers, John, Jr., clergy	New London, CT	disrupted worship	arrest
11/1712	Rogers, John, Jr., clergy	New London, CT	riot	jail
7/26/1725	Rogers, John, Jr., clergy	Groton, CT	broke the Sabbath	prison, fine
1676	Rogers, John, Sr., clergy	New London, CT	broke the Sabbath	prison, fine
3/1694	Rogers, John, Sr., clergy	New London, CT	blasphemy	fine
3/26/1712	Rogers, John, Sr., clergy	New London, CT	contempt of court	jail, fled
after 1718	Rogers, John, Sr., clergy	New London, CT	riot, resisted arrest	arrest
1676	Rogers, Jonathan	New London, CT	broke the Sabbath	prison, fine
ca. 1690s	Rogers, Mary Ransford	New London, CT	assaulted an officer	arrest
1679–1680	Russell, John, Jr., cobbler, clergy	Woburn, MA	distributed pamphlets	scorn, abuse
6/3/1658	Scott, Katherine Marbury	Salem, MA	protest	lashed, prison
4/1675	Screven, William, clergy	Kittery, ME	religious unorthodoxy	jail, fine
7/6/1675	Screven, William, clergy	York, ME	broke the Sabbath	charged
7/1682	Screven, William, clergy	York, ME	broke the Sabbath	banished
1658	Shattuck, Samuel	Salem, MA	fed prisoners	
9/1773	Smith, Ebenezer, clergy	Chelmsford, MA	demanded rights	
6/1650	Smith, Edward	Swansea, MA	religious unorthodoxy	arrest
7/26/1725	Smith, James	Groton, CT	broke the Sabbath	prison, fine
6/1650	Smith, Mrs. Edward	Swansea, MA	religious unorthodoxy	arrest
1658	Southwick, Cassandra Burnell	Salem, MA	Quaker convert	jail
3/11/1659	Southwick, Josiah	Salem, MA	blasphemy	lashed, jail
1658	Southwick, Laurence	Salem, MA	Quaker convert	jail
5/31/1651	Spur, John	Lynn, MA	religious nonconformity	jail, fine, lashed to death
1751	Streeter, John	Sturbridge, MA	religious unorthodoxy	confiscation
1663	Tanner, Nicholas, lawyer	Rehoboth, MA	preached	expelled
7/2/1667	Tanner, Nicholas, lawyer	Rehoboth, MA	preached	fine
10/30/1667	Tanner, Nicholas, lawyer	Rehoboth, MA	preached	expelled
1663	Tomkins, Mary	Dover, NH	preached	stripped, lashed
6/1650	Torrey, Greene	Swansea, MA	religious unorthodoxy	arrest
6/1650	Torrey, Joseph	Swansea, MA	religious unorthodoxy	arrest
1790s	Vaughan, Joshua, clergy	Philadelphia	religious unorthodoxy	threat
1765	Waller, John, clergy	Culpeper, VA	preached	jail, harassment
7/26/1769	Waller, John, clergy	Middlesex, VA	religious unorthodoxy	jail
8/1771	Waller, John, clergy	Culpeper, VA	preached	prison, choking, assault, lashed
8/1777	Ware, James	Culpeper, VA	religious unorthodoxy	prison
7/26/1769	Ware, Robert	Middlesex, VA	religious unorthodoxy	jail
7/26/1725	Waterhouse, John	Groton, CT	broke the Sabbath	prison, fine
4/14/1685	Way, Joanna	New London, CT	disrupted worship	lashed
1773	Weatherford, John	Pittsylvania, VA	preached	jail, knife attack, fine
7/26/1769	Webber, William	Middlesex, VA	religious unorthodoxy	jail
11/3/1659	Wharton, Edward	Plymouth, MA	protest	lashed, fine

Target of Act/Date	Name, Occupation	Location	Act	Consequence
11/11/1656	Wickenden, William, clergy	Providence, RI	religious unorthodoxy	exile
1659	Wright, Hannah	Boston	protest	
7/8/1677	Wright, Lydia	Boston	wore sackcloth and ash	lashed
1659	Wright, Mary	Boston	protest	
8/1771	Young, John, clergy	Culpeper, VA	preached	prison

Revolutionary War

Target of Act/Date	Name, Occupation	Location	Act	Consequence
1770s	Baker, John, farmer	Connecticut	refused to serve	
1770s	Barrell, Colburn, merchant	Boston	refused to serve	house rifled, confiscation, wife threatened, exile
1770s	Barrell, Nathaniel, merchant	Boston	refused to serve	
1770s	Benedict, Comfort	Danbury, CT	refused to serve	prison
7/1777	Brown, William	Philadelphia	refused to serve	ridicule
1770s	Capen, Hopestill, cloth dealer	Boston	refused to serve	jail
1777	Compton, William	Philadelphia	refused to serve	prison, threat
17770s	Davis, Benjamin, Sr., merchant	Boston	refused to serve	bankrupt, exile
1770s	Estabrook, E., Baptist clergy	New Hampshire	refused to serve	
7/20/1775	Foster, Edward, blacksmith	Attleboro, MA	refused to serve	home rifled
11/16/1777	Gawthorp, James	Frederick County, VA	refused to serve	forced march
1770s	Giering, Andrew, shoemaker	Emmaus, PA	refused to serve	
1770s	Gregory, Munson	Danbury, CT	refused to serve	
1770s	Healy, Joseph, shoemaker	Litchfield, CT	refused to serve	
1770s	Lee, Jesse, Methodist clergy	Bertie, NC	refused to serve	
7/1777	Masterman, Thomas	Philadelphia	refused to serve	ridicule
8/28/1777	Pemberton, Israel, Jr., merchant	Philadelphia	refused to serve	
1770s	Sparhawk, John	Danbury, CT	refused to serve	jail
1778–1779	Watson, Sarah Woolston	Middletown, PA	protest	
1778–1779	Watson, Thomas, farmer	Middletown, PA	refused paper currency	sentenced to death
7/1777	Wayne, William	Philadelphia	refused to serve	ridicule
7/1777	Wells, Edward	Philadelphia	refused to serve	prison
1770s	Whipple, Jonathan, teacher	Quakertown, CT	refused to serve	threats, confiscation
1770s	Whipple, Noah, mason	Quakertown, CT	refused to serve	threats, confiscation
1770s	White, Ebenezer	Hebron, CT	refused to serve	
1770s	Winslow, Isaac, Jr., distiller	Roxbury, MA	refused to serve	home burned
1770s	Zubly, John Joachim, clergy	Savannah, GA	refused to serve	

ROTC

Target of Act/Date	Name, Occupation	Location	Act	Consequence
4/30/2001	Almenas, Pedro Colón, student	Rio Piedras, Puerto Rico	struck an officer	prison
11/18/2005	Cohen, Karla, activist	Eugene, OR	chained to ROTC classroom entrance	arrest
5/9/1972	Fonda, Jane, actor	Los Angeles	denounced military	
9/29/2005	Jacobs, Lana, activist	Columbia, MO	destroyed property	fine, arrest
9/29/2005	Jacobs, Steve, activist	Columbia, MO	destroyed property	fine, arrest

Target of Act/Date	Name, Occupation	Location	Act	Consequence
9/29/2005	Khan, Tariq, activist	Fairfax, VA	demonstration	police brutality
5/5/1970	Kogan, Larry, student	St. Louis, MO	demonstration	prison
5/5/1970	Mechanic, Howard, student	St. Louis, MO	demonstration	prison
11/18/2005	Tabor, Dorene O. Ewing, writer	Eugene, OR	chained to ROTC classroom entrance	arrest
1960	Theroux, Paul Edward, student	Amherst, MA	refused training	
5/21/2000	Vaughn, Emiliano Huet, student	Kansas City, KS	protest	

Sacco and Vanzetti death sentence

8/1927	Black, Helen	New York City		arrest
8/1927	Craton, Ann Washington, reformer	New York City		arrest
4/8/1927	Dewey, John, educator	New York City	protest	
7/14/1920	Dos Passos, John, writer	New York City	protest	
7/14/1920	Flynn, Elizabeth Gurley, activist	New York City	protest	
7/14/1920	Frankfurter, Felix, jurist	Washington, DC	protest	
4/8/1927	Gold, Michael, journalist	Boston	procession	arrest
4/8/1927	Guthrie, Woody, folksinger	Boston	protest	
4/8/1927	Lippmann, Walter, critic	Boston	protest	
7/14/1920	Mencken, H.L., editor	Baltimore	protest	
8/1927	Millay, Edna St. Vincent, poet	Dedham, MA	procession	arrest
8/1927	Parker, Dorothy Rothschild, satirist	Boston	procession	arrest
4/8/1927	Porter, Katherine Anne, writer	Boston	protest	
4/8/1927	Schlesinger, Arthur, Sr.	Boston	protest	
4/8/1927	Shahn, Ben, artist	Boston	protest	
4/8/1927	Sinclair, Upton, writer	Boston	protest	

School of the Americas

11/21/2005	Bell, Buddy, student	Fort Benning, GA	trespass	arrest
9/1997	Bichsel, Bill, priest	Fort Benning, GA	trespass	prison
11/1997	Bichsel, Bill, priest	Fort Benning, GA	trespass	prison, fine
8/1990	Bourgeois, Roy, priest	Fort Benning, GA	trespass	prison
1994	Bourgeois, Roy, priest	Fort Benning, GA	trespass	prison
1995	Bourgeois, Roy, priest	Fort Benning, GA	trespass	prison
11/1997	Bourgeois, Roy, priest	Fort Benning, GA	trespass	prison, fine
11/19/2006	Bourgeois, Roy, priest	Fort Benning, GA	trespass	prison
11/21/2005	Brancel, Fred, dairier	Fort Benning, GA	trespass	arrest
11/21/2005	Bryant-Gainer, Margaret, activist	Fort Benning, GA	trespass	arrest
11/19/2006	Bryant-Gainer, Margaret, activist	Fort Benning, GA	die-in	arrest
11/21/2005	Busch-Nema, Tina	Fort Benning, GA	trespass	arrest
11/19/2006	Busch-Nema, Tina	Fort Benning, GA	die-in	arrest
11/21/2005	Call, Robert St. Clair, priest	Fort Benning, GA	trespass	arrest
9/1997	Cardell, Nicholas, priest	Fort Benning, GA	trespass	prison
11/1997	Cardell, Nicholas, priest	Fort Benning, GA	trespass	prison, fine
11/21/2005	Carney, Charles, landscaper	Fort Benning, GA	trespass	arrest

Target of Act/Date	Name, Occupation	Location	Act	Consequence
11/21/2005	Clemens, Stephen, activist	Fort Benning, GA	trespass	arrest
11/21/2005	Coleman, Don, clergy	Fort Benning, GA	trespass	arrest
11/19/2006	Coleman, Don, clergy	Fort Benning, GA	die-in	arrest
11/21/2005	Cowan, Joanne, accountant	Fort Benning, GA	trespass	arrest
11/21/2005	Dempsky, Scott, janitor	Fort Benning, GA	trespass	arrest
11/21/2005	DeRaymond, Joe, nurse	Fort Benning, GA	trespass	arrest
11/1997	Early, Mary, teacher	Fort Benning, GA	trespass	prison, fine
9/1997	Eilerman, Marge, nun	Fort Benning, GA	trespass	prison
11/1997	Eilerman, Marge, nun	Fort Benning, GA	trespass	prison, fine
11/19/2006	Fillenwarth, Valerie	Fort Benning, GA	die-in	arrest
11/1997	Flanigan, Mary Kay, nun	Fort Benning, GA	trespass	prison, fine
9/1997	Foster, Sam, retiree	Fort Benning, GA	trespass	arrest
11/19/2006	Gates, Philip, educator	Fort Benning, GA	die-in	arrest
11/21/2005	Gayman, Michael, student	Fort Benning, GA	trespass	arrest
11/19/2006	Gerard, Alice, journalist	Fort Benning, GA	die-in	arrest
11/21/2005	Harper, Sarah, landscaper	Fort Benning, GA	trespass	arrest
11/19/2006	Harris, Joshua, student	Fort Benning, GA	die-in	arrest
11/19/2006	Helman, Melissa, student	Fort Benning, GA	die-in	arrest
11/1997	Herman, Ann, reformer	Fort Benning, GA	trespass	prison, fine
11/21/2005	Hosking, Jan, activist	Fort Benning, GA	trespass	arrest
11/1997	Inman, Paddy, farmer	Fort Benning, GA	trespass	prison, fine
11/2001	Jacobs, Lana, activist	Fort Benning, GA	trespass	arrest
11/2001	Jacobs, Steve, activist	Fort Benning, GA	trespass	arrest
11/1997	Jones, Christopher, student	Fort Benning, GA	trespass	prison, fine
11/1997	Kennon, Ken, clergy	Fort Benning, GA	trespass	prison, fine
9/1997	Kinane, Ed, writer	Fort Benning, GA	trespass	prison
11/1997	Kinane, Ed, writer	Fort Benning, GA	trespass	prison, fine
11/21/2005	LaForge, John, writer	Fort Benning, GA	trespass	arrest
11/1997	Lawton, Dwight, retired	Fort Benning, GA	trespass	prison, fine
11/19/2006	Leforce, Martina, student	Fort Benning, GA	die-in	arrest
11/21/2005	Lentsch, Mary Dennis, nun	Fort Benning, GA	trespass	arrest
11/21/2005	Lewinson, Ed, teacher	Fort Benning, GA	trespass	prison
11/21/2005	Lloyd, Robin, filmmaker	Fort Benning, GA	trespass	arrest
11/1997	Lucey, Rita, retired	Fort Benning, GA	trespass	prison, fine
11/21/2005	Mashburn, Linda, nurse	Fort Benning, GA	trespass	arrest
11/1997	McNulty, Bill, teacher	Fort Benning, GA	trespass	prison, fine
11/19/2006	Oldfield, Julienne, activist	Fort Benning, GA	die-in	arrest
11/21/2005	Parker, Dorothy, counselor	Fort Benning, GA	trespass	arrest
11/21/2005	Phares, Gail, activist	Fort Benning, GA	trespass	arrest
11/19/2006	Ray, Katherine Whitney, student	Fort Benning, GA	die-in	arrest
11/1997	Rice, Megan, nun	Fort Benning, GA	trespass	prison, fine
11/1997	Richardson, Carol, clergy	Fort Benning, GA	trespass	prison, fine
11/21/2005	Ruland, Judith, nurse	Fort Benning, GA	trespass	arrest
9/1997	Rumpf, Kathleen, activist	Fort Benning, GA	trespass	prison, fine
11/1997	Rumpf, Kathleen, activist	Fort Benning, GA	trespass	prison, fine

Target of Act/Date	Name, Occupation	Location	Act	Consequence
11/1997	Sage, Dan, teacher	Fort Benning, GA	trespass	prison, fine
11/1997	Sage, Doris, teacher	Fort Benning, GA	trespass	prison, fine
11/19/2006	Salmon, Sheila, nun	Fort Benning, GA	die-in	arrest
11/21/2005	Schwaller, Delmar, alderman	Fort Benning, GA	trespass	arrest
11/1997	Serraglio, Randy, activist	Fort Benning, GA	trespass	prison, fine
11/21/2000	Sheen, Martin, actor	Fort Benning, GA	sprinkled blood	
11/19/2006	Slater, Nathan, activist	Fort Benning, GA	die-in	arrest
11/21/2005	Smith, Donte, student	Fort Benning, GA	trespass	arrest
11/21/2005	Smith, Edward, activist	Fort Benning, GA	trespass	arrest
11/21/2005	Sommers, Cheryl, activist	Fort Benning, GA	trespass	arrest
11/1997	Steinhagen, Rita, nun	Fort Benning, GA	trespass	prison, fine
11/1997	Streb, Richard, teacher	Fort Benning, GA	trespass	prison, fine
11/21/2005	Sylvester, David, writer	Fort Benning, GA	trespass	arrest
11/1997	Tiffany, Ann, counselor	Fort Benning, GA	trespass	prison, fine
11/21/2005	Treska, Priscilla, teacher	Fort Benning, GA	trespass	arrest
9/1997	Trotochaud, Mary, potter	Fort Benning, GA	trespass	prison
11/1997	Trotochaud, Mary, potter	Fort Benning, GA	trespass	prison, fine
11/21/2005	Vitale, Louis, priest	Fort Benning, GA	trespass	prison
11/19/2006	Vosburg-Casey, Mike, piano tuner	Fort Benning, GA	die-in	arrest
11/21/2005	Walters, Jamie, activist	Fort Benning, GA	trespass	arrest
11/19/2006	Ward, Graymon, activist	Fort Benning, GA	die-in	arrest
11/19/2006	Webster, Cathy, activist	Fort Benning, GA	die-in	arrest
11/1997	Williams, Judith, music therapist	Fort Benning, GA	trespass	prison, fine
11/1997	Woodring, Ruthy, student	Fort Benning, GA	trespass	prison, fine
11/21/2005	Woolever, Frank, priest	Fort Benning, GA	trespass	arrest
11/21/2005	Zawada, Jerome, priest	Fort Benning, GA	trespass	arrest

segregation

Target of Act/Date	Name, Occupation	Location	Act	Consequence
6/2/1961	Abernathy, Ralph David, clergy	Montgomery, AL	lunch counter sit-in	arrest
8/8/1963	Allen, Ralph W., III, student	Americus, GA	protest march	arrest
2/1/1960	Blair, Ezell A., Jr., student	Greensboro, NC	sit-in	
5/14/1963	Booth, Mabel St. Clair, activist	Cambridge, MD	sit-in	jail
1960	Brown, Hubert G., student	Baton Rouge, LA	promoted integration	suspended
3/1965	Brown, Hubert G., activist	Selma, AL	promoted integration	
6/23/1957	Clyburn, Mary Elizabeth	Durham, NC	sit-in	jail, fine
1961	Coffin, William Sloane, Jr., clergy	Baltimore	protest	arrest
1961	Coffin, William Sloane, Jr., clergy	St. Augustine, FL	protest	arrest
6/2/1961	Coffin, William Sloane, Jr., clergy	Montgomery, AL	lunch counter sit-in	arrest
5/14/1963	Cromwell, Dwight, student	Cambridge, MD	sit-in	jail
10/19/1960	Edelman, Marian Wright, educator	Atlanta, GA	sit-in	arrest
1957	Farmer, James Leonard, clergy	Greensboro, NC	sit-in	
5/24/1961	Farmer, James Leonard, clergy	Jackson, MS	Freedom Rider	jail
5/29/1961	Farmer, James Leonard, clergy	Jackson, MS	integrated a bus station	jail
2/1961	Finney, Ernest, lawyer	Sumter, SC	defended sit-ins	

Target of Act/Date	Name, Occupation	Location	Act	Consequence
3/15/1960	Gaither, Thomas, student	Orangeburg, SC	sit-in, trespass	arraigned
1/31/1961	Gaither, Thomas, student	Rock Hill, SC	sit-in	
6/23/1957	Glenn, Claude Edward	Durham, NC	sit-in	jail, fine
6/23/1957	Gray, Jesse Willard	Durham, NC	sit-in	jail, fine
8/8/1963	Harris, Don, activist	Americus, GA	protest march	arrest
1954	Hawkins, Reginald Armistice, dentist	Charlotte, NC	sit-in	
5/4/1945	James, Daniel, Jr., soldier	Seymour, IN	sit-in	arrest
2/1961	Jones, J. Charles, lawyer	Rock Hill, SC	sit-in	jail
6/23/1957	Jones, Vivian Elaine	Durham, NC	sit-in	jail, fine
10/19/1960	King, Martin Luther, Jr., clergy	Atlanta, GA	restaurant sit-in	prison
4/12/1963	King, Martin Luther, Jr., clergy	Birmingham, AL	contempt of court	jail
6/11/1964	King, Martin Luther, Jr., clergy	St. Augustine, FL	integrated a restaurant	arrest
1961	Lawson, James, student	Nashville, TN	sit-in	expelled
6/2/1961	Lee, Bernard Scott, activist	Montgomery, AL	lunch counter sit-in	arrest
8/19/1958	Luper, Clara, teacher	Oklahoma City, OK	sit-in	
2/9/1960	Matthews, Carl Wesley, activist	Winston-Salem, NC	sit-in	
2/1/1960	McCain, Franklin, student	Greensboro, NC	sit-in	
6/23/1957	McKissick, Floyd B., Sr., lawyer	Durham, NC	sit-in	jail, fine
2/1/1960	McNeil, Joseph, student	Greensboro, NC	sit-in	
6/23/1957	Moore, Douglas E., clergy	Durham, NC	sit-in	jail, fine
1960	Motley, Constance Baker, lawyer	New Haven, CT	abetted sit-ins	
7/4/1963	Perdew, John, student	Americus, GA	integrated a restaurant	mob violence
8/8/1963	Perdew, John, student	Americus, GA	protest march	arrest
8/19/1958	Posey, Barbara, student	Oklahoma City, OK	sit-in	
5/14/1963	Richardson, Gloria, piano teacher, activist	Cambridge, MD	sit-in	jail
2/1/1960	Richmond, David, student	Greensboro, NC	sit-in	
1942	Rustin, Bayard Taylor, activist	Nashville, TN	integrated a bus	arrest, police brutality
6/2/1961	Shuttlesworth, Fred Lee, clergy	Montgomery, AL	lunch counter sit-in	arrest
1/31/1961	Smith, Ruby Doris, student	Rock Hill, SC	sit-in	jail
1/3/1961	Taylor, Charles, student	Rock Hill, SC	sit-in	fine
7/19/1958	Walters, Ronald, student	Wichita, KS	lunch counter sit-in	
5/14/1963	White, Reva Dinez, student	Cambridge, MD	sit-in	jail
2/1/1960	Wilkins, Roy, activist	Greensboro, NC	promoted sit-ins	
6/23/1957	Willis, Melvin Haywood	Durham, NC	sit-in	jail, fine
6/11/1964	Young, Andrew Jackson, Jr.	St. Augustine, FL	integrated a restaurant	arrest

slave education ban

12/1841	Adams, Henry, clergy	Louisville, KY	educated slaves	
1825	Auld, Sophia Keithley	Baltimore	educated slaves	
1835–1865	Beasley, Mary, educator	Savannah, GA	educated slaves	patrols
1770	Benezet, Anthony, teacher	Philadelphia	educated slaves	threats
1807	Bonneau, Thomas Siah, teacher	Charleston, SC	educated slaves	
1860	Bouguille, Ludger, teacher	New Orleans, LA	tutored a slave boy	
1851	Brown, Emma V., teacher's aide	Washington, DC	educated slaves	

Target of Act/Date	Name, Occupation	Location	Act	Consequence
1838	Butler, Fanny Kemble, actor	St. Simon's, GA	educated slaves	divorce, loss of children
1808–1832	Chavis, John, teacher	Raleigh, NC	educated slaves	criminalized
1851	Clapp, Margaret, teacher	Washington, DC	educated slaves	
1851	Conway, Moncure Daniel, lecturer	Washington, DC	educated slaves	
1855	Cook, John F., Jr., teacher	Washington, DC	educated slaves	warning
1859	Cook, John F., Jr., teacher	New Orleans, LA	educated slaves	warnings
1838	Cooper, Elizabeth Hodgson, teacher	Williamson, NY	tutored slaves	
1831	Crandall, Prudence, teacher	Canterbury, CT	educated slaves	arson, jail
1861	Crouch, Jane A., educator	Alexandria, VA	educated slaves	
1833–1839	Darlington, Phoebe, teacher	West Chester, PA	educated slaves	
ca. 1820	Delany, Pati Peace, seamstress, laundress	Charlestown, WV	educated slaves, bought a textbook	arrest
1842	Delille, Henriette, nun	New Orleans, LA	educated slaves	
1835–1865	Deveaux, Catherine, educator	Savannah, GA	educated slaves	patrols
1835–1865	Deveaux, Jane, educator	Savannah, GA	educated slaves	patrols
1/1813	Dorfeuille, Godefroy, teacher	New Orleans, LA	educated slaves	
1853	Douglass, Margaret Crittenden, seamstress, educator	Alexandria, VA	educated slaves	arrest, persecution, fine, jail
1853	Douglass, Rosa, educator	Alexandria, VA	educated slaves	arrest, persecution, fine, jail
1851	Edmondson, Emily, teacher's aide	Washington, DC	educated slaves	
1818–1844	Fromantin, Jean Julien, educator	Savannah, GA	educated slaves	
1842	Gaudin, Juliette, nun	New Orleans, LA	educated slaves	
1860s	Granson, Milla, teacher	Natchez, MS	educated slaves	
1861	Gray, Sarah, educator	Alexandria, VA	educated slaves	
1802	Haines, Ann, teacher	New York City	educated slaves	
1802	Haines, Jane Bowne, teacher	New York City	educated slaves	
1829	Harvey, Elizabeth Burgess, educator	Harveysburg, OH	educated slaves	
1829	Harvey, Jesse, educator	Harveysburg, OH	educated slaves	
1861	Herbert, Peter, teacher	Hampton, VA	educated slaves	
1824	Himrod, William, iron manufacturer	Erie, PA	educated slaves	
1857–1859	Howland, Emily, administrator	Washington, DC	educated slaves	
1851	Inman, Anna, French teacher	Washington, DC	educated slaves	
1849	Jane Frances, nun	Savannah, GA	educated slaves	
1851	Johnson, Nancy M., member of school board	Washington, DC	educated slaves	
1851	Johnson, Walter W., lecturer	Washington, DC	educated slaves	
1851	Jones, Anna, teacher's aide	Washington, DC	educated slaves	
1847	Lanusse, Armand, headmaster	New Orleans, LA	educated slaves	
1851	Madden, Matilda Jones, student aide	Washington, DC	educated slaves	
1851	Mann, Lydia B., superintendent	Washington, DC	educated slaves	
1840s	Maudlin, Wright	Bourbon County, KY	abolitionist spy	
1840s–1850s	Meachum, John Berry, preacher	St. Louis, MO	educated slaves	
1840s–1850s	Meachum, Mary, teacher	St. Louis, MO	educated slaves	
1820s	Mendenhall, George C., lawyer	Jamestown, NC	educated slaves	

Target of Act/Date	Name, Occupation	Location	Act	Consequence
1820s	Mendenhall, Richard, tanner	Jamestown, NC	educated slaves	
1863	Merrick, Chloe	Fernandina, FL	educated slave, ran an orphanage and depot	
7/1846	Miner, Myrtilla, educator	Whitesville, MS	educated slaves	threats
1850s	Miner, Myrtilla, educator	Washington, DC	educated slaves	harassment, arson
1851	Moore, Helen, educator	Washington, DC	educated slaves	
1826–1847	Morris, Sylvia, educator	Alexandria, VA	educated slaves	intimidation
1837–1843	Parry, Alfred, teacher	Alexandria, VA	educated slaves	
ca. 1820	Peace, Graci	Charlestown, WV	educated slaves	
9/17/1861	Peake, Mary Smith Kelsey, teacher	Hampton, VA	educated slaves	
1840s	Porter, James, educator	Savannah, GA	educated slaves	police raid
1841	Porter, Sarah, teacher	Nashville, TN	educated slaves	
ca. 1860	Purdy, Edwin, clergy	Augusta, GA	educated slaves	jail, fine, lashed
1850s	Rogers, Stephen Walter, clergy	Mobile, AL	educated slaves	
1830s	Rotch, Charity Rodman	Kendal, OH	educated slaves	
1851	Searing, Anna Hutchinson, doctor	Washington, DC	educated slaves	
1860s	Simms, James Meriles, teacher, clergy	Savannah, GA	educated slaves	lashed, fine
1854–1863	Skipworth, Lucy, teacher	Hopewell, AL	educated slaves	threats
1857	Stanley, Frances Griffith, teacher	Cleveland, OH	educated slaves	
1830–1857	Stanley, John Stewart, teacher	New Bern, NC	educated slaves	forced out
7/9/1848	Stanton, Elizabeth Cady	Waterloo, NY	conspiracy	
3/1833	Sumner, Alphonso M,. teacher	Nashville, TN	educated slaves	beaten
1830s	Swisshelm, Jane Grey Cannon, educator, author	Louisville, KY	educated slaves	mob violence
1797	Thomas, Avis Stanton	Mount Pleasant, OH	ran a safehouse	
1797	Thomas, Jesse, Jr., farmer	Mount Pleasant, OH	ran a safehouse	
1842; 1862	Wadkins, Daniel, teacher	Nashville, TN	educated slaves	threats
1856	Wadkins, Daniel, teacher	Louisville, KY	educated slaves	
1851	Weaver, Amanda, educator	Washington, DC	educated slaves	
1835–1865	Woodhouse, Mary, educator	Savannah, GA	educated slaves	
1850s	Woodhouse, Mary Jane, educator	Savannah, GA	educated slaves	
1829–1860s	Wright, Phebe Wierman	South Mountain, PA	educated slaves	
1829–1860s	Wright, William	South Mountain, PA	educated slaves	
1/1838	Yandle, John, teacher	Nashville, TN	educated slaves	

slave recapture

9/23/1859	Abbott, James Burnett	Wakarusa, KS	jailbreak	
1830s–1840s	Adams, Robert S., bookseller	Fall River, MA	sheltered slaves	
10/16/1830	Alcott, Amos Bronson, educator	Concord, MA	recruiter	
1840s–1850s	Alcott, Amos Bronson, educator	Concord, MA	sheltered slaves	
1840s–1850s	Alcott, Louisa May, author	Concord, MA	sheltered slaves	
1840s	Allinson, William J., druggist	Burlington, NJ	sheltered slaves	
1840s	Alston, John	Middletown, DE	sheltered slaves	
10/1/1851	Ames, Amy Perkins	Mexico, NY	slave transport	
10/15/1851	Ames, Leonard, Jr.	Oswego, NY	slave transport	

Target of Act/Date	Name, Occupation	Location	Act	Consequence
10/1/1851	Ames, Orson	Mexico, NY	slave transport	
1837–1861	Anderson, Elijah, blacksmith	Madison, IN	slave relay	died in prison
4/3/1851	Andrew, John Albion, attorney	Boston	slave rescue	
3/11/1854	Angove, James S., carpenter	Milwaukee, WI	jailbreak	
1820s–1830s	Anthony, Elihu	Greenfield, NY	slave relay	
1820s–1830s	Anthony, Mason	Greenfield, NY	slave relay	
1810s	Anthony, Susan Brownell, orator	Rochester, NY	propaganda	
1857	Arnold, Joseph, miller	Linnville, IA	slave relay	
1857	Arnold, Tacy Smith	Linnville, IA	slave relay	
9/13/1858	Backus, Franklin T., lawyer	Cleveland, OH	defended slave rescue	
4/15/1848	Bailey, Gamaliel, editor	Washington, DC	complicity in slave escape	mob violence
1840s–1860s	Baltimore, Priscilla	St. Louis, MO	slave rescue	
1834–1860s	Barker, David	Niagara, NY	ran a safehouse	
1834–1865	Barker, Elizabeth Hazard	New Orleans, LA	ran a safehouse	
1834–1865	Barker, Jacob	New Orleans, LA	ran a safehouse	
1834–1860s	Barker, Pennsylvania Herendeen	Niagara, NY	ran a safehouse	
1860s	Barnard, Eusebius, clergy	Pocopsin, PA	slave relay	
9/13/1858	Bartlett, James, cobbler	Oberlin, OH	impeded arrest	jail
9/13/1858	Bartlett, James H., Jr., cobbler	Oberlin, OH	impeded arrest	jail
1840s–1860s	Battin, Marshall	Elklands, PA	slave relay	
1840s–1860s	Baylis, William, sea captain	Wilmington, DE	sea transport	
1830s–1860s	Bearse, Austin, sea captain	New Bedford, MA	sea transport	
10/1/1851	Beebe, Asa, deacon	Mexico, NY	slave concealment	
10/1/1851	Beebe, Mary Whipple	Mexico, NY	slave concealment	
10/15/1851	Beebe, Winsor	Mexico, NY	slave transport	
1847	Beecher, Henry Ward, clergy	Brooklyn, NY	ran a depot	threats
4/15/1848	Beecher, Henry Ward, clergy	Washington, DC	protest, fund-raising	
9/25/1857	Bell, Charles A.	Mauckport, IN	slave rescue ferry	kidnap, jail
4/15/1848	Bell, Daniel	Washington, DC	sea transport	
1829	Bell, David Williamson, ferryman	Mauckport, IN	slave rescue ferry	
9/25/1857	Bell, David Williamson, ferryman	Mauckport, IN	slave rescue ferry	kidnap, jail
1829	Bell, Elizabeth Wright	Mauckport, IN	slave rescue ferry	
9/25/1857	Bell, Horace	Mauckport, IN	slave rescue ferry	kidnap, jail
1780s–1830s	Bell, James Patterson, soldier	Colerain, PA	sheltered slaves	
1847	Benson, George W.	Brooklyn, CT	conspiracy to rescue	
1860s	Bickerdyke, Mary Ann, nurse	Tennessee	sheltered slaves	
2/16/1851	Bigelow, Ann Hager	Concord, MA	sheltered slaves	
2/16/1851	Bigelow, Francis Edwin, blacksmith	Concord, MA	sheltered slaves, transport	
9/13/1858	Boies, Eli, doctor	Oberlin, OH	impeded arrest	jail
1840s	Bonsall, Susan P. Johnson	Wagontown, PA	sheltered slaves	
1840s–1850s	Bonsall, Thomas	Wagontown, PA	sheltered slaves	
3/11/1854	Booth, Sherman Miller, editor	Milwaukee, WI	jailbreak	
10/1/1851	Brigham, J.B.	Syracuse, NY	jailbreak	tried
1840s–1850s	Brooks, Mary Merrick	Concord, MA	ran a safehouse	
2/16/1851	Brooks, Nathan, lawyer	Concord, MA	defended slave rescue	

Target of Act/Date	Name, Occupation	Location	Act	Consequence
1810s	Brown, Ann Kirk	Fulton, PA	sheltered slaves	
1855	Brown, Frederick	Lawrence, KS	border clashes	
1810s–1850s	Brown, Jeremiah	Fulton, PA	sheltered slaves	
1825–1835	Brown, John, tanner	Randolph, PA	slave relay	
1835	Brown, John, tanner	Tabor, PA	slave transport	
1851	Brown, John	Springfield, MA	ran a street patrol	
1855	Brown, John, tanner	Lawrence, KS	border clashes	
5/21/1856	Brown, John, tanner	Lawrence, KS	border clashes	injured in sword fight
12/20/1858	Brown, John, tanner	Missouri	slave transport	
1833–1885	Brown, Mary McClanahan, peddler	Henderson County, KY	spying, slave transport	prison
1766	Brown, Moses, entrepreneur	Providence, RI	ran a safehouse	
1855	Brown, Oliver	Lawrence, KS	border clashes	
1855	Brown, Owen	Lawrence, KS	border clashes	
1766	Brown, Phebe Waterman	Providence, RI	ran a safehouse	
1800s–1820s	Brown, Rachel Milner	Little Britain, PA	sheltered slaves	
1820	Brown, Randall, financier	Charleston, WV	slave rescue	
1855	Brown, Salmon	Lawrence, KS	border clashes	
1833–1885	Brown, Thomas, peddler	Henderson County, KY	spying, slave transport	banished
1800s–1820s	Brown, William	Little Britain, PA	sheltered slaves	
1840s	Brown, William Wells, lake pilot	Cleveland, OH	lake transport	
8/15/1858	Buckner, Dick	Louisville, KY	slave rescue	prison
4/3/1851	Buffum, James Needham, financier	Lynn, MA	fund-raising	
6/1825	Bulla, William	Wayne County, IN	slave recovery	lawsuit
7/1841	Burr, James E.	Palmyra, MO	slave conductor	prison at hard labor, maimed
1840s–1850s	Burroughs, George L., rail laborer	Cairo, IL	slave transport	
1767	Burt, Elijah	East Longmeadow, MA	sheltered slaves	
4/3/1851	Burton, Alexander P.	Boston	jailbreak	tried
4/15/1848	Bush, Linda Clark, innkeeper	Washington, DC	sea transport	
4/15/1848	Bush, William, innkeeper	Washington, DC	sea transport	
9/13/1858	Bushnell, Simeon Martin, printer	Oberlin, OH	impeded arrest	jail
1810s–1860s	Bushong, Henry	Quarryville, PA	sheltered slaves	
1830s	Butler, Benjamin Franklin, general	Fort Monroe, VA	sheltered slaves	
5/13/1861	Butterworth, Henry Thomas	Lebanon, OH	ran a safehouse	
1830s	Butterworth, Nancy Irvin Wales	Lebanon, OH	ran a safehouse	
1850s	Cain, Augustus Way, doctor	Sadsbury, PA	slave rescue	
1850s	Cain, Lydia Ann Dickinson	Sadsbury, PA	slave rescue	
1830s–1860s	Carpenter, Joseph	New Rochelle, NY	slave rescue	
1830s–1860s	Carpenter, Margaret W. Cornell	New Rochelle, NY	slave rescue	
1830s	Cattell, Jonas	Salem, OH	ran a safehouse	
1840s–1860s	Chace, Elizabeth Buffum	Valley Falls, RI	forgery	
1830	Chandler, Elizabeth Margaret, author	Tecumseh, MI	recruiter	
4/15/1848	Chaplin, William Lawrence, orator	Washington, DC	sea transport, assault	prison

Target of Act/Date	Name, Occupation	Location	Act	Consequence
7/6/1859	Chase, Salmon Portland, lawyer	Washington, DC	propaganda, defended civil disobedience	
1830s	Child, David Lee, publisher	New York City	abetted slave rescue	
5/9/1837	Child, Lydia Maria Francis, publisher	New York City	abetted slave rescue, propaganda	
1860	Child, Lydia Maria Francis, publisher	New York City	abetted slave rescue	
8/2/1839	Cinqué, Joseph, slave	Montauk, NY	murder, piracy	jail
1850–1861	Clark, Jonas W., clothier	Boston	ran a street patrol	
10/15/1851	Clarke, Charlotte Ambler	Oswego, NY	slave concealment	
10/15/1851	Clarke, Edwin W., lawyer	Oswego, NY	slave concealment	
1840s	Clay, Cassius Marcellus, publisher	Jeffersonville, IN	abetted slave rescue	
1840s–1850s	Coates, Deborah T. Simmons	Sadsbury, PA	slave rescue	
1840s–1850s	Coates, Lindley	Sadsbury, PA	slave rescue	
10/1/1851	Cobb, Ira	Syracuse, NY	jailbreak	tried
12/15/1851	Coburn, John P.	Boston	jailbreak	tried
1854	Coburn, John P.	Boston	ran a street patrol	
1840s–1860s	Coffin, Alfred V.	Guilford County, NC	conspiracy	
1826–1847	Coffin, Catherine White, merchant	Newport, IN	slave relay	
1847–1861	Coffin, Catherine White, merchant	Cincinnati, OH	slave relay	
1826–1847	Coffin, Levi, merchant	Newport, IN	slave relay, recruiter	
1847–1861	Coffin, Levi, merchant	Cincinnati, OH	slave relay, recruiter	
11/9/1851	Coffin, Levi, merchant	Cincinnati, OH	fund-raising	
1862	Conway, Ellen Davis Dana	Falmouth, VA	slave relay	mob violence
1862	Conway, Moncure Daniel, clergy	Falmouth, VA	slave relay	mob violence
1858	Cook, John E.	Harpers Ferry, VA	spying, supplied anarchists	executed
9/13/1858	Copeland, John Anthony, Jr., carpenter	Oberlin, OH	impeded arrest	jail
1755	Corbet, Daniel	Smyrna, DE	sheltered slaves	
1755	Corbet, Mary Brinton	Smyrna, DE	sheltered slaves	
1784	Cowles, Polly Gleason	Farmington, CT	ran a safehouse	
1784	Cowles, Solomon	Farmington, CT	ran a safehouse	
1838	Cox, Hannah Peirce	Longwood, PA	slave relay	
1838	Cox, John, farmer	Longwood, PA	slave relay	
1838	Cox, John William, farmer	Longwood, PA	slave relay	
5/1850	Crooks, Adam, missionary	Jamestown, NC	distributed literature	mob violence, arrest
1783	Cuffe, Paul, whaler	Westport, MA	sea relay	
9/13/1858	Cummings, Robert L.	Oberlin, OH	impeded arrest	jail
1820s	Curry, Vina, laundress	Guilford County, NC	conspiracy	
10/1/1851	Davis, James	Saratoga, NY	slave transport	
1850s	DeBaptiste, George	Madison, IN	slave rescue, anarchy	
1830s	Delany, Martin Robinson, doctor	Pittsburgh	recruiter	
4/29/1861	De Mortie, Mark	Boston	ran a street patrol	
9/13/1858	De Wolfe, Matthew, lawyer	Oberlin, OH	impeded arrest	jail
1850s–1860s	Dickson, Moses, clergy	St. Louis, MO	conspiracy, slave rescue	
12/5/1848	Dillingham, Richard	Nashville, TN	slave relay	died in prison at hard labor

Target of Act/Date	Name, Occupation	Location	Act	Consequence
1858	Donnell, Luther A.	Clarksburg, IN	slave relay	lawsuit
11/9/1851	Doram, Catherine	Cincinnati, OH	fund-raising	
9/1851	Douglass, Anna Murray, cobbler	Rochester, NY	slave rescue	
9/1851	Douglass, Frederick, editor, orator	Rochester, NY	slave rescue	
1830s–1860s	Dow, Cornelia Durant Maynard	Portland, ME	slave refuge	
1830s–1860s	Dow, Neal	Portland, ME	slave refuge	
4/29/1861	Downing, George T.	Boston	ran a street patrol	
1854	Doy, Charles	Deer Creek, KS	slave transport	jail, threat
1/1859	Doy, Charles	St. Louis, MO	slave transport	jail, threat
1854	Doy, John W., homeopath	Deer Creek, KS	slave transport	jail, threat
1/1859	Doy, John W., homeopath	St. Louis, MO	slave transport	jail, threat
8/5/1848	Doyle, Edward James, student	Danville, KY	slave rescue	died in prison at hard labor
2/16/1851	Drake, Frances Hills Wilder	Leominster, MA	slave harboring	
2/16/1851	Drake, Jonathan	Leominster, MA	slave harboring	
4/15/1848	Drayton, Daniel, sea captain	Washington, DC	sea transport	knifed, prison, fine, suicide
4/15/1848	Ducket, Thomas	Washington, DC	sea transport	
1846	Dyer, Charles Volney, surgeon	Chicago	slave rescue	knife fight
1840s	Eells, Erastus, mortician	Lisbon, OH	slave concealment, relay	
1792	Ellis, Mercy Cox	Muncy, PA	ran a safehouse	
1792	Ellis, William, realtor	Muncy, PA	ran a safehouse	
1859	Ellyson, Zachariah, mechanic, mill-wright	Pleasant Plain, IA	slave rescue	
1850	Emerson, Lydia Jackson	Concord, MA	slave transport, fund-raising	
1850	Emerson, Ralph Waldo, philosopher	Concord, MA	slave transport, fund-raising	
1840s	Eshleman, Jacob K, doctor	Strasburg, PA	slave rescue	
1830s–1840s	Evans, David	Greenwich, NJ	slave rescue	shunning
9/13/1858	Evans, Henry, cabinetmaker	Oberlin, OH	impeded arrest	jail
1830s–1840s	Evans, Nathan, farmer	Greenwich, NJ	slave rescue	shunning
9/13/1858	Evans, Wilson Bruce, carpenter	Oberlin, OH	impeded arrest	jail
1830s–1840s	Evans, Zillah Maule	Greenwich, NJ	slave rescue	shunning
1837	Fairbank, Calvin, clergy	Cincinnati, OH	slave transport	
9/28/1844	Fairbank, Calvin, clergy	Lexington, KY	slave liberation	mob violence, prison at hard labor
11/9/1851	Fairbank, Calvin, clergy	Louisville, KY	slave rescue	prison
9/13/1858	Fairchild, James Harris	Oberlin, OH	slave rescue	
9/13/1858	Fairchild, Mary Fletcher Kellogg	Oberlin, OH	slave rescue	
10/1855	Fairweather, James	New Bedford, MA	ran a street patrol	
1830s	Falls, William S., druggist	Burlington, NJ	sheltered slaves	
11/9/1851	Fee, Gregg, clergy	Louisville, KY	supported slave rescue	
1820s–1840s	Fish, Benjamin	Rochester, NY	slave rescue	shunning
1820s–1840s	Fish, Catharine Ann	Rochester, NY	slave rescue	shunning
1820s–1840s	Fish, Mary Braithwaite	Rochester, NY	slave rescue	shunning
1820s–1840s	Fish, Sarah Davids Bill	Rochester, NY	slave rescue	shunning
9/13/1858	Fitch, James M., bookseller	Oberlin, OH	impeded arrest	jail

Target of Act/Date	Name, Occupation	Location	Act	Consequence
1840s	Ford, Cyrus, orchardist	Cleveland, OH	lake relay	
1840s	Ford, Darius, orchardist	Cleveland, OH	lake relay	
1840s–1850s	Ford, Horatio Clark	Cleveland, OH	lake relay	
9/13/1858	Fox, Jeremiah, teamster	Oberlin, OH	impeded arrest	jail
4/14/1775	Franklin, Benjamin, publisher	Philadelphia	organized abolitionists	
1833–1840s	Frazier, Anna Joy	Salem, IA	protest	ousted by Quakers
1833–1840s	Frazier, Stephen	Salem, IA	protest	ousted by Quakers
1841–1851	Freeman, Amos Noah, clergy	Portland, ME	depot conductor	
10/1/1851	Fuller, James Canning, Jr., druggist	Skaneateles, NY	jailbreak	
10/15/1851	Fuller, James Canning, Jr., druggist	Skaneateles, NY	slave transport	
1820s–1850s	Fuller, James Canning, Sr.	Skaneateles, NY	slave relay	
1820s–1850s	Fuller, Lydia Charleton	Skaneateles, NY	slave relay	
1850s–1860s	Fuller, Sam, oysterman	Middletown, DE	slave smuggling	
9/11/1851	Fussell, Bartholomew, doctor	Kennett Square, PA	slave rescue, transport	
1842–1860s	Fussell, Edwin, doctor	Pendleton, IN	slave rescue	
1842–1860s	Fussell, Emma Jane	Pendleton, IN	slave rescue	acid in the face
1842–1860s	Fussell, Rebecca Lewis	Pendleton, IN	slave rescue	
1840s	Gansey, Isaac, waterman	Norfolk, VA	slave transport	
1850s–1860s	Gardner, Eliza	Douglas County, KS	ran a safehouse	
1850s–1860s	Gardner, Joseph	Douglas County, KS	ran a safehouse	
8/1859	Gardner, Joseph	Vinland, KS	jailbreak	
9/23/1859	Gardner, Joseph	Vinland, KS	jailbreak	
9/23/1859	Gardner, Joseph	Vinland, KS	jailbreak	
6/9/1860	Gardner, Joseph	Vinland, KS	slave rescue	wanted criminal, gunfight
1840s–1850s	Gardner, Mary Ann Price	Worthington, OH	ran a safehouse	
1840s–1850s	Gardner, Ozem, brickmaker	Worthington, OH	ran a safehouse	
6/9/1860	Gardner, Theodore	Vinland, KS	slave rescue	gunfight
1/30/1856	Garner, Margaret	Mill Creek, OH	murder of a child	re-enslaved
8/21/1843	Garnet, Henry Highland, clergy	Troy, NY	slave relay, sabotage	
1848	Garrett, Rachel Mendenhall	Wilmington, DE	slave rescue, disguise	
1848	Garrett, Thomas, ironworker, hardware dealer	Wilmington, DE	slave relay	lawsuit, price on his head
1818	Garrison, William Lloyd, child	Newburyport, MA	propaganda	
1829	Garrison, William Lloyd, editor	Baltimore	propaganda	jail
1/1/1831	Garrison, William Lloyd, editor	Boston	propaganda	
1835	Garrison, William Lloyd, editor	Boston	propaganda	mob violence
1/1836	Garrison, William Lloyd, editor	New York City	trained agents	
1842	Garrison, William Lloyd, editor	Annapolis, MD	spying	jail
2/21/1851	Garrison, William Lloyd, editor	Boston	propaganda	
4/3/1851	Garrison, William Lloyd, editor	Boston	slave rescue	
1840s	Garvey, Edward Christie Kerr, editor	Topeka, KS	sheltered slaves	
8/1/1857	Gaul, Lewis	Boston	ran a street patrol	
1845	Gay, Elizabeth J. Neall	Staten Island, NY	conspiracy	
9/13/1858	Gena, Thomas, fugitive slave	Oberlin, OH	impeded arrest	jail

Target of Act/Date	Name, Occupation	Location	Act	Consequence
1836	Gibbons, Abigail Hopper	New York City	slave conducting	ousted by Quakers
1800s–1850s	Gibbons, Daniel	Bird-in-Hand, PA	slave rescue	
1800s–1850s	Gibbons, Hannah Wierman	Bird-in-Hand, PA	nursed fleeing slaves	
1836	Gibbons, James Sloan	New York City	slave conducting	ousted by Quakers
1840s	Gibbs, Jonathan C., clergy	Troy, NY	sheltered slaves	
10/1855	Gibson, Robert	New Bedford, MA	ran a street patrol	
1841	Giddings, Joshua Reed, lawyer, legislator	Jefferson, OH	abetted slave transport	congressional censure
4/15/1848	Giddings, Joshua Reed, lawyer, legislator	Washington, DC	defended slave transport	
9/13/1858	Gillett, Matthew M., farmer	Oberlin, OH	impeded arrest	jail
1852	Gillette, Francis, senator	Bloomfield, CT	slave rescue, transport	
8/1843	Goodnow, Lyman	Prairieville, WI	slave relay	
1838–1860	Goodwin, Abigail	Salem, NJ	slave rescue, disguise	
1838–1860	Goodwin, Elizabeth	Salem, NJ	slave rescue, disguise	
9/13/1858	Goodyear, Chauncey	Oberlin, OH	impeded arrest	jail
5/4/1840	Gray, Greenburg	Anne Arundel County, MD	forgery	prison
11/1856	Green, Samuel, Jr., clergy	Indian Creek, MD	slave harboring	arrest, book confiscation, prison
4/29/1842	Green, Wesley, farmer	Anne Arundel County, MD	slave rescue	died in prison
1853	Greenebaum, Michael G., lawyer	Chicago	protest, jailbreak	
1830s–1850s	Grew, Mary	Philadelphia	slave rescue	
8/1860	Grey, Emily O. Goodridge	St. Anthony Falls, MN	sheltered slaves	mob violence
4/3/1851	Grimes, Archibald, clergy	Boston	slave rescue	
1832–1850s	Grimes, John	Boonton, NJ	slave rescue	
3/1839	Grimes, Leonard Andrew, cabman	Washington, DC	slave transport	prison
1845	Grimké, Angelina Emily, orator	Staten Island, NY	conspiracy	
1845	Grimké, Sarah Moore	Staten Island, NY	conspiracy	
1853	Grinnell, Josiah Bushnell, clergy	Grinnell, IA	slave relay	
1853	Grinnell, Julia Ann Chapin	Grinnell, IA	slave relay	
9/13/1858	Griswold, Seneca O., lawyer	Cleveland, OH	defended slave rescue	
1/24/1859	Grover, Emily Jane Hunt	Lawrenceville, KS	slave rescue	
1/24/1859	Grover, Joel	Lawrenceville, KS	slave rescue	
10/1855	Guinn, Isaac	New Bedford, MA	ran a street patrol	
1842	Hadley, Deborah D., quilter	Springfield, OH	coded quilt	ousted from Quakers
1842	Hadley, Lydia D., quilter	Springfield, OH	coded quilt	ousted from Quakers
1842	Hadley, Rebecca Harvey, quilter	Springfield, OH	coded quilt	ousted from Quakers
1840s–1860s	Haines, Jacob A.	Muncy, PA	slave relay	
1840s–1860s	Haines, Jesse	Muncy, PA	slave relay	
1840s–1860s	Haines, Rachel Ellis	Muncy, PA	slave relay	
1820s–1840s	Haines, Sarah Brown	Fulton, PA	slave rescue	
1820s–1840s	Haines, Timothy	Fulton, PA	slave rescue	
4/3/1851	Hale, John Parker, lawyer	Boston	defended slave rescue	

Target of Act/Date	Name, Occupation	Location	Act	Consequence
1850–1865	Hanover, John T., naturalist	Gibson County, IN	route planning	
9/11/1851	Hanway, Castner, miller	Christiana, PA	slave rescue	shoot-out, arrest
1830s	Harris, Hazzard	Harford County, MD	water relay	
9/13/1858	Hartwell, John, fugitive slave	Oberlin, OH	impeded arrest	jail
1840s	Hatfield, John, clergy	Cincinnati, OH	slave transport	
1845	Haviland, Laura Smith	Raisin, MI	refugee orphanage	threats
4/3/1851	Hayden, Harriet Bell	Boston	slave harboring	
2/15/1851	Hayden, Lewis	Boston	jailbreak	
4/3/1851	Hayden, Lewis	Boston	jailbreak, slave harboring	tried
4/29/1861	Hayden, Lewis	Boston	ran a street patrol	
1826–1847	Haydock, Hannah Thompson	Newport, IN	slave conductor	
1826–1847	Haydock, Thomas Thompson	Newport, IN	slave conductor	
1854–1861	Heineman, Emil S.	Detroit, MI	slave transport	
1854–1861	Heineman, Fanny Butzel	Detroit, MI	slave transport	
9/28/1844	Helm, James, waterman	Lexington, KY	slave transport	
1840s	Hickok, James Butler "Wild Bill"	Homer, IL	slave relay	
1830s	Hickok, Polly Butler	Homer, IL	slave relay	
1830s	Hickok, William Alonzo	Homer, IL	slave relay	
1824	Hicks, Elias, preacher	Cass County, MI	sheltered, hired slaves	threat
1851	Hicks, Hannah	Long Island, NY	slave rescue	
1810s	Hicks, Mary Underhill Mott	New York City	slave rescue	
1810s	Hicks, Rachel Seaman, orator	Westbury, NY	propaganda	
5/26/1854	Higginson, Thomas Wentworth, clergy	Boston	jailbreak	hurt, indicted
1840s–1860s	Hill, John	Elklands, PA	slave relay	
9/13/1858	Hines, Lewis, farmer	Oberlin, OH	impeded arrest	jail
9/11/1851	Hood, Caleb C., farmer	Bart, PA	slave rescue	
9/11/1851	Hood, Joseph, farmer	Bart, PA	slave rescue	
6/1825	Hoover, Andrew	Wayne County, IN	slave recovery	lawsuit
9/11/1851	Hopkins, Henry C., farmer	Christiana, PA	slave rescue	shoot-out
1801	Hopper, Isaac Tatem, bookseller	Philadelphia	child recovery	
1836	Hopper, Isaac Tatem, bookseller	New York City	slave conductor	expelled from Quakers
1836	Hopper, Sarah Tatum Hopper	New York City	slave conductor	
1830s	Hossack, John, lumberman	Ottawa, IL	slave rescue	
10/1/1851	Hoyt, Jason Sylvester	Saratoga, NY	slave transport	
1830s–1850s	Huber, Charles Boerstler, tanner	Bethel, OH	sheltered slaves	
4/21/1839	Hudson, Sally	Ripley, OH	slave rescue	shot
7/9/1848	Hunt, Jane Clothier Master	Waterloo, NY	slave concealment	
8/1/1847	Hussey, Sylvanus Erastus Fuller, farmer	Plymouth, MI	slave rescue	threat
4/15/1848	Jackson, Francis, historian	Washington, DC	defended slave rescue	
4/3/1851	Jackson, Francis, historian	Boston	slave rescue	
9/11/1851	Johnson, Abraham, farmer	Christiana, PA	slave rescue	shoot-out
10/1855	Johnson, Henry	New Bedford, MA	ran a street patrol	
1812	Jones, Absalom, activist	Philadelphia	paramilitary	
1850s	Jones, John Tecumseh "Ottawa"	Ottawa, KS	slave rescue	shot at; home, store burned

Target of Act/Date	Name, Occupation	Location	Act	Consequence
1853	Kayer, Leopold	Chicago	protest, jailbreak	
1851	Ketcham, Rebecca	Long Island, NY	slave rescue	
1840s	Knoefel, August, druggist	New York City	slave rescue	
1820s–1840s	Lane, Hester, interior decorator	New York City	slave rescue	
until 1854	Lane, James Henry, orator	Lawrenceburg, IN	guerrilla war	
9/13/1858	Langston, Charles Henry, lawyer	Oberlin, OH	impeded arrest	jail, fine
7/6/1859	Langston, Charles Henry, lawyer	Washington, DC	propaganda, defended civil disobedience	
9/13/1858	Leary, Lewis Sheridan, saddler	Oberlin, OH	impeded arrest	jail
1840s	Lewelling, Henderson W., tree grafter	Salem, IA	ran a depot	ousted by Quakers
1840s	Lewelling, Jane Elizabeth Presnall	Salem, IA	ran a depot	ousted by Quakers
9/11/1851	Lewis, Elijah, farmer	Christiana, PA	slave rescue	shoot-out, arrest
1853	Lewis, Elizabeth R.	Kimberton, PA	slave rehabilitation	
1853	Lewis, Esther Fussell	Kimberton, PA	slave rehabilitation	
9/13/1858	Lewis, Franklin	Oberlin, OH	impeded arrest	jail
1853	Lewis, Graceanna	Kimberton, PA	slave rehabilitation	
1853	Lewis, Mariann	Kimberton, PA	slave rehabilitation	
1830s–1850s	Lewis, Pompey	Small Gloucester, NJ	slave rescue	
9/1851	Lewis, Samuel	Norristown, PA	slave rescue	shoot-out
9/1851	Lewis, William	Norristown, PA	slave transport	
8/15/1858	Lewis, William	Louisville, KY	slave rescue	
9/13/1858	Lincoln, William E, student	Oberlin, OH	impeded arrest	jail
1860s	Livermore, Mary Ashton Rice, nurse	St. Louis, MO	sheltered slaves	
1853	Loeb, Adolph	Chicago	protest, jailbreak	
1837–1861	Loguen, Jermaine Wesley, clergy	Rochester, NY	slave rescue, propaganda	
10/1/1851	Loguen, Jermaine Wesley, clergy	Syracuse, NY	jailbreak	fled
4/3/1851	Loring, Ellis Gray, lawyer	Boston	slave rescue	
9/13/1858	Loveland, Abner, farmer	Oberlin, OH	impeded arrest	jail
1819	Lundy, Benjamin, editor	Mount Pleasant, OH	propaganda	
1829	Lundy, Benjamin, editor	Mount Pleasant, OH	recruiter	
9/13/1858	Lyman, Ansel Wright, customs agent	Oberlin, OH	impeded arrest	jail
1830s–1840s	Magill, Edward Hicks, teacher	Langhorne, PA	slave relay	
1830s–1840s	Magill, Jonathan Paxson, teacher	Solebury, PA	slave relay	
1830s–1840s	Magill, Watson P.	Solebury, PA	slave relay	
1839	Mahan, John Bennington, clergy	Sardinia, OH	incited a riot	fine; jail on bread, water
1844	Mahan, John Bennington, clergy	Sardinia, OH	rescue operation	threat of kidnap or murder, died from prison at hard labor
1844	Mahan, William Jacob, carpenter	Sardinia, OH	rescue operation	ousted by Methodists
9/13/1858	Mandeville, John, brickmaker	Oberlin, OH	impeded arrest	jail
1840s–1850s	Mann, Horace, educator	Boston	sheltered slaves	
4/15/1848	Mann, Horace, educator	Washington, DC	defended slave rescue	
1833	Manuel	Elizabeth City, NC	forgery	
1841	Marriot, Charles	Hudson, NY	slave conducting	expelled from Quakers
1820s–1840s	Marsh, Gravner	Caln, PA	slave relay	

Target of Act/Date	Name, Occupation	Location	Act	Consequence
1820s–1840s	Marsh, Hannah	Caln, PA	slave relay	
1840s–1850s	Marsh, Sarah, wagoneer	Caln, PA	slave relay	
10/1857	Maxson, Delilah Bowland	Cedar County, IA	slave rescue	
10/1857	Maxson, William	Cedar County, IA	slave rescue	
10/16/1830	May, Samuel Joseph, clergy	Syracuse, NY	recruiter	
5/1850	McBride, Jesse, missionary	Jamestown, NC	distributed literature	mob violence, arrest
7/9/1948	M'Clintock, Mary Ann Wilson	Waterloo, NY	conspiracy	
10/5/1851	M'Clintock, Mary Ann Wilson	Waterloo, NY	jailbreak	
10/5/1851	M'Clintock, Thomas, chemist	Waterloo, NY	jailbreak	
10/1/1851	McHenry, William "Jerry," cooper	Syracuse, NY	jailbreak	
7/3/1859	McIntosh, Henson, ropemaker	New Albany, IN	slave conducting, spying	prison
1841	McKay, Jean Gray	Macomb County, MI	slave rescue	
1841	McKay, Robert, stockman	Macomb County, MI	slave rescue	
10/5/1851	McKim, James Miller, clergy	Philadelphia	conspiracy	
1830s	McWhorter, Francis "Free Frank," gunpowder manufacturer	New Philadelphia, IL	slave rescue	
1840s–1850s	Meachum, John Berry, preacher	St. Louis, MO	river transport	
1840s–1850s	Meachum, Mary	St. Louis, MO	river transport	
1840s–1850s	Meachum, Mary	St. Louis, MO	impeded police	
5/1850	Mendenhall, George C.	Logan County, OH	slave transport	
9/11/1851	Mendenhall, Isaac	Kennett Square, PA	slave rescue	
10/1/1851	Merrick, Charles	Syracuse, NY	jailbreak, sheltered slaves	
1863	Merrick, Chloe	Fernandina, FL	slave transport, depot, orphanage operator	
10/1/1851	Merrick, Sylvanus	Syracuse, NY	jailbreak, harbored slaves	fled
3/11/1854	Messinger, John A., brickmaker	Milwaukee, WI	jailbreak	
2/15/1851	Minkins, Fredric "Shadrach," slave	Boston	jailbreak	fled
1800s	Monroe, David, carriage maker	Chillicothe, OH	slave rescue, transport	price on his head
until 1854	Montgomery, James	Ashtabula, OH	led militia	
1830s–1860s	Moore, Elizabeth W. Ely	Christiana, PA	slave rescue	
1830s–1860s	Moore, Jeremiah	Christiana, PA	slave rescue	
2/12/1851	Morris, Robert, lawyer	Boston	conspiracy, jailbreak	tried
1763	Mott, James	Oyster Bay, NY	aided runaways	
1800s	Mott, James, Jr.	Philadelphia	slave rescue	
1800s	Mott, Lucretia Coffin, orator	Philadelphia	slave rescue, propaganda	
5/9/1837	Mott, Lucretia Coffin, orator	New York City	abetted slave rescue	
1845	Mott, Lucretia Coffin, orator	Staten Island, NY	conspiracy	
7/9/1848	Mott, Lucretia Coffin, orator	Philadelphia	planned routes	
1763	Mott, Mary Underhill	Oyster Bay, NY	aided runaways	
1780s	Mott, Richard, clergy	Mamaroneck, NY	slave rescue	
1790s	Mott, Samuel, shipper	Cowneck, NY	slave rescue	
1812	Murrow, Andrew Caldwell, trader	New Garden, NC	slave transport	
1858	Nast, Thomas, cartoonist	New York City	abetted slave rescue	
1816	Nelson, David	Marion County, MO	sheltered slaves	threats
1740s	Nicholls, Edward, soldier	Prospect Bluff, FL	sheltered slaves	

Target of Act/Date	Name, Occupation	Location	Act	Consequence
9/13/1858	Niles, Henry D., lawyer	Oberlin, OH	impeded arrest	jail
10/1/1951	Norton, Jo, ex-slave	Washington, DC	jailbreak	fled
2/24/1859	Nute, Ephraim, clergy	Lawrence, KS	slave rescue, fund-raising	
1816	Osborn, Charles Worth, publisher	Mount Pleasant, OH	propaganda	
1830s–1850s	Osborn, Josiah	Calvin, MI	slave relay	
1830s–1850s	Osborn, Mary Barnard	Calvin, MI	slave relay	
6/1862	Paine, Halbert Eleazer, soldier	Baton Rouge, LA	slave harboring	
3/31/1845	Paine, Lewis W., loom repairman	Milledgeville, GA	aided flight	prison at hard labor, confiscation
9/11/1851	Parker, Eliza Ann Elizabeth Howard	Christiana, PA	slave rescue	shoot-out, jail
5/26/1854	Parker, Theodore, clergy	Boston	jailbreak	
9/11/1851	Parker, William	Christiana, PA	slave rescue	shoot-out
9/11/1851	Paxson, Jacob Longstreth	Christiana, PA	slave rescue	
1811	Paxton, James Alexander, lawyer, innkeeper	Maysville, KY	slave hiding, conspiracy	
1811	Paxton, Maria Keith Marshall, innkeeper	Maysville, KY	slave hiding, conspiracy	
1840s	Pearson, Benjamin Franklin, mason	Keosauqua, IA	slave rescue	
1830s–1860s	Peart, Lewis	Lampeter, PA	slave rescue	
9/13/1858	Peck, Henry Everard, clergy	Oberlin, OH	impeded arrest	jail
4/14/1775	Pemberton, James, publisher	Philadelphia	abolitionism	
1829	Pennington, James William Charles	New York City	slave rescue	
1830s–1850s	Pennypacker, Elijah Funk, teacher, surveyor	Phoenixville, PA	slave rescue, transport	
1830s–1850s	Pennypacker, Hannah Adamson	Phoenixville, PA	slave rescue, transport	
1830s–1841	Pennypacker, Sarah W. Coates	Phoenixville, PA	slave rescue, transport	
1850s	Peoria, Baptiste, translator, guide	Ottawa, KS	slave conducting, plotted a raid	
11/1857	Peoria, Baptiste, translator, guide	Paola, KS	abetted anarchy	
1839	Pettijohn, Amos	Brown County, OH	impeded police, incited a riot	fine; jail on bread, water
6/25/1831	Pettijohn, Eleanor Northcutt	Clay, OH	slave rescue	stripped naked
1839	Pettijohn, Joseph	Brown County, OH	impeded police, incited a riot	fine; jail on bread, water
6/25/1831	Pettijohn, Lewis	Clay, OH	slave rescue	clubbed
1845	Phillips, Wendell Addison, orator	Staten Island, NY	conspiracy, propaganda	
4/3/1851	Phillips, Wendell Addison, orator	Boston	jailbreak	
5/26/1854	Phillips, Wendell Addison, orator	Boston	jailbreak	indicted
8/4/1860	Pickett, Armine	Winnebago, WI	jailbreak	
9/23/1859	Pike, Joshua A.	Vinland, KS	jailbreak	
6/30/1868	Pillsbury, Parker, editor	Philadelphia	conspiracy, propaganda	
1850s–1860s	Pinkerton, Allan, detective	Chicago	slave transport	
1850s–1860s	Pinkerton, Joan Carfrae	Chicago	slave transport	
9/11/1851	Pinkney, Alexander, farmer	Christiana, PA	slave rescue	shoot-out
9/11/1851	Pinkney, Mrs. Alexander	Christiana, PA	slave rescue	shoot-out, jail
9/13/1858	Plumb, Ralph, lawyer	Oberlin, OH	impeded arrest	jail
1840	Porter, Eliza Emily Chappell	Green Bay, WI	slave rescue	threatened

Target of Act/Date	Name, Occupation	Location	Act	Consequence
1840	Porter, Jeremiah, clergy	Green Bay, WI	slave rescue	threatened
1850–1865	Posey, John Wesley	McComb, IN	spying	
1810s	Post, Amy Kirby, orator	Rochester, NY	propaganda	
1851	Post, Mary W.	Long Island, NY	slave rescue	
9/11/1851	Pownall, Levi, farmer	Bucks County, PA	slave rescue	shoot-out
9/11/1851	Pownall, Sarah Henderson	Bucks County, PA	slave rescue	shoot-out
1850s	Pownall, Thomas	Bucks County, PA	sheltered slaves, disguise	
9/13/1858	Price, John, slave	Oberlin, OH	jailbreak	fled
5/16/1838	Pugh, Sarah, teacher	Philadelphia	impeded police	
1845	Purvis, Robert, organizer	Staten Island, NY	conspiracy	
6/25/1859	Putnam, David, Jr.	Wood County, VA	slave rescue	lawsuit
1840s–1860s	Quinn, William Paul, clergy	Terre Haute, IN	slave rescue	
1840s–1860s	Rakestraw, William H.	Bart, PA	slave rescue	
9/28/1844	Rankin, Jean	Ripley, OH	sheltered slaves	
11/25/1835	Rankin, John, clergy	Ripley, OH	protest, conspiracy	
1838	Rankin, John, clergy	Ripley, OH	slave rescue	
9/28/1844	Rankin, John, clergy	Ripley, OH	sheltered slaves	
10/1/1851	Reed, Enoch	Syracuse, NY	jailbreak	tried
4/29/1861	Remond, Charles Lenox, barber	Boston	ran a street patrol	
1844	Rhodes, John, slave	Hamilton County, IN	flight	tried
1844	Rhodes, Rhuann, slave	Hamilton County, IN	flight	tried
9/13/1858	Riddle, Albert G., lawyer	Cleveland, OH	defended slave rescue	
12/1858	Ritchie, John, frontiersman	Holton, KS	slave transport	
9/18/1859	Ritchie, John, frontiersman	Topeka, KS	violence, conspiracy, highway robbery	charged
1830s–1840s	Robinson, Rachel Gilpin	Ferrisburg, VT	ran a depot	
1830s–1840s	Robinson, Rowland Thomas	Ferrisburg, VT	ran a depot	
1853	Rosenthal, Julius	Chicago	protest, jailbreak	
1835	Ruggles, David	New York City	ran a street patrol	
1840s–1860s	Russell, Amelia Kirk	East Drumore, PA	slave rescue	
1840s–1860s	Russell, John Neal	East Drumore, PA	slave rescue	
3/11/1854	Rycraft, John	Milwaukee, WI	jailbreak	
10/1/1851	Salmon, William Lyman, currier, tanner	Granby, NY	jailbreak	tried
4/15/1848	Sayer, Edward, sea captain	Washington, DC	sea transport	prison, fine
9/11/1851	Scarlett, Joseph P., farmer, miller	Christiana, PA	slave rescue	shoot-out, arrest
1853	Schneider, George	Chicago	protest, jailbreak	
9/13/1858	Sciples, William	Oberlin, OH	impeded arrest	jail
4/3/1851	Scott, James, cobbler	Boston	jailbreak	tried
9/13/1858	Scott, John H., saddler	Oberlin, OH	impeded arrest	jail
9/13/1858	Scrimgeour, William E., student	Oberlin, OH	impeded arrest	jail
1851	Seaman, Elizabeth H.	Long Island, NY	slave rescue	
11/1775	Sears, Isaac, merchant	New York City	jailbreak	
9/23/1859	Senix, Jacob	Vinland, KS	jailbreak	
10/16/1830	Sewall, Samuel Edmund, lawyer	Boston	recruiter	
4/3/1851	Sewall, Samuel Edmund, lawyer	Boston	jailbreak	

Target of Act/Date	Name, Occupation	Location	Act	Consequence
10/1/1851	Seward, Frances Miller	Auburn, NY	abetted jailbreak	
4/15/1848	Seward, William Henry, politician	Cayuga, NY	fund-raising	
10/1/1851	Seward, William Henry, politician	Auburn, NY	jailbreak, conspiracy	indicted
1857	Seward, William Henry, politician	Auburn, NY	backer	
1830s–1850s	Sharper, Jubilee	Small Gloucester, NJ	slave rescue	
1838	Shaw, Chance, shore patrol	Ripley, OH	slave rescue	
9/13/1858	Shepard, James R.	Oberlin, OH	impeded arrest	jail
9/13/1858	Shipherd, Jacob Rudd, historian	Oberlin, OH	impeded arrest	jail
1860s	Shipman, Charles, clergy	Girard, PA	recruiter	
1850s	Simmons, J.J.	New York City	ran a street patrol	
9/23/1859	Simmons, Thomas	Vinland, KS	jailbreak	
4/3/1851	Sims, Thomas M.	Boston	jailbreak	
1855	Sirwell, William	Pittsburgh	ran a street patrol	
8/21/1843	Smith, Gerrit, politician	Troy, NY	slave relay, sabotage, propaganda	
10/1/1851	Smith, Gerrit, politician	New York City	jailbreak	
2/15/1851	Smith, John J., barber	Boston	jailbreak	
4/3/1851	Smith, John J., barber	Boston	jailbreak, slave transport	
1840s–1850s	Smith, Joseph	Drumore, PA	slave rescue	
1840s–1850s	Smith, Tacy Shoemaker	Drumore, PA	slave rescue	
2/16/1851	Snow, Benjamin, Jr., industrialist	West Fitchburg, MA	slave harboring	
2/16/1851	Snow, Mary Baldwin Boutolle	West Fitchburg, MA	slave harboring	
1847	Sojourner Truth, domestic, orator	Brooklyn, CT	conspiracy	
1854	Soule, Amasa R.	Lawrence, KS	slave rescue	arson, mob violence
9/23/1859	Soule, Silas Stillman	Vinland, KS	jailbreak	
9/13/1858	Soules, Walter, farmer	Oberlin, OH	impeded arrest	jail
9/13/1858	Spalding, Rufus P., lawyer	Cleveland, OH	defended slave rescue	
1861	Sparrow, Thomas	Washington, DC	ran a street patrol	
4/3/1851	Spear, John Murray, clergy	Boston	jailbreak	
1841	Stanton, Benjamin, doctor	Newport, IN	propaganda	Quaker schism
9/23/1859	Stewart, John E.	Wakarusa, KS	jailbreak	
1832–1840	Stowe, Harriet Beecher, author	Cincinnati, OH	slave rescue, propaganda	
1853	Strother, David Hunter, cartoonist	New York City	abetted slave rescue	
9/1838	Taber, William Congdon	New Bedford, MA	slave conducting	
1830s	Taylor, Joseph C., farm merchant	Little Britain, PA	retrieved kidnapped child	
1850s	Teesdale, John, editor	Iowa City, IA	slave relay	
1797	Thomas, Avis Stanton	Mount Pleasant, OH	ran a safehouse	
1797	Thomas, Jesse, Jr., farmer	Mount Pleasant, OH	ran a safehouse	
10/1/1851	Thomas, John, journalist	Syracuse, NY	jailbreak	
1797	Thomas, Joseph Stanton, farmer	Mount Pleasant, OH	slave relay	
1830	Thomas, Nathan Muncie, doctor	Schoolcraft, MI	slave relay	
7/1841	Thompson, George	Palmyra, MO	slave conducting	prison at hard labor
1850s	Thoreau, Cynthia Dunbar	Concord, MA	ran a safehouse	
1850s	Thoreau, Helen	Concord, MA	ran a safehouse	
1840s	Thoreau, Henry David, philosopher	Concord, MA	slave relay, propaganda	jail

Target of Act/Date	Name, Occupation	Location	Act	Consequence
1850s	Thoreau, Sophia	Concord, MA	ran a safehouse	
11/1857	Todd, John	Tabor, IA	stored weapons	
1842	Torrey, Charles Turner, clergy	Annapolis, MD	spying	jail
12/1850	Tubman, Harriet, hotel cook	Baltimore	slave transport	
1/1851	Tubman, Harriet, hotel cook	Bucktown, MD	slave transport	wanted criminal
fall 1851	Tubman, Harriet	Bucktown, MD	slave transport	
12/1851	Tubman, Harriet	Bucktown, MD	slave transport	
fall 1852	Tubman, Harriet	Bucktown, MD	slave transport	
11/15/1856	Tubman, Harriet	Indian Creek, MD	slave transport	
12/1856	Tubman, Harriet	Bucktown, MD	slave transport	
4/27/1860	Tubman, Harriet	Troy, NY	jailbreak	fled
12/1860	Tubman, Harriet	Bucktown, MD	slave transport	
1863	Tubman, Harriet, nurse, spy	Fort Monroe, VA	slave transport	
1737	Underhill, Ann Carpenter	Musketa Cove, NY	slave rescue	
1737	Underhill, Samuel	Musketa Cove, NY	slave rescue	
1843	Van Zandt, John, clergy	Glendale, OH	slave rescue	lawsuit, excommunication
10/1/1851	Vashon, George Boye, lawyer	Pittsburgh	jailbreak	
1810s–1840s	Vickers, Abigail Paxson	Wagontown, PA	slave rescue	
1810s–1840s	Vickers, John	Wagontown, PA	slave rescue	
9/13/1858	Wadsworth, Loring, lawyer	Oberlin, OH	impeded arrest	jail
1/24/1859	Wagoner, Henry O., entrepreneur	Chicago	slave rescue	
1783	Wainer, Thomas, sea captain	Westport, MA	sea relay	
6/23/1844	Walker, Jonathan, sea captain	Pensacola, FL	sea rescue	solitary cell, confiscation, fine, branding
9/13/1858	Wall, Orindatus Simon Bolivar, cobbler, leather worker	Oberlin, OH	impeded arrest	jail
10/1/1851	Ward, Samuel Ringgold, educator	New York City	jailbreak	
1830s	Waters, Hamilton E., barber	Erie, PA	sheltered slaves	
10/1/1851	Watkins, Susan	Syracuse, NY	jailbreak	
9/13/1858	Watson, David, farmer	Oberlin, OH	impeded arrest	jail
9/13/1858	Watson, John, grocer	Oberlin, OH	impeded arrest	jail
9/13/1858	Watson, William, clerk	Oberlin, OH	impeded arrest	jail
1826–1847	Way, Henry H., doctor, publisher	Newport, IN	propaganda, medical care	Quaker schism
1850s	Webber, George E., ironworker	Hinkley, OH	sheltered slaves	
1840	Webster, David	Wellington, OH	slave rescue	
9/28/1844	Webster, Delia Ann, teacher	Lexington, KY	slave liberation	mob violence, prison
11/1852	Webster, Delia Ann, orator	Trimble County, KY	recruiting	mob violence, vandalism, jail
1840	Webster, Hannah Post	Wellington, OH	slave rescue	
1860s	Weld, Angelina Emily Grimké	Suffolk, MA	recruiter	
1/1836	Weld, Theodore Dwight	New York City	training agents	
1860s	Weld, Theodore Dwight	Suffolk, MA	recruiter	
9/11/1851	West, J. Pierce	Christiana, PA	slave relay	
9/11/1851	West, Thomas	Christiana, PA	slave relay	

Target of Act/Date	Name, Occupation	Location	Act	Consequence
10/1/1851	Wheaton, Charles Augustus, hardware dealer	Syracuse, NY	jailbreak	
1839–1860s	Whinery, John Carroll, dentist	Salem, OH	ran a safehouse	
1830s	White, Horace, executive	Syracuse, NY	sheltered slaves	
1830s–1860s	Whitson, Martha Hobson	Bart, PA	slave rescue	
1830s–1860s	Whitson, Thomas	Bart, PA	slave rescue	
1842	Whittier, John Greenleaf, editor	Annapolis, MD	spying	jail
9/28/1844	Whittier, John Greenleaf, editor	Staten Island, NY	propaganda	
1845	Whittier, John Greenleaf, editor	Staten Island, NY	conspiracy	
9/13/1858	Williams, Daniel, farmer	Oberlin, OH	impeded arrest	jail
1858	Williams, George	Ripley, OH	slave rescue	died in prison
1851	Willets, Mary W.	Long Island, NY	slave rescue	
1851	Willets, Phebe	Long Island, NY	slave rescue	
9/23/1859	Willis, S.J.	Vinland, KS	jailbreak	
1820s	Wilson, James, cabdriver	Baltimore	slave transport	
9/13/1858	Windsor, Robert	Oberlin, OH	impeded arrest	jail
9/13/1858	Winsor, Richard, student	Oberlin, OH	impeded arrest	jail
1840s–1860s	Wood, Day	Fulton, PA	slave rescue	
1840s–1860s	Wood, Eliza Jackson	Fulton, PA	slave rescue	
7/1841	Work, Alanson	Palmyra, MO	slave conductor	prison at hard labor
1830s	Worthington, William	Harford County, MD	coded messages	
1852	Wright, Elizur, editor	Boston	slave rescue	tried
7/9/1848	Wright, Martha Coffin Pelham	Waterloo, NY	conspiracy	
11/1857	Wright, Owell	Mauckport, IN	slave transport	kidnap, jail
1829–1860s	Wright, Phebe Wierman	South Mountain, PA	slave rescue	
1830–1863	Wright, Samuel Guild, clergy	Peoria, IL	conspiracy	
1829–1860s	Wright, William	South Mountain, PA	slave rescue	

slavery

1854–1861	Adler, Leibman, rabbi	Detroit, MI	protest	
1820s	Allen, Abraham	Wilmington, OH	protest	
1840s	Allen, Samuel, farmer	Mercer County, PA	protest	
10/16/1859	Anderson, Jeremiah Goldsmith	Harpers Ferry, VA	guerrilla war	bayoneted
10/16/1859	Anderson, John	Harpers Ferry, VA	guerrilla war	killed
10/16/1859	Anderson, Osborne, printer	Harpers Ferry, VA	guerrilla war	fled
until 1854	Anthony, Daniel Read, Sr., editor	Leavenworth, KS	guerrilla war	
1810s	Atcheson, George, lumberman	Green, PA	protest	
1840s–1860s	Barnard, Vincent S., botanist	Kennett Square, PA	conspiracy	
1850s	Benjamin, Jacob	Lawrence, KS	protest	
3/11/1854	Bingham, George	Milwaukee, WI	jailbreak	
1833	Birney, James Gillespie	Cincinnati, OH	protest, conspiracy	
1850s	Bondi, August, printer	Lawrence, KS	protest	
1850s	Bondi, Henrietta Einstein	Lawrence, KS	protest	
10/16/1859	Brown, John, tanner	Harpers Ferry, VA	sedition	hanged
10/16/1859	Brown, Oliver	Harpers Ferry, VA	guerrilla war	killed

Target of Act/Date	Name, Occupation	Location	Act	Consequence
10/16/1859	Brown, Owen	Harpers Ferry, VA	guerrilla war	fled
10/16/1859	Brown, Watson	Harpers Ferry, VA	guerrilla war	killed
1833	Buffum, Arnold	Providence, RI	protest, conspiracy	
1835	Burleigh, Charles Callistus, lawyer	Boston	protest, propaganda	mob violence
1810s	Campbell, Alexander, senator	Ripley, OH	protest	
1830s–1860s	Chapman, Maria Weston, editor	Boston	propaganda	
1847	Chase, Salmon Portland, lawyer	Washington, DC	fund-raising	
4/15/1848	Chase, Salmon Portland, lawyer	Washington, DC	defended slave rescue	
6/15/1849	Clay, Cassius Marcellus, publisher	Jeffersonville, IN	speech	stabbed
until 1826	Coffin, Catherine White, merchant	New Garden, NC	conspiracy	
1813–1826	Coffin, Levi, merchant	New Garden, NC	conspiracy	
1847	Coffin, Levi, merchant	Cincinnati, OH	fund-raising	
2/1856	Coffin, Levi, merchant	Cincinnati, OH	slave defense	
1830s	Comstock, Elizabeth Leslie Rous	Rollin, MI	protest	
10/16/1859	Cook, John E.	Harpers Ferry, VA	guerrilla war	hanged
10/16/1859	Copeland, John Anthony, Jr., carpenter	Harpers Ferry, VA	guerrilla war	shot
10/16/1859	Coppoc, Barclay	Harpers Ferry, VA	guerrilla war	fled
10/16/1859	Coppoc, Edwin	Harpers Ferry, VA	guerrilla war	hanged
1850s	Curtis, Annie Fenner	Lewisburg, PA	protest	
1830s	Curtis, Thomas F., clergy	Lewisburg, PA	protest	
10/1851	Cuyler, Theodore, attorney	Philadelphia	conspiracy	
1830s–1860s	Dickinson, Anna Elizabeth, writer	Philadelphia	propaganda	
1834	Dresser, Amos, student	Cincinnati, OH	protest	expelled, lashed
1833	Forten, James	Philadelphia	protest, conspiracy	
1833	Forten, Margaretta, activist	Philadelphia	protest, conspiracy	
1838	Foster, Abigail Kelley, orator	Worcester, MA	broke the Sabbath	
1846	Foster, Abigail Kelley, orator	Worcester, MA	propaganda	arrest
1838	Foster, Stephen Symons, orator	Worcester, MA	broke the Sabbath	
1846	Foster, Stephen Symons, orator	Worcester, MA	propaganda	arrest
1830s–1860s	Garrison, Helen Eliza Benson	Boston	fund-raising	
1829	Garrison, William Lloyd, publisher	Boston	libel	jail
1840s	Garvey, Edward Christie Kerr, editor	Topeka, KS	protest, propaganda	
1840s	Graue, Frederick, miller	Fullersburg, IL	protest	
1841–1863	Greeley, Horace, editor	New York City	propaganda	
1793	Green, Beriah, clergy	Whitesboro, NY	protest	
10/16/1859	Green, Shields	Harpers Ferry, VA	guerrilla war	hanged
1853	Greenebaum, Sarah Spiegel	Chicago	protest	
1830s–1860s	Harper, Frances Ellen Watkins, poet	Baltimore	propaganda	
1850s–1860s	Hayes, Rutherford Birchard, lawyer	Cincinnati, OH	conspiracy	
10/16/1859	Hazlett, Albert	Harpers Ferry, VA	guerrilla war	hanged
1850s	Hazlett, Hugh, lawyer	Dorcester County, MD	protest	
1840s–1860s	Helper, Hinton Rowan, agitator	New York City	conspiracy	
1/1857	Higginson, Thomas Wentworth, clergy	Boston	fund-raising	
1811–1860s	Higley, Erastus, judge	Fairhaven, VT	protest	

Target of Act/Date	Name, Occupation	Location	Act	Consequence
1850s	Hinton, Richard Josiah, journalist	New York City	protest	
1840s	Holmes, George Young, Sr., clergy	Claysville, NY	protest	
1840s–1850s	Howe, Julia Ward, songwriter	Boston	conspiracy	
4/15/1848	Howe, Samuel Gridley, lawyer	Boston	fund-raising	
1/1857	Howe, Samuel Gridley, lawyer	Boston	fund-raising	
until 1854	Jennison, Charles Ransford, doctor	Mound City, KS	guerrilla war	
1830s–1860s	Johnson, Oliver, editor	Boston	propaganda	
2/1856	Joliffe, John, lawyer	Cincinnati, OH	slave defense	
9/18/1859	Kagi, John Henry, lawyer	Topeka, KS	jayhawking, highway robbery, conspiracy	charged
10/16/1859	Kagi, John Henry, lawyer	Harpers Ferry, VA	guerrilla war	shot
1840s	Kelley, John J., priest	Albany, NY	protest	
1834–1849	Kemble, Fanny, actor	St. Simons, GA	conspiracy	
1840s	Langston, George R.	Howard County, MO	protest	
1731–1759	Lay, Benjamin, activist	Abington, PA	assault, trespass, disturbing the peace	
1770s	Lay, Benjamin, activist	Abington, PA	kidnap	
10/16/1859	Leary, Lewis Sheridan, saddler	Harpers Ferry, VA	guerrilla war	shot
1793	Lee, Luther, clergy	Plymouth, NY	protest	
10/16/1859	Leeman, William H.	Harpers Ferry, VA	guerrilla war	killed
1830s	Lind, Sylvester, carpenter	Lake Forest, IL	protest	
1780s	Lott, Hendrick I., farmer	Brooklyn, NY	protest	
1790s	Lott, Mary Brownjohn	Brooklyn, NY	protest	
11/1837	Lovejoy, Elijah Parish, editor	Alton, IL	propaganda	shot
1820s	Magoffin, Grace Elizabeth Mitcheltree	Mercerville, PA	protest	
1820s	Magoffin, James, Jr., doctor	Mercerville, PA	protest	
1820s	Marshall, Samuel, judge	Connoquenessing, PA	protest	
1840s	McAndrew, Helen Walker, doctor	Ypsilanti, MI	protest	
1840s	McAndrew, William, carpenter	Ypsilanti, MI	protest	
1841	McKay, Jean Gray	Macomb County, MI	protest	
1841	McKay, Robert, stockman	Macomb County, MI	protest	
1820s	McKeever, Jane Campbell	West Middletown, PA	protest	
1770s	McKeever, William, hatter	West Middletown, PA	protest	
7/9/1848	McKim, James Miller, clergy	Philadelphia	protest	
10/16/1859	Merriam, Francis Jackson	Harpers Ferry, VA	conspiracy, financial support	fled
1830s	Mihills, Uriah Dimond, town supervisor	Keene, NY	protest	
4/15/1848	Morris, Robert, lawyer	Washington, DC	defended slave rescue	
1833	Mott, Lucretia Coffin, orator	Philadelphia	protest, conspiracy, propaganda	
4/15/1851	Nell, William Cooper, printer	Boston	propaganda	charged
10/16/1859	Newby, Dangerfield	Harpers Ferry, VA	guerrilla war	shot
10/1857	Painter, Edith Dean	Springdale, IA	sheltered anarchists	

Target of Act/Date	Name, Occupation	Location	Act	Consequence
10/1857	Painter, John H., peace officer	Springdale, IA	sheltered anarchists	
1820s	Palmer, Elizabeth Ward	Weller, OH	protest	
1820s	Palmer, John Edgerton, merchant	Weller, OH	protest	
1/1857	Parker, Theodore, clergy	Boston	fund-raising	
1688	Pastorius, Francis Daniel	Germantown, PA	protest	
1850s	Pinner, Moritz, editor	Kansas City, KS	protest	
4/3/1851	Pitts, Coffin	Boston	fund-raising	
1830s	Powell, Thomas Howells	Coshocton County, OH	protest	
1830s	Pritchett, Edward Corrie, clergy	Union Village, NY	protest	
1830s	Purvis, Robert, backer	Philadelphia	protest	
1847–1861	Remond, Charles Lenox, barber	Boston	conspiracy	
1830s	Robinson, Marius R., editor	Salem, OH	admired oratory	tarred, feathered
1850s	Ross, Alexander Milton, ornithologist	Detroit, MI	protest	
1830s	Sardou, Charles, sailor	Topeka, KS	protest	
1840s	Scholes, Thomas Coggin	West Burlington, IA	protest	
4/15/1848	Sewall, Samuel Edmund, lawyer	Washington, DC	defended slave rescue	
1850s	Shaw, Anna Howard, clergy	New Bedford, MA	protest	
1840s–1850s	Shaw, Nicolas Stott	New Bedford, MA	protest	
1840s–1850s	Shaw, Thomas	New Bedford, MA	protest	
1854–1861	Sloman, Mark, furrier	Detroit, MI	protest	
1830s	Smith, Gerrit, politician	New York City	conspiracy, propaganda	
1830s	Stauffer, Daniel, cooper	Zelienople, PA	protest	
1/1857	Stearns, George Luther, merchant	Medford, MA	fund-raising	
1830s	Steel, William, Sr., merchant	Stafford, OH	protest	
10/16/1859	Stevens, Aaron Dwight	Harpers Ferry, VA	guerrilla war	hanged
10/1851	Stevens, Thaddeus, lawyer	Philadelphia	conspiracy	
1800s	Stewart, Peter, engineer	Downer's Grove, IL	protest	
1833	Still, William	Philadelphia	protest, conspiracy	
2/1856	Stone, Lucy, orator	Cincinnati, OH	slave defense	
10/1/1851	Tappan, Arthur, merchant	New York City	protest	
10/1/1851	Tappan, Lewis, merchant	New York City	protest	
10/16/1859	Taylor, Stewart	Harpers Ferry, VA	guerrilla war	killed
1854	Thacker, Henry L.W., waiter	Boston	conspiracy, financial support	
10/16/1859	Thompson, Dauphin Adolphus	Harpers Ferry, VA	guerrilla war	killed
1855	Thompson, Henry	Lawrence, KS	paramilitary	
10/16/1859	Thompson, William	Harpers Ferry, VA	guerrilla war	killed
1840s	Thoreau, Henry David, philosopher	Concord, MA	protest	
1849	Thoreau, Henry David, philosopher	Concord, MA	propaganda	
10/30/1859	Thoreau, Henry David, philosopher	Concord, MA	abetted anarchy	
10/16/1859	Tidd, Charles Plummer	Harpers Ferry, VA	guerrilla war	fled
1840s	Vincent, James, publisher	Tabor, IA	protest	
1829	Walker, David, tractarian	Boston	propaganda	poisoned
1830s	Walter, Albert G., orthopedist	Pittsburgh	protest	
1854	Washington, George, barber	Boston	conspiracy	

Target of Act/Date	Name, Occupation	Location	Act	Consequence
2/4/1853	Watkins, William J., teacher	Boston	conspiracy	
1830s	Weldon, Bridget Mead	Plainfield, IL	protest	
1830s	Weldon, John, farmer	Plainfield, IL	protest	
1800s	Wells, John Howard, Sr., merchant	Richland, NY	protest	
1830s	Wheeler, James Taylor, clergy	Kane County, IL	protest	
1840s	Wheeler, Jerusha A. Young	Kane County, IL	protest	
1842	Whittier, John Greenleaf, editor	New York City	protest	
1855–1856	Wiener, Theodore, merchant	St. Louis, MO	protest	
1830s–1860s	Winslow, Comfort Hussey	Portland, ME	financial support	
1830s–1860s	Winslow, Nathan, hardware dealer	Portland, ME	financial support	

Spanish-American War

Target of Act/Date	Name, Occupation	Location	Act	Consequence
1898	Love, Alfred Henry, merchant	Philadelphia	opposed	burned in effigy

surveillance

Target of Act/Date	Name, Occupation	Location	Act	Consequence
1885	Hampton, Brigham Young, memoirist	Salt Lake City	sting operation	

taxation

Target of Act/Date	Name, Occupation	Location	Act	Consequence
1/16/1943	Alcott, Amos Bronson, educator	Concord, MA	tax resistance	jail
1787	Austin, Abigail	Concord, MA	jailbreak	
10/15/1752	Backus, Elizabeth Tracy, widow	Norwich, CT	tax resistance	jail
1773	Backus, Isaac, clergy	Boston	tax resistance	jail
10/15/1752	Backus, Samuel	Norwich, CT	tax resistance	
1/1968	Baldwin, James, author	New York City	tax resistance	
9/12/1786	Bardwell, Perez	Concord, MA	paramilitary leader	debtors' prison
12/6/1786	Bly, John, laborer	Berkshire County, MA	paramilitary	hanged
7/16/1794	Bradford, David, politician	Allegheny, PA	tax revolt	
7/16/1794	Bradford, William	Allegheny, PA	robbed mail	
1920s	Carner, Lucy Perkins, sociologist	York, PA	antitax speech	
1948	Champney, Horace, activist	Cleveland, OH	tax resistance	
1990s	Corner, Betsy, activist	Colrain, MA	tax resistance	eviction
1780	Cuffe, Paul	Cuttyhunk Island, MA	tax resistance	
1760s	Dawson, William	Cambridge, MD	refused religious tax	jail
9/12/1786	Day, Luke	West Springfield, MA	paramilitary	debtors' prison
1676	Fox, Bathsheba Rogers	New London, CT	tax resistance	
11/16/1777	Gawthorp, James	Frederick County, VA	tax resistance	
2005	Graves, Bruce, activist	Ann Arbor, MI	picketed federal building	
2005	Graves, Ruth, activist	Ann Arbor, MI	picketed federal building	
1939	Gregg, Richard Bartlett, ethicist	Putney, VT	propaganda	
1958	Harper, Robin, activist	Wallingford, PA	resisted war tax	threats
1961	Hennacy, Ammon, activist	Salt Lake City	tax resistance	
2003	Hill, Julia Butterfly, activist	Mount Vernon, MO	tax resistance	

Target of Act/Date	Name, Occupation	Location	Act	Consequence
1786–1787	Holcroft, John, distiller	Bedford, PA	paramilitary	
1990s	Kehler, Randy, activist	Colrain, MA	tax resistance	eviction
9/12/1786	Kelsey, John, town clerk	Concord, MA	paramilitary leader	
10/1787	Manning, William	Concord, MA	paramilitary	prison at hard labor
7/16/1794	Marshall, James, soldier	Allegheny, PA	tax revolt	
1681	Maule, Thomas, publisher	Salem, MA	tax resistance	fine, lashed, jail
3/1777	McClunn, Thomas	Frederick County, VA	tax resistance	
5/1961	McCrackin, Maurice, clergy	Cincinnati, OH	tax resistance	
7/16/1794	McFarlane, James	Allegheny, PA	tax revolt	
7/16/1794	Miller, Oliver	Allegheny, PA	tax revolt	shot
7/16/1794	Mitchell, John	Allegheny, PA	robbed mail	
1952	Muste, Abraham Johannes, activist	New York City	tax resistance	
1/1968	Olsen, Tillie, writer	New York City	tax resistance	
9/12/1786	Page, Benjamin	Concord, MA	paramilitary leader	
1/1968	Paley, Grace, author	New York City	tax resistance	
9/12/1786	Parker, Oliver	Concord, MA	paramilitary leader	
1786–1787	Parmenter, Jason	Berkshire County, MA	paramilitary	jail
9/12/1786	Parsons, Eli	Chicopee, MA	paramilitary	
8/9/1757	Pemberton, Israel, Jr., merchant	Philadelphia	tax resistance	
8/9/1757	Pemberton, John, trader, clergy	Philadelphia	tax resistance	
1676	Rogers, Bathsheba	New London, CT	tax resistance	fine, jail
1676	Rogers, Elizabeth Rowland	New London, CT	tax resistance	fine, jail
1676	Rogers, James, commissioner	New London, CT	tax resistance	fine, jail
1676	Rogers, James, cooper	New London, CT	tax resistance	fine, jail
1676	Rogers, John, Sr., clergy	New London, CT	tax resistance	fine, jail
9/1677	Rogers, John, Sr., clergy	New London, CT	tax resistance	
1676	Rogers, Jonathan	New London, CT	tax resistance	fine, jail
12/6/1786	Rose, Charles, laborer	Berkshire County, MA	paramilitary	hanged
1/1968	Rukeyser, Muriel, poet	New York City	tax resistance	
9/12/1786	Shattuck, Job	Concord, MA	paramilitary leader	slashed
9/12/1786	Shays, Daniel Patrick	Pelham, MA	paramilitary leader	
6/18/2004	Sheehan, Cindy Lee Miller, activist	Fort Lewis, WA	tax resistance	
11/5/1873	Smith, Abigail Hadassah, orator	Glastonbury, CT	tax resistance	
1769	Smith, Chileab	Ashfield, MA	tax resistance	confiscation
1769	Smith, Ebenezer	Ashfield, MA	tax resistance	confiscation
11/5/1873	Smith, Julia Evelina, scholar	Glastonbury, CT	tax resistance	
9/12/1786	Smith, Nathan	Concord, MA	paramilitary leader	
1/1968	Sontag, Susan, essayist	New York City	tax resistance	
1/1968	Steinem, Gloria, journalist	New York City	tax resistance	
1858	Stone, Lucy, orator	Boston	tax resistance	
1/1968	Styron, William, novelist	New York City	tax resistance	
7/1846	Thoreau, Henry David, philosopher	Concord, MA	tax resistance	jail
1/1968	Vonnegut, Kurt, Jr., novelist	New York City	tax resistance	

Target of Act/Date	Name, Occupation	Location	Act	Consequence
1660s	White, Esther	Raynham, MA	tax resistance	prison
9/12/1786	Wilcox, Peter, Jr.	Berkshire County, MA	paramilitary leader	jail
1787	Wilcox, Polly	Concord, MA	jailbreak	
8/9/1757	Woolman, John, tailor, philosopher	Mount Holly, PA	tax resistance	
1/1968	Zinn, Howard, historian	New York City	tax resistance	

taxes, corruption

Target of Act/Date	Name, Occupation	Location	Act	Consequence
5/9/1771	Alexander, William, farmer	Concord, NC	destroyed supplies	
5/9/1771	Ashmore, James Samuel, farmer	Concord, NC	destroyed supplies	
5/16/1771	Brown, William	Alamance, NC	paramilitary	
1770s	Butler, William, songwriter	Orange County, NC	paramilitary	
5/9/1771	Caruthers, Robert, farmer	Concord, NC	destroyed supplies	
5/9/1771	Cockerham, Benjamin	Concord, NC	destroyed supplies	
5/16/1771	Copeland, James, Jr.	Alamance, NC	paramilitary	
5/16/1771	Cox, Harmon	Alamance, NC	paramilitary	
5/9/1771	Davis, Robert, farmer	Concord, NC	destroyed supplies	
5/16/1771	Emerson, James, Sr.	Alamance, NC	paramilitary	
5/16/1771	Few, James	Alamance, NC	paramilitary	hanged
5/9/1771	Hadley, Joshua	Concord, NC	destroyed supplies	
1770s	Howell, Rednap, balladeer	Orange County, NC	paramilitary	
1770s	Hunter, James, orator	Brunswick, NC	paramilitary	
5/16/1771	Hunter, James, orator	Alamance, NC	paramilitary	house burned
1770	Husband, Herman, tractarian	Brunswick, NC	propaganda	arrest
5/16/1771	Husband, Herman, tractarian	Alamance, NC	paramilitary leader	fled, house burned
6/19/1771	Matear, Robert, merchant	Hillsborough, NC	paramilitary	hanged
6/19/1771	Mercer, Forrester	Hillsborough, NC	paramilitary	
6/19/1771	Merrill, Benjamin, planter	Hillsborough, NC	paramilitary leader	hanged
5/16/1771	Messer, Robert	Alamance, NC	paramilitary	chained, dragged, hanged
5/16/1771	Pugh, James	Alamance, NC	paramilitary	hanged
5/16/1771	Stewart, James, clergy	Alamance, NC	paramilitary	
5/16/1771	Thompson, Robert	Alamance, NC	paramilitary	killed
5/9/1771	Waddell, Hugh, soldier	Concord, NC	destroyed supplies	
5/9/1771	White, James	Concord, NC	destroyed supplies	
5/9/1771	White, John, Jr.	Concord, NC	destroyed supplies	
5/9/1771	White, William	Concord, NC	destroyed supplies	
5/9/1771	White, William, Jr.	Concord, NC	destroyed supplies	

torture

Target of Act/Date	Name, Occupation	Location	Act	Consequence
9/19/2006	Barrios, Luis, priest	New York City	protest	police brutality

travel restrictions due to terrorism

Target of Act/Date	Name, Occupation	Location	Act	Consequence
10/20/2003	Heatwole, Nathaniel, student	Damascus, MD	concealed weapon	fine

Target of Act/Date	Name, Occupation	Location	Act	Consequence
unemployment				
5/1/1854	Browne, Carl Dryden, patent medicine dealer	Washington, DC	march	police brutality, jail
5/1/1854	Cantwell, Jumbo	Washington, DC	march	jail
2/12/1938	Chinn, Genevieve, organizer	Harlem, NY	boycott	
5/1/1854	Coxey, Henrietta	Washington, DC	march	
5/1/1854	Coxey, Jacob Sechier, politician	Washington, DC	march	police brutality, arrest
5/1/1854	Coxey, Legal Tender	Washington, DC	march	
5/1/1854	Coxey, Mamie	Washington, DC	march	
2/12/1938	Ford, James W., organizer	Harlem, NY	boycott	
5/1/1854	Fry, Lewis C., soldier	Washington, DC	march	
2/12/1938	Imes, William Lloyd, clergy	Harlem, NY	boycott	
2/12/1938	Johnson, Arnold Samuel, agitator	Harlem, NY	boycott	
4/30/1894	Jones, Mary "Mother," labor organizer	Washington, DC	march	
2/12/1938	Powell, Adam Clayton, Jr., clergy, politician	Harlem, NY	boycott	
5/1/1854	Shepard, Henry, surveyor	Washington, DC	march	
veterans hospital inadequacy				
1974	Kovic, Ronald L., disabled veteran	Los Angeles	fast, trespass	
Vieques destruction				
2/18/1971	Berríos-Martínez, Rubén Ángel, lawyer	Culebra, Puerto Rico	trespass	jail
5/8/1999	Berríos-Martínez, Rubén Ángel, lawyer	Vieques, Puerto Rico	camp-in	
5/4/2000	Berríos-Martínez, Rubén Ángel, lawyer	Vieques, Puerto Rico	camp-in	arrest
5/1/2001	Berríos-Martínez, Rubén Ángel, lawyer	Vieques, Puerto Rico	trespass	arrest
5/1/2001	Bhatia-Gautier, Eduardo, senator	Vieques, Puerto Rico	trespass	arrest
5/1/2001	Burgos-Andújar, Norma E., senator	Vieques, Puerto Rico	trespass	arrest
1/10/2003	Cardona, Gustavo Dásvila, student	Vieques, Puerto Rico	trespass	
1/10/2003	Cepeda, Feliciano Rivera, retiree	Vieques, Puerto Rico	trespass	
1/10/2003	Cristóbal, Ángel Rodríguez	Vieques, Puerto Rico	trespass	prison
5/1/2001	Feliciano, José, singer	Vieques, Puerto Rico	trespass	
5/19/1979	Ferrer, Leonardo Estrada, sociologist	Vieques, Puerto Rico	trespass	
1/10/2003	Ferrer, Leonardo Estrada, sociologist	Vieques, Puerto Rico	trespass	
5/21/1979	Guadalupe-Ortiz, Ismael, teacher	Vieques, Puerto Rico	trespass	prison
4/21/1999	Guadalupe-Ortiz, Ismael, teacher	Vieques, Puerto Rico	trespass	
1/10/2003	Guadalupe-Ortiz, Ismael, teacher	Vieques, Puerto Rico	trespass	prison
5/1/2001	Gutiérrez, Luis Vicente, senator	Vieques, Puerto Rico	trespass	arrest
5/1/2001	Jackson, Jacqueline Lavinia Brown, activist	Vieques, Puerto Rico	trespass	arrest, solitary confinement
4/21/1999	Kayak, Tito, activist	Vieques, Puerto Rico	trespass	
11/5/2000	Kayak, Tito, activist	New York City	protest flag	
5/1/2001	Kayak, Tito, activist	Vieques, Puerto Rico	trespass	arrest
5/1/2001	Kennedy, Robert F., Jr., investor	Vieques, Puerto Rico	trespass	arrest

Target of Act/Date	Name, Occupation	Location	Act	Consequence
6/1/2000	Lebron, Lolita	Vieques, Puerto Rico	halted army maneuvers	arrest
5/1/2001	Martin, Ricky, singer	Vieques, Puerto Rico	trespass	
5/1/2001	Menchú, Rigoberta, activist	Vieques, Puerto Rico	trespass	
1/10/2003	Morales, Orlando, soldier	Vieques, Puerto Rico	trespass	
5/1/2001	Olmos, Edward James, actor	Vieques, Puerto Rico	trespass	arrest
5/19/1979	Parrilla-Bonilla, Antulio, bishop	Vieques, Puerto Rico	trespass, said Mass	fine, marshal brutality
5/1/2001	Rangel, Charles Bernard, politician	Vieques, Puerto Rico	trespass	
5/1/2001	Rivera, Dennis, civil servant	Vieques, Puerto Rico	trespass	arrest
5/1/2001	Rivera, Jose, politician	Vieques, Puerto Rico	trespass	arrest
5/1/2001	Rodriguez, Chi Chi, athlete	Vieques, Puerto Rico	trespass	arrest
5/1/2001	Rosa, Robi Draco, musician	Vieques, Puerto Rico	trespass	arrest
5/1/2001	Sanes-Rodríquez, Mirta	Vieques, Puerto Rico	trespass	arrest, trial
5/1/2001	Santiago, Rafael Cordero, mayor	Vieques, Puerto Rico	trespass	arrest
5/1/2001	Sharpton, Charles Alfred, clergy	Vieques, Puerto Rico	trespass, hunger strike	arrest, prison
5/1/2001	Sheen, Martin, actor	Vieques, Puerto Rico	trespass	arrest
5/11/2000	Suárez-Franceschi, Antonio, professor	Vieques, Puerto Rico	trespass	tried
5/1/2001	Trinidad, Félix, athlete	Vieques, Puerto Rico	trespass	arrest
1/10/2003	Vázquez, Grego Marcano, activist	Vieques, Puerto Rico	trespass	
5/1/2001	Velázquez, Nydia Margarita, legislator	Vieques, Puerto Rico	trespass	arrest

Vietnam War

Target of Act/Date	Name, Occupation	Location	Act	Consequence
10/9/1968	Abdoo, Jayma, librarian	Catonsville, MD	sabotage	
1966	Ali, Muhammad, boxer	Louisville, KY	refused to serve	
5/22/1968	Amick, Dan, soldier	Fort Ord, CA	distributed literature	prison at hard labor
10/9/1968	Anderson, William, doctor	Catonsville, MD	sabotage	
12/25/1965	Aptheker, Herbert, historian	Hanoi, Vietnam	passport violation	
5/1972	Aptheker, Herbert, historian	Hanoi, Vietnam	protest	vilification
8/1965	Baez, Joan, folksinger	Washington, DC	picketed	
10/1967	Baez, Joan, folksinger	Oakland, CA	sit-in	jail
12/1967	Baez, Joan, folksinger	Oakland, CA	sit-in	jail
1970s	Baez, Joan, folksinger	Los Altos, CA	tax resistance	
1970s	Baldwin, James, novelist	New York City	tax resistance	
1967	Beaumont, Florence	Los Angeles	self-immolation	
3/22/1969	Begin, Robert T., priest	Washington, DC	sabotage	
1/1968	Berrigan, Daniel, priest	New York City	tax resistance	
5/17/1968	Berrigan, Daniel, priest	Catonsville, MD	arson	prison
10/27/1967	Berrigan, Philip, priest	Baltimore	destroyed files	arrest
1/1968	Berrigan, Philip, priest	New York City	tax resistance	
10/9/1968	Billman, George Milo, clergy	Catonsville, MD	sabotage	
1967	Boardman, Elizabeth Jelinek	Danang, South Vietnam	obstructed blockade	arrest
1967	Braxton, John Worth, scientist	Danang, South Vietnam	obstructed blockade	arrest
1970	Braxton, John Worth, scientist	Petersburg, VA	draft evasion	prison

Target of Act/Date	Name, Occupation	Location	Act	Consequence
10/9/1968	Buckalew, Terry, court clerk	Catonsville, MD	sabotage	
1967	Carner, Lucy Perkins, sociologist	York, PA	propaganda	
1967	Champney, Horace	Danang, South Vietnam	obstructed blockade	arrest
1/5/1968	Coffin, William Sloane, Jr., clergy	New Haven, CT	conspiracy	prison
10/9/1968	Couming, Paul, activist	Catonsville, MD	sabotage	
12/7/1967	Daniels, George, soldier	Portsmouth, NH	denunciation	prison at hard labor
5/17/1968	Darst, David A., teacher	Catonsville, MD	arson	prison
1965	Davis, Angela, student	Frankfurt, Germany	picketed	lost job
8/25/1968	Davis, Renard Cordon, activist	Chicago	conspiracy, riot	arrest
1960s	Day, Dorothy, reformer, editor	New York City	protest	jail
8/25/1968	Dellinger, David T., activist	Chicago	conspiracy, riot	arrest
10/9/1968	Dixon, Eugene, factory supervisor	Catonsville, MD	sabotage	
3/22/1969	Dougherty, Michael R., priest	Washington, DC	sabotage	
10/9/1968	Doyle, Michael, priest	Catonsville, MD	sabotage	
1967	Drath, Phil	Danang, South Vietnam	obstructed blockade	arrest
10/9/1968	Dunham, Ann, church worker	Catonsville, MD	sabotage	
1/1968	Dworkin, Andrea, activist	New York City	tax resistance	
1967	Eaton, Bob	Danang, South Vietnam	obstructed blockade	arrest
10/27/1967	Eberhardt, David, poet	Baltimore	destroyed files	arrest
6/13/1971	Ellsberg, Daniel, consultant	Washington, DC	whistle-blowing	arrest
1/5/1968	Ferber, Michael, teacher	New Haven, CT	conspiracy	prison
4/1970	Fonda, Jane, actor	Fort Mead, MD	protest	arrest
5/1970	Fonda, Jane, actor	Fort Bragg, NC	distributed pamphlets	arrest
2/1971	Fonda, Jane, actor	Valley Forge, PA	rally	
5/1972	Fonda, Jane, actor	Hanoi, Vietnam	protest	vilification
10/9/1968	Fordi, Peter D., priest	Catonsville, MD	sabotage	
10/9/1968	Forsyth, Keith, cab driver	Catonsville, MD	sabotage	
1/1968	Friedan, Betty, social activist	New York City	tax resistance	
10/9/1968	Geddes, Maggie, activist	New York City	sabotage	
5/14/1970	Gibbs, Phillip Lafayette, student	Jackson, MS	incited a riot	shot
1965	Ginsberg, Allen, poet	Oakland, CA	march	
12/5/1967	Ginsberg, Allen, poet	New York City	demonstration, conspiracy	
1/1968	Ginsberg, Allen, poet	New York City	tax resistance	
10/9/1968	Giocondo, Michael, monk	Catonsville, MD	sabotage	
10/9/1968	Good, Robert, student	Catonsville, MD	sabotage	
1/5/1968	Goodman, Mitchell, writer	New Haven, CT	conspiracy	arrest
10/9/1968	Grady, John, sociologist	Catonsville, MD	sabotage	
1970s	Graves, Bruce, activist	Ann Arbor, MI	resisted war taxes	
1970s	Graves, Ruth, activist	Ann Arbor, MI	resisted war taxes	
5/14/1970	Green, James Earl, student	Jackson, MS	incited a riot	shot
1/1968	Greenberg, Daniel, teacher	New York City	tax resistance	
7/15/1969	Harris, David, activist	Fresno, CA	draft evasion	prison

Target of Act/Date	Name, Occupation	Location	Act	Consequence
12/7/1967	Harvey, William L., soldier	Portsmouth, NH	denunciation	prison at hard labor
12/25/1965	Hayden, Thomas Emmett, activist	Hanoi, Vietnam	passport violation	
8/25/1968	Hayden, Thomas Emmett, activist	Chicago	conspiracy, riot	arrest
5/1972	Hayden, Thomas Emmett, activist	Hanoi, Vietnam	protest	vilification
11/2/1965	Herz, Alice	Washington, DC	self-immolation	
8/25/1968	Hoffman, Abbott Howard, salesman	Chicago	conspiracy, riot	arrest
5/17/1968	Hogan, John, monk	Catonsville, MD	arson	prison
11/ 6/1965	Howe, Henry H., Jr., soldier	El Paso, TX	carried a placard	prison at hard labor
10/9/1968	Innes, Margaret, nun	Catonsville, MD	sabotage	
6/30/1966	Johnson, James, soldier	Fort Hood, TX	refused assignment	prison at hard labor
1967	Kehler, Randy	Colrain, MA	refused draft card	prison
10/1967	Kepler, Roy	Oakland, CA	obstructed sidewalk	jail
12/1967	Kepler, Roy	Oakland, CA	obstructed sidewalk	arrest
4/4/1967	King, Martin Luther, Jr., clergy	New York City	preached	
5/4/1970	Krause, Alison, student	Kent, OH	demonstration	shot
1967	Lakey, George	Danang, South Vietnam	obstructed blockade	arrest
11/9/1965	LaPorte, Roger Allen	New York City	self-immolation	
1960s	Lawson, James, Jr., clergy	Oberlin, OH	refused to register	prison
6/2/1967	Levy, Howard B., doctor	Fort Jackson, SC	refused to train medics	prison at hard labor
10/27/1967	Lewis, Tom, poet	Baltimore	destroyed files	arrest
5/17/1968	Lewis, Tom, poet	Catonsville, MD	arson	prison
12/25/1965	Lynd, Staughton, professor	Hanoi, Vietnam	passport violation	
3/22/1969	Malone, Joann, nun	Washington, DC	sabotage	
1967	Massar, Ivan	Danang, South Vietnam	obstructed blockade	arrest
10/9/1968	McGowan, Edward, priest	Catonsville, MD	sabotage	
10/9/1968	Melmadden, Francis, priest	Catonsville, MD	sabotage	
3/22/1969	Melville, Arthur G.	Washington, DC	sabotage	
3/22/1969	Melville, Catherine	Washington, DC	sabotage	
5/17/1968	Melville, Marjorie Bradford, nun	Catonsville, MD	arson	prison
5/17/1968	Melville, Thomas, priest	Catonsville, MD	arson	prison
10/27/1967	Mengel, James L., missionary	Baltimore	destroyed files	arrest
3/22/1969	Meyer, Bernard, clergy	Washington, DC	sabotage	
10/15/1965	Miller, David J., student	Syracuse, NY	burned draft card	
5/4/1970	Miller, Jeffrey Glen, student	Kent, OH	demonstration	shot
5/17/1968	Mische, George, labor organizer	Catonsville, MD	arson	prison
3/20/1965	Mitchell, David Henry, III, student	New Canaan, CT	draft evasion	prison, fine
10/9/1968	Moccia, Lianne, student	Catonsville, MD	sabotage	
3/22/1969	Moloney, Dennis J., clergy	Washington, DC	sabotage	
6/30/1966	Mora, Dennis, soldier	Fort Hood, TX	refused assignment	prison at hard labor
11/2/1965	Morrison, Norman R.	Washington, DC	self-immolation	
12/1967	Mott, Jeremy	Chicago	burned draft card	prison
5/17/1968	Moylan, Mary, nurse-midwife	Catonsville, MD	arson	prison
1/1963	Muhammad, Wallace D., clergy	Hamtramck, MI	refused to serve	prison

Target of Act/Date	Name, Occupation	Location	Act	Consequence
10/9/1968	Murphy, Edward, priest	Catonsville, MD	sabotage	
10/9/1968	Musi, Barry, counselor	Catonsville, MD	sabotage	
3/8/1968	Noye, Dale H., psychologist	Colorado Springs, CO	refused an order	prison
3/22/1969	O'Rourke, Michael J., priest	Washington, DC	sabotage	threat
10/9/1968	Pommersheim, Frank, lawyer	Catonsville, MD	sabotage	
1960s	Powell, Adam Clayton, Jr., clergy, politician	Washington, DC	protest	
1/1968	Rankin, Jeannette, politician	Washington, DC	march	
4/12/1971	Rankin, Jeannette, politician	Washington, DC	march	
1/5/1968	Raskin, Marcus, political aide	New Haven, CT	conspiracy	arrest
10/9/1968	Reilly, Joan, student	Catonsville, MD	sabotage	
10/9/1968	Reilly, Rosemary, activist	Catonsville, MD	sabotage	
1967	Reynolds, Barbara Leonard	Danang, South Vietnam	obstructed blockade	arrest
1967	Reynolds, Earle, anthropologist	Danang, South Vietnam	obstructed blockade	arrest
10/9/1968	Ricci, Anita, student	Catonsville, MD	sabotage	
10/9/1968	Ridolfi, Kathleen, student	Catonsville, MD	sabotage	
8/25/1968	Rubin, Jerry, writer	Chicago	conspiracy, riot	arrest
6/30/1966	Samas, David, soldier	Fort Hood, TX	refused assignment	prison at hard labor
5/4/1970	Scheuer, Sandra, student	Kent, OH	demonstration	shot
10/12/1968	Schnall, Susan, nurse	Oakland, CA	distributed literature	prison at hard labor
5/4/1970	Schroeder, William, student	Kent, OH	demonstration	shot
8/25/1968	Seale, Robert George, activist	Chicago	conspiracy, riot, contempt of court	prison
10/9/1968	Shemeley, Martha, reformer	Catonsville, MD	sabotage	
3/22/1969	Slaski, Michael, activist	Washington, DC	sabotage	
10/20/1967	Spock, Benjamin, doctor	Arlington, VA	conspiracy	prison
12/5/1967	Spock, Benjamin, doctor	New York City	demonstration, conspiracy	
1/5/1968	Spock, Benjamin, doctor	New Haven, CT	conspiracy	
5/22/1968	Stolte, Ken, soldier	Fort Ord, CA	distributed literature	prison at hard labor
10/9/1968	Swinglish, John, activist	Catonsville, MD	sabotage	
1968	Thomas, Norman, socialist	New Haven, CT	protest, conspiracy	
10/9/1968	Tosi, Sara, church worker	Catonsville, MD	sabotage	
10/9/1968	Williamson, Robert, reformer	Catonsville, MD	sabotage	
5/10/1970	Winne, George, Jr., student	San Diego, CA	self-immolation	

voter intimidation

Target of Act/Date	Name, Occupation	Location	Act	Consequence
12/15/1961	Abernathy, Ralph David, clergy	Albany, GA	obstructed sidewalk, counseled volunteers	jail
8/8/1963	Allen, Ralph W., III, activist	Albany, GA	protest march, assault	jail, prison
11/5/1872	Anthony, Charlotte Bolles, teacher	Rochester, NY	voted	arraigned
11/5/1872	Anthony, Mary Stafford	Rochester, NY	voted	arraigned
11/5/1872	Anthony, Susan Brownell, orator	Rochester, NY	voted	handcuffed, fine
10–11/1960	Ashley, Stephen, activist	Magnolia, MS	registered voters	jail

Target of Act/Date	Name, Occupation	Location	Act	Consequence
11/5/1872	Baker, Ellen S., teacher	Rochester, NY	voted	arraigned
10–11/1960	Bennett, Myrtis, activist	Magnolia, MS	registered voters	jail
12/1961	Blackwell, Unita, author	Lula, MS	registered voters	death threat, arrest
3/1965	Boynton, Amelia Platts, activist	Selma, AL	promoted integration	assault
9/5/1961	Britt, Travis	Tylertown, MS	registered voters	assault
7/1967	Brown, Hubert G., activist	Cambridge, MD	promoted integration	shot, fled
10–11/1960	Campbell, Janie, activist	Magnolia, MS	registered voters	jail
12/1961	Carmichael, Stokely, activist	Lowndes County, MS	registered voters	
11/5/1872	Chapman, Nancy M.	Rochester, NY	voted	arraigned
11/5/1872	Chatfield, Hannah M., seamstress	Rochester, NY	voted	arraigned
11/5/1872	Cogswell, Jane M.	Rochester, NY	voted	arraigned
8/13/1965	Daniels, Jonathan Myrick, student	Fort Deposit, AL	protected a child protester	shot
11/5/1872	De Garmo, Rhoda	Rochester, NY	voted	arraigned
10–11/1960	Diggs, Ivory, activist	Magnolia, MS	registered voters	jail
8/8/1963	Durham, Sallie Mae, activist	Americus, GA	assaulted an officer	jail
1964	Farmer, James Leonard, clergy	Mississippi	registered voters	
10/16/1995	Farrakhan, Louis, activist	Washington, DC	march	
6/4/1963	Guyot, Lawrence, student	Winona, MS	investigated brutality	police brutality
8/31/1962	Hamer, Fannie Lou, activist	Indianola, MS	registered voters	jail
6/3/1963	Hamer, Fannie Lou, activist	Winona, MS	registered voters	jail, assault
9/7/1961	Hardy, John, activist	Tylertown, MS	registered voters	pistol-whipped
12/1961	Hardy, John, activist	Magnolia, MS	registered voters	
8/8/1963	Harris, Don, activist	Albany, GA	registered voters	jail
11/5/1872	Hebard, Mary S., activist	Rochester, NY	voted	arraigned
11/5/1872	Hough, Susan M.	Rochester, NY	voted	arraigned
2/18/1965	Jackson, Jimmy Lee, farmhand	Marion, AL	protected voters	shot
12/15/1961	King, Martin Luther, Jr., clergy	Albany, GA	obstructed sidewalk, prayed, counseled volunteers	jail
1/18/1965	King, Martin Luther, Jr., clergy	Selma, AL	registered to vote	attacked
2/2/1965	King, Martin Luther, Jr., clergy	Selma, AL	demanded voter rights	arrest
3/1965	Lafayette, Bernard, clergy	Selma, AL	promoted integration	
3/1965	Lafayette, Colia Liddell	Selma, AL	promoted integration	
10–11/1960	Lewis, Isaac, activist	Magnolia, MS	registered voters	jail
8/30/1961	Lewis, Isaac, activist	McComb, MS	impeded an officer	jail
11/5/1872	Leyden, Margaret Leora Garrigues	Rochester, NY	voted	arraigned
8/8/1963	McDaniel, Thomas, activist	Americus, GA	assaulted an officer	jail
10–11/1960	McDew, Charles, activist	Magnolia, MS	registered voters	jail
11/5/1872	McLean, Guelma Penn Anthony	Rochester, NY	voted	arraigned
10/15/1872	Minor, Virginia Louisa, suffragist	St. Louis, MO	registered to vote	
8/15/1961	Moses, Robert Parris, teacher	Amite County, MS	impeded police	fine, jail
12/1961	Moses, Robert Parris, teacher	Amite County, MS	registered voters	shot at
11/5/1872	Mosher, Hannah Lapham Anthony	Rochester, NY	voted	arraigned
10–11/1960	Muhammad, Curtis Hayes, activist	Magnolia, MS	registered voters	jail
10/16/1995	Parks, Rosa, seamstress	Washington, DC	march	
8/8/1963	Perdew, John, activist	Albany, GA	registered voters	jail

Target of Act/Date	Name, Occupation	Location	Act	Consequence
6/3/1963	Ponder, Annelle, activist	Winona, MS	registered voters	jail, assault
11/5/1872	Pulver, Mary Elizabeth Miller	Rochester, NY	voted	arraigned
10–11/1960	Robinson, Harold, activist	Magnolia, MS	registered voters	jail
12/1961	Robinson, Reginald L., activist	Magnolia, MS	registered voters	
12/3/1964	Savio, Mario, student	Berkeley, CA	registered voters	banned from campus, jail
3/1873	Smith, Abigail Hadassah, orator	Glastonbury, CT	registered voters	confiscation
3/1873	Smith, Julia Evelina, scholar	Glastonbury, CT	registered voters	confiscation
10–11/1960	Talbert, Robert, activist	Magnolia, MS	registered voters	jail
8/30/1961	Talbert, Robert, activist	McComb, MS	impeded an officer	jail
8/30/1961	Travis, Brenda, activist	McComb, MS	impeded an officer	jail
11/5/1872	Truesdale, Sarah Cole	Rochester, NY	voted	arraigned
10–11/1960	Vick, Lee Chester, activist	Magnolia, MS	registered voters	jail
10–11/1960	Watkins, Hollis, activist	Magnolia, MS	registered voters	jail
10–11/1960	Wells, James, activist	Magnolia, MS	registered voters	jail

war

12/23/1963	Deming, Barbara, writer	Albany, GA	protest, fast	jail
12/23/1963	Havice, Harriet Katherine, student	Albany, GA	protest, fast	jail
12/23/1963	Robinson, Ray, activist	Albany, GA	protest, fast	jail
11/12/1960	Scott, Lawrence, activist	Arlington, VA	sit-in	
11/12/1960	Scott, Viola Maria Standley, activist	Arlington, VA	sit-in	
1958	Whitney, Norman Jehiel, teacher	Cheyenne, WY	trespass	

war bond sale

1917	Benner, Rhine Wiegner, clergy	Job, WV	protest	fine, arrest
1917	Heatwole, Lewis James, bishop	Harrisonburg, VA	protest	fine, arrest

War of 1812

10/1/1812	Baxter, Robert, soldier	Union Village, OH	desertion	forced march
10/1/1812	Davis, Rufus E.	Union Village, OH	desertion	forced march
10/1/1812	Davis, William, Jr.	Union Village, OH	desertion	forced march
10/1/1812	Gallaher, Adam	Union Village, OH	desertion	forced march
10/1/1812	McClelland, Samuel Swan	Union Village, OH	desertion	forced march
6/1/1812	McNemar, Richard, clergy	Union Village, OH	protest	
6/1/1812	Rollins, Samuel	Union Village, OH	protest	
10/1/1812	Rollins, Samuel	Union Village, OH	desertion	forced march
10/1/1812	Spinning, David	Union Village, OH	desertion	forced march
1812	Whipple, Jonathan	Ipswich, MA	refused to serve	threat, fine

white-owned business

3/19/1937	Powell, Adam Clayton, Jr., clergy, politician	Harlem, NY	riot	

Target of Act/Date	Name, Occupation	Location	Act	Consequence

wilderness destruction

Target of Act/Date	Name, Occupation	Location	Act	Consequence
5/23/1990	Bari, Judith Beatrice, activist	Oakland, CA	recruiter	
5/24/1990	Cherney, Darryl, activist	Oakland, CA	tree-sitting	pipe bomb
1979	Foreman, Dave, conservationist	Siskiyou, OR	sabotage	
1983	Foreman, Dave, conservationist	Siskiyou, OR	sabotage	injured
12/10/1997	Hill, Julia Butterfly, activist	Arcata, CA	tree-sitting	intimidation, violence
7/20/1985	Huber, Ron, environmentalist	Corvallis, OR	tree-sitting	violence
5/23/1990	Littletree, Alicia, environmentalist	Albion, CA	tree-sitting	pipe bomb
1992	Littletree, Alicia, environmentalist	Albion, CA	tree-sitting	death threat, assault
1979	Wolke, Howie, conservationist	Grayback Ridge, WY	sabotage	
1984	Wolke, Howie, conservationist	Grayback Ridge, WY	sabotage	

women's disenfranchisement

Target of Act/Date	Name, Occupation	Location	Act	Consequence
9/4/1917	Adams, Pauline Forstall Colclough, suffragist	Washington, DC	obstructed traffic	arrest
2/9/1919	Adams, Pauline Forstall Colclough, suffragist	Washington, DC	burned an effigy	arrest
9/1917	Ainge, Edith, suffragist	Washington, DC	picketed	workhouse
8/1918	Ainge, Edith, suffragist	Washington, DC	demonstration	arrest
2/1919	Ainge, Edith, suffragist	Washington, DC	burned an effigy	arrest
1840s–1850s	Anthony, Susan Brownell, orator	Rochester, NY	promoted activism	
6/30/1868	Anthony, Susan Brownell, orator	Philadelphia	protest	
7/4/1876	Anthony, Susan Brownell, orator	Philadelphia	protest	
6/27/1917	Arniel, Annie M. Clarke, suffragist	Washington, DC	picketed	workhouse
11/1917	Arniel, Annie M. Clarke, suffragist	Washington, DC	picketed	workhouse
2/1919	Arnold, Berthe, teacher	Washington, DC	burned an effigy	arrest
6/27/1917	Arnold, Virginia Josephine, student	Washington, DC	picketed	workhouse
8/1918	Ascough, Lillian, suffragist	Washington, DC	demonstration	arrest
2/1919	Ascough, Lillian, suffragist	Washington, DC	burned an effigy	arrest
6/27/1917	Baird, Margaret Frances, artist	Washington, DC	picketed	workhouse
9/1917	Baker, Abby Scott, suffragist	Washington, DC	picketed	workhouse
9/1917	Blumberg, Hilda, teacher	Washington, DC	picketed	workhouse
11/10/1917	Blumberg, Hilda, teacher	Washington, DC	picketed	workhouse
1/10/1917	Branham, Lucy Gwynne, suffragist	Washington, DC	picketed	workhouse
9/1917	Branham, Lucy Gwynne, suffragist	Washington, DC	picketed	workhouse
7/14/1917	Brannan, Eunice Mignon Dana, publisher	Washington, DC	picketed	workhouse
11/10/1917	Brannan, Eunice Mignon Dana, publisher	Washington, DC	picketed	workhouse
11/1913	Burns, Lucy, editor	Washington, DC	wrote on a sidewalk	fine
6/22/1917	Burns, Lucy, editor	Washington, DC	picketed	jail, stripped, workhouse, force-feeding
9/1917	Burns, Lucy, editor	Washington, DC	picketed	workhouse
11/10/1917	Burns, Lucy, editor	Washington, DC	picketed	workhouse, brutality, force-feeding
8/15/1918	Burns, Lucy, editor	Washington, DC	speech	arrest

Target of Act/Date	Name, Occupation	Location	Act	Consequence
1/1919	Burns, Lucy, editor	Washington, DC	picketed	workhouse
7/4/1917	Calderhead-Walker, Iris Gallant	Washington, DC	picketed	workhouse
2/1919	Colvin, Sarah Tarleton, memoirist	Washington, DC	burned an effigy	arrest
11/10/1917	Cosu, Alice M. Claressi, suffragist	Washington, DC	picketed	workhouse
8/17/1917	Crocker, Gertrude L., clerk	Washington, DC	picketed	workhouse
8/1918	Crocker, Gertrude L., clerk	Washington, DC	demonstration	arrest
2/1919	Crocker, Gertrude L., clerk	Washington, DC	burned an effigy	arrest
11/10/1917	Day, Dorothy, reformer, editor	Washington, DC	picketed	workhouse
6/30/1868	Dickinson, Anna Elizabeth, orator	Philadelphia	protest	
8/14/1917	Dixon, Edna, teacher	Washington, DC	picketed	workhouse
11/10/1917	Dixon, Mary Bartlett, backer	Washington, DC	picketed	workhouse
6/27/1917	Dock, Lavinia Lloyd, nurse	Washington, DC	picketed	workhouse
8/17/1917	Dock, Lavinia Lloyd, nurse	Washington, DC	picketed	workhouse, brutalized
1/6/1919	Dubrow, Mary, teacher	Washington, DC	burned an effigy	arrest
11/10/1917	Emory, Julia	Washington, DC	picketed	workhouse
8/1918	Emory, Julia	Washington, DC	demonstration	arrest
1/7/1919	Emory, Julia	Washington, DC	burned an effigy	arrest
8/17/1917	Ewing, Lucy Hyde, suffragist	Washington, DC	picketed	workhouse
1/1919	Fendall, Mary Gertrude	Washington, DC	burned an effigy	arrest
8/16/1917	Flanagan, Catherine M., secretary	Washington, DC	picketed	workhouse
7/14/1917	Fotheringham, Janet, teacher	Washington, DC	picketed	workhouse
10/2/1914	Funk, Antoinette, lawyer	Minot, ND	street speech	jail, fine
7/4/1876	Gage, Matilda Joslyn, orator	Philadelphia	protest	
7/14/1917	Gardner, Matilda Hall, publisher	Washington, DC	picketed	workhouse
1/13/1919	Gardner, Matilda Hall, publisher	Washington, DC	picketed	
12/1919	Goldman, Emma, orator	New York City	protest	deported
11/10/1917	Gram, Betty, publisher	Washington, DC	picketed	workhouse
8/17/1917	Gray, Natalie Hoyt, student	Washington, DC	picketed	workhouse
9/22/1917	Hara, Ernestine	Washington, DC	picketed	workhouse
2/10/1919	Havemeyer, Louisine Waldron Elder, art expert	Washington, DC	burned an effigy	arrest
10/15/1917	Heffelfinger, Kate, student	Washington, DC	picketed	workhouse
8/1918	Heffelfinger, Kate, student	Washington, DC	demonstration	arrest
1/1919	Heffelfinger, Kate, student	Washington, DC	burned an effigy	arrest
10/6/1917	Hennessy, Minnie, suffragist	Washington, DC	picketed	suspended sentence
10/8/1917	Hennessy, Minnie, suffragist	Washington, DC	picketed	workhouse
8/1918	Hill, Elsie Mary, suffragist	Washington, DC	demonstration	arrest
2/1919	Hill, Elsie Mary, suffragist	Washington, DC	burned an effigy	arrest
6/27/1917	Hilles, Florence Bayard, suffragist	Washington, DC	picketed	workhouse
7/14/1917	Hopkins, Alison Turnbull	Washington, DC	picketed	workhouse
11/10/1917	Hunkins-Hallinan, Hazel, professor	Washington, DC	picketed	workhouse
8/1919	Hunkins-Hallinan, Hazel, professor	Washington, DC	demonstration	arrest
7/14/1917	Hurlbut, Julia, suffragist	Washington, DC	unlawful assembly	workhouse
11/10/1917	Jakobi, Paula, playwright	Washington, DC	picketed	workhouse
6/27/1917	Jamison, Maud, suffragist	Washington, DC	picketed	workhouse

Target of Act/Date	Name, Occupation	Location	Act	Consequence
11/10/1917	Juengling, Amy, suffragist	Washington, DC	picketed	workhouse
12/16/1918	Kalb, Elizabeth Green, librarian	Washington, DC	demonstration	arrest
1/1919	Kalb, Elizabeth Green, librarian	Washington, DC	burned an effigy	arrest
11/10/1917	Kendall, Ada Davenport, journalist	Washington, DC	picketed	workhouse
11/10/1917	Kent, Elizabeth Thatcher, conservationist	Washington, DC	picketed	workhouse
11/10/1917	Kinkead, Beatrice, writer	Washington, DC	picketed	workhouse
6/30/1868	Kirk, Eleanor, journalist	Philadelphia	protest	
11/10/1917	Kruger, Hattie, nurse	Washington, DC	picketed	workhouse
6/27/1917	Lewis, Dora Kelly, suffragist	Washington, DC	picketed	workhouse
7/1917	Lewis, Dora Kelly, suffragist	Washington, DC	picketed	workhouse
11/10/1917	Lewis, Dora Kelly, suffragist	Washington, DC	picketed	workhouse
8/15/1918	Lewis, Dora Kelly, suffragist	Washington, DC	speech	arrest
1/1919	Lewis, Dora Kelly, suffragist	Washington, DC	burned an effigy	arrest
6/30/1868	Lozier, Clemence Sophia, doctor	Philadelphia	protest	
7/14/1917	Martin, Anne, professor	Washington, DC	picketed	workhouse
11/10/1917	Martinette, Catherine, suffragist	Washington, DC	picketed	workhouse
11/10/1917	McShane, Elizabeth, businesswoman	Washington, DC	picketed	workhouse
2/1919	Mercer, Nell, businesswoman	Washington, DC	burned an effigy	arrest
7/4/1917	Milholland, Vida, singer	Washington, DC	picketed	workhouse
1/1919	Moller, Bertha C. Berglin, lawyer	Washington, DC	burned an effigy	arrest
6/22/1917	Morey, Katherine, suffragist	Washington, DC	picketed	jail
11/10/1917	Morey, Mary Agnes Hosmer, memoirist	Washington, DC	picketed	workhouse
11/10/1917	Nolan, Mary A., librarian	Washington, DC	picketed	workhouse
1/1919	Nolan, Mary A., librarian	Washington, DC	burned an effigy	arrest
1/10/1917	Paul, Alice, suffragist	Washington, DC	picketed	arrest
3/4/1917	Paul, Alice, suffragist	Washington, DC	chained to a fence	warning
10/20/1917	Paul, Alice, suffragist	Washington, DC	picketed	workhouse
11/1917	Paul, Alice, suffragist	Washington, DC	picketed	workhouse, torture, asylum, force-feeding, solitary confinement
8/15/1918	Paul, Alice, suffragist	Washington, DC	speech	arrest
11/10/1917	Quay, Minnie	Washington, DC	picketed	workhouse
7/14/1917	Rogers, Elizabeth Selden White, suffragist	Washington, DC	picketed	workhouse
9/1917	Samarodin, Nina, teacher	Washington, DC	picketed	workhouse
11/10/1917	Scott, Phoebe Persons, suffragist	Washington, DC	picketed	workhouse
3/1873	Smith, Abigail Hadassah, orator	Glastonbury, CT	tax resistance	
3/1873	Smith, Julia Evelina, scholar	Glastonbury, CT	tax resistance	
6/30/1868	Smith, Susan A., doctor	Philadelphia	protest	
10/20/1917	Spencer, Caroline E., doctor	Washington, DC	picketed	workhouse
1/13/1919	Spencer, Caroline E., doctor	Washington, DC	burned an effigy	arrest
6/30/1868	Stanton, Elizabeth Cady, essayist	Philadelphia	protest	
1913	Stevens, Doris, suffragist	Washington, DC	protest	
1858	Stone, Lucy, orator	Boston	tax resistance	

Target of Act/Date	Name, Occupation	Location	Act	Consequence
7/14/1917	Stuyvesant, Elizabeth, dancer	Washington, DC	picketed	workhouse
6/27/1917	Vernon, Mabel, orator	Washington, DC	picketed	workhouse
8/17/1917	Watson, Madeleine	Washington, DC	picketed	workhouse
8/1918	Watson, Madeleine	Washington, DC	demonstration	arrest
7/4/1917	Weed, Helena Charlotte Hill, suffragist	Washington, DC	picketed	workhouse
1/1918	Weed, Helena Charlotte Hill, suffragist	Washington, DC	picketed	workhouse
8/1918	Weed, Helena Charlotte Hill, suffragist	Washington, DC	picketed	workhouse
11/10/1917	White, Sue Shelton, suffragist	Washington, DC	picketed	workhouse
11/10/1917	Wiley, Anna Kelton, suffragist	Washington, DC	picketed	workhouse
10/15/1917	Winslow, Rose, weaver	Washington, DC	picketed	workhouse
9/1917	Winsor, Mary, orator	Washington, DC	picketed	workhouse
1/1919	Winsor, Mary, orator	Washington, DC	burned an effigy	arrest
6/27/1917	Youmans, Florence L., suffragist	Washington, DC	picketed	workhouse
8/17/1917	Young, Matilda, suffragist	Washington, DC	picketed	workhouse
11/10/1917	Young, Matilda, suffragist	Washington, DC	picketed	workhouse
1/1919	Young, Matilda, suffragist	Washington, DC	burned an effigy	arrest
7/4/1917	Young-Rogers, Joy, editor	Washington, DC	picketed	workhouse

worker endangerment

Target of Act/Date	Name, Occupation	Location	Act	Consequence
11/1909	Beard, Mary Ritter, activist, labor organizer	New York City	strike	jail
1894	Jones, Mary "Mother," labor organizer	Tuscaloosa, AL	protest	
11/1909	O'Reilly, Leonora, activist	New York City	strike	jail

World War I

Target of Act/Date	Name, Occupation	Location	Act	Consequence
8/1914	Addams, Jane, reformer	Chicago	sheltered draft evaders	
6/1918	Adkisson, Bliss	Heber Springs, AR	draft evasion	prison
6/1918	Adkisson, Hardy	Heber Springs, AR	draft evasion	prison at hard labor
6/1918	Adkisson, Tom, Jr.	Heber Springs, AR	draft evasion	prison at hard labor
6/1918	Adkisson, Tom, Sr.	Heber Springs, AR	abetted draft evasion	prison
8/1914	Balch, Emily Greene, professor	Jamaica Plains, MA	demonstration	
8/30/1918	Baldazzi, Giovanni, writer	Chicago	draft evasion	prison
1918	Baldwin, Roger Nash	Atlanta, GA	refused physical	prison
4/30/1918	Basinger, David W.	Chillicothe, OH	refused uniform	
1918	Becker, Henry J., barber	Fort Leavenworth, KS	refused to break the Sabbath	prison at hard labor
6/1918	Blakely, Jesse Jewel	Heber Springs, AR	draft evasion	prison at hard labor
6/1918	Blakely, Jim	Heber Springs, AR	draft evasion	prison at hard labor
6/1918	Blakely, Lum	Heber Springs, AR	draft evasion	prison at hard labor
1917	Blickenstaff, L.C., clergy	Fort Leavenworth, KS	refused a uniform	prison
1917–1920	Briehl, Fred	Fort Leavenworth, KS	conscientious objection	expelled from school, prison
5/1918	Buller, Henry B.	Buhler, KS	conscientious objection	forced to plant trees
9/7/1917	Buller, Herman H.	Buhler, KS	refused a rifle	guardhouse

Target of Act/Date	Name, Occupation	Location	Act	Consequence
1918	Burke, Frank L.	Fort Leavenworth, KS	conscientious objection	jail
1918	Cameron, Holland William	Salem, OH	refused a uniform	forced to serve
1918	Caughron, Benjamin Curl	Mena, AR	armed resistance	electric chair
6/27/1918	Claassen, Menno	Fort Riley, KS	refused a uniform	
8/1918	Conrad, Orie Martin	Fort Lewis, WA	refused a weapon	torture
1918	DeRosa, Ulysses	Fort Riley, KS	draft evasion	prison
1918	Eash, Reuben J.	Fort Leavenworth, KS	conscientious objection	jail
1917	Eichel, David	Camp Upton, NY	conscientious objection	prison
11/2/1918	Eichel, Julius, chemist	Camp Upton, NY	conscientious objection	prison at hard labor
1918	Enfield, Orville E., lawyer	Arnett, OK	conspiracy	arrest
11/1918	Firestone, Julius	Camp Hancock, GA	conscientious objection	tarred, feathered
1914	Fitzgerald, Mary Eleanor, activist	Deerfield, WI	aided draft evaders	
1918	Flory, Daniel B.	Fort Leavenworth, KS	conscientious objection	jail
1918	Franz, Heinrich F.	Fort Leavenworth, KS	conscientious objection	jail
1917	Gaeddert, Gustav Raymond, teacher	Fort Riley, KS	conscientious objection	prison, asylum
1918	Gellert, Ernest, artist	Fort Hancock, NJ	conscientious objection	forced to dig his grave, shot
1917	Getts, Clark H., journalist	New York City	conscientious objection	prison, asylum
8/1914	Goldman, Emma, lecturer	New York City	sheltered draft evaders	
6/15/1917	Goldman, Emma, lecturer	New York City	conspiracy	prison, deportation
1918	Gray, Harold S.	Fort Leavenworth, KS	conscientious objection	prison
4/25/1918	Grosser, Philip	Boston	draft evasion	mock hanging
6/22/1918	Haessler, Carl, teacher	Camp Sheridan, AL	refused to serve, led prison revolt	prison at hard labor
9/1917	Haywood, William Dudley, labor organizer	Chicago	opposed war	arrest
4/5/1917	Hennacy, Ammon, activist	Atlanta, GA	draft evasion	prison
1918	Hess, Maurice, scholar	Fort Leavenworth, KS	conscientious objection	solitary confinement on bread and water
4/21/1918	Hicks, William Madison, lecturer	Elk City, OK	conspiracy	tarred, feathered
5/24/1918	Hofer, David	Fort Leavenworth, KS	conscientious objection	prison, torture
5/24/1918	Hofer, Josef	Fort Leavenworth, KS	conscientious objection	torture, died in prison
5/24/1918	Hofer, Michael	Fort Leavenworth, KS	conscientious objection	prison, torture,
1918	James, William Oral	St. Louis, MO	conscientious objection, prison revolt	prison
7/2/1918	Kantor, William Marx	Camden, NJ	conscientious objection	prison, threat, ridicule
1918	Klassen, Johannes M.	Fort Leavenworth, KS	conscientious objection	prison
7/1918	Leatherman, Noah	Camp Dodge, IA	conscientious objection	solitary cell

Target of Act/Date	Name, Occupation	Location	Act	Consequence
1918	Lehane, Cornelius	Bridgeport, CT	conscientious objection	prison
1917	Liechty, Elmer, plumber	Fort Leavenworth, KS	conscientious objection	prison
10/15/1918	Lunde, Erling H.	Chicago	conscientious objection	prison
1918	Magon, Ricardo Flores	Fort Leavenworth, KS	conscientious objection	prison
6/1918	Martin, Leo Douglas	Heber Springs, AR	draft evasion	prison at hard labor
8/1918	McTimmonds, Elmer Tracy	Fort Lewis, WA	refused a weapon	torture
1917	Meyer, Ernest L., journalist	Fort Leavenworth, KS	conscientious objection	expelled from university, prison
1917	Moore, Howard W., farmer	Camp Upton, NY	conscientious objection	prison
1917	Mummaw, Adam H.	Louisville, KY	conscientious objection	prison
7/29/1917	O'Hare, Kate Richards, orator	Bowman, ND	promoted pacifism	
6/1918	Osbourne, Houston Earl	Heber Springs, AR	protest	
6/1918	Owen, Chandler, journalist	Cleveland, OH	antiwar speech	jail for sedition
11/1918	Pankratz, Peter W., carpenter	Del Rio, TX	conscientious objection	prison
6/1918	Penrod, John	Heber Springs, AR	draft evasion	prison at hard labor
11/1/1917	Quiring, Peter J.	Camp Travis, TX	refused a uniform	prison at hard labor
6/1918	Randolph, Asa Philip, editor	Cleveland, OH	antiwar speech	jail for sedition, surveillance
4/2/1917	Rankin, Jeannette, politician	Washington, DC	protest	
1917	Richards, Edward C.M., forester	West Chester, PA	conscientious objection	
1918	Salmon, Benjamin J.	Denver, CO	denounced war	prison on bread and water, asylum
1918	Schwartz, Jacob	Bellevue, WA	conscientious objection	prison
1918	Seidenberg, Roderick, architect	Camp Upton, NY	conscientious objection	prison
7/22/1917	Siemens, Leonard	Camp Funston, KS	conscientious objection	prison
1918	Skedine, Van	Bridewell, IL	conscientious objection	prison
1917	Soldner, Tilman, dentist	Camp Taylor, KY	conscientious objection	prison
1918	Sprunger, Walter	Monroe, IN	conscientious objection	prison
6/1918	Sweeten, Eli Jackson	Heber Springs, AR	protest	
1918	Teuscher, Daniel E.	Fort Leavenworth, KS	conscientious objection	prison
11/2/1918	Thomas, Evan, teacher	Camp Upton, NY	conscientious objection	life in prison, bread and water
1918	Thomas, Mark R.	Fort Leavenworth, KS	conscientious objection	prison
9/1918	Vogt, Jacob Willard	Camp Logan, TX	conscientious objection	abuse
1917	Voth, Albert Cornelius	Camp Travis, TX	refused orders	prison
8/1914	Wald, Lillian, nurse	New York City	sheltered draft evaders	
1918	Wallace, Daniel H.	Davenport, IA	conscientious objection	prison
8/1917	Waltner, Edward J.B.	Camp Cody, NM	refused to drill	prison
1918	Wells, Ernest D.	Fort Leavenworth, KS	conscientious objection	prison
1918	Wipf, Jacob	Fort Leavenworth, KS	conscientious objection	prison
1918	Wolfe, John M.	Fort Riley, KS	conscientious objection	prison

Target of Act/Date	Name, Occupation	Location	Act	Consequence
1918	Wortsman, Jacob	Fort Leavenworth, KS	conscientious objection	prison
1918	Yoder, Daniel S.	Fort Leavenworth, KS	conscientious objection	prison

World War II

Target of Act/Date	Name, Occupation	Location	Act	Consequence
1944	Anderson, William	St. Paul, MN	conscientious objection	engaged in starvation experiment
1944	Andresen, Bent	Kane, PA	protest	prison, tube-feeding
4/1943	Andrews, Bennett W.	Danbury, CT	pacifism	prison
7/1943	Ball, James W.		draft evasion	prison
1943	Bishop, Corbett, chemist	New York City	left a camp	prison, torture, tube-feeding
1944	Blickenstaff, Harold, teacher	St. Paul, MN	conscientious objection	engaged in starvation experiment
1943	Bofman, Albert	Sandstone, MN	protest	prison
1944	Burrous, Wendell, miner	St. Paul, MN	conscientious objection	engaged in starvation experiment
4/6/1943	Butcher, Charles, businessman	Cambridge, MA	draft evasion	prison in irons
4/6/1943	Clark, Bronson P., activist	Cambridge, MA	draft evasion	prison in irons
1944	Cowles, Edward	St. Paul, MN	conscientious objection	engaged in starvation experiment
6/28/1943	Darrow, Gerald Pittman	California	draft evasion	prison
9/28/1943	Dellinger, David T., student	Wakefield, MA	refused to register	prison
1943	DiGia, Ralph	Danbury, CT	refused to register	prison
9/28/1943	Dixon, Jack	Lewisburg, PA	protest	prison
1942	Dole, Arthur A., student	Yellow Springs, OH	refused classification	prison
6/28/1943	Dolve, Philip Curtis	California	draft evasion	prison
1941	Doty, Hiram	Chicago	refused to serve	prison
5/28/1943	Drumheller, Leland W.	Philadelphia	conscientious objection	indicted
11/1944	Dyer, Henry	Sandstone, MN	left camp	prison, tube-feeding
1944	Ebeling, George, actor	St. Paul, MN	conscientious objection	engaged in starvation experiment
10/1942	Elder, George	Philadelphia	conscientious objection	asylum
1944	Frederick, Carlyle	St. Paul, MN	conscientious objection	engaged in starvation experiment
1942	Gara, Larry, teacher	Lewisburg, PA	refused to serve	prison
1944	Garner, Jasper H.B., biologist	St. Paul, MN	conscientious objection	engaged in starvation experiment
1944	Glick, Lester, college dean	St. Paul, MN	conscientious objection	engaged in starvation experiment
1944	Graham, James, teacher	St. Paul, MN	conscientious objection	engaged in starvation experiment
7/9/1942	Griffith, John H., camp counselor	Columbia, SC	refused to register	jail
1945	Haney, George L.	Chicago	refused to register	prison
1944	Heckman, Earl	St. Paul, MN	conscientious objection	engaged in starvation experiment

Target of Act/Date	Name, Occupation	Location	Act	Consequence
10/1943	Hewelcke, John	Denver, CO	draft resistance	prison
1944	Hinkle, Roscoe C., sociologist	St. Paul, MN	conscientious objection	engaged in starvation experiment
1940	Houser, George M.	Norwood, CO	refused to register	humiliation
1944	Kampelman, Max, teacher, writer	St. Paul, MN	conscientious objection	engaged in starvation experiment
1943	Kepler, Earl, Jr.	Denver, CO	pacifism	prison
1943	Kepler, Roy	Denver, CO	pacifism	prison
9/28/1943	Kuenning, William Houston	Du Page, IL	protest	prison
1944	Legg, Sam, college director	St. Paul, MN	conscientious objection	engaged in starvation experiment
1944	Liljengren, Philip	St. Paul, MN	conscientious objection	engaged in starvation experiment
1942	Lohmann, Henry, student	Minneapolis, MN	conscientious objection	
9/28/1943	Lovett, William	Fallsington, PA	protest	prison
1940s	Lowell, Robert, poet	New York City	abetted draft resistance	prison
1944	Lutz, Howard	St. Paul, MN	conscientious objection	engaged in starvation experiment
5/13/1943	Man, Albon Platt, Jr.	Lewisburg, PA	protest	prison
1944	McCullagh, Robert	St. Paul, MN	conscientious objection	engaged in starvation experiment
1944	McReynolds, William	St. Paul, MN	conscientious objection	engaged in starvation experiment
1944	Miller, Dan	St. Paul, MN	conscientious objection	engaged in starvation experiment
1944	Miller, L. Wesley	St. Paul, MN	conscientious objection	engaged in starvation experiment
6/29/1945	Moorman, Albert E.	North Dakota	draft resistance	prison
1944	Mundy, Richard	St. Paul, MN	conscientious objection	engaged in starvation experiment
1943	Murphy, Stanley Thomas	Danbury, CT	conscientious objection	prison, tube-feeding, asylum
1943	Nelson, Wallace Floyd	Coshocton, OH	fled work camp	prison
11/1944	Newton, David	Sandstone, MN	conscientious objection	prison, tube feeding
7/21/1944	Omura, James M., journalist	Heart Mountain, WY	conspiracy	arrest
1940s	Parker, Malcolm "Max"	Sandstone, MN	protest	prison
1944	Peacock, Daniel	St. Paul, MN	conscientious objection	engaged in starvation experiment
1943	Phillips, Randolph Godfrey, lawyer	New York City	conscientious objection	guardhouse, asylum
1944	Plaugher, James	St. Paul, MN	conscientious objection	engaged in starvation experiment
1940s	Powers, J.F., novelist	New York City	abetted draft resistance	prison
9/28/1943	Price, Paton	Lewisburg, PA	protest	prison
1944	Rainwater, Woodrow	St. Paul, MN	conscientious objection	engaged in starvation experiment
4/1942	Richards, Frederick Howard, student	West Chester, PA	draft evasion	prison
5/1942	Richards, William Lippincott, student	West Chester, PA	refused to enlist	prison
8/1942	Roberts, William P., Jr.	Ashland, KY	refused to register	prison

Target of Act/Date	Name, Occupation	Location	Act	Consequence
1943	Roodenko, Igal	New York City	draft resistance	forced labor
1944	Rustin, Bayard Taylor	Lewisburg, PA	protest	prison
1944	Sanders, Daniel	St. Paul, MN	conscientious objection	engaged in starvation experiment
11/26/1944	Satterthwait, Arnold Chase, student	Reading, PA	refused to register	prison
6/28/1943	Scaff, Lloyd	California	draft evasion	prison
1944	Scholberg, Cedric, librarian	St. Paul, MN	conscientious objection	engaged in starvation experiment
1943	Shubin, John	California	conscientious objection	prison, beaten
1944	Smith, Charles	St. Paul, MN	conscientious objection	engaged in starvation experiment
10/14/1942	Sparling, Fred M.		draft evasion	
1944	Stanton, William Macy, Jr.	St. Paul, MN	conscientious objection	engaged in starvation experiment
1942	Stern, Thomas Noel, professor	Pittsburgh	conscientious objection	
1944	Summers, Raymond	St. Paul, MN	conscientious objection	engaged in starvation experiment
5/13/1943	Sutherland, William H., Jr.	Lewisburg, PA	draft evasion	prison
1944	Sutton, Marshall O.	St. Paul, MN	conscientious objection	engaged in starvation experiment
1943	Taylor, Louis	Danbury, CT	conscientious objection	prison, tube-feeding, asylum
7/1942	Templin, Lawrence, teacher	New York City	conscientious objection	jail
1944	Tuttle, Kenneth	St. Paul, MN	conscientious objection	engaged in starvation experiment
3/4/1944	Vetter, Herbert F., Jr., clergy	Bedford, VA	abandoned work assignment	
1944	Villwock, Robert	St. Paul, MN	conscientious objection	engaged in starvation experiment
1940s	Walker, Charles C.	Petersburg, VA	abandoned work assignment	prison
1944	Wallace, William Vincent	St. Paul, MN	conscientious objection	engaged in starvation experiment
1944	Watkins, Franklin, organist, linguist	St. Paul, MN	conscientious objection	engaged in starvation experiment
1943	Weatherbee, Herbert	Monterey, CA	draft resistance	life in prison
2/2/1945	Weber, Henry	Camp Roberts, CA	refused assignment	threat of hanging, prison
1944	Weygandt, W. Earl, grocery clerk	St. Paul, MN	conscientious objection	engaged in starvation experiment
1943	Wieck, David Thoreau, journalist	New York City	refused to register	prison
1944	Willoughby, Robert, teacher	St. Paul, MN	conscientious objection	engaged in starvation experiment
1944	Wilsnack, Gerald	St. Paul, MN	conscientious objection	engaged in starvation experiment
1/1941	Wilson, Winslow	Sandstone, MN	protest	prison
11/1944	Wiser, Art	Sandstone, MN	conscientious objection	prison, tube-feeding
9/28/1943	Woodman, Thomas	Lewisburg, PA	protest	prison
6/28/1943	Worley, Charles Vincent	California	protest	prison, tube-feeding
1942	Yamada, George	Minatare, NE	conscientious objection	prison

Acts of Conscience and Civil Disobedience, by Location

(Note: Some acts were committed outside of the United States.)

State/Target of Act	Date	Name	Location	Act	Consequence
Alabama					
slave education ban	1850s	Rogers, Stephen Walter	Mobile	educated slaves	
Fugitive Slave Law of 1850	1851	Concklin, Seth	Florence	slave rescue	
slave education ban	1854–1863	Skipworth, Lucy	Hopewell	educated slaves	threats
black rights	12/24/1864	Crowe, James Rankin	Sheffield	paramilitary	
black rights	12/24/1864	McCord, Frank Owen	Moulton	paramilitary	
child labor	1894	Jones, Mary "Mother"	Birmingham	protest	
worker endangerment	1894	Jones, Mary "Mother"	Tuscaloosa	protest	
World War I	6/22/1918	Haessler, Carl	Camp Sheridan	refused to serve	prison at hard labor, prison revolt
racism	1944	Parks, Rosa	Montgomery	integrated a bus	ejected
racism	1955	Colvin, Claudette	Montgomery	integrated a bus	arrest
racism	1955	Smith, Mary Louise	Montgomery	integrated a bus	arrest
racism	12/1955	Robinson, Jo Ann Gibson	Montgomery	protest	
racism	12/1/1955	Abernathy, Ralph David	Montgomery	abetted bus protest	
racism	12/1/1955	King, Martin Luther, Jr.	Montgomery	abetted bus protest	
racism	12/1/1955	Parks, Raymond	Montgomery	protest	lost job
racism	12/1/1955	Parks, Rosa	Montgomery	integrated a bus	arrest, lost job
racism	12/1/1955	Rustin, Bayard Taylor	Montgomery	abetted bus protest	
racism	1/26/1956	King, Martin Luther, Jr.	Montgomery	led a procession	arrest
racism	1/30/1956	King, Martin Luther, Jr.	Montgomery	church meeting	home bombed
racism	1/27/1957	King, Martin Luther, Jr.	Montgomery	protest	unexploded bomb
racism	9/3/1958	King, Martin Luther, Jr.	Montgomery	loitering	police brutality
racism	5/21/1960	King, Martin Luther, Jr.	Montgomery	rally	stoned, teargassed
racism	5/21/1960	Shuttlesworth, Fred Lee	Montgomery	rally	stoned, teargassed
racism	5/20/1961	Barbee, William	Montgomery	Freedom Rider	injured
racism	5/20/1961	Lewis, John Robert	Montgomery	Freedom Rider	injured
racism	5/20/1961	Zweng, Jim	Montgomery	Freedom Rider	beaten
racism	5/21/1961	King, Martin Luther, Jr.	Montgomery	Freedom Rider	threats
racism	5/21/1961	Shuttlesworth, Fred Lee	Montgomery	Freedom Rider	threats
racism	5/24/1961	Lewis, John Robert	Montgomery	Freedom Rider	injured
segregation	6/2/1961	Abernathy, Ralph David	Montgomery	lunch counter sit-in	arrest
segregation	6/2/1961	Coffin, William Sloane, Jr.	Montgomery	lunch counter sit-in	arrest
segregation	6/2/1961	Lee, Bernard Scott	Montgomery	lunch counter sit-in	arrest
segregation	6/2/1961	Shuttlesworth, Fred Lee	Montgomery	lunch counter sit-in	arrest
racism	3/25/1963	Baez, Joan	Selma	march	mob attack
racism	4/12/1963	Abernathy, Ralph David	Birmingham	contempt of court	jail, fine

State/Target of Act	Date	Name	Location	Act	Consequence
segregation	4/12/1963	King, Martin Luther, Jr.	Birmingham	contempt of court	jail
racism	9/1963	Lewis, John Robert	Selma	protest	jail
voter intimidation	1/18/1965	King, Martin Luther, Jr.	Selma	registered to vote	attacked
racism	2/2/1965	Baez, Joan	Selma	march	
voter intimidation	2/2/1965	King, Martin Luther, Jr.	Selma	demanded voter rights	arrest
voter intimidation	2/18/1965	Jackson, Jimmy Lee	Marion	protected voters	shot
voter intimidation	3/1965	Boynton, Amelia Platts	Selma	promoted integration	assault
segregation	3/1965	Brown, Hubert G.	Selma	promoted integration	
voter intimidation	3/1965	Lafayette, Bernard	Selma	promoted integration	
voter intimidation	3/1965	Lafayette, Colia Liddell	Selma	promoted integration	
racism	3/1965	Lewis, John Robert	Montgomery	march	assault
racism	3/15/1965	Wilkins, Roy	Selma	march	
racism	3/25/1965	Abernathy, Ralph David	Selma	march	mob attack
racism	3/25/1965	Berrigan, Philip	Selma	march	mob attack, jail
racism	3/25/1965	Bunche, Ralph	Selma	march	mob attack
racism	3/25/1965	Heschel, Abraham Joshua	Selma	march	mob attack
racism	3/25/1965	King, Martin Luther, Jr.	Selma	march	mob attack
racism	3/25/1965	Young, Andrew	Selma	march	mob attack
voter intimidation	8/13/1965	Daniels, Jonathan Myrick	Fort Deposit	protected a child protester	shot
voter intimidation	7/1967	Brown, Hubert G.	Cambridge	promoted integration	shot, fled
segregation	10/30/1967	King, Martin Luther, Jr.	Birmingham	contempt of court	jail

Alaska

State/Target of Act	Date	Name	Location	Act	Consequence
nuclear power	11/5/1971	Watson, Paul	Amchitka	protest	
marijuana ban	1/24/2002	Frederick, Joseph	Juneau	promarijuana banner	suspension

Arizona

State/Target of Act	Date	Name	Location	Act	Consequence
labor organization ban	2/20/1906	Jones, Mary "Mother"	Bisbee	public harangue	
polygamy ban	12/1935	Johnson, Price William	Lees Ferry	plural marriage	raid, prison
polygamy ban	12/1935	Spencer, Isaac Carling	Short Creek	plural marriage	raid, prison
World War II	1943	Tallis, Manuel	Tucson	protest	prison
polygamy ban	3/7/1944	Darger, David Brigham	Colorado City	plural marriage	prison
polygamy ban	3/7/1944	Dockstader, Theral	Colorado City	plural marriage	prison
polygamy ban	3/7/1944	Jessop, Vergel Yeates	Colorado City	plural marriage	prison
polygamy ban	3/7/1944	Stubbs, Lawrence Ritchie	Colorado City	plural marriage	prison
polygamy ban	5/12/1945	Barlow, John Yates	Short Creek	plural marriage	prison

State/ Target of Act	Date	Name	Location	Act	Consequence
alien refugee abuse	1980s	Aguilar, María del Socorro Pardo de	Tucson	alien asylum, transport	charged
alien refugee abuse	1980s	Clark, Anthony	Tucson	alien asylum, transport	
alien refugee abuse	1980s	Elford, Ricardo	Tucson	alien asylum, transport	
alien refugee abuse	1980s	Espinosa, Mary Kay Dean	Tucson	alien asylum, transport	
alien refugee abuse	1980s	Flaherty, Katherine	Tucson	alien asylum	
alien refugee abuse	1980s	Hutchinson, Peggy	Tucson	alien asylum, transport	
alien refugee abuse	1980s	LeWin, Wendy	Tucson	alien asylum, transport	
alien refugee abuse	1980s	MacDonald, Nena	Tucson	alien asylum, transport	
alien refugee abuse	1980s	Nicgorski, Darlene	Tucson	alien asylum, transport	
alien refugee abuse	1980s	Priester, Anna	Tucson	alien asylum, transport	charged
alien refugee abuse	1980s	Quiñones, Ramón Dagoberto	Tucson	alien asylum, transport	
alien refugee abuse	1980s	Waddell, Mary	Tucson	alien asylum, transport	charged
alien refugee abuse	1980s	Weizenbaum, Joseph	Tucson	alien asylum, transport	
alien refugee abuse	1980s	Willis-Conger, Philip	Tucson	alien asylum, transport	
alien refugee abuse	5/4/1981	Corbett, James A.	Tucson	alien asylum, transport	
alien refugee abuse	5/4/1981	Corbett, Patricia Collins	Tucson	alien asylum, transport	
alien refugee abuse	1982	Kennon, Ken	Tucson	alien asylum, transport	
alien refugee abuse	3/24/1982	Carr, Nan	Tucson	alien asylum	
alien refugee abuse	3/24/1982	Fife, John M.	Tucson	alien asylum, recruitment	
alien refugee abuse	3/24/1982	Mann, Hilda	Tucson	alien asylum	
alien refugee abuse	1984	Elder, John A.	Tucson	alien asylum, transport	
alien refugee abuse	1987	Ufford-Chase, Rick	Tucson	alien asylum, transport	
labor organization ban	8/1988	Sheen, Martin	Phoenix	promoted unions	
peyote ban	1995	Mercado, Leonard	Kearny	peyote growing	arrest
peyote ban	1995	Mercado, Raven	Kearny	peyote growing	arrest
peyote ban	1/8/1999	Mercado, Leonard	Kearny	peyote growing	arrest, prison
animal rights	12/2/2004	Coronado, Rodney Adam	Sabino Canyon	destroyed property	
animal rights	12/2/2004	Crozier, Matthew	Sabino Canyon	destroyed property	
alien refugees	1/1/2005	Gilchrist, Jim	Tombstone	paramilitary	

State/ Target of Act	Date	Name	Location	Act	Consequence
alien refugees	1/1/2005	Simcox, Chris	Tombstone	paramilitary	
polygamy ban	7/2006	Barlow, Dale Evans	Colorado City	sex with a minor	prison
polygamy ban	7/2006	Barlow, David Romaine	Colorado City	sex with a minor	prison
polygamy ban	7/2006	Barlow, Donald Robert	Colorado City	sex with a minor	prison
polygamy ban	7/2006	Barlow, Randolph Joseph	Colorado City	sex with a minor	prison
polygamy ban	7/2006	Barlow, Terry Darger	Colorado City	sex with a minor	prison
polygamy ban	7/2006	Bateman, David Romaine	Colorado City	sex with a minor	prison
polygamy ban	7/2006	Fischer, Kelly	Colorado City	sex with a minor	prison
polygamy ban	7/2006	Holm, Rodney Hans	Colorado City	sex with a minor	prison
polygamy ban	7/2006	Jessop, Vergel Bryce	Colorado City	child abuse	prison

Arkansas

draft	11/15/1917	Ellis, J.H.	Newport	draft protest	assault, jail
World War I	1918	Caughron, Benjamin Curl	Mena	armed resistance	electric chair
draft	3/28/1918	Oberlee, Frank	Clarksville	draft protest	tarred, feathered
World War I	6/1918	Adkisson, Bliss	Heber Springs	draft evasion	prison
World War I	6/1918	Adkisson, Hardy	Heber Springs	draft evasion	prison at hard labor
World War I	6/1918	Adkisson, Tom, Jr.	Heber Springs	draft evasion	prison at hard labor
World War I	6/1918	Adkisson, Tom, Sr.	Heber Springs	abetted draft evasion	prison
World War I	6/1918	Blakely, Jesse Jewel	Heber Springs	draft evasion	prison at hard labor
World War I	6/1918	Blakely, Jim	Heber Springs	draft evasion	prison at hard labor
World War I	6/1918	Blakely, Lum	Heber Springs	draft evasion	prison at hard labor
World War I	6/1918	Martin, Leo Douglas	Heber Springs	draft evasion	prison at hard labor
World War I	6/1918	Osbourne, Houston Earl	Heber Springs	protest	
World War I	6/1918	Penrod, John	Heber Springs	draft evasion	prison at hard labor
World War I	6/1918	Sweeten, Eli Jackson	Heber Springs	protest	
religious persecution	7/1918	Burleson, George	Heber Springs	contraband literature	charged
World War II	1940s	Johnson, Paul	Texarkana	opposed the draft	prison
segregation	1957	Bates, Daisy Lee Gatson	Little Rock	promoted integration	threats

California

Asian workers	1877	Kearney, Dennis	San Francisco	arson, assault	
labor organization ban	11/3/1877	Kearney, Dennis	San Francisco	public speech	arrest
free speech ban	4/1908	Goldman, Emma	San Francisco	conspiracy	banned

State/ Target of Act	Date	Name	Location	Act	Consequence
free speech ban	4/26/1908	Buwalda, William	San Francisco	attended a speech	court-martial, prison at hard labor
free speech ban	1/14/1909	Buwalda, William	San Francisco	unlawful assembly	jail
free speech ban	1/17/1909	Goldman, Emma	San Francisco	unlawful assembly	jail
free speech ban	1/17/1909	Reitman, Ben	San Francisco	unlawful assembly	jail
free speech ban	5/29/1912	Goldman, Emma	Oakland	conspiracy	banned
free speech ban	5/30/1913	Goldman, Emma	San Diego	conspiracy	arrest
labor exploitation	3/1914	Keller, Helen Adams	Sacramento	promoted unions	
police brutality	3/1914	Keller, Helen Adams	Sacramento	denunciation	
draft	12/17/1917	Ryland, Edwin P.	Hollywood	draft protest	fired
draft	5/1/1918	Han, George W.	Berkeley	draft protest	expelled from school
draft	5/24/1918	Brueger, Mary	Los Angeles	draft protest	fired
draft	6/26/1918	Levin, Rose	San Francisco	draft protest	denied a diploma
draft	7/11/1918	Varrelman, F. Alfred	San Francisco	draft protest	fired
labor organization ban	11/1924	Valdane, Robert	Los Angeles	distributed literature	prison, exile
labor exploitation	1934	Olsen, Jack	San Francisco	strike	jail
labor exploitation	1934	Olsen, Tillie Lerner	San Francisco	strike	jail
Japanese internment	5/30/1942	Korematsu, Fred Toyosaburo	San Leandro	defied curfew	
Japanese internment	12/5/1942	Tayama, Fred	Manzanar	uprising	beaten
World War II	1943	Shubin, John	California	conscientious objection	prison, beaten
World War II	1943	Weatherbee, Herbert	Monterey	draft resistance	life in prison
World War II	6/28/1943	Darrow, Gerald Pittman	California	draft evasion	prison
World War II	6/28/1943	Dolve, Philip Curtis	California	draft evasion	prison
World War II	6/28/1943	Scaff, Lloyd	California	draft evasion	prison
World War II	6/28/1943	Worley, Charles Vincent	California	draft protest	prison, tube-feeding
racism	1944	Chávez, César	Delano	sit-in	arrest
World War II	2/2/1945	Weber, Henry	Camp Roberts	refused assignment	threat of hanging, prison
House Committee on Un-American Activities	1947	Kelson, Perl	Hollywood	contempt of Congress	blacklist
House Committee on Un-American Activities	1947	Morley, Karen	Hollywood	contempt of Congress	blacklist
House Committee on Un-American Activities	1947	Parks, Larry	Hollywood	contempt of Congress	blacklist
House Committee on Un-American Activities	1948	Durr, Clifford	Hollywood	contempt of Congress	blacklist
House Committee on Un-American Activities	1948	Welles, Orson	Hollywood	contempt of Congress	blacklist, exile
House Committee on Un-American Activities	1948	White, Josh	Hollywood	contempt of Congress	blacklist
House Committee on Un-American Activities	1949	Adler, Larry	Hollywood	contempt of Congress	exile

State/ Target of Act	Date	Name	Location	Act	Consequence
House Committee on Un-American Activities	1949	Lee, Canada	Hollywood	contempt of Congress	blacklist
House Committee on Un-American Activities	1949	Robinson, Earl Hawley	Hollywood	contempt of Congress	blacklist
House Committee on Un-American Activities	1950s	Brecht, Bertolt	Hollywood	contempt of Congress	exile
House Committee on Un-American Activities	1950s	Butler, Hugo	Hollywood	contempt of Congress	blacklist
House Committee on Un-American Activities	1950s	Cobb, Lee J.	Hollywood	contempt of Congress	
House Committee on Un-American Activities	1950s	Comingore, Dorothy	Hollywood	contempt of Congress	ruin
House Committee on Un-American Activities	1950s	Crum, Bartley Cavanaugh	Hollywood	contempt of Congress	smeared, suicide
House Committee on Un-American Activities	1950s	Dassin, Jules	Hollywood	contempt of Congress	ruin
House Committee on Un-American Activities	1950s	Eisler, Hanns	Hollywood	contempt of Congress	blacklist, exile
House Committee on Un-American Activities	1950s	Garfield, John	Hollywood	contempt of Congress	
House Committee on Un-American Activities	1950s	Gordon, Bernard	Hollywood	contempt of Congress	
House Committee on Un-American Activities	1950s	Lawrence, Marc	Hollywood	contempt of Congress	
House Committee on Un-American Activities	1950s	Losey, Joseph	Hollywood	contempt of Congress	blacklist
House Committee on Un-American Activities	1950s	Ornitz, Samuel	Hollywood	contempt of Congress	prison, fine, blacklist
House Committee on Un-American Activities	1950s	Stander, Lionel Jay	Hollywood	whistled "The Internationale"	libel
House Committee on Un-American Activities	1950	Bessie, Alvah	Hollywood	contempt of Congress	prison, fine, blacklist, ruin
House Committee on Un-American Activities	1950	Biberman, Herbert J.	Hollywood	contempt of Congress	prison, fine, exile
House Committee on Un-American Activities	1950	Cole, Lester	Hollywood	contempt of Congress	prison, fine, exile
House Committee on Un-American Activities	1950	Dmytryk, Edward	Hollywood	contempt of Congress	prison
House Committee on Un-American Activities	1950	Fast, Howard	Hollywood	contempt of Congress	blacklist, prison
House Committee on Un-American Activities	1950	Hobart, Rose	Hollywood	contempt of Congress	blacklist
House Committee on Un-American Activities	1950	Holliday, Judy	Hollywood	contempt of Congress	blacklist
House Committee on Un-American Activities	1950	Lardner, Ring, Jr.	Hollywood	contempt of Congress	blacklist, prison, fine
House Committee on Un-American Activities	1950	Lawson, John Howard	Hollywood	contempt of Congress	prison, exile, blacklist, fine
House Committee on Un-American Activities	1950	Loeb, Philip	Hollywood	contempt of Congress	blacklist, suicide

State/ Target of Act	Date	Name	Location	Act	Consequence
House Committee on Un-American Activities	1950	Maltz, Albert	Hollywood	contempt of Congress	blacklist, prison, fine
House Committee on Un-American Activities	1950	Meredith, Burgess	Hollywood	contempt of Congress	blacklist
House Committee on Un-American Activities	1950	Morgan, Henry	Hollywood	contempt of Congress	blacklist
House Committee on Un-American Activities	1950	Mostel, Zero	Hollywood	contempt of Congress	blacklist
House Committee on Un-American Activities	1950	Parker, Dorothy	Hollywood	contempt of Congress	blacklist
House Committee on Un-American Activities	1950	Robeson, Paul	Hollywood	contempt of Congress	blacklist, exile
House Committee on Un-American Activities	1950	Scott, Adrian	Hollywood	contempt of Congress	prison, fine, blacklist
House Committee on Un-American Activities	1950	Scott, Hazel	Hollywood	contempt of Congress	censored
House Committee on Un-American Activities	1950	Shirer, William Lawrence	Hollywood	contempt of Congress	blacklist
House Committee on Un-American Activities	1950	Sondergaard, Gale	Hollywood	contempt of Congress	exile
House Committee on Un-American Activities	1951	Bernstein, Walter	Hollywood	contempt of Congress	blacklist
House Committee on Un-American Activities	1951	Blitzstein, Marc	Hollywood	contempt of Congress	blacklist, exile
House Committee on Un-American Activities	1951	Brand, Phoebe	Hollywood	contempt of Congress	blacklist
House Committee on Un-American Activities	1951	Carnovsky, Morris	Hollywood	contempt of Congress	blacklist
House Committee on Un-American Activities	1951	Da Silva, Howard	Hollywood	contempt of Congress	blacklist
House Committee on Un-American Activities	1951	Foreman, Carl	Hollywood	contempt of Congress	blacklist, exile
House Committee on Un-American Activities	1951	Grant, Lee	Hollywood	contempt of Congress	blacklist
House Committee on Un-American Activities	1951	Hammett, Dashiell	Hollywood	contempt of Congress	jail
House Committee on Un-American Activities	1951	Shaw, Irwin	Hollywood	contempt of Congress	blacklist, exile
House Committee on Un-American Activities	1951	Trumbo, Dalton	Hollywood	contempt of Congress	prison, fine, blacklist
House Committee on Un-American Activities	1952	Chaplin, Charles	Hollywood	contempt of Congress	visa denied
House Committee on Un-American Activities	1952	Gough, Lloyd	Hollywood	contempt of Congress	blacklist
House Committee on Un-American Activities	1952	Hellman, Lillian	Hollywood	contempt of Congress	blacklist, jail
House Committee on Un-American Activities	1952	Holliday, Judy	Hollywood	contempt of Congress	smeared
House Committee on Un-American Activities	1952	Hunt, Marsha	Hollywood	contempt of Congress	blacklist

State/ Target of Act	Date	Name	Location	Act	Consequence
House Committee on Un-American Activities	1952	Jaffe, Sam	Hollywood	contempt of Congress	blacklist
House Committee on Un-American Activities	1952	Revere, Anne	Hollywood	contempt of Congress	blacklist
House Committee on Un-American Activities	1952	Wanamaker, Sam	Hollywood	contempt of Congress	blacklist, exile
House Committee on Un-American Activities	1953	Copland, Aaron	Hollywood	contempt of Congress	blacklist, censored
House Committee on Un-American Activities	1953	Hughes, Langston	Hollywood	contempt of Congress	smeared
House Committee on Un-American Activities	1953	Palca, Alfred	Hollywood	contempt of Congress	blacklist, censored
House Committee on Un-American Activities	1953	Shaw, Artie	Hollywood	contempt of Congress	
House Committee on Un-American Activities	1954	Miller, Arthur	Hollywood	contempt of Congress	passport cancelled
House Committee on Un-American Activities	1956	Seeger, Pete	Hollywood	contempt of Congress	convicted, blacklist
free press ban	3/25/1957	Ferlinghetti, Lawrence	San Francisco	sold a poem, obscenity	arrest
free press ban	3/25/1957	Murao, Shigeyoshi	San Francisco	sold a poem, obscenity	arrest
free speech ban	10/4/1961	Bruce, Lenny	San Francisco	comic act	arrest
peyote ban	4/28/1962	Anderson, Leon B.	Needles	peyote worship	arrest
peyote ban	4/28/1962	Nez, Dan Dee	Needles	peyote worship	arrest
peyote ban	4/28/1962	Woody, John	Needles	peyote worship	arrest
nuclear power	5/27/1962	Baez, Joan	San Francisco	demonstration	jail
nuclear power	5/27/1962	Merton, Thomas	San Francisco	denunciation	
nuclear power	5/27/1962	Stallings, Harold	Sausalito	contempt of court	jail
nuclear power	7/4/1962	Zahn, Franklin	Los Angeles	contempt of court	jail
free speech ban	10/20/1962	Bruce, Lenny	West Hollywood	comic act	arrest
free speech ban	1963	Zappa, Frank	Los Angeles	obscenity	arrest
racism	3/7/1964	Savio, Mario	Berkeley	sit-in	arrest
racism	3/7/1964	Weinberg, Jack	Berkeley	sit-in	arrest
free speech ban	12/3/1964	Savio, Mario	Berkeley	voter registration	campus ban, jail
Vietnam War	1965	Ginsberg, Allen	Oakland	march	
labor organization ban	9/16/1965	Chávez, César	Delano	violated a court order	
labor organization ban	1966	Baez, Joan	Santa Monica	demonstration	
labor organization ban	3/1966	Chávez, César	Sacramento	march	
Indian displacement	12/25/1966	Baez, Joan	San Quentin	picket	
Vietnam War	1967	Beaumont, Florence	Los Angeles	self-immolation	
Vietnam War	10/1967	Baez, Joan	Oakland	sit-in	jail
Vietnam War	10/1967	Kepler, Roy	Oakland	obstructed a sidewalk	jail
Vietnam War	12/1967	Baez, Joan	Oakland	sit-in	jail

State/ Target of Act	Date	Name	Location	Act	Consequence
Vietnam War	12/1967	Kepler, Roy	Oakland	obstructed sidewalk	arrest
Vietnam War	5/22/1968	Amick, Dan	Fort Ord	distributed literature	prison at hard labor
Vietnam War	5/22/1968	Stolte, Ken	Fort Ord	distributed literature	prison at hard labor
Vietnam War	10/12/1968	Schnall, Susan	Oakland	information campaign	prison at hard labor
Vietnam War	7/15/1969	Harris, David	Fresno	draft evasion	prison
Indian displacement	11/14/1969	Anderson, Wallace Mad Bear	Alcatraz	trespass	
Indian displacement	11/14/1969	Banks, Dennis James	Alcatraz	trespass	
Indian displacement	11/14/1969	Bellecourt, Clyde	Alcatraz	trespass	
Indian displacement	11/14/1969	Bergen, Candace	Alcatraz	trespass	
Indian displacement	11/14/1969	Brando, Marlon	Alcatraz	trespass	
Indian displacement	11/14/1969	Drath, Marjorie	Alcatraz	trespass	
Indian displacement	11/14/1969	Drath, Phillip	Alcatraz	trespass	
Indian displacement	11/14/1969	Fonda, Jane	Alcatraz	trespass	
Indian displacement	11/14/1969	Oakes, Richard	Alcatraz	trespass	
Indian displacement	11/14/1969	Quinn, Anthony	Alcatraz	trespass	
Indian displacement	11/14/1969	Trudell, John	Alcatraz	trespass	
Indian displacement	11/14/1969	Trudell, Lou	Alcatraz	trespass	
nuclear power	1970s	Baez, Joan	Los Altos	tax resistance	
Vietnam War	1970s	Baez, Joan	Los Altos	tax resistance	
Vietnam War	5/10/1970	Winne, George, Jr.	San Diego	self-immolation	
labor organization ban	6/1970	Chávez, César	Delano	strike, boycott	
labor organization ban	12/10/1970	Baez, Joan	Salinas	abetted picket	
labor organization ban	12/10/1970	Chávez, César	Salinas	picket	jail, death threats
ROTC	5/9/1972	Fonda, Jane	Los Angeles	denounced military	
labor organization ban	8/1973	Chávez, César	Delano	picket, refused to leave cell	jail
labor organization ban	8/1973	Day, Dorothy	Delano	organizing	jail
veterans hospital inadequacy	1974	Kovic, Ronald L.	Los Angeles	fast, trespass	
labor organization ban	2/1975	Chávez, César	Delano	boycott	
gay persecution	1978	Feinstein, Diane	San Francisco	support	
gay persecution	1978	Fonda, Jane	San Francisco	support	
gay persecution	11/27/1978	Milk, Harvey	San Francisco	lawmaking	shot
gay persecution	11/27/1978	Moscone, George	San Francisco	lawmaking	shot
police brutality	1981	Hernandez, Crosby Wilfredo Orantes	Culver City	sought asylum	pistol-whipped
alien refugee abuse	1981–1990	Olivares, Luis	Los Angeles	abetted alien asylum	
labor organization ban	9/21/1983	Lopez, Rene	Fresno	voted in a union election	shot
AIDS neglect	1984	Corti, Jim	Los Angeles	bootleg drugs	
AIDS neglect	1984	Delaney, Martin	Sausalito	bootleg drugs	

State/ Target of Act	Date	Name	Location	Act	Consequence
AIDS neglect	1985	Brewer, Joe	San Francisco	bootleg drugs	
labor organization ban	1986	Chávez, César	Delano	boycott, fast	
labor organization ban	1988	Huerta, Dolores	San Francisco	picket	clubbed
labor organization ban	7/1988	Chávez, César	Delano	boycott, fast	
labor organization ban	7/1988	Goldberg, Whoopi	Delano	boycott, fast	
labor organization ban	7/1988	Jackson, Jesse Louis	Delano	boycott, fast	
labor organization ban	7/1988	Olmos, Edward James	Delano	boycott, fast	
labor organization ban	7/1988	Sheen, Martin	Delano	boycott, fast	
labor organization ban	7/1988	Simon, Carly	Delano	boycott, fast	
AIDS neglect	5/1989	Huseman, Clark	San Francisco	bootleg drugs	
AIDS neglect	5/1989	Levin, Alan	San Francisco	bootleg drugs	
AIDS neglect	5/1989	McGrath, Michael S.	San Francisco	bootleg drugs	
AIDS neglect	5/1989	Waites, Lawrence	San Francisco	bootleg drugs	
wilderness destruction	5/23/1990	Bari, Judith Beatrice	Oakland	recruitment	
wilderness destruction	5/23/1990	Littletree, Alicia	Albion	tree-sitting	pipe bomb
wilderness destruction	5/24/1990	Cherney, Darryl	Oakland	tree-sitting	injured by pipe bomb
labor organization ban	9/1990	Chávez, César	Los Angeles	violated a court order	arrest
wilderness destruction	1992	Littletree, Alicia	Albion	tree-sitting	death threat, assault
wilderness destruction	12/10/1997	Hill, Julia Butterfly	Arcata	tree-sitting	intimidation, violence
animal rights	1/2000	Ferdin, Pamelyn	Woodland Hills	contraband weapon	jail
nuclear power	10/8/2000	Sheen, Martin	Santa Barbara	trespass	arrest
nuclear power	10/8/2000	Turk, Lawrence	Santa Barbara	trespass	arrest
marijuana ban	8/2002	Epis, Bryan James	Butte County	grew marijuana	prison
female genital mutilation	1/2004	Bertrang, Todd Cameron	Santa Clarita	conspiracy	
female genital mutilation	1/2004	Faulkinbury, Robyn	Santa Clarita	conspiracy	
death penalty	2/4/2004	Carlstadt, Hal	San Quentin	obstructed traffic	arrest
death penalty	2/4/2004	Romney, Hugh	San Quentin	obstructed traffic	arrest
death penalty	2/4/2004	Sawyer, Paul	San Quentin	obstructed traffic	arrest
death penalty	2/4/2004	Vitale, Louis	San Quentin	obstructed traffic	arrest
death penalty	1/18/2005	Blair, Steven	San Quentin	protest	
death penalty	1/18/2005	Farrell, Mike	San Quentin	protest	
dress code	9/2005	Scott, Toni Kay	Napa	wore Tigger socks	detained
alien refugee abuse	1/2006	Velásquez, David	Maywood	alien asylum	
prison conditions	3/2006	Mahony, Roger	Los Angeles	protest	
alien refugee abuse	2007	Coskey, Laurie	San Diego	alien asylum	
alien refugee abuse	2007	Estrada, Richard	Los Angeles	alien asylum	
Iraq War	5/2007	Cantu, Ronn	Los Angeles	protest	
alien refugee abuse	5/9/2007	Salvatierra, Alexia	Los Angeles	alien rescue	
alien refugee abuse	5/9/2007	Swilley, Reginald	San Jose	alien rescue	
Iraq War	6/2007	Ergo, Mike	Walnut Creek	e-mail protest	

State/ Target of Act	Date	Name	Location	Act	Consequence
Iraq War	6/2007	Magruder, Jabar	Walnut Creek	anti-enlistment protest	
Iraq War	6/2007	O'Neill, Sean	Walnut Creek	anti-enlistment protest	

Colorado

labor organization ban	12/30/1905	Haywood, William Dudley	Denver	murder	tried
free speech ban	4/1910	Goldman, Emma	Denver	conspiracy	arrest
free speech ban	4/1910	Reitman, Ben L.	Denver	conspiracy	arrest
labor organization ban	1/4/1914	Jones, Mary "Mother"	Trinidad	abetted insurrection	deported
labor organization ban	1/12/1914	Jones, Mary "Mother"	Trinidad	abetted insurrection	deported
labor organization ban	3/1/1914	Jones, Mary "Mother"	Trinidad	abetted insurrection	deported
labor organization ban	3/22/1914	Jones, Mary "Mother"	Walsenburg	strike	jail
labor organization ban	4/20/1914	Jones, Mary "Mother"	Ludlow	fund-raising	arrest
draft	12/4/1917	Dutsch, Henry	Hugo	draft protest	tarred, feathered
World War I	1918	Salmon, Benjamin J.	Denver	denounced war	prison on bread, water; asylum
draft	2/13/1918	Kennan, Ellen	Denver	draft protest	fired
draft	2/13/1918	Nafe, Gertrude	Denver	draft protest	fired
World War II	1940	Houser, George M.	Norwood	refused to register	humiliation
World War II	1943	Kepler, Earl, Jr.	Denver	pacifism	prison
World War II	1943	Kepler, Roy	Denver	pacifism	prison
World War II	10/1943	Hewelcke, John	Denver	draft resistance	prison
peyote ban	1960s	Martinez, Lorenzo	Grand Junction	peyote worship	
Vietnam War	3/8/1968	Noye, Dale H.	Colorado Springs	refused an order	prison
nuclear power	6/14/1978	Ginsberg, Allen	Boulder	blocked a train	jail
nuclear power	6/14/1978	Orlovsky, Peter	Boulder	blocked a train	jail
nuclear power	1989	Tchozewski, Darrell Chet	Rocky Flats	demonstration	
nuclear power	8/6/2000	Kabat, Carl	Weld County	sabotage	arrest
gun carry ban	12/15/2001	Stanley, Richard Eugene	Denver	contraband weapon	confiscation
gun carry ban	9/2002	Stanley, Richard Eugene	Denver	contraband weapon	confiscation, jail, fine
nuclear power	10/6/2002	Gilbert, Carol	Greeley	sabotage	prison
nuclear power	10/6/2002	Hudson, Jackie	Greeley	sabotage	prison
nuclear power	10/6/2002	Platt, Ardeth	Greeley	sabotage	prison
nuclear power	4/9/2004	Kabat, Carl	New Raymer	sabotage	arrest
Indian displacement	10/9/2004	Morris, Glenn T.	Denver	protest	
Indian displacement	10/11/2004	Badhand, Yank	Denver	protest	
Indian displacement	10/11/2004	Dann, Carrie	Denver	protest	
Indian displacement	10/11/2004	Tinker, George Edward	Denver	protest	

State/ Target of Act	Date	Name	Location	Act	Consequence
Connecticut					
heresy	1657	Smith, Bathsheba	New London	defied Puritans	threat
heresy	1658	Dyer, Mary Barrett	New Haven	defied Puritans	exile
taxation	1676	Fox, Bathsheba Rogers	New London	tax resistance	
religious persecution	1676	Rogers, Bathsheba	New London	broke the Sabbath	prison, fine
taxation	1676	Rogers, Bathsheba	New London	tax resistance	fine, jail
religious persecution	1676	Rogers, Elizabeth Rowland	New London	broke the Sabbath	prison, fine
taxation	1676	Rogers, Elizabeth Rowland	New London	tax resistance	fine, jail
religious persecution	1676	Rogers, James	New London	broke the Sabbath	prison, fine
taxation	1676	Rogers, James	New London	tax resistance	fine, jail
nonattendance of church	1676	Rogers, John, Jr.	New London	avoided Puritan service	arrest
religious persecution	1676	Rogers, John, Sr.	New London	broke the Sabbath	prison, fine
taxation	1676	Rogers, John, Sr.	New London	tax resistance	fine, jail
religious persecution	1676	Rogers, Jonathan	New London	broke the Sabbath	prison, fine
taxation	1676	Rogers, Jonathan	New London	tax resistance	fine, jail
nonattendance of church	1676	Rogers, Mary Jordan	New London	avoided Puritan service	arrest
taxation	9/1677	Rogers, John, Sr.	New London	tax resistance	
religious persecution	4/14/1685	Beebe, Samuel, Jr.	New London	disrupted worship	lashed
religious persecution	4/14/1685	Prentis, Elizabeth Rogers	New London	disrupted worship	
religious persecution	4/14/1685	Rogers, James	New London	disrupted worship	lashed
religious persecution	4/14/1685	Rogers, John, Jr.	New London	disrupted worship	arrest
religious persecution	4/14/1685	Way, Joanna	New London	disrupted worship	lashed
religious persecution	ca. 1690s	Rogers, Mary Ransford	New London	assaulted an officer	arrest
religious persecution	3/1694	Rogers, John, Sr.	New London	blasphemy	fine
religious persecution	3/26/1712	Rogers, John, Sr.	New London	contempt of court	unheated, dark jail; fled
religious persecution	11/1712	Rogers, John, Jr.	New London	riot	jail
religious persecution	after 1718	Rogers, John, Sr.	New London	riot, resisted arrest	arrest
religious persecution	7/26/1725	Bolles, John	Groton	broke the Sabbath	prison, fine
religious persecution	7/26/1725	Bolles, Joseph	Groton	broke the Sabbath	prison, fine
religious persecution	7/26/1725	Culver, John	Groton	broke the Sabbath	prison, fine
religious persecution	7/26/1725	Culver, Sarah Hibbard	Groton	broke the Sabbath	prison, fine
religious persecution	7/26/1725	Davis, Andrew	Groton	broke the Sabbath	prison, fine
religious persecution	7/26/1725	Rogers, John, Jr.	Groton	broke the Sabbath	prison, fine
religious persecution	7/26/1725	Smith, James	Groton	broke the Sabbath	prison, fine
religious persecution	7/26/1725	Waterhouse, John	Groton	broke the Sabbath	prison, fine
religious persecution	2/1744	Buckley, Job	Saybrook	religious unorthodoxy	prison
taxation	10/15/1752	Backus, Elizabeth Tracy	Norwich	tax resistance	jail
taxation	10/15/1752	Backus, Samuel	Norwich	tax resistance	
colonial taxation	1765	Butler, Zebulon	Norwich	paramilitary	

State/ Target of Act	Date	Name	Location	Act	Consequence
colonial taxation	1765	Dyer, Eliphalet	Norwich	paramilitary recruiter	
colonial taxation	1765	Foote, Abigail	Colchester	backed paramilitary	
colonial taxation	1765	Griswold, Matthew	Lyme	paramilitary organizer	
colonial taxation	1765	Harvey, Benjamin	Norwich	paramilitary	
colonial taxation	8/1765	Huntington, Samuel	Norwich	burned tea	
colonial taxation	8/1765	Johnson, Stephen	Lyme	paramilitary organizer	
colonial taxation	8/1765	Perry, David	Killingly	burned tea	
colonial taxation	8/1765	Trumbull, Jonathan	Lebanon	paramilitary recruiter	
colonial taxation	8/1765	Sturges, Jonathan	Fairfield	paramilitary organizer	
colonial taxation	fall 1765	Huntington, Jedediah	Norwich	paramilitary	
colonial taxation	9/19/1765	Durkee, John	Windham	commander	
colonial taxation	9/19/1765	Ledlie, Hugh	New London	backed paramilitary	
colonial taxation	9/19/1765	Putnam, Israel	Pomfret	paramilitary leader	
Revolutionary War	1770s	Baker, John		refused to serve	
Revolutionary War	1770s	Benedict, Comfort	Danbury	refused to serve	prison
Revolutionary War	1770s	Gregory, Munson	Danbury	refused to serve	
Revolutionary War	1770s	Healy, Joseph	Litchfield	refused to serve	
Revolutionary War	1770s	Sparhawk, John	Danbury	refused to serve	jail
Revolutionary War	1770s	Whipple, Jonathan	Quakertown	refused to serve	threats, confiscation
Revolutionary War	1770s	Whipple, Noah	Quakertown	refused to serve	threats, confiscation
Revolutionary War	1770s	White, Ebenezer	Hebron	refused to serve	
colonial taxation	7/4/1774	Backus, Ebenezer	Windham	harassment	
colonial taxation	7/4/1774	Bissell, Hezekiah	Windham	intimidation	
colonial taxation	7/4/1774	Huntington, Simeon	Windham	harassment	
colonial taxation	7/4/1774	Larrabee, Timothy	Windham	intimidation	
colonial taxation	7/4/1774	Lathrop, Benjamin	Windham	intimidation	
colonial taxation	7/4/1774	Warren, Nathaniel	Windham	intimidation	
slave recapture	1784	Cowles, Polly Gleason	Farmington	ran a safehouse	
slave recapture	1784	Cowles, Solomon	Farmington	ran a safehouse	
slave education ban	1831	Crandall, Prudence	Canterbury	educated slaves	arson, jail
slave recapture	1847	Benson, George W.	Brooklyn	conspiracy to rescue	
slave recapture	1847	Sojourner Truth	Brooklyn	conspiracy	
slave recapture	1852	Gillette, Francis	Bloomfield	slave rescue, transport	
taxation	3/1873	Smith, Abigail Hadassah	Glastonbury	tax resistance	
voter intimidation	3/1873	Smith, Abigail Hadassah	Glastonbury	voter registration	confiscation
taxation	3/1873	Smith, Julia Evelina	Glastonbury	tax resistance	

State/ Target of Act	Date	Name	Location	Act	Consequence
voter intimidation	3/1873	Smith, Julia Evelina	Glastonbury	voter registration	confiscation
taxation	11/5/1873	Smith, Abigail Hadassah	Glastonbury	tax resistance	
taxation	11/5/1873	Smith, Julia Evelina	Glastonbury	tax resistance	
free speech ban	5/14/1909	Goldman, Emma	New Haven	conspiracy	banned
World War I	1918	Lehane, Cornelius	Bridgeport	conscientious objection	prison
draft	1/5/1918	Von Hoegen, Maximilian	Hartford	draft protest	assault
World War II	1943	DiGia, Ralph	Danbury	refused to register	prison
World War II	1943	Murphy, Stanley Thomas	Danbury	conscientious objection	prison, tube-feeding, asylum
World War II	1943	Taylor, Louis	Danbury	conscientious objection	prison, tube-feeding, asylum
World War II	4/1943	Andrews, Bennett W.	Danbury	pacifism	prison
segregation	1960	Motley, Constance Baker	New Haven	abetted sit-ins	
Vietnam War	3/20/1965	Mitchell, David Henry, III	New Canaan	draft evasion	prison, fine
Comstock Act	6/7/1965	Buxton, Charles Lee	Hartford	birth control information	jail, fine
free speech ban	6/7/1965	Griswold, Estelle Trebert	Hartford	birth control information	jail, fine
draft	10/16/1967	Coffin, William Sloane, Jr.	New Haven	conspiracy	charged
draft	10/16/1967	Ferber, Michael	New Haven	conspiracy	charged
draft	10/16/1967	Goodman, Mitchell	New Haven	conspiracy	charged
draft	10/16/1967	Raskin, Marcus	New Haven	conspiracy	charged
draft	10/16/1967	Spock, Benjamin	New Haven	conspiracy	charged
draft	10/16/1967	Thomas, Norman	New Haven	conspiracy	charged
Vietnam War	1968	Thomas, Norman	New Haven	protest, conspiracy	
Vietnam War	1/5/1968	Coffin, William Sloane, Jr.	New Haven	conspiracy	prison
Vietnam War	1/5/1968	Ferber, Michael	New Haven	conspiracy	prison
Vietnam War	1/5/1968	Goodman, Mitchell	New Haven	conspiracy	arrest
Vietnam War	1/5/1968	Raskin, Marcus	New Haven	conspiracy	arrest
Vietnam War	1/5/1968	Spock, Benjamin	New Haven	conspiracy	
U.S. interference in Nicaragua	1981	Coffin, William Sloane, Jr.	New Haven	protest, sanctuary	
Iraq War	2005	Lynd, Staughton	New Haven	sued Pentagon	

Cuba

Guantánamo prison	2007	Zewawai, Zohra	Guantánamo	protest	

Delaware

slave recapture	1755	Corbet, Daniel	Smyrna	harbored slaves	
slave recapture	1755	Corbet, Mary Brinton	Smyrna	harbored slaves	
slave recapture	1840s	Alston, John	Middletown	harbored slaves	

State/ Target of Act	Date	Name	Location	Act	Consequence
slave recapture	1840s–1860s	Baylis, William	Wilmington	sea transport	
slave recapture	1848	Garrett, Rachel Mendenhall	Wilmington	slave disguise, rescue	
slave recapture	1848	Garrett, Thomas	Wilmington	slave relay	lawsuit, wanted criminal
slave recapture	1850s–1860s	Fuller, Sam	Middletown	slave smuggling	

Florida

State/ Target of Act	Date	Name	Location	Act	Consequence
slave recapture	1740s	Nicholls, Edward	Prospect Bluff	harbored slaves	
slave recapture	6/23/1844	Walker, Jonathan	Pensacola	sea rescue	solitary cell, confiscation, fine, branded
slave education ban	1863	Merrick, Chloe	Fernandina	educated slaves, ran an orphanage and depot	
segregation	1961	Coffin, William Sloane, Jr.	St. Augustine	segregation protest	arrest
segregation	6/11/1964	King, Martin Luther, Jr.	St. Augustine	integrated restaurant	arrest
segregation	6/11/1964	Young, Andrew Jackson, Jr.	St. Augustine	integrated restaurant	arrest
racism	7/11/1964	King, Martin Luther, Jr.	St. Augustine	protest	
free speech ban	11/15/1969	Joplin, Janis	Tampa	obscenity	arrest
abortion	1985	Andrews, Joan	Broward County	destroyed property	prison
Indian grave robbery	1985	Murphy, Sheridan	Tampa	protest	
AIDS neglect	5/1989	Ellis, Paul	Miami	bootleg drugs	
free speech ban	3/1994	Diana, Mike	Largo	obscenity	arrest
Indian grave robbery	10/30/1999	Beaulieu, Ruby	New Port Richey	protest	
rainforest pillaging	5/17/2004	Anderson, Scott	Miami	boarded a vessel	prison
rainforest pillaging	5/17/2004	Hosta, Hillary	Miami	boarded a vessel	prison
rainforest pillaging	5/17/2004	Paul, Scott	Miami	boarded a vessel	prison

Georgia

State/ Target of Act	Date	Name	Location	Act	Consequence
colonial taxation	1765	Cuyler, Jane Latouche	Savannah	paramilitary host	
colonial taxation	11/4/1765	Bryan, Jonathan	Savannah	paramilitary	
colonial taxation	11/4/1765	Bulloch, Archibald	Savannah	backed paramilitary	
colonial taxation	11/4/1765	Houstoun, John	Savannah	paramilitary organizer	
colonial taxation	11/4/1765	Jones, Noble Wimberley	Savannah	backed paramilitary	
colonial taxation	11/4/1765	MacHenry, James	Savannah	paramilitary host	
colonial taxation	11/4/1765	Walton, George	Savannah	backed paramilitary	
colonial taxation	9/12/1769	Bryan, Jonathan	Savannah	boycott on goods	
Revolutionary War	1770s	Zubly, John Joachim	Savannah	refused to serve	

State/ Target of Act	Date	Name	Location	Act	Consequence
colonial taxation	7/27/1774	Telfair, Edward	Savannah	condemned port bill	
colonial taxation	7/27/1774	Tondee, Peter	Savannah	condemned port bill	
colonial taxation	5/11/1775	Telfair, Edward	Savannah	raid	
colonial taxation	5/11/1775	Tondee, Peter	Savannah	raid	
slave education ban	1818–1844	Fromantin, Jean Julien	Savannah	educated slaves	
slave recapture	1834–1849	Kemble, Fanny	St. Simons	conspiracy	
slave education ban	1835–1865	Beasley, Mary	Savannah	educated slaves	surveillance
slave education ban	1835–1865	Deveaux, Catheriner	Savannah	educated slaves	surveillance
slave education ban	1835–1865	Deveaux, Jane	Savannah	educated slaves	surveillance
slave education ban	1835–1865	Woodhouse, Mary	Savannah	educated slaves	
slave education ban	1838	Butler, Fanny Kemble	St. Simons	educated slaves	divorce, lost custody of children
slave education ban	1840s	Porter, James	Savannah	educated slaves	police raid
slave recapture	3/31/1845	Paine, Lewis W.	Milledgeville	aided flight	prison at hard labor, confiscation
slave education ban	1849	Jane Frances	Savannah	educated slaves	
slave education ban	1850s	Woodhouse, Mary Jane	Savannah	educated slaves	
slave education ban	ca. 1860	Purdy, Edwin	Augusta	educated slaves	jail, fine, lashed
slave education ban	1860s	Simms, James Meriles	Savannah	educated slaves	lashed, fine
black rights	1915	Simmons, William Joseph	Stone Mountain	paramilitary organizer	
World War I	4/5/1917	Hennacy, Ammon	Atlanta	draft evasion	prison
World War I	1918	Baldwin, Roger Nash	Atlanta	refused physical	prison
World War I	11/1918	Firestone, Julius	Camp Hancock	conscientious objection	tarred, feathered
segregation	10/19/1960	Edelman, Marian Wright	Atlanta	sit-in	arrest
segregation	10/19/1960	King, Martin Luther, Jr.	Atlanta	restaurant sit-in	prison
racism	11/1961	Reagon, Bernice Johnson	Albany	Freedom Rider	jail
racism	12/15/1961	Abernathy, Ralph David	Albany	abetted Freedom Rides	jail
voter intimidation	12/15/1961	Abernathy, Ralph David	Albany	obstructed sidewalk	jail
racism	12/15/1961	King, Martin Luther, Jr.	Albany	abetted Freedom Rides	jail
segregation	7/4/1963	Perdew, John	Americus	integrated a restaurant	mob violence
segregation	8/8/1963	Allen, Ralph W., III	Americus	protest march	arrest
voter intimidation	8/8/1963	Allen, Ralph W., III	Albany	protest march, assault	jail, prison
voter intimidation	8/8/1963	Durham, Sallie Mae	Americus	assaulted an officer	jail
segregation	8/8/1963	Harris, Don	Americus	protest march	arrest
voter intimidation	8/8/1963	Harris, Don	Albany	voter registration	jail
voter intimidation	8/8/1963	McDaniel, Thomas	Americus	assaulted an officer	jail

State/ Target of Act	Date	Name	Location	Act	Consequence
segregation	8/8/1963	Perdew, John	Americus	protest march	arrest
voter intimidation	8/8/1963	Perdew, John	Albany	voter registration	jail
free speech ban	11/9/1963	Dellinger, David T.	Griffin	war protest	
free speech ban	11/9/1963	Lyttle, Bradford	Griffin	war protest	
free speech ban	11/19/1963	Dellinger, David T.	Macon	war protest	arrest
free speech ban	11/19/1963	Lyttle, Bradford	Macon	war protest	arrest
war	12/23/1963	Deming, Barbara	Albany	protest, fast	jail
war	12/23/1963	Havice, Harriet Katherine	Albany	protest, fast	jail
war	12/23/1963	Robinson, Ray	Albany	protest, fast	jail
free speech ban	2/1964	Dellinger, David T.	Albany	war protest	arrest
free speech ban	2/1964	Lyttle, Bradford	Albany	war protest	arrest
free speech ban	2/1964	Muste, Abraham Johannes	Albany	war protest	
racism	3/1970	Day, Dorothy	Americus	protest	drive-by shooting
racism	3/1970	Morgan, Elizabeth	Americus	protest	drive-by shooting
School of the Americas	8/1990	Bourgeois, Roy	Fort Benning	trespass	prison
School of the Americas	1994	Bourgeois, Roy	Fort Benning	trespass	prison
School of the Americas	1995	Bourgeois, Roy	Fort Benning	trespass	prison
School of the Americas	9/1997	Bichsel, Bill	Fort Benning	trespass	prison
School of the Americas	9/1997	Cardell, Nicholas	Fort Benning	trespass	prison
School of the Americas	9/1997	Eilerman, Marge	Fort Benning	trespass	prison
School of the Americas	9/1997	Foster, Sam	Fort Benning	trespass	arrest
School of the Americas	9/1997	Kinane, Ed	Fort Benning	trespass	prison
School of the Americas	9/1997	Rumpf, Kathleen	Fort Benning	trespass	prison, fine
School of the Americas	9/1997	Trotochaud, Mary	Fort Benning	trespass	prison
School of the Americas	11/1997	Bichsel, Bill	Fort Benning	trespass	prison, fine
School of the Americas	11/1997	Bourgeois, Roy	Fort Benning	trespass	prison, fine
School of the Americas	11/1997	Cardell, Nicholas	Fort Benning	trespass	prison, fine
School of the Americas	11/1997	Early, Mary	Fort Benning	trespass	prison, fine
School of the Americas	11/1997	Eilerman, Marge	Fort Benning	trespass	prison, fine
School of the Americas	11/1997	Flanigan, Mary Kay	Fort Benning	trespass	prison, fine
School of the Americas	11/1997	Herman, Ann	Fort Benning	trespass	prison, fine
School of the Americas	11/1997	Inman, Paddy	Fort Benning	trespass	prison, fine
School of the Americas	11/1997	Jones, Christopher	Fort Benning	trespass	prison, fine
School of the Americas	11/1997	Kennon, Ken	Fort Benning	trespass	prison, fine
School of the Americas	11/1997	Kinane, Ed	Fort Benning	trespass	prison, fine
School of the Americas	11/1997	Lawton, Dwight	Fort Benning	trespass	prison, fine
School of the Americas	11/1997	Lucey, Rita	Fort Benning	trespass	prison, fine
School of the Americas	11/1997	McNulty, Bill	Fort Benning	trespass	prison, fine
School of the Americas	11/1997	Rice, Megan	Fort Benning	trespass	prison, fine
School of the Americas	11/1997	Richardson, Carol	Fort Benning	trespass	prison, fine
School of the Americas	11/1997	Rumpf, Kathleen	Fort Benning	trespass	prison, fine
School of the Americas	11/1997	Sage, Dan	Fort Benning	trespass	prison, fine
School of the Americas	11/1997	Sage, Doris	Fort Benning	trespass	prison, fine

State/ Target of Act	Date	Name	Location	Act	Consequence
School of the Americas	11/1997	Serraglio, Randy	Fort Benning	trespass	prison, fine
School of the Americas	11/1997	Steinhagen, Rita	Fort Benning	trespass	prison, fine
School of the Americas	11/1997	Streb, Richard	Fort Benning	trespass	prison, fine
School of the Americas	11/1997	Tiffany, Ann	Fort Benning	trespass	prison, fine
School of the Americas	11/1997	Trotochaud, Mary	Fort Benning	trespass	prison, fine
School of the Americas	11/1997	Williams, Judith	Fort Benning	trespass	prison, fine
School of the Americas	11/1997	Woodring, Ruthy	Fort Benning	trespass	prison, fine
School of the Americas	11/21/2000	Sheen, Martin	Fort Benning	sprinkled blood	
female genital mutilation	3/29/2001	Adem, Khalid	Gwinnett County	maimed his child	prison
School of the Americas	11/2001	Jacobs, Lana	Fort Benning	trespass	arrest
School of the Americas	11/2001	Jacobs, Steve	Fort Benning	trespass	arrest
School of the Americas	11/21/2005	Bell, Buddy	Fort Benning	trespass	arrest
School of the Americas	11/21/2005	Brancel, Fred	Fort Benning	trespass	arrest
School of the Americas	11/21/2005	Bryant-Gainer, Margaret	Fort Benning	trespass	arrest
School of the Americas	11/21/2005	Busch-Nema, Tina	Fort Benning	trespass	arrest
School of the Americas	11/21/2005	Call, Robert St. Clair	Fort Benning	trespass	arrest
School of the Americas	11/21/2005	Carney, Charles	Fort Benning	trespass	arrest
School of the Americas	11/21/2005	Clemens, Stephen	Fort Benning	trespass	arrest
School of the Americas	11/21/2005	Coleman, Don	Fort Benning	trespass	arrest
School of the Americas	11/21/2005	Cowan, Joanne, accountant	Fort Benning	trespass	arrest
School of the Americas	11/21/2005	Dempsky, Scott	Fort Benning	trespass	arrest
School of the Americas	11/21/2005	DeRaymond, Joe	Fort Benning	trespass	arrest
School of the Americas	11/21/2005	Gayman, Michael	Fort Benning	trespass	arrest
School of the Americas	11/21/2005	Harper, Sarah	Fort Benning	trespass	arrest
School of the Americas	11/21/2005	Hosking, Jan	Fort Benning	trespass	arrest
School of the Americas	11/21/2005	LaForge, John	Fort Benning	trespass	arrest
School of the Americas	11/21/2005	Lentsch, Mary Dennis	Fort Benning	trespass	arrest
School of the Americas	11/21/2005	Lewinson, Ed	Fort Benning	trespass	prison
School of the Americas	11/21/2005	Lloyd, Robin	Fort Benning	trespass	arrest
School of the Americas	11/21/2005	Mashburn, Linda	Fort Benning	trespass	arrest
School of the Americas	11/21/2005	Parker, Dorothy	Fort Benning	trespass	arrest
School of the Americas	11/21/2005	Phares, Gail	Fort Benning	trespass	arrest
School of the Americas	11/21/2005	Ruland, Judith	Fort Benning	trespass	arrest
School of the Americas	11/21/2005	Schwaller, Delmar	Fort Benning	trespass	arrest
School of the Americas	11/21/2005	Smith, Donte	Fort Benning	trespass	arrest
School of the Americas	11/21/2005	Smith, Edward	Fort Benning	trespass	arrest
School of the Americas	11/21/2005	Sommers, Cheryl	Fort Benning	trespass	arrest
School of the Americas	11/21/2005	Sylvester, David	Fort Benning	trespass	arrest
School of the Americas	11/21/2005	Treska, Priscilla	Fort Benning	trespass	arrest
School of the Americas	11/21/2005	Vitale, Louis	Fort Benning	trespass	prison
School of the Americas	11/21/2005	Walters, Jamie	Fort Benning	trespass	arrest
School of the Americas	11/21/2005	Woolever, Frank	Fort Benning	trespass	arrest

State/ Target of Act	Date	Name	Location	Act	Consequence
School of the Americas	11/21/2005	Zawada, Jerome	Fort Benning	trespass	arrest
School of the Americas	11/19/2006	Bourgeois, Roy	Fort Benning	trespass	prison
School of the Americas	11/19/2006	Bryant-Gainer, Margaret	Fort Benning	die-in	arrest
School of the Americas	11/19/2006	Busch-Nema, Tina	Fort Benning	die-in	arrest
School of the Americas	11/19/2006	Coleman, Don	Fort Benning	die-in	arrest
School of the Americas	11/19/2006	Fillenwarth, Valerie	Fort Benning	die-in	arrest
School of the Americas	11/19/2006	Gates, Philip	Fort Benning	die-in	arrest
School of the Americas	11/19/2006	Gerard, Alice	Fort Benning	die-in	arrest
School of the Americas	11/19/2006	Harris, Joshua	Fort Benning	die-in	arrest
School of the Americas	11/19/2006	Helman, Melissa	Fort Benning	die-in	arrest
School of the Americas	11/19/2006	Leforce, Martina	Fort Benning	die-in	arrest
School of the Americas	11/19/2006	Oldfield, Julienne	Fort Benning	die-in	arrest
School of the Americas	11/19/2006	Ray, Katherine Whitney	Fort Benning	die-in	arrest
School of the Americas	11/19/2006	Salmon, Sheila	Fort Benning	die-in	arrest
School of the Americas	11/19/2006	Slater, Nathan	Fort Benning	die-in	arrest
School of the Americas	11/19/2006	Vosburg-Casey, Mike	Fort Benning	die-in	arrest
School of the Americas	11/19/2006	Ward, Graymon	Fort Benning	die-in	arrest
School of the Americas	11/19/2006	Webster, Cathy	Fort Benning	die-in	arrest

Germany

State/ Target of Act	Date	Name	Location	Act	Consequence
Vietnam War	1965	Davis, Angela	Frankfurt	picket	lost job

Hawaii

State/ Target of Act	Date	Name	Location	Act	Consequence
Kaho'Olawe destruction	8/30/1975	DeFries, Emma	Kaho'Olawe	conspiracy	
Kaho'Olawe destruction	8/30/1975	Hanchett, Barbara	Kaho'Olawe	conspiracy	
Kaho'Olawe destruction	8/30/1975	Kanakaole, Edith	Kaho'Olawe	conspiracy	
Kaho'Olawe destruction	8/30/1975	Kapuni, Lani	Kaho'Olawe	conspiracy	
Kaho'Olawe destruction	8/30/1975	Ku, Clara	Kaho'Olawe	trespass	
Kaho'Olawe destruction	8/30/1975	Lee, Mary	Kaho'Olawe	conspiracy	
Kaho'Olawe destruction	8/30/1975	Maxwell, Charles Kauluwehi, Sr.	Kaho'Olawe	trespass	
Kaho'Olawe destruction	8/30/1975	Wainui, Rose	Kaho'Olawe	conspiracy	
Kaho'Olawe destruction	1/6/1976	Aluli, Kimo	Kaho'Olawe	trespass	
Kaho'Olawe destruction	1/6/1976	Aluli, Noa Emmett	Kaho'Olawe	trespass	arrest
Kaho'Olawe destruction	1/6/1976	Helm, George Jarrett, Jr.	Kaho'Olawe	trespass	
Kaho'Olawe destruction	1/6/1976	Kealoha, Sam	Kaho'Olawe	trespass	fine, prison
Kaho'Olawe destruction	1/6/1976	Lind, Ian	Kaho'Olawe	trespass	
Kaho'Olawe destruction	1/6/1976	Maxwell, Charles Kauluwehi, Sr.	Kaho'Olawe	trespass	
Kaho'Olawe destruction	1/6/1976	Miles, Ellen	Kaho'Olawe	trespass	
Kaho'Olawe destruction	1/6/1976	Mitchell, Kimo	Kaho'Olawe	trespass	
Kaho'Olawe destruction	1/6/1976	Morse, Stephen	Kaho'Olawe	trespass	
Kaho'Olawe destruction	1/6/1976	Mowat, Karl	Kaho'Olawe	trespass	fine, prison

State/ Target of Act	Date	Name	Location	Act	Consequence
Kaho'Olawe destruction	1/6/1976	Prejean, Gail Kawaipuna	Kaho'Olawe	trespass	
Kaho'Olawe destruction	1/6/1976	Ritte, Walter, Jr.	Kaho'Olawe	trespass	fine, prison
Kaho'Olawe destruction	1/6/1976	Sawyer, Richard	Kaho'Olawe	trespass	fine, prison
Kaho'Olawe destruction	1/6/1976	Villalba, Karla	Kaho'Olawe	trespass	
Kaho'Olawe destruction	2/2/1977	Helm, George Jarrett, Jr.	Kaho'Olawe	trespass	
Kaho'Olawe destruction	2/2/1977	Ka'uhane, Francis	Kaho'Olawe	trespass	
Kaho'Olawe destruction	2/2/1977	Ritte, Walter, Jr.	Kaho'Olawe	trespass	
Kaho'Olawe destruction	2/2/1977	Sawyer, Richard	Kaho'Olawe	trespass	
Kaho'Olawe destruction	2/2/1977	Warrington, Charles	Kaho'Olawe	trespass	
Kaho'Olawe destruction	3/7/1977	Helm, George Jarrett, Jr.	Kaho'Olawe	trespass	drowned
Kaho'Olawe destruction	3/7/1977	Mitchell, Billy	Kaho'Olawe	trespass	
Kaho'Olawe destruction	3/7/1977	Mitchell, Kimo	Kaho'Olawe	trespass	drowned
animal rights	5/29/1977	LeVasseur, Kenneth W.	Honolulu	freed animals	
animal rights	5/29/1977	Sipman, Steve	Honolulu	freed animals	
animal rights	1982	Cate, Dexter	Kaho'Olawe	trespass	
animal rights	1982	Leaman, Denver	Kaho'Olawe	trespass	
Kaho'Olawe destruction	4/16/1982	Mitchell, Harry Kunihi	Kaho'Olawe	trespass	
Kaho'Olawe destruction	1990	Saiki, Patricia Fukuda	Kaho'Olawe	protest	
Kaho'Olawe destruction	1995	Maxwell, Charles Kauluwehi, Sr.	Kaho'Olawe	protest	
Iraq War	1/2006	Vadim, Vanessa	Honolulu	refused deployment	demotion
Iraq War	6/22/2006	Watada, Ehren	Honolulu	refused deployment	charged

Illinois

slavery	1800s	Stewart, Peter	Downer's Grove	protest	
slave recapture	1830–1863	Wright, Samuel Guild	Peoria	conspiracy	
slave recapture	1830s	Hickok, Polly Butler	Homer	slave relay	
slave recapture	1830s	Hickok, William Alonzo	Homer	slave relay	
slave recapture	1830s	Hossack, John	Ottawa	slave rescue	
slavery	1830s	Lind, Sylvester	Lake Forest	protest	
slave recapture	1830s	McWhorter, Francis "Free Frank"	New Philadelphia	slave rescue	
slavery	1830s	Weldon, Bridget Mead	Plainfield	protest	
slavery	1830s	Weldon, John	Plainfield	protest	
slavery	1830s	Wheeler, James Taylor	Kane County	protest	
slavery	11/1837	Lovejoy, Elijah Parish	Alton	propaganda	shot
slavery	1840s	Graue, Frederick	Fullersburg	protest	
slave recapture	1840s	Hickok, James Butler "Wild Bill"	Homer	slave relay	
slavery	1840s	Wheeler, Jerusha A. Young	Kane County	protest	
slave recapture	1840s– 1850s	Burroughs, George L.	Cairo	slave relay	

State/ Target of Act	Date	Name	Location	Act	Consequence
polygamy ban	6/27/1844	Smith, Hyrum	Carthage	plural marriage	assassinated
polygamy ban	6/27/1844	Smith, Joseph, Jr.	Carthage	plural marriage	assassinated
slave recapture	1846	Dyer, Charles Volney	Chicago	slave rescue	knife fight
slave recapture	1850s–1860s	Pinkerton, Allan	Chicago	slave transport	
slave recapture	1850s–1860s	Pinkerton, Joan Carfrae	Chicago	slave transport	
Fugitive Slave Law of 1850	1853	Greenebaum, Michael G.	Chicago	protest	
slave recapture	1853	Greenebaum, Michael G.	Chicago	jailbreak	
slavery	1853	Greenebaum, Sarah Spiegel	Chicago	protest	
Fugitive Slave Law of 1850	1853	Kayer, Leopold	Chicago	protest	
slave recapture	1853	Kayer, Leopold	Chicago	jailbreak	
Fugitive Slave Law of 1850	1853	Loeb, Adolph	Chicago	protest	
slave recapture	1853	Loeb, Adolph	Chicago	jailbreak	
Fugitive Slave Law of 1850	1853	Rosenthal, Julius	Chicago	protest	
slave recapture	1853	Rosenthal, Julius	Chicago	jailbreak	
Fugitive Slave Law of 1850	1853	Schneider, George	Chicago	protest	
slave recapture	1853	Schneider, George	Chicago	jailbreak	
slave recapture	1/24/1859	Wagoner, Henry O.	Chicago	slave rescue	
labor exploitation	5/4/1886	Engel, George	Chicago	strike	hanged
labor exploitation	5/4/1886	Fielden, Samuel	Chicago	factory strike	prison
labor exploitation	5/4/1886	Fischer, Adolph	Chicago	promoted unions	hanged
labor exploitation	5/4/1886	Lingg, Louis	Chicago	factory strike	prison
labor exploitation	5/4/1886	Neebe, Oscar William	Chicago	factory strike	prison
labor exploitation	5/4/1886	Parsons, Albert Richard	Chicago	promoted unions	hanged
labor exploitation	5/4/1886	Parsons, Lucy Gonzalez	Chicago	factory strike	
labor exploitation	5/4/1886	Schwab, Michael	Chicago	factory strike	prison
labor exploitation	5/4/1886	Spies, August Vincent Theodore	Chicago	distributed pamphlets	hanged
Pullman Palace Car Company	May–August 1894	Curtis, Jennie	Chicago	protest	
Pullman Palace Car Company	May–August 1894	Debs, Eugene Victor	Chicago	contempt of court	jail
Pullman Palace Car Company	May–August 1894	Howard, George W.	Chicago	contempt of court	jail
Pullman Palace Car Company	May–August 1894	Jones, Mary "Mother"	Chicago	propaganda	
Pullman Palace Car Company	May–August 1894	Keliher, Sylvester	Chicago	contempt of court	jail
Pullman Palace Car Company	May–August 1894	Rogers, Lewis W.	Chicago	contempt of court	jail
alcohol sale and consumption	1897	Kepley, Ada Harriet Miser	Effingham	destroyed property	fine, beating
Comstock Act	1902	Craddock, Ida C.	Chicago	birth control information	suicide

State/ Target of Act	Date	Name	Location	Act	Consequence
free speech ban	3/1908	Goldman, Emma	Chicago	conspiracy	fine
free speech ban	2/1910	Goldman, Emma	Springfield	conspiracy	intimidation
free speech ban	3/5/1911	Goldman, Emma	Staunton	conspiracy	intimidation
World War I	8/1914	Addams, Jane	Chicago	sheltered draft evaders	
labor exploitation	1917	Flynn, Elizabeth Gurley	Chicago	defense of Industrial Workers of the World	arrest
World War I	9/1917	Haywood, William Dudley	Chicago	opposed war	arrest
World War I	1918	Skedine, Van	Bridewell	conscientious objection	prison
draft	2/12/1918	Metzen, John L.	Staunton	draft protest	assault, tarred
draft	3/23/1918	Kovalsky, John	Christopher	draft protest	tarred, feathered
draft	3/25/1918	Bergen, Frances	Benton	draft protest	banished
World War I	8/30/1918	Baldazzi, Giovanni	Chicago	draft evasion	prison
draft	8/31/1918	Oberden, Severino	Staunton	draft protest	assault, tarred
World War I	10/15/1918	Lunde, Erling H.	Chicago	conscientious objection	prison
draft	11/8/1918	Lunde, Theo H.	Chicago	draft protest	confiscation
labor organization ban	1921	Day, Dorothy	Chicago	organizing	charged with prostitution
labor exploitation	1921	Haywood, William Dudley	Chicago	promoted unions	fled on bail
labor exploitation	7/1925	Randolph, Asa Philip	Chicago	promoted unions	
draft	5/24/1929	Schwimmer, Rosika	Chicago	protest	citizenship revoked
labor exploitation	1937	Seidman, Joel	Chicago	propaganda	
World War II	1941	Doty, Hiram	Chicago	refused to serve	prison
draft	1942	Muste, Abraham Johannes,	Chicago	supported draft evasion	
racism	1943	Randolph, Asa Philip	Chicago	rally	
World War II	9/28/1943	Kuenning, William Houston	Du Page	war protest	prison
World War II	1945	Haney, George L.	Chicago	refused to register	prison
labor organization ban	1946	Alinsky, Saul David	Chicago	promoted unions	prison
free speech ban	12/4/1962	Bruce, Lenny	Chicago	comic act	jail
free speech ban	12/4/1962	Carlin, George	Chicago	comic act	jail
racism	1963	Gregory, Dick	Chicago	promoted integration	
free speech ban	6/4/1963	Hefner, Hugh	Chicago	obscenity	arrest
racism	1/22/1966	Abernathy, Ralph David	Chicago	rally	threats
racism	1/22/1966	King, Martin Luther, Jr.	Chicago	rally	threats
racism	8/5/1966	Abernathy, Ralph David	Chicago	rally	stoned
racism	8/5/1966	King, Martin Luther, Jr.	Chicago	rally	
Vietnam War	12/1967	Mott, Jeremy	Chicago	burned draft card	prison
Vietnam War	8/25/1968	Davis, Renard Cordon	Chicago	conspiracy, riot	arrest
Vietnam War	8/25/1968	Dellinger, David T.	Chicago	conspiracy, riot	arrest

State/ Target of Act	Date	Name	Location	Act	Consequence
Vietnam War	8/25/1968	Hayden, Thomas Emmett	Chicago	conspiracy, riot	arrest
Vietnam War	8/25/1968	Hoffman, Abbott Howard	Chicago	conspiracy, riot	arrest
Vietnam War	8/25/1968	Rubin, Jerry	Chicago	conspiracy, riot	arrest
Vietnam War	8/25/1968	Seale, Robert George	Chicago	conspiracy, riot, contempt of court	prison
free speech ban	8/28/1968	Hoffman, Abbie	Chicago	obscenity	arrest
racism	10/13/1970	Poindexter, David R.	Chicago	aided a felon	jail
nuclear power	12/1/1992	Sellers, John	Chicago	trespass	
Iraq War	3/20/2003	Diaz, Jennifer	Chicago	vigil, demonstration	
Iraq War	3/20/2003	Ritscher, Mark David "Malachi"	Chicago	self-immolation	
animal rights	8/2005	Deardorff, Eric	Peoria	public nudity	arrest
animal rights	8/2005	Sehgal, Melissa	Peoria	public nudity	arrest
alien refugee abuse	5/9/2007	Bobo, Kim	Chicago	alien asylum	

Indiana

State/ Target of Act	Date	Name	Location	Act	Consequence
slave recapture	6/1825	Bulla, William	Wayne County	slave recovery	lawsuit
slave recapture	6/1825	Hoover, Andrew	Wayne County	slave recovery	lawsuit
slave recapture	1826–1847	Coffin, Catherine White	Newport	slave relay	
slave recapture	1826–1847	Coffin, Levi	Newport	slave relay, recruitment	
slave recapture	1826–1847	Haydock, Hannah Thompson	Newport	slave conductor	
slave recapture	1826–1847	Haydock, Thomas Thompson	Newport	slave conductor	
slave recapture	1826–1847	Way, Henry H.	Newport	propaganda, medical care	Quaker schism
slave recapture	1829	Bell, David Williamson	Mauckport	slave rescue ferry	
slave recapture	1829	Bell, Elizabeth Wright	Mauckport	slave rescue ferry	
slave recapture	1837–1861	Anderson, Elijah	Madison	slave relay	prison
slave recapture	1840s	Clay, Cassius Marcellus	Jeffersonville	abetted slave rescue	
slave recapture	1840s– 1860s	Quinn, William Paul	Terre Haute	slave rescue	
slave recapture	1841	Stanton, Benjamin	Newport	propaganda	Quaker schism
slave recapture	1842–1860s	Fussell, Edwin	Pendleton	slave rescue	
slave recapture	1842–1860s	Fussell, Emma Jane	Pendleton	slave rescue	acid in the face
slave recapture	1842–1860s	Fussell, Rebecca Lewis	Pendleton	slave rescue	
slave recapture	1844	Rhodes, John	Hamilton County	flight	tried
slave recapture	1844	Rhodes, Rhuann	Hamilton County	flight	tried
slavery	6/15/1849	Clay, Cassius Marcellus	Jeffersonville	speech	stabbed

State/ Target of Act	Date	Name	Location	Act	Consequence
slave recapture	1850s	DeBaptiste, George	Madison	slave rescue, anarchy	
slave recapture	1850–1865	Hanover, John T.	Gibson County	route planning	
slave recapture	1850–1865	Posey, John Wesley	McComb	spying	
slave recapture	1854	Lane, James Henry	Lawrenceburg	guerrilla war	
slave recapture	9/25/1857	Bell, Charles A.	Mauckport	slave rescue ferry	kidnap, jail
slave recapture	9/25/1857	Bell, David Williamson	Mauckport	slave rescue ferry	kidnap, jail
slave recapture	9/25/1857	Bell, Horace	Mauckport	slave rescue ferry	kidnap, jail
slave recapture	11/1857	Wright, Owell	Mauckport	slave relay	kidnap, jail
slave recapture	1858	Donnell, Luther A.	Clarksburg	slave relay	lawsuit
slave recapture	7/3/1859	McIntosh, Henson	New Albany	slave conducting, spying	prison twice
Civil War	1863	Macy, Jesse	Knightstown	refused to serve	forced into army
Comstock Act	1876	Farr, H. Gustavus	Indiana	sale of contraceptives	arrest
free speech ban	11/1910	Goldman, Emma	Indianapolis	conspiracy	banned
draft	1917	Herschberger, Guy Franklin	Goshen	protest	
draft	11/3/1917	Lamonte, Frank S.	Evansville	draft protest	disbarred
draft	12/27/1917	Baumann, Charles W.	Indianapolis	draft protest	fired
draft	12/31/1917	Best, Charles W.	Indianapolis	draft protest	fired
World War I	1918	Sprunger, Walter	Monroe	conscientious objection	prison
segregation	5/4/1945	James, Daniel, Jr.	Seymour	sit-in	arrest
draft	10/1982	Schmucker, Mark A.	Goshen	refused to register	fine

Iowa

State/ Target of Act	Date	Name	Location	Act	Consequence
slave recapture	1833–1840s	Frazier, Anna Joy	Salem	protest	ousted by Quakers
slave recapture	1833–1840s	Frazier, Stephen	Salem	protest	ousted by Quakers
slave recapture	1840s	Lewelling, Henderson W.	Salem	ran a depot	ousted by Quakers
slave recapture	1840s	Lewelling, Jane Elizabeth Presnall	Salem	ran a depot	ousted by Quakers
slave recapture	1840s	Pearson, Benjamin Franklin	Keosauqua	slave rescue	
slavery	1840s	Scholes, Thomas Coggin	West Burlington	protest	
slavery	1840s	Vincent, James	Tabor	protest	
slave recapture	1850s	Teesdale, John	Iowa City	slave relay	
slave recapture	1853	Grinnell, Julia Ann Chapin	Grinnell	slave relay	
slave recapture	1857	Arnold, Joseph	Linnville	slave relay	
slave recapture	1857	Arnold, Tacy Smith	Linnville	slave relay	
slave recapture	10/1857	Maxson, Delilah Bowland	Cedar County	slave rescue	
slave recapture	10/1857	Maxson, William	Cedar County	slave rescue	

State/ Target of Act	Date	Name	Location	Act	Consequence
slavery	10/1857	Painter, Edith Dean	Springdale	sheltered anarchists	
slavery	10/1857	Painter, John H.	Springdale	sheltered anarchists	
slavery	11/1857	Todd, John	Tabor	stored weapons	
slave recapture	1859	Ellyson, Zachariah	Pleasant Plain	slave rescue	
draft	12/18/1917	Starck, W.A.	Audubon	draft protest	assault, nearly lynched
draft	12/18/1917	Tennegkeit, Fred	Audubon	draft protest	assault, nearly lynched
World War I	1918	Wallace, Daniel H.	Davenport	conscientious objection	prison
draft	3/13/1918	Battig, Leon	Ottumwa	draft protest	painted yellow
World War I	7/1918	Leatherman, Noah	Camp Dodge	conscientious objection	solitary cell
dress code	12/16/1965	Eckhardt, Christopher	Des Moines	wore black armband	suspended
dress code	12/16/1965	Tinker, John F.	Des Moines	wore black armband	suspended
dress code	12/16/1965	Tinker, Mary Beth	Des Moines	wore black armband	suspended

Iraq

Iraq War	2006	Bazzi, Zack	Fallujah	protest film	
Iraq War	2006	Moriarty, Mike	Fallujah	protest film	
Iraq War	2006	Pink, Steven	Fallujah	protest film	

Kansas

slavery	1830s	Sardou, Charles	Topeka	protest	
slave recapture	1840s	Garvey, Edward Christie Kerr	Topeka	protest, propaganda, harbored slaves	
slave recapture	1854	Anthony, Daniel Read, Sr.	Leavenworth	guerrilla war	
slave recapture	1854	Jennison, Charles Ransford	Mound City	guerrilla war	
slavery	1850s	Benjamin, Jacob	Lawrence	protest	
slavery	1850s	Bondi, August	Lawrence	protest	
slavery	1850s	Bondi, Henrietta Einstein	Lawrence	protest	
slave recapture	1850s	Jones, John Tecumseh "Ottawa"	Ottawa	slave rescue	shot at, home and store burned
slave recapture	1850s	Peoria, Baptiste	Ottawa	slave conducting, violence	
slavery	1850s	Pinner, Moritz	Kansas City	protest	
slave recapture	1850s–1860s	Gardner, Eliza	Douglas County	ran a safehouse	
slave recapture	1850s–1860s	Gardner, Joseph	Douglas County	ran a safehouse	
slave recapture	1854	Doy, Charles	Deer Creek	slave relay	jail, threat

State/ Target of Act	Date	Name	Location	Act	Consequence
slave recapture	1854	Doy, John W.	Deer Creek	slave relay	jail, threat
slave recapture	1854	Soule, Amasa R.	Lawrence	slave rescue	arson, mob violence
slave recapture	1855	Brown, Frederick	Lawrence	border clashes	
slave recapture	1855	Brown, John	Lawrence	border clashes	
slave recapture	1855	Brown, Oliver	Lawrence	border clashes	
slave recapture	1855	Brown, Owen	Lawrence	border clashes	
slave recapture	1855	Brown, Salmon	Lawrence	border clashes	
Fugitive Slave Law of 1850	8/20/1855	Kelley, J.W.B.	Atchison	protest	stoned, tarred
Fugitive Slave Law of 1850	1856	Mitchell, William	Wamego	protest, skirmish	
slave recapture	5/21/1856	Brown, John	Lawrence	border clashes	sword fight
Fugitive Slave Law of 1850	7/1856	Tappan, Samuel Forster, Jr.	Lawrence	gun running	
slave recapture	11/1857	Peoria, Baptiste	Paola	abetted anarchy	
slave recapture	12/1858	Ritchie, John	Holton	slave relay	
slave recapture	1/24/1859	Grover, Emily Jane Hunt	Lawrenceville	slave rescue	
slave recapture	1/24/1859	Grover, Joel	Lawrenceville	slave rescue	
slave recapture	2/24/1859	Nute, Ephraim	Lawrence	slave rescue, fund-raising	
slave recapture	8/1859	Gardner, Joseph	Vinland	jailbreak	
slave recapture	9/18/1859	Kagi, John Henry	Topeka	violence, highway robbery, conspiracy	charged
slave recapture	9/18/1859	Ritchie, John	Topeka	violence, conspiracy, highway robbery	charged
slave recapture	9/23/1859	Abbott, James Burnett	Wakarusa	jailbreak	
slave recapture	9/23/1859	Gardner, Joseph	Vinland	jailbreak	
slave recapture	9/23/1859	Pike, Joshua A.	Vinland	jailbreak	
slave recapture	9/23/1859	Senix, Jacob	Vinland	jailbreak	
slave recapture	9/23/1859	Simmons, Thomas	Vinland	jailbreak	
slave recapture	9/23/1859	Soule, Silas Stillman	Vinland	jailbreak	
slave recapture	9/23/1859	Stewart, John E.	Wakarusa	jailbreak	
slave recapture	9/23/1859	Willis, S.J.	Vinland	jailbreak	
slave recapture	6/9/1860	Gardner, Joseph	Vinland	slave rescue	wanted criminal, gunfight
slave recapture	6/9/1860	Gardner, Theodore	Vinland	slave rescue	gunfight
marriage laws	1886	Harman, Lillian	Valley Falls	cohabitation	prison
marriage laws	1886	Walker, Edwin Cox	Valley Falls	cohabitation	prison
Comstock Act	2/23/1887	Harman, Moses	Valley Falls	birth control information	jail
Comstock Act	5/1/1890	Harman, Moses	Valley Falls	birth control information	jail, fine
Comstock Act	6/1895	Harman, Moses	Valley Falls	birth control information	prison at hard labor
alcohol sale and consumption	12/27/1900	Nation, Carry Amelia Moore	Wichita	destroyed property	jail

State/ Target of Act	Date	Name	Location	Act	Consequence
alcohol sale and consumption	2/5/1901	Nation, Carry Amelia Moore	McKane	destroyed property	arrest
alcohol sale and consumption	4/1901	Nation, Carry Amelia Moore	Kansas City	obstructed traffic	arrest
alcohol sale and consumption	7/1901	Nation, Carry Amelia Moore	Topeka	destroyed property	jail
alcohol sale and consumption	9/28/1904	McHenry, Myra Gains Warren	Wichita	destroyed property	jail
alcohol sale and consumption	9/28/1904	Muntz, Lydia, crusader	Wichita	destroyed property	jail
alcohol sale and consumption	9/28/1904	Nation, Carry Amelia Moore	Wichita	destroyed property	jail
alcohol sale and consumption	9/28/1904	Wilhoite, Lucy	Wichita	destroyed property	jail
World War I	1917	Blickenstaff, L.C.	Fort Leavenworth	refused a uniform	prison
World War I	1917	Gaeddert, Gustav Raymond	Fort Riley	conscientious objection	prison, asylum
World War I	1917	Liechty, Elmer	Fort Leavenworth	conscientious objection	prison
World War I	1917	Meyer, Ernest L.	Fort Leavenworth	conscientious objection	expelled, prison
World War I	1917–1920	Briehl, Fred	Fort Leavenworth	conscientious objection	expelled from school, prison
World War I	7/22/1917	Siemens, Leonard	Camp Funston	conscientious objection	prison
World War I	9/7/1917	Buller, Herman H.	Buhler	refused a rifle	guardhouse
World War I	1918	Becker, Henry J.	Fort Leavenworth	refused to break the Sabbath	prison at hard labor
World War I	1918	Burke, Frank L.	Fort Leavenworth	conscientious objection	jail
World War I	1918	DeRosa, Ulysses		draft evasion	prison
World War I	1918	Eash, Reuben J.	Fort Leavenworth	conscientious objection	jail
World War I	1918	Flory, Daniel B.	Fort Leavenworth	conscientious objection	jail
World War I	1918	Franz, Heinrich F.	Fort Leavenworth	conscientious objection	jail
World War I	1918	Gray, Harold S.	Fort Leavenworth	conscientious objection	prison
World War I	1918	Hess, Maurice	Fort Leavenworth	conscientious objection	solitary cell on bread and water
World War I	1918	Klassen, Johannes M.	Fort Leavenworth	conscientious objection	prison
draft	1918	Magon, Ricardo Flores	Fort Leavenworth	conscientious objection	prison
World War I	1918	Teuscher, Daniel E.	Fort Leavenworth	conscientious objection	prison
World War I	1918	Thomas, Mark R.	Fort Leavenworth	conscientious objection	prison

State/ Target of Act	Date	Name	Location	Act	Consequence
World War I	1918	Wells, Ernest D.	Fort Leavenworth	conscientious objection	prison
World War I	1918	Wipf, Jacob	Fort Leavenworth	conscientious objection	prison
World War I	1918	Wolfe, John M.	Fort Riley	conscientious objection	prison
World War I	1918	Wortsman, Jacob	Fort Leavenworth	conscientious objection	prison
World War I	1918	Yoder, Daniel S.	Fort Leavenworth	conscientious objection	prison
World War I	5/1918	Buller, Henry B.	Buhler	conscientious objection	forced to plant trees
World War I	5/24/1918	Hofer, David	Fort Leavenworth	conscientious objection	prison, torture
World War I	5/24/1918	Hofer, Josef	Fort Leavenworth	conscientious objection	torture, prison
World War I	5/24/1918	Hofer, Michael	Fort Leavenworth	conscientious objection	torture, prison
World War I	6/27/1918	Claassen, Menno	Fort Riley	refused a uniform	
labor exploitation	1932	Olsen, Tillie Lerner	Kansas City	distributed leaflets	jail
segregation	7/19/1958	Walters, Ronald	Wichita	lunch counter sit-in	
ROTC	5/21/2000	Vaughn, Emiliano Huet	Kansas City	protest	
anti-abortion laws	7/19/2001	Klein, Joshua	Wichita	battery	arrest
anti-abortion laws	7/19/2001	Rose, Karen	Wichita	battery	arrest
abortion	7/21/2001	Stanfield, Kevin	Wichita	blocked traffic	arrest
abortion	7/21/2001	Thompson, Daniel	Wichita	blocked traffic	arrest

Kentucky

State/ Target of Act	Date	Name	Location	Act	Consequence
slave recapture	1811	Paxton, James Alexander	Maysville	slave hiding, conspiracy	
slave recapture	1811	Paxton, Maria Keith Marshall	Maysville	slave hiding, conspiracy	
slave education ban	1830s	Swisshelm, Jane Grey Cannon	Louisville	educated slaves	mob violence
slave recapture	1833–1885	Brown, Mary McClanahan	Henderson County	spying, slave relay	prison
slave recapture	1833–1885	Brown, Thomas	Henderson County	spying, slave relay	banished
slave recapture	1840s	Maudlin, Wright	Bourbon County	spying	
slave education ban	12/1841	Adams, Henry	Louisville	educated slaves	
slave recapture	9/28/1844	Fairbank, Calvin	Lexington	slave liberation	mob violence, prison at hard labor
slave recapture	9/28/1844	Helm, James	Lexington	slave relay	
slave recapture	9/28/1844	Webster, Delia Ann	Lexington	slave liberation	mob violence, prison
slave recapture	8/5/1848	Doyle, Edward James	Danville	slave rescue	prison at hard labor

State/ Target of Act	Date	Name	Location	Act	Consequence
slave recapture	11/9/1851	Fairbank, Calvin	Louisville	slave rescue	prison
slave recapture	11/9/1851	Fee, Gregg	Louisville	abetted slave rescue	
slave recapture	11/1852	Webster, Delia Ann	Trimble County	recruitment	mob violence, vandalism, jail
slave education ban	1856	Wadkins, Daniel	Louisville	educated slaves	
slave recapture	8/15/1858	Buckner, Dick	Louisville	slave rescue	prison
slave recapture	8/15/1858	Lewis, William	Louisville	slave rescue	
Fugitive Slave Law of 1850	9/13/1858	Swisshelm, Jane Grey Cannon	Louisville	protest	
Civil War	1861–1863	Eads, Harvey L.	South Union	protest	
Civil War	1861–1863	Rankin, John N.	South Union	protest	
World War I	1917	Mummaw, Adam H.	Louisville	conscientious objection	prison
World War I	1917	Soldner, Tilman	Camp Taylor	conscientious objection	prison
draft	10/30/1917	Bigelow, Herbert Seely	Newport	draft protest	kidnap, lashed
World War II	8/1942	Roberts, William P., Jr.	Ashland	refused to register	prison
draft	11/1943	Rustin, Bayard Taylor	Ashland	refused draft	prison
Vietnam War	1966	Ali, Muhammad	Louisville	refused to serve	
Indian grave robbery	1987	Banks, Dennis James	Uniontown	protest	

Louisiana

State/ Target of Act	Date	Name	Location	Act	Consequence
slave education ban	1/1813	Dorfeuille, Godefroy	New Orleans	educated slaves	
slave recapture	1834–1865	Barker, Elizabeth Hazard	New Orleans	ran a safehouse	
slave recapture	1834–1865	Barker, Jacob	New Orleans	ran a safehouse	
slave education ban	1842	Delille, Henriette	New Orleans	educated slaves	
slave education ban	1842	Gaudin, Juliette	New Orleans	educated slaves	
slave education ban	1847	Lanusse, Armand	New Orleans	educated slaves	
slave education ban	1859	Cook, John F., Jr.	New Orleans	educated slaves	warnings
slave education ban	1860	Bouguille, Ludger	New Orleans	tutored a slave	
Civil War	1861–1863	Guillory, Martin	Bois Mallet	refused to serve	shot
slave recapture	6/1862	Paine, Halbert Eleazer	Baton Rouge	harbored slaves	
Civil War	1863–1865	Carrière, Hilaire	Bois Mallet	refused to serve	shot
Civil War	1863–1865	Carrière, Ozémé	Bois Mallet	refused to serve	shot
Civil War	1863–1865	Carrière, Ursin	Bois Mallet	refused to serve	shot
Civil War	1863–1865	Saunier, Carmelite Carrière	Bois Mallet	abetted draft evaders	shot
segregation	1960	Brown, Hubert G.	Baton Rouge	promoted integration	suspended from school
racism	8/28/1963	Farmer, James Leonard	Plaquemine	activism	stalked, jail, death threat
black rights	1974	Duke, David Ernest	Lafayette	mail and tax fraud	prison
genetic food engineering	11/19/1996	Johnson, Teri	Destrehan	demonstration	
animal rights	6/2001	Lieberman, Cynthia	Shreveport	mockery	arrest

State/ Target of Act	Date	Name	Location	Act	Consequence
Maine					
religious persecution	4/1675	Screven, William	Kittery	religious unorthodoxy	jail, fine
nonattendance of church	7/6/1675	Screven, William	York	avoided Puritan services	charged
religious persecution	7/6/1675	Screven, William	York	broke the Sabbath	charged
religious persecution	7/1682	Screven, William	York	broke the Sabbath	banished
colonial taxation	1765	Burton, Benjamin	York	led protest	
colonial taxation	1765	Simpson, Benjamin	York	led protest	
colonial taxation	1765	Watson, James	York	led protest	
colonial taxation	3/19/1766	Burbank, Silas	Scarborough	rifled a residence	
colonial taxation	10/1773	Rice, Thomas	Wiscasset	harbor violence	
colonial taxation	10/1773	Wood, Abiel	Wiscasset	harbor violence	
colonial taxation	6/12/1775	Foster, Benjamin	Machias	seized a ship	
colonial taxation	6/12/1775	O'Brien, Dennis	Machias	seized a ship	
colonial taxation	6/12/1775	O'Brien, Gideon	Machias	seized a ship	
colonial taxation	6/12/1775	O'Brien, Jeremiah	Machias	seized a ship	
colonial taxation	6/12/1775	O'Brien, John	Machias	seized a ship	
colonial taxation	6/12/1775	O'Brien, Joseph	Machias	seized a ship	
colonial taxation	6/12/1775	O'Brien, William	Machias	seized a ship	
land profiteering	1790s	Ely, Samuel	Northport	paramilitary leader	
land profiteering	1790s	Shurtleff, James	Litchfield	paramilitary leader	lynched
land profiteering	1/1808	Brackett, Daniel	Fairfax	paramilitary leader	
land profiteering	1/1808	Brackett, Thomas	Falmouth	jailbreak	
property rights	4/1808	Barlow, Nathan	Fairfax	assault	
property rights	4/1808	Brackett, Thomas	Fairfax	assault	
land profiteering	5/1808	Barlow, Nathan	Albion	jailbreak, assault	prison at hard labor
slave recapture	1830s–1860s	Dow, Cornelia Durant Maynard	Portland	slave refuge	
slave recapture	1830s–1860s	Dow, Neal	Portland	slave refuge	
slave recapture	1830s–1860s	Winslow, Comfort Hussey	Portland	financial support	
slave recapture	1830s–1860s	Winslow, Nathan	Portland	financial support	
slave recapture	1841–1851	Freeman, Amos Noah	Portland	depot conductor	
draft	3/9/1918	Walz, William Emanuel	Bangor	draft protest	fired
nuclear power	3/31/1991	Berrigan, Philip	Bath	sabotage	
nuclear power	3/31/1991	Lewis, Tom	Bath	sabotage	
nuclear power	2/12/1997	Baggerly, Steve J.	Bath	sabotage	prison
nuclear power	2/12/1997	Berrigan, Philip	Bath	sabotage	prison
nuclear power	2/12/1997	Colville, Mark	Bath	sabotage	prison
nuclear power	2/12/1997	Crane, Susan	Bath	sabotage	prison
nuclear power	2/12/1997	Kelly, Steven	Bath	sabotage	prison
nuclear power	2/12/1997	Lewis, Tom	Bath	sabotage	prison

State/ Target of Act	Date	Name	Location	Act	Consequence
Marshall Islands					
nuclear power	5/1/1958	Bigelow, Albert S.	Eniwetok Atoll	contempt of court	jail
nuclear power	5/1/1958	Huntington, William Reed	Eniwetok Atoll	contempt of court	jail
nuclear power	5/1/1958	Peck, James	Eniwetok Atoll	contempt of court	jail
nuclear power	5/1/1958	Sherwood, Orion W.	Eniwetok Atoll	contempt of court	jail
nuclear power	5/1/1958	Willoughby, George	Eniwetok Atoll	contempt of court	jail
nuclear power	6/4/1958	Bigelow, Albert S.	Eniwetok Atoll	contempt of court	jail
nuclear power	6/4/1958	Huntington, William Reed	Eniwetok Atoll	contempt of court	jail
nuclear power	6/4/1958	Peck, James	Eniwetok Atoll	contempt of court	jail
nuclear power	6/4/1958	Sherwood, Orion W.	Eniwetok Atoll	contempt of court	jail
nuclear power	6/4/1958	Willoughby, George	Eniwetok Atoll	contempt of court	jail
Maryland					
militia service	1658	Keene, Richard, Sr.	Calvert County	refused to serve	struck with a saber
taxation	1760s	Dawson, William	Cambridge	refused religious tax	jail
colonial taxation	1765	Adair, Robert	Baltimore	paramilitary	
colonial taxation	1765	Aisquith, William	Baltimore	paramilitary	
colonial taxation	1765	Alexander, Robert	Baltimore	paramilitary	
colonial taxation	1765	Allen, Michael	Baltimore	paramilitary	
colonial taxation	1765	Baker, William	Baltimore	paramilitary	
colonial taxation	1765	Bowly, Daniel	Baltimore	paramilitary	
colonial taxation	1765	Buchanan, Archibald	Baltimore	paramilitary	
colonial taxations	1765	Buchanan, William	Baltimore	paramilitary	
colonial taxation	1765	Calhoun, James	Baltimore	paramilitary	
colonial taxation	1765	Chamier, Daniel	Baltimore	paramilitary	
colonial taxation	1765	Clemm, William	Baltimore	paramilitary	
colonial taxation	1765	Courtney, Hercules	Baltimore	paramilitary	
colonial taxation	1765	Cox, James	Baltimore	paramilitary	
colonial taxation	1765	Cresap, Thomas	Oldtown	paramilitary organizer	
colonial taxation	1765	Dever, John	Baltimore	paramilitary	
colonial taxation	1765	Duvall, George	Baltimore	paramilitary	
colonial taxation	1765	Franciscus, George	Baltimore	paramilitary	
colonial taxation	1765	Griest, Isaac	Baltimore	paramilitary	
colonial taxation	1765	Griffith, Benjamin	Baltimore	paramilitary	
colonial taxation	1765	Hall, Caleb	Baltimore	paramilitary	
colonial taxation	1765	Hollingsworth, Stephen	Baltimore	paramilitary	
colonial taxation	1765	Hopkins, Gerard	Baltimore	paramilitary	
colonial taxation	1765	Keener, Melchior	Baltimore	paramilitary	
colonial taxation	1765	Leverly, George	Baltimore	paramilitary	

State/ Target of Act	Date	Name	Location	Act	Consequence
colonial taxation	1765	Levington, Aaron	Baltimore	paramilitary	
colonial taxation	1765	Lindenberger, George Ernst	Baltimore	paramilitary	
colonial taxation	1765	Lux, William	Baltimore	paramilitary	
colonial taxation	1765	Lyon, William	Baltimore	paramilitary	
colonial taxation	1765	McLane, John	Baltimore	paramilitary	
colonial taxation	1765	Patton, George	Baltimore	paramilitary	
colonial taxation	1765	Purviance, Samuel, Jr.	Baltimore	paramilitary	
colonial taxation	1765	Rusk, David	Baltimore	paramilitary	
colonial taxation	1765	Savery, William	Baltimore	paramilitary	
colonial taxation	1765	Shields, David	Baltimore	paramilitary	
colonial taxation	1765	Smith, John	Baltimore	paramilitary	
colonial taxation	1765	Smith, William	Baltimore	paramilitary	
colonial taxation	1765	Spear, William	Baltimore	paramilitary	
colonial taxation	1765	Sterrett, James	Baltimore	paramilitary	
colonial taxation	1765	Sterrett, John	Baltimore	paramilitary	
colonial taxation	1765	Uhler, Erasmus	Baltimore	paramilitary	
colonial taxation	1765	Warfield, Charles Alexander	Baltimore	paramilitary	
colonial taxation	1765	Wells, Cyprian	Baltimore	paramilitary	
colonial taxation	1765	Wells, George	Baltimore	paramilitary	
colonial taxation	1765	Willson, William	Baltimore	paramilitary	
colonial taxation	1765	Winters, Elisha	Baltimore	paramilitary	
colonial taxation	3/1/1766	Chase, Samuel	Annapolis	denounced poll tax	
colonial taxation	3/1/1766	Lendrum, Andrew	Annapolis	paramilitary leader	
colonial taxation	3/1/1766	Nicholson, Joseph Hopper	Annapolis	paramilitary leader	
colonial taxation	3/1/1766	Paca, William	Annapolis	denounced poll tax	
colonial taxation	3/8/1766	Chase, Thomas	Baltimore	paramilitary, orator	
colonial taxation	1768	Dickinson, John	Talbot	paramilitary	
colonial taxation	10/19/1774	Carroll, Charles	Annapolis	arson	
slave recapture	1820s	Wilson, James	Baltimore	slave relay	
slave education ban	1825	Auld, Sophia Keithley	Baltimore	educated slaves	
slavery	1829	Garrison, William Lloyd	Baltimore	propaganda	jail
slave recapture	1830s	Harris, Hazzard	Harford County	water relay	
slave recapture	1830s	Worthington, William	Harford County	coded messages	
slavery	1830s–1860s	Harper, Frances Ellen Watkins	Baltimore	propaganda	
free speech ban	5/22/1839	Wilson, Sherry	Queen Anne's County	abolitionism	prison
slave recapture	1842	Garrison, William Lloyd	Annapolis	spying	jail
slave recapture	1842	Torrey, Charles Turner	Annapolis	spying	jail
slave recapture	1842	Whittier, John Greenleaf	Annapolis	spying	jail

State/ Target of Act	Date	Name	Location	Act	Consequence
slave recapture	4/29/1842	Green, Wesley	Anne Arundel County	slave rescue	died in prison
slave recapture	5/4/1847	Gray, Greenburg	Anne Arundel County	forgery	prison
slavery	1850s	Hazlett, Hugh	Dorcester County	protest	
slave recapture	12/1850	Tubman, Harriet	Baltimore	slave relay	
slave recapture	1/1851	Tubman, Harriet	Bucktown	slave relay	wanted criminal
slave recapture	fall 1851	Tubman, Harriet	Bucktown	slave relay	
slave recapture	12/1851	Tubman, Harriet	Bucktown	slave relay	
slave recapture	fall 1852	Tubman, Harriet	Bucktown	slave relay	
slave recapture	11/1856	Green, Samuel, Jr.	Indian Creek	harbored slaves	arrest, prison, confiscation
slave recapture	11/15/1856	Tubman, Harriet	Indian Creek	slave relay	
slave recapture	12/1856	Tubman, Harriet	Bucktown	slave relay	
slave recapture	12/1860	Tubman, Harriet	Bucktown	slave relay	
draft	12/18/1863	Moore, Benjamin P., Jr.	Bel Air	draft evasion	
free speech ban	12/1910	Goldman, Emma	Baltimore	conspiracy	intimidation
draft	8/27/1918	Jordan, David Starr	Baltimore	protest	assault
Sacco and Vanzetti death sentence	7/14/1920	Mencken, H.L.,	Baltimore	protest	
biological warfare	7/1/1959	Scott, Lawrence	Fort Detrick	sit-in	
nuclear power	7/1/1959	Scott, Lawrence	Fort Detrick	protest	
biological warfare	7/1/1959	Scott, Viola Maria Standley	Fort Detrick	sit-in	
nuclear power	7/1/1959	Scott, Viola Maria Standley	Fort Detrick	protest	
biological warfare	7/1/1959	Walker, Charles C.	Fort Detrick	sit-in	
nuclear power	7/1/1959	Walker, Charles C.	Fort Detrick	protest	
segregation	1961	Coffin, William Sloane, Jr.	Baltimore	protest	arrest
racism	1962	Grubb, Enez Stafford	Cambridge	protest	
racism	1963	Powell, Adam Clayton, Jr.	Cambridge	defended sit-ins	
segregation	5/14/1963	Booth, Mabel St. Clair	Cambridge	restaurant sit-in	jail
segregation	5/14/1963	Cromwell, Dwight	Cambridge	sit-in	jail
segregation	5/14/1963	Richardson, Donna	Cambridge	restaurant sit-in	jail
segregation	5/14/1963	Richardson, Gloria	Cambridge	restaurant sit-in	jail
segregation	5/14/1963	White, Reva Dinez	Cambridge	restaurant sit-in	reformatory
racism	5/17/1963	Richardson, Gloria	Cambridge	plotted a riot	arrest
racism	6/11/1964	Richardson, Gloria	Cambridge	picket	arrest
voter intimidation	7/1967	Brown, Hubert G.	Cambridge	promoted integration	shot, fled
Vietnam War	10/27/1967	Berrigan, Philip	Baltimore	destroyed files	arrest
Vietnam War	10/27/1967	Eberhardt, David	Baltimore	destroyed files	arrest
Vietnam War	10/27/1967	Lewis, Tom	Baltimore	destroyed files	arrest

State/Target of Act	Date	Name	Location	Act	Consequence
Vietnam War	10/27/1967	Mengel, James L.	Baltimore	destroyed files	arrest
nuclear power	5/17/1968	Berrigan, Daniel	Catonsville	sabotage	prison
Vietnam War	5/17/1968	Berrigan, Daniel	Catonsville	arson	prison
Vietnam War	5/17/1968	Darst, David A.	Catonsville	arson	prison
Vietnam War	5/17/1968	Hogan, John	Catonsville	arson	prison
Vietnam War	5/17/1968	Lewis, Tom	Catonsville	arson	prison
Vietnam War	5/17/1968	Melville, Marjorie Bradford	Catonsville	arson	prison
Vietnam War	5/17/1968	Melville, Thomas	Catonsville	arson	prison
Vietnam War	5/17/1968	Mische, George	Catonsville	arson	prison
Vietnam War	5/17/1968	Moylan, Mary	Catonsville	arson	prison
Vietnam War	10/9/1968	Abdoo, Jayma	Catonsville	sabotage	
Vietnam War	10/9/1968	Anderson, William	Catonsville	sabotage	
Vietnam War	10/9/1968	Billman, George Milo	Catonsville	sabotage	
Vietnam War	10/9/1968	Buckalew, Terry	Catonsville	sabotage	
Vietnam War	10/9/1968	Couming, Paul	Catonsville	sabotage	
Vietnam War	10/9/1968	Dixon, Eugene	Catonsville	sabotage	
Vietnam War	10/9/1968	Doyle, Michael	Catonsville	sabotage	
Vietnam War	10/9/1968	Dunham, Ann	Catonsville	sabotage	
Vietnam War	10/9/1968	Fordi, Peter D.	Catonsville	sabotage	
Vietnam War	10/9/1968	Forsyth, Keith	Catonsville	sabotage	
Vietnam War	10/9/1968	Giocondo, Michael	Catonsville	sabotage	
Vietnam War	10/9/1968	Good, Robert	Catonsville	sabotage	
Vietnam War	10/9/1968	Grady, John	Catonsville	sabotage	
Vietnam War	10/9/1968	Innes, Margaret	Catonsville	sabotage	
Vietnam War	10/9/1968	McGowan, Edward	Catonsville	sabotage	
Vietnam War	10/9/1968	Melmadden, Francis	Catonsville	sabotage	
Vietnam War	10/9/1968	Moccia, Lianne	Catonsville	sabotage	
Vietnam War	10/9/1968	Murphy, Edward	Catonsville	sabotage	
Vietnam War	10/9/1968	Musi, Barry	Catonsville	sabotage	
Vietnam War	10/9/1968	Pommersheim, Frank	Catonsville	sabotage	
Vietnam War	10/9/1968	Reilly, Joan	Catonsville	sabotage	
Vietnam War	10/9/1968	Reilly, Rosemary	Catonsville	sabotage	
Vietnam War	10/9/1968	Ricci, Anita	Catonsville	sabotage	
Vietnam War	10/9/1968	Ridolfi, Kathleen	Catonsville	sabotage	
Vietnam War	10/9/1968	Shemeley, Martha	Catonsville	sabotage	
Vietnam War	10/9/1968	Swinglish, John	Catonsville	sabotage	
Vietnam War	10/9/1968	Tosi, Sara	Catonsville	sabotage	
Vietnam War	10/9/1968	Williamson, Robert	Catonsville	sabotage	
Vietnam War	4/1970	Fonda, Jane	Fort Mead	protest	arrest
biological warfare	1971	Carner, Lucy Perkins	Fort Detrick	blocked a gate	
biological warfare	1971	Scott, Lawrence	Fort Detrick	blocked a gate	
animal rights	10/1981	Pacheco, Alex	Silver Spring	spying	death threats

State/ Target of Act	Date	Name	Location	Act	Consequence
nuclear power	12/20/1999	Berrigan, Philip	Middle River	sabotage	prison
nuclear power	12/20/1999	Crane, Susan	Middle River	sabotage	prison
nuclear power	12/20/1999	Kelly, Steven	Middle River	sabotage	prison
nuclear power	12/20/1999	Walz, Elizabeth	Middle River	sabotage	prison
travel restrictions due to terrorism	10/20/2003	Heatwole, Nathaniel	Damascus	concealed weapon	fine

Massachusetts

heresy	1634	Williams, Roger	Salem	preached	ousted
religious persecution	1637	Gorton, Samuel	Boston	blasphemy	prison, exile
religious persecution	1637	King, William	Salem	sheltered Quakers	exile, confiscation
heresy	1638	Dyer, Mary Barrett	Boston	defied Puritans	exile
heresy	1638	Dyer, William	Boston	defied Puritans	exile
religious persecution	1638	Gorton, Samuel	Plymouth	blasphemy	prison, exile
heresy	3/22/1638	Hawkins, Jane	Boston	feminist teachings	banished
heresy	3/22/1638	Hutchinson, Anne Marbury	Boston	feminist teachings	banished
religious persecution	1643	Gorton, Samuel	Boston	blasphemy	hard labor
religious persecution	1650	Buell, Mary Post	Swansea	religious unorthodoxy	arrest
religious persecution	1650	Newman, Samuel	Swansea	religious unorthodoxy	harassment
religious persecution	6/1650	Buell, William	Swansea	religious unorthodoxy	arrest
religious persecution	6/1650	Hazel, John	Swansea	religious unorthodoxy	arrest
religious persecution	6/1650	Holmes, Obadiah	Swansea	religious unorthodoxy	arrest
religious persecution	6/1650	Mann, Mrs. James	Swansea	religious unorthodoxy	arrest
religious persecution	6/1650	Smith, Edward	Swansea	religious unorthodoxy	arrest
religious persecution	6/1650	Smith, Mrs. Edward	Swansea	religious unorthodoxy	arrest
religious persecution	6/1650	Torrey, Greene	Swansea	religious unorthodoxy	arrest
religious persecution	5/31/1651	Clarke, John	Lynn	religious nonconformity	jail, fine
religious persecution	5/31/1651	Crandall, John	Lynn	religious nonconformity	jail, fine
religious persecution	5/31/1651	Hazel, John	Lynn	religious unorthodoxy	jail, fine, lash
religious persecution	5/31/1651	Holmes, Obadiah	Lynn	religious unorthodoxy	jail, fine, lash
religious persecution	5/31/1651	Spur, John	Lynn	religious nonconformity	jail, fine, lashed to death
religious persecution	9/28/1653	Dunster, Henry	Cambridge	refused infant baptism	lost job, exile

State/ Target of Act	Date	Name	Location	Act	Consequence
illegal assembly	1654	Gaunt, Lydia Hampton	Sandwich	Quaker worship	fine
illegal assembly	1654	Gaunt, Peter	Sandwich	Quaker worship	fine
religious persecution	7/1656	Austin, Ann	Boston	blasphemy	books burned, prison
religious persecution	7/1656	Fisher, Mary	Boston	blasphemy	books burned, prison
heresy	8/1656	Waugh, Dorothy	Boston	proselytized	jail on low rations, exile
heresy	8/9/1656	Brend, William	Salem	Quaker worship	jail
heresy	8/9/1656	Copeland, John	Salem	Quaker worship	jail
heresy	8/9/1656	Gibbons, Sarah	Boston	Quaker worship	jail
heresy	8/9/1656	Holder, Christopher	Salem	Quaker worship	jail
heresy	8/9/1656	Prince, Mary	Boston	Quaker worship	jail
heresy	8/9/1656	Thurston, Thomas	Boston	Quaker worship	jail
heresy	8/9/1656	Waugh, Dorothy	Boston	Quaker worship	jail
heresy	8/9/1656	Weatherhead, Mary	Boston	Quaker worship	jail
religious persecution	fall 1656	Locke, Robert	Boston	contempt of court	jail
jail rules	10/14/1656	Upsal, Nicholas	Boston	fed prisoners	fine, jail
heresy	1657	Allen, William	Sandwich	Quaker worship	warning
exile	1657	Burden, Anne	Boston	ignored banishment	prison in the dark, confiscation
heresy	1657	Burden, Anne	Boston	preached	exile
religious persecution	1657	Clark, Mary	Boston	blasphemy	scourged
heresy	1657	Dowdney, Richard	Dedham	delivered a message	
heresy	1657	Dowdney, Richard	Boston	Quaker worship	lashed, exile, confiscation
exile	1657	Dyer, Mary Barrett	Boston	ignored banishment	prison in the dark, confiscation
heresy	1657	Dyer, Mary Barrett	Boston	preached	exile
religious persecution	1657	Howland, Arthur	Plymouth	refused bond	prison
heresy	1657	Newland, John	Sandwich	Quaker worship	warning
heresy	1658	Brend, William	Sandwich	refused an oath	flogged
loyalty oath	1658	Brend, William	Salem	refused loyalty oath	lashed
heresy	1658	Brown, Judith	Plymouth	Quaker worship	lashed
heresy	1658	Copeland, John	Salem	defied Puritans	jail
death penalty	1658	Davis, Nicholas	Barnstable	protest	
heresy	1658	Davis, Nicholas	Plymouth	Quaker worship	prison, exile
death penalty	1658	Dyer, Mary Barrett	Boston	protest	
heresy	1658	Harris, Thomas	Boston	preached	prison, lashed, low rations
heresy	1658	Holder, Christopher	Salem	defied Puritans	throttled, jail
heresy	1658	Leddra, William	Plymouth	Quaker worship	prison
heresy	1658	Pearson, Peter	Plymouth	Quaker worship	prison, lashed
death penalty	1658	Robinson, William	Boston	protest	
heresy	1658	Shattuck, Samuel	Salem	aided Quakers	jail, flogged, exile

State/ Target of Act	Date	Name	Location	Act	Consequence
heresy	1658	Southwick, Cassandra Burnell	Salem	defied Puritans	jail, threat
religious persecution	1658	Southwick, Cassandra Burnell	Salem	Quaker convert	jail
heresy	1658	Southwick, Laurence	Salem	defied Puritans	jail, threat
religious persecution	1658	Southwick, Laurence	Salem	Quaker convert	jail
death penalty	1658	Stephenson, Marmaduke	Boston	protest	
religious persecution	3/2/1658	Howland, Arthur	Plymouth	seditious letter	prison, fine
heresy	4/15/1658	Copeland, John	Cape Cod	defied Puritans	scourged
heresy	4/15/1658	Holder, Christopher	Cape Cod	defied Puritans	scourged
heresy	4/15/1658	Holder, Mary Scott	Cape Cod	defied Puritans	prison
heresy	4/15/1658	Scott, Katherine Marbury	Cape Cod	defied Puritans	flogged, prison
heresy	4/15/1658	Scott, Patience	Cape Cod	defied Puritans	prison
heresy	6/3/1658	Holder, Christopher	Cape Cod	defied Puritans	ear lopped
religious persecution	6/3/1658	Scott, Katherine Marbury	Salem	protest	lashed, prison
heresy	1659	Dyer, Mary Barrett	Boston	visited Quakers	jail
religious persecution	1659	Dyer, Mary Barrett	Boston	contempt of court	hanged
heresy	1659	Greenfield, Thomas	Boston	refused to testify	jail
religious persecution	1659	Harper, Deborah Perry	Boston	claimed a Quaker corpse	prison, exile
religious persecution	1659	Harper, Robert	Boston	claimed a Quaker corpse	prison, exile
religious persecution	1659	Wright, Hannah	Boston	protest	
religious persecution	1659	Wright, Mary	Boston	protest	
religious persecution	3/11/1659	Buffum, Joshua	Salem	blasphemy	
religious persecution	3/11/1659	Phelps, Nicholas	Salem	blasphemy	threat
religious persecution	3/11/1659	Southwick, Josiah	Salem	blasphemy	lashed, jail
heresy	10/6/1659	Howland, Henry	Plymouth	Quaker worship	fine, confiscation
religious persecution	10/6/1659	Howland, Henry	Plymouth	refused jury duty	
heresy	10/19/1659	Dyer, Mary Barrett	Boston	defied Puritans	death sentence
heresy	10/27/1659	Robinson, William	Boston	preached, sacrilege	confiscation, exile, hanged
heresy	10/27/1659	Stephenson, Marmaduke	Boston	preached	exile, hanged
heresy	11/3/1659	Wharton, Edward	Boston	defied Puritans	scourged, fine
religious persecution	11/3/1659	Wharton, Edward	Plymouth	protest	lashed, fine
taxation	1660s	White, Esther	Raynham	tax resistance	prison
religious persecution	5/1/1660	Howland, Henry	Plymouth	illegal meetings	fine
heresy	6/1/1660	Dyer, Mary Barrett	Boston	defied Puritans	hanged
heresy	10/1660	Harper, Deborah Perry	Plymouth	aided Quakers	prison, exile
heresy	10/1660	Harper, Robert	Plymouth	aided Quakers	prison, exile
religious persecution	10/2/1660	Howland, Henry	Plymouth	illegal meetings	fine, confiscation
heresy	1661	Christopherson, Wenlock	Boston	defied Puritans	exile

State/ Target of Act	Date	Name	Location	Act	Consequence
religious persecution	1661	Christopherson, Wenlock	Boston	blasphemy	exile
religious persecution	1661	Gaunt, Lydia Hampton	Sandwich	housed missionaries	confiscation
religious persecution	1661	Gaunt, Peter	Sandwich	housed missionaries	confiscation
heresy	1661	Norton, Humphrey	Boston	Quaker worship	lashed, jail, starved
religious persecution	1661	Norton, Humphrey	Boston	blasphemy	jail
heresy	3/14/1661	Leddra, William	Boston	Quaker worship	shackled, prison, hanged
religious persecution	1662	Hooton, Elizabeth	Boston	visited Quaker prisoners	abandoned
religious persecution	1663	Alby, Benjamin	Rehoboth	preached	expelled
religious persecution	1663	Brown, James	Rehoboth	preached	expelled
religious persecution	1663	Butterworth, John	Rehoboth	preached	expelled
religious persecution	1663	Carpenter, James	Rehoboth	preached	expelled
religious persecution	1663	Kingsley, Eldad	Rehoboth	preached	fine
religious persecution	1663	Myles, John	Rehoboth	religious unorthodoxy	exile
religious persecution	1663	Tanner, Nicholas	Rehoboth	preached	expelled
heresy	ca. 1665	Hooton, Elizabeth	Cambridge	professed Quaker creed	whipped, abandoned
religious persecution	11/1665	Howland, Henry	Plymouth	harbored Quakers	fine, confiscation
heresy	1666	Farnum, John	Boston	preached	jail, exile
religious persecution	1666	Farnum, John	Boston	religious unorthodoxy	jail
heresy	1666	George, John	Boston	defied Puritans	jail
heresy	1666	Goold, Thomas	Boston	defied Puritans	jail
religious persecution	1666	Goold, Thomas	Boston	flight from arrest	
heresy	1666	Osborne, Priscilla Brighton	Boston	defied Puritans	ousted
religious persecution	1666	Osborne, Priscilla Brighton	Boston	religious unorthodoxy	excommunicated
heresy	1666	Osborne, Thomas	Boston	defied Puritans	jail
religious persecution	1666	Osborne, Thomas	Boston	religious unorthodoxy	jail
religious persecution	7/2/1667	Brown, James	Rehoboth	preached	fine, expelled
religious persecution	7/2/1667	Myles, John	Rehoboth	preached	fine
religious persecution	7/2/1667	Tanner, Nicholas	Rehoboth	preached	fine
religious persecution	10/30/1667	Alby, Benjamin	Rehoboth	preached	expelled
religious persecution	10/30/1667	Brown, James	Rehoboth	preached	
religious persecution	10/30/1667	Butterworth, John	Rehoboth	preached	expelled
religious persecution	10/30/1667	Carpenter, James	Rehoboth	preached	expelled
religious persecution	10/30/1667	Kingsley, Eldad	Rehoboth	preached	expelled
religious persecution	10/30/1667	Myles, John	Rehoboth	preached	expelled
religious persecution	10/30/1667	Tanner, Nicholas	Rehoboth	preached	expelled

State/Target of Act	Date	Name	Location	Act	Consequence
religious persecution	3/1668	Goold, Thomas	Boston	religious unorthodoxy	tried
heresy	1669	Robinson, William	Salem	aided a heretic	fine, exile
heresy	1669	Shattuck, Samuel	Salem	aided a heretic	fine, exile
religious persecution	3/1671	Maule, Thomas	Salem	broke the Sabbath	lashed
religious persecution	7/8/1677	Bowers, Elizabeth	Boston	wore sackcloth and ash	lashed
religious persecution	7/8/1677	Brewster, Margaret	Boston	wore sackcloth and ash	lashed
religious persecution	7/8/1677	Easton, John, Jr.	Boston	wore sackcloth and ash	lashed
religious persecution	7/8/1677	Miles, Mary	Boston	wore sackcloth and ash	lashed
religious persecution	7/8/1677	Wright, Lydia	Boston	wore sackcloth and ash	lashed
religious persecution	1679–1680	Russell, John, Jr.	Woburn	distributed pamphlets	scorn, abuse
militia service	1681	Maule, Thomas	Salem	refused to serve	
taxation	1681	Maule, Thomas	Salem	tax resistance	fine, lashed, jail
free speech ban	12/12/1695	Maule, Thomas	Salem	sold tracts	books burned
Indian wars	1703	Macomber, Thomas	Taunton	draft evasion	prison
Indian wars	1703	Smith, John	Bristol	draft evasion	prison
religious persecution	1751	Barstow, Jeremiah	Sturbridge	religious unorthodoxy	confiscation, prison
religious persecution	1751	Bloyce, Abraham	Sturbridge	religious unorthodoxy	confiscation
religious persecution	1751	Blunt, John	Sturbridge	religious unorthodoxy	confiscation
religious persecution	1751	Coller, Phineas	Sturbridge	religious unorthodoxy	confiscation
religious persecution	1751	Corey, John	Sturbridge	religious unorthodoxy	prison
religious persecution	1751	Draper, John	Sturbridge	religious unorthodoxy	confiscation, prison
religious persecution	1751	Fisk, Henry	Sturbridge	religious unorthodoxy	confiscation, prison
religious persecution	1751	Morse, David	Sturbridge	religious unorthodoxy	confiscation
religious persecution	1751	Moulton, Elder	Sturbridge	religious unorthodoxy	prison, exile
religious persecution	1751	Newell, John	Sturbridge	religious unorthodoxy	confiscation
religious persecution	1751	Perry, Jonathan	Sturbridge	religious unorthodoxy	confiscation
religious persecution	1751	Perry, Josiah	Sturbridge	religious unorthodoxy	prison
religious persecution	1751	Pike, John	Sturbridge	religious unorthodoxy	confiscation

State/ Target of Act	Date	Name	Location	Act	Consequence
religious persecution	1751	Robbins, Benjamin	Sturbridge	religious unorthodoxy	confiscation
religious persecution	1751	Streeter, John	Sturbridge	religious unorthodoxy	confiscation
colonial taxation	1760s–1770s	Whiting, Daniel	Dover	paramilitary host	
religious persecution	1762	Rich, Elisha	Royalston	refused to renounce faith	threat
religious persecution	1764	Harvey, Samuel	Montague	religious unorthodoxy	confiscation
religious persecution	1764	Montague, Richard	North Leverett	religious unorthodoxy	jail, confiscation
colonial taxation	8/1765	Adams, John	Boston	paramilitary organizer	
colonial taxation	8/1765	Adams, Samuel	Boston	paramilitary	
colonial taxation	8/1765	Avery, John	Boston	paramilitary	
colonial taxation	8/1765	Bradlee, Nathaniel	Boston	paramilitary	
colonial taxation	8/1765	Cushing, Thomas	Boston	informant	
colonial taxation	8/1765	Daws, Tom	Boston	paramilitary	
colonial taxation	8/1765	Edes, Benjamin	Boston	paramilitary	
colonial taxation	8/1765	Hancock, John	Boston	paramilitary	
colonial taxation	8/1765	Mackintosh, Ebenezer	Boston	rifled a residence	
colonial taxation	8/1765	Otis, James	Boston	organized paramilitary	
colonial taxation	8/1765	Revere, Paul	Boston	paramilitary	
colonial taxation	8/1765	Swift, Henry	Boston	paramilitary	
colonial taxation	8/1765	Thomas, Isaiah	Boston	paramilitary	
colonial taxation	8/1765	Tuckerman, Edward	Boston	paramilitary	
colonial taxation	8/1765	Warren, Joseph	Boston	paramilitary	
colonial taxation	8/1765	Warren, Mercy Otis	Boston	propaganda	
colonial taxation	8/1765	Winthrop, Hannah Fayerweather Tolman	Cambridge	propaganda	
colonial taxation	8/1765	Young, Thomas	Boston	paramilitary	
colonial taxation	4/13/1766	Edes, Thomas	Boston	delivered messages	
slave recapture	1767	Burt, Elijah	East Longmeadow	harbored slaves	
taxation	1769	Smith, Chileab	Ashfield	tax resistance	confiscation
taxation	1769	Smith, Ebenezer	Ashfield	tax resistance	confiscation
colonial taxation	8/14/1769	Adams, John	Boston	paramilitary	
Revolutionary War	1770s	Barrell, Colburn	Boston	refused to serve	house rifled, confiscation, exile, wife threatened
Revolutionary War	1770s	Capen, Hopestill	Boston	refused to serve	jail
Revolutionary War	1770s	Davis, Benjamin, Sr.	Boston	refused to serve	bankruptcy, exile
Revolutionary War	1770s	Winslow, Isaac, Jr.	Roxbury	refused to serve	home burned
colonial taxation	1770	Thomas, Isaiah	Boston	paramilitary	

State/ Target of Act	Date	Name	Location	Act	Consequence
colonial taxation	1/1770	Warren, Joseph	Boston	raid	
colonial taxation	2/22/1770	Clarke, Charity	Marlborough	mock funeral procession	
colonial taxation	2/22/1770	Foote, Betsy	Marlborough	mock funeral procession	
colonial taxation	2/22/1770	Winslow, Anna	Marlborough	mock funeral procession	
religious persecution	1773	Backus, Isaac	Middleborough	demanded rights	
taxation	1773	Backus, Isaac	Boston	tax resistance	jail
religious persecution	9/1773	Fletcher, Asaph	Chelmsford	demanded rights	
religious persecution	9/1773	Smith, Ebenezer	Chelmsford	demanded rights	
colonial taxation	12/16/1773	Adams, Samuel	Boston	sabotage	
colonial taxation	12/16/1773	Akeley, Francis	Boston	sabotage	
colonial taxation	12/16/1773	Barber, Nathaniel	Boston	sabotage	
colonial taxation	12/16/1773	Barnard, Samuel	Boston	sabotage	
colonial taxation	12/16/1773	Bass, Henry	Boston	sabotage	
colonial taxation	12/16/1773	Bassett, Joseph	Boston	sabotage	
colonial taxation	12/16/1773	Bates, Edward	Boston	sabotage	
colonial taxation	12/16/1773	Beals, Adam, Jr.	Boston	sabotage	
colonial taxation	12/16/1773	Bolter, Thomas	Boston	sabotage	
colonial taxation	12/16/1773	Bradlee, Ann Dunlap	Boston	sabotage	
colonial taxation	12/16/1773	Bradlee, David	Boston	sabotage	
colonial taxation	12/16/1773	Bradlee, James	Boston	sabotage	
colonial taxation	12/16/1773	Bradlee, Josiah	Boston	sabotage	
colonial taxation	12/16/1773	Bradlee, Nathaniel	Boston	sabotage	
colonial taxation	12/16/1773	Bradlee, Thomas	Boston	sabotage	
colonial taxation	12/16/1773	Brewer, James	Boston	sabotage	
colonial taxation	12/16/1773	Brown, John	Boston	sabotage	
colonial taxation	12/16/1773	Brown, Seth Ingersoll	Boston	sabotage	
colonial taxation	12/16/1773	Bruse, Stephen	Boston	sabotage	
colonial taxation	12/16/1773	Burton, Benjamin	Boston	sabotage	
colonial taxation	12/16/1773	Campbell, Nicholas	Boston	sabotage	
colonial taxation	12/16/1773	Carleton, George	Boston	sabotage	
colonial taxation	12/16/1773	Chase, Thomas	Boston	sabotage	
colonial taxation	12/16/1773	Child, Nathaniel	Boston	sabotage	
colonial taxation	12/16/1773	Clark, Jonathan	Boston	sabotage	
colonial taxation	12/16/1773	Clarke, Benjamin	Boston	sabotage	
colonial taxation	12/16/1773	Cochran, John	Boston	sabotage	
colonial taxation	12/16/1773	Colesworthy, Gilbert	Boston	sabotage	
colonial taxation	12/16/1773	Collidge, S.	Boston	sabotage	
colonial taxation	12/16/1773	Collier, Gershom (or Gersham)	Boston	sabotage	

State/ Target of Act	Date	Name	Location	Act	Consequence
colonial taxation	12/16/1773	Collson, Adam	Boston	sabotage	
colonial taxation	12/16/1773	Condy, James Foster	Boston	sabotage	
colonial taxation	12/16/1773	Coolidge, Daniel	Boston	sabotage	
colonial taxation	12/16/1773	Coolidge, Joseph	Boston	sabotage	
colonial taxation	12/16/1773	Coolidge, Samuel	Boston	sabotage	
colonial taxation	12/16/1773	Cooper, Samuel	Boston	sabotage	
colonial taxation	12/16/1773	Cox, William	Boston	sabotage	
colonial taxation	12/16/1773	Crafts, Thomas, Jr.	Boston	sabotage	
colonial taxation	12/16/1773	Crane, John	Boston	sabotage	
colonial taxation	12/16/1773	Crockett	Boston	sabotage	
colonial taxation	12/16/1773	Curtis, Obadiah	Boston	sabotage	
colonial taxation	12/16/1773	Dana, Thomas, Jr.	Boston	sabotage	
colonial taxation	12/16/1773	Davis, Robert	Boston	sabotage	
colonial taxation	12/16/1773	DeCarteret, John	Boston	sabotage	
colonial taxation	12/16/1773	Decker, David	Boston	sabotage	
colonial taxation	12/16/1773	Dickman, John	Boston	sabotage	
colonial taxation	12/16/1773	Dolbeare, Edward	Boston	sabotage	
colonial taxation	12/16/1773	Dolbeare, Samuel	Boston	sabotage	
colonial taxation	12/16/1773	Duton, George	Boston	sabotage	
colonial taxation	12/16/1773	Dyar, John, Jr.	Boston	sabotage	
colonial taxation	12/16/1773	Eaton, Joseph Eaton	Boston	sabotage	
colonial taxation	12/16/1773	Eckley, Joseph Eayres	Boston	sabotage	
colonial taxation	12/16/1773	Edes, Benjamin	Boston	sabotage	
colonial taxation	12/16/1773	Etheridge, George	Boston	sabotage	
colonial taxation	12/16/1773	Etheridge, William	Boston	sabotage	
colonial taxation	12/16/1773	Fenno, Samuel	Boston	sabotage	
colonial taxation	12/16/1773	Foster, Samuel	Boston	sabotage	
colonial taxation	12/16/1773	Fracker, Thomas	Boston	sabotage	
colonial taxation	12/16/1773	Frothingham, Nathaniel, Jr.	Boston	sabotage	
colonial taxation	12/16/1773	Fulton, John	Boston	sabotage	
colonial taxation	12/16/1773	Fulton, Sarah Bradlee	Boston	abetted sabotage	
colonial taxation	12/16/1773	Gammell, John	Boston	sabotage	
colonial taxation	12/16/1773	Gay, Eliazar	Boston	sabotage	
colonial taxation	12/16/1773	Gerrish, Thomas	Boston	sabotage	
colonial taxation	12/16/1773	Gill, John	Boston	sabotage	
colonial taxation	12/16/1773	Gore, Samuel	Boston	sabotage	
colonial taxation	12/16/1773	Grant, Moses	Boston	sabotage	
colonial taxation	12/16/1773	Greene, Nathaniel	Boston	sabotage	
colonial taxation	12/16/1773	Greenleaf, John	Boston	sabotage	
colonial taxation	12/16/1773	Guy, Timothy	Boston	sabotage	
colonial taxation	12/16/1773	Hammond, Samuel	Boston	sabotage	

State/ Target of Act	Date	Name	Location	Act	Consequence
colonial taxation	12/16/1773	Hancock, John	Boston	sabotage	
colonial taxation	12/16/1773	Harrington, Peter	Boston	sabotage	
colonial taxation	12/16/1773	Haskins, William	Boston	sabotage	
colonial taxation	12/16/1773	Hendley, William	Boston	sabotage	
colonial taxation	12/16/1773	Hewes, George R.T.	Boston	sabotage	
colonial taxation	12/16/1773	Hicks, John	Boston	sabotage	
colonial taxation	12/16/1773	Hobbs, Samuel	Boston	sabotage	
colonial taxation	12/16/1773	Hooten, John	Boston	sabotage	
colonial taxation	12/16/1773	Horton, Elisha	Boston	sabotage	
colonial taxation	12/16/1773	Houghton, Elijah	Boston	sabotage	
colonial taxation	12/16/1773	Howard, Samuel	Boston	sabotage	
colonial taxation	12/16/1773	Howe, Edward Compton	Boston	sabotage	
colonial taxation	12/16/1773	Hunnewell, Jonathan	Boston	sabotage	
colonial taxation	12/16/1773	Hunnewell, Richard	Boston	sabotage	
colonial taxation	12/16/1773	Hunnewell, Richard, Jr.	Boston	sabotage	
colonial taxation	12/16/1773	Hunstable, Thomas	Boston	sabotage	
colonial taxation	12/16/1773	Hunt, Abraham	Boston	sabotage	
colonial taxation	12/16/1773	Ingersoll, Daniel	Boston	sabotage	
colonial taxation	12/16/1773	Jameson, Charles	Boston	sabotage	
colonial taxation	12/16/1773	Jameson, Robert	Boston	sabotage	
colonial taxation	12/16/1773	Joy, Jared	Boston	sabotage	
colonial taxation	12/16/1773	Kinnison, David	Boston	sabotage	
colonial taxation	12/16/1773	Lash, Robert	Boston	sabotage	
colonial taxation	12/16/1773	Learned, Amariah	Boston	sabotage	
colonial taxation	12/16/1773	Lee, Joseph	Boston	sabotage	
colonial taxation	12/16/1773	Lee, Nathaniel	Boston	sabotage	
colonial taxation	12/16/1773	Lincoln, Amos	Boston	sabotage	
colonial taxation	12/16/1773	Locke, John	Boston	sabotage	
colonial taxation	12/16/1773	Loring, Mathew	Boston	sabotage	
colonial taxation	12/16/1773	Lovering, Joseph	Boston	sabotage	
colonial taxation	12/16/1773	Ludden, Joseph	Boston	sabotage	
colonial taxation	12/16/1773	Lyon, David	Boston	sabotage	
colonial taxation	12/16/1773	Machin, Thomas	Boston	sabotage	
colonial taxation	12/16/1773	Macintosh, Peter	Boston	sabotage	
colonial taxation	12/16/1773	Mackintosh, Ebenezer	Boston	sabotage	arrest
colonial taxation	12/16/1773	MacNeill, Archibald	Boston	sabotage	
colonial taxation	12/16/1773	Marston, John	Boston	sabotage	
colonial taxation	12/16/1773	Martin, John	Boston	sabotage	
colonial taxation	12/16/1773	Martin, William P.	Boston	sabotage	
colonial taxation	12/16/1773	Maxwell, Thomas	Boston	sabotage	
colonial taxation	12/16/1773	May, John	Boston	sabotage	
colonial taxation	12/16/1773	Mead, John	Boston	sabotage	

State/ Target of Act	Date	Name	Location	Act	Consequence
colonial taxation	12/16/1773	Mellius, Henry	Boston	sabotage	
colonial taxation	12/16/1773	Melville, Thomas	Boston	sabotage	
colonial taxation	12/16/1773	Miller, Aaron John	Boston	sabotage	
colonial taxation	12/16/1773	Mills, John	Boston	sabotage	
colonial taxation	12/16/1773	Molineux, William	Boston	sabotage	
colonial taxation	12/16/1773	Moore, Francis	Boston	sabotage	
colonial taxation	12/16/1773	Moore, Thomas	Boston	sabotage	
colonial taxation	12/16/1773	Morse, Anthony	Boston	sabotage	
colonial taxation	12/16/1773	Mountford, Joseph	Boston	sabotage	
colonial taxation	12/16/1773	Newell, Eliphelet	Boston	sabotage	
colonial taxation	12/16/1773	Nicholls, Joseph	Boston	sabotage	
colonial taxation	12/16/1773	Nowell, Samuel	Boston	sabotage	
colonial taxation	12/16/1773	Palmer, Joseph Pease	Boston	sabotage	
colonial taxation	12/16/1773	Parker, Jonathan	Boston	sabotage	
colonial taxation	12/16/1773	Payson, Joseph	Boston	sabotage	
colonial taxation	12/16/1773	Pearce, William	Boston	sabotage	
colonial taxation	12/16/1773	Peck, Samuel	Boston	sabotage	
colonial taxation	12/16/1773	Peters, John	Boston	sabotage	
colonial taxation	12/16/1773	Pitman, Isaac	Boston	sabotage	
colonial taxation	12/16/1773	Pitts, Lendall	Boston	sabotage	
colonial taxation	12/16/1773	Pitts, Samuel	Boston	sabotage	
colonial taxation	12/16/1773	Porter, Thomas	Boston	sabotage	
colonial taxation	12/16/1773	Prentiss, Henry	Boston	sabotage	
colonial taxation	12/16/1773	Prentiss, Nathaniel Surtees	Boston	sabotage	
colonial taxation	12/16/1773	Prince, John	Boston	sabotage	
colonial taxation	12/16/1773	Proctor, Edward	Boston	sabotage	
colonial taxation	12/16/1773	Purkitt, Henry	Boston	sabotage	
colonial taxation	12/16/1773	Putnam, Seth	Boston	sabotage	
colonial taxation	12/16/1773	Quincy, Josiah, II	Boston	sabotage	
colonial taxation	12/16/1773	Randall, John	Boston	sabotage	
colonial taxation	12/16/1773	Reed, Joseph	Boston	sabotage	
colonial taxation	12/16/1773	Revere, Paul	Boston	sabotage	
colonial taxation	12/16/1773	Rice, Benjamin	Boston	sabotage	
colonial taxation	12/16/1773	Robins, Jonathan Dorby	Boston	sabotage	
colonial taxation	12/16/1773	Roby, Joseph	Boston	sabotage	
colonial taxation	12/16/1773	Russell, John	Boston	sabotage	
colonial taxation	12/16/1773	Russell, William	Boston	sabotage	
colonial taxation	12/16/1773	Sawtelle, Jonathan	Boston	sabotage	
colonial taxation	12/16/1773	Sayward, George	Boston	sabotage	
colonial taxation	12/16/1773	Sears, Edmund	Boston	sabotage	
colonial taxation	12/16/1773	Sessions, Robert	Boston	sabotage	

State/ Target of Act	Date	Name	Location	Act	Consequence
colonial taxation	12/16/1773	Shed, Joseph	Boston	sabotage	
colonial taxation	12/16/1773	Simpson, Benjamin	Boston	sabotage	
colonial taxation	12/16/1773	Slater, Peter, Jr.	Boston	sabotage	
colonial taxation	12/16/1773	Slope, Samuel	Boston	sabotage	
colonial taxation	12/16/1773	Smith, Ephraim	Boston	sabotage	
colonial taxation	12/16/1773	Snelling, Josiah	Boston	sabotage	
colonial taxation	12/16/1773	Spear, Thomas	Boston	sabotage	
colonial taxation	12/16/1773	Sprague, Samuel	Boston	sabotage	
colonial taxation	12/16/1773	Spurr, John	Boston	sabotage	
colonial taxation	12/16/1773	Starr, James	Boston	sabotage	
colonial taxation	12/16/1773	Stearns, Phineas	Boston	sabotage	
colonial taxation	12/16/1773	Stevens, Ebenezer	Boston	sabotage	
colonial taxation	12/16/1773	Stoddard, James	Boston	sabotage	
colonial taxation	12/16/1773	Story, Elisha	Boston	sabotage	
colonial taxation	12/16/1773	Swan, James	Boston	sabotage	
colonial taxation	12/16/1773	Tower, Abraham	Boston	sabotage	
colonial taxation	12/16/1773	Trow, Bartholomew, Jr.	Boston	sabotage	
colonial taxation	12/16/1773	Truman, John	Boston	sabotage	
colonial taxation	12/16/1773	Tucker, Benjamin, Jr.	Boston	sabotage	
colonial taxation	12/16/1773	Urann, Thomas	Boston	sabotage	
colonial taxation	12/16/1773	Warren, Joseph	Boston	sabotage	
colonial taxation	12/16/1773	Watson, James	Boston	sabotage	
colonial taxation	12/16/1773	Wells, Henry	Boston	sabotage	
colonial taxation	12/16/1773	Wells, Thomas	Boston	sabotage	
colonial taxation	12/16/1773	Wheeler, Josiah	Boston	sabotage	
colonial taxation	12/16/1773	White, Thomas	Boston	sabotage	
colonial taxation	12/16/1773	Whitehead, John	Boston	sabotage	
colonial taxation	12/16/1773	Williams, David	Boston	sabotage	
colonial taxation	12/16/1773	Williams, Isaac	Boston	sabotage	
colonial taxation	12/16/1773	Williams, Jeremiah	Boston	sabotage	
colonial taxation	12/16/1773	Williams, Thomas	Boston	sabotage	
colonial taxation	12/16/1773	Willis, Charles	Boston	sabotage	
colonial taxation	12/16/1773	Willis, Nathaniel	Boston	sabotage	
colonial taxation	12/16/1773	Wyeth, Joshua	Boston	sabotage	
colonial taxation	12/16/1773	Young, Thomas	Boston	sabotage	
religious persecution	1774	Backus, Isaac	Boston	demanded rights	
Revolutionary War	7/20/1775	Foster, Edward	Attleboro	refused to serve	home rifled
taxation	1780	Cuffe, Paul	Cuttyhunk Island	tax resistance	
slave recapture	1783	Cuffe, Paul	Westport	sea relay	
slave recapture	1783	Wainer, Thomas	Westport	sea relay	
taxation	9/12/1786	Bardwell, Perez	Concord	paramilitary leader	debtors' prison

State/ Target of Act	Date	Name	Location	Act	Consequence
taxation	9/12/1786	Day, Luke	West Springfield	paramilitary	debtors' prison
taxation	9/12/1786	Kelsey, John	Concord	paramilitary leader	
taxation	9/12/1786	Page, Benjamin	Concord	paramilitary leader	
taxation	9/12/1786	Parker, Oliver	Concord	paramilitary leader	
taxation	9/12/1786	Parsons, Eli	Chicopee	paramilitary	
taxation	9/12/1786	Shattuck, Job	Concord	paramilitary leader	slashed
taxation	9/12/1786	Shays, Daniel Patrick	Pelham	paramilitary leader	
taxation	9/12/1786	Smith, Nathan	Concord	paramilitary leader	
taxation	9/12/1786	Wilcox, Peter, Jr.	Berkshire County	paramilitary leader	jail
taxation	12/6/1786	Bly, John	Berkshire County	paramilitary	hanged
taxation	12/6/1786	Rose, Charles	Berkshire County	paramilitary	hanged
debt	1786–1787	Bardwell, Perez	Williamsburg	paramilitary	
taxation	1786–1787	Parmenter, Jason	Berkshire County	paramilitary	jail
debt, taxation	1787	Austin, Abigail	Concord	jailbreak	
debt, taxation	1787	Wilcox, Polly Mansfield	Berkshire County	jailbreak	
taxation	10/1787	Manning, William	Concord	paramilitary	prison at hard labor
War of 1812	1812	Whipple, Jonathan	Ipswich	refused to serve	threat, fine
slavery	1818	Garrison, William Lloyd	Newburyport	propaganda	
slavery	1829	Garrison, William Lloyd	Boston	libel	jail
slavery	1829	Walker, David	Boston	propaganda	poisoned
slave recapture	1830s–1840s	Adams, Robert S.	Fall River	harbored slaves	
slave recapture	1830s–1850s	Sharper, Jubilee	Small Gloucester	slave rescue	
slave recapture	1830s–1860s	Bearse, Austin	New Bedford	sea transport	
slavery	1830s–1860s	Chapman, Maria Weston	Boston	propaganda	
slavery	1830s–1860s	Garrison, Helen Eliza Benson	Boston	fund-raising	
slavery	1830s–1860s	Johnson, Oliver	Boston	propaganda	
slave recapture	10/16/1830	Alcott, Amos Bronson	Concord	recruitment	
slave recapture	10/16/1830	Sewall, Samuel Edmund	Boston	recruitment	
slavery	1/1/1831	Garrison, William Lloyd	Boston	propaganda	
slavery	1835	Burleigh, Charles Callistus	Boston	protest, propaganda	mob violence
slavery	1835	Garrison, William Lloyd	Boston	propaganda	mob violence
slavery	1838	Foster, Abigail Kelley	Worcester	broke the Sabbath	
slavery	1838	Foster, Stephen Symons	Worcester	broke the Sabbath	
slave recapture	9/1838	Taber, William Congdon	New Bedford	slave conducting	
Mexican-American War	1840s	Thoreau, Henry David	Concord	resisted taxes	jail

State/ Target of Act	Date	Name	Location	Act	Consequence
slavery	1840s	Thoreau, Henry David	Concord	protest	
slave recapture	1840s	Thoreau, Henry David	Concord	slave relay, propaganda	
slave recapture	1840s–1850s	Alcott, Amos Bronson	Concord	harbored slaves	
slave recapture	1840s–1850s	Alcott, Louisa May	Concord	harbored slaves	
slave recapture	1840s–1850s	Brooks, Mary Merrick	Concord	ran a safehouse	
slave recapture	1840s–1850s	Howe, Julia Ward	Boston	conspiracy	
slave recapture	1840s–1850s	Mann, Horace	Boston	harbored slaves	
slavery	1840s–1850s	Shaw, Nicolas Stott	New Bedford	protest	
slavery	1840s–1850s	Shaw, Thomas	New Bedford	protest	
taxation	1/16/1843	Alcott, Amos Bronson	Concord	tax resistance	jail
slavery	1846	Foster, Abigail Kelley	Worcester	propaganda	arrest
slavery	1846	Foster, Stephen Symons	Worcester	propaganda	arrest
taxation	7/1846	Thoreau, Henry David	Concord	tax resistance	jail
slave recapture	1847–1861	Remond, Charles Lenox	Boston	conspiracy	
slavery	4/15/1848	Howe, Samuel Gridley	Boston	fund-raising	
slavery	1849	Thoreau, Henry David	Concord	propaganda	
Fugitive Slave Law of 1850	1850s	Emerson, Lydia Jackson	Concord	slave rescue, recruitment	
slavery	1850s	Shaw, Anna Howard	New Bedford	protest	
slave recapture	1850s	Thoreau, Cynthia Dunbar	Concord	ran a safehouse	
slave recapture	1850s	Thoreau, Helen	Concord	ran a safehouse	
slave recapture	1850s	Thoreau, Sophia	Concord	ran a safehouse	
slave recapture	1850	Emerson, Lydia Jackson	Concord	slave relay, fund-raising	
slave recapture	1850	Emerson, Ralph Waldo	Concord	slave relay, fund-raising	
slave recapture	1850–1861	Clark, Jonas W.	Boston	ran a street patrol	
Fugitive Slave Law of 1850	9/1850	Parker, Theodore	Boston	protest	
slave recapture	1851	Brown, John	Springfield	ran a street patrol	
slave recapture	2/12/1851	Morris, Robert	Boston	conspiracy, jailbreak	tried
Fugitive Slave Law of 1850	2/15/1851	Hayden, Harriet Bell	Boston	harbored slaves	
Fugitive Slave Law of 1850	2/15/1851	Hayden, Jo	Boston	harbored slaves	
Fugitive Slave Law of 1850	2/15/1851	Hayden, Lewis	Boston	harbored slaves	tried
slave recapture	2/15/1851	Hayden, Lewis	Boston	jailbreak	
slave recapture	2/15/1851	Minkins, Fredric "Shadrach"	Boston	jailbreak	fled
slave recapture	2/15/1851	Smith, John J.	Boston	jailbreak	
slave recapture	2/16/1851	Bigelow, Ann Hager	Concord	harbored slaves	
slave recapture	2/16/1851	Bigelow, Francis Edwin	Concord	harbored and relayed slaves	
slave recapture	2/16/1851	Brooks, Nathan	Concord	defended slave rescue	

State/ Target of Act	Date	Name	Location	Act	Consequence
slave recapture	2/16/1851	Drake, Frances Hills Wilder	Leominster	harbored slaves	
slave recapture	2/16/1851	Drake, Jonathan	Leominster	harbored slaves	
slave recapture	2/16/1851	Snow, Benjamin, Jr.	West Fitchburg	harbored slaves	
slave recapture	2/16/1851	Snow, Mary Baldwin Boutolle	West Fitchburg	harbored slaves	
slavery	2/21/1851	Garrison, William Lloyd	Boston	propaganda	
Fugitive Slave Law of 1850	3/1851	French, Rodney	New Bedford	halted slave recapture	
slave recapture	4/3/1851	Andrew, John Albion	Boston	slave rescue	
slave recapture	4/3/1851	Buffum, James Needham	Lynn	fund-raising	
slave recaptures	4/3/1851	Burton, Alexander P.	Boston	jailbreak	tried
Fugitive Slave Law of 1850	4/3/1851	Dana, Richard Henry, Jr.	Boston	jailbreak	
Fugitive Slave Law of 1850	4/3/1851	Emerson, Ralph Waldo	Concord	slave relay, recruitment	
slave recapture	4/3/1851	Garrison, William Lloyd	Boston	jailbreak	denounced
Fugitive Slave Law of 1850	4/3/1851	Grimes, Archibald	Boston	jailbreak	
slave recapture	4/3/1851	Grimes, Archibald	Boston	slave rescue	
slave recapture	4/3/1851	Hale, John Parker	Boston	defended slave rescue	
slave recapture	4/3/1851	Hayden, Harriet Bell	Boston	harbored slaves	
slave recapture	4/3/1851	Hayden, Lewis	Boston	jailbreak, harbored slaves	tried
slave recapture	4/3/1851	Jackson, Francis	Boston	jailbreak	
slave recapture	4/3/1851	Loring, Ellis Gray	Boston	jailbreak	
Fugitive Slave Law of 1850	4/3/1851	Parker, Theodore	West Fitchburg	protest	
slave recapture	4/3/1851	Phillips, Wendell Addison	Boston	jailbreak	
slavery	4/3/1851	Pitts, Coffin	Boston	fund-raising	
slave recapture	4/3/1851	Scott, James	Boston	jailbreak	tried
Fugitive Slave Law of 1850	4/3/1851	Sewall, Samuel Edmund	Boston	jailbreak	
slave recapture	4/3/1851	Sims, Thomas M.	Boston	jailbreak	
slave recapture	4/3/1851	Smith, John J.	Boston	jailbreak, slave relay	
slave recapture	4/3/1851	Spear, John Murray	Boston	jailbreak	
Fugitive Slave Law of 1850	4/3/1851	Thoreau, Henry David	Concord	protest	
slavery	4/15/1851	Nell, William Cooper	Boston	propaganda	charged
Fugitive Slave Law of 1850	9/1851	Garrison, William Lloyd	Boston	conspiracy, propaganda	
slave recapture	12/15/1851	Coburn, John P.	Boston	jailbreak	tried
slave recapture	1852	Wright, Elizur	Boston	slave rescue	tried
slave recapture	2/4/1853	Watkins, William J.	Boston	conspiracy	
slave recapture	1854	Coburn, John P.	Boston	ran a street patrol	
slave recapture	1854	Thacker, Henry L.W.	Boston	backer, conspiracy	

State/ Target of Act	Date	Name	Location	Act	Consequence
slave recapture	1854	Washington, George	Boston	backer, conspiracy	
slavery	1854–1861	Adler, Leibman	Detroit	protest	
slavery	1854–1861	Sloman, Mark	Detroit	protest	
slave recapture	5/26/1854	Higginson, Thomas Wentworth	Boston	jailbreak	indicted
slave recapture	5/26/1854	Parker, Theodore	Boston	jailbreak	
slave recapture	5/26/1854	Phillips, Wendell Addison	Boston	protest, jailbreak	indicted
Fugitive Slave Law of 1850	6/1854	Parker, Theodore	Boston	protest	
slave recapture	10/1855	Fairweather, James	New Bedford	ran a street patrol	
slave recapture	10/1855	Gibson, Robert	New Bedford	ran a street patrol	
slave recapture	10/1855	Guinn, Isaac	New Bedford	ran a street patrol	
slave recapture	10/1855	Johnson, Henry	New Bedford	ran a street patrol	
Fugitive Slave Law of 1850	7/4/1856	Phillips, Wendell Addison	Boston	protest	
slavery	1/1857	Higginson, Thomas Wentworth	Boston	fund-raising	
slavery	1/1857	Howe, Samuel Gridley	Boston	fund-raising	
slavery	1/1857	Parker, Theodore	Boston	fund-raising	
slavery	1/1857	Stearns, George Luther	Medford	fund-raising	
slave recapture	8/1/1857	Gaul, Lewis	Boston	ran a street patrol	
women's disenfranchisement	1858	Stone, Lucy	Boston	tax resistance	
slave recapture	10/30/1859	Thoreau, Henry David	Concord	abetted anarchy	
Civil War	1860s	Prouty, Lorenzo D.	Shirley	refused to serve	
Civil War	1860s	Prouty, Nathan Converse	Shirley	refused to serve	guardhouse
slave recapture	1860s	Weld, Angelina Emily Grimké	Suffolk	recruitment	
Civil War	1860s	Weld, Charles Stewart	Suffolk	refused to serve	humiliation
slave recapture	1860s	Weld, Theodore Dwight	Suffolk	recruitment	
draft	1861	Emerson, Ralph Waldo	Concord	supported pacifism	
draft	1861	Phillips, Wendell Addison	Boston	supported pacifism	
draft	1861	Sumner, Charles	Boston	supported pacifism	
slave recapture	4/29/1861	De Mortie, Mark	Boston	ran a street patrol	
slave recapture	4/29/1861	Downing, George T.	Boston	ran a street patrol	
slave recapture	4/29/1861	Hayden, Lewis	Boston	ran a street patrol	
slave recapture	4/29/1861	Remond, Charles Lenox	Boston	ran a street patrol	
draft	1862	Swift, Henry D.	South Dedham	draft protest	
draft	1863	Prouty, Lorenzo D.	Shirley	draft protest	
draft	1863	Prouty, Nathan Converse	Shirley	draft protest	
Civil War	1863	Swift, Henry D.	South Dedham	refused to serve	stockade

State/ Target of Act	Date	Name	Location	Act	Consequence
draft	7/30/1863	Royce, Samuel	Boston	abetted draft evasion	
Comstock Act	11/3/1877	Heywood, Angela Fiducia Tilton	Princeton	mailed pamphlets	
Comstock Act	11/3/1877	Heywood, Ezra Hervey	Boston	mailed pamphlets	prison at hard labor
Comstock Act	11/3/1877	Ingersoll, Robert Green	Princeton	birth control information	arraigned
Comstock Act	5/1890	Heywood, Ezra Hervey	Princeton	mailed pamphlets	prison
free speech ban	9/8/1909	Goldman, Emma	Worcester	conspiracy	banned
labor exploitation	1/1912	Flynn, Elizabeth Gurley	Lawrence	mill strike	jail
labor exploitation	1/1912	Haywood, William Dudley	Lawrence	mill strike	jail
labor exploitation	1/29/1912	Caruso, Joseph	Lawrence	strike	prison
labor exploitation	1/29/1912	Ettor, Joseph	Lawrence	murder	charged
labor exploitation	1/29/1912	Giovannitti, Arturo M.	Lawrence	strike	prison
labor exploitation	1/29/1912	LoPizzo, Anna	Lawrence	strike	shot
World War I	8/1914	Balch, Emily Greene	Jamaica Plains	demonstration	
World War I	4/25/1918	Grosser, Philip	Boston	draft evasion	mock hanging
Sacco and Vanzetti death sentence	4/8/1927	Gold, Michael	Boston	procession	arrest
Sacco and Vanzetti death sentence	4/8/1927	Guthrie, Woody	Boston	protest	
Sacco and Vanzetti death sentence	4/8/1927	Lippmann, Walter	Boston	protest	
Sacco and Vanzetti death sentence	4/8/1927	Porter, Katherine Anne	Boston	protest	
Sacco and Vanzetti death sentence	4/8/1927	Schlesinger, Arthur, Sr.	Boston	protest	
Sacco and Vanzetti death sentence	4/8/1927	Shahn, Ben	Boston	protest	
Sacco and Vanzetti death sentence	4/8/1927	Sinclair, Upton	Boston	protest	
Sacco and Vanzetti death sentence	8/1927	Millay, Edna St. Vincent	Dedham	procession	arrest
Sacco and Vanzetti death sentence	8/1927	Parker, Dorothy Rothschild	Boston	procession	arrest
Comstock Act	1928	Dennett, Mary Coffin Ware	Worcester	birth control information	arrest
Comstock Act	2/1928	Konikow, Antoinette Kay Bucholz	Boston	birth control information	jail, torture
World War II	4/6/1943	Butcher, Charles	Cambridge	draft evasion	prison in irons
World War II	4/6/1943	Clark, Bronson P.	Cambridge	draft evasion	prison in irons
World War II	9/28/1943	Dellinger, David T.	Wakefield	refused to register	prison
ROTC	1960	Theroux, Paul Edward	Amherst	refused training	
draft	3/31/1966	O'Brien, David Paul	Boston	burned draft card	prison
Vietnam War	1967	Kehler, Randy	Colrain	refused draft card	prison
anti-abortion laws	10/2/1973	Edelin, Kenneth C.	Boston	manslaughter	tried
taxation	1990s	Corner, Betsy	Colrain	tax resistance	eviction

State/ Target of Act	Date	Name	Location	Act	Consequence
taxation	1990s	Kehler, Randy	Colrain	tax resistance	eviction
campaign finance corruption	11/15/1999	Kehler, Randy	Boston	sit-in	

Michigan
(* indicates multiple acts on same date)
(** indicates body left at emergency room)

State/ Target of Act	Date	Name	Location	Act	Consequence
slave recapture	1824	Hicks, Elias	Cass County	harbored slaves, hired slaves	threat
slavery	1830s	Comstock, Elizabeth Leslie Rous	Rollin	protest	
slave recapture	1830s–1850s	Osborn, Josiah	Calvin	slave relay	
slave recapture	1830s–1850s	Osborn, Mary Barnard	Calvin	slave relay	
slave recapture	1830	Chandler, Elizabeth Margaret	Tecumseh	recruitment	
slave recapture	1830	Thomas, Nathan Muncie	Schoolcraft	slave relay	
slavery	1840s	McAndrew, Helen Walker	Ypsilanti	protest	
slavery	1840s	McAndrew, William	Ypsilanti	protest	
slave recapture	1841	McKay, Jean Gray	Macomb County	slave rescue	
slave recapture	1841	McKay, Robert	Macomb County	slave rescue	
slave recapture	1845	Haviland, Laura Smith	Raisin	refugee orphanage	threats
slave recapture	8/1/1847	Hussey, Sylvanus Erastus Fuller	Plymouth	slave rescue	threat
slavery	1850s	Ross, Alexander Milton	Detroit	protest	
slave recapture	1854–1861	Heineman, Emil S.	Detroit	slave relay	
slave recapture	1854–1861	Heineman, Fanny Butzel	Detroit	slave relay	
free speech ban	3/16/1907	Goldman, Emma	Detroit	conspiracy	banned
draft	3/13/1918	Dieterle, John	Ann Arbor	draft protest	fired
draft	3/13/1918	Ficken, Richard O.	Ann Arbor	draft protest	fired
draft	3/13/1918	Florer, Warren W.	Ann Arbor	draft protest	fired
draft	3/13/1918	Kostermann, W.W.	Ann Arbor	draft protest	fired
draft	3/13/1918	Wiegand, Henry J.	Ann Arbor	draft protest	fired
labor organization ban	11/17/1936	Frankensteen, Richard	Detroit	sit-down strike	
labor organization ban	11/28/1936	Reuther, Roy	Detroit	sit-down strike	
labor organization ban	11/28/1936	Reuther, Victor George	Detroit	sit-down strike	
labor organization ban	11/28/1936	Reuther, Walter Philip	Detroit	sit-down strike	
labor organization ban	12/29/1936	Addes, George	Flint	promoted unions	
labor organization ban	12/29/1936	Dale, Ralph	Flint	promoted unions	
labor organization ban	12/29/1936	DeLong, Earl	Flint	promoted unions	shot
labor organization ban	12/29/1936	Dollinger, Genora Johnson	Flint	promoted unions	

State/Target of Act	Date	Name	Location	Act	Consequence
labor organization ban	12/29/1936	Hapgood, Mary Donovan	Flint	promoted unions	
labor organization ban	12/29/1936	Hapgood, William Powers	Flint	promoted unions	
labor organization ban	12/29/1936	Hendricks, Nellie Besson	Flint	promoted unions	
labor organization ban	12/29/1936	Johnson, Kermit	Flint	promoted unions	
labor organization ban	12/29/1936	Kraus, Henry	Flint	promoted unions	
labor organization ban	12/29/1936	Krause, Charles I.	Flint	promoted unions	
labor organization ban	12/29/1936	Lewis, John Llewellyn	Flint	promoted unions	
labor organization ban	12/29/1936	Martin, Homer	Flint	promoted unions	
labor organization ban	12/29/1936	Pitts, Ruth	Flint	blocked gates	
labor organization ban	12/29/1936	Reuther, Fania Sankin	Flint	sit-down strike	
labor organization ban	12/29/1936	Roy, Tekla	Flint	blocked gates	
labor organization ban	12/29/1936	Travis, Bob	Flint	promoted unions	
labor organization ban	12/29/1936	Van Zandt, Roscoe	Flint	promoted unions	
labor organization ban	12/29/1936	Walker, Teeter	Flint	promoted unions	
labor organization ban	1/1937	Coburn, William	Flint	strike	killed
Vietnam War	1/1963	Muhammad, Wallace D.	Hamtramck	refused to serve	prison
Vietnam War	1970s	Graves, Bruce	Ann Arbor	resisted war taxes	
Vietnam War	1970s	Graves, Ruth	Ann Arbor	resisted war taxes	
busing	9/1971	Miles, Robert	Pontiac	firebombing	prison
euthanasia ban	6/4/1990	Kevorkian, Murad "Jack"	Holly	lethal IV	injunction
euthanasia ban	10/23/1991	Kevorkian, Murad "Jack"	Sodus	lethal IV	
euthanasia ban	10/23/1991	Kevorkian, Murad "Jack"	Roseville	lethal gas	
animal rights	2/28/1992	Coronado, Rodney Adam	East Lansing	arson, looted	lawsuit
euthanasia ban	5/15/1992	Kevorkian, Murad "Jack"	Clawson	lethal gas	
euthanasia ban	9/26/1992	Kevorkian, Murad "Jack"	Waterford	lethal gas	
euthanasia ban	11/23/1992	Kevorkian, Murad "Jack"	Waterford	lethal gas	
euthanasia ban	12/15/1992*	Kevorkian, Murad "Jack"	Auburn Hills	lethal gas	
euthanasia ban	12/15/1992*	Kevorkian, Murad "Jack"	Auburn Hills	lethal gas	
euthanasia ban	1/20/1993	Kevorkian, Murad "Jack"	Huron	lethal gas	
euthanasia ban	2/4/1993*	Kevorkian, Murad "Jack"	Leland	lethal gas	
euthanasia ban	2/4/1993*	Kevorkian, Murad "Jack"	Leland	lethal gas	

State/ Target of Act	Date	Name	Location	Act	Consequence
euthanasia ban	2/12/1993	Kevorkian, Murad "Jack"	Southfield	lethal gas	
euthanasia ban	2/15/1993	Kevorkian, Murad "Jack"	Roseville	lethal gas	
euthanasia ban	2/18/1993*	Kevorkian, Murad "Jack"	Waterford	lethal gas	
euthanasia ban	2/18/1993*	Kevorkian, Murad "Jack"	Waterford	lethal gas	
euthanasia ban	5/16/1993	Kevorkian, Murad "Jack"	Detroit	lethal gas	
euthanasia ban	8/4/1993	Kevorkian, Murad "Jack"	Detroit	lethal gas	
euthanasia ban	9/9/1993	Kevorkian, Murad "Jack"	Redford	euthanasia	
euthanasia ban	10/22/1993	Kevorkian, Murad "Jack"	Royal Oak	lethal gas	
euthanasia ban	11/22/1993	Kevorkian, Murad "Jack"	Royal Oak	lethal gas	
euthanasia ban	11/26/1994	Kevorkian, Murad "Jack"	Royal Oak	lethal gas	
euthanasia ban	5/8/1995	Kevorkian, Murad "Jack"	Royal Oak	lethal gas	
euthanasia ban	5/12/1995	Kevorkian, Murad "Jack"	Pontiac	lethal gas	
euthanasia ban	6/26/1995	Kevorkian, Murad "Jack"	Springfield	lethal gas	
euthanasia ban	11/8/1995*	Kevorkian, Murad "Jack"	Pontiac	lethal gas	
euthanasia ban	11/8/1995*	Kevorkian, Murad "Jack"	Pontiac	lethal gas	
euthanasia ban	1/29/1996	Kevorkian, Murad "Jack"	Oakland	lethal gas	
euthanasia ban	5/7/1996	Kevorkian, Murad "Jack"	Farmington Hills	euthanasia	
euthanasia ban	6/10/1996	Kevorkian, Murad "Jack"	Pontiac	lethal gas	
euthanasia ban	6/18/1996	Kevorkian, Murad "Jack"	Pontiac	lethal gas	
euthanasia ban	6/21/1996	Kevorkian, Murad "Jack"	Pontiac	lethal gas	
euthanasia ban	7/5/1996	Kevorkian, Murad "Jack"	Royal Oak	lethal injection	
euthanasia ban	7/9/1996	Kevorkian, Murad "Jack"	Pontiac	lethal injection	
euthanasia ban	8/7/1996	Kevorkian, Murad "Jack"	Pontiac	lethal injection	
euthanasia ban	8/17/1996	Kevorkian, Murad "Jack"	Pontiac	lethal injection	
euthanasia ban	8/20/1996	Kevorkian, Murad "Jack"	Ionia	euthanasia	

State/ Target of Act	Date	Name	Location	Act	Consequence
euthanasia ban	8/22/1996	Kevorkian, Murad "Jack"	location unknown**	lethal injection	
euthanasia ban	8/23/1996	Kevorkian, Murad "Jack"	location unknown**	lethal injection	
euthanasia ban	9/2/1996	Kevorkian, Murad "Jack"	location unknown**	lethal injection	
euthanasia ban	9/7/1996	Kevorkian, Murad "Jack"	location unknown**	euthanasia	
euthanasia ban	9/29/1996	Kevorkian, Murad "Jack"	location unknown**	euthanasia	
euthanasia ban	10/10/1996	Kevorkian, Murad "Jack"	location unknown**	euthanasia	
euthanasia ban	10/17/1996	Kevorkian, Murad "Jack"	Pontiac	euthanasia	
euthanasia ban	10/24/1996	Kevorkian, Murad "Jack"	Pontiac	euthanasia	
euthanasia ban	2/2/1997*	Kevorkian, Murad "Jack"	Pontiac	lethal injection	
euthanasia ban	2/2/1997*	Kevorkian, Murad "Jack"	Pontiac	lethal injection	
euthanasia ban	3/7/1997	Kevorkian, Murad "Jack"	Romulus	euthanasia	
euthanasia ban	3/19/1997	Kevorkian, Murad "Jack"	Livonia	euthanasia	
euthanasia ban	3/23/1997	Kevorkian, Murad "Jack"	Warren	euthanasia	
euthanasia ban	4/8/1997	Kevorkian, Murad "Jack"	Romulus	euthanasia	
euthanasia ban	5/3/1997	Kevorkian, Murad "Jack"	Detroit	lethal IV	
euthanasia ban	6/25/1997	Kevorkian, Murad "Jack"	Southfield	lethal gas	
euthanasia ban	7/3/1997	Kevorkian, Murad "Jack"	Macomb	euthanasia	
euthanasia ban	7/3/1997	Kevorkian, Murad "Jack"	Wayne	euthanasia	
euthanasia ban	8/13/1997	Kevorkian, Murad "Jack"	Farmington Hills	lethal injection	
euthanasia ban	8/26/1997	Kevorkian, Murad "Jack"	Farmington Hills	lethal injection	
euthanasia ban	8/29/1997	Kevorkian, Murad "Jack"	Farmington Hills	euthanasia	
euthanasia ban	9/3/1997	Kevorkian, Murad "Jack"	Bloomfield	lethal injection	
euthanasia ban	9/8/1997	Kevorkian, Murad "Jack"	Romulus	euthanasia	
euthanasia ban	9/21/1997	Kevorkian, Murad "Jack"	Bloomfield	euthanasia	
euthanasia ban	9/29/1997	Kevorkian, Murad "Jack"	Detroit	euthanasia	

State/ Target of Act	Date	Name	Location	Act	Consequence
euthanasia ban	10/3/1997	Kevorkian, Murad "Jack"	Oakland	euthanasia	
euthanasia ban	10/8/1997	Kevorkian, Murad "Jack"	Bloomfield	euthanasia	
euthanasia ban	10/9/1997	Kevorkian, Murad "Jack"	Oakland	lethal injection	
animal rights	10/24/1997	Samuel, Justin Clayton, activist	Sheboygan	freed animals	
animal rights	10/24/1997	Young, Peter Daniel, activist	Sheboygan	freed animals	
euthanasia ban	10/30/1997	Kevorkian, Murad "Jack"	Detroit	euthanasia	
euthanasia ban	11/14/1997	Kevorkian, Murad "Jack"	Detroit	lethal gas	
euthanasia ban	11/23/1997	Kevorkian, Murad "Jack"	Pontiac	euthanasia	
euthanasia ban	11/23/1997	Kevorkian, Murad "Jack"	Detroit	euthanasia	
euthanasia ban	12/3/1997	Kevorkian, Murad "Jack"	Detroit	euthanasia	
euthanasia ban	12/11/1997	Kevorkian, Murad "Jack"	Romulus	lethal injection	
euthanasia ban	12/16/1997	Kevorkian, Murad "Jack"	Allen Park	euthanasia	
euthanasia ban	12/16/1997	Kevorkian, Murad "Jack"	Pontiac	euthanasia	
euthanasia ban	12/27/1997	Kevorkian, Murad "Jack"	Pontiac	euthanasia	
euthanasia ban	12/27/1997	Kevorkian, Murad "Jack"	Pontiac	euthanasia	
euthanasia ban	1/8/1998	Kevorkian, Murad "Jack"	Pontiac	euthanasia	
euthanasia ban	1/18/1998	Kevorkian, Murad "Jack"	Pontiac	lethal injection	
euthanasia ban	2/3/1998	Kevorkian, Murad "Jack"	Pontiac	euthanasia	
euthanasia ban	2/23/1998	Kevorkian, Murad "Jack"	Royal Oak	euthanasia	
euthanasia ban	2/26/1998	Kevorkian, Murad "Jack"	Southfield	lethal injection	
euthanasia ban	3/5/1998*	Kevorkian, Murad "Jack"	Pontiac	lethal injection	
euthanasia ban	3/5/1998*	Kevorkian, Murad "Jack"	Pontiac	lethal injection	
euthanasia ban	3/13/1998	Kevorkian, Murad "Jack"	Detroit	euthanasia	
euthanasia ban	3/28/1998	Kevorkian, Murad "Jack"	Southfield	euthanasia	
euthanasia ban	4/9/1998	Kevorkian, Murad "Jack"	Huron	lethal injection	

State/ Target of Act	Date	Name	Location	Act	Consequence
euthanasia ban	4/13/1998	Kevorkian, Murad "Jack"	Pontiac	lethal injection	
euthanasia ban	4/16/1998*	Kevorkian, Murad "Jack"	Oakland	lethal injection	
euthanasia ban	4/16/1998*	Kevorkian, Murad "Jack"	Oakland	lethal injection	
euthanasia ban	4/24/1998	Kevorkian, Murad "Jack"	Rochester Hills	cyanide	
euthanasia ban	5/7/1998	Kevorkian, Murad "Jack"	Royal Oak	euthanasia	
euthanasia ban	5/19/1998	Kevorkian, Murad "Jack"	Royal Oak	euthanasia	
euthanasia ban	6/7/1998	Kevorkian, Murad "Jack"	Oakland	assault, resisted arrest	fine
euthanasia ban	6/7/1998	Reding, George	Oakland	assault, resisted arrest	fine
euthanasia ban	11/22/1998	Kevorkian, Murad "Jack"	Oakland	lethal injection, murder	prison
taxation	2005	Graves, Bruce	Ann Arbor	picketed federal building	
taxation	2005	Graves, Ruth	Ann Arbor	picketed federal building	

Minnesota

State/ Target of Act	Date	Name	Location	Act	Consequence
slave recapture	8/1860	Grey, Emily O. Goodridge	St. Anthony Falls	harbored slaves	mob violence
labor exploitation	1916	Flynn, Elizabeth Gurley	Mesaba	strike	arrest
labor exploitation	4/1917	Flynn, Elizabeth Gurley	Duluth	pacifism	banished
draft	7/1917	Webster, Frank A.	St. Paul	draft protest	fired
draft	11/22/1917	Stratemeyer, E.H.	Osakis	draft protest	tarred, feathered
draft	2/11/1918	Ackerman, Ralph	New Ulm	draft protest	forced to resign
draft	3/25/1918	Lundin, Gust	Duluth	draft protest	tarred, feathered
draft	9/15/1918	Schaper, William August	Minneapolis	draft protest	fired
draft	12/19/1918	Criseler, George P	Rochester	draft protest	fired
World War II	1940s	Parker, Malcolm "Max"	Sandstone	war protest	prison
World War II	1/1941	Wilson, Winslow	Sandstone	draft protest	prison
World War II	1942	Lohmann, Henry	Minneapolis	alternate service	
World War II	1943	Bofman, Albert	Sandstone	war protest	prison
World War II	1944	Anderson, William	St. Paul	conscientious objection	engaged in starvation experiment
World War II	1944	Blickenstaff, Harold	St. Paul	conscientious objection	engaged in starvation experiment
World War II	1944	Burrous, Wendell	St. Paul	conscientious objection	engaged in starvation experiment

State/ Target of Act	Date	Name	Location	Act	Consequence
World War II	1944	Cowles, Edward	St. Paul	conscientious objection	engaged in starvation experiment
World War II	1944	Ebeling, George	St. Paul	conscientious objection	engaged in starvation experiment
World War II	1944	Frederick, Carlyle	St. Paul	conscientious objection	engaged in starvation experiment
World War II	1944	Garner, Jasper H.B.	St. Paul	conscientious objection	engaged in starvation experiment
World War II	1944	Glick, Lester	St. Paul	conscientious objection	engaged in starvation experiment
World War II	1944	Graham, James	St. Paul	conscientious objection	engaged in starvation experiment
World War II	1944	Heckman, Earl	St. Paul	conscientious objection	engaged in starvation experiment
World War II	1944	Hinkle, Roscoe C.	St. Paul	conscientious objection	engaged in starvation experiment
World War II	1944	Kampelman, Max	St. Paul	conscientious objection	engaged in starvation experiment
World War II	1944	Legg, Sam	St. Paul	conscientious objection	engaged in starvation experiment
World War II	1944	Liljengren, Philip	St. Paul	conscientious objection	engaged in starvation experiment
World War II	1944	Lutz, Howard	St. Paul	conscientious objection	engaged in starvation experiment
World War II	1944	McCullagh, Robert	St. Paul	conscientious objection	engaged in starvation experiment
World War II	1944	McReynolds, William	St. Paul	conscientious objection	engaged in starvation experiment
World War II	1944	Miller, Dan	St. Paul	conscientious objection	engaged in starvation experiment
World War II	1944	Miller, L. Wesley	St. Paul	conscientious objection	engaged in starvation experiment
World War II	1944	Mundy, Richard	St. Paul	conscientious objection	engaged in starvation experiment

State/ Target of Act	Date	Name	Location	Act	Consequence
World War II	1944	Peacock, Daniel	St. Paul	conscientious objection	engaged in starvation experiment
World War II	1944	Plaugher, James	St. Paul	conscientious objection	engaged in starvation experiment
World War II	1944	Rainwater, Woodrow	St. Paul	conscientious objection	engaged in starvation experiment
World War II	1944	Sanders, Daniel	St. Paul	conscientious objection	engaged in starvation experiment
World War II	1944	Scholberg, Cedric	St. Paul	conscientious objection	engaged in starvation experiment
World War II	1944	Smith, Charles	St. Paul	conscientious objection alternate service	engaged in starvation experiment
World War II	1944	Stanton, William Macy, Jr.	St. Paul	conscientious objection	engaged in starvation experiment
World War II	1944	Summers, Raymond	St. Paul	conscientious objection	engaged in starvation experiment
World War II	1944	Sutton, Marshall O.	St. Paul	conscientious objection	engaged in starvation experiment
World War II	1944	Tuttle, Kenneth	St. Paul	conscientious objection	engaged in starvation experiment
World War II	1944	Villwock, Robert	St. Paul	conscientious objection alternate service	engaged in starvation experiment
World War II	1944	Wallace, William Vincent	St. Paul	conscientious objection	engaged in starvation experiment
World War II	1944	Watkins, Franklin	St. Paul	conscientious objection	engaged in starvation experiment
World War II	1944	Weygandt, W. Earl	St. Paul	conscientious objection	engaged in starvation experiment
World War II	1944	Willoughby, Robert	St. Paul	conscientious objection	engaged in starvation experiment
World War II	1944	Wilsnack, Gerald	St. Paul	conscientious objection	engaged in starvation experiment
World War II	11/1944	Dyer, Henry	Sandstone	left camp	prison, tube-feeding
World War II	11/1944	Newton, David	Sandstone	conscientious objection	prison, tube-feeding

State/ Target of Act	Date	Name	Location	Act	Consequence
World War II	11/1944	Wiser, Art	Sandstone	conscientious objection	prison, tube-feeding
anti-abortion laws	1970	Hodgson, Jane	St. Paul	performed abortion	lost license
animal rights	1/18/2006	Cho, Michelle Y.	Minneapolis	public nudity	arrest

Mississippi

State/ Target of Act	Date	Name	Location	Act	Consequence
slave education ban	7/1846	Miner, Myrtilla	Whitesville	educated slaves	threats
slave education ban	1860s	Granson, Milla	Natchez	educated slaves	
voter intimidation	10–11/1960	Ashley, Stephen	Magnolia	registered voters	jail
voter intimidation	10–11/1960	Bennett, Myrtis	Magnolia	registered voters	jail
voter intimidation	10–11/1960	Campbell, Janie	Magnolia	registered voters	jail
voter intimidation	10–11/1960	Diggs, Ivory	Magnolia	registered voters	jail
voter intimidation	10–11/1960	Lewis, Isaac	Magnolia	registered voters	jail
voter intimidation	10–11/1960	McDew, Charles	Magnolia	registered voters	jail
voter intimidation	10–11/1960	Muhammad, Curtis Hayes	Magnolia	registered voters	jail
voter intimidation	10–11/1960	Robinson, Harold	Magnolia	registered voters	jail
voter intimidation	10–11/1960	Talbert, Robert	Magnolia	registered voters	jail
voter intimidation	10–11/1960	Vick, Lee Chester	Magnolia	registered voters	jail
voter intimidation	10–11/1960	Watkins, Hollis	Magnolia	registered voters	jail
voter intimidation	10–11/1960	Wells, James	Magnolia	registered voters	jail
racism	5/14/1961	Britt, Travis	Jackson	Freedom Rider	jail
racism	5/24/1961	Farmer, James Leonard	Jackson	Freedom Rider	jail
racism	5/24/1961	Mahoney, William	Sunflower County	Freedom Rider	torture
racism	5/24/1961	Singer, Felix	Sunflower County	Freedom Rider	torture
racism	5/24/1961	Sullivan, Terry	Sunflower County	Freedom Rider	torture
segregation	5/29/1961	Farmer, James Leonard	Jackson	integrated a bus station	jail
voter intimidation	8/15/1961	Moses, Robert Parris	Amite County	impeded police	fine, jail
racism	8/26/1961	Hayes, Elmer	McComb	sit-in	jail
racism	8/26/1961	Watkins, Hollis	McComb	sit-in	jail
racism	8/29/1961	Bryant, Curtis Conway	McComb	encouraged a teen to protest	arrest
racism	8/29/1961	Reagan, Cordelle	McComb	encouraged a teen to protest	arrest
racism	8/30/1961	Lewis, Isaac	McComb	sit-in	jail
voter intimidation	8/30/1961	Lewis, Isaac	McComb	impeded an officer	jail
racism	8/30/1961	Talbert, Robert	McComb	sit-in	jail
voter intimidation	8/30/1961	Talbert, Robert	McComb	impeded an officer	jail
racism	8/30/1961	Travis, Brenda	McComb	sit-in	
voter intimidation	8/30/1961	Travis, Brenda	McComb	impeded an officer	jail
racism	9/1961	Britt, Travis	Liberty	Freedom Rider	beaten
voter intimidation	9/5/1961	Britt, Travis	Tylertown	registered voters	assault

State/ Target of Act	Date	Name	Location	Act	Consequence
voter intimidation	9/7/1961	Hardy, John	Tylertown	voter registration	pistol-whipped
racism	9/24/1961	Lee, Herbert	Liberty	sat in a truck	shot
voter intimidation	12/1961	Blackwell, Unita	Lula	voter registration	death threat, arrest
voter intimidation	12/1961	Carmichael, Stokely	Lowndes County	voter registration	
voter intimidation	12/1961	Hardy, John	Magnolia	voter registration	
voter intimidation	12/1961	Moses, Robert Parris	Amite County	registered voters	shot at
voter intimidation	12/1961	Robinson, Reginald L.	Magnolia	voter registration	
voter intimidation	8/31/1962	Hamer, Fannie Lou	Indianola	voter registration	jail
voter intimidation	6/3/1963	Hamer, Fannie Lou	Winona	voter registration	jail, assault
voter intimidation	6/3/1963	Ponder, Annelle	Winona	voter registration	jail, assault
voter intimidation	6/4/1963	Guyot, Lawrence	Winona	investigated brutality	police brutality
racism	1964	Farmer, James Leonard	Mississippi	investigated church arson	
voter intimidation	1964	Farmer, James Leonard	Mississippi	registered voters	
racism	1/31/1964	Allen, Louis	Liberty	murder witness	shot
racism	6/21/1964	Chaney, James	Meridian	protest	shot
racism	6/21/1964	Goodman, Andrew	Meridian	protest	shot
racism	6/21/1964	Schwerner, Michael	Meridian	protest	shot
Vietnam War	5/14/1970	Gibbs, Phillip Lafayette	Jackson	incited a riot	shot
Vietnam War	5/14/1970	Green, James Earl	Jackson	incited a riot	shot

Missouri

State/ Target of Act	Date	Name	Location	Act	Consequence
slave recapture	1816	Nelson, David	Marion County	harbored slaves	threats
slavery	1840s	Langston, George R.	Howard County	protest	
slave education ban	1840s–1850s	Meachum, John Berry	St. Louis	educated slaves	
slave recapture	1840s–1850s	Meachum, John Berry	St. Louis	river transport	
slave education ban	1840s–1850s	Meachum, Mary	St. Louis	educated slaves	
slave recapture	1840s–1850s	Meachum, Mary	St. Louis	river transport, impeded police	
slave recapture	1840s–1860s	Baltimore, Priscilla	St. Louis	slave rescue	
slave recapture	7/1841	Burr, James E.	Palmyra	slave conducting	prison at hard labor, maiming
slave recapture	7/1841	Thompson, George	Palmyra	slave conducting	prison at hard labor
slave recapture	7/1841	Work, Alanson	Palmyra	slave conducting	prison at hard labor
Fugitive Slave Law of 1850	1850s	Gibson, John	Jefferson City	conducted slaves	died in prison
slave recapture	1850s–1860s	Dickson, Moses	St. Louis	conspiracy, slave rescue	
slavery	1855–1856	Wiener, Theodore	St. Louis	protest	
rape	6/23/1855	Celia	Fulton	manslaughter	executed
slave recapture	12/20/1858	Brown, John	Missouri	slave relay	
slave recapture	1/1859	Doy, Charles	St. Louis	slave relay	jail, threat
slave recapture	1/1859	Doy, John W.	St. Louis	slave relay	jail, threat

State/ Target of Act	Date	Name	Location	Act	Consequence
slave recapture	1860s	Livermore, Mary Ashton Rice	St. Louis	harbored slaves	
women's disenfranchisement	10/15/1872	Minor, Virginia Louisa	St. Louis	registered to vote	
alcohol sale and consumption	9/1904	McHenry, Myra Gains Warren	Hannibal	destroyed property	jail
alcohol sale and consumption	9/1904	Muntz, Lydia	Hannibal	destroyed property	jail
alcohol sale and consumption	9/1904	Nation, Carry Amelia Moore	Hannibal	destroyed property	jail
alcohol sale and consumption	9/1904	Wilhoite, Lucy	Hannibal	destroyed property	jail
free speech ban	1/1910	Goldman, Emma	Hannibal	conspiracy	intimidation
free press ban	1911	Gompers, Samuel	St. Louis	published a list	limited speech
free speech ban	7/9/1917	Goldman, Emma	Jefferson City	conspiracy	prison
draft	12/10/1917	Oburn, Emmett A.	St. Louis	draft protest	assault
World War I	1918	James, William Oral	St. Louis	conscientious objection, prison revolt	prison
draft	10/26/1918	Hieminz, Frank X.	St. Louis	draft protest	saloon closed
ROTC	5/5/1970	Kogan, Larry	St. Louis	demonstration	prison
ROTC	5/5/1970	Mechanic, Howard	St. Louis	demonstration	prison
taxation	2003	Hill, Julia Butterfly	Mount Vernon	tax resistance	
ROTC	9/29/2005	Jacobs, Lana	Columbia	destroyed property	fine, arrest
ROTC	9/29/2005	Jacobs, Steve	Columbia	destroyed property	fine, arrest

Montana

State/ Target of Act	Date	Name	Location	Act	Consequence
labor exploitation	9/28/1908	Flynn, Elizabeth Gurley	Missoula	street speech	arrest
labor exploitation	8/1/1917	Little, Frank	Butte	union organizing	lynched
peyote ban	1923	Bird Above	Bighorn	peyote worship	arrest
peyote ban	1926	Bethune, Frank	Reno	peyote worship	
peyote ban	1926	Big Sheep	Lodge Grass	peyote use	shackled
peyote ban	1926	Stewart, Tom	Grass Lodge	peyote worship	
peyote ban	1960s	Old Coyote, Barney	Bighorn	peyote worship	

Nebraska

State/ Target of Act	Date	Name	Location	Act	Consequence
polygamy ban	1874	Reynolds, George	Lincoln	plural marriage	prison
Indian displacement	1/1879	Bear Shield	Omaha	left reservation	
Indian displacement	1/1879	Prairie Flower	Omaha	left reservation	
Indian displacement	1/1879	Primo, Suzette	Omaha	left reservation	arrest
Indian displacement	1/1879	Standing Bear	Omaha	left reservation	arrest
Indian displacement	1/1879	Standing Bear, Fanny	Omaha	left reservation	arrest
peyote ban	1900s	Rave, John	Thurston	peyote worship	
free speech ban	11/7/1908	Goldman, Emma	Omaha	conspiracy	locked out
draft	3/5/1918	Larson, Esther	Omaha	draft protest	fired

State/ Target of Act	Date	Name	Location	Act	Consequence
draft	6/19/1918	Hopt, Erwin B.	Lincoln	draft protest	forced out of job
draft	6/19/1918	Lucker, G.W.A.	Lincoln	draft protest	forced out of job
draft	6/19/1918	Persinger, Edward B.	Lincoln	draft protest	forced to resign
World War II	1942	Yamada, George	Minatare	conscientious objection	prison
nuclear power	6/20/1959	Muste, Abraham Johannes	Omaha	blocked traffic, trespass	jail
nuclear power	7/1/1959	Muste, Abraham Johannes	Omaha	blocked traffic, trespass	jail, fine
nuclear power	7/6/1959	Meyer, Karl	Omaha	trespass	jail, prison
nuclear power	7/6/1959	Wyman, David S.	Omaha	trespass	jail
nuclear power	7/6/1959	Young, Wilmer Job	Omaha	trespass	jail
nuclear power	7/21/1959	Muste, Abraham Johannes	Omaha	trespass	jail
nuclear power	7/21/1959	Swann, Marjorie	Omaha	trespass	jail
peyote ban	4/1993	Snake, Reuben A., Jr.	Winnebago	peyote use	

Nevada

draft	12/11/1917	Adams, Dorothy	Carson City	draft protest	fired
draft	3/20/1918	White, Elmer	Yerington	draft protest	lashed
nuclear power	8/6/1957	Bigelow, Albert S.	Yucca Flats	demonstration	
nuclear power	8/6/1957	Choate, Prentiss	Yucca Flats	demonstration	arrest
nuclear power	8/6/1957	Muste, Abraham Johannes	Las Vegas	blocked traffic	jail
nuclear power	8/6/1957	Peck, James	Yucca Flats	demonstration	arrest
nuclear power	8/6/1957	Peterson, Gonar	Yucca Flats	demonstration	arrest
nuclear power	8/6/1957	Pickus, Robert	Yucca Flats	demonstration	arrest
nuclear power	8/6/1957	Scott, Lawrence	Yucca Flats	demonstration	arrest
nuclear power	8/6/1957	Willoughby, Lillian	Yucca Flats	demonstration	arrest
racism	2/1971	Abernathy, Ralph David	Las Vegas	march	
racism	2/1971	Chávez, César	Las Vegas	march	
racism	2/1971	Spock, Benjamin	Las Vegas	march	
racism	2/1971	Sutherland, Donald	Las Vegas	march	
nuclear power	3/20/1988	Blake, Robert	Las Vegas	trespass	
nuclear power	3/20/1988	Coffin, William Sloane, Jr.	Las Vegas	trespass	
nuclear power	3/20/1988	Ellsberg, Daniel	Las Vegas	trespass	
nuclear power	3/20/1988	Garr, Teri	Las Vegas	trespass	
nuclear power	3/20/1988	Kasem, Casey	Las Vegas	trespass	
nuclear power	3/20/1988	Knight, Shirley	Las Vegas	trespass	
free speech ban	6/10/1992	Sturman, Reuben	Las Vegas	obscenity	arrest
nuclear power	4/17/1993	Mento, Jack	Beatty	camp-in	
nuclear power	4/17/1993	Vitale, Louis	Beatty	camp-in	
polygamy ban	8/2006	Jeffs, Warren Steed	Las Vegas	abetted rape	prison

State/ Target of Act	Date	Name	Location	Act	Consequence
nuclear power	4/1/2007	Dunn, Carrie	Mercury	trespass	arrest
nuclear power	4/1/2007	Sheen, Martin	Mercury	trespass	arrest
nuclear power	4/1/2007	Vitale, Louis	Mercury	trespass	arrest
nuclear power	4/1/2007	Wright, Ann	Mercury	trespass	arrest

New Hampshire

State/ Target of Act	Date	Name	Location	Act	Consequence
heresy	1663	Ambrose, Alice	Dover	preached	stripped, lashed
heresy	1663	Coleman, Anna	Dover	preached	stripped, lashed
heresy	1663	Tomkins, Mary	Dover	preached	stripped, lashed
Revolutionary War	1770s	Estabrook, E.	New Hampshire	refused to serve	
colonial taxation	1773	Kelley, Moses	Goffstown	paramilitary host	
colonial emancipation	1774	Wright, Zadock	Canterbury	loyalty to England	fled, jail
colonial taxation	12/14/1774	Langdon, John	Portsmouth	paramilitary raider	
colonial taxation	12/14/1774	Revere, Paul	Portsmouth	paramilitary raider	
colonial taxation	12/14/1774	Sullivan, John	Portsmouth	paramilitary raider	
colonial taxation	8/1765	Cutt, Samuel	Portsmouth	paramilitary	
colonial taxation	8/1765	Davenport, John	Portsmouth	paramilitary	
colonial taxation	8/1765	Gains, George	Portsmouth	paramilitary	
colonial taxation	8/1765	Langdon, Samuel	Portsmouth	paramilitary leader	
colonial taxation	8/1765	Manning, Thomas	Portsmouth	paramilitary	
Civil War	1860s	Taber, Horace S.	Temple	refused to serve	forced into army
Vietnam War	12/7/1967	Daniels, George	Portsmouth	denunciation	prison at hard labor
Vietnam War	12/7/1967	Harvey, William L.	Portsmouth	denunciation	prison at hard labor

New Jersey

State/ Target of Act	Date	Name	Location	Act	Consequence
militia service	1704	Matthews, Samuel	Cape May	refused to serve	fine
colonial taxation	8/1765	Hendrickson, Daniel	Freehold	paramilitary raider	
colonial taxation	8/1765	Livingston, William	Elizabethtown	paramilitary coordinator	
colonial taxation	11/22/1774	Elmer, Ebenezer	Greenwich	destroyed tea	
colonial taxation	11/22/1774	Fithian, Philip Vickers	Greenwich	destroyed tea	
slave recapture	1830s–1840s	Evans, David	Greenwich	slave rescue	shunned
slave recapture	1830s–1840s	Evans, Nathan	Greenwich	slave rescue	shunned
slave recapture	1830s–1840s	Evans, Zillah Maule	Greenwich	slave rescue	shunned
slave recapture	1830s–1850s	Lewis, Pompey	Small Gloucester	slave rescue	
slave recapture	1832–1850s	Grimes, John	Boonton	slave rescue	
slave recapture	1838–1860	Goodwin, Abigail	Salem	slave rescue, disguise	
slave recapture	1838–1860	Goodwin, Elizabeth	Salem	slave rescue, disguise	
draft	1863	Taber, Horace S.	Temple	protest	
free speech ban	6/8/1909	Goldman, Emma	East Orange	conspiracy	banned
labor exploitation	2/25/1913	Boyd, Frederick Sumner	Paterson	mill strike	prison
free speech ban	2/25/1913	Flynn, Elizabeth Gurley	Paterson	abetted a strike	arrest

State/ Target of Act	Date	Name	Location	Act	Consequence
labor exploitation	2/25/1913	Flynn, Elizabeth Gurley	Paterson	mill strike	arrest
labor exploitation	2/25/1913	Quinlan, Patrick J.	Paterson	mill strike	prison
labor exploitation	2/25/1913	Tresca, Carlo	Paterson	mill strike	
labor organization ban	2/25/1913	Tresca, Carlo	Paterson	labor organizing	arrest
free speech ban	12/15/1913	Goldman, Emma	Paterson	conspiracy	banned
World War I	12/17/1917	Canter, Albert M.	Clayton	protest	banished
World War I	1918	Cameron, Holland William	Salem	refused a uniform	forced to serve
World War I	1918	Gellert, Ernest	Fort Hancock	conscientious objection	forced to dig his grave, shot
prison conditions	2/25/1918	Reed, John	Paterson	protest	jail
draft	5/13/1918	Wusterbarth, Fred W.	Newark	protest	citizenship revoked
World War I	7/2/1918	Kantor, William Marx	Camden	conscientious objection	prison, threat, ridicule
draft	1966	Mott, Jeremy	Ridgewood	burned draft card	
free speech ban	1966	Mott, Jeremy	Ridgewood	burned draft card	prison

New Mexico

World War I	8/1917	Waltner, Edward J.B.	Camp Cody	refused to drill	prison
labor organization ban	1934	Pallares, Jesus	Gallup	promoted unions	deported
Hispanic displacement	6/5/1967	Tijerina, Reies López	Echo Park	sought land rights	
euthanasia ban	8/30/1998	Reding, George	Albuquerque	euthanasia	
nuclear power	8/9/1999	Sheen, Martin	Los Alamos	prayer, trespass	arrest

New York

religious persecution	1653	Doughty, Francis	Flushing	religious unorthodoxy	exile
religious persecution	11/11/1656	Hallett, William	Flushing	religious unorthodoxy	fired, fine
heresy	8/1657	Hodgson, Robert	Long Island	preached	jail, lashed, fine, prison at hard labor
heresy	8/1657	Waugh, Dorothy	New Amsterdam	defied Puritans	jail
heresy	8/1657	Weatherhead, Mary	New Amsterdam	defied Puritans	jail
heresy	10/1660	Wright, Mary	Oyster Bay	defied Puritans	jail
heresy	1661	Bowne, John	Flushing	Quaker worship, protest	arrest, exile
religious persecution	1661	Bowne, John	Flushing	worship	banished, fine
free press ban	11/17/1734	Alexander, James	New York City	libel	disbarment
free press ban	11/17/1734	Smith, William	New York City	libel	disbarment
free press ban	11/17/1734	Zenger, Peter	New York City	libel	jail
slave recapture	1737	Underhill, Ann Carpenter	Musketa Cove	slave rescue	
slave recapture	1737	Underhill, Samuel	Musketa Cove	slave rescue	
colonial taxation	1760–1770s	Holt, John	New York City	propaganda	
slave recapture	1763	Mott, James	Oyster Bay	aided slaves	
slave recapture	1763	Mott, Mary Underhill	Oyster Bay	aided slaves	

State/ Target of Act	Date	Name	Location	Act	Consequence
colonial taxation	1765	McDougall, Hannah Roe Bostwick	New York City	paramilitary	
colonial taxation	2/1765	Allicocke, Joseph	New York City	paramilitary	
colonial taxation	2/1765	Bancker, Flores	New York City	paramilitary	
colonial taxation	2/1765	Brush, Thomas	Huntington	paramilitary	
colonial taxation	2/1765	Chambers, Rowland	Oyster Bay	paramilitary	
Stamp Act	2/1765	Colden, Alexander	New York City	paramilitary	
colonial taxation	2/1765	Conklin, Cornelius	Huntington	paramilitary	
colonial taxation	2/1765	Delancey, James	New York City	paramilitary	
colonial taxation	2/1765	Dow, Volkert P.	Albany	paramilitary	
colonial taxation	2/1765	Fonda, Jelles Douwe	Albany	paramilitary	
colonial taxation	2/1765	Henry, Robert	Albany	paramilitary	
colonial taxation	2/1765	Hobart, John Sloss	Huntington	paramilitary	
colonial taxation	2/1765	Hughes, Hugh	New York City	paramilitary	
colonial taxation	2/1765	Ketcham, John	New York City	paramilitary	
colonial taxation	2/1765	Laight, Edward	New York City	paramilitary	
colonial taxation	2/1765	Lamb, John	New York City	paramilitary	
colonial taxation	2/1765	McDougall, Alexander	New York City	paramilitary	
colonial taxation	2/1765	Mott, Gershom	New York City	paramilitary	
colonial taxation	2/1765	Mulligan, Hercules	New York City	paramilitary	
colonial taxation	2/1765	Mulligan, Hugh	New York City	paramilitary	
colonial taxation	2/1765	Nicoll, Charles	New York City	paramilitary	
colonial taxation	2/1765	Potter, Gilbert	Huntington	paramilitary	
colonial taxation	2/1765	Quackenbos, Walter	New York City	paramilitary	
colonial taxation	2/1765	Robinson, Thomas	New York City	paramilitary	
colonial taxation	2/1765	Roseboom, Myndert	Albany	paramilitary	
colonial taxation	2/1765	Scott, John Morin	New York City	paramilitary	
colonial taxation	2/1765	Sears, Isaac	New York City	paramilitary	
colonial taxation	2/1765	Sneething, Barak	Oyster Bay	paramilitary	
colonial taxation	2/1765	Solomon, Haym	New York City	paramilitary	
colonial taxation	2/1765	Ten Eyck, Abraham	Albany	paramilitary treasurer	
colonial taxation	2/1765	Townsend, Benjamin	Oyster Bay	paramilitary	
colonial taxation	2/1765	Townsend, George	Oyster Bay	paramilitary	
colonial taxation	2/1765	Van Rensselaer, Jeremiah	Albany	paramilitary	
colonial taxation	2/1765	Weekes, George	Oyster Bay	paramilitary	
colonial taxation	2/1765	Weekes, Michael	Oyster Bay	paramilitary	
colonial taxation	2/1765	Wiley, William	New York City	paramilitary	
colonial taxation	2/1765	Willett, Marinus	New York City	paramilitary	
colonial taxation	2/1765	Williams, Nathan	Huntington	paramilitary	
colonial taxation	2/1765	Young, Thomas	Albany	paramilitary	
colonial taxation	10/31/1765	Ketcham, John	New York City	threats	
colonial taxation	11/1/1765	Sears, Isaac	New York City	paramilitary leader	
colonial taxation	5/1766	Howard, Richard	Huntington	paramilitary host	

State/ Target of Act	Date	Name	Location	Act	Consequence
colonial taxation	6/1767	Sears, Isaac	New York City	raised a Liberty Pole	
Quartering Act	12/16/1769	McDougall, Alexander	New York City	propaganda	arrest
Quartering Act	12/16/1769	McDougall, Hannah Roe Bostwick	New York City	protest	
colonial taxation	1770	Delancey, James	New York City	paramilitary organizer	
colonial taxation	1770	Hamilton, Alexander	New York City	spying	
colonial taxation	1770	Mulligan, Hercules	New York City	spying	
colonial taxation	1770	Mulligan, Hugh	New York City	spying	
colonial taxation	1770	Solomon, Haym	New York City	spying	
colonial taxation	1/13/1770	Mulligan, Hercules	New York City	brawl	
religious persecution	1774	Lee, Ann	Albany	blasphemy	jail
colonial taxation	1774	McDougall, Alexander	New York City	destroyed tea	
colonial taxation	4/1774	Sears, Isaac	New York City	closed harbor	
colonial taxation	4/22/1774	Hamilton, Alexander	New York City	spying, destroyed tea	
colonial taxation	4/22/1774	Mulligan, Hercules	New York City	destroyed tea	
colonial taxation	11/1775	Sears, Isaac	New York City	destroyed a press	jail
slave recapture	11/1775	Sears, Isaac	New York City	jailbreak	
slavery	1780s	Lott, Hendrick I.	Brooklyn	protest	
slave recapture	1780s	Mott, Richard	Mamaroneck	slave rescue	
colonial emancipation	7/1780	Hammond, Hezekiah	Albany	loyalty to England	jail
Colonial emancipation	7/1780	Harlow, Calvin	Albany	loyalty to England	jail
colonial emancipation	7/1780	Hocknell, John	Albany	loyalty to England	jail
colonial emancipation	7/1780	Lee, Ann	Albany	loyalty to England	jail, threats
colonial emancipation	7/1780	Lee, William	Albany	loyalty to England	jail
colonial emancipation	7/1780	Meachum, Joseph, Jr.	Albany	loyalty to England	jail
colonial emancipation	7/1780	Partington, Mary	Albany	loyalty to England	jail
colonial emancipation	7/1780	Pratt, Joel	Albany	loyalty to England	jail
colonial emancipation	7/1780	Whittaker, James	Albany	loyalty to England	jail
slavery	1790s	Lott, Mary Brownjohn	Brooklyn	protest	
slave recapture	1790s	Mott, Samuel	Cowneck	slave rescue	
slavery	1793	Green, Beriah	Whitesboro	protest	
slavery	1793	Lee, Luther	Plymouth	protest	
slave recapture	1800s	Wells, John Howard, Sr.	Richland	protest	
slave education ban	1802	Haines, Ann	New York City	educated slaves	
slave education ban	1802	Haines, Jane Bowne	New York City	educated slaves	
slave recapture	1810s	Anthony, Susan Brownell	Rochester	propaganda	
slave recapture	1810s	Hicks, Mary Underhill Mott	New York City	slave rescue	
slave recapture	1810s	Hicks, Rachel Seaman	Westbury	propaganda	
slave recapture	1810s	Post, Amy Kirby	Rochester	propaganda	
slave recapture	1820s–1830s	Anthony, Elihu	Greenfield	slave relay	
slave recapture	1820s–1830s	Anthony, Mason	Greenfield	slave relay	

State/ Target of Act	Date	Name	Location	Act	Consequence
slave recapture	1820s–1840s	Fish, Benjamin	Rochester	slave rescue	shunned
slave recapture	1820s–1840s	Fish, Catharine Ann	Rochester	slave rescue	shunned
slave recapture	1820s–1840s	Fish, Mary Braithwaite	Rochester	slave rescue	shunned
slave recapture	1820s–1840s	Fish, Sarah Davids Bill	Rochester	slave rescue	shunned
slave recapture	1820s–1840s	Lane, Hester	New York City	slave rescue	
slave recapture	1820s–1850s	Fuller, James Canning, Sr.	Skaneateles	slave relay	
slave recapture	1820s–1850s	Fuller, Lydia Charleton	Skaneateles	slave relay	
slave recapture	1829	Pennington, James William Charles	New York City	slave rescue	
slave recapture	1830s	Child, David Lee	New York City	abetted slave rescue	
slavery	1830s	Mihills, Uriah Dimond	Keene	protest	
slavery	1830s	Pritchett, Edward Corrie	Union Village	protest	
slavery	1830s	Smith, Gerrit	New York City	conspiracy, propaganda	
slave recapture	1830s	White, Horace	Syracuse	sheltered slaves	
slave recapture	1830s–1860s	Carpenter, Joseph	New Rochelle	slave rescue	
slave recapture	1830s–1860s	Carpenter, Margaret W. Cornell	New Rochelle	rescued orphaned slaves	
slave recapture	10/16/1830	May, Samuel Joseph	Syracuse	recruitment	
slave recapture	1834–1860s	Barker, David	Niagara	ran a safehouse	
slave recapture	1834–1860s	Barker, Pennsylvania Herendeen	Niagara	ran a safehouse	
slave recapture	1835	Ruggles, David	New York City	ran a street patrol	
slave recapture	1836	Gibbons, Abigail Hopper	New York City	slave conductor	ousted by Quakers
slave recapture	1836	Gibbons, James Sloan	New York City	slave conductor	ousted by Quakers
slave recapture	1836	Hopper, Isaac Tatem	New York City	slave conductor	expelled from Quakers
slave recapture	1836	Hopper, Sarah Tatum Hopper	New York City	slave conductor	
slave recapture	1/1836	Garrison, William Lloyd	New York City	trained agents	
slave recapture	1/1836	Weld, Theodore Dwight	New York City	trained agents	
slave recapture	1837–1861	Loguen, Jermaine Wesley	Rochester	slave rescue, propaganda	
slave recapture	5/9/1837	Child, Lydia Maria Francis	New York City	abetted slave rescue, propaganda	
slavery	5/9/1837	Mott, Lucretia Coffin	New York City	abetted slave rescue	
slave education ban	1838	Cooper, Elizabeth Hodgson	Williamson	tutored slaves	
slavery	8/2/1839	Cinqué, Joseph	Montauk	murder, piracy	jail
slavery	1840s–1860s	Helper, Hinton Rowan	New York City	conspiracy	
slave recapture	1840s	Gibbs, Jonathan C.	Troy	sheltered slaves	
slavery	1840s	Holmes, George Young, Sr.	Claysville	protest	

State/ Target of Act	Date	Name	Location	Act	Consequence
slavery	1840s	Kelley, John J.	Albany	protest	
slave recapture	1840s	Knoefel, August	New York City	slave rescue	
women's disenfranchisement	1840s–1850s	Anthony, Susan Brownell	Rochester	activism for women	
slave recapture	1841	Marriot, Charles	Hudson	slave conductor	expelled from Quakers
slavery	1841–1863	Greeley, Horace	New York City	propaganda, backed UGRR	
slave recapture	1842	Whittier, John Greenleaf	New York City	protest	
slave recapture	8/21/1843	Garnet, Henry Highland	Troy	slave relay, sabotage	
slave recapture	8/21/1843	Smith, Gerrit	Troy	slave relay, sabotage, propaganda	
slave recapture	9/28/1844	Whittier, John Greenleaf	Staten Island	propaganda	
slave recapture	1845	Gay, Elizabeth J. Neall	Staten Island	conspiracy	
slave recapture	1845	Grimké, Angelina Emily	Staten Island	conspiracy	
slave recapture	1845	Grimké, Sarah Moore	Staten Island	conspiracy	
slave recapture	1845	Mott, Lucretia Coffin	Staten Island	conspiracy	
slave recapture	1845	Phillips, Wendell Addison	Staten Island	conspiracy, propaganda	
slave recapture	1845	Purvis, Robert	Staten Island	conspiracy	
slave recapture	1845	Whittier, John Greenleaf	Staten Island	conspiracy	
slave recapture	1847	Beecher, Henry Ward	Brooklyn	ran a depot	threats
slave recapture	4/15/1848	Seward, William Henry	Cayuga	fund-raising	
slave education ban	7/9/1848	Hunt, Jane Clothier Master	Waterloo	conspiracy	
slave education ban	7/9/1848	M'Clintock, Mary Ann Wilson	Waterloo	conspiracy	
slave education ban	7/9/1848	Stanton, Elizabeth Cady	Waterloo	conspiracy	
slave recapture	7/9/1848	Wright, Martha Coffin Pelham	Waterloo	conspiracy	
slavery	1850s	Hinton, Richard Josiah	New York City	protest	
slave recapture	1850s	Simmons, J.J.	New York City	ran a street patrol	
Fugitive Slave Law of 1850	1850s	Torrey, Charles Turner	Albany	spying, conspiracy	
slave recapture	1851	Hicks, Hannah	Long Island	slave rescue	
slave recapture	1851	Ketcham, Rebecca	Long Island	slave rescue	
slave recapture	1851	Post, Mary W.	Long Island	slave rescue	
slave recapture	1851	Seaman, Elizabeth H.	Long Island	slave rescue	
slave recapture	1851	Willets, Mary W.	Long Island	slave rescue	
slave recapture	1851	Willets, Phebe	Long Island	slave rescue	
Fugitive Slave Law of 1850	5/1851	Smith, Gerrit	Syracuse	public harangue	
slave recapture	9/1851	Douglass, Anna Murray	Rochester	slave rescue	
slave recapture	9/1851	Douglass, Frederick	Rochester	slave rescue	

State/ Target of Act	Date	Name	Location	Act	Consequence
slave recapture	10/1/1851	Ames, Amy Perkins	Mexico	slave relay	
slave recapture	10/1/1851	Ames, Orson	Mexico	slave relay	
slave recapture	10/1/1851	Beebe, Asa	Mexico	slave concealment	
slave recapture	10/1/1851	Beebe, Mary Whipple	Mexico	slave concealment	
slave recapture	10/1/1851	Brigham, J.B.	Syracuse	jailbreak	tried
slave recapture	10/1/1851	Cobb, Ira	Syracuse	jailbreak	tried
slave recapture	10/1/1851	Davis, James	Saratoga	slave relay	
Fugitive Slave Law of 1850	10/1/1851	Fuller, James Canning, Jr.	Skaneateles	jailbreak	
slave recapture	10/1/1851	Fuller, James Canning, Jr.	Skaneateles	slave relay	
Fugitive Slave Law of 1850	10/1/1851	Gibbs, Leonard Dean	Union Village	denunciation	
Fugitive Slave Law of 1850	10/1/1851	Hoyt, Hiram	Syracuse	jailbreak	
slave recapture	10/1/1851	Hoyt, Jason Sylvester	Saratoga	slave relay	
Fugitive Slave Law of 1850	10/1/1851	Loguen, Jermaine Wesley	Syracuse	jailbreak	fled
slave recapture	10/1/1851	McHenry, William "Jerry"	Syracuse	jailbreak	
slave recapture	10/1/1851	Merrick, Charles	Syracuse	jailbreak, sheltered slaves	
Fugitive Slave Law of 1850	10/1/1851	Merrick, Montgomery	Syracuse	jailbreak	
slave recapture	10/1/1851	Merrick, Sylvanus	Syracuse	jailbreak, sheltered slaves	fled
slave recapture	10/1/1851	Reed, Enoch	Syracuse	jailbreak	tried
Fugitive Slave Law of 1850	10/1/1851	Salmon, William Lyman	Granby	jailbreak	tried
slavery	10/1/1851	Seward, Frances Miller	Auburn	abetted jailbreak	
slave recapture	10/1/1851	Seward, William Henry	Auburn	jailbreak, conspiracy	indicted
Fugitive Slave Law of 1850	10/1/1851	Smith, Gerrit	Peterboro	protest	
slave recapture	10/1/1851	Smith, Gerrit	New York City	jailbreak	
slave recapture	10/1/1851	Tappan, Arthur	New York City	protest	
slave recapture	10/1/1851	Tappan, Lewis	New York City	protest	
slave recapture	10/1/1851	Thomas, John	Syracuse	jailbreak	
slave recapture	10/1/1851	Ward, Samuel Ringgold	New York City	jailbreak	
slave recapture	10/1/1851	Watkins, Susan	Syracuse	jailbreak	
Fugitive Slave Law of 1850	10/1/1851	Wheaton, Charles Augustus	Syracuse	jailbreak	
slave recapture	10/5/1851	M'Clintock, Mary Ann Wilson	Waterloo	jailbreak	
slave recapture	10/5/1851	M'Clintock, Thomas	Waterloo	jailbreak	
slave recapture	10/15/1851	Ames, Leonard, Jr.	Oswego	slave relay	
slave recapture	10/15/1851	Beebe, Winsor	Mexico	slave relay	
slave recapture	10/15/1851	Clarke, Charlotte Ambler	Oswego	slave concealment	
slave recapture	10/15/1851	Clarke, Edwin W.	Oswego	slave concealment	
Fugitive Slave Law of 1850	11/1/1851	May, Samuel Joseph, clergy	Syracuse	protest, recruitment	

State/ Target of Act	Date	Name	Location	Act	Consequence
Fugitive Slave Law of 1850	10/1/1852	Douglass, Frederick	Syracuse	public harangue	
Fugitive Slave Law of 1850	10/1/1852	Higgins, Thomas Wentworth	Syracuse	public harangue	
Fugitive Slave Law of 1850	10/1/1852	Smith, Gerrit	Syracuse	public harangue	
slave recapture	1853	Strother, David Hunter	New York City	abetted slave rescue	
slave recapture	1857	Seward, William Henry	Auburn	backer	
slavery	1858	Nast, Thomas	New York City	abetted slave rescue	
Civil War	1860s	Benedict, Judson D.	Aurora	refused to serve	prison
slave recapture	1860	Child, Lydia Maria Francis	New York City	abetted slave rescue	
slave recapture	4/27/1860	Tubman, Harriet	Troy	jailbreak	fled
draft	1861	Beecher, Henry Ward	Brooklyn	supported pacifism	
draft	1861	Greeley, Horace	New York City	supported pacifism	
free press ban	8/19/1862	Greeley, Horace	New York City	protest	
draft	8/1/1863	Evans, Frederick W.	New Lebanon	supported pacifism	
draft	8/1/1863	Gates, Benjamin	New Lebanon	supported pacifism	
Comstock Act	1872	Sickel, Morris	New York City	made contraceptives	jail, fine
Comstock Act	3/6/1872	Mancher, Charles	New York City	sold contraceptives	
free press ban	11/2/1872	Claflin, Tennessee Celeste	New York City	obscenity	arrest
Comstock Act	11/2/1872	Train, George Francis	New York City	obscenity	jail
free press ban	11/2/1872	Woodhull, Victoria Claflin	New York City	obscenity	arrest
voter intimidation	11/5/1872	Anthony, Charlotte Bolles	Rochester	voted	arraigned
voter intimidation	11/5/1872	Anthony, Mary Stafford	Rochester	voted	arraigned
voter intimidation	11/5/1872	Anthony, Susan Brownell	Rochester	voted	handcuffed, fine
voter intimidation	11/5/1872	Baker, Ellen S.	Rochester	voted	arraigned
voter intimidation	11/5/1872	Chapman, Nancy M.	Rochester	voted	arraigned
voter intimidation	11/5/1872	Chatfield, Hannah M.	Rochester	voted	arraigned
voter intimidation	11/5/1872	Cogswell, Jane M.	Rochester	voted	arraigned
voter intimidation	11/5/1872	De Garmo, Rhoda	Rochester	voted	arraigned
voter intimidation	11/5/1872	Hebard, Mary S.	Rochester	voted	arraigned
voter intimidation	11/5/1872	Hough, Susan M.	Rochester	voted	arraigned
voter intimidation	11/5/1872	Leyden, Margaret Leora Garrigues	Rochester	voted	arraigned
voter intimidation	11/5/1872	McLean, Guelma Penn Anthony	Rochester	voted	arraigned
voter intimidation	11/5/1872	Mosher, Hannah Lapham Anthony	Rochester	voted	arraigned
voter intimidation	11/5/1872	Pulver, Mary Elizabeth Miller	Rochester	voted	arraigned
voter intimidation	11/5/1872	Truesdale, Sarah Cole	Rochester	voted	arraigned

State/ Target of Act	Date	Name	Location	Act	Consequence
Comstock Act	1874	Bass, Morris	New York City	sold contraceptives	impounded
anti-abortion laws	1878	Lohman, Ann Trow	New York City	performed abortion	charged
Comstock Act	1878	Lohman, Ann Trow	New York City	sold contraceptives	charged
Comstock Act	1878	Soule, Asa Titus	Rochester	birth control information	fine
Comstock Act	6/1878	Chase, Sarah Blakeslee	New York City	sold contraceptives	charged
Comstock Act	12/10/1878	Bennett, DeRobigne Mortimer	New York City	birth control treatise	fine, prison at hard labor
Comstock Act	12/19/1878	Heywood, Ezra Hervey	New York City	mailed pamphlets	
Comstock Act	1887	Knoedler, Herman	New York City	sold art nudes	jail, fine
anti-abortion laws	1893	Chase, Sarah Blakeslee	New York City	lectured, sold birth control devices	prison
fishing ban	1901	Kennedy, Fayette	Cattaraugus	spear-fished	arrest
fishing ban	1901	Kennedy, Warren	Cattaraugus	spear-fished	arrest
fishing ban	1901	White, Willis, Jr.	Cattaraugus	spear-fished	arrest
alcohol sale and consumption	6/1902	Nation, Carry Amelia Moore	Coney Island	destroyed property	jail, battery
labor exploitation	1905	Flynn, Elizabeth Gurley	Schenectady	blocked traffic	arrest
Comstock Act	1905	MacFadden, Bernarr	New York City	nude photos	confiscation
labor exploitation	1906	Flynn, Elizabeth Gurley	New York City	street corner speech	arrest
free speech ban	10/30/1906	Goldman, Emma	New York City	riot	arrest
free speech ban	11/23/1906	Goldman, Emma	New York City	conspiracy	
free speech ban	1/6/1907	Berkman, Alexander	New York City	conspiracy	arrest
free speech ban	9/7/1908	Edelsohn, Becky	New York City	conspiracy	jail
free speech ban	9/7/1908	Goldman, Emma	New York City	conspiracy	jail
free speech ban	9/7/1908	Reitman, Ben L.	New York City	conspiracy	arrest
free speech ban	5/28/1909	Goldman, Emma	Brooklyn	conspiracy	banned
free speech ban	8/11/1909	Goldman, Emma	New York City	conspiracy	banned
worker endangerment	11/1909	Beard, Mary Ritter	New York City	strike	jail
worker endangerment	11/1909	O'Reilly, Leonora	New York City	strike	jail
free speech ban	10/13/1911	Goldman, Emma	New York City	conspiracy	intimidation
labor exploitation	1912	Flynn, Elizabeth Gurley	New York City	hotel strike	arrest
labor exploitation	1913	Keller, Helen Adams	New York City	promoted unions	
Comstock Act	1913	Ortiz, Philippe	New York City	displayed nude art	threat
free press ban	2/9/1913	Sanger, Margaret Louise Higgins	New York City	birth control information	
World War I	8/1914	Goldman, Emma	New York City	sheltered draft evaders	
Comstock Act	8/1914	Sanger, Margaret Louise Higgins	New York City	birth control information	arrest, fled
free press ban	8/1914	Sanger, Margaret Louise Higgins	New York City	birth control information	arrest, fled
World War I	8/1914	Wald, Lillian	New York City	sheltered draft evaders	
labor organization ban	1915	Jones, Mary "Mother"	New York City	public harangue	

State/ Target of Act	Date	Name	Location	Act	Consequence
free press ban	9/10/1915	Sanger, William	New York City	birth control information	arrest, jail
free speech ban	2/11/1916	Goldman, Emma	New York City	birth control lecture	arrest, prison
Comstock Act	2/11/1916	Reitman, Ben L.	New York City	birth control leaflets	jail
Comstock Act	5/20/1916	Ashley, Jessie	New York City	birth control information	arrest
Comstock Act	5/20/1916	Eastman, Ida Rauh	New York City	birth control information	arrest
free speech ban	5/20/1916	Goldman, Emma	New York City	birth control information	arrest
free speech ban	5/20/1916	Hall, Bolton	New York City	birth control information	arrest
Comstock Act	5/20/1916	Stokes, Rose Pastor	New York City	birth control information	arrest
Comstock Act	7/1916	Allison, Van Kleek	New York City	birth control information	arrest
Comstock Act	7/1916	Marion, Katharina Schafer	New York City	birth control information	arrest
Comstock Act	7/1916	Smedley, Agnes	New York City	birth control information	arrest
Comstock Act	10/20/1916	Goldman, Emma	New York City	obscenity	arrest
Comstock Act	10/27/1916	Byrne, Ethel Higgins	New York City	birth control information	workhouse, force-feeding
Comstock Act	10/27/1916	Mindall, Fania	New York City	birth control information	arrest
free press ban	10/27/1916	Sanger, Margaret Louise Higgins	New York City	birth control information	workhouse
Comstock Act	12/15/1916	Reitman, Ben L.	Rochester	birth control leaflets	arrest
World War I	1917	Eichel, David	Camp Upton	conscientious objection	prison
World War I	1917	Getts, Clark H.	New York City	conscientious objection	prison, asylum
loyalty oath	1917	McDowell, Mary Stone	Brooklyn	refused pledge	fired
World War I	1917	Moore, Howard W.	Camp Upton	conscientious objection	prison
food prices	2/20/1917	Harris, Ida	New York City	riot	
free speech ban	7/15/1917	Goldman, Emma	New York City	conspiracy	office closed
free speech ban	8/1917	Goldman, Emma	New York City	conspiracy	impounded
free speech ban	9/11/1917	Goldman, Emma	New York City	conspiracy	banned
draft	10/1917	Cattell, J. McKeen	New York City	protest	fired
draft	10/1917	Dana, Henry Wadsworth Longfellow	New York City	protest	fired
draft, free press ban	10/30/1917	Binder, Stephen	Brooklyn	protest	confiscation
free speech ban	10/30/1917	Goldman, Emma	New York City	conspiracy	prison
free speech ban	12/14/1917	Goldman, Emma	New York City	conspiracy	prison

State/Target of Act	Date	Name	Location	Act	Consequence
World War I	1918	Seidenberg, Roderick	Camp Upton	conscientious objection	prison
free press ban	5/8/1918	Rutherford, Joseph Franklin	New York	distributed tracts	prison
draft	8/31/1918	Nelles, Walter	New York City	protest	raided
World War I	11/2/1918	Eichel, Julius	Camp Upton	conscientious objection	prison at hard labor
World War I	11/2/1918	Thomas, Evan	Camp Upton	conscientious objection	life in prison, bread and water
women's disenfranchisement	12/1919	Goldman, Emma	New York City	protest	deported
World War I, free speech ban	12/1919	Goldman, Emma	New York City	conspiracy, protested draft	prison
Sacco and Vanzetti death sentence	7/14/1920	Dos Passos, John	New York City	protest	
Sacco and Vanzetti death sentence	7/14/1920	Flynn, Elizabeth Gurley	New York City	protest	
Comstock Act, free speech ban	11/1921	Sanger, Margaret Louise Higgins	New York City	birth control lecture	arrest
Comstock Act	11/1921	Winsor, Mary	New York City	birth control information	arrest
Sacco and Vanzetti death sentence	4/8/1927	Dewey, John	New York City	protest	
Sacco and Vanzetti death sentence	8/1927	Black, Helen	New York City	protest	arrest
Sacco and Vanzetti death sentence	8/1927	Craton, Ann Washington	New York City	protest	arrest
Comstock Act	1929	Stone, Hannah Mayer	New York City	birth control information	confiscation
homelessness, racism	1930s	Phillips, Donnellan	Harlem	protest	
lynching	1930s	Powell, Adam Clayton, Jr.	Harlem	propaganda	
racism	4/21/1930	Powell, Adam Clayton, Jr.	Harlem	protest	
racism	3/25/1931	Powell, Adam Clayton, Jr.	Harlem	protest	
racism	1933	Powell, Adam Clayton, Jr.	Harlem	picket	
Olympics	1936	Powell, Adam Clayton, Jr.	Harlem	propaganda	
white-owned business	3/19/1937	Powell, Adam Clayton, Jr.	Harlem	riot	
unemployment	2/12/1938	Chinn, Genevieve	Harlem	boycott	
unemployment	2/12/1938	Ford, James W.	Harlem	boycott	
unemployment	2/12/1938	Imes, William Lloyd	Harlem	boycott	
unemployment	2/12/1938	Johnson, Arnold Samuel	Harlem	boycott	
unemployment	2/12/1938	Powell, Adam Clayton, Jr.	Harlem	boycott	
racism	1939	Paige, Myles A.	Harlem	picket	

State/ Target of Act	Date	Name	Location	Act	Consequence
racism	1939	Powell, Adam Clayton, Jr.	Harlem	picket, boycott	
World War II	1940s	Lowell, Robert	New York City	abetted draft resistance	prison
World War II	1940s	Powers, J.F.	New York City	abetted draft resistance	prison
racism	1941	Powell, Adam Clayton, Jr.	New York City	march	
racism	1941	Quill, Michael J.	New York City	march	
World War II	7/1942	Templin, Lawrence	New York City	conscientious objection	jail
World War II	1943	Bishop, Corbett	New York City	left a camp	prison, torture, tube-feeding
World War II	1943	Phillips, Randolph Godfrey	New York City	conscientious objection	guardhouse, asylum
racism	1943	Randolph, Asa Philip	New York City	rally	
World War II	1943	Roodenko, Igal	New York City	resisted draft	forced labor
World War II	1943	Wieck, David Thoreau	New York City	refused to register	prison
police brutality	6/1943	Powell, Adam Clayton, Jr.	New York City	propaganda	
draft	1947	Randolph, Asa Philip	Albany	protest	
draft	1947	Reynolds, Grant	Albany	protest	
draft	1948	Dellinger, David T.	New York City	protest	assault
draft	1948	Rustin, Bayard Taylor	New York City	protest	assault
Korean War	1950	Norton, Edgar R.	Glen Falls	pacifism	
taxation	1952	Muste, Abraham Johannes	New York City	tax resistance	
nuclear power	6/15/1955	Day, Dorothy	New York City	protest	jail
nuclear power	6/15/1955	Muste, Abraham Johannes	New York City	protest	jail
nuclear power	1956	Day, Dorothy	New York City	protest	jail
nuclear power	1959	Day, Dorothy	New York City	protest	jail
Vietnam War	1960s	Day, Dorothy	New York City	protest	jail
draft	1960	Day, Dorothy	New York City	protest	jail
police brutality	1/1960	Powell, Adam Clayton, Jr.	New York City	rally	
free speech ban	1961	Miller, Henry	New York City	obscenity	arrest
racism	1962	Farmer, James Leonard	New York City	picket	
nuclear power	4/26/1962	Becker, Norma	New York City	march	
racism	9/28/1963	Farmer, James Leonard	New York City	sit-in	arrest
free speech ban	3/31/1964	Bruce, Lenny	New York City	comic act	workhouse
free speech ban	3/31/1964	Solomon, Howard	New York City	comic act	workhouse
racism	4/23/1964	Fruchter, Norman D.	New York City	sit-in	arrest
racism	4/23/1964	Harrington, Edward Michael	New York City	sit-in	arrest
racism	4/23/1964	Rustin, Bayard Taylor	New York City	sit-in	arrest
racism	7/18/1964	King, Martin Luther, Jr	Harlem	demonstration	stoned

State/Target of Act	Date	Name	Location	Act	Consequence
draft, Vietnam War	10/15/1965	Miller, David J.	Syracuse	burned draft card	
Vietnam War	11/9/1965	LaPorte, Roger Allen	New York City	self-immolation	
racism, Vietnam War	4/4/1967	King, Martin Luther, Jr.	New York City	denounced draft, war	
Vietnam War	12/5/1967	Ginsberg, Allen	New York City	demonstration, conspiracy	
Vietnam War	12/5/1967	Spock, Benjamin	New York City	demonstration, conspiracy	
taxation	1/1968	Baldwin, James	New York City	tax resistance	
Vietnam War	1/1968	Berrigan, Daniel	New York City	tax resistance	
Vietnam War	1/1968	Berrigan, Philip	New York City	tax resistance	
Vietnam War	1/1968	Dworkin, Andrea	New York City	tax resistance	
Vietnam War	1/1968	Friedan, Betty	New York City	tax resistance	
Vietnam War	1/1968	Ginsberg, Allen	New York City	tax resistance	
Vietnam War	1/1968	Greenberg, Daniel	New York City	tax resistance	
taxation	1/1968	Olsen, Tillie	New York City	tax resistance	
taxation	1/1968	Paley, Grace	New York City	tax resistance	
taxation	1/1968	Rukeyser, Muriel	New York City	tax resistance	
taxation	1/1968	Sontag, Susan	New York City	tax resistance	
taxation	1/1968	Steinem, Gloria	New York City	tax resistance	
taxation	1/1968	Styron, William	New York City	tax resistance	
taxation	1/1968	Vonnegut, Kurt, Jr.	New York City	tax resistance	
taxation	1/1968	Zinn, Howard	New York City	tax resistance	
Vietnam War	10/9/1968	Geddes, Maggie	New York City	sabotage	
draft, war	7/3/1969	Boskey, Jill Ann	New York City	destroyed property	arrest
draft, war	7/3/1969	Czarnik, Kathy	New York City	destroyed property	arrest
draft, war	7/3/1969	Geddes, Maggie	New York City	destroyed property	arrest
draft, war	7/3/1969	Green, Valentine	New York City	destroyed property	arrest
draft, war	7/3/1969	Kennedy, Pat	New York City	destroyed property	arrest
taxation	1970s	Baldwin, James	New York City	tax resistance	
racism	3/18/1970	Brownmiller, Susan	New York City	intimidation	
racism	3/18/1970	Firestone, Shulamith	New York City	intimidation	
racism	3/18/1970	Hammer, Signe	New York City	intimidation	
pornography, rape	4/1970	Atkinson, Ti-Grace	New York City	intimidation	
pornography, rape	4/1970	Morgan, Robin	New York City	intimidation	
gay persecution	5/1/1970	Falstein, Jesse	New York City	sit-in	arrest
gay persecution	5/1/1970	Griffo, Michaela	New York City	sit-in	arrest
racism	10/13/1970	Angelou, Maya	New York City	protest	
racism	10/13/1970	Baldwin, James	New York City	protest	
racism	10/13/1970	Bambara, Toni Cade	New York City	protest	
racism	10/13/1970	Davis, Angela	New York City	conspiracy, kidnap, violence	jail
racism	10/13/1970	Franklin, Aretha	New York City	protest	
racism	10/13/1970	Giovanni, Nikki	New York City	protest	
racism	10/13/1970	Jagger, Mick	New York City	protest	

State/Target of Act	Date	Name	Location	Act	Consequence
racism	10/13/1970	Lennon, John	New York City	protest	
racism	10/13/1970	Sanchez, Sonia	New York City	protest	
free speech ban	1972	Lovelace, Linda	Binghamton	obscenity	arrest
free speech ban	1972	Reems, Harry	Binghamton	obscenity	arrest
nuclear power	1980s	Coffin, William Sloane, Jr.	New York City	protest	
nuclear power	11/24/1983	Berrigan, Elizabeth McAlister	Rome	sabotage	jail
nuclear power	1986	Bergin, Patrick	New York City	blocked a door	
nuclear power	1986	Costner, Pat	New York City	blocked a door	home burned
nuclear power	1986	Sheen, Martin	New York City	blocked a door	
AIDS neglect	1987	Bordowitz, Gregg	New York City	protest	
AIDS neglect	1987	Kramer, Larry	New York City	protest	
AIDS neglect	1987	Northrop, Ann	New York City	protest	
AIDS neglect	1987	Sikorowski, Mark	New York City	protest	
AIDS neglect	1987	Woodard, Ken	New York City	protest	
AIDS neglect	3/24/1987	Staley, Peter	New York City	sit-in	
AIDS neglect	1/1/1988	Banzhaf, Marion D.	New York City	disrupted office	
AIDS neglect	1/1/1988	Maggenti, Maria	New York City	disrupted office	
park curfew	8/6/1988	Ginsberg, Allen	New York City	protest	black eye
Persian Gulf War	3/31/1990	Eichman, Shawn D.	New York City	burned flag	arrest
Persian Gulf War	3/31/1990	Urgo, Joseph R.	New York City	burned flag	arrest
flag burning ban	8/2/1990	Eichman, Shawn D.	New York City	burned flag	fine, community service
flag burning ban	8/2/1990	Urgo, Joseph R.	New York City	burned flag	fine, community service
AIDS neglect	1/22/1991	Weir, John	New York City	disrupted television broadcast	
nuclear power	10/31/1991	Connett, Paul	New York City	sang, trespassed	arrest
nuclear power	10/31/1991	Sheen, Martin	New York City	sang, trespassed	arrest
AIDS neglect	1997	Sawyer, Eric	New York City	march	
Vieques destruction	11/5/2000	Kayak, Tito	New York City	protest flag	
AIDS neglect	8/26/2004	Lugg, Amanda	New York City	nude protest	
AIDS neglect	8/26/2004	Smith, Eustacia	New York City	nude protest	
AIDS neglect	9/1/2005	Hermes, Kris	New York City	assault, incited a riot	arrest, police brutality
Iraq War	3/6/2006	Benjamin, Medea	New York City	protest	arrest
Iraq War	3/6/2006	Sheehan, Cindy	New York City	blocked an entrance	arrest
gay torture	9/19/2006	Barrios, Luis	New York City	protest	police brutality
gay persecution	11/3/2006	Ciervo, Clare	New York City	sit-in	arrest
gay persecution	11/3/2006	Golomb, Julia	New York City	sit-in	arrest
gay persecution	11/3/2006	Hamilton, Leslie	New York City	sit-in	arrest
gay persecution	11/3/2006	Peterson, Curt	New York City	sit-in	arrest
gay persecution	11/3/2006	Rodriguez, David	New York City	sit-in	arrest
gay persecution	11/3/2006	Whinn, Peter	New York City	sit-in	arrest

State/ Target of Act	Date	Name	Location	Act	Consequence
Iraq War	2/11/2007	Barrios, Luis	New York City	protest	arrest
Iraq War	2/13/2007	Barrios, Luis	New York City	protest	arrest
alien refugee abuse	5/9/2007	Ruiz, Juan Carlos	New York City	alien rescue	

North Carolina

State/ Target of Act	Date	Name	Location	Act	Consequence
colonial taxation	1765	Ashe, John Baptiste	Wilmington	underground leader	
colonial taxation	1765	Harnett, Cornelius, Jr.	Wilmington	paramilitary organizer	
colonial taxation	10/1765	Hunter, James	Brunswick	paramilitary organizer	
colonial taxation	10/1765	Husband, Herman	Brunswick	paramilitary organizer	
colonial taxation	11/1765	Waddell, Hugh	Wilmington	ship seizure	
colonial taxation	2/19/1766	Harnett, Cornelius, Jr.	Brunswick	burned an effigy, reopened port	
taxes, corruption	1770s	Butler, William	Orange County	paramilitary	
taxes, corruption	1770s	Howell, Rednap	Orange County	paramilitary	
taxes, corruption	1770s	Hunter, James	Brunswick	paramilitary	
Revolutionary War	1770s	Lee, Jesse	Bertie County	refused to serve	
taxes, corruption	1770	Husband, Herman	Brunswick	propaganda	arrest
colonial taxation	4/12/1770	Harnett, Cornelius, Jr.	Brunswick	paramilitary leader	
colonial taxation	1771	Rowan, Robert	Cumberland County	paramilitary leader	
colonial taxation	5/9/1771	Alexander, William	Rocky River	spying	
taxes, corruption	5/9/1771	Alexander, William	Concord	destroyed supplies	
colonial taxation	5/9/1771	Ashmore, James Samuel	Rocky River	spying	
taxes, corruption	5/9/1771	Ashmore, James Samuel	Concord	destroyed supplies	
colonial taxation	5/9/1771	Caruthers, Robert	Rocky River	sabotage	
taxes, corruption	5/9/1771	Caruthers, Robert	Concord	destroyed supplies	
colonial taxation	5/9/1771	Cockerham, Benjamin	Rocky River	sabotage	
taxes, corruption	5/9/1771	Cockerham, Benjamin	Concord	destroyed supplies	
colonial taxation	5/9/1771	Davis, Robert, farmer	Rocky River	sabotage	
taxes, corruption	5/9/1771	Davis, Robert, Farmer	Concord	destroyed supplies	
colonial taxation	5/9/1771	Hadley, Joshua	Rocky River	sabotage	
taxes, corruption	5/9/1771	Hadley, Joshua	Concord	destroyed supplies	
taxes, corruption	5/9/1771	Waddell, Hugh	Concord	destroyed supplies	
taxes, corruption	5/9/1771	White, James	Concord	destroyed supplies	
colonial taxation	5/9/1771	White, James, Jr.	Rocky River	sabotage	
colonial taxation	5/9/1771	White, John, Jr.	Rocky River	sabotage	
taxes, corruption	5/9/1771	White, John, Jr.	Concord	destroyed supplies	
colonial taxation	5/9/1771	White, William	Rocky River	sabotage	
taxes, corruption	5/9/1771	White, William	Concord	destroyed supplies	
colonial taxation	5/9/1771	White, William, Jr.	Rocky River	sabotage	
taxes, corruption	5/9/1771	White, William, Jr.	Concord	destroyed supplies	
taxes, corruption	5/16/1771	Copeland, James, Jr.	Alamance	paramilitary	

State/ Target of Act	Date	Name	Location	Act	Consequence
taxes, corruption	5/16/1771	Brown, William	Alamance	paramilitary	
taxes, corruption	5/16/1771	Cox, Harmon	Alamance	paramilitary	
taxes, corruption	5/16/1771	Emerson, James, Sr.	Alamance	paramilitary	
taxes, corruption	5/16/1771	Few, James	Alamance	paramilitary	hanged
taxes, corruption	5/16/1771	Hunter, James	Alamance	paramilitary	house burned
taxes, corruption	5/16/1771	Husband, Herman	Alamance	paramilitary leader	fled, house burned
taxes, corruption	5/16/1771	Messer, Robert	Alamance	paramilitary	chained, dragged, hanged
taxes, corruption	5/16/1771	Pugh, James	Alamance	paramilitary	hanged
taxes, corruption	5/16/1771	Stewart, James	Alamance	paramilitary	
taxes, corruption	5/16/1771	Thompson, Robert	Alamance	paramilitary	killed
colonial taxation	6/19/1771	Brown, William	Hillsborough	paramilitary	
taxes, corruption	6/19/1771	Matear, Robert	Hillsborough	paramilitary	hanged
taxes, corruption	6/19/1771	Mercer, Forrester	Hillsborough	paramilitary	
taxes, corruption	6/19/1771	Merrill, Benjamin	Hillsborough	paramilitary leader	hanged
colonial taxation	6/19/1771	Pugh, James	Hillsborough	paramilitary	hanged
colonial taxation	10/25/1774	Barker, Penelope	Edenton	denounced British goods	
colonial taxation	10/25/1774	King, Elizabeth	Edenton	paramilitary host	
colonial taxation	1775	Hadley, Joshua	Fayetteville	paramilitary organizer	
slave education ban	1808–1832	Chavis, John	Raleigh	educated slaves	criminalized
slave recapture	1810	Murrow, Andrew Caldwell	New Garden	slave relay	
slave recapture	1813–1826	Coffin, Catherine White	New Garden	conspiracy	
slave recapture	1813–1826	Coffin, Levi	New Garden	conspiracy	
slave recapture	1820s	Curry, Vina	Guilford County	conspiracy	
slave education ban	1820s	Mendenhall, George C.	Jamestown	educated slaves	
slave education ban	1820s	Mendenhall, Richard	Jamestown	educated slaves	
slave education ban	1830–1857	Stanley, John Stewart	New Bern	educated slaves	forced out of job
slave recapture	1833	Manuel	Elizabeth City	forgery	
slave recapture	1840s–1860s	Coffin, Alfred V.	Guilford County	conspiracy	
slave recapture	5/1850	Crooks, Adam	Jamestown	distributed literature	mob violence, jail
slave recapture	5/1850	McBride, Jesse	Jamestown	distributed literature	mob violence, jail
slave recapture	5/1850	Mendenhall, George C.	Jamestown	slave rescue	
Civil War	1861–1863	Dobbins, Jesse Virgil	Yadkin County	refused to serve	fled
Civil War	1861–1863	Dobbins, William	Yadkin County	refused to serve	fled
Civil War	1863	Hockett, Himelius Mendenhall	Guilford	refused to serve	torture
Civil War	1863	Hockett, Jesse Davis	Guilford	refused to serve	torture
Civil War	1863	Hockett, William B.	Guilford	refused to serve	torture
Civil War	1863	Laughlin, Seth Wade	Randolph	refused to serve	beaten to death
Civil War	1863	Macon, Gideon	Concord	refused to serve	threat of hanging
racism	4/9/1947	Adams, Louis	Greensboro	integrated a bus	

State/ Target of Act	Date	Name	Location	Act	Consequence
racism	4/12/1947	Johnson, Andrew	Durham	integrated a bus	arrest
racism	4/12/1947	Peck, James	Chapel Hill	integrated a bus	battery
racism	4/12/1947	Peck, James	Durham	integrated a bus	arrest
racism	4/12/1947	Rustin, Bayard Taylor	Durham	integrated a bus	arrest
racism	4/13/1947	Felmet, Joseph	Chapel Hill	integrated a bus	arrest
racism	4/13/1947	Johnson, Andrew	Chapel Hill	integrated a bus	arrest
racism	4/13/1947	Jones, Charles M.	Chapel Hill	abetted integration	death threat, lost job
racism	4/13/1947	Roodenko, Igal	Chapel Hill	integrated a bus	arrest
racism	4/13/1947	Rustin, Bayard Taylor	Chapel Hill	integrated a bus	arrest, chain gang
racism	4/15/1947	Banks, Dennis	Asheville	integrated a bus	fine
segregation	1954	Hawkins, Reginald Armistice	Charlotte	sit-in	
racism	4/15/1957	Peck, James	Asheville	integrated a bus	fine
racism	1957	Farmer, James Leonard	Raleigh	conference	
segregation	1957	Farmer, James Leonard	Greensboro	sit-in	
racism	1957	King, Martin Luther, Jr.	Raleigh	conference	
racism	1957	Lewis, John Robert	Raleigh	conference	
racism	1957	Randolph, Asa Philip	Raleigh	conference	
racism	1957	Wilkins, Roy	Raleigh	conference	
racism	1957	Young, Whitney Moore, Jr.	Raleigh	conference	
segregation	6/23/1957	Clyburn, Mary Elizabeth	Durham	sit-in	jail, fine
segregation	6/23/1957	Glenn, Claude Edward	Durham	sit-in	jail, fine
segregation	6/23/1957	Gray, Jesse Willard	Durham	sit-in	jail, fine
segregation	6/23/1957	Jones, Vivian Elaine	Durham	sit-in	jail, fine
segregation	6/23/1957	McKissick, Floyd B., Sr.	Durham	sit-in	jail, fine
segregation	6/23/1957	Moore, Douglas E.	Durham	sit-in	jail, fine
segregation	6/23/1957	Willis, Melvin Haywood	Durham	sit-in	jail, fine
segregation	2/1/1960	Blair, Ezell A., Jr.	Greensboro	sit-in	
segregation	2/1/1960	McCain, Franklin	Greensboro	sit-in	
segregation	2/1/1960	McNeil, Joseph	Greensboro	sit-in	
segregation	2/1/1960	Richmond, David	Greensboro	sit-in	
segregation	2/1/1960	Wilkins, Roy	Greensboro	promoted sit-ins	
segregation	2/9/1960	Matthews, Carl Wesley	Winston-Salem	sit-in	
racism	4/15/1960	Baker, Ella	Raleigh	protest	
racism	8/2/1961	Forman, James	Monroe	Freedom Rider	police brutality, jail
Vietnam War	5/1970	Fonda, Jane	Fort Bragg	distributed pamphlets	arrest
racism	11/3/1979	Cauce, César	Greensboro	protest	shot
black rights	11/3/1979	Dawson, Edward	Greensboro	paramilitary spy	
black rights	11/3/1979	Hennis, E.H.	Greensboro	paramilitary spy	
racism	11/3/1979	Nathan, Michael Ronald	Greensboro	protest	shot
racism	11/3/1979	Samson, William Evan	Greensboro	protest	shot
racism	11/3/1979	Smith, Sandi Neely	Greensboro	protest	shot

State/ Target of Act	Date	Name	Location	Act	Consequence
racism	11/3/1979	Waller, James Michael	Greensboro	protest	shot
nuclear power	12/7/1993	Berrigan, Philip	Goldsboro	sabotage	jail
nuclear power	12/7/1993	Dear, John	Goldsboro	sabotage	jail
nuclear power	12/7/1993	Fredriksson, Lynn	Goldsboro	sabotage	jail
nuclear power	12/7/1993	Friedrich, Bruce	Goldsboro	sabotage	jail
black rights	2/2007	Fincher, Edward	Gastonia	paramilitary officer	
black rights	2/2007	Griffin, Virgil	Gastonia	anti-Latino leader	

North Dakota

World War I	10/2/1914	Funk, Antoinette	Minot	street speech	jail, fine
World War I	7/29/1917	O'Hare, Kate Richards	Bowman	promoted pacifism	
World War II	6/29/1945	Moorman, Albert E.	North Dakota	draft resistance	prison

Ohio

slave rescue	1797	Thomas, Avis Stanton	Mount Pleasant	ran a safehouse	
slave rescue	1797	Thomas, Jesse, Jr.	Mount Pleasant	ran a safehouse	
slave rescue	1797	Thomas, Joseph Stanton	Mount Pleasant	slave relay	
slave rescue	1800s	Monroe, David	Chillicothe	slave rescue, transport	wanted criminal
slavery	1810s	Campbell, Alexander	Ripley	protest	
War of 1812	6/1/1812	McNemar, Richard	Union Village	protest	
War of 1812	6/1/1812	Rollins, Samuel	Union Village	protest	
War of 1812	10/1/1812	Baxter, Robert	Union Village	deserted	forced march
War of 1812	10/1/1812	Davis, Rufus E.	Union Village	deserted	forced march
War of 1812	10/1/1812	Davis, William, Jr.	Union Village	deserted	forced march
War of 1812	10/1/1812	Gallaher, Adam	Union Village	deserted	forced march
War of 1812	10/1/1812	McClelland, Samuel Swan	Union Village	deserted	forced march
War of 1812	10/1/1812	Rollins, Samuel	Union Village	deserted	forced march
War of 1812	10/1/1812	Spinning, David	Union Village	deserted	forced march
slavery	1816	Osborn, Charles Worth	Mount Pleasant	propaganda	
slave recapture	1819	Lundy, Benjamin	Mount Pleasant	propaganda	
slavery	1820s	Allen, Abraham	Wilmington	protest	
slavery	1820s	Palmer, Elizabeth Ward	Weller	protest	
slavery	1820s	Palmer, John Edgerton	Weller	protest	
slave education ban	1829	Harvey, Elizabeth Burgess	Harveysburg	educated slaves	
slave education ban	1829	Harvey, Jesse	Harveysburg	educated slaves	
slave recapture	1829	Lundy, Benjamin	Mount Pleasant	recruitment	
slave recapture	1830s	Butterworth, Nancy Irvin Wales	Lebanon	ran a safehouse	
slave recapture	1830s	Cattell, Jonas	Salem	ran a safehouse	
slavery	1830s	Powell, Thomas Howells	Coshocton County	protest	
slavery	1830s	Robinson, Marius R.	Salem	admired oratory	tarred, feathered

State/Target of Act	Date	Name	Location	Act	Consequence
slave education ban	1830s	Rotch, Charity Rodman	Kendal	educated slaves	
slavery	1830s	Steel, William, Sr.	Stafford	protest	
slave recapture	1830s–1850s	Huber, Charles Boerstler	Bethel	sheltered slaves	
slave recapture	6/25/1831	Pettijohn, Eleanor Northcutt	Clay	slave rescue	stripped naked
slave recapture	6/25/1831	Pettijohn, Lewis	Clay	slave rescue	clubbed
slave recapture	1832–1840	Stowe, Harriet Beecher	Cincinnati	slave rescue, propaganda	
slave recapture	1833	Birney, James Gillespie	Cincinnati	protest, conspiracy	
free speech ban	1834	Dresser, Amos	Cincinnati	abolitionism	expelled, lashed
slavery	11/25/1835	Rankin, John	Ripley	protest, conspiracy	
slave recapture	1837	Fairbank, Calvin	Cincinnati	slave relay	
slave recapture	1838	Rankin, John	Ripley	slave rescue	
slave recapture	1838	Shaw, Chance	Ripley	slave rescue	
slave recapture	1839	Mahan, John Bennington	Sardinia	incited a riot	fine, jail on bread and water
slave recapture	1839	Pettijohn, Amos	Brown County	impeded police, incited a riot	fine, jail on bread and water
slave recapture	1839	Pettijohn, Joseph	Brown County	impeded police, incited a riot	fine, jail on bread and water
slave recapture	4/21/1839	Hudson, Sally	Ripley	slave rescue	shot
slave recapture	1839–1860s	Whinery, John Carroll	Salem	ran a safehouse	
slave recapture	1840s	Brown, William Wells	Cleveland	lake relay	
slave recapture	1840s	Eells, Erastus	Lisbon	slave concealment, relay	
slave recapture	1840s	Ford, Cyrus	Cleveland	lake relay	
slave recapture	1840s	Ford, Darius	Cleveland	lake relay	
slave recapture	1840s	Hatfield, John	Cincinnati	slave relay	
slave recapture	1840s–1850s	Ford, Horatio Clark	Cleveland	lake relay	
slave recapture	1840s–1850s	Gardner, Mary Ann Price	Worthington	ran a safehouse	
slave recapture	1840s–1850s	Gardner, Ozem	Worthington	ran a safehouse	
slave recapture	1840	Webster, David	Wellington	slave rescue	
slave recapture	1840	Webster, Hannah Post	Wellington	slave rescue	
slave recapture	1841	Giddings, Joshua Reed	Jefferson	abetted slave relay	congressional censure
slave recapture	1842	Hadley, Deborah D.	Springfield	coded quilt	ousted from Quakers
slave recapture	1842	Hadley, Lydia D.	Springfield	coded quilt	ousted from Quakers
slave recapture	1842	Hadley, Rebecca Harvey	Springfield	coded quilt	ousted from Quakers
polygamy ban	1843	Rigson, Sidney	Hiram	bigamy	killed
polygamy ban	1843	Smith, Joseph, Jr.	Hiram	bigamy	tarred, feathered
slave recapture	1843	Van Zandt, John	Glendale	slave rescue	lawsuit, excommunication

State/ Target of Act	Date	Name	Location	Act	Consequence
slave recapture	1844	Mahan, John Bennington	Sardinia	rescue operation	threat of kidnap or murder, died in prison at hard labor
slave recapture	1844	Mahan, William Jacob	Sardinia	rescue operation	ousted by Methodists
slave recapture	9/28/1844	Rankin, Jean	Ripley	sheltered slaves	
slave recapture	9/28/1844	Rankin, John	Ripley	sheltered slaves	
slavery	1847	Coffin, Levi	Cincinnati	fund-raising	
slave recapture	1847–1861	Coffin, Catherine White	Cincinnati	slave relay	
slave recapture	1847–1861	Coffin, Levi	Cincinnati	slave relay, recruitment	
free press ban	4/22/1848	Crooks, Adam	Columbiana	abolitionist pamphlet	jail
free press ban	4/22/1848	McBride, Jesse	Columbiana	abolitionist pamphlet	jail
free press ban	4/22/1848	Robinson, Marius Racine, editor	Mahoning County	editorial	tarred, feathered
slave recapture	1850s	Webber, George E.	Hinckley	sheltered slaves	
slavery	1850s–1860s	Hayes, Rutherford Birchard	Cincinnati	conspiracy	
slave recapture	5/1850	Mendenhall, George C.	Logan County	slave transport	
Fugitive Slave Law of 1850	9/1850	Monroe, James	Oberlin	slave rescue	
Fugitive Slave Law of 1850	9/1850	Peck, Henry Everard	Oberlin	slave rescue	
slave recapture	11/9/1851	Coffin, Levi	Cincinnati	fund-raising	
slave recapture	11/9/1851	Doram, Catherine	Cincinnati	fund-raising	
slave recapture	1854	Montgomery, James	Ashtabula	led militia	
slavery	1/30/1856	Garner, Margaret	Mill Creek	murdered a child	re-enslaved
slavery	2/1856	Coffin, Levi	Cincinnati	slave defense	
slavery	2/1856	Joliffe, John	Cincinnati	slave defense	
slavery	2/1856	Stone, Lucy	Cincinnati	slave defense	
slave recapture	1857	Stanley, Frances Griffith	Cleveland	educated slaves	
slave recapture	1858	Williams, George	Ripley	slave rescue	prison
slave recapture	9/13/1858	Backus, Franklin T.	Cleveland	defended slave rescue	
slave recapture	9/13/1858	Bartlett, James	Oberlin	impeded arrest	jail
slave recapture	9/13/1858	Bartlett, James H., Jr.	Oberlin	impeded arrest	jail
slave recapture	9/13/1858	Boies, Eli	Oberlin	impeded arrest	jail
slave recapture	9/13/1858	Bushnell, Simeon Martin	Oberlin	impeded arrest	jail
slave recapture	9/13/1858	Copeland, John Anthony, Jr.	Oberlin	impeded arrest	jail
slave recapture	9/13/1858	Cummings, Robert L.	Oberlin	impeded arrest	jail
slave recapture	9/13/1858	De Wolfe, Matthew	Oberlin	impeded arrest	jail
slave recapture	9/13/1858	Evans, Henry	Oberlin	impeded arrest	jail
slave recapture	9/13/1858	Evans, Wilson Bruce	Oberlin	impeded arrest	jail
slave recapture	9/13/1858	Fairchild, James Harris	Oberlin	slave rescue	

State/ Target of Act	Date	Name	Location	Act	Consequence
slave recapture	9/13/1858	Fairchild, Mary Fletcher Kellogg	Oberlin	slave rescue	
slave recapture	9/13/1858	Fitch, James M.	Oberlin	impeded arrest	jail
slave recapture	9/13/1858	Fox, Jeremiah	Oberlin	impeded arrest	jail
slave recapture	9/13/1858	Gena, Thomas	Oberlin	impeded arrest	jail
slave recapture	9/13/1858	Gillett, Matthew M.	Oberlin	impeded arrest	jail
slave recapture	9/13/1858	Goodyear, Chauncey	Oberlin	impeded arrest	jail
slave recapture	9/13/1858	Griswold, Seneca O.	Cleveland	defended slave rescue	
slave recapture	9/13/1858	Hartwell, John	Oberlin	impeded arrest	jail
slave recapture	9/13/1858	Hines, Lewis	Oberlin	impeded arrest	jail
slave recapture	9/13/1858	Langston, Charles Henry	Oberlin	impeded arrest	jail, fine
slave recapture	9/13/1858	Leary, Lewis Sheridan	Oberlin	impeded arrest	jail
slave recapture	9/13/1858	Lewis, Franklin	Oberlin	impeded arrest	jail
slave recapture	9/13/1858	Lincoln, William E.	Oberlin	impeded arrest	jail
slave recapture	9/13/1858	Loveland, Abner	Oberlin	impeded arrest	jail
slave recapture	9/13/1858	Lyman, Ansel Wright	Oberlin	impeded arrest	jail
slave recapture	9/13/1858	Mandeville, John	Oberlin	impeded arrest	jail
slave recapture	9/13/1858	Niles, Henry D.	Oberlin	impeded arrest	jail
slave recapture	9/13/1858	Peck, Henry Everard	Oberlin	impeded arrest	jail
slave recapture	9/13/1858	Plumb, Ralph	Oberlin	impeded arrest	jail
slave recapture	9/13/1858	Price, John	Oberlin	jailbreak	fled
slave recapture	9/13/1858	Riddle, Albert G.	Cleveland	defended slave rescue	
slave recapture	9/13/1858	Sciples, William	Oberlin	impeded arrest	jail
slave recapture	9/13/1858	Scott, John H.	Oberlin	impeded arrest	jail
slave recapture	9/13/1858	Scrimgeour, William E.	Oberlin	impeded arrest	jail
slave recapture	9/13/1858	Shepard, James R.	Oberlin	impeded arrest	jail
slave recapture	9/13/1858	Shipherd, Jacob Rudd	Oberlin	impeded arrest	jail
slave recapture	9/13/1858	Soules, Walter	Oberlin	impeded arrest	jail
slave recapture	9/13/1858	Spalding, Rufus P.	Cleveland	defended slave rescue	
slave recapture	9/13/1858	Wadsworth, Loring	Oberlin	impeded arrest	jail
slave recapture	9/13/1858	Wall, Orindatus Simon Bolivar	Oberlin	impeded arrest	jail
slave recapture	9/13/1858	Watson, David	Oberlin	impeded arrest	jail
slave recapture	9/13/1858	Watson, John	Oberlin	impeded arrest	jail
slave recapture	9/13/1858	Watson, William	Oberlin	impeded arrest	jail
slave recapture	9/13/1858	Williams, Daniel	Oberlin	impeded arrest	jail
slave recapture	9/13/1858	Windsor, Robert	Oberlin	impeded arrest	jail
slave recapture	9/13/1858	Winsor, Richard	Oberlin	impeded arrest	jail
draft	1861	Giddings, Joshua Reed	Jefferson	supported pacifism	
slave recapture	5/13/1861	Butterworth, Henry Thomas	Lebanon	ran a safehouse	
Civil War	5/1863	Vallandigham, Clement Laird	Dayton	refused to serve	prison

State/ Target of Act	Date	Name	Location	Act	Consequence
draft	5/1863	Vallandigham, Clement Laird	Dayton	incited draft evasion	prison
alcohol sale and consumption	4/1874	Leavitt, Emily Wilder Sherman	Cincinnati	obstructed a sidewalk	arrest
labor organization ban	1/22/1890	Jones, Mary "Mother"	Columbus	public harangue	
free press ban	3/9/1907	Goldman, Emma	Columbus	conspiracy	banned
free speech ban	1/17/1911	Goldman, Emma	Columbus	conspiracy	banned
free speech ban	12/12/1916	Reitman, Ben L.	Cleveland	birth control leaflets	jail
draft	8/10/1917	Martin, M.L.	Marion	protest	fired
World War I	4/30/1918	Basinger, David W.	Chillicothe	refused uniform	
World War I	6/1918	Owen, Chandler	Cleveland	antiwar speech	jail for sedition
World War I	6/1918	Randolph, Asa Philip	Cleveland	antiwar speech	jail for sedition, surveillance
draft	6/12/1918	Albrink, Fred	Columbus	protest	suspended
black rights	1920	Effinger, Virgil Hubert	Lima	anti-Semitic leader	
black rights	1920	Shepard, William Jacob	Bellaire	paramilitary leader	
World War II	1942	Dole, Arthur A.	Yellow Springs	refused classification	prison
World War II	1943	Nelson, Wallace Floyd	Coshocton	fled work camp	prison
racism	4/19/1947	Houser, George	Cincinnati	integrated a bus	threat
taxation	1948	Champney, Horace	Cleveland	tax resistance	
racism	4/19/1957	Worthy, William	Cincinnati	integrated a bus	
Korean War	1960s	Lawson, James, Jr.	Massillon	refused to register	prison
taxation	5/1961	McCrackin, Maurice	Cincinnati	tax resistance	
Vietnam War	5/4/1970	Krause, Alison	Kent	demonstration	shot
Vietnam War	5/4/1970	Miller, Jeffrey Glen	Kent	demonstration	shot
Vietnam War	5/4/1970	Scheuer, Sandra	Kent	demonstration	shot
Vietnam War	5/4/1970	Schroeder, William, student	Kent	demonstration	shot
free press ban	5/1976	Flynt, Larry	Dayton	obscenity	arrest

Oklahoma

Indian displacement	1879	Big Snake	Baxter Springs	left a reservation	shot
peyote ban	1900s	Parker, Quanah	Fort Sill	peyote worship	
peyote ban	1900s	Whiteman, John	Apache	peyote worship	
draft	8/2/1917	Benefield, William L.	Sasakwa	conspiracy, vandalism	
draft	8/2/1917	Crane, Roy	Sasakwa	conspiracy, vandalism	prison
draft	8/2/1917	Harjo, John	Sasakwa	conspiracy, vandalism	
draft	8/2/1917	Martin, William M.	Sasakwa	conspiracy, vandalism	prison
draft	8/2/1917	Munson, H.H. "Rube"	Sasakwa	conspiracy, vandalism	prison

State/ Target of Act	Date	Name	Location	Act	Consequence
draft	8/2/1917	Spence, Homer Carlos	Sasakwa	conspiracy, vandalism	
World War I	1918	Enfield, Orville E.	Arnett	conspiracy	arrest
draft	3/21/1918	Hoffman, Henry	Altus	protest	assault, tarred, feathered
draft	3/21/1918	Westbrook, O.F.	Altus	protest	assault, tarred, feathered
World War I	4/21/1918	Hicks, William Madison	Elk City	conspiracy	tarred, feathered
segregation	8/19/1958	Luper, Clara	Oklahoma City	sit-in	
segregation	8/19/1958	Posey, Barbara	Oklahoma City	sit-in	

Oregon

State/ Target of Act	Date	Name	Location	Act	Consequence
free press ban	8/6/1915	Goldman, Emma	Portland	birth control information	fine
free press ban	8/6/1915	Reitman, Ben L.	Portland	birth control information	fine
draft	5/11/1918	Kimmons, I.	Portland	protest	fired
draft	9/13/1918	Park, Alice	Portland	protest	confiscation
debt	5/1932	Waters, Walter Willis	Portland	paramilitary	
Japanese internment	3/28/1942	Yasui, Minoru	Hood River	defied curfew	lost citizenship
wilderness destruction	1979	Foreman, Dave	Siskiyou	sabotage	
wilderness destruction	1983	Foreman, Dave	Siskiyou	sabotage	injured
wilderness destruction	7/20/1985	Huber, Ron	Corvallis	tree-sitting	violence
peyote ban	1990	Black, Galen	Douglas County	peyote worship	lost job
peyote ban	1990	Smith, Alfred	Douglas County	peyote worship	lost job
ROTC	11/18/2005	Cohen, Karla	Eugene	chained to ROTC classroom entrance	arrest
ROTC	11/18/2005	Tabor, Dorene O. Ewing	Eugene	chained to ROTC classroom entrance	arrest

Pennsylvania

State/ Target of Act	Date	Name	Location	Act	Consequence
slavery	1688	Pastorius, Francis Daniel	Germantown	protest	
draft	1689	Penn, William	Philadelphia	refused to institute draft	
slavery	1731–1759	Lay, Benjamin	Abington	assault, trespass, disturbing the peace	
Indian wars	1743	Woolman, John	Northampton	protested usurpation	
French and Indian War	1/12/1755	Woolman, John	Northampton	aided Indian refugees	
French and Indian War	12/16/1755	Armitt, John	Philadelphia	aided Indian refugees	
French and Indian War	12/16/1755	Bartram, James	Philadelphia	aided Indian refugees	
French and Indian War	12/16/1755	Benezet, Anthony	Philadelphia	aided Indian refugees	

State/ Target of Act	Date	Name	Location	Act	Consequence
French and Indian War	12/16/1755	Brown, Thomas	Philadelphia	aided Indian refugees	
French and Indian War	12/16/1755	Brown, William	Philadelphia	aided Indian refugees	
French and Indian War	12/16/1755	Carleton, Thomas	Philadelphia	aided Indian refugees	
French and Indian War	12/16/1755	Churchman, John	Philadelphia	aided Indian refugees	
French and Indian War	12/16/1755	Eastburn, Samuel	Philadelphia	aided Indian refugees	
French and Indian War	12/16/1755	Ely, Joshua	Philadelphia	aided Indian refugees	
French and Indian War	12/16/1755	Evans, John	Philadelphia	aided Indian refugees	
French and Indian War	12/16/1755	Farrington, Abraham	Philadelphia	aided Indian refugees	
French and Indian War	12/16/1755	Fothergill, Sam	Philadelphia	aided Indian refugees	
French and Indian War	12/16/1755	Horne, William	Philadelphia	aided Indian refugees	
French and Indian War	12/16/1755	Jackson, William	Philadelphia	aided Indian refugees	
French and Indian War	12/16/1755	Pemberton, John	Philadelphia	protest	
French and Indian War	12/16/1755	Scarborough, John	Philadelphia	aided Indian refugees	
French and Indian War	12/16/1755	Stanton, Daniel	Philadelphia	aided Indian refugees	
French and Indian War	12/16/1755	Trotter, Benjamin	Philadelphia	aided Indian refugees	
French and Indian War	12/16/1755	White, Joseph	Philadelphia	aided Indian refugees	
French and Indian War	12/16/1755	Yarnell, Mordecai	Philadelphia	aided Indian refugees	
French and Indian War	12/16/1755	Zane, Isaac	Philadelphia	aided Indian refugees	
taxation	8/9/1757	Pemberton, Israel, Jr.	Philadelphia	tax resistance	
taxation	8/9/1757	Pemberton, John	Philadelphia	tax resistance	
taxation	8/9/1757	Woolman, John	Mount Holly	tax resistance	
quartering of troops	4/4/1758	Woolman, John, tailor	Philadelphia	refused payment	
colonial taxation	1765	Allen, William	Philadelphia	propaganda	
colonial taxation	1765	Bayard, John Bubenheim	Philadelphia	protest	
colonial taxation	1765	Bradford, William	Philadelphia	propaganda	
colonial taxation	1768	Franklin, Benjamin	Philadelphia	propaganda	
colonial taxation	1768	Griffits, Hannah	Philadelphia	paramilitary	
colonial taxation	1768	Moore, Milcah Martha	Philadelphia	propaganda	
Revolutionary War	1770s	Giering, Andrew	Emmaus	refused to serve	
slavery	1770s	Lay, Benjamin	Abington	kidnap	
slavery	1770s	McKeever, William	West Middletown	protest	

State/ Target of Act	Date	Name	Location	Act	Consequence
slave education ban	1770	Benezet, Anthony	Philadelphia	educated slaves	threats
colonial taxation	1774	Mifflin, Thomas	Philadelphia	paramilitary organizer	
colonial taxation	1774	Reed, Joseph	Philadelphia	paramilitary organizer	
colonial taxation	1774	Thomson, Charles	Philadelphia	paramilitary organizer	
slavery	4/14/1775	Franklin, Benjamin	Philadelphia	organized abolitionists	
slave recapture	4/14/1775	Pemberton, James	Philadelphia	abolitionism	
Revolutionary War	1777	Compton, William	Philadelphia	refused to serve	prison, threat
Revolutionary War	7/1777	Brown, William	Philadelphia	refused to serve	ridicule
Revolutionary War	7/1777	Masterman, Thomas	Philadelphia	refused to serve	ridicule
Revolutionary War	7/1777	Wayne, William	Philadelphia	refused to serve	ridicule
Revolutionary War	7/1777	Wells, Edward	Philadelphia	refused to serve	prison
loyalty oath	8/28/1777	Affleck, Isabella	Philadelphia	agitation	
loyalty oath	8/28/1777	Affleck, Thomas	Philadelphia	treason	prison
loyalty oath	8/28/1777	Asheton, Robert	Philadelphia	treason	prison
loyalty oath	8/28/1777	Ashton, Thomas	Philadelphia	treason	prison
loyalty oath	8/28/1777	Ayres, E.	Philadelphia	treason	prison
loyalty oath	8/28/1777	Bond, Phineas	Philadelphia	treason	exile
loyalty oath	8/28/1777	Brown, Elijah, Sr.	Philadelphia	treason	parole
loyalty oath	8/28/1777	Brown, Mary Armitt	Philadelphia	agitation	
loyalty oath	8/28/1777	Chew, Benjamin	Philadelphia	treason	banished
loyalty oath	8/28/1777	Coombe, Thomas	Philadelphia	treason	exile
loyalty oath	8/28/1777	Drinker, Elizabeth	Philadelphia	agitation	
loyalty oath	8/28/1777	Drinker, Henry	Philadelphia	treason	prison
loyalty oath	8/28/1777	Eddy, Charles	Philadelphia	treason	prison, bankrupt
loyalty oath	8/28/1777	Emlen, Caleb	Philadelphia	treason	prison
loyalty oath	8/28/1777	Emlen, Samuel, Jr.	Philadelphia	treason	prison
loyalty oath	8/28/1777	Fisher, Esther	Philadelphia	agitation	
loyalty oath	8/28/1777	Fisher, Joshua	Philadelphia	treason	prison, bankrupt
loyalty oath	8/28/1777	Fisher, Miers	Philadelphia	treason	prison
loyalty oath	8/28/1777	Fisher, Samuel Rowland	Philadelphia	treason	prison
loyalty oath	8/28/1777	Fisher, Sarah Logan	Philadelphia	agitation	
loyalty oath	8/28/1777	Fisher, Sarah Redwood	Philadelphia	agitation	
loyalty oath	8/28/1777	Fisher, Thomas	Philadelphia	treason	prison
loyalty oath	8/28/1777	Fox, Joseph	Philadelphia	treason	prison
loyalty oath	8/28/1777	Galloway, John	Philadelphia	treason	prison
loyalty oath	8/28/1777	Gilpin, Thomas	Philadelphia	treason	died in prison
loyalty oath	8/28/1777	Hollingshead, William	Philadelphia	treason	prison
loyalty oath	8/28/1777	Hunt, John	Philadelphia	treason	forcible arrest, died in prison
loyalty oath	8/28/1777	Hunt, Rachel	Philadelphia	agitation	
loyalty oath	8/28/1777	Imlay, William	Philadelphia	treason	prison
loyalty oath	8/28/1777	Jackson, Samuel	Philadelphia	treason	prison

State/ Target of Act	Date	Name	Location	Act	Consequence
loyalty oath	8/28/1777	James, Abel	Philadelphia	treason	prison
loyalty oath	8/28/1777	James, John	Philadelphia	treason	fled
loyalty oath	8/28/1777	Jervis, Charles	Philadelphia	treason	prison
loyalty oath	8/28/1777	Jervis, Elizabeth Walton	Philadelphia	agitation	
loyalty oath	8/28/1777	Jervis, Rebecca	Philadelphia	agitation	
loyalty oath	8/28/1777	Jones, Owen, Jr.	Philadelphia	treason	prison
loyalty oath	8/28/1777	Jones, Susanna Evans	Philadelphia	agitation	
loyalty oath	8/28/1777	Kuhn, Adam	Philadelphia	treason	prison
loyalty oath	8/28/1777	Lennox, William, Jr.	Philadelphia	treason	prison
loyalty oath	8/28/1777	Lenox, David	Philadelphia	treason	prison
loyalty oath	8/28/1777	Livezey, Thomas	Philadelphia	treason	prison
loyalty oath	8/28/1777	Murdoch, Samuel	Philadelphia	treason	prison
loyalty oath	8/28/1777	Pemberton, Hannah Zane	Philadelphia	agitation	
loyalty oath	8/28/1777	Pemberton, Israel, Jr.	Philadelphia	treason	forcible arrest
Revolutionary War	8/28/1777	Pemberton, Israel, Jr.	Philadelphia	refused to serve	
loyalty oath	8/28/1777	Pemberton, James	Philadelphia	treason	prison
loyalty oath	8/28/1777	Pemberton, John	Philadelphia	treason	prison
loyalty oath	8/28/1777	Pemberton, Mary Stansbury	Philadelphia	agitation	
loyalty oath	8/28/1777	Pemberton, Phebe Lewis	Philadelphia	agitation	
loyalty oath	8/28/1777	Penn, John, Sr.	Philadelphia	treason	banished
loyalty oath	8/28/1777	Pennington, Edward	Philadelphia	treason	prison, vandalism
loyalty oath	8/28/1777	Pennington, Sarah Shoemaker	Philadelphia	agitation	
loyalty oath	8/28/1777	Pike, Thomas	Philadelphia	treason, violated curfew	house arrest
loyalty oath	8/28/1777	Pleasants, Mary Pemberton	Philadelphia	agitation	
loyalty oath	8/28/1777	Pleasants, Samuel	Philadelphia	treason	forcible arrest, prison
loyalty oath	8/28/1777	Roberts, George	Philadelphia	treason	prison
loyalty oath	8/28/1777	Roberts, Hugh	Philadelphia	treason	prison
loyalty oath	8/28/1777	Shoemaker, Samuel	Philadelphia	treason	prison
loyalty oaths	8/28/1777	Smith, Elizabeth	Philadelphia	agitation	
loyalty oath	8/28/1777	Smith, William	Philadelphia	treason	exile
loyalty oath	8/28/1777	Smith, William Drewit	Philadelphia	treason	prison
loyalty oath	8/28/1777	Starr, James	Philadelphia	treason	stoned
loyalty oath	8/28/1777	Stedman, Alexander	Philadelphia	treason	prison
loyalty oath	8/28/1777	Stedman, Charles, Jr.	Philadelphia	treason	prison
loyalty oath	8/28/1777	Warder, Jeremiah	Philadelphia	treason	prison
loyalty oath	8/28/1777	Wharton, Rachel Midcalf	Philadelphia	agitation	
loyalty oath	8/28/1777	Wharton, Thomas, Sr.	Philadelphia	treason	prison, land confiscated

State/ Target of Act	Date	Name	Location	Act	Consequence
loyalty oath	8/28/1777	Zane, Isaac	Philadelphia	treason	stoned
Revolutionary War	1778–1779	Watson, Sarah Woolston	Middletown	protest	
Revolutionary War	1778–1779	Watson, Thomas	Middletown	refused paper currency	sentenced to death
loyalty oath	7/15/1779	Drinker, Henry	Philadelphia	treason	jail
loyalty oath	7/15/1779	Fisher, Samuel Rowland	Philadelphia	treason	jail
slave recapture	1780s–1830s	Bell, James Patterson	Colerain	sheltered slaves	
taxation	1786–1787	Holcroft, John	Bedford	paramilitary	
religious persecution	1790s	Vaughan, Joshua	Philadelphia	religious unorthodoxy	threat
debt	1791–1794	Holcroft, John	Bedford	paramilitary leader	
slave recapture	1792	Ellis, Mercy Cox	Muncy	ran a safehouse	
slave recapture	1792	Ellis, William	Muncy	ran a safehouse	
debt	1794	Marshall, James	Indiana County	paramilitary	
debt	7/1794	Mitchell, John	Mingo	mail theft	martial law
debt	7/1794	Bradford, William	Mingo	mail theft	martial law
taxation	7/16/1794	Bradford, David	Allegheny	tax revolt	
taxation	7/16/1794	Bradford, William	Allegheny	robbed mail	
taxation	7/16/1794	Marshall, James	Allegheny	tax revolt	
debt	7/16/1794	McFarlane, James	Allegheny	paramilitary leader	shot
taxation	7/16/1794	McFarlane, James	Allegheny	tax revolt	
debt	7/16/1794	Miller, Oliver	Allegheny	paramilitary	shot
taxation	7/16/1794	Miller, Oliver	Allegheny	tax revolt	shot
taxation	7/16/1794	Mitchell, John	Allegheny	robbed mail	
debt	10/19/1794	Black, John	Bedford	paramilitary	
debt	10/19/1794	Bolton, Daniel	Bedford	paramilitary	
debt	10/19/1794	Bonham, William	Bedford	paramilitary	
debt	10/19/1794	Bradford, David	Bedford	paramilitary	fled
debt	10/19/1794	Burnett, John	Bedford	paramilitary	
debt	10/19/1794	Burney, Thomas	Bedford	paramilitary	
debt	10/19/1794	Corbley, John	Bedford	paramilitary	
debt	10/19/1794	Crawford, William	Bedford	paramilitary	
debt	10/19/1794	Criswell, John	Bedford	paramilitary	
debt	10/19/1794	Curtis, Marmaduke	Bedford	paramilitary	
debt	10/19/1794	Hamilton, John	Bedford	paramilitary	
debt	10/19/1794	Husband, Herman	Bedford	paramilitary	
debt	10/19/1794	Kerr, James	Bedford	paramilitary	
debt	10/19/1794	Lockery, John	Bedford	paramilitary	
debt	10/19/1794	Lucas, George	Bedford	paramilitary	
debt	10/19/1794	Mounts, Caleb	Bedford	paramilitary	
debt	10/19/1794	Nye, Samuel	Bedford	paramilitary	
debt	10/19/1794	Parry, Joseph	Bedford	paramilitary	
debt	10/19/1794	Philson, Robert	Bedford	paramilitary	
debt	10/19/1794	Porter, Robert	Bedford	paramilitary	

State/ Target of Act	Date	Name	Location	Act	Consequence
debt	10/19/1794	Scott, Joseph	Bedford	paramilitary	
debt	10/19/1794	Sedgwick, Thomas	Bedford	paramilitary	
debt	10/19/1794	Stewart, James	Bedford	paramilitary	
debt	10/19/1794	Vigol, Philip	Bedford	paramilitary	
debt	10/19/1794	Walker, Isaac	Bedford	paramilitary	
debt	10/19/1794	Wisegarver, George	Bedford	paramilitary	
slave recapture	1800s	Mott, James, Jr.	Philadelphia	slave rescue	
slave recapture	1800s	Mott, Lucretia Coffin	Philadelphia	slave rescue, propaganda	
slave recapture	1800s–1820s	Brown, Rachel Milner	Little Britain	sheltered slaves	
slave recapture	1800s–1820s	Brown, William	Little Britain	sheltered slaves	
slave recapture	1800s–1850s	Gibbons, Daniel	Bird-in-Hand	slave rescue	
slave recapture	1800s–1850s	Gibbons, Hannah Wierman	Bird-in-Hand	nursed slave	censure
slave recapture	1801	Hopper, Isaac Tatem	Philadelphia	child recovery	
slavery	1810s	Atcheson, George	Green	protest	
slave recapture	1810s	Brown, Ann Kirk	Fulton	sheltered slaves	
slave recapture	1810s–1840s	Vickers, Abigail Paxson	Wagontown	slave rescue	
slave recapture	1810s–1840s	Vickers, John	Wagontown	slave rescue	
slave recapture	1810s–1850s	Brown, Jeremiah	Fulton	sheltered slaves	
slave recapture	1810s–1860s	Bushong, Henry	Quarryville	sheltered slaves	
slave recapture	1812	Jones, Absalom	Philadelphia	paramilitary	
slavery	1820s	Magoffin, Grace Elizabeth Mitcheltree	Mercerville	protest	
slavery	1820s	Magoffin, James, Jr.	Mercerville	protest	
slavery	1820s	Marshall, Samuel	Connoquenessing	protest	
slavery	1820s	McKeever, Jane Campbell	West Middletown	protest	
slave recapture	1820s–1840s	Haines, Sarah Brown	Fulton	slave rescue	
slave recapture	1820s–1840s	Haines, Timothy	Fulton	slave rescue	
slave recapture	1820s–1840s	Marsh, Gravner	Caln	slave relay	
slave recapture	1820s–1840s	Marsh, Hannah	Caln	slave relay	
slave education ban	1824	Himrod, William	Erie	educated slaves	
slave recapture	1825–1835	Brown, John	Randolph	slave relay	
slave education ban	1829–1860s	Wright, Phebe Wierman	South Mountain	educated slaves	
slave recapture	1829–1860s	Wright, Phebe Wierman	South Mountain	slave rescue	
slave education ban	1829–1860s	Wright, William	South Mountain	educated slaves	
slave recapture	1829–1860s	Wright, William	South Mountain	slave rescue	
slavery	1830s	Curtis, Thomas F.	Lewisburg	protest	
slave recapture	1830s	Delany, Martin Robinson	Pittsburgh	recruitment	
slavery	1830s	Purvis, Robert	Philadelphia	protest	
slavery	1830s	Stauffer, Daniel	Zelienople	protest	
slave recapture	1830s	Taylor, Joseph C.	Little Britain	retrieved kidnapped child	
slavery	1830s	Walter, Albert G.	Pittsburgh	protest	

State/ Target of Act	Date	Name	Location	Act	Consequence
slave recapture	1830s	Waters, Hamilton E.	Erie	sheltered slaves	
slave recapture	1830s–1840s	Magill, Edward Hicks	Langhorne	slave relay	
slave recapture	1830s–1840s	Magill, Jonathan Paxson	Solebury	slave relay	
slave recapture	1830s–1840s	Magill, Watson P.	Solebury	slave relay	
slave recapture	1830s–1841	Pennypacker, Sarah W. Coates	Phoenixville	slave rescue, relay	
slave recapture	1830s–1850s	Grew, Mary	Philadelphia	slave rescue	
slave recapture	1830s–1850s	Pennypacker, Elijah Funk	Phoenixville	slave rescue, relay	
slave recapture	1830s–1850s	Pennypacker, Hannah Adamson	Phoenixville	slave rescue, relay	
slavery	1830s–1860s	Dickinson, Anna Elizabeth	Philadelphia	propaganda	
slave recapture	1830s–1860s	Moore, Elizabeth W. Ely	Christiana	slave rescue	
slave recapture	1830s–1860s	Moore, Jeremiah	Christiana	slave rescue	
slave recapture	1830s–1860s	Peart, Lewis	Lampeter	slave rescue	
slave recapture	1830s–1860s	Whitson, Martha Hobson	Bart	slave rescue	
slave recapture	1830s–1860s	Whitson, Thomas	Bart	slave rescue	
slave rescue	1833	Forten, James	Philadelphia	protest, conspiracy	
slave rescue	1833	Forten, Margaretta	Philadelphia	protest, conspiracy	
slave rescue	1833	Mott, Lucretia Coffin	Philadelphia	protest, conspiracy, propaganda	
slave rescue	1833	Still, William	Philadelphia	protest, conspiracy	
slave education ban	1833–1839	Darlington, Phoebe	West Chester	educated slaves	
slave recapture	1835	Brown, John	Tabor	slave relay	
slave recapture	1838	Cox, Hannah Peirce	Longwood	slave relay	
slave recapture	1838	Cox, John	Longwood	slave relay	
slave recapture	1838	Cox, John William	Longwood	slave relay	
slave recapture	5/16/1838	Pugh, Sarah	Philadelphia	impeded police	
slavery	1840s	Allen, Samuel	Mercer County	protest	
slave recapture	1840s	Bonsall, Susan P. Johnson	Wagontown	sheltered slaves	
slave recapture	1840s	Eshleman, Jacob K.	Strasburg	slave rescue	
slave recapture	1840s–1850s	Bonsall, Thomas	Wagontown	sheltered slaves	
slave recapture	1840s–1850s	Coates, Deborah T. Simmons	Sadsbury	slave rescue	
slave recapture	1840s–1850s	Coates, Lindley	Sadsbury	slave rescue	
slave recapture	1840s–1850s	Marsh, Sarah	Caln	slave relay	
slave recapture	1840s–1850s	Smith, Joseph	Drumore	slave rescue	
slave recapture	1840s–1850s	Smith, Tacy Shoemaker	Drumore	slave rescue	
slave rescue	1840s–1860s	Barnard, Vincent S.	Kennett Square	conspiracy	
slave recapture	1840s–1860s	Battin, Marshall	Elklands	slave relay	
slave recapture	1840s–1860s	Haines, Jacob A.	Muncy	slave relay	
slave recapture	1840s–1860s	Haines, Jesse	Muncy	slave relay	

State/ Target of Act	Date	Name	Location	Act	Consequence
slave recapture	1840s–1860s	Haines, Rachel Ellis	Muncy	slave relay	
slave recapture	1840s–1860s	Hill, John	Elklands	slave relay	
slave recapture	1840s–1860s	Rakestraw, William H.	Bart	slave rescue	
slave recapture	1840s–1860s	Russell, Amelia Kirk	East Drumore	slave rescue	
slave recapture	1840s–1860s	Russell, John Neal	East Drumore	slave rescue	
slave recapture	1840s–1860s	Wood, Day	Fulton	slave rescue	
slave recapture	1840s–1860s	Wood, Eliza Jackson	Fulton	slave rescue	
slave rescue	7/9/1848	McKim, James Miller	Philadelphia	protest, conspiracy	
slave recapture	7/9/1848	Mott, Lucretia Coffin	Philadelphia	route planning	
slave recapture	1850s	Cain, Augustus Way	Sadsbury	slave rescue	
slave recapture	1850s	Cain, Lydia Ann Dickinson	Sadsbury	slave rescue	
slavery	1850s	Curtis, Annie Fenner	Lewisburg	protest	
slave recapture	1850s	Pownall, Thomas	Bucks County	sheltered slaves, disguise	
slave recapture	9/1851	Lewis, Samuel	Norristown	slave rescue	shoot-out
slave recapture	9/1851	Lewis, William	Norristown	slave relay	
Fugitive Slave Law of 1850	9/1851	Mott, Lucretia Coffin	Philadelphia	denunciation	
slave recapture	9/11/1851	Fussell, Bartholomew	Kennett Square	slave rescue, relay	
slave recapture	9/11/1851	Hanway, Castner	Christiana	slave rescue	shoot-out, arrest
slave recapture	9/11/1851	Hood, Caleb C.	Bart	slave rescue	
slave recapture	9/11/1851	Hood, Joseph	Bart	slave rescue	
slave recapture	9/11/1851	Hopkins, Henry C.	Christiana	slave rescue	shoot-out
slave recapture	9/11/1851	Johnson, Abraham	Christiana	slave rescue	shoot-out
slave recapture	9/11/1851	Lewis, Elijah	Christiana	slave rescue	shoot-out, arrest
Fugitive Slave Law of 1850	9/11/1851	Mendenhall, Dinah Hannum	Kennett Square	slave rescue	
slave recapture	9/11/1851	Mendenhall, Isaac	Kennett Square	slave rescue	
slave recapture	9/11/1851	Parker, Eliza Ann Elizabeth Howard	Christiana	slave rescue	shoot-out, jail
slave recapture	9/11/1851	Parker, William	Christiana	slave rescue	shoot-out
slave recapture	9/11/1851	Paxson, Jacob Longstreth	Christiana	slave rescue	
slave recapture	9/11/1851	Pinkney, Alexander	Christiana	slave rescue	shoot-out
slave recapture	9/11/1851	Pinkney, Mrs. Alexander	Christiana	slave rescue	shoot-out, jail
slave recapture	9/11/1851	Pownall, Levi	Bucks County	slave rescue	shoot-out
slave recapture	9/11/1851	Pownall, Sarah Henderson	Bucks County	slave rescue	shoot-out
slave recapture	9/11/1851	Scarlett, Joseph P.	Christiana	slave rescue	shoot-out, arrest
slave recapture	9/11/1851	West, J. Pierce	Christiana	slave relay	
slave recapture	9/11/1851	West, Thomas	Christiana	slave relay	
slave rescue	10/1851	Cuyler, Theodore	Philadelphia	conspiracy	
slave rescue	10/1851	Stevens, Thaddeus	Philadelphia	conspiracy	
slave rescue	10/1/1851	Vashon, George Boye	Pittsburgh	jailbreak	
slave rescue	10/5/1851	McKim, James Miller	Philadelphia	conspiracy	

State/ Target of Act	Date	Name	Location	Act	Consequence
slave recapture	1853	Lewis, Elizabeth R.	Kimberton	slave rehabilitation	
slave recapture	1853	Lewis, Esther Fussell	Kimberton	slave rehabilitation	
slave recapture	1853	Lewis, Graceanna	Kimberton	slave rehabilitation	
slave recapture	1853	Lewis, Mariann	Kimberton	slave rehabilitation	
slave rescue	1855	Sirwell, William	Pittsburgh	ran a street patrol	
slave recapture	1860s	Barnard, Eusebius	Pocopsin	slave relay	
Civil War	1860s	Moore, Rachel W.	Philadelphia	refused to serve	threats
slave recapture	1860s	Shipman, Charles	Girard	recruitment	
draft	1860s	Smedley, Edwin	Philadelphia	protest	
draft	1860s	Smedley, William H.	Philadelphia	protest	
Civil War	1861	Barnard, Vincent S.	Kennett Square	refused to serve	scorn
Civil War	1863	Smedley, Edwin	Philadelphia	refused to serve	forced march
Civil War	1863	Smedley, William H.	Philadelphia	refused to serve	forced march
Civil War	7/21/1863	Love, Alfred Henry	Philadelphia	refused to profiteer	lost business
draft	8/22/1863	Gerhard, Benjamin	Philadelphia	supported pacifism	
genocide	1866	Love, Alfred Henry	Philadelphia	protest	lost business
abandonment	2/8/1868	Vaughan, Hester	Philadelphia	infanticide	pardoned
women's disenfranchisement	6/30/1868	Anthony, Susan Brownell	Philadelphia	protest	
women's disenfranchisement	6/30/1868	Dickinson, Anna Elizabeth	Philadelphia	protest	
women's disenfranchisement	6/30/1868	Kirk, Eleanor	Philadelphia	protest	
women's disenfranchisement	6/30/1868	Lozier, Clemence Sophia	Philadelphia	protest	
women's disenfranchisement	6/30/1868	Pillsbury, Parker	Philadelphia	propaganda	
women's disenfranchisement	6/30/1868	Smith, Susan A	Philadelphia	protest	
women's disenfranchisement	6/30/1868	Stanton, Elizabeth Cady	Philadelphia	protest	
women's disenfranchisement	7/4/1876	Anthony, Susan Brownell	Philadelphia	protest	
women's disenfranchisement	7/4/1876	Gage, Matilda Joslyn	Philadelphia	protest	
free speech ban	1894	Goldman, Emma, lecturer	Homestead	conspiracy	prison
labor organization ban	6/15/1895	Jones, Mary "Mother"	Philadelphia	public harangue	
labor exploitation	9/10/1897	Futa, John	Lattimer	march	shot
labor exploitation	9/10/1897	Jurich, Steve	Lattimer	march	shot
Spanish-American War	1898	Love, Alfred Henry	Philadelphia	opposed	burned in effigy
labor organization ban	11/1899	Jones, Mary "Mother"	Arnot	public rally, march	
labor organization ban	2/18/1901	Jones, Mary "Mother"	Scranton	public rally, march	
free speech ban	4/1901	Goldman, Emma	Philadelphia	conspiracy	arrest
labor organization ban	1902	Jones, Mary "Mother"	Manayunk	public harangue	
free speech ban	mid-1902	Goldman, Emma	McKeesport	conspiracy	banned
free speech ban	mid-1902	Goldman, Emma	Wilkes-Barre	conspiracy	banned

State/ Target of Act	Date	Name	Location	Act	Consequence
child labor	1903	Jones, Mary "Mother"	Kensington	public march	
alcohol sale and consumption	1/14/1904	Nation, Carry Amelia Moore	Philadelphia	destroyed property	jail, battery
labor exploitation	1909	Flynn, Elizabeth Gurley	Philadelphia	demonstration	arrest
free speech ban	9/24/1909	Goldman, Emma	Philadelphia	conspiracy	banned
labor exploitation	1911	Flynn, Elizabeth Gurley	Philadelphia	strike speech	arrest
labor organization ban	6/1912	Jones, Mary "Mother"	Greensburg	promoted solidarity	
free speech ban	1/4/1914	Goldman, Emma	Philadelphia	conspiracy	intimidation
free speech ban	3/9/1914	Goldman, Emma	Philadelphia	conspiracy	intimidation
World War I	1917	Richards, Edward C.M.	West Chester	conscientious objection	
draft	1/13/1918	Beilfuss, Paul	Philadelphia	protest	nearly lynched
draft	2/14/1918	Liebig, H.C.	Harrisburg	protest	fired
draft	4/22/1918	Hang, Christy	Connellsville	protest	confiscation
draft	4/22/1918	Hang, William	Connellsville	protest	confiscation
labor organization ban	8/20/1919	Jones, Mary "Mother"	Homestead	speech	arrest, fine
labor organization ban	9/1919	Foster, William Z.	Duquesne	labor assembly	jail
labor organization ban	9/1919	Jones, Mary "Mother"	Duquesne	labor assembly	jail
taxation	1920s	Carner, Lucy Perkins	York	antitax speech	
flag saluting	10/23/1935	Gobitas, Lillian	Minersville	disobeyed teacher	expelled
flag saluting	10/23/1935	Gobitas, William H.	Minersville	disobeyed teacher	expelled
draft	1939	Gregg, Richard Bartlett	Pendle Hill	denounced war	
racism	1940s	Carner, Lucy Perkins	York	sit-ins	
World War II	1942	Gara, Larry	Lewisburg	refused to serve	prison
World War II	1942	Stern, Thomas Noel	Pittsburgh	conscientious objection	
World War II	4/1942	Richards, Frederick Howard	West Chester	draft evasion	prison
World War II	5/1942	Richards, William Lippincott	West Chester	refused to enlist	prison
World War II	10/1942	Elder, George	Philadelphia	conscientious objection	asylum
World War II	5/13/1943	Man, Albon Platt, Jr.	Lewisburg	protest	prison
World War II	5/13/1943	Sutherland, William H., Jr.	Lewisburg	draft evasion	prison
World War II	5/28/1943	Drumheller, Leland W.	Philadelphia	conscientious objection	indicted
World War II	7/1943	Ball, James W.		draft evasion	prison
World War II	9/28/1943	Dixon, Jack	Lewisburg	protest	prison
World War II	9/28/1943	Lovett, William	Fallsington	protest	prison
World War II	9/28/1943	Price, Paton	Lewisburg	protest	prison
World War II	9/28/1943	Woodman, Thomas	Lewisburg	protest	prison
World War II	1944	Andresen, Bent	Kane	protest	prison, tube-feeding
World War II	1944	Rustin, Bayard Taylor	Lewisburg	protest	prison
World War II	11/26/1944	Satterthwait, Arnold Chase	Reading	refused to register	prison

State/ Target of Act	Date	Name	Location	Act	Consequence
nuclear power	1948	Carner, Lucy Perkins	York	protested bombs	
Korean War	1948	Palmer, T. Vail	Concordville	refused to register	prison
racism	1948	Randolph, Asa Philip	Philadelphia	protest	
Korean War	1/1951	Seaver, David	Haverford	refused to register	prison
Korean War	1/1951	Seaver, Paul	Haverford	refused to register	prison
taxation	1958	Harper, Robin	Wallingford	resisted war tax	threats
Vietnam War	1967	Carner, Lucy Perkins	York	propaganda	
Vietnam War	2/1971	Fonda, Jane	Valley Forge	rally	
nuclear power	9/9/1980	Berrigan, Philip	King of Prussia	sabotage	prison
nuclear power	9/9/1980	Hammer, Dean	King of Prussia	sabotage	prison
nuclear power	9/9/1980	Kabat, Carl	King of Prussia	sabotage	prison
nuclear power	9/9/1980	Mass, Elmer	King of Prussia	sabotage	prison
nuclear power	9/9/1980	Montgomery, Anne	King of Prussia	sabotage	prison
nuclear power	9/9/1980	Rush, Molly	King of Prussia	sabotage	prison
nuclear power	9/9/1980	Schuchardt, John	King of Prussia	sabotage	prison
hazardous waste	4/30/1991	Eisen, Audrey Louise	Bath	protest	arraigned
hazardous waste	4/30/1991	Sellers, John	Bath	protest	arraigned
death penalty	10/19/1998	Garis, Jeffrey	Scranton	obstructed justice	arrest
death penalty	10/19/1998	Pickard, William	Scranton	obstructed justice	arrest
death penalty	10/31/2000	Kaufman, Sarah	Philadelphia	sit-in	arrest
death penalty	10/31/2000	Macomber, Amanda	Philadelphia	sit-in	arrest
death penalty	10/31/2000	Tankel, Jared	Philadelphia	sit-in	arrest
Iraq War	3/21/2003	Eisenberg-Guyot, Nadja	Philadelphia	blocked a building	
Iraq War	3/21/2003	Ford, Dana	Philadelphia	blocked a building	
Iraq War	3/21/2003	Hanlon-Smith, Jamie	Philadelphia	blocked a building	
Iraq War	3/21/2003	Liem, Elizabeth	Philadelphia	blocked a building	
Iraq War	3/21/2003	Morris, Sarah	Philadelphia	blocked a building	
Iraq War	3/21/2003	Noterman, Elsa	Philadelphia	blocked a building	
Iraq War	6/28/2006	Brix, Michael	Philadelphia	blocked doors	jail, fine
Iraq War	6/28/2006	Brown, Marion	Philadelphia	blocked doors	jail, fine
Iraq War	6/28/2006	Fultz, Jason	Philadelphia	blocked doors	jail, fine
Iraq War	6/28/2006	Haw, Cassandra Haino	Philadelphia	blocked doors	jail, fine
Iraq War	6/28/2006	Haw, Christopher	Philadelphia	blocked doors	jail, fine
Iraq War	6/28/2006	Metzler, Sylvia	Philadelphia	blocked doors	jail, fine
Iraq War	6/28/2006	Sanchez, Sonia	Philadelphia	trespass	arrest
Iraq War	6/28/2006	Willoughby, Lillian	Philadelphia	blocked doors	jail, fine

Puerto Rico

State/ Target of Act	Date	Name	Location	Act	Consequence
Vieques destruction	2/18/1971	Berríos-Martínez, Rubén Ángel	Culebra	trespass	jail
Vieques destruction	5/19/1979	Ferrer, Leonardo Estrada	Vieques	trespass	
Vieques destruction	5/19/1979	Parrilla-Bonilla, Antulio	Vieques	trespass, said Mass	fine, marshal brutality
Vieques destruction	5/21/1979	Guadalupe-Ortiz, Ismael	Vieques	trespass	prison

State/ Target of Act	Date	Name	Location	Act	Consequence
Vieques destruction	4/21/1999	Guadalupe-Ortiz, Ismael	Vieques	trespass	
Vieques destruction	4/21/1999	Kayak, Tito	Vieques	trespass	
Vieques destruction	5/8/1999	Berríos-Martínez, Rubén Ángel	Vieques	camp-in	
Vieques destruction	5/4/2000	Berríos-Martínez, Rubén Ángel	Vieques	camp-in	arrest
Vieques destruction	5/11/2000	Suárez-Franceschi, Antonio	Vieques	trespass	tried
Vieques destruction	6/1/2000	Lebron, Lolita	Vieques	halted army maneuvers	arrest
ROTC	4/30/2001	Almenas, Pedro Colón	Rio Piedras	struck an officer	prison
Vieques destruction	5/1/2001	Berríos-Martínez, Rubén Ángel	Vieques	trespass	arrest
Vieques destruction	5/1/2001	Bhatia-Gautier, Eduardo	Vieques	trespass	arrest
Vieques destruction	5/1/2001	Burgos-Andújar, Norma E.	Vieques	trespass	arrest
Vieques destruction	5/1/2001	Feliciano, José	Vieques	trespass	
Vieques destruction	5/1/2001	Gutiérrez, Luis Vicente	Vieques	trespass	arrest
Vieques destruction	5/1/2001	Jackson, Jacqueline Lavinia Brown	Vieques	trespass	arrest, solitary confinement
Vieques destruction	5/1/2001	Kayak, Tito	Vieques	trespass	arrest
Vieques destruction	5/1/2001	Kennedy, Robert F., Jr.	Vieques	trespass	arrest
Vieques destruction	5/1/2001	Martin, Ricky	Vieques	trespass	
Vieques destruction	5/1/2001	Menchú, Rigoberta	Vieques	trespass	
Vieques destruction	5/1/2001	Olmos, Edward James	Vieques	trespass	arrest
Vieques destruction	5/1/2001	Rangel, Charles Bernard	Vieques	trespass	
Vieques destruction	5/1/2001	Rivera, Dennis	Vieques	trespass	arrest
Vieques destruction	5/1/2001	Rivera, Jose	Vieques	trespass	arrest
Vieques destruction	5/1/2001	Rodriguez, Chi Chi	Vieques	trespass	arrest
Vieques destruction	5/1/2001	Rosa, Robi Draco	Vieques	trespass	arrest
Vieques destruction	5/1/2001	Sanes-Rodríquez, Mirta	Vieques	trespass	arrest, trial
Vieques destruction	5/1/2001	Santiago, Rafael Cordero	Vieques	trespass	arrest
Vieques destruction	5/1/2001	Sharpton, Charles Alfred	Vieques	trespass, fast	arrest, prison
Vieques destruction	5/1/2001	Sheen, Martin	Vieques	trespass	arrest
Vieques destruction	5/1/2001	Trinidad, Félix	Vieques	trespass	arrest
Vieques destruction	5/1/2001	Velázquez, Nydia Margarita	Vieques	trespass	arrest
Vieques destruction	1/10/2003	Cardona, Gustavo Dásvila	Vieques	trespass	
Vieques destruction	1/10/2003	Cepeda, Feliciano Rivera	Vieques	trespass	
Vieques destruction	1/10/2003	Cristóbal, Ángel Rodríguez	Vieques	trespass	prison

State/ Target of Act	Date	Name	Location	Act	Consequence
Vieques destruction	1/10/2003	Ferrer, Leonardo Estrada	Vieques	trespass	
Vieques destruction	1/10/2003	Guadalupe-Ortiz, Ismael	Vieques	trespass	prison
Vieques destruction	1/10/2003	Morales, Orlando	Vieques	trespass	
Vieques destruction	1/10/2003	Vázquez, Grego Marcano	Vieques	trespass	

Rhode Island

State/ Target of Act	Date	Name	Location	Act	Consequence
religious persecution	1639	Gorton, Samuel	Newport	blasphemy	pillory, lashed
religious persecution	11/11/1656	Wickenden, William	Providence	religious unorthodoxy	exile
death penalty	1658	Scott, Patience	Providence	protest	
impressment at sea	1704	Anthony, Thomas	Portsmouth	refused to serve	confined
impressment at sea	1704	Smith, John	Portsmouth	refused to serve	confined
slave recapture	1766	Brown, Moses	Providence	ran a safehouse	
slave recapture	1766	Brown, Phebe Waterman	Providence	ran a safehouse	
colonial taxation	1766	Frye, Eleanor	East Greenwich	paramilitary organizer	
colonial taxation	1766	Lawton, Mary Easton	Newport	paramilitary host	
colonial taxation	1766	Lawton, Robert	Newport	paramilitary host	
colonial taxation	7/25/1768	Downer, Silas	Providence	demonstration	
colonial taxation	6/9/1772	Allen, Paul	Providence	arson, looted	
colonial taxation	6/9/1772	Bowen, Ephraim	Providence	arson, looted	
colonial taxation	6/9/1772	Briggs, Aaron	Providence	arson, looted	
colonial taxation	6/9/1772	Brown, Abial	Providence	arson, looted	
colonial taxation	6/9/1772	Brown, John	Providence	arson, looted	
colonial taxation	6/9/1772	Brown, Joseph	Providence	arson, looted	
colonial taxation	6/9/1772	Bucklin, Joseph	Providence	arson, looted	
colonial taxation	6/9/1772	Dunn, Samuel	Providence	arson, looted	
colonial taxation	6/9/1772	Easterbrooks, Abe	Providence	arson, looted	
colonial taxation	6/9/1772	Easterbrooks, Nathaniel	Providence	arson, looted	
colonial taxation	6/9/1772	Godfrey, Caleb	Providence	arson, looted	
colonial taxation	6/9/1772	Godfrey, Samuel	Providence	arson, looted	
colonial taxation	6/9/1772	Greene, Rufus, Jr.	Providence	arson, looted	
colonial taxation	6/9/1772	Greenwood, John	Providence	arson, looted	
colonial taxation	6/9/1772	Hammond, Benjamin	Providence	arson, looted	
colonial taxation	6/9/1772	Harris, Joseph	Providence	arson, looted	
colonial taxation	6/9/1772	Hopkins, John B.	Providence	arson, looted	
colonial taxation	6/9/1772	Jacobs, Justin	Providence	arson, looted	
colonial taxation	6/9/1772	Jencks, Joseph	Providence	arson, looted	
colonial taxation	6/9/1772	Kilton, John Jenckes	Providence	arson, looted	
colonial taxation	6/9/1772	Kinnicut, Hezekiah	Providence	arson, looted	
colonial taxation	6/9/1772	Lindsey, Benjamin	Newport	sabotage	

State/ Target of Act	Date	Name	Location	Act	Consequence
colonial taxation	6/9/1772	Luther, Abner	Providence	arson, looted	
colonial taxation	6/9/1772	Mawney, John	Providence	arson, looted	
colonial taxation	6/9/1772	Olney, Simeon Hunt	Providence	arson, looted	
colonial taxation	6/9/1772	Ormsbee, Ezra	Providence	arson, looted	
colonial taxation	6/9/1772	Page, Benjamin	Providence	arson, looted	
colonial taxation	6/9/1772	Pearce, Daniel	Newport	sabotage	
colonial taxation	6/9/1772	Potter, Simeon	Providence	arson, looted	
colonial taxation	6/9/1772	Salisbury, Nathan	Providence	arson, looted	
colonial taxation	6/9/1772	Sheldon, Christopher	Providence	arson, looted	
colonial taxation	6/9/1772	Shepard, Benjamin	Providence	arson, looted	
colonial taxation	6/9/1772	Smith, James	Providence	arson, looted	
colonial taxation	6/9/1772	Smith, Turpin	Providence	arson, looted	
colonial taxation	6/9/1772	Sutton, Robert	Providence	arson, looted	
colonial taxation	6/9/1772	Swan, Thomas	Providence	arson, looted	
colonial taxation	6/9/1772	Sylvester, Amos	Providence	arson, looted	
colonial taxation	6/9/1772	Tillinghest, Joseph	Providence	arson, looted	
colonial taxation	6/9/1772	Whipple, Abraham	Providence	arson, looted	
slavery	1833	Buffum, Arnold	Providence	protest, conspiracy	
slave recapture	1840s–1860s	Chace, Elizabeth Buffum	Valley Falls	forgery	
animal rights	12/2005	Cho, Michelle Y.	Providence	public nudity	arrest
animal rights	12/2005	Valladolid, Brandi	Providence	public nudity	arrest

South Carolina

State/ Target of Act	Date	Name	Location	Act	Consequence
colonial taxation	8/1765	Gadsden, Christopher	Charleston	paramilitary organizer	
colonial taxation	9/28/1765	Timothy, Peter	Charleston	propaganda	
colonial taxation	11/1/1765	Gadsden, Christopher	Charleston	paramilitary organizer	
bureaucracy, colonial	1767	Calhoun, Patrick	Abbeville	paramilitary	
bureaucracy, colonial	1767	Kirkland, Moses	Abbeville	paramilitary	
bureaucracy, colonial	7/1768	Gibson, Gideon	Liberty County	paramilitary leader	
bureaucracy, colonial	5/1769	Gilbert, Jonathan	Beaverdam Creek	paramilitary	
bureaucracy, colonial	5/1769	Musgrove, John	Saluda	paramilitary	
colonial taxation	7/1770	Timothy, Peter	Charleston	propaganda	
colonial taxation	11/21/1772	Alexander, Alexander	Charleston	paramilitary	
colonial taxation	11/21/1772	Ash, Cato	Charleston	paramilitary	
colonial taxation	11/21/1772	Barlow, J.	Charleston	paramilitary	
colonial taxation	11/21/1772	Beekman, Bernard	Charleston	paramilitary	
colonial taxation	11/21/1772	Berwick, Simon, Jr.	Charleston	paramilitary	
colonial taxation	11/21/1772	Bookless, Henry Y.	Charleston	paramilitary	
colonial taxation	11/21/1772	Brown, James	Charleston	paramilitary	
colonial taxation	11/21/1772	Calvert, John	Charleston	paramilitary	
colonial taxation	11/21/1772	Cannon, Daniel	Charleston	paramilitary	

State/ Target of Act	Date	Name	Location	Act	Consequence
colonial taxation	11/21/1772	Coleman, Thomas	Charleston	paramilitary	
colonial taxation	11/21/1772	Dill, Joseph	Charleston	paramilitary	
colonial taxation	11/21/1772	Edwards, William	Charleston	paramilitary	
colonial taxation	11/21/1772	Field, William	Charleston	paramilitary	
colonial taxation	11/21/1772	Flagg, George	Charleston	paramilitary	prison
colonial taxation	11/21/1772	Fullerton, John	Charleston	paramilitary	
colonial taxation	11/21/1772	Gadsden, Christopher	Charleston	street patrol leader	prison
colonial taxation	11/21/1772	Hall, John	Charleston	paramilitary	
colonial taxation	11/21/1772	Hall, William	Charleston	paramilitary	
colonial taxation	11/21/1772	Hawes, Benjamin	Charleston	paramilitary	
colonial taxation	11/21/1772	Howard, Robert	Charleston	paramilitary	
colonial taxation	11/21/1772	Johnson, William	Charleston	paramilitary	prison
colonial taxation	11/21/1772	Jones, Robert	Charleston	paramilitary	
colonial taxation	11/21/1772	Laughton, John	Charleston	paramilitary	
colonial taxation	11/21/1772	Laughton, William	Charleston	paramilitary	
colonial taxation	11/21/1772	Lebby, Nathaniel	Charleston	paramilitary	
colonial taxation	11/21/1772	Lockwood, Joshua	Charleston	propagandist	
colonial taxation	11/21/1772	Matthews, John	Charleston	paramilitary	
colonial taxation	11/21/1772	Mazyck, Isaac	Charleston	paramilitary host	
colonial taxation	11/21/1772	Moncrief, Richard	Charleston	paramilitary	
colonial taxation	11/21/1772	Morris, Mark	Charleston	propaganda	
colonial taxation	11/21/1772	Munclean, Peter	Charleston	paramilitary	
colonial taxation	11/21/1772	Nightingale, Thomas	Charleston	paramilitary	
colonial taxation	11/21/1772	Rogers, Uzziah	Charleston	paramilitary	
colonial taxation	11/21/1772	Saunders, Peter	Charleston	paramilitary	
colonial taxation	11/21/1772	Sheed, George	Charleston	paramilitary	
colonial taxation	11/21/1772	Swarle, Thomas	Charleston	paramilitary	
colonial taxation	11/21/1772	Tebout, Tunis	Charleston	paramilitary	
colonial taxation	11/21/1772	Trezevant, Theodore	Charleston	paramilitary	
colonial taxation	11/21/1772	Trusler, William	Charleston	paramilitary	
colonial taxation	11/21/1772	Verree, Joseph	Charleston	propagandist	
colonial taxation	11/21/1772	Weyman, Edward	Charleston	paramilitary	
colonial taxation	11/21/1772	Wilkes, John	Charleston	paramilitary	
colonial taxation	11/21/1772	Young, Thomas	Charleston	paramilitary	
colonial taxation	4/21/1775	Weyman, Edward	Charleston	raid	
colonial taxation	11/15/1780	Weyman, Edward	Charleston	raid	prison
slave education ban	1807	Bonneau, Thomas Siah	Charleston	educated slaves	
draft	8/23/1917	Sims, W.T.	York	protest	lynched
World War II	7/9/1942	Griffith, John H.	Columbia	refused to register	jail
segregation	3/15/1960	Gaither, Thomas	Orangeburg	sit-in, trespass	arraigned
racism	1/1961	Barry, Marion Shepilov	Rock Hill	Freedom Rider	arrest
segregation	1/31/1961	Gaither, Thomas	Rock Hill	sit-in	
racism	1/31/1961	Smith, Ruby Doris	Rock Hill	sit-in	jail
segregation	1/31/1961	Taylor, Charles	Rock Hill	sit-in	fine

State/ Target of Act	Date	Name	Location	Act	Consequence
racism	2/1961	Bevel, James	Rock Hill	Freedom Rider	arrest
segregation	2/1961	Finney, Ernest	Sumter	defended sit-ins	
segregation	2/1961	Jones, J. Charles	Rock Hill	sit-in	jail
racism	2/1961	Nash, Diane	Rock Hill	lunch counter sit-in	jail
segregation	2/1961	Nash, Diane	Rock Hill	organized Freedom Ride	arrest
racism	2/1961	Smith, Ruby Doris	Rock Hill	Freedom Rider	firebombed, jail
Vietnam War	6/2/1967	Levy, Howard B.	Fort Jackson	refused to train medics	prison at hard labor

South Dakota

State/ Target of Act	Date	Name	Location	Act	Consequence
World War I	1/22/1918	Rempfer, William C.	Mitchell	protest	deported
World War I	3/16/1918	Friederich, August	Scotland	protest	banished
World War I	3/16/1918	Rempfer, William C.	Scotland	protest	banished
peyote ban	1960s	Crow Dog, Leonard	Rosebud	peyote worship	
Indian displacement	9/1971	Brightman, Lehman L.	Mount Rushmore	paramilitary	
Indian displacement	2/27/1973	Aquash, Anna Mae	Wounded Knee	paramilitary	arrest, killed
Indian displacement	2/27/1973	Aquash, Nogeeshik	Wounded Knee	paramilitary	
Indian displacement	2/27/1973	Bear Runner	Wounded Knee	paramilitary	
Indian displacement	2/27/1973	Hat, Sally	Wounded Knee	paramilitary	
peyote ban	1990	Blue Bird, James	Medicine Root	peyote worship	
peyote ban	1993	Cook, Loretta Afraid-of-Bear	Slim Butte	peyote use	

Tennessee

State/ Target of Act	Date	Name	Location	Act	Consequence
slave education ban	3/1833	Sumner, Alphonso M.	Nashville	educated slaves	beaten
slave education ban	1/1838	Yandle, John	Nashville	educated slaves	
slave education ban	1841	Porter, Sarah	Nashville	educated slaves	
slave education ban	1842	Wadkins, Daniel	Nashville	educated slaves	threats
slave recapture	12/5/1848	Dillingham, Richard	Nashville	slave relay	died in prison at hard labor
Fugitive Slave Law of 1850	1859–1863	Burkle, Jacob	Memphis	slave relay	
slave recapture	1860s	Bickerdyke, Mary Ann	Tennessee	sheltered slaves	
slave education ban	1862	Wadkins, Daniel	Nashville	educated slaves	threats
black rights	12/24/1864	Forrest, Nathan Bedford	Chapel Hill	paramilitary leader	
black rights	12/24/1864	Gordon, George Washington	Pulaski	paramilitary organizer	
black rights	12/24/1864	Jones, J. Calvin	Pulaski	paramilitary	
black rights	12/24/1864	Kennedy, John B.	Lawrenceburg	paramilitary	
black rights	12/24/1864	Lester, John Calhoun, lawyer	Giles	paramilitary	
black rights	12/24/1864	Reed, Richard Robert	Giles	paramilitary	
debt	1894	Jones, Mary "Mother"	Gibson	protest	

State/ Target of Act	Date	Name	Location	Act	Consequence
evolutionism ban	5/7/1925	Baldwin, Roger Nash	Dayton	abetted teaching of evolutionism	
evolutionism ban	5/7/1925	Rappleyea, George Washington	Dayton	abetted teaching of evolutionism	
evolutionism ban	5/7/1925	Scopes, John Thomas	Dayton	taught evolutionism	fine
segregation	1942	Rustin, Bayard Taylor	Nashville	integrated a bus	arrest, police brutality
segregation	1961	Lawson, James	Nashville	sit-in	expelled
racism	6/7/1966	Carmichael, Stokely	Memphis	march	
racism	6/7/1966	King, Martin Luther, Jr.	Memphis	march	stoned
racism	6/7/1966	McKissick, Floyd	Memphis	march	
labor organization ban	3/28/1968	King, Martin Luther, Jr.	Memphis	march	shot, tear-gassed
labor organization ban	4/8/1968	King, Coretta Scott, activist	Memphis	protest	

Texas

State/ Target of Act	Date	Name	Location	Act	Consequence
Hispanic displacement	7/13/1859	Cortina, Juan Nepomuceno	Brownsville	shot at a marshal	
Hispanic displacement	9/28/1859	Cabrera, Tomás	Brownsville	paramilitary	pistol-whipped
Hispanic displacement	9/28/1859	Cortina, Juan Nepomuceno	Brownsville	jailbreak	
Hispanic displacement	5/1861	Cortina, Juan Nepomuceno	Brownsville	rebellion	house arrest
free speech ban	3/14/1909	Goldman, Emma	El Paso	conspiracy	banned
World War I	1917	Voth, Albert Cornelius	Camp Travis	refused orders	prison
World War I	11/1/1917	Quiring, Peter J.	Camp Travis	refused a uniform	prison at hard labor
World War I	9/1918	Vogt, Jacob Willard	Camp Logan	conscientious objection	abuse
World War I	11/1918	Pankratz, Peter W.	Del Rio	conscientious objection	prison
labor organization ban	1932	Tenayuca, Emma Zepeda	San Antonio	picket	jail
labor organization ban	1/31/1938	Tenayuca, Emma Zepeda	San Antonio	strike	police brutality, jail, death threat
labor organization ban	8/25/1939	Tenayuca, Emma Zepeda	San Antonio	promoted unions	mob violence
Vietnam War	11/6/1965	Howe, Henry H., Jr.	El Paso	carried a placard	prison at hard labor
Vietnam War	6/30/1966	Johnson, James	Fort Hood	refused assignment	prison at hard labor
Vietnam War	6/30/1966	Mora, Dennis	Fort Hood	refused assignment	prison at hard labor
Vietnam War	6/30/1966	Samas, David	Fort Hood	refused assignment	prison at hard labor
alien refugee abuse	1980s	Fitzpatrick, John Joseph	Brownsville	alien asylum	

State/ Target of Act	Date	Name	Location	Act	Consequence
flag burning ban	8/22/1984	Johnson, Gregory Lee	Dallas	protest	fine, prison
alien refugee abuse	2/1984	Merkt, Stacy Lynn	Brownsville	alien asylum	prison
alien refugee abuse	2/1984	Muhlenkamp, Diane	Brownsville	alien asylum	prison
Iraq War	3/2003	Benderman, Kevin	Fort Hood	defied orders	prison
Iraq War	2005	Asner, Ed	Crawford	protest	
Iraq War	2005	Baez, Joan	Crawford	protest	
Iraq War	2005	Ellsberg, Daniel	Crawford	protest	
Iraq War	8/6/2005	Sheehan, Cindy	Crawford	vigil	
Iraq War	8/28/2005	Sheen, Martin	Crawford	protest	
death penalty	12/1/2005	Bonowitz, Abraham J.	Austin	protest	charged
Iraq War	2006	Fonda, Jane	Crawford	protest	
polygamy	5/6/2008	Neison, Wendell Loy	Eldorado	bigamy	

Utah

State/ Target of Act	Date	Name	Location	Act	Consequence
polygamy ban	1840s	Woodruff, Wilford	Salt Lake City	bigamy	fled
polygamy ban	1846	Hyde, Orson	Spring City	bigamy	
polygamy ban	1846	Young, Brigham	Salt Lake City	bigamy	
polygamy ban	1847	Taylor, John	Salt Lake City	bigamy	exile
polygamy ban	1860s	Pratt, Orson	Salt Lake City	bigamy	lost wives
polygamy ban	1862	Ogston, Cyril	Salt Lake City	bigamy	exile
polygamy ban	1878	Smith, Eliza Roxey Snow	Salt Lake City	cohabitation	
polygamy ban	1880s	Smith, Joseph Fielding	Salt Lake City	bigamy	exile
polygamy ban	1882	Snow, Erastus	Salt Lake City	bigamy	exile
polygamy ban	8/1882	Clawson, Lydia Spencer	Salt Lake City	cohabitation	prison, fine
polygamy ban	8/1882	Clawson, Rudger Judd	Salt Lake City	bigamy	prison, fine
polygamy ban	1884	Clawson, Lydia Spencer	Salt Lake City	cohabitation	prison, fine
polygamy ban	1884	Connelly, Annie Gallifant	Salt Lake City	cohabitation	prison, fine
polygamy ban	1884	Merrill, Isabella Maria Harris	Salt Lake City	cohabitation	prison, fine
polygamy ban	1884	Musser, Amos Milton	Salt Lake City	bigamy	prison, fine
polygamy ban	1884	Newsome, Lucy Maria Devereux	Salt Lake City	cohabitation	prison, fine
polygamy ban	1884	Roundy, Nellie White	Salt Lake City	cohabitation	prison, fine
polygamy ban	1884	Snell, Eliza Shafer	Salt Lake City	cohabitation	prison, fine
polygamy ban	1884	White, Elizabeth Ann Starkey	Salt Lake City	cohabitation	prison, fine
entrapment	1885	Hampton, Brigham Young	Salt Lake City	sting operation	
polygamy ban	1885	Tanner, Joseph Marion	Provo	bigamy	forced to resign from job
polygamy ban	1/19/1885	Cannon, Angus Munn	St. George	bigamy	prison, fine
polygamy ban	5/1885	Brown, Francis Almond	Ogden	bigamy	prison, fine
polygamy ban	5/1885	Miner, Aurelius	Salt Lake City	bigamy	prison, fine
polygamy ban	9/1885	Cannon, Angus Munn	St. George	bigamy	prison, fine

State/ Target of Act	Date	Name	Location	Act	Consequence
polygamy ban	11/20/1885	Snow, Lorenzo	Ogden	bigamy	prison, fine
polygamy ban	1886	Penrose, Charles William	Salt Lake City	bigamy	exile
polygamy ban	1/1886	Cannon, George Quayle	Salt Lake City	bigamy	prison, fine
polygamy ban	2/1886	Lyman, Francis Marion	Provo	bigamy	prison, fine
polygamy ban	3/1887	John, David	Salt Lake City	bigamy	prison, fine
polygamy ban	9/1888	Cannon, George Quayle	Salt Lake City	bigamy	prison, fine
polygamy ban	1889	Roberts, Brigham Henry	Salt Lake City	bigamy	prison, ousted from Congress
polygamy ban	1893	Woolley, Lorin Calvin	Salt Lake City	bigamy	
polygamy ban	1899	Grant, Heber Jeddy	Salt Lake City	bigamy	prison, fine
polygamy ban	1902	Musser, Joseph White	Salt Lake City	bigamy	prison
labor organization ban	4/24/1904	Jones, Mary "Mother"	Helper	public harangue	arson, jail
labor exploitation	1914	Flynn, Elizabeth Gurley	Salt Lake City	defense of Joe Hill	arrest
polygamy ban	1915	Broadbent, Joseph Leslie	Lehi	bigamy	
labor exploitation	11/19/1915	Hill, Joe	Salt Lake City	supported unions	shot
polygamy ban	9/1939	Jessop, Fred	St. George	bigamy	prison
polygamy ban	9/1939	Jessop, Richard Seth	St. George	bigamy	prison
polygamy ban	1944	Steed, Rulon Timpson	Salt Lake City	bigamy	prison
polygamy ban	5/12/1945	Kelsch, Louis Alma	Salt Lake City	cohabitation	prison
polygamy ban	5/12/1945	Musser, Joseph White	Salt Lake City	marriage to minors	
polygamy ban	5/12/1945	Timpson, Alma Willard	Salt Lake City	cohabitation	prison
polygamy ban	5/12/1945	Zitting, Charles Frederick	Harrisville	bigamy	prison
taxation	1961	Hennacy, Ammon	Salt Lake City	tax resistance	
peyote ban	1/2001	Mooney, James	Benjamin	peyote worship	
peyote ban	1/2001	Mooney, Linda	Benjamin	peyote worship	
polygamy ban	6/24/2002	Green, Thomas Arthur	Joab County	child rape, bigamy	prison
polygamy ban	6/24/2002	Hampton, Brigham Young	Salt Lake City	bigamy	

Vermont

State/ Target of Act	Date	Name	Location	Act	Consequence
colonial taxation	8/1765	Smith, Richard, Jr.	Burlington	led revolt	
slavery	1811–1860s	Higley, Erastus	Fairhaven	protest	
slave recapture	1830s	Falls, William S.	Burlington	sheltered slaves	
slave recapture	1830s–1840s	Robinson, Rachel Gilpin	Ferrisburg	ran a depot	
slave recapture	1830s–1840s	Robinson, Rowland Thomas	Ferrisburg	ran a depot	
slave recapture	1840s	Allinson, William J.	Burlington	sheltered slaves	
Civil War	1863	Dakin, Peter	Ferrisburg	refused to serve	stockade, torture
Civil War	1863	Macomber, Lindley M.	Grande Isle	refused to serve	stockade, torture
Civil War	1863–1865	Stevens, William Byrd	Montpelier	refused to serve	
Civil War	7/13/1863	Pringle, Cyrus Guernsey	Charlotte	refused to serve	stockade, torture
free speech ban	9/3/1909	Goldman, Emma	Burlington	conspiracy	banned

State/ Target of Act	Date	Name	Location	Act	Consequence
taxation	1939	Gregg, Richard Bartlett	Putney	propaganda	
gay persecution	1987	Coffin, William Sloane, Jr.	Strafford	demonstration	

Vietnam

Vietnam War	12/25/1965	Aptheker, Herbert	Hanoi	passport violation	
Vietnam War	12/25/1965	Hayden, Thomas Emmett	Hanoi	passport violation	
Vietnam War	12/25/1965	Lynd, Staughton	Hanoi	passport violation	
Vietnam War	1967	Boardman, Elizabeth Jelinek	Danang	breached blockade	arrest
Vietnam War	1967	Braxton, John Worth	Danang	breached blockade	arrest
Vietnam War	1967	Champney, Horace	Danang	breached blockade	arrest
Vietnam War	1967	Drath, Phil	Danang	breached blockade	arrest
Vietnam War	1967	Eaton, Bob	Danang	breached blockade	arrest
Vietnam War	1967	Lakey, George	Danang	breached blockade	arrest
Vietnam War	1967	Massar, Ivan	Danang	breached blockade	arrest
Vietnam War	1967	Reynolds, Barbara Leonard	Danang	breached blockade	arrest
Vietnam War	1967	Reynolds, Earle	Danang	breached blockade	arrest
prisoners of war	1/1968	Berrigan, Daniel	Hanoi	passport violation	
prisoners of war	1/1968	Zinn, Howard	Hanoi	passport violation	
Vietnam War	5/1972	Aptheker, Herbert	Hanoi	protested bombing	vilification
Vietnam War	5/1972	Fonda, Jane	Hanoi	protested bombing	vilification
Vietnam War	5/1972	Hayden, Thomas Emmett	Hanoi	protested bombing	vilification
draft	9/25/1972	Coffin, William Sloane, Jr.	Hanoi	protest	
prisoners of war	12/25/1972	Baez, Joan	Hanoi	prison visit	

Virginia

heresy	1662	Wilson, George	Jamestown	Quaker worship	shackled, died in jail
French and Indian War	1756	Standley, William	Loudon County	refused to serve	lashed, prison at hard labor
religious persecution	1765	Childs, James	Culpeper	preached	harassment, jail
religious persecution	1765	Craig, Elijah	Culpeper	preached	jail on bread and water
religious persecution	1765	Craig, John	Lexington	religious unorthodoxy	stalked, ridicule
religious persecution	1765	Craig, Lewis	Culpeper	preached	jail, harassment
religious persecution	1765	Harris, Samuel	Culpeper	preached	jail, harassment
religious persecution	1765	Ireland, James	Culpeper	preached	jail, attempted assassination
religious persecution	1765	Marsh, William	Culpeper	preached	jail, harassment
religious persecution	1765	Read, James	Culpeper	preached	jail, harassment

State/ Target of Act	Date	Name	Location	Act	Consequence
religious persecution	1765	Waller, John	Culpeper	preached	jail, harassment
colonial taxation	8/1765	Henry, Patrick	Red Hill	spokesman	
colonial taxation	8/1765	Randolph, Peyton	Williamsburg	paramilitary	
colonial taxation	9/1765	Lee, Richard Henry	Williamsburg	protest	
colonial taxation	3/31/1766	Curle, William Roscoe Wilson	Norfolk	paramilitary organizer	
religious persecution	1767	Lane, Dutton	Meherrin	religious unorthodoxy	silenced
religious persecution	7/26/1769	Greenwood, James	Middlesex	religious unorthodoxy	jail
religious persecution	7/26/1769	Waller, John	Middlesex	religious unorthodoxy	jail
religious persecution	7/26/1769	Ware, Robert	Middlesex	religious unorthodoxy	jail
religious persecution	7/26/1769	Webber, William	Middlesex	religious unorthodoxy	jail
religious persecution	8/1771	Burrus, John	Culpeper	preached	prison
religious persecution	8/1771	Cheming, Bartholomew	Culpeper	preached	prison
religious persecution	8/1771	Craig, Lewis	Culpeper	preached	prison
religious persecution	8/1771	Goodrick, James	Culpeper	preached	prison
religious persecution	8/1771	Herndon, Edward	Culpeper	preached	prison
religious persecution	8/1771	Pitman, James	Culpeper	religious unorthodoxy	prison
religious persecution	8/1771	Waller, John	Culpeper	preached	prison, choked, assault, lashed
religious persecution	8/1771	Young, John	Culpeper	preached	prison
religious persecution	7/1/1773	Barrow, David	Portsmouth	preached	torture
religious persecution	7/1/1773	Mintz, Edward	Portsmouth	preached	torture
religious persecution	1773	Weatherford, John	Pittsylvania	preached	jail, knife attack, fine
colonial taxation	11/1774	Cary, Archibald	Williamsburg	intimidation	
taxation	3/1777	McClunn, Thomas	Frederick County	tax resistance	
religious persecution	8/1777	Ware, James	Culpeper	religious unorthodoxy	prison
Revolutionary War	11/16/1777	Gawthorp, James	Frederick County	refused to serve	forced march
taxation	11/16/1777	Gawthorp, James	Frederick County	tax resistance	
slave education ban	1826–1847	Morris, Sylvia	Alexandria	educated slaves	intimidation
slave recapture	1830s	Butler, Benjamin Franklin	Fort Monroe	sheltered slaves	
slave education ban	1837–1843	Parry, Alfred	Alexandria	educated slaves	
slave recapture	1840s	Gansey, Isaac	Norfolk	slave relay	
slave education ban	1853	Douglass, Margaret Crittenden	Alexandria	educated slaves	arrest, jail, persecution, fine
slave education ban	1853	Douglass, Rosa	Alexandria	educated slaves	arrest, persecution, fine, jail

State/ Target of Act	Date	Name	Location	Act	Consequence
slave recapture	1858	Cook, John E.	Harpers Ferry	spying, supplied anarchists	executed
slave recapture	6/25/1859	Putnam, David, Jr.	Wood County	slave rescue	lawsuit
slavery	10/16/1859	Anderson, Jeremiah Goldsmith	Harpers Ferry	guerrilla war	bayoneted
slavery	10/16/1859	Anderson, John	Harpers Ferry	guerrilla war	killed
slavery	10/16/1859	Anderson, Osborne	Harpers Ferry	guerrilla war	fled
slavery	10/16/1859	Brown, John	Harpers Ferry	sedition	hanged
slavery	10/16/1859	Brown, Oliver	Harpers Ferry	guerrilla war	killed
slavery	10/16/1859	Brown, Owen	Harpers Ferry	guerrilla war	fled
slavery	10/16/1859	Brown, Watson	Harpers Ferry	guerrilla war	killed
slavery	10/16/1859	Cook, John E.	Harpers Ferry	guerrilla war	hanged
slavery	10/16/1859	Copeland, John Anthony, Jr.	Harpers Ferry	guerrilla war	shot
slavery	10/16/1859	Coppoc, Barclay	Harpers Ferry	guerrilla war	fled
slavery	10/16/1859	Coppoc, Edwin	Harpers Ferry	guerrilla war	hanged
slavery	10/16/1859	Green, Shields	Harpers Ferry	guerrilla war	hanged
slavery	10/16/1859	Hazlett, Albert	Harpers Ferry	guerrilla war	hanged
slavery	10/16/1859	Kagi, John Henry	Harpers Ferry	guerrilla war	shot
slavery	10/16/1859	Leary, Lewis Sheridan	Harpers Ferry	guerrilla war	shot
slavery	10/16/1859	Leeman, William H.	Harpers Ferry	guerrilla war	killed
slavery	10/16/1859	Merriam, Francis Jackson	Harpers Ferry	conspiracy, financial support	fled
slavery	10/16/1859	Newby, Dangerfield	Harpers Ferry	guerrilla war	shot
slavery	10/16/1859	Stevens, Aaron Dwight	Harpers Ferry	guerrilla war	hanged
slavery	10/16/1859	Taylor, Stewart	Harpers Ferry	guerrilla war	killed
slavery	10/16/1859	Thompson, Dauphin Adolphus	Harpers Ferry	guerrilla war	killed
slavery	10/16/1859	Thompson, William	Harpers Ferry	guerrilla war	killed
slavery	10/16/1859	Tidd, Charles Plummer	Harpers Ferry	guerrilla war	fled
slave education ban	1861	Crouch, Jane A.	Alexandria	educated slaves	
slave education ban	1861	Gray, Sarah	Alexandria	educated slaves	
slave education ban	1861	Herbert, Peter	Hampton	educated slaves	
slave education ban	9/17/1861	Peake, Mary Smith Kelsey	Hampton	educated slaves	
slave recapture	1862	Conway, Ellen Davis Dana	Falmouth	slave relay	mob violence
slave recapture	1862	Conway, Moncure Daniel	Falmouth	slave relay	mob violence
Civil War	1863	Conway, Moncure Daniel	Falmouth	refused to serve	exile
slave recapture	1863	Tubman, Harriet	Fort Monroe	slave relay	
food prices	4/2/1863	Jackson, Mary	Richmond	rioted, looted	charged
food prices	4/2/1863	Meredith, Minerva	Richmond	looted	charged
draft	8/31/1863	Dakin, Peter	Culpeper	protest	
draft	8/31/1863	Macomber, Lindley M.	Culpeper	protest	

State/ Target of Act	Date	Name	Location	Act	Consequence
draft	8/31/1863	Pringle, Cyrus Guernsey	Culpeper	protest	
draft	6/15/1864	Kline, John	Broadway	protest	shot
labor organization ban	7/15/1877	Jones, Mary "Mother"	Norton	public harangue	
labor organization ban	1891	Hado, Dud	Norton	concealed weapon	fine
labor organization ban	1891	Jones, Mary "Mother"	Norton	public harangue	death threat
war bond sale	1917	Heatwole, Lewis James	Harrisonburg	protest	fine, arrest
draft	11/25/1917	Whipple, Leonidas Rutledge	Charlottesville	protest	fired
World War II	1940s	Walker, Charles C.	Petersburg	left work	prison
World War II	3/4/1944	Vetter, Herbert F., Jr.	Bedford	abandoned work	
nuclear power	6/30/1946	Man, Albon Platt, Jr.	Arlington	picket	
racism	4/11/1947	Rustin, Bayard Taylor	Petersburg	freedom ride	
racism	4/20/1947	Bromley, Ernest	Roanoke	freedom ride	
racism	4/22/1947	Nelson, Wallace Floyd	Amherst		threat, arrest
racism	4/23/1947	Banks, Dennis	Culpeper	freedom ride	arrest
war	11/12/1960	Scott, Lawrence	Arlington	sit-in	
war	11/12/1960	Scott, Viola Maria Standley	Arlington	sit-in	
draft, war	10/21/1967	Baez, Joan	Arlington	blocked an entrance	arrest
draft, war	10/21/1967	Chomsky, Noam	Arlington	trespass, blocked traffic	arrest
draft, war	10/21/1967	Davis, Angela	Arlington	blocked an entrance	arrest
draft, war	10/21/1967	Deming, Barbara	Arlington	trespass, blocked traffic	arrest
draft, war	10/21/1967	Dohrn, Bernadine	Arlington	blocked an entrance	arrest
draft, war	10/21/1967	Fonda, Jane	Arlington	blocked an entrance	arrest
draft, war	10/21/1967	Lens, Sidney	Arlington	trespass, blocked traffic	arrest
draft, war	10/21/1967	Levertov, Denise	Arlington	trespass, blocked traffic	arrest
draft, war	10/21/1967	Lowell, Robert	Arlington	trespass, blocked traffic	arrest
draft, war	10/21/1967	Macdonald, Dwight	Arlington	trespass, blocked traffic	arrest
draft	10/21/1967	Spock, Benjamin	Arlington	blocked an entrance	arrest
Vietnam War	10/21/1967	Spock, Benjamin	Arlington	conspiracy	prison
draft, war	10/21/1967	Spock, Jane Cheney	Arlington	trespass, blocked traffic	arrest
Vietnam War	1970	Braxton, John Worth	Petersburg	draft evasion	prison
animal rights	1980	Newkirk, Ingrid	Norfolk	protest	
animal rights	1980	Pacheco, Alex	Norfolk	protest	
nuclear power	4/3/1988	Berrigan, Philip	Norfolk	sabotage	prison
nuclear power	4/3/1988	Boertje, Gregory	Norfolk	sabotage	prison

State/ Target of Act	Date	Name	Location	Act	Consequence
nuclear power	4/3/1988	Lawrence, Andrew	Norfolk	sabotage	prison
nuclear power	4/3/1988	McKenna, Margaret	Norfolk	sabotage	prison
ROTC	9/29/2005	Khan, Tariq	Fairfax	demonstration	police brutality

Washington

State/ Target of Act	Date	Name	Location	Act	Consequence
free speech ban	3/1908	Reitman, Ben L.	Bellingham	conspiracy	banned
free speech ban	12/13/1908	Goldman, Emma	Everett	conspiracy	banned
free speech ban	12/14/1908	Goldman, Emma	Bellingham	conspiracy	arrest, exile
free speech ban	12/14/1908	Reitman, Ben L.	Bellingham	conspiracy	banned
labor exploitation	11/28/1909	Filigno, Charley	Spokane	union organizing	prison
labor exploitation	11/28/1909	Flynn, Elizabeth Gurley	Spokane	chained to a lamppost	arrest
labor exploitation	11/28/1909	Little, Frank	Spokane	union organizing	prison
labor organization ban	11/30/1909	Filigno, Charley	Spokane	conspiracy	prison
free speech ban	11/30/1909	Flynn, Elizabeth Gurley	Spokane	disorderly conduct	arrest
labor organization ban	11/30/1909	Little, Frank	Spokane	conspiracy	prison
free speech ban	8/9/1913	Goldman, Emma	Seattle	conspiracy	arrest
free speech ban	8/9/1913	Reitman, Ben L.	Seattle	conspiracy	arrest
labor exploitation	1916	Flynn, Elizabeth Gurley	Spokane	protest	arrest
World War I	1918	Schwartz, Jacob	Bellevue	conscientious objection	died in prison
draft	6/17/1918	Carr, C.R.	Olympia	protest	fired
World War I	8/1918	Conrad, Orie Martin	Fort Lewis	refused a weapon	torture
World War I	8/1918	McTimmonds, Elmer Tracy	Fort Lewis	refused a weapon	torture
draft	8/27/1918	Irvin, Clara M.	Spokane	protest	confiscation
labor exploitation	11/11/1919	Everett, Wesley	Centralia	union organizing	lynched
fishing ban	5/6/1939	Spedis, Martin	Celilo Falls	gill-netted	arrest
fishing ban	5/6/1939	Switzler, William	Celilo Falls	gill-netted	arrest
fishing ban	5/6/1939	Tulee, Sampson	Celilo Falls	netted	arrest
Japanese internment	10/20/1942	Hirabayashi, Gordon Kiyoshi	Seattle	defied curfew	
fishing ban	12/1945	Frank, Billy, Jr.	Frank's Landing	gill-netted	raid
fishing ban	7/1960	McCoy, Joseph	Skagit River	gill-netted	arrest
fishing ban	1/1961	Starr, James	Green River	gill-netted	arrest
fishing ban	1/1961	Starr, Louis, Jr.	Green River	gill-netted	arrest
fishing ban	1/1961	Wayne, Leonard	Green River	gill-netted	arrest
fishing ban	3/2/1964	Brando, Marlon	Seattle	fished	
fishing ban	3/2/1964	Gregory, Dick	Seattle	fished	
fishing ban	3/2/1964	Satiacum, Bob	Seattle	fished	jail
fishing ban	3/2/1964	Wright, Reuben	Seattle	fished	jail
fishing ban	3/2/1964	Yaryan, John J.	Seattle	fished	
fishing ban	4/21/1964	Weeks, Madeline Alexander	Cook's Landing	fished	boat rammed
fishing ban	9/21/1964	Satiacum, Clara	Tacoma	outran police	arrest

State/ Target of Act	Date	Name	Location	Act	Consequence
fishing ban	9/21/1964	Satiacum, Susan	Tacoma	outran police	arrest
fishing ban	10/7/1965	Bridges, Alvin	Frank's Landing	fished	raid
fishing ban	10/7/1965	Frank, Billy, Jr.	Frank's Landing	gill-netted	seized, canoe confiscated
fishing ban	10/13/1965	Gregory, Dick	Frank's Landing	fish-in	arrest
fishing ban	10/13/1965	Gregory, Lillian Smith	Frank's Landing	fish-in	arrest
fishing ban	10/13/1965	McCloud, Donald	Frank's Landing	fished illegally	canoe crushed
fishing ban	10/13/1965	McCloud, Janet Renecker	Frank's Landing	resisted arrest	attacked
fishing ban	10/13/1965	McCloud, Jeffrey	Frank's Landing	fish-in	canoe crushed
fishing ban	10/13/1965	Roberts, Evan, Jr.	Frank's Landing	attended fish-in	raid
fishing ban	10/13/1965	Sanchez, Dorian	Frank's Landing	fish-in	canoe crushed
fishing ban	10/13/1965	Satiacum, Susan	Frank's Landing	resisted arrest	arrest
fishing ban	10/26/1965	Wright, Elaine	Nisqually	fish-in	
fishing ban	11/1965	Bridges, Alvin	Frank's Landing	fish-in	
fishing ban	11/1965	McCloud, Janet Renecker	Frank's Landing	fish-in	
fishing ban	2/6/1966	Gregory, Dick	Frank's Landing	rally	jail
fishing ban	2/6/1966	Gregory, Lillian Smith	Frank's Landing	rally	jail
fishing ban	3/1/1966	McCloud, Edith	Frank's Landing	fished illegally	canoe crushed
fishing ban	3/1/1966	McCloud, Janet Renecker	Frank's Landing	fish-in	
Indian displacement	1970	Bennett, Ramona	Tacoma	defied officers	arrest, threat
Indian displacement	3/8/1970	Fonda, Jane	Fort Lawton	protest	
Indian displacement	3/8/1970	Peltier, Leonard	Fort Lawton	protest	
Indian displacement	3/8/1970	Satiacum, Bob	Fort Lawton	protest	
Indian displacement	3/8/1970	Whitebear, Bernie Reyes	Fort Lawton	protest	
fishing ban	9/9/1970	Frank, Tobin	Frank's Landing	fished	raid
fishing ban	1981	Sohappy, David	Harrah	sold fish	arrest
fishing ban	1981	Sohappy, David, Jr.	Harrah	sold fish	arrest
gay persecution	1989	Cammermeyer, Margarethe	Seattle	admitted homosexuality	ousted from military
flag burning ban	10/30/1989	Eichman, Shawn D.	Seattle	burned flag	arrest
peyote ban	1993	Strong, Ted	Satus	peyote use	
taxation	6/18/2004	Sheehan, Cindy	Fort Lewis	tax resistance	

State/ Target of Act	Date	Name	Location	Act	Consequence
alien refugee abuse	4/2007	Ramos, Michael	Seattle	alien asylum	
alien refugee abuse	4/2007	Ray, Roberta	Seattle	alien asylum	

Washington, DC

State/ Target of Act	Date	Name	Location	Act	Consequence
slave recapture	3/1839	Grimes, Leonard Andrew		slave relay	prison
slave recapture	1847	Chase, Salmon Portland		fund-raising	
slave recapture	4/15/1848	Bailey, Gamaliel		sea relay	mob violence
slave recapture	4/15/1848	Beecher, Henry Ward		protest, fund-raising	
slave recapture	4/15/1848	Bell, Daniel		sea relay	
slave recapture	4/15/1848	Bush, Linda Clark		sea relay	
slave recapture	4/15/1848	Bush, William		sea relay	
slave recapture	4/15/1848	Chaplin, William Lawrence		sea relay, assault	prison
slave recapture	4/15/1848	Chase, Salmon Portland		defended slave rescue	
slave recapture	4/15/1848	Drayton, Daniel		sea relay	knifing, prison, fine, suicide
slave recapture	4/15/1848	Ducket, Thomas		sea relay	
slave recapture	4/15/1848	Giddings, Joshua Reed		defended slave relay	
slave recapture	4/15/1848	Jackson, Francis		defended slave rescue	
slave recapture	4/15/1848	Mann, Horace		defended slave rescue	
slave recapture	4/15/1848	Morris, Robert		defended slave rescue	
slave recapture	4/15/1848	Sayer, Edward		sea relay	prison, fine
slave recapture	4/15/1848	Sewall, Samuel Edmund		defended slave rescue	
Fugitive Slave Law of 1850	1850s	Chaplin, William Lawrence		spying, conspiracy	
slave education ban	1850s	Miner, Myrtilla		educated slaves	harassment, arson
slave education ban	1851	Brown, Emma V.		educated slaves	
slave education ban	1851	Clapp, Margaret		educated slaves	
slave education ban	1851	Conway, Moncure Daniel		educated slaves	
slave education ban	1851	Edmondson, Emily		educated slaves	
slave education ban	1851	Inman, Anna		educated slaves	
slave education ban	1851	Johnson, Nancy M.		educated slaves	
slave education ban	1851	Johnson, Walter W.		educated slaves	
slave education ban	1851	Jones, Anna		educated slaves	
slave education ban	1851	Madden, Matilda Jones		educated slaves	
slave education ban	1851	Mann, Lydia B.		educated slaves	
slave education ban	1851	Moore, Helen		educated slaves	

State/ Target of Act	Date	Name	Location	Act	Consequence
slave education ban	1851	Searing, Anna Hutchinson		educated slaves	
slave education ban	1851	Weaver, Amanda		educated slaves	
slave recapture	10/1/1851	Norton, Jo		jailbreak	fled
unemployment	5/1/1854	Browne, Carl Dryden		march	police brutality, jail
unemployment	5/1/1854	Cantwell, Jumbo		march	jail
unemployment	5/1/1854	Coxey, Henrietta		march	
unemployment	5/1/1854	Coxey, Jacob Sechier		march	police brutality, arrest
unemployment	5/1/1854	Coxey, Legal Tender		march	
unemployment	5/1/1854	Coxey, Mamie		march	
unemployment	5/1/1854	Fry, Lewis C.		march	
unemployment	5/1/1854	Shepard, Henry		march	
slave education ban	1855	Cook, John F., Jr.		educated slaves	warning
slave education ban	1857–1859	Howland, Emily		educated slaves	
slave recapture	7/6/1859	Chase, Salmon Portland		propaganda, defended civil disobedience	
slave recapture	7/6/1859	Langston, Charles Henry		propaganda, defended civil disobedience	
slave recapture	1861	Sparrow, Thomas		ran a street patrol	
unemployment	4/30/1894	Jones, Mary "Mother"		march	
free speech ban	11/1910	Goldman, Emma		conspiracy	banned
Mexican Revolution	1911	Jones, Mary "Mother"		protest	
women's disenfranchisement	1913	Stevens, Doris		protest	
women's disenfranchisement	11/1913	Burns, Lucy		wrote on sidewalk	fine
women's disenfranchisement	1/10/1917	Branham, Lucy Gwynne		picketed	workhouse
women's disenfranchisement	1/10/1917	Paul, Alice		picketed	arrest
women's disenfranchisement	3/4/1917	Paul, Alice		chained to a fence	warning
World War I	4/2/1917	Rankin, Jeannette		protest	
women's disenfranchisement	6/22/1917	Burns, Lucy		picketed	workhouse, force-feeding, stripped
women's disenfranchisement	6/22/1917	Morey, Katherine		picketed	jail
women's disenfranchisement	6/27/1917	Arniel, Annie M. Clarke		picketed	workhouse
women's disenfranchisement	6/27/1917	Arnold, Virginia Josephine		picketed	workhouse
women's disenfranchisement	6/27/1917	Baird, Margaret Frances		picketed	workhouse

State/ Target of Act	Date	Name	Location	Act	Consequence
women's disenfranchisement	6/27/1917	Dock, Lavinia Lloyd		picketed	workhouse
women's disenfranchisement	6/27/1917	Hilles, Florence Bayard		picketed	workhouse
women's disenfranchisement	6/27/1917	Jamison, Maud		picketed	workhouse
women's disenfranchisement	6/27/1917	Lewis, Dora Kelly		picketed	workhouse
women's disenfranchisement	6/27/1917	Vernon, Mabel		picketed	workhouse
women's disenfranchisement	6/27/1917	Youmans, Florence L.		picketed	workhouse
women's disenfranchisement	7/1917	Lewis, Dora Kelly		picketed	workhouse
women's disenfranchisement	7/4/1917	Calderhead-Walker, Iris Gallant		picketed	workhouse
women's disenfranchisement	7/4/1917	Milholland, Vida		picketed	workhouse
women's disenfranchisement	7/4/1917	Weed, Helena Charlotte		picketed	workhouse
women's disenfranchisement	7/4/1917	Young-Rogers, Joy		picketed	workhouse
women's disenfranchisement	7/14/1917	Brannan, Eunice Mignon Dana		picketed	workhouse
women's disenfranchisement	7/14/1917	Fotheringham, Janet		picketed	workhouse
women's disenfranchisement	7/14/1917	Gardner, Matilda Hall		picketed	workhouse
women's disenfranchisement	7/14/1917	Hopkins, Alison Turnbull		picketed	workhouse
women's disenfranchisement	7/14/1917	Hurlbut, Julia		unlawful assembly	workhouse
women's disenfranchisement	7/14/1917	Martin, Anne		picketed	workhouse
women's disenfranchisement	7/14/1917	Rogers, Elizabeth Selden White		picketed	workhouse
women's disenfranchisement	7/14/1917	Stuyvesant, Elizabeth		picketed	workhouse
women's disenfranchisement	8/14/1917	Dixon, Edna		picketed	workhouse
women's disenfranchisement	8/16/1917	Flanagan, Catherine M.		picketed	workhouse
women's disenfranchisement	8/17/1917	Crocker, Gertrude L.		picketed	workhouse
women's disenfranchisement	8/17/1917	Dock, Lavinia Lloyd		picketed	workhouse, brutalized
women's disenfranchisement	8/17/1917	Ewing, Lucy Hyde		picketed	workhouse
women's disenfranchisement	8/17/1917	Gray, Natalie Hoyt		picketed	workhouse

State/ Target of Act	Date	Name	Location	Act	Consequence
women's disenfranchisement	8/17/1917	Watson, Madeleine		picketed	workhouse
women's disenfranchisement	8/17/1917	Young, Matilda		picketed	workhouse
women's disenfranchisement	9/1917	Ainge, Edith		picketed	workhouse
women's disenfranchisement	9/1917	Baker, Abby Scott		picketed	workhouse
women's disenfranchisement	9/1917	Blumberg, Hilda		picketed	workhouse
women's disenfranchisement	9/1917	Branham, Lucy Gwynne		picketed	workhouse
women's disenfranchisement	9/1917	Burns, Lucy		picketed	workhouse
women's disenfranchisement	9/1917	Samarodin, Nina		picketed	workhouse
women's disenfranchisement	9/1917	Winsor, Mary		picketed	workhouse
women's disenfranchisement	9/4/1917	Adams, Pauline Forstall Colclough		obstructed traffic	arrest
women's disenfranchisement	9/22/1917	Hara, Ernestine		picketed	workhouse
women's disenfranchisement	10/6/1917	Hennessy, Minnie		picketed	workhouse
women's disenfranchisement	10/8/1917	Hennessy, Minnie		picketed	workhouse
women's disenfranchisement	10/15/1917	Heffelfinger, Kate		picketed	workhouse
women's disenfranchisement	10/15/1917	Winslow, Rose		picketed	workhouse
women's disenfranchisement	10/20/1917	Paul, Alice		picketed	workhouse
women's disenfranchisement	10/20/1917	Spencer, Caroline E.		picketed	workhouse
women's disenfranchisement	11/1917	Arniel, Annie M. Clarke		picketed	workhouse
women's disenfranchisement	11/1917	Emory, Julia		picketed	workhouse
women's disenfranchisement	11/1917	Paul, Alice		picketed	workhouse, torture, asylum, force-feeding, solitary
women's disenfranchisement	11/10/1917	Blumberg, Hilda		picketed	workhouse
women's disenfranchisement	11/10/1917	Brannan, Eunice Mignon Dana		picketed	workhouse
women's disenfranchisement	11/10/1917	Burns, Lucy		picketed	workhouse, brutality, force-feeding

State/ Target of Act	Date	Name	Location	Act	Consequence
women's disenfranchisement	11/10/1917	Cosu, Alice M. Claressi		picketed	workhouse
women's disenfranchisement	11/10/1917	Day, Dorothy		picketed	workhouse
women's disenfranchisement	11/10/1917	Dixon, Mary Bartlett		picketed	workhouse
women's disenfranchisement	11/10/1917	Emory, Julia		picketed	workhouse
women's disenfranchisement	11/10/1917	Gram, Betty		picketed	workhouse
women's disenfranchisement	11/10/1917	Hunkins-Hallinan, Hazel		picketed	workhouse
women's disenfranchisement	11/10/1917	Jakobi, Paula		picketed	workhouse
women's disenfranchisement	11/10/1917	Juengling, Amy		picketed	workhouse
women's disenfranchisement	11/10/1917	Kendall, Ada Davenport		picketed	workhouse
women's disenfranchisement	11/10/1917	Kent, Elizabeth Thatcher		picketed	workhouse
women's disenfranchisement	11/10/1917	Kinkead, Beatrice		picketed	workhouse
women's disenfranchisement	11/10/1917	Kruger, Hattie		picketed	workhouse
women's disenfranchisement	11/10/1917	Lewis, Dora Kelly		picketed	workhouse
women's disenfranchisement	11/10/1917	Martinette, Catherine		picketed	workhouse
women's disenfranchisement	11/10/1917	McShane, Elizabeth		picketed	workhouse
women's disenfranchisement	11/10/1917	Morey, Mary Agnes Hosmer		picketed	workhouse
women's disenfranchisement	11/10/1917	Nolan, Mary A.		picketed	workhouse
women's disenfranchisement	11/10/1917	Quay, Minnie		picketed	workhouse
women's disenfranchisement	11/10/1917	Scott, Phoebe Persons		picketed	workhouse
women's disenfranchisement	11/10/1917	White, Sue Shelton		picketed	workhouse
women's disenfranchisement	11/10/1917	Wiley, Anna Kelton		picketed	workhouse
women's disenfranchisement	11/10/1917	Young, Matilda		picketed	workhouse
women's disenfranchisement	1/1918	Weed, Helena Charlotte Hill		picketed	workhouse
draft	6/8/1918	Abbe, Cleveland, Jr.		protest	fired
women's disenfranchisement	8/1918	Ainge, Edith		demonstration	arrest

State/ Target of Act	Date	Name	Location	Act	Consequence
women's disenfranchisement	8/1918	Ascough, Lillian		demonstration	arrest
women's disenfranchisement	8/1918	Crocker, Gertrude L.		demonstration	arrest
women's disenfranchisement	8/1918	Emory, Julia		demonstration	arrest
women's disenfranchisement	8/1918	Heffelfinger, Kate		demonstration	arrest
women's disenfranchisement	8/1918	Hill, Elsie Mary		demonstration	arrest
women's disenfranchisement	8/1918	Watson, Madeleine		demonstration	arrest
women's disenfranchisement	8/1918	Weed, Helena Charlotte Hill		picketed	workhouse
women's disenfranchisement	8/15/1918	Burns, Lucy		speech	arrest
women's disenfranchisement	8/15/1918	Lewis, Dora Kelly		speech	arrest
women's disenfranchisement	8/15/1918	Paul, Alice		speech	arrest
women's disenfranchisement	12/16/1918	Kalb, Elizabeth Green		demonstration	arrest
women's disenfranchisement	1/1919	Burns, Lucy		picketed	workhouse
women's disenfranchisement	1/1919	Fendall, Mary Gertrude		burned an effigy	arrest
women's disenfranchisement	1/1919	Heffelfinger, Kate		burned an effigy	arrest
women's disenfranchisement	1/1919	Kalb, Elizabeth Green		burned an effigy	arrest
women's disenfranchisement	1/1919	Lewis, Dora Kelly		burned an effigy	arrest
women's disenfranchisement	1/1919	Moller, Bertha C. Berglin		burned an effigy	arrest
women's disenfranchisement	1/1919	Nolan, Mary A.		burned an effigy	arrest
women's disenfranchisement	1/1919	Winsor, Mary		burned an effigy	arrest
women's disenfranchisement	1/1919	Young, Matilda		burned an effigy	arrest
women's disenfranchisement	1/6/1919	Dubrow, Mary		burned an effigy	arrest
women's disenfranchisement	1/7/1919	Emory, Julia		burned an effigy	arrest
women's disenfranchisement	1/13/1919	Gardner, Matilda Hall		picketed	
women's disenfranchisement	1/13/1919	Spencer, Caroline E.		burned an effigy	arrest
women's disenfranchisement	2/1919	Ainge, Edith		burned an effigy	arrest

State/ Target of Act	Date	Name	Location	Act	Consequence
women's disenfranchisement	2/1919	Arnold, Berthe		burned an effigy	arrest
women's disenfranchisement	2/1919	Ascough, Lillian		burned an effigy	arrest
women's disenfranchisement	2/1919	Colvin, Sarah Tarleton		burned an effigy	arrest
women's disenfranchisement	2/1919	Crocker, Gertrude L.		burned an effigy	arrest
women's disenfranchisement	2/1919	Hill, Elsie Mary		burned an effigy	arrest
women's disenfranchisement	2/1919	Mercer, Nell		burned an effigy	arrest
women's disenfranchisement	2/9/1919	Adams, Pauline Forstall Colclough		burned an effigy	arrest
women's disenfranchisement	2/10/1919	Havemeyer, Louisine Waldron Elder		burned an effigy	arrest
women's disenfranchisement	8/1919	Hunkins-Hallinan, Hazel		demonstration	arrest
Sacco and Vanzetti death sentence	7/14/1920	Frankfurter, Felix		protest	
draft	4/1922	O'Hare, Kate Richards		protest march	
debt	5/1932	Butler, Smedley Darlington		paramilitary	
debt	7/28/1932	Carlson, Eric		paramilitary	killed
debt	7/28/1932	Hushka, William		paramilitary	killed
lynching	11/1934	Dorsey, Emmett		paraded illegally	arrest
lynching	11/1934	Lovett, Edward P.		paraded illegally	arrest
lynching	11/1934	Murphy, George B., Jr.		paraded illegally	arrest
lynching	11/1934	Wilkins, Roy.		paraded illegally	arrest
racism	1940	Powell, Adam Clayton, Jr.		trespass	arrest
racism	6/1941	Bethune, Mary McLeod		conspiracy	
racism	6/1941	Powell, Adam Clayton, Jr.		conspiracy	
racism	6/1941	Randolph, Asa Philip		conspiracy	
racism	4/9/1947	Baker, Ella		integrated a bus	
racism	4/9/1947	Farmer, James Leonard		integrated a bus	
racism	4/9/1947	Lynn, Conrad J.	Petersburg	integrated a bus	threats, arrest
racism	4/9/1947	Moorman, Natalie		integrated a bus	
racism	4/9/1947	Murray, Pauli		integrated a bus	
racism	4/9/1947	Muste, Abraham Johannes		integrated a bus	
draft	1948	Peck, James		chained to a fence	
racism	1948	Randolph, Asa Philip		protest	
lynching	8/28/1955	Powell, Adam Clayton, Jr.		rally	
Vietnam War	1960s	Powell, Adam Clayton, Jr.		protest	

State/ Target of Act	Date	Name	Location	Act	Consequence
racism	1960	Wilkins, Roy		march	
racism	4/15/1960	Carmichael, Stokely		protest	
racism	1961	Aaron, Julian		Freedom Rider	
racism	1961	Blankenheim, Edward		Freedom Rider	
racism	1961	Burks, Catherine		Freedom Rider	
racism	1961	Carmichael, Stokely		Freedom Rider	
racism	1961	Castle, Jean		Freedom Rider	
racism	1961	Chatham, Price		Freedom Rider	
racism	1961	Coffin, William Sloan		Freedom Rider	
racism	1961	Collins, Lucretia		Freedom Rider	
racism	1961	Cox, Benjamin Elton		Freedom Rider	
racism	1961	Dennis, David		Freedom Rider	
racism	1961	Diederich, Paul		Freedom Rider	
racism	1961	Dolan, John Luther		Freedom Rider	
racism	1961	Fankhouser, David Brokaw		Freedom Rider	
racism	1961	Farmer, James Leonard		Freedom Rider	
racism	1961	Gordon, Albert		Freedom Rider	
racism	1961	Green, Stephen		Freedom Rider	
racism	1961	Herrman, Susan		Freedom Rider	
racism	1961	Lafayette, Bernard, Jr.		Freedom Rider	
racism	1961	Lane, Mark		Freedom Rider	
racism	1961	Lawson, James Morris		organized Freedom Ride	job threat, expelled
racism	1961	Leonard, Frederic		Freedom Rider	
racism	1961	Levine, Eugene		Freedom Rider	
racism	1961	McNichols, Steve		Freedom Rider	
racism	1961	Moody, John, Jr.		Freedom Rider	
racism	1961	Mulholland, Joan Trumpower		Freedom Rider	
racism	1961	Nelson, Frank		Freedom Rider	
racism	1961	Nixon, Sandra		Freedom Rider	
racism	1961	O'Neal, Helen		Freedom Rider	
racism	1961	Peck, James		Freedom Rider	beaten
racism	1961	Shilman, Kenneth		Freedom Rider	
racism	1961	Singleton, Helen		Freedom Rider	
racism	1961	Singleton, Robert		Freedom Rider	
racism	1961	Smith, George Bundy		Freedom Rider	
racism	1961	Smith, Jerome		Freedom Rider	
racism	1961	Steward, Richard		Freedom Rider	
racism	1961	Teale, Buron Lewis		Freedom Rider	
racism	1961	Walker, Wyatt Tee		Freedom Rider	
racism	1961	Wilbur, Susan		Freedom Rider	
racism	2/1961	Baker, Ella		organized Freedom Ride	

State/Target of Act	Date	Name	Location	Act	Consequence
racism	2/1961	Lee, Bernard Scott		Freedom Rider	
racism	2/1961	Moses, Robert Parris		Freedom Rider	
racism	2/1961	Nash, Diane		organized Freedom Ride	
Cuban invasion	5/1961	Dellinger, David T.		fast, vigil	jail, intimidation
Cuban invasion	5/1961	Steed, Bob		fast, vigil	jail, intimidation
racism	5/4/1961	Bigelow, Albert		Freedom Rider	beaten
racism	5/4/1961	Lewis, John Robert		Freedom Rider	beaten
racism	5/4/1961	Thomas, Henry		Freedom Rider	mob threat
racism	5/17/1961	Shuttlesworth, Fred Lee		Freedom Rider	arrested
racism	5/20/1961	Sieganthaler, John, Sr.		Freedom Rider	injured
racism	3/18/1963	Lewis, John Robert		protest	
racism	8/28/1963	Baez, Joan		demonstration	
racism	8/28/1963	Dylan, Bob		demonstration	
racism	8/28/1963	Randolph, Asa Philip		march	
racism	8/28/1963	Rustin, Bayard Taylor		demonstration	
nuclear power	11/1/1964	Abzug, Bella Savitsky		demonstration	
nuclear power	11/1/1964	Allen, Donna		march	
nuclear power	11/1/1964	Wilson, Dagmar		demonstration	
House Committee on Un-American Activities	12/4/1964	Allen, Donna		contempt of Congress	
House Committee on Un-American Activities	12/4/1964	Wilson, Dagmar		contempt of Congress	
Vietnam War	8/1965	Baez, Joan		picket	
Vietnam War	11/2/1965	Herz, Alice		self-immolation	
Vietnam War	11/2/1965	Morrison, Norman R.		self-immolation	
Vietnam War	1/1968	Rankin, Jeannette		march	
Vietnam War	3/22/1969	Begin, Robert T.		sabotage	
Vietnam War	3/22/1969	Dougherty, Michael R.		sabotage	
Vietnam War	3/22/1969	Malone, Joann		sabotage	
Vietnam War	3/22/1969	Melville, Arthur G.		sabotage	
Vietnam War	3/22/1969	Melville, Catherine		sabotage	
Vietnam War	3/22/1969	Meyer, Bernard		sabotage	
Vietnam War	3/22/1969	Moloney, Dennis J.		sabotage	
Vietnam War	3/22/1969	O'Rourke, Michael J.		sabotage	threat
Vietnam War	3/22/1969	Slaski, Michael		sabotage	
Vietnam War	4/12/1971	Rankin, Jeannette		march	
Vietnam War	6/13/1971	Ellsberg, Daniel		whistleblowing	arrest
marijuana ban	1975	Randall, Robert		marijuana use	arrest
nuclear power	5/6/1979	Fonda, Jane		rally	
nuclear power	5/6/1979	Mitchell, Joni		rally	
nuclear power	5/6/1979	Nader, Ralph		rally	
nuclear power	4/28/1980	Dellinger, David T.		blocked a heliport	arrest
nuclear power	4/28/1980	McReynolds, David		blocked a heliport	arrest

State/ Target of Act	Date	Name	Location	Act	Consequence
nuclear power	4/28/1980	Paley, Grace		blocked a heliport	arrest
nuclear power	4/28/1980	Spock, Benjamin		blocked a heliport	arrest
apartheid	11/24/1984	Berry, Mary Frances		unlawful entry	arrest, handcuffed
apartheid	11/24/1984	Conyers, John		unlawful entry	
apartheid	11/24/1984	Dellums, Ronald Verni		unlawful entry	
apartheid	11/24/1984	Fauntroy, Walter Edward		unlawful entry	arrest, handcuffed
apartheid	11/24/1984	Hayes, Charles Arthur		unlawful entry	
apartheid	11/24/1984	Lowery, Joseph Echols		unlawful entry	
apartheid	11/24/1984	Norton, Eleanor Holmes		unlawful entry	
apartheid	11/24/1984	Rangel, Charles Bernard		unlawful entry	
apartheid	11/24/1984	Robinson, Randall		unlawful entry	arrest, handcuffed
farm debt	9/1985	Field, Sally		protest	
farm debt	9/1985	Fonda, Jane		protest	
farm debt	9/1985	Lange, Jessica		protest	
farm debt	9/1985	Spacek, Sissy		protest	
alien refugee abuse	1986	Romagoza, Juan		alien rescue	
homelessness	10/7/1989	Snyder, Mitch		march, trespass	arrest
voter intimidation	10/16/1995	Farrakhan, Louis		march	
voter intimidation	10/16/1995	Parks, Rosa		march	
death penalty	1/17/1997	Bonowitz, Abraham J.		protest	intimidation
Kosovo bombing	6/8/1999	Legg, Sam		protest	arrest
campaign finance corruption	10/26/1999	Corner, Betsy		rally, protest banner	arrest
campaign finance corruption	10/26/1999	Crowe, Frances		rally, protest banner	arrest
campaign finance corruption	10/26/1999	Kehler, Randy		rally, protest banner	arrest
gay persecution	11/13/2000	Coffin, William Sloane, Jr.		blocked an entrance	arrest, handcuffed
gay persecution	11/13/2000	Taft, Fran		blocked an entrance	arrest, handcuffed
gay persecution	11/13/2000	White, Mel		blocked an entrance	arrest, handcuffed
marijuana ban	9/23/2002	McVay, Doug		handcuffed to a fence	arrest
marijuana ban	9/23/2002	Thomas, Charles		handcuffed to a fence	arrest
Iraq War	2004	Coffin, William Sloane, Jr.		protest	
genocide	7/13/2004	Cohen, Ben		blocked an entrance	arrest
genocide	7/13/2004	Edgar, Robert W. "Bob"		blocked an entrance	arrest
genocide, human rights abuse in Sudan	7/13/2004	Fauntroy, Walter Edward		blocked an entrance	arrest
genocide	7/13/2004	Greenfield, Jerry		blocked an entrance	arrest

State/ Target of Act	Date	Name	Location	Act	Consequence
genocide	7/13/2004	Gregory, Dick		blocked an entrance	arrest
genocide	7/13/2004	Hoeffel, Joseph M.		blocked an entrance	arrest
genocide	7/13/2004	Madison, Joe		blocked an entrance	arrest
genocide, human rights abuse in Sudan	7/13/2004	Rangel, Charles Bernard		blocked an entrance	arrest
human rights abuse in Sudan	7/13/2004	Robinson, Randall		felonious entry	arrest
genocide	7/13/2004	Rush, Bobby Lee		blocked an entrance	arrest
Iraq War	9/26/2005	Baez, Joan		protest	
Iraq War	9/26/2005	Bond, Julian		protest	
Iraq War	9/26/2005	Jackson, Jesse		protest	
Iraq War	9/26/2005	Sharpton, Al		protest	
Iraq War	9/26/2005	Sheehan, Cindy		tied to a fence	arrest
Iraq War	1/31/2006	Sheehan, Cindy		wore protest T-shirt	charged
genocide	4/28/2006	Lantos, Tom		protest	arrest
genocide	4/28/2006	Lee, Sheila		protest	arrest
genocide	4/28/2006	McGovern, James P.		protest	arrest
genocide	4/28/2006	Moran, Jim		protest	arrest
genocide	4/28/2006	Olver, John Walter		protest	arrest
genocide	5/1/2006	Clooney, George		protest	
genocide	5/1/2006	Rusesabagina, Paul		protest	
Iraq War	5/14/2006	Adams, Hunter Campbell		march	
Iraq War	5/14/2006	Sarandon, Susan		demonstration	
Iraq War	5/14/2006	Sheehan, Cindy		demonstration	
genocide	5/16/2006	Watt, Melvin Luther		protest	
Iraq War	7/4/2006	Jon-Paul, Chloe		rally	arrest
Iraq War	7/4/2006	Mallard, Geoffrey		rally	arrest
Guantánamo Prison	1/10/2007	Ki-moon, Ban		protest	
Guantánamo Prison	1/10/2007	Sheehan, Cindy		protest	
Guantánamo Prison	1/10/2007	Zewawai, Zohra		protest	
Guantánamo Prison	1/11/2007	Iqbal, Asif		protest	
Iraq War	1/27/2007	Ensler, Eve		protest	
Iraq War	1/27/2007	Fonda, Jane		protest	
Iraq War	1/27/2007	Glover, Danny		protest	
Iraq War	1/27/2007	Penn, Sean		protest	
Iraq War	1/27/2007	Robbins, Tim		protest	
Iraq War	1/27/2007	Sarandon, Susan		protest	
Iraq War	1/27/2007	Waters, Maxine		protest	
Iraq War	1/27/2007	Woolsey, Lynn		protest	
Iraq War	2/2007	Kelly, Kathy		sit-in	prison
Iraq War	7/23/2007	McGovern, Raymond		sit-in	arrest, fine

State/ Target of Act	Date	Name	Location	Act	Consequence
Iraq War	7/23/2007	Sheehan, Cindy		sit-in	arrest, fine
Iraq War	7/23/2007	Yearwood, Lennox, Jr.		sit-in	arrest, fine
Iraq War	9/10/2007	Sheehan, Cindy		shouted	arrest

West Virginia

slave recapture	1820	Brown, Randall	Charleston	slave rescue	
slave education ban	ca. 1820	Delany, Pati Peace	Charlestown	educated slaves, bought a textbook	arrest
slave education ban	ca. 1820	Peace, Graci	Charlestown	educated slaves	
Civil War	1863	Pratt, John Wesley	Tyler	refused to serve	forced into army
labor organization ban	6/20/1902	Hagerty, Thomas J.	Clarksburg	violated an injunction	arraigned
labor organization ban	6/20/1902	Jones, Mary "Mother"	Clarksburg	violated an injunction	arraigned
labor organization ban	2/13/1913	Boswell, Charles H.	Charleston	promoted solidarity	arrest
labor organization ban	2/13/1913	Jones, Mary "Mother"	Charleston	promoted solidarity	arrest
war bond sale	1917	Benner, Rhine Wiegner	Job	protest	fine, arrest
draft	1/22/1918	Keenan, L.H.	Elkins	protest	tarred, feathered
prison conditions	1919	Jones, Mary "Mother"	Kanawha County	public harangue	
labor exploitation	8/1/1921	Chambers, Ed	Matewan	abetted unionism	assassinated
labor exploitation	8/1/1921	Hatfield, Albert Sidney	Matewan	abetted unionism	assassinated
labor organization ban	8/1/1921	Jones, Mary "Mother"	Mingo County	conspiracy	
labor exploitation	9/2/1921	Blizzard, Bill	Matewan	strike, murder	jail
labor exploitation	9/2/1921	Keeney, Frank	Matewan	strike, murder	arrest
labor exploitation	9/2/1921	Mooney, Fred	Matewan	strike, murder	arrest
prison conditions	1923	Jones, Mary "Mother"	Logan County	protest	
flag saluting	1942	Barnett, Gathie	Charleston	disobeyed teacher	expelled
flag saluting	1942	Barnett, Marie	Charleston	disobeyed teacher	expelled

Wisconsin

slave recapture	1840	Porter, Eliza Emily Chappell	Green Bay	slave rescue	threatened
slave recapture	1840	Porter, Jeremiah	Green Bay	slave rescue	threatened
slave recapture	8/1843	Goodnow, Lyman	Prairieville	slave relay	
slave recapture	3/11/1854	Angove, James S.	Milwaukee	jailbreak	
slave recapture	3/11/1854	Bingham, George	Milwaukee	jailbreak	
slave recapture	3/11/1854	Booth, Sherman Miller	Milwaukee	jailbreak	
slave recapture	3/11/1854	Messinger, John A.	Milwaukee	jailbreak	
slave recapture	3/11/1854	Rycraft, John	Milwaukee	jailbreak	
slave recapture	8/4/1860	Pickett, Armine	Winnebago	jailbreak	
fishing ban	1901	Blackbird, John	Bad River	gill-netted	arrest
labor organization ban	1910	Jones, Mary "Mother"	Milwaukee	promoted solidarity	
World War I	1914	Fitzgerald, Mary Eleanor	Deerfield	aided draft evaders	

State/ Target of Act	Date	Name	Location	Act	Consequence
peyote ban	2/14/1914	Neck, Mitchell	Phlox	received peyote	arrest
draft	3/31/1918	Schimmel, E.A.	Ashland	protest	tarred, feathered
peyote ban	1960s	Prescott, Thomas	Wittenberg	peyote worship	
free speech ban	1972	Carlin, George	Milwaukee	obscenity	arrest
fishing ban	3/8/1974	Tribble, Frederick	Hayward	spear-fished	arrest
fishing ban	3/8/1974	Tribble, Michael	Hayward	spear-fished	arrest
alien refugee abuse	1983	Weakland, Rembert	Milwaukee	alien asylum, relay	
fishing ban	1/1993	Wilbur, Tony	Wolf River	fished	
animal rights	1/20/2006	Cho, Michelle Y.	Madison	public nudity	arrest

Wyoming

State/ Target of Act	Date	Name	Location	Act	Consequence
Japanese internment	7/21/1944	Omura, James M.	Heart Mountain	protest	charged
World War II	7/21/1944	Omura, James M.	Heart Mountain	conspiracy	arrest
nuclear power	1958	Lyttle, Bradford	Cheyenne	protest	
nuclear power	1958	Whitney, Norman Jehiel	Cheyenne	protest, trespass	
wilderness destruction	1979	Wolke, Howie	Grayback Ridge	sabotage	
wilderness destruction	1984	Wolke, Howie	Grayback Ridge	sabotage	
peyote ban	1994	Spotted Elk, Abraham	Ethete	peyote worship	

Documents

Documents

Association of the Sons of Liberty in New York (December 15, 1773)

The Sons of Liberty was a network of secret associations established throughout the American colonies in November 1765 to oppose the Stamp Act and subsequent actions by the British Parliament. Although the New York Sons promise in the following document to "use all lawful endeavours" to oppose British abuses, the association frequently resorted to extralegal measures as well. Notable also in this document is the series of resolutions regarding the treatment of colonials who oppose the Sons' cause.

The following association is signed by a great number of the principal gentlemen of the city, merchants, lawyers, and other inhabitants of all ranks, and it is still carried about the city to give an opportunity to those who have not yet signed, to unite with their fellow citizens, to testify their abhorrence to the diabolical project of enslaving America.

The Association of the Sons of Liberty of New York

It is essential to the freedom and security of a free people, that no taxes be imposed upon them but by their own consent, or their representatives. For "What property have they in that which another may, by right, take when he pleases to himself?" The former is the undoubted right of Englishmen, to secure which they expended millions and sacrificed the lives of thousands. And yet, to the astonishment of all the world, and the grief of America, the Commons of Great Britain, after the repeal of the memorable and detestable Stamp Act, reassumed the power of imposing taxes on the American colonies; and insisting on it as a necessary badge of parliamentary supremacy, passed a bill, in the seventh year of his present Majesty's reign, imposing duties on all glass, painters' colours, paper, and teas, that should, af-

ter the 20th of November, 1767, be "imported from Great Britain into any colony or plantation in America." This bill, after the concurrence of the Lords, obtained the royal assent. And thus they who, from time immemorial, have exercised the right of giving to, or withholding from the crown, their aids and subsidies, according to their own free will and pleasure, signified by their representatives in Parliament, do, by the Act in question, deny us, their brethren in America, the enjoyment of the same right. As this denial, and the execution of that Act, involves our slavery, and would sap the foundation of our freedom, whereby we should become slaves to our brethren and fellow subjects, born to no greater stock of freedom than the Americans—the merchants and inhabitants of this city, in conjunction with the merchants and inhabitants of the ancient American colonies, entered into an agreement to decline a part of their commerce with Great Britain, until the above mentioned Act should be totally repealed. This agreement operated so powerfully to the disadvantage of the manufacturers of England that many of them were unemployed. To appease their clamours, and to provide the subsistence for them, which the nonimportation had deprived them of, the Parliament, in 1770, repealed so much of the Revenue Act as imposed a duty on glass, painters' colours, and paper, and left the duty on tea, as a test of the parliamentary right to tax us. The merchants of the cities of New York and Philadelphia, having strictly adhered to the agreement, so far as it is related to the importation of articles subject to an American duty, have convinced the ministry, that some other measures must be adopted to execute parliamentary supremacy over this country, and to remove the distress brought on the East India Company, by the ill policy of that Act. Accordingly, to increase the temptation to the shippers of tea from England, an Act of Parliament passed the last session, which gives the whole duty on tea, the company were subject to pay, upon the importation of it into England, to the purchasers and exporters; and when the company have ten millions of pounds of tea in their warehouses exclusive of the quantity they may want to ship, they are allowed to export tea, discharged from the payment of that duty with which they were before chargeable. In hopes of aid in the execution of this project, by the influence of the owners of the American ships, application was made by the company to the captains of those ships to take the tea on freight; but they virtuously rejected it. Still determined on the scheme, they have chartered ships to bring the tea to this country, which may be hourly expected, to make an important trial of our virtue. If they succeed in the sale of that tea, we shall have no property that we can call our own, and then we may bid adieu to American liberty. Therefore, to prevent a calamity which, of all others, is the most to be dreaded—slavery and its terrible concomitants—we, the subscribers, being influenced from a regard to liberty, and disposed to use all lawful endeavours in our power, to defeat the pernicious project, and to transmit to our posterity those blessings of freedom which our ancestors have handed down to us; and to contribute to the support of the common liberties of America, which are in danger to be subverted, do, for those important purposes, agree to associate together, under the name and style of the sons of New York, and engage our honour to, and with each other faithfully to observe and perform the following resolutions, viz.

1st. Resolved, that whoever shall aid or abet, or in any manner assist, in the introduction of tea from any place whatsoever, into this colony, while it is subject, by a British Act of Parliament, to the payment of a duty, for the purpose of raising a revenue in America, he shall be deemed an enemy to the liberties of America.

2d. Resolved, that whoever shall be aiding, or assisting, in the landing, or carting of such tea, from any ship, or vessel, or shall hire any house, storehouse, or cellar or any place whatsoever, to deposit the tea, subject to a duty as aforesaid, he shall be deemed an enemy to the liberties of America.

3d. Resolved, that whoever shall sell, or buy, or in any manner contribute to the sale, or purchase of tea, subject to a duty as aforesaid, or

shall aid, or abet, in transporting such tea, by land or water, from this city, until the 7th George III, chap. 46, commonly called the Revenue Act, shall be totally and clearly repealed, he shall be deemed an enemy to the liberties of America.

4th. Resolved, that whether the duties on tea, imposed by this Act, be paid in Great Britain or in America, our liberties are equally affected.

5th. Resolved, that whoever shall transgress any of these resolutions, we will not deal with, or employ, or have any connection with him.

The Liberator: Inaugural Editorial, William Lloyd Garrison (January 1, 1831)

In the inaugural issue of the anti-abolitionist newspaper The Liberator, *Boston publisher William Lloyd Garrison set an ardent tone for his publication and declared an uncompromising campaign against slavery. In the consequences-be-damned spirit of civil disobedience, he defends the "precipitancy of my measures" and swears ever to "oppose and thwart, with heart and hand" the brutality of human oppression.*

To the Public

In the month of August, I issued proposals for publishing "THE LIBERATOR" in Washington city; but the enterprise, though hailed in different sections of the country, was palsied by public indifference. Since that time, the removal of the *Genius of Universal Emancipation* [Benjamin Lundy's antislavery newspaper] to the Seat of Government has rendered less imperious the establishment of a similar periodical in that quarter.

During my recent tour for the purpose of exciting the minds of the people by a series of discourses on the subject of slavery, every place that I visited gave fresh evidence of the fact, that a greater revolution in public sentiment was to be effected in the free States—*and particularly in New-England*—than at the south. I found contempt more bitter, opposition more active, detraction more relentless, prejudice more stubborn, and apathy more frozen, than among slave owners themselves. Of course, there were individual exceptions to the contrary. This state of things afflicted, but did not dishearten me. I determined, at every hazard, to lift up the standard of emancipation in the eyes of the nation, *within sight of Bunker Hill and in the birth place of liberty.* That standard is now unfurled; and long may it float, unhurt by the spoliations of time or the missiles of a desperate foe—yea, till every chain be broken, and every bondman set free! Let southern oppressors tremble—let their secret abettors tremble—let their northern apologists tremble—let all the enemies of the persecuted blacks tremble.

I deem the publication of my original Prospectus unnecessary, as it has obtained a wide circulation. The principles therein inculcated will be steadily pursued in this paper, excepting that I shall not array myself as the political partisan of any man. In defending the great cause of human rights, I wish to derive the assistance of all religions and of all parties.

Assenting to the "self-evident truth" maintained in the American Declaration of Independence, "that all men are created equal, and endowed by their Creator with certain inalienable rights—among which are life, liberty and the pursuit of happiness," I shall strenuously contend for the immediate enfranchisement of our slave population. In Park-street Church, on the Fourth of July, 1829, in an address on slavery, I unreflectingly assented to the popular but pernicious doctrine of gradual abolition. I seize this opportunity to make a full and unequivocal recantation, and thus publicly to ask pardon of my God, of my country, and of my brethren the poor slaves, for having uttered a sentiment so full of timidity, injustice and absurdity. A similar recantation, from my pen, was published in the *Genius of Universal Emancipation* at Baltimore, in September, 1829. My conscience in now satisfied.

I am aware, that many object to the severity of my language; but is there not cause for severity? I *will* be as harsh as truth, and as uncompromising as justice. On this subject, I do not wish to think, or speak, or write, with moderation. No! no! Tell a man whose house is on fire, to give a moderate alarm; tell him to moderately rescue his wife from the hand of the ravisher; tell the mother to gradually extricate her babe from the fire into which it has fallen;—but urge me not to use moderation in a cause like the present. I am in earnest—I will not equivocate—I will not excuse—I will not retreat a single inch—AND I WILL BE HEARD. The apathy of the people is

enough to make every statue leap from its pedestal, and to hasten the resurrection of the dead.

It is pretended, that I am retarding the cause of emancipation by the coarseness of my invective, and the precipitancy of my measures. The *charge is not true.* On this question my influence—humble as it is—is felt at this moment to a considerable extent, and shall be felt in coming years—not perniciously, but beneficially—not as a curse, but as a blessing; and posterity will bear testimony that I was right. I desire to thank God, that he enables me to disregard "the fear of man which bringeth a snare," and to speak his truth in its simplicity and power. And here I close with this fresh dedication:

> Oppression! I have seen thee, face to face,
> And met thy cruel eye and cloudy brow;
> But thy soul-withering glance I fear not
>   now—
> For dread to prouder feelings doth give
>   place
> Of deep abhorrence! Scorning the disgrace
> Of slavish knees that at thy footstool bow,
> I also kneel—but with far other vow
> Do hail thee and thy hord of hirelings
>   base:—
> I swear, while life-blood warms my throb-
>   bing veins,
> Still to oppose and thwart, with heart and
>   hand,
> Thy brutalising sway—till Afric's chains
> Are burst, and Freedom rules the rescued
>   land,—
> Trampling Oppression and his iron rod:
> *Such is the vow I take*—SO HELP ME GOD!

Source: The Liberator, 1:1 (January 1, 1831).

On Civil Disobedience (1849), Henry David Thoreau

Henry David Thoreau's essay "Civil Disobedience" is generally regarded as the classic exposition on the subject. He wrote the piece in disgust after spending a night in jail for refusing to pay his poll tax as a protest against slavery. (His aunt bailed him out, over his objections.) The essay was first published in 1849 under the title "Resistance to Civil Government" in a magazine called Aesthetic Papers. *It was reprinted in a posthumous collection in 1866 as "Civil Disobedience," the title by which the essay is commonly known.*

I heartily accept the motto, "That government is best which governs least"; and I should like to see it acted up to more rapidly and systematically. Carried out, it finally amounts to this, which also I believe—"That government is best which governs not at all"; and when men are prepared for it, that will be the kind of government which they will have. Government is at best but an expedient; but most governments are usually, and all governments are sometimes, inexpedient. The objections which have been brought against a standing army, and they are many and weighty, and deserve to prevail, may also at last be brought against a standing government. The standing army is only an arm of the standing government. The government itself, which is only the mode which the people have chosen to execute their will, is equally liable to be abused and perverted before the people can act through it. Witness the present Mexican war, the work of comparatively a few individuals using the standing government as their tool; for in the outset, the people would not have consented to this measure.

This American government—what is it but a tradition, though a recent one, endeavoring to transmit itself unimpaired to posterity, but each instant losing some of its integrity? It has not the vitality and force of a single living man; for a single man can bend it to his will. It is a sort of wooden gun to the people themselves. But it is not the less necessary for this; for the people must have some complicated machinery or other, and hear its din, to satisfy that idea of government which they have. Governments show thus how successfully men can be imposed upon, even impose on themselves, for their own advantage. It is excellent, we must all allow. Yet this government never of itself furthered any enterprise, but by the alacrity with which it got out of its way. *It* does not keep the country free. *It* does not settle the West. *It* does not educate. The character inherent in the American people has done all that has been accomplished; and it would have done somewhat more, if the government had not sometimes got in its way. For government is an expedient, by which men would fain succeed in letting one another alone; and, as has been said, when it is most expedient, the governed are most let alone by it. Trade and commerce, if they were not made of India rubber, would never manage to bounce over obstacles which legislators are continually putting in their way; and if one were to judge these men wholly by the effects of their actions and not partly by their intentions, they would deserve to be classed and punished with those mischievous persons who put obstructions on the railroads.

But, to speak practically and as a citizen, unlike those who call themselves no-government men, I ask for, not at once no government, but at once a better government. Let every man make known what kind of government would command his respect, and that will be one step toward obtaining it.

After all, the practical reason why, when the power is once in the hands of the people, a majority are permitted, and for a long period continue, to rule is not because they are most likely to be in the right, nor because this seems fairest to the minority, but because they are physically the strongest. But a government in which the majority rule in all cases can not be based on justice, even as far as men understand it. Can there not be a government in which the majorities do not virtually decide right and wrong, but conscience?—in which majorities decide only those questions to which the rule of expediency is applicable? Must the citizen ever for a moment, or in the least degree, resign his conscience to the legislator? Why has every man a conscience then? I think that we should be men first, and subjects afterward. It is not desirable to cultivate a respect for the law, so much as for the right. The only obligation which I have a right to assume is to do at any time what I think right. It is truly enough said that a corporation has no conscience; but a corporation of conscientious men is a corporation *with* a conscience. Law never made men a whit more just; and, by means of their respect for it, even the well-disposed are daily made the agents on injustice. A common and natural result of an undue respect for the law is, that you may see a file of soldiers, colonel, captain, corporal, privates, powder-monkeys, and all, marching in admirable order over hill and dale to the wars, against their wills, ay, against their common sense and consciences, which makes it very steep marching indeed, and produces a palpitation of the heart. They have no doubt that it is a damnable business in which they are concerned; they are all peaceably inclined. Now, what are they? Men at all? or small movable forts and magazines, at the service of some unscrupulous man in power? Visit the Navy Yard, and behold a marine, such a man as an American government can make, or such as it can make a man with its black arts—a mere shadow and reminiscence of humanity, a man laid out alive and standing, and already, as one may say, buried under arms with funeral accompaniment, though it may be,

"Not a drum was heard, not a funeral note,
As his corse to the rampart we hurried;
Not a soldier discharged his farewell shot
O'er the grave where out hero was buried."

The mass of men serve the state thus, not as men mainly, but as machines, with their bodies. They are the standing army, and the militia, jailers, constables, *posse comitatus*, etc. In most cases there is no free exercise whatever of the judgement or of the moral sense; but they put themselves on a level with wood and earth and stones; and wooden men can perhaps be manufactured that will serve the purpose as well. Such command no more respect than men of straw or a lump of dirt. They have the same sort of worth only as horses and dogs. Yet such as these even are commonly esteemed good citizens. Others—as most legislators, politicians, lawyers, ministers, and office-holders—serve the state chiefly with their heads; and, as they rarely make any moral distinctions, they are as likely to serve the devil, without *intending* it, as God. A very few—as heroes, patriots, martyrs, reformers in the great sense, and *men*—serve the state with their consciences also, and so necessarily resist it for the most part; and they are commonly treated as enemies by it. A wise man will only be useful as a man, and will not submit to be "clay," and "stop a hole to keep the wind away," but leave that office to his dust at least:

"I am too high born to be propertied,
To be a second at control,
Or useful serving-man and instrument
To any sovereign state throughout the
    world."

He who gives himself entirely to his fellow men appears to them useless and selfish; but he who gives himself partially to them is pronounced a benefactor and philanthropist.

How does it become a man to behave toward the American government today? I answer, that

he cannot without disgrace be associated with it. I cannot for an instant recognize that political organization as *my* government which is the *slave's* government also.

All men recognize the right of revolution; that is, the right to refuse allegiance to, and to resist, the government, when its tyranny or its inefficiency are great and unendurable. But almost all say that such is not the case now. But such was the case, they think, in the Revolution of '75. If one were to tell me that this was a bad government because it taxed certain foreign commodities brought to its ports, it is most probable that I should not make an ado about it, for I can do without them. All machines have their friction; and possibly this does enough good to counter-balance the evil. At any rate, it is a great evil to make a stir about it. But when the friction comes to have its machine, and oppression and robbery are organized, I say, let us not have such a machine any longer. In other words, when a sixth of the population of a nation which has undertaken to be the refuge of liberty are slaves, and a whole country is unjustly overrun and conquered by a foreign army, and subjected to military law, I think that it is not too soon for honest men to rebel and revolutionize. What makes this duty the more urgent is that fact that the country so overrun is not our own, but ours is the invading army.

Paley, a common authority with many on moral questions, in his chapter on the "Duty of Submission to Civil Government," resolves all civil obligation into expediency; and he proceeds to say that "so long as the interest of the whole society requires it, that is, so long as the established government cannot be resisted or changed without public inconvenience, it is the will of God . . . that the established government be obeyed—and no longer. This principle being admitted, the justice of every particular case of resistance is reduced to a computation of the quantity of the danger and grievance on the one side, and of the probability and expense of redressing it on the other." Of this, he says, every man shall judge for himself. But Paley appears never to have contemplated those cases to which the rule of expediency does not apply, in which a people, as well as an individual, must do justice, cost what it may. If I have unjustly wrested a plank from a drowning man, I must restore it to him though I drown myself. This, according to Paley, would be inconvenient. But he that would save his life, in such a case, shall lose it. This people must cease to hold slaves, and to make war on Mexico, though it cost them their existence as a people.

In their practice, numerous nations agree with Paley; but does anyone think that Massachusetts does exactly what is right at the present crisis?

> "A drab of stat,
> a cloth-o'-silver slut,
> To have her train borne up,
> and her soul trail in the dirt."

Practically speaking, the opponents to a reform in Massachusetts are not a hundred thousand politicians at the South, but a hundred thousand merchants and farmers here, who are more interested in commerce and agriculture than they are in humanity, and are not prepared to do justice to the slave and to Mexico, *cost what it may.* I quarrel not with far-off foes, but with those who, near at home, co-operate with, and do the bidding of, those far away, and without whom the latter would be harmless. We are accustomed to say, that the mass of men are unprepared; but improvement is slow, because the few are not as materially wiser or better than the many. It is not so important that many should be good as you, as that there be some absolute goodness somewhere; for that will leaven the whole lump. There are thousands who are *in opinion* opposed to slavery and to the war, who yet in effect do nothing to put an end to them; who, esteeming themselves children of Washington and Franklin, sit down with their hands in their pockets, and say that they know not what to do, and do nothing; who even postpone the question of freedom to the question of free trade, and quietly read the prices-current along with the latest advices from Mexico, after dinner, and, it may be, fall asleep over them both. What is the price-current of an honest man and patriot today? They hesitate, and they regret, and sometimes they petition; but they do nothing in earnest and with effect. They will wait, well disposed, for other to remedy the evil, that they may no longer have it to regret. At most, they give up only a cheap vote, and a feeble countenance and Godspeed, to the right, as it goes by

them. There are nine hundred and ninety-nine patrons of virtue to one virtuous man. But it is easier to deal with the real possessor of a thing than with the temporary guardian of it.

All voting is a sort of gaming, like checkers or backgammon, with a slight moral tinge to it, a playing with right and wrong, with moral questions; and betting naturally accompanies it. The character of the voters is not staked. I cast my vote, perchance, as I think right; but I am not vitally concerned that that right should prevail. I am willing to leave it to the majority. Its obligation, therefore, never exceeds that of expediency. Even *voting for the right* is *doing* nothing for it. It is only expressing to men feebly your desire that it should prevail. A wise man will not leave the right to the mercy of chance, nor wish it to prevail through the power of the majority. There is but little virtue in the action of masses of men. When the majority shall at length vote for the abolition of slavery, it will be because they are indifferent to slavery, or because there is but little slavery left to be abolished by their vote. *They* will then be the only slaves. Only *his* vote can hasten the abolition of slavery who asserts his own freedom by his vote.

I hear of a convention to be held at Baltimore, or elsewhere, for the selection of a candidate for the Presidency, made up chiefly of editors, and men who are politicians by profession; but I think, what is it to any independent, intelligent, and respectable man what decision they may come to? Shall we not have the advantage of this wisdom and honesty, nevertheless? Can we not count upon some independent votes? Are there not many individuals in the country who do not attend conventions? But no: I find that the respectable man, so called, has immediately drifted from his position, and despairs of his country, when his country has more reasons to despair of him. He forthwith adopts one of the candidates thus selected as the only *available* one, thus proving that he is himself *available* for any purposes of the demagogue. His vote is of no more worth than that of any unprincipled foreigner or hireling native, who may have been bought. O for a man who is a man, and, as my neighbor says, has a bone in his back which you cannot pass your hand through! Our statistics are at fault: the population has been returned too large. How many *men* are there to a square thousand miles in the country? Hardly one. Does not America offer any inducement for men to settle here? The American has dwindled into an Odd Fellow—one who may be known by the development of his organ of gregariousness, and a manifest lack of intellect and cheerful self-reliance; whose first and chief concern, on coming into the world, is to see that the almshouses are in good repair; and, before yet he has lawfully donned the virile garb, to collect a fund to the support of the widows and orphans that may be; who, in short, ventures to live only by the aid of the Mutual Insurance company, which has promised to bury him decently.

It is not a man's duty, as a matter of course, to devote himself to the eradication of any, even to most enormous wrong; he may still properly have other concerns to engage him; but it is his duty, at least, to wash his hands of it, and, if he gives it no thought longer, not to give it practically his support. If I devote myself to other pursuits and contemplations, I must first see, at least, that I do not pursue them sitting upon another man's shoulders. I must get off him first, that he may pursue his contemplations too. See what gross inconsistency is tolerated. I have heard some of my townsmen say, "I should like to have them order me out to help put down an insurrection of the slaves, or to march to Mexico—see if I would go"; and yet these very men have each, directly by their allegiance, and so indirectly, at least, by their money, furnished a substitute. The soldier is applauded who refuses to serve in an unjust war by those who do not refuse to sustain the unjust government which makes the war; is applauded by those whose own act and authority he disregards and sets at naught; as if the state were penitent to that degree that it hired one to scourge it while it sinned, but not to that degree that it left off sinning for a moment. Thus, under the name of Order and Civil Government, we are all made at last to pay homage to and support our own meanness. After the first blush of sin comes its indifference; and from immoral it becomes, as it were, unmoral, and not quite unnecessary to that life which we have made.

The broadest and most prevalent error requires the most disinterested virtue to sustain it. The slight reproach to which the virtue of patriotism is commonly liable, the noble are most likely to incur. Those who, while they disap-

prove of the character and measures of a government, yield to it their allegiance and support are undoubtedly its most conscientious supporters, and so frequently the most serious obstacles to reform. Some are petitioning the State to dissolve the Union, to disregard the requisitions of the President. Why do they not dissolve it themselves—the union between themselves and the State—and refuse to pay their quota into its treasury? Do not they stand in same relation to the State that the State does to the Union? And have not the same reasons prevented the State from resisting the Union which have prevented them from resisting the State?

How can a man be satisfied to entertain an opinion merely, and enjoy *it?* Is there any enjoyment in it, if his opinion is that he is aggrieved? If you are cheated out of a single dollar by your neighbor, you do not rest satisfied with knowing you are cheated, or with saying that you are cheated, or even with petitioning him to pay you your due; but you take effectual steps at once to obtain the full amount, and see to it that you are never cheated again. Action from principle, the perception and the performance of right, changes things and relations; it is essentially revolutionary, and does not consist wholly with anything which was. It not only divided States and churches, it divides families; ay, it divides the *individual,* separating the diabolical in him from the divine.

Unjust laws exist: shall we be content to obey them, or shall we endeavor to amend them, and obey them until we have succeeded, or shall we transgress them at once? Men, generally, under such a government as this, think that they ought to wait until they have persuaded the majority to alter them. They think that, if they should resist, the remedy would be worse than the evil. But it is the fault of the government itself that the remedy is worse than the evil. *It* makes it worse. Why is it not more apt to anticipate and provide for reform? Why does it not cherish its wise minority? Why does it cry and resist before it is hurt? Why does it not encourage its citizens to put out its faults, and *do* better than it would have them? Why does it always crucify Christ and excommunicate Copernicus and Luther, and pronounce Washington and Franklin rebels?

One would think, that a deliberate and practical denial of its authority was the only offense never contemplated by its government; else, why has it not assigned its definite, its suitable and proportionate, penalty? If a man who has no property refuses but once to earn nine shillings for the State, he is put in prison for a period unlimited by any law that I know, and determined only by the discretion of those who put him there; but if he should steal ninety times nine shillings from the State, he is soon permitted to go at large again.

If the injustice is part of the necessary friction of the machine of government, let it go, let it go: perchance it will wear smooth—certainly the machine will wear out. If the injustice has a spring, or a pulley, or a rope, or a crank, exclusively for itself, then perhaps you may consider whether the remedy will not be worse than the evil; but if it is of such a nature that it requires you to be the agent of injustice to another, then I say, break the law. Let your life be a counter-friction to stop the machine. What I have to do is to see, at any rate, that I do not lend myself to the wrong which I condemn.

As for adopting the ways of the State has provided for remedying the evil, I know not of such ways. They take too much time, and a man's life will be gone. I have other affairs to attend to. I came into this world, not chiefly to make this a good place to live in, but to live in it, be it good or bad. A man has not everything to do, but something; and because he cannot do *everything*, it is not necessary that he should be doing *something* wrong. It is not my business to be petitioning the Governor or the Legislature any more than it is theirs to petition me; and if they should not hear my petition, what should I do then? But in this case the State has provided no way: its very Constitution is the evil. This may seem to be harsh and stubborn and unconciliatory; but it is to treat with the utmost kindness and consideration the only spirit that can appreciate or deserves it. So is all change for the better, like birth and death, which convulse the body.

I do not hesitate to say, that those who call themselves Abolitionists should at once effectually withdraw their support, both in person and property, from the government of Massachusetts, and not wait till they constitute a majority of one, before they suffer the right to prevail through them. I think that it is enough if they have God on their side, without waiting for that other one.

Moreover, any man more right than his neighbors constitutes a majority of one already.

I meet this American government, or its representative, the State government, directly, and face to face, once a year—no more—in the person of its tax-gatherer; this is the only mode in which a man situated as I am necessarily meets it; and it then says distinctly, Recognize me; and the simplest, the most effectual, and, in the present posture of affairs, the indispensablest mode of treating with it on this head, of expressing your little satisfaction with and love for it, is to deny it then. My civil neighbor, the tax-gatherer, is the very man I have to deal with—for it is, after all, with men and not with parchment that I quarrel—and he has voluntarily chosen to be an agent of the government. How shall he ever know well that he is and does as an officer of the government, or as a man, until he is obliged to consider whether he will treat me, his neighbor, for whom he has respect, as a neighbor and well-disposed man, or as a maniac and disturber of the peace, and see if he can get over this obstruction to his neighborliness without a ruder and more impetuous thought or speech corresponding with his action. I know this well, that if one thousand, if one hundred, if ten men whom I could name—if ten *honest* men only—ay, if *one* HONEST man, in this State of Massachusetts, *ceasing to hold slaves,* were actually to withdraw from this co-partnership, and be locked up in the county jail therefor, it would be the abolition of slavery in America. For it matters not how small the beginning may seem to be: what is once well done is done forever. But we love better to talk about it: that we say is our mission. Reform keeps many scores of newspapers in its service, but not one man. If my esteemed neighbor, the State's ambassador, who will devote his days to the settlement of the question of human rights in the Council Chamber, instead of being threatened with the prisons of Carolina, were to sit down the prisoner of Massachusetts, that State which is so anxious to foist the sin of slavery upon her sister—though at present she can discover only an act of inhospitality to be the ground of a quarrel with her—the Legislature would not wholly waive the subject of the following winter.

Under a government which imprisons unjustly, the true place for a just man is also a prison. The proper place today, the only place which Massachusetts has provided for her freer and less despondent spirits, is in her prisons, to be put out and locked out of the State by her own act, as they have already put themselves out by their principles. It is there that the fugitive slave, and the Mexican prisoner on parole, and the Indian come to plead the wrongs of his race should find them; on that separate but more free and honorable ground, where the State places those who are not *with* her, but *against* her—the only house in a slave State in which a free man can abide with honor. If any think that their influence would be lost there, and their voices no longer afflict the ear of the State, that they would not be as an enemy within its walls, they do not know by how much truth is stronger than error, nor how much more eloquently and effectively he can combat injustice who has experienced a little in his own person. Cast your whole vote, not a strip of paper merely, but your whole influence. A minority is powerless while it conforms to the majority; it is not even a minority then; but it is irresistible when it clogs by its whole weight. If the alternative is to keep all just men in prison, or give up war and slavery, the State will not hesitate which to choose. If a thousand men were not to pay their tax bills this year, that would not be a violent and bloody measure, as it would be to pay them, and enable the State to commit violence and shed innocent blood. This is, in fact, the definition of a peaceable revolution, if any such is possible. If the tax-gatherer, or any other public officer, asks me, as one has done, "But what shall I do?" my answer is, "If you really wish to do anything, resign your office." When the subject has refused allegiance, and the officer has resigned from office, then the revolution is accomplished. But even suppose blood should flow. Is there not a sort of blood shed when the conscience is wounded? Through this wound a man's real manhood and immortality flow out, and he bleeds to an everlasting death. I see this blood flowing now.

I have contemplated the imprisonment of the offender, rather than the seizure of his goods—though both will serve the same purpose—because they who assert the purest right, and consequently are most dangerous to a corrupt State, commonly have not spent much time in accumulating property. To such the State renders comparatively small service, and a slight tax is wont to appear exorbitant, particularly if they are obliged to earn it by special labor with their hands. If there were one who lived wholly without the use of money, the State itself would hesitate to demand it of him. But the rich man—not to make any invidious comparison—is always sold to the institution which makes him rich. Absolutely speaking, the more money, the less virtue; for money comes between a man and his objects, and obtains them for him; it was certainly no great virtue to obtain it. It puts to rest many questions which he would otherwise be taxed to answer; while the only new question which it puts is the hard but superfluous one, how to spend it. Thus his moral ground is taken from under his feet. The opportunities of living are diminished in proportion as that are called the "means" are increased. The best thing a man can do for his culture when he is rich is to endeavor to carry out those schemes which he entertained when he was poor. Christ answered the Herodians according to their condition. "Show me the tribute-money," said he—and one took a penny out of his pocket—if you use money which has the image of Caesar on it, and which he has made current and valuable, that is, *if you are men of the State,* and gladly enjoy the advantages of Caesar's government, then pay him back some of his own when he demands it. "Render therefore to Caesar that which is Caesar's and to God those things which are God's"—leaving them no wiser than before as to which was which; for they did not wish to know.

When I converse with the freest of my neighbors, I perceive that, whatever they may say about the magnitude and seriousness of the question, and their regard for the public tranquillity, the long and the short of the matter is, that they cannot spare the protection of the existing government, and they dread the consequences to their property and families of disobedience to it. For my own part, I should not like to think that I ever rely on the protection of the State. But, if I deny the authority of the State when it presents its tax bill, it will soon take and waste all my property, and so harass me and my children without end. This is hard. This makes it impossible for a man to live honestly, and at the same time comfortably, in outward respects. It will not be worth the while to accumulate property; that would be sure to go again. You must hire or squat somewhere, and raise but a small crop, and eat that soon. You must live within yourself, and depend upon yourself always tucked up and ready for a start, and not have many affairs. A man may grow rich in Turkey even, if he will be in all respects a good subject of the Turkish government. Confucius said: "If a state is governed by the principles of reason, poverty and misery are subjects of shame; if a state is not governed by the principles of reason, riches and honors are subjects of shame." No: until I want the protection of Massachusetts to be extended to me in some distant Southern port, where my liberty is endangered, or until I am bent solely on building up an estate at home by peaceful enterprise, I can afford to refuse allegiance to Massachusetts, and her right to my property and life. It costs me less in every sense to incur the penalty of disobedience to the State than it would to obey. I should feel as if I were worth less in that case.

Some years ago, the State met me in behalf of the Church, and commanded me to pay a certain sum toward the support of a clergyman whose preaching my father attended, but never I myself. "Pay," it said, "or be locked up in the jail." I declined to pay. But, unfortunately, another man saw fit to pay it. I did not see why the schoolmaster should be taxed to support the priest, and not the priest the schoolmaster; for I was not the State's schoolmaster, but I supported myself by voluntary subscription. I did not see why the lyceum should not present its tax bill, and have the State to back its demand, as well as the Church. However, at the request of the selectmen, I condescended to make some such statement as this in writing: "Know all men by these presents, that I, Henry Thoreau, do not wish to be regarded as a member of any incorporated society which I have not joined." This I gave to the town clerk; and he has it. The State, having thus learned that I did not wish to be regarded as a member of that church, has never made a like demand on me since; though it said that it must adhere to its original presumption that time. If I had known how to name them, I should then have signed off in detail from all the societies which I never signed on to; but I did not know where to find such a complete list.

I have paid no poll tax for six years. I was put into a jail once on this account, for one night; and, as I stood considering the walls of solid stone, two or three feet thick, the door of wood and iron, a foot thick, and the iron grating which strained the light, I could not help being struck with the foolishness of that institution which treated me as if I were mere flesh and blood and bones, to be locked up. I wondered that it should have concluded at length that this was the best use it could put me to, and had never thought to avail itself of my services in some way. I saw that, if there was a wall of stone between me and my townsmen, there was a still more difficult one to climb or break through before they could get to be as free as I was. I did not for a moment feel confined, and the walls seemed a great waste of stone and mortar. I felt as if I alone of all my townsmen had paid my tax. They plainly did not know how to treat me, but behaved like persons who are underbred. In every threat and in every compliment there was a blunder; for they thought that my chief desire was to stand the other side of that stone wall. I could not but smile to see how industriously they locked the door on my meditations, which followed them out again without let or hindrance, and *they* were really all that was dangerous. As they could not reach me, they had resolved to punish my body; just as boys, if they cannot come at some person against whom they have a spite, will abuse his dog. I saw that the State was half-witted, that it was timid as a lone woman with her silver spoons, and that it did not know its friends from its foes, and I lost all my remaining respect for it, and pitied it.

Thus the state never intentionally confronts a man's sense, intellectual or moral, but only his body, his senses. It is not armed with superior wit or honesty, but with superior physical strength. I was not born to be forced. I will breathe after my own fashion. Let us see who is the strongest. What force has a multitude? They only can force me who obey a higher law than I. They force me to become like themselves. I do not hear of *men* being *forced* to live this way or that by masses of men. What sort of life were that to live? When I meet a government which says to me, "Your money or your life," why should I be in haste to give it my money? It may be in a great strait, and not know what to do: I cannot help that. It must help itself; do as I do. It is not worth the while to snivel about it. I am not responsible for the successful working of the machinery of society. I am not the son of the engineer. I perceive that, when an acorn and a chestnut fall side by side, the one does not remain inert to make way for the other, but both obey their own laws, and spring and grow and flourish as best they can, till one, perchance, overshadows and destroys the other. If a plant cannot live according to nature, it dies; and so a man.

The night in prison was novel and interesting enough. The prisoners in their shirtsleeves were enjoying a chat and the evening air in the doorway, when I entered. But the jailer said, "Come, boys, it is time to lock up"; and so they dispersed, and I heard the sound of their steps returning into the hollow apartments. My room-mate was introduced to me by the jailer as "a first-rate fellow and clever man." When the door was locked, he showed me where to hang my hat, and how he managed matters there. The rooms were whitewashed once a month; and this one, at least, was the whitest, most simply furnished, and probably neatest apartment in town. He naturally wanted to know where I came from, and what brought me there; and, when I had told him, I asked him in my turn how he came there, presuming him to be an honest man, of course; and as the world goes, I believe he was. "Why," said he, "they accuse me of burning a barn; but I never did it." As near as I could discover, he had probably gone to bed in a barn when drunk, and smoked his pipe there; and so a barn was burnt. He had the reputation of being a clever man, had been there some three months waiting for his trial to come on, and would have to wait as much longer; but he was quite domesticated and contented, since he got his board for nothing, and thought that he was well treated.

He occupied one window, and I the other; and I saw that if one stayed there long, his principal business would be to look out the window. I had soon read all the tracts that were left there, and examined where former prisoners had broken out, and where a grate had been sawed off, and heard the history of the various occupants of that room; for I found that even there there was a history and a gossip which never circulated beyond the walls of the jail. Probably this is the only house in the town where verses are composed, which are afterward printed in a circular form, but not published. I was shown quite

a long list of young men who had been detected in an attempt to escape, who avenged themselves by singing them.

I pumped my fellow-prisoner as dry as I could, for fear I should never see him again; but at length he showed me which was my bed, and left me to blow out the lamp.

It was like travelling into a far country, such as I had never expected to behold, to lie there for one night. It seemed to me that I never had heard the town clock strike before, nor the evening sounds of the village; for we slept with the windows open, which were inside the grating. It was to see my native village in the light of the Middle Ages, and our Concord was turned into a Rhine stream, and visions of knights and castles passed before me. They were the voices of old burghers that I heard in the streets. I was an involuntary spectator and auditor of whatever was done and said in the kitchen of the adjacent village inn—a wholly new and rare experience to me. It was a closer view of my native town. I was fairly inside of it. I never had seen its institutions before. This is one of its peculiar institutions; for it is a shire town. I began to comprehend what its inhabitants were about.

In the morning, our breakfasts were put through the hole in the door, in small oblong-square tin pans, made to fit, and holding a pint of chocolate, with brown bread, and an iron spoon. When they called for the vessels again, I was green enough to return what bread I had left, but my comrade seized it, and said that I should lay that up for lunch or dinner. Soon after he was let out to work at haying in a neighboring field, whither he went every day, and would not be back till noon; so he bade me good day, saying that he doubted if he should see me again.

When I came out of prison—for some one interfered, and paid that tax—I did not perceive that great changes had taken place on the common, such as he observed who went in a youth and emerged a gray-headed man; and yet a change had come to my eyes come over the scene—the town, and State, and country, greater than any that mere time could effect. I saw yet more distinctly the State in which I lived. I saw to what extent the people among whom I lived could be trusted as good neighbors and friends; that their friendship was for summer weather only; that they did not greatly propose to do right; that they were a distinct race from me by their prejudices and superstitions, as the Chinamen and Malays are; that in their sacrifices to humanity they ran no risks, not even to their property; that after all they were not so noble but they treated the thief as he had treated them, and hoped, by a certain outward observance and a few prayers, and by walking in a particular straight though useless path from time to time, to save their souls. This may be to judge my neighbors harshly; for I believe that many of them are not aware that they have such an institution as the jail in their village.

It was formerly the custom in our village, when a poor debtor came out of jail, for his acquaintances to salute him, looking through their fingers, which were crossed to represent the jail window, "How do ye do?" My neighbors did not thus salute me, but first looked at me, and then at one another, as if I had returned from a long journey. I was put into jail as I was going to the shoemaker's to get a shoe which was mended. When I was let out the next morning, I proceeded to finish my errand, and, having put on my mended shoe, joined a huckleberry party, who were impatient to put themselves under my conduct; and in half an hour—for the horse was soon tackled—was in the midst of a huckleberry field, on one of our highest hills, two miles off, and then the State was nowhere to be seen.

This is the whole history of "My Prisons."

I have never declined paying the highway tax, because I am as desirous of being a good neighbor as I am of being a bad subject; and as for supporting schools, I am doing my part to educate my fellow countrymen now. It is for no particular item in the tax bill that I refuse to pay it. I simply wish to refuse allegiance to the State, to withdraw and stand aloof from it effectually. I do not care to trace the course of my dollar, if I could, till it buys a man or a musket to shoot one with—the dollar is innocent—but I am concerned to trace the effects of my allegiance. In fact, I quietly declare war with the State, after my fashion, though I will still make use and get what advantages of her I can, as is usual in such cases.

If others pay the tax which is demanded of me, from a sympathy with the State, they do but what they have already done in their own case, or rather they abet injustice to a greater extent than the State requires. If they pay the tax from a mistaken interest in the individual taxed, to save his property, or prevent his going to jail, it is because they have not considered wisely how far they let their private feelings interfere with the public good.

This, then, is my position at present. But one cannot be too much on his guard in such a case, lest his actions be biased by obstinacy or an undue regard for the opinions of men. Let him see that he does only what belongs to himself and to the hour.

I think sometimes, Why, this people mean well, they are only ignorant; they would do better if they knew how: why give your neighbors this pain to treat you as they are not inclined to? But I think again, This is no reason why I should do as they do, or permit others to suffer much greater pain of a different kind. Again, I sometimes say to myself, When many millions of men, without heat, without ill will, without personal feelings of any kind, demand of you a few shillings only, without the possibility, such is their constitution, of retracting or altering their present demand, and without the possibility, on your side, of appeal to any other millions, why expose yourself to this overwhelming brute force? You do not resist cold and hunger, the winds and the waves, thus obstinately; you quietly submit to a thousand similar necessities. You do not put your head into the fire. But just in proportion as I regard this as not wholly a brute force, but partly a human force, and consider that I have relations to those millions as to so many millions of men, and not of mere brute or inanimate things, I see that appeal is possible, first and instantaneously, from them to the Maker of them, and, secondly, from them to themselves. But if I put my head deliberately into the fire, there is no appeal to fire or to the Maker of fire, and I have only myself to blame. If I could convince myself that I have any right to be satisfied with men as they are, and to treat them accordingly, and not according, in some respects, to my requisitions and expectations of what they and I ought to be, then, like a good Mussulman and fatalist, I should endeavor to be satisfied with things as they are, and say it is the will of God. And, above all, there is this difference between resisting this and a purely brute or natural force, that I can resist this with some effect; but I cannot expect, like Orpheus, to change the nature of the rocks and trees and beasts.

I do not wish to quarrel with any man or nation. I do not wish to split hairs, to make fine distinctions, or set myself up as better than my neighbors. I seek rather, I may say, even an excuse for conforming to the laws of the land. I am but too ready to conform to them. Indeed, I have reason to suspect myself on this head; and each year, as the tax-gatherer comes round, I find myself disposed to review the acts and position of the general and State governments, and the spirit of the people to discover a pretext for conformity.

> "We must affect our country as our parents,
> And if at any time we alienate
> Out of love or industry from doing it honor,
> We must respect effects and teach the soul
> Matter of conscience and religion,
> And not desire of rule or benefit."

I believe that the State will soon be able to take all my work of this sort out of my hands, and then I shall be no better patriot than my fellow-countrymen. Seen from a lower point of view, the Constitution, with all its faults, is very good; the law and the courts are very respectable; even this State and this American government are, in many respects, very admirable, and rare things, to be thankful for, such as a great many have described them; seen from a higher still, and the highest, who shall say what they are, or that they are worth looking at or thinking of at all?

However, the government does not concern me much, and I shall bestow the fewest possible thoughts on it. It is not many moments that I live under a government, even in this world. If a man is thought-free, fancy-free, imagination-free, that which *is not* never for a long time appearing *to be* to him, unwise rulers or reformers cannot fatally interrupt him.

I know that most men think differently from myself; but those whose lives are by profession devoted to the study of these or kindred subjects content me as little as any. Statesmen and legislators, standing so completely within the institution, never distinctly and nakedly behold it. They speak of moving society, but have no resting-place without it. They may be men of a certain experience and discrimination, and have no doubt in-vented ingenious and even useful systems, for which we sincerely thank them; but all their wit and usefulness lie within certain not very wide limits. They are wont to forget that the world is not governed by policy and expediency. Webster never goes behind government, and so cannot speak with authority about it. His words are wisdom to those legislators who contemplate no essential reform in the existing government; but for thinkers, and those who legislate for all time, he never once glances at the subject. I know of those whose serene and wise speculations on this theme would soon reveal the limits of his mind's range and hospitality. Yet, compared with the cheap professions of most reformers, and the still cheaper wisdom and eloquence of politicians in general, his are almost the only sensible and valuable words, and we thank Heaven for him. Comparatively, he is always strong, original, and, above all, practical. Still, his quality is not wisdom, but prudence. The lawyer's truth is not Truth, but consistency or a consistent expediency. Truth is always in harmony with herself, and is not concerned chiefly to reveal the justice that may consist with wrong-doing. He well deserves to be called, as he has been called, the Defender of the Constitution. There are really no blows to be given him but defensive ones. He is not a leader, but a follower. His leaders are the men of '87. "I have never made an effort," he says, "and never propose to make an effort; I have never countenanced an effort, and never mean to countenance an effort, to disturb the arrangement as originally made, by which various States came into the Union." Still thinking of the sanction which the Constitution gives to slavery, he says, "Because it was part of the original compact—let it stand." Notwithstanding his special acuteness and ability, he is unable to take a fact out of its merely political relations, and behold it as it lies absolutely to be disposed of by the intellect—what, for instance, it behooves a man to do here in America today with regard to slavery—but ventures, or is driven, to make some such desperate answer to the following, while professing to speak absolutely, and as a private man—from which what new and singular of social duties might be inferred? "The manner," says he, "in which the governments of the States where slavery exists are to regulate it is for their own consideration, under the responsibility to their constituents, to the general laws of propriety, humanity, and justice, and to God. Associations formed elsewhere, springing from a feeling of humanity, or any other cause, have nothing whatever to do with it. They have never received any encouragement from me and they never will."

They who know of no purer sources of truth, who have traced up its stream no higher, stand, and wisely stand, by the Bible and the Constitution, and drink at it there with reverence and humanity; but they who behold where it comes trickling into this lake or that pool, gird up their loins once more, and continue their pilgrimage toward its fountainhead.

No man with a genius for legislation has appeared in America. They are rare in the history of the world. There are orators, politicians, and eloquent men, by the thousand; but the speaker has not yet opened his mouth to speak who is capable of settling the much-vexed questions of the day. We love eloquence for its own sake, and not for any truth which it may utter, or any heroism it may inspire. Our legislators have not yet learned the comparative value of free trade and of freedom, of union, and of rectitude, to a nation. They have no genius or talent for comparatively humble questions of taxation and finance, commerce and manufactures and agriculture. If we were left solely to the wordy wit of legislators in Congress for our guidance, uncorrected by the seasonable experience and the effectual complaints of the people, America would not long retain her rank among the nations. For eighteen hundred years, though perchance I have no right to say it, the New Testament has been written; yet where is the legislator who has wisdom and practical talent enough to avail himself of the light which it sheds on the science of legislation?

The authority of government, even such as I am willing to submit to—for I will cheerfully obey those who know and can do better than I, and in many things even those who neither know nor can do so well—is still an impure one: to be strictly just, it must have the sanction and consent of the governed. It can have no pure right over my person and property but what I concede to it. The progress from an absolute to a limited monarchy, from a limited monarchy to a democracy, is a progress toward a true respect for the individual. Even the Chinese philosopher was wise enough to regard the individual as the basis of the empire. Is a democracy, such as we know it, the last improvement possible in government? Is it not possible to take a step further towards recognizing and organizing the rights of man? There will never be a really free and enlightened State until the State comes to recognize the individual as a higher and independent power, from which all its own power and authority are derived, and treats him accordingly. I please myself with imagining a State at last which can afford to be just to all men, and to treat the individual with respect as a neighbor; which even would not think it inconsistent with its own repose if a few were to live aloof from it, not meddling with it, nor embraced by it, who fulfilled all the duties of neighbors and fellow men. A State which bore this kind of fruit, and suffered it to drop off as fast as it ripened, would prepare the way for a still more perfect and glorious State, which I have also imagined, but not yet anywhere seen.

John Brown's Final Speech (November 2, 1859)

In the fall of 1859, radical abolitionist John Brown was tried by the Commonwealth of Virginia on charges of treason for leading an insurrection against a federal arsenal at Harpers Ferry (now located in West Virginia). Brown's purpose in organizing the raid was to spark a slave uprising and establish a free state to which blacks could escape. Found guilty on November 2, Brown defended his actions in a final address to the court. He characterized his efforts as an expression of divine justice—for which he was willing to give up his life.

I have, may it please the court, a few words to say.

In the first place, I deny everything but what I have all along admitted,—the design on my part to free the slaves. I intended certainly to have made a clean thing of that matter, as I did last winter, when I went into Missouri and there took slaves without the snapping of a gun on either side, moved them through the country, and finally left them in Canada. I designed to do the same thing again, on a larger scale. That was all I intended. I never did intend murder, or treason, or the destruction of property, or to excite or incite slaves to rebellion, or to make insurrection.

I have another objection; and that is, it is unjust that I should suffer such a penalty. Had I interfered in the manner which I admit, and which I admit has been fairly proved (for I admire the truthfulness and candor of the greater portion of the witnesses who have testified in this case),—had I so interfered in behalf of the rich, the powerful, the intelligent, the so-called great, or in behalf of any of their friends—either father, mother, brother, sister, wife, or children, or any of that class—and suffered and sacrificed what I have in this interference, it would have been all right; and every man in this court would have deemed it an act worthy of reward rather than punishment.

This court acknowledges, as I suppose, the validity of the law of God. I see a book kissed here which I suppose to be the Bible, or at least the New Testament. That teaches me that all things whatsoever I would that men should do to me, I should do even so to them. It teaches me, further, to "remember them that are in bonds, as bound with them." I endeavored to act up to that instruction. I say, I am yet too young to understand that God is any respecter of persons. I believe that to have interfered as I have done—as I have always freely admitted I have done—in behalf of His despised poor, was not wrong, but right. Now, if it is deemed necessary that I should forfeit my life for the furtherance of the ends of justice, and mingle my blood further with the blood of my children and with the blood of millions in this slave country whose rights are disregarded by wicked, cruel, and unjust enactments—I submit; so let it be done!

Let me say one word further.

I feel entirely satisfied with the treatment I have received on my trial. Considering all the circumstances, it has been more generous than I expected. I feel no consciousness of guilt. I have stated that from the first what was my intention, and what was not. I never had any design against the life of any person, nor any disposition to commit treason, or excite slaves to rebel, or make any general insurrection. I never encouraged any man to do so, but always discouraged any idea of that kind.

Let me say also, a word in regard to the statements made by some of those connected with me. I hear it has been stated by some of them that I have induced them to join me. But the contrary is true. I do not say this to injure them, but as regretting their weakness. There is not one of them but joined me of his own accord, and the greater part of them at their own expense. A number of them I never saw, and never had a word of conversation with, till the day they came to me; and that was for the purpose I have stated.

Now I have done.

Trial Remarks of Susan B. Anthony (1873)

In 1872, suffragist Susan Brownell Anthony was arrested in Rochester, New York, for voting illegally in the presidential election. In a courtroom exchange with Justice Ward Hunt on June 19, 1873, Anthony stated her case for claiming full citizenship under the Bill of Rights and declared her refusal to pay any fine or be swayed by any other penalty. The following exchange, variously recorded, is based on her personal account.

Judge Hunt (ordering the defendant to stand up): Has the prisoner anything to say why sentence shall not be pronounced?

Miss Anthony: Yes, your honor, I have many things to say; for in your ordered verdict of guilty, you have trampled under foot every vital principle of our government. My natural rights, my civil rights, my political rights, my judicial rights, are all alike ignored. Robbed of the fundamental privilege of citizenship, I am degraded from the status of a citizen to that of a subject; and not only myself individually, but all of my sex, are, by your honor's verdict, doomed to political subjection under this, so-called, form of government.

Judge Hunt: The Court cannot listen to a rehearsal of arguments the prisoner's counsel has already consumed three hours in presenting.

Miss Anthony: May it please your honor, I am not arguing the question, but simply stating the reasons why sentence cannot, in justice, be pronounced against me. Your denial of my citizen's right to vote, is the denial of my right of consent as one of the governed, the denial of my right of representation as one of the taxed, the denial of my right to a trial by a jury of my peers as an offender against law, therefore, the denial of my sacred rights to life, liberty, property and—

Judge Hunt: The Court cannot allow the prisoner to go on.

Miss Anthony: But your honor will not deny me this one and only poor privilege of protest against this high-handed outrage upon my citizen's rights. May it please the Court to remember that since the day of my arrest last November, this is the first time that either myself or any person of my disfranchised class has been allowed a word of defense before judge or jury—

Judge Hunt: The prisoner must sit down. The Court cannot allow it.

Miss Anthony: All of my prosecutors, from the 8th ward corner grocery politician, who entered the complaint, to the United States Marshal, Commissioner, District Attorney, District Judge, your honor on the bench, not one is my peer, but each and all are my political sovereigns; and had your honor submitted my case to the jury, as was clearly your duty, even then I should have had just cause of protest for not one of those men was my peer; but, native or foreign born, white or black, rich or poor, educated or ignorant, awake or asleep, sober or drunk, each and every man of them was my political superior; hence, in no sense, my peer. Even, under such circumstances, a commoner of England, tried before a jury of Lords, would have far less cause to complain than should I, a woman, tried before a jury of men. Even my counsel, the Hon. Henry R. Selden, who has argued my cause so ably, so earnestly, so unanswerably before your honor, is my political sovereign. Precisely as no disfranchised person is entitled to sit upon a jury, and no woman is entitled to the franchise, so, none but a regularly admitted lawyer is allowed to practice in the courts, and no woman can gain admission to the bar hence, jury, judge, counsel, must all be of the superior class.

Judge Hunt: The Court must insist the prisoner has been tried according to the established forms of law.

Miss Anthony: Yes, your honor, but by forms of law all made by men, interpreted by men, administered by men, in favor of men, and against women; and hence, your honor's ordered verdict of guilty, against a United States citizen for the exercise of *"that citizen's right to vote,"* simply because that citizen was a woman and not a man.

But, yesterday, the same man-made forms of law, declared it a crime punishable with $1,000 fine and six months' imprisonment, for you, or me, or any of us, to give a cup of cold water, a crust of bread, or a night's shelter to a panting fugitive as he was tracking his way to Canada. And every man or woman in whose veins coursed a drop of human sympathy violated that wicked law, reckless of consequences, and was justified in so doing. As then, the slaves who got their freedom must take it over, or under, or through the unjust forms of law, precisely so, now, must women, to get their right to a voice in this government, take it; and I have taken mine, and mean to take it at every possible opportunity.

Judge Hunt: The Court orders the prisoner to sit down. It will not allow another word.

Miss Anthony: When I was brought before your honor for trial, I hoped for a broad and liberal interpretation of the Constitution and its recent amendments, that should declare all United States citizens under its protecting aegis that should declare equality of rights the national guarantee to all persons born or naturalized in the United States. But failing to get this justice—failing, even, to get a trial by a jury not of my peers—I ask not leniency at your hands—but rather the full rigors of the law.

Judge Hunt: The Court must insist—
(Here the prisoner sat down.)

Judge Hunt: The prisoner will stand up.
(Here Miss Anthony arose again.)

The sentence of the Court is that you pay a fine of one hundred dollars and the costs of the prosecution.

Miss Anthony: May it please your honor, I shall never pay a dollar of your unjust penalty. All the stock in trade I possess is a $10,000 debt, incurred by publishing my paper—*The Revolution*—four years ago, the sole object of which was to educate all women to do precisely as I have done, rebel against your man-made, unjust, unconstitutional forms of law, that tax, fine, imprison and hang women, while they deny them the right of representation in the government; and I shall work on with might and main to pay every dollar of that honest debt, but not a penny shall go to this unjust claim. And I shall earnestly and persistently continue to urge all women to the practical recognition of the old revolutionary maxim, that "Resistance to tyranny is obedience to God."

Judge Hunt: Madam, the Court will not order you committed until the fine is paid.

Source: An Account of the Proceedings on the Trial of Susan B. Anthony on the Charge of Illegal Voting... (Rochester, NY, 1874), 81–85.

No-Conscription League Manifesto (1917), Emma Goldman

After U.S. entry into World War I in April 1917 and passage of the Selective Service Act the following month, President Woodrow Wilson established June 4 as Registration Day for men between the ages of 21 and 31. In response, anarchist Emma Goldman and colleague Alexander Berkman founded the No-Conscription League in New York City and organized a series of antiwar draft rallies, at which the league's manifesto was distributed. Goldman and Berkman were promptly arrested and charged with conspiracy to obstruct the draft. Found guilty, they served two years in prison and were deported to the Soviet Union in 1919.

NO CONSCRIPTION!

CONSCRIPTION has now become a fact in this country. It took England fully 18 months after she engaged in the war to impose compulsory military service on her people. It was left for "free" America to pass a conscription bill six weeks after she declared war against Germany.

What becomes of the patriotic boast of America to have entered the European war in behalf of the principle of democracy? But that is not all. Every country in Europe has recognized the right of conscientious objectors—of men who refuse to engage in war on the ground that they are opposed to taking life. Yet this democratic country makes no such provision for those who will not commit murder at the behest of the war profiteers. Thus the "land of the free and the home of the brave" is ready to coerce free men into the military yoke.

No one to whom the fundamental principle of liberty and justice is more than an idle phrase, can help realize that the patriotic clap-trap now shouted by press, pulpit and the authorities, betrays a desperate effort of the ruling class in this country to throw sand in the eyes of the masses and to blind them to the real issue confronting them. That issue is the Prussianizing of America so as to destroy whatever few liberties the people have achieved through an incessant struggle of many years.

Already all labor protective laws have been abrogated, which means that while husbands, fathers and sons are butchered on the battlefield, the women and children will be exploited in our industrial bastiles to the heart's content of the American patriots for gain and power.

Freedom of speech, of press and assembly is about to be thrown upon the dungheap of political guarantees. But crime of all crimes, the flower of the country is to be forced into murder whether or not they believe in war or in the efficacy of saving democracy in Europe by the destruction of democracy at home.

Liberty of conscience is the most fundamental of all human rights, the pivot of all progress. No man may be deprived of it without losing every vestige of freedom of thought and action. In these days when every principle and conception of democracy and individual liberty is being cast overboard under the pretext of democratizing Germany, it behooves every liberty-loving man and woman to insist on his or her right of individual choice in the ordering of his life and actions.

The NO-CONSCRIPTION LEAGUE has been formed for the purpose of encouraging conscientious objectors to affirm their liberty of conscience and to make their objection to human slaughter effective by refusing to participate in the killing of their fellow men. The NO-CONSCRIPTION LEAGUE is to be the voice of protest against the coercion of conscientious objectors to participate in the war. Our platform may be summarized as follows:

We oppose conscription because we are internationalists, anti-militarists, and opposed to all wars waged by capitalistic governments.

We will fight for what we choose to fight for; we will never fight simply because we are ordered to fight.

We believe that the militarization of America is an evil that far outweighs, in its anti-social and anti-libertarian effects, any good that may come from America's participation in the war.

We will resist conscription by every means in our power, and we will sustain those who, for similar reasons, refuse to be conscripted.

We are not unmindful of the difficulties in our way. But we have resolved to go ahead and spare no effort to make the voice of protest a moral force in the life of this country. The initial efforts of the conscientious objectors in England were fraught with many hardships and danger, but finally the government of Great Britain was forced to give heed to the steadily increasing volume of public protest against the coercion of conscientious objectors. So we, too, in America, will doubtless meet the full severity of the government and the condemnation of the war-mad jingoes, but we are nevertheless determined to go ahead. We feel confident in arousing thousands of people who are conscientious objectors to the murder of their fellowmen and to whom a principle represents the most vital thing in life.

Resist conscription. Organize meetings. Join our League. Send us money. Help us to give assistance to those who come in conflict with the government. Help us to publish literature against militarism and against conscription.

NO-CONSCRIPTION LEAGUE
20 East 125th St., New York

Source: Records of the Department of War and Military Intelligence Division, Record Group 165, National Archives. Available at Berkeley Digital Library, http://sunsite.berkeley.edu.

John Lewis Remembers the Nashville Sit-Ins (1960)

In the spring of 1960, John Lewis—who would later become a major figure in the civil rights movement and a U.S. congressman from Georgia—was a 20-year-old student at the American Baptist Theological Seminary in Memphis, Tennessee. A devout follower of the Reverend Martin Luther King, Jr., and his principle of nonviolence, Lewis helped organize the historic sit-in campaign to combat segregation at lunch counters throughout the South. He recounts the events in Nashville that spring in his memoir, Walking with the Wind *(1998).*

This is what we had prepared for. That night Bernard [Lafayette] and I let ourselves into the [American Baptist Theological Seminary] ad-

ministration building . . . and "liberated" a ream of mimeograph paper. Though many of the students who would be sitting in the next day had been trained, our numbers were swelling so fast that there were hundreds who had not. So I wrote up a basic list of dos and don'ts to be distributed the next day:

DO NOT:

1. Strike back nor curse if abused.
2. Laugh out.
3. Hold conversations with floor walker.
4. Leave your seat until your leader has given you permission to do so.
5. Block entrances to stores outside nor the aisles inside.

DO:

1. Show yourself friendly and courteous at all times.
2. Sit straight; always face the counter.
3. Report all serious incidents to your leader.
4. Refer information seekers to your leader in a polite manner.
5. Remember the teachings of Jesus Christ, Mahatma Gandhi and Martin Luther King.

Love and nonviolence is the way.

MAY GOD BLESS EACH OF YOU

Bernard and I, with the help of a young administrative secretary, made five hundred copies of the leaflet that night. Then we locked up and left. . . .

There was no question we would continue, no debate, no protest from any of the adults. We knew that sooner or later the stakes would be raised. It was a natural step in the process, a step we had practiced and prepared for. Our workshops had been like little laboratories in human behavior and response to nonviolent protest. Now we were seeing real humans respond in almost exactly the same ways Jim Lawson had taught us they would. The danger waiting for us this day was to be expected, which didn't mean I wasn't a little bit nervous. But by now I was so committed deep inside to the sureness and sanctity of the nonviolent way, and I was so calmed by the sense that the Spirit of History was with us, that the butterflies were gone by the time we left the church and headed downtown. . . .

As soon as my group entered our target store, Woolworth's, we were confronted with a group of young white men shouting, "Go home, nigger!" and "Get back to Africa!" They jabbed us as we passed and chided us for not fighting back. "What's the matter? You *chicken?*" they teased, trying to force the situation onto terms they were comfortable with—fists and fighting.

We weren't playing by those rules, of course, and that infuriated them even further. No sooner did we take our seats at the upstairs counter than some of these young men began pushing the group at the downstairs restaurant off their stools, shoving them against the counter, punching them.

We immediately went down to join our brothers and sisters, taking seats of our own. I was hit in the ribs, not too hard, but enough to knock me over. Down the way I could see one of the white men stubbing a lit cigarette against the back of a guy in our group, though I couldn't tell who it was in the swirl of the action.

I got back on my stool and sat there, not saying a word. The others did the same. Violence does beget violence, but the opposite is just as true. Hitting someone who does not hit back can last only so long. Fury spends itself pretty quickly when there's no fury facing it. We could see in the mirror on the wall in front of us the crowd gathered at our backs. They continued trying to egg us on, but the beating subsided. . . .

At the same time, we would learn later, the same thing was happening in the other stores. Yellow mustard was squeezed onto the head of one black male student in Kress's while the crowd hooted and laughed. Ketchup was poured down the shirt of another. Paul LaPrad, being white, attracted particularly brutal attention over at McClellan's. He was pulled off his stool, beaten and kicked by a group of young whites with the word "Chattanooga" written on their jackets—a reference to recent white-on-black attacks in that city that had followed a series of sit-ins there.

A television camera crew was at McClellan's, recording the scene as LaPrad's attackers spent themselves. It filmed Paul—bloody and bruised and silent—pulling himself back on to his chair. When the footage aired that night on national television, it marked one of the earliest instances where Americans were shown firsthand the kind of anger and ugliness that the peaceful movement for civil rights was prompting in the South. Many viewers were sickened by what they saw. They would see more in the years to come.

We didn't sit there long before the police, conspicuous by their absence during the attacks, arrived. I didn't imagine they had come to arrest anyone for assault, and I was right. As the young men who had beaten us looked on and cheered, we were told that we were under arrest for "disorderly conduct." . . .

But I felt no shame or disgrace. I didn't feel fear, either. As we were led out of the store single file, singing "We Shall Overcome," I felt exhilarated. As we passed through a cheering crowd gathered on the sidewalk outside, I felt high, almost giddy with joy. As we approached the open rear doors of a paddy wagon, I felt elated.

It was really happening, what I'd imagined for so long, the drama of good and evil playing itself out on the stage of the living, breathing world. It felt holy, and noble, and good.

That paddy wagon—crowded, cramped, dirty, with wire cage windows and doors—seemed like a chariot to me, a freedom vehicle carrying me across a threshold. I had wondered all along, as anyone would, how I would handle the reality of what I had studied and trained and prepared for for so long, what it would be like to actually face pain and rage and the power of uniformed authority.

Now I knew. Now I had crossed over, I had stepped through the door into total, unquestioning commitment. This wasn't just about that moment or that day. This was about forever. It was like deliverance. I had, as they say in Christian circles when a person accepts Jesus Christ into his heart, come home. But this was not Jesus I had come home to. It was the purity and utter certainty of the nonviolent path.

When we got to the city jail, the place was awash with a sense of jubilation. With all these friends, these familiar faces piling out of those wagons, it felt like a crusade, as if we were prisoners in a holy war. We sang as we were led into cells much too small for our numbers, which would total eighty-two by the end of the day. Cubicles built for three or four prisoners were jammed with fifteen to twenty of us each. The police could hardly keep up with the waves of students who were replacing one another back at those lunch counters. No sooner would one group be arrested than another would take its place. Once word would spread back to the campuses what was happening downtown, students arrived at First Baptist literally by the hundreds, angry, outraged, and ready to put their own bodies on the line. Even the adults stood ready to join. C.T. Vivian, an ABT graduate who was now pastor of a small church near Fisk [University], urged his fellow NCLC [Nashville Christian Leadership Conference] members to join him on the sit-in line. "We'll let our vacant pulpits be our testimony tomorrow morning," he proclaimed.

But by then word had come that the police had stopped the arrests. They couldn't deal with the numbers they were facing. And there was no more room at the jail. . . .

It didn't take Nashville's powers-that-be long to realize it was fruitless to try forcing us to pay our way out. At eleven that night, after about six hours behind bars, we were released into the custody of the president of Fisk, Dr. Stephen J. Wright. With him were reporters and about two hundred cheering students. We were exultant. Those six hours had been an act of baptism for all involved. . . .

The next day we went to court—the eighty-two who had been arrested, along with more than two thousand supporters. . . . The judge then found us all guilty. He gave us the option of paying a $50 fine each or serving thirty days in the county workhouse. . . .

The following day, March 3, the mayor of Nashville, Ben West, ordered our release. . . . What West did was name a biracial committee to study the situation of segregation in the city. He asked us to halt the sit-ins while the committee looked into the problem, and we agreed. . . .

It had begun quietly, almost invisibly, in late March. No one knew quite where it started, but it became organized and communicated through the churches. "Don't buy Downtown" was the simple slogan, and it was amazingly effective. Estimates were that black Nashville spent as much as $60 million a year in the city, a figure which meant even more to downtown merchants who had seen many of their white customers move to the suburbs in recent years and were depending increasingly on the black buyers who remained.

By the beginning of April, those stores stood virtually empty. One leader at a local black Baptist church asked every person in the congregation who had not spent a penny downtown in the previous two weeks to stand. Everyone in the room rose.

White people, too, were staying away. Some were wary of the violence and disturbances caused by the sit-ins. Others joined the boycott as a sign of support for our cause. A few white women went down to their favorite Nashville stores and made a visible show of turning in their credit cards as their own act of protest. . . .

[T]he next night . . . Thurgood Marshall, who was seven years away from becoming the nation's first black U.S. Supreme Court justice, arrived at the Fisk gymnasium to address an audience of more than four thousand. The atmosphere was intense as Marshall began by praising what we had accomplished with our sit-ins. But then he told us we were making a mistake by staying in jail and refusing bail. The way to change America, Marshall maintained, was the way the country's black power structure had been doing it since the 1940s—through the courts. . . . It was clear to me that evening that Thurgood Marshall, along with so many of his generation, just did not understand the essence of what we, the younger blacks of America, were doing. . . . Thurgood Marshall was a good man, a historic figure, but watching him speak on that April evening in Nashville convinced me more than ever that our revolt was as much against this nation's traditional black leadership structure as it was against racial segregation and discrimination. Five days after Marshall's speech we resumed our sit-ins. . . .

By noon, nearly two thousand students, faculty and townspeople had gathered at Tennessee State to march on city hall. We . . . had decided that morning to march and had sent the mayor a telegram telling him we were on our way.

I had never seen anything like the scene as we moved toward city hall that day. The nation had never seen anything like it. This was the first such mass march in the history of America, the first civil rights assault on such a scale. People kept coming and coming. The newspapers said there were three thousand of us, but I think that figure is low. I'm certain the number was closer to five thousand.

We walked three and four abreast in complete silence, blacks and whites, ten miles through the heart of Nashville. People came out of their homes to join us. Cars drove beside us, moving slowly, at the speed of our footsteps. The line looked as if it went on forever. Everyone was very intense, but very disciplined and very orderly. It was a stupendous scene. There was some singing at first, but as we neared city hall it stopped. The last mile or so, the only sound was the sound of our footsteps, all those feet.

When we reached city hall, Mayor West, in his bow tie and hat, came down the steps out front to meet us. [He] made a plea with us to be peaceful.

"You all have the power to destroy this city," he said. "So let's not have any mobs."

He went on to say he would enforce the laws without prejudice, but that he had no power to force restaurant owners to serve anyone they did not want to. Then he said, "We are all Christians together. Let us pray together."

To which one student shouted, "How about eating together?"

Then Diane [Nash] stepped forward. She held a typed list of questions, which we'd come up with that morning. When she asked West if he would use "the prestige of your office to appeal to the citizens to stop racial discrimination," his answer was succinct.

"I appeal to all citizens," said the mayor, "to end discrimination, to have no bigotry, no bias, no hatred."

Then Diane asked the million-dollar question, pushing the mayor to be specific.

"Do you mean that to include lunch counters?" . . .

"Yes," said West.

The crowd exploded, cheering and applauding.

Source: John Lewis, with Michael D'Orso, *Walking with the Wind: A Memoir of the Movement* (New York: Simon & Schuster, 1998). Copyright © 1998 by John Lewis. Abridged by permission of Simon & Schuster Adult Publishing Group.

Student Nonviolent Coordinating Committee Founding Statement (1960)

In April 1960, after the historic lunch counter sit-ins and other direct-action demonstrations against segregation across the South, a group of student activists led by Ella Baker organized a conference at Shaw University in Raleigh, North Carolina, to advance the cause. The outcome of the meeting was the establishment of the Student Nonviolent Coordinating Committee (SNCC), based on the following declaration of nonviolence, conscience, and core beliefs.

We affirm the philosophical or religious ideal of nonviolence as the foundation of our purpose, the presupposition of our belief, and the manner of our action.

Nonviolence, as it grows from the Judeo-Christian tradition, seeks a social order of justice permeated by love. Integration of human endeavor represents the crucial first step towards such a society.

Through nonviolence, courage displaces fear. Love transcends hate. Acceptance dissipates prejudice; hope ends despair. Faith reconciles doubt. Peace dominates war. Mutual regards cancel enmity. Justice for all overthrows injustice. The redemptive community supersedes immoral social systems.

By appealing to conscience and standing on the moral nature of human existence, nonviolence nurtures the atmosphere in which reconciliation and justice become actual possibilities.

Although each local group in this movement must diligently work out the clear meaning of this statement of purpose, each act or phase of our corporate effort must reflect a genuine spirit of love and good-will.

Source: "Student Nonviolent Coordinating Committee Founding Statement." The Sixties Project. Available at http://www3.iath.virginia.edu/sixties/HTML_docs/Sixties.html.

Letter from Birmingham Jail, Martin Luther King, Jr. (April 16, 1963)

Reflecting his dedication to the principle of nonviolent civil disobedience, the Reverend Martin Luther King, Jr.'s "Letter from Birmingham Jail" also marked a philosophical and strategic turning point in the civil rights movement of the 1960s. Dr. King wrote the long, open letter—in which he declared a "moral responsibility to disobey unjust laws"—after his arrest for protesting segregation in Birmingham, Alabama. Specifically, the text was a response to a "Call for Unity" on the part of eight white Alabama clergymen.

My Dear Fellow Clergyman:

While confined here in the Birmingham City Jail, I came across your recent statement calling our present activities "unwise and untimely." Seldom, if ever, do I pause to answer criticism of my work and ideas. If I sought to answer all the criticisms that cross my desk, my secretaries would be engaged in little else in the course of the day, and I would have no time for constructive work. But since I feel that you are men of genuine goodwill and your criticisms are sincerely set forth, I would like to answer your statement in what I hope will be patient and reasonable terms.

I think I should give the reason for my being in Birmingham, since you have been influenced by the argument of "outsiders coming in." I have the honor of serving as president of the Southern Christian Leadership Conference, an organization operating in every Southern state, with headquarters in Atlanta, Georgia. We have some eighty-five affiliate organizations all across the South—one being the Alabama Christian Movement for Human Rights. Whenever necessary and possible we share staff, educational and financial resources with our affiliates. Several months ago our local affiliate here in Birmingham invited us to be on call to engage in a nonviolent direct action program if such were deemed necessary. We readily consented and when the hour came we lived up to our promises. So I am here, along with several members of my staff, because I have basic organizational ties here.

Beyond this, I am in Birmingham because injustice is here. Just as the eighth century prophets left their little villages and carried their "thus saith the Lord" far beyond the boundaries of their home towns; and just as the Apostle Paul left his little village of Tarsus and carried the gospel of Jesus Christ to practically every hamlet and city of the Graeco-Roman world, I too am compelled to carry the gospel of freedom beyond my particular home town. Like Paul, I must constantly respond to the Macedonian call for aid.

Moreover, I am cognizant of the interrelatedness of all communities and states. I cannot sit idly by in Atlanta and not be concerned about what happens in Birmingham. Injustice anywhere is a threat to justice everywhere. We are caught in an inescapable network of mutuality, tied in a single garment of destiny. Whatever affects one directly affects all indirectly. Never again can we afford to live with the narrow, provincial "outside agitator" idea. Anyone who lives inside the United States can never be considered an outsider anywhere in this country.

You deplore the demonstrations that are presently taking place in Birmingham. But I am sorry that your statement did not express a similar concern for the conditions that brought the demonstrations into being. I am sure that each of you would want to go beyond the superficial social analyst who looks merely at effects, and does not grapple with underlying causes. I would not hesitate to say that it is unfortunate that so-called demonstrations are taking place in Birmingham at this time, but I would say in more emphatic terms that it is even more unfortunate that the white power structure of this city left the Negro community with no other alternative.

In any nonviolent campaign there are four basic steps: 1) Collection of the facts to determine whether injustices are alive. 2) Negotiation. 3) Self-purification and 4) Direct action. We have gone through all of these steps in Birmingham. There can be no gainsaying of the fact that racial injustice engulfs this community.

Birmingham is probably the most thoroughly segregated city in the United States. Its ugly record of police brutality is known in every section of this country. Its unjust treatment of Negroes in the courts is a notorious reality. There have been more unsolved bombings of Negro homes and churches in Birmingham than any city in this nation. These are the hard, brutal and unbelievable facts. On the basis of these conditions, Negro leaders sought to negotiate with the city fathers. But the political leaders consistently refused to engage in good faith negotiation.

Then came the opportunity last September to talk with some of the leaders of the economic community. In these negotiating sessions certain promises were made by the merchants—such as the promise to remove the humiliating racial signs from the stores. On the basis of these promises Rev. [Fred] Shuttlesworth and the leaders of the Alabama Christian Movement for Human Rights agreed to call a moratorium on any type of demonstrations. As the weeks and months unfolded we realized that we were the victims of a broken promise. The signs remained. Like so many experiences of the past we were confronted with blasted hopes, and the dark shadow of a deep disappointment settled upon us. So we had no alternative except that of preparing for direct action, whereby we would present our very bodies as a means of laying our case before the conscience of the local and national community. We were not unmindful of the difficulties involved. So we decided to go through a process of self-purification. We started having workshops on nonviolence and repeatedly asked ourselves the questions: "Are you able to accept blows without retaliating?" "Are you able to endure the ordeals of jail?" We decided to set our direct-action program around the Easter season, realizing that with the exception of Christmas, this was the largest shopping period of the year. Knowing that a strong economic withdrawal program would be the by-product of direct action, we felt that this was the best time to bring pressure on the merchants for the needed changes. Then it occurred to us that the March election was ahead and so we speedily decided to postpone action until after election day. When we discovered that Mr. [Eugene "Bull"] Connor was in the run-off, we decided again to postpone action so that the demonstrations could not be used to cloud the issues. At this time we agreed to begin our nonviolent witness the day after the run-off.

This reveals that we did not move irresponsibly into direct action. We too wanted to see Mr. Connor defeated; so we went through postponement after postponement to aid in this community need. After this we felt that direct action could be delayed no longer.

You may well ask: "Why direct action? Why sit-ins, marches, etc.? Isn't negotiation a better path?" You are exactly right in your call for negotiation. Indeed, this is the purpose of direct action. Nonviolent direct action seeks to create such a crisis and establish such creative tension that a community that has constantly refused to negotiate is forced to confront the issue. It seeks so to dramatize the issue that it can no longer be ignored. I just referred to the creation of tension as a part of the work of the nonviolent resister. This may sound rather shocking. But I must confess that I am not afraid of the word tension. I have earnestly worked and preached against violent tension, but there is a type of constructive nonviolent tension that is necessary for growth. Just as Socrates felt that it was necessary to create a tension in the mind so that individuals could rise from the bondage of myths and half-truths to the unfettered realm of creative analysis and objective appraisal, we must see the need of having nonviolent gadflies to create the kind of tension in society that will help men to rise from the dark depths of prejudice and racism to the majestic heights of understanding and brotherhood. So the purpose of the direct action is to create a situation so crisis-packed that it will inevitably open the door to negotiation. We, therefore, concur with you in your call for negotiation. Too long has our beloved Southland been bogged down in the tragic attempt to live in monologue rather than dialogue.

One of the basic points in your statement is that our acts are untimely. Some have asked, "Why didn't you give the new administration time to act?" The only answer that I can give to this inquiry is that the new Birmingham administration must be prodded about as much as the outgoing one before it acts. We will be sadly mistaken if we feel that the election of Mr. [Albert] Boutwell will bring the millennium to Birmingham. While Mr. Boutwell is much more articulate and gentle than Mr. Connor, they are both segregationists, dedicated to the task of maintaining the status quo. The hope I see in Mr. Boutwell is that he will be reasonable enough to see the futility of massive resistance to desegregation. But he will not see this without pressure from the devotees of civil rights. My friends, I must say to you that we have not made a single gain in civil rights without determined legal and nonviolent pressure. History is the long and tragic story of the fact that privileged groups seldom give up their privileges voluntarily. Individuals may see the moral light and voluntarily give up their unjust posture; but as Reinhold Niebuhr has reminded us, groups are more immoral than individuals.

We know through painful experience that freedom is never voluntarily given by the oppressor; it must be demanded by the oppressed. Frankly, I have never yet engaged in a direct action movement that was "well timed," according to the timetable of those who have not suffered unduly from the disease of segregation. For years now I have heard the words [sic] "Wait!" It rings in the ear of every Negro with a piercing familiarity. This "Wait" has almost always meant "Never." We must come to see with the distinguished jurist of yesterday that "justice too long delayed is justice denied."

We have waited for more than three hundred and forty years for our constitutional and God-given rights. The nations of Asia and Africa are moving with jet-like speed toward the goal of political independence, and we still creep at horse and buggy pace toward the gaining of a cup of coffee at a lunch counter. I guess it is easy for those who have never felt the stinging darts of segregation to say, "Wait." But when you have seen vicious mobs lynch your mothers and fathers at will and drown your sisters and brothers at whim; when you have seen hate filled policemen curse, kick, brutalize and even kill your black brothers and sisters with impunity; when you see the vast majority of your twenty million Negro brothers smothering in an airtight cage of poverty in the midst of an affluent society; when you suddenly find your tongue twisted and your speech stammering as you seek to explain to your six-year-old daughter why she can't go to the public amusement park that has just been advertised on television, and see tears welling up in her eyes when she is told that Funtown is closed to colored children, and see the depressing clouds of inferiority begin to form in her little mental sky, and see her begin to distort her little personality by unconsciously developing a bitterness toward white people; when you have to concoct an answer for a five-year-old son asking in agonizing pathos: "Daddy, why do white people treat colored people so mean?"; when you take a cross-country drive and find it necessary to sleep night after night in the uncomfortable corners of your automobile because no motel will accept you; when you are humiliated day in and day out by nagging signs reading "white" and "colored"; when your first name becomes "nigger," your middle name becomes "boy" (however old you are) and your last name becomes "John," and your wife and mother are never given the respected title "Mrs."; when you are harried by day and haunted by night by the fact that you are a Negro, living constantly at tip-toe stance never quite knowing what to expect next, and plagued with inner fears and outer resentments; when you are forever fight-

ing a degenerating sense of "nobodiness"; then you will understand why we find it difficult to wait. There comes a time when the cup of endurance runs over, and men are no longer willing to be plunged into an abyss of despair. I hope, sirs, you can understand our legitimate and unavoidable impatience.

You express a great deal of anxiety over our willingness to break laws. This is certainly a legitimate concern. Since we so diligently urge people to obey the Supreme Court's decision of 1954 outlawing segregation in the public schools, it is rather strange and paradoxical to find us consciously breaking laws. One may well ask: "How can you advocate breaking some laws and obeying others?" The answer is found in the fact that there are two types of laws: There are *just* and there are *unjust* laws. I would agree with Saint Augustine that "An unjust law is no law at all."

Now, what is the difference between the two? How does one determine when a law is just or unjust? A just law is a man-made code that squares with the moral law or the law of God. An unjust law is a code that is out of harmony with the moral law. To put it in the terms of Saint Thomas Aquinas, an unjust law is a human law that is not rooted in eternal and natural law. Any law that uplifts human personality is just. Any law that degrades human personality is unjust. All segregation statutes are unjust because segregation distorts the soul and damages the personality. It gives the segregator a false sense of superiority, and the segregated a false sense of inferiority. To use the words of Martin Buber, the Jewish philosopher, segregation substitutes an "I-it" relationship for an "I-thou" relationship, and ends up relegating persons to the status of things. So segregation is not only politically, economically and sociologically unsound, but it is morally wrong and sinful. Paul Tillich has said that sin is separation. Isn't segregation an existential expression of man's tragic separation, an expression of his awful estrangement, his terrible sinfulness? So I can urge men to disobey segregation ordinances because they are morally wrong.

Let us turn to a more concrete example of just and unjust laws. An unjust law is a code that a majority inflicts on a minority that is not binding on itself. This is difference made legal. On the other hand a just law is a code that a majority compels a minority to follow that it is willing to follow itself. This is sameness made legal.

Let me give another explanation. An unjust law is a code inflicted upon a minority which that minority had no part in enacting or creating because they did not have the unhampered right to vote. Who can say that the legislature of Alabama which set up the segregation laws was democratically elected? Throughout the state of Alabama all types of conniving methods are used to prevent Negroes from becoming registered voters and there are some counties without a single Negro registered to vote despite the fact that the Negro constitutes a majority of the population. Can any law set up in such a state be considered democratically structured?

These are just a few examples of unjust and just laws. There are some instances when a law is just on its face and unjust in its application. For instance, I was arrested Friday on a charge of parading without a permit. Now there is nothing wrong with an ordinance which requires a permit for a parade, but when the ordinance is used to preserve segregation and to deny citizens the First-Amendment privilege of peaceful assembly and peaceful protest, then it becomes unjust.

I hope you can see the distinction I am trying to point out. In no sense do I advocate evading or defying the law as the rabid segregationist would do. This would lead to anarchy. One who breaks an unjust law must do it *openly, lovingly,* (not hatefully as the white mothers did in New Orleans when they were seen on television screaming "nigger, nigger, nigger") and with a willingness to accept the penalty. I submit that an individual who breaks a law that conscience tells him is unjust, and willingly accepts the penalty by staying in jail to arouse the conscience of the community over its injustice, is in reality expressing the very highest respect for law.

Of course, there is nothing new about this kind of civil disobedience. It was seen sublimely in the refusal of Shadrach, Meshach and Abednego to obey the laws of Nebuchadnezzar because a higher moral law was involved. It was practiced superbly by the early Christians who were willing to face hungry lions and the excruciating pain of chopping blocks, before submitting to certain unjust laws of the Roman empire.

To a degree academic freedom is a reality today because Socrates practiced civil disobedience.

We can never forget that everything Hitler did in Germany was "legal" and everything the Hungarian freedom fighters did in Hungary was "illegal." It was "illegal" to aid and comfort a Jew in Hitler's Germany. But I am sure that if I had lived in Germany during that time I would have aided and comforted my Jewish brothers even though it was illegal. If I lived in a Communist country today where certain principles dear to the Christian faith are suppressed, I believe I would openly advocate disobeying these anti-religious laws. I must make two honest confessions to you, my Christian and Jewish brothers. First, I must confess that over the last few years I have been gravely disappointed with the white moderate. I have almost reached the regrettable conclusion that the Negro's great stumbling block in the stride toward freedom is not the White Citizen's Counciler or the Ku Klux Klanner, but the white moderate who is more devoted to "order" than to justice; who prefers a negative peace which is the absence of tension to a positive peace which is the presence of justice; who constantly says "I agree with you in the goal you seek, but I can't agree with your methods of direct action;" who paternalistically feels he can set the timetable for another man's freedom; who lives by the myth of time and who constantly advises the Negro to wait until a "more convenient season." Shallow understanding from people of goodwill is more frustrating than absolute misunderstanding from people of ill will. Lukewarm acceptance is much more bewildering than outright rejection.

I had hoped that the white moderate would understand that law and order exist for the purpose of establishing justice, and that when they fail to do this they become dangerously structured dams that block the flow of social progress. I had hoped that the white moderate would understand that the present tension in the South is merely a necessary phase of the transition from an obnoxious negative peace, where the Negro passively accepted his unjust plight, to a substance-filled positive peace, where all men will respect the dignity and worth of human personality. Actually, we who engage in nonviolent direct action are not the creators of tension. We merely bring to the surface the hidden tension that is already alive. We bring it out in the open where it can be seen and dealt with. Like a boil that can never be cured as long as it is covered up but must be opened with all its pus-flowing ugliness to the natural medicines of air and light, injustice must likewise be exposed, with all of the tension its exposing creates, to the light of human conscience and the air of national opinion before it can be cured.

In your statement you asserted that our actions, even though peaceful, must be condemned because they precipitate violence. But can this assertion be logically made? Isn't this like condemning the robbed man because his possession of money precipitated the evil act of robbery? Isn't this like condemning Socrates because his unswerving commitment to truth and his philosophical delvings precipitated the misguided popular mind to make him drink the hemlock? Isn't this like condemning Jesus because His unique God-Consciousness and never-ceasing devotion to His will precipitated the evil act of crucifixion? We must come to see, as the federal courts have consistently affirmed, that it is immoral to urge an individual to withdraw his efforts to gain his basic constitutional rights because the quest precipitates violence. Society must protect the robbed and punish the robber.

I had also hoped that the white moderate would reject the myth of time. I received a letter this morning from a white brother in Texas which said: "All Christians know that the colored people will receive equal rights eventually, but it is possible that you are in too great of a religious hurry. It has taken Christianity almost 2000 years to accomplish what it has. The teachings of Christ take time to come to earth." All that is said here grows out of a tragic misconception of time. It is the strangely irrational notion that there is something in the very flow of time that will inevitably cure all ills. Actually time is neutral. It can be used either destructively or constructively. I am coming to feel that the people of ill-will have used time much more effectively than the people of good will. We will have to repent in this generation not merely for the vitriolic words and actions of the bad people, but for the appalling silence of the good people. We must come to see that human progress never rolls in on wheels of inevitability. It comes through the tireless efforts and persistent work of men willing to be co-

workers with God, and without this hard work time itself becomes an ally of the forces of social stagnation. We must use time creatively, and forever realize that the time is always ripe to do right. Now is the time to make real the promise of democracy, and transform our pending national elegy into a creative psalm of brotherhood. Now is the time to lift our national policy from the quicksand of racial injustice to the solid rock of human dignity.

You spoke of our activity in Birmingham as extreme. At first I was rather disappointed that fellow clergymen would see my nonviolent efforts as those of the extremist. I started thinking about the fact that I stand in the middle of two opposing forces in the Negro community. One is a force of complacency made up of Negroes who, as a result of long years of oppression, have been so completely drained of self-respect and a sense of "somebodiness" that they have adjusted to segregation, and, of a few Negroes in the middle class who, because of a degree of academic and economic security, and because at points they profit by segregation, have unconsciously become insensitive to the problems of the masses. The other force is one of bitterness, and hatred comes perilously close to advocating violence. It is expressed in the various black nationalist groups that are springing up over the nation, the largest and best-known being Elijah Muhammad's Muslim movement. This movement is nourished by the contemporary frustration over the continued existence of racial discrimination. It is made up of people who have lost faith in America, who have absolutely repudiated Christianity, and who have concluded that the white man is an incurable "devil." I have tried to stand between these two forces saying that we need not follow the "do-nothingism" of the complacent or the hatred and despair of the black nationalist. There is the more excellent way of love and nonviolent protest. I'm grateful to God that, through the Negro church, the dimension of nonviolence entered our struggle. If this philosophy had not emerged, I am convinced that by now many streets of the South would be flowing with floods of blood. And I am further convinced that if our white brothers dismiss as "rabble rousers" and "outside agitators" those of us who are working through the channels of nonviolent direct action and refuse to support our nonviolent efforts, millions of Negroes, out of frustration and despair, will seek solace and security in black-nationalist ideologies, a development that will lead inevitably to a frightening racial nightmare.

Oppressed people cannot remain oppressed forever. The urge for freedom will eventually come. This is what happened to the American Negro. Something within has reminded him of his birthright of freedom; something without has reminded him that he can gain it. Consciously and unconsciously, he has been swept in by what the Germans call the *Zeitgeist,* and with his black brothers of Africa, and his brown and yellow brothers of Asia, South America and the Caribbean, he is moving with a sense of cosmic urgency toward the promised land of racial justice. Recognizing this vital urge that has engulfed the Negro community, one should readily understand public demonstrations. The Negro has many pent up resentments and latent frustrations. He has to get them out. So let him march sometime; let him have his prayer pilgrimages to the city hall; understand why he must have sit-ins and freedom rides. If his repressed emotions do not come out in these nonviolent ways, they will come out in ominous expressions of violence. This is not a threat; it is a fact of history. So I have not said to my people "get rid of your discontent." But I have tried to say that this normal and healthy discontent can be channelized through the creative outlet of nonviolent direct action. Now this approach is being dismissed as extremist. I must admit that I was initially disappointed in being so categorized.

But as I continued to think about the matter I gradually gained a bit of satisfaction from being considered an extremist. Was not Jesus an extremist for love—"Love your enemies, bless them that curse you, pray for them that despitefully use you." Was not Amos an extremist for justice—"Let justice roll down like waters and righteousness like a mighty stream." Was not Paul an extremist for the gospel of Jesus Christ—"I bear in my body the marks of the Lord Jesus." Was not Martin Luther an extremist—"Here I stand; I can do none other so help me God." Was not John Bunyan an extremist—"I will stay in jail to the end of my days before I make a butchery of my conscience." Was not Abraham Lincoln an extremist—"This nation cannot survive half slave and half free." Was not Thomas Jefferson an extremist—"We hold these truths to be self-evident, that all men are created equal." So the question is not whether we will be extremist but what kind of extremist will we be. Will we be extremists for hate or will we be extremists for love? Will we be extremists for the preservation of injustice—or will we be extremists for the cause of justice? In that dramatic scene on Calvary's hill, three men were crucified. We must not forget that all three were crucified for the same crime—the crime of extremism. Two were extremists for immorality, and thusly fell below their environment. The other, Jesus Christ, was an extremist for love, truth and goodness, and thereby rose above his environment. So, after all, maybe the South, the nation and the world are in dire need of creative extremists.

I had hoped that the white moderate would see this. Maybe I was too optimistic. Maybe I expected too much. I guess I should have realized that few members of a race that has oppressed another race can understand or appreciate the deep groans and passionate yearnings of those that have been oppressed and still fewer have the vision to see that injustice must be rooted out by strong, persistent and determined action. I am thankful, however, that some of our white brothers have grasped the meaning of this social revolution and committed themselves to it. They are still all too small in quantity, but they are big in quality. Some like Ralph McGill, Lillian Smith, Harry Golden and James Dabbs have written about our struggle in eloquent, prophetic and understanding terms. Others have marched with us down nameless streets of the South. They have languished in filthy roach-infested jails, suffering the abuse and brutality of angry policemen who see them as "dirty nigger lovers." They, unlike so many of their moderate brothers and sisters, have recognized the urgency of the moment and sensed the need for powerful "action" antidotes to combat the disease of segregation.

Let me rush on to mention my other disappointment. I have been so greatly disappointed with the white church and its leadership. Of course, there are some notable exceptions. I am not unmindful of the fact that each of you has taken some significant stands on this issue.

I commend you, Rev. [Earl] Stallings, for your Christian stand on this past Sunday, in welcoming Negroes to your worship service on a non-segregated basis. I commend the Catholic leaders of this state for integrating Spring Hill College several years ago.

But despite these notable exceptions I must honestly reiterate that I have been disappointed with the church. I do not say that as one of those negative critics who can always find something wrong with the church. I say it as a minister of the gospel, who loves the church; who was nurtured in its bosom; who has been sustained by its spiritual blessings and who will remain true to it as long as the cord of life shall lengthen.

I had the strange feeling when I was suddenly catapulted into the leadership of the bus protest in Montgomery several years ago, that we would have the support of the white church. I felt that the white ministers, priests and rabbis of the South would be some of our strongest allies. Instead, some have been outright opponents, refusing to understand the freedom movement and misrepresenting its leaders; all too many others have been more cautious than courageous and have remained silent behind the anesthetizing security of the stained-glass windows.

In spite of my shattered dreams of the past, I came to Birmingham with the hope that the white religious leadership of this community would see the justice of our cause, and with deep moral concern, serve as the channel through which our just grievances would get to the power structure. I had hoped that each of you would understand. But again I have been disappointed. I have heard numerous religious leaders of the South call upon their worshippers to comply with a desegregation decision because it is the *law*, but I have longed to hear white ministers say, "follow this decree because integration is morally *right* and the Negro is your brother." In the midst of blatant injustices inflicted upon the Negro, I have watched white churches stand on the sideline and merely mouth pious irrelevancies and sanctimonious trivialities. In the midst of a mighty struggle to rid our nation of racial and economic injustice, I have heard so many ministers say, "Those are social issues with which the gospel has no real concern." And I have watched so many churches commit themselves to a completely other-worldly religion which

made a strange distinction between body and soul, the sacred and the secular.

So here we are moving toward the exit of the twentieth century with a religious community largely adjusted to the status quo, standing as a tail-light behind other community agencies rather than a headlight leading men to higher levels of justice.

I have traveled the length and breadth of Alabama, Mississippi and all the other southern states. On sweltering summer days and crisp autumn mornings I have looked at her beautiful churches with their lofty spires pointing heavenward. I have beheld the impressive outlay of her massive religious education buildings. Over and over again I have found myself asking: "What kind of people worship here? Who is their God? Where were their voices when the lips of Governor Barnett dripped with words of interposition and nullification? Where were they when Governor Wallace gave the clarion call for defiance and hatred? Where were their voices of support when tired, bruised and weary Negro men and women decided to rise from the dark dungeons of complacency to the bright hills of creative protest?"

Yes, these questions are still in my mind. In deep disappointment, I have wept over the laxity of the church. But be assured that my tears have been tears of love. There can be no deep disappointment where there is not deep love. Yes, I love the church; I love her sacred walls. How could I do otherwise? I am in the rather unique position of being the son, the grandson and the great-grandson of preachers. Yes, I see the church as the body of Christ. But, oh! How we have blemished and scarred that body through social neglect and fear of being nonconformists.

There was a time when the church was very powerful. It was during that period when the early Christians rejoiced when they were deemed worthy to suffer for what they believed. In those days the church was not merely a thermometer that recorded the ideas and principles of popular opinion; it was a thermostat that transformed the mores of society. Whenever the early Christians entered a town the power structure got disturbed and immediately sought to convict them for being "disturbers of the peace" and "outside agitators." But they went on with the conviction that they were "a colony of heaven," and had to obey God rather than man. They were small in number but big in commitment. They were too God-intoxicated to be "astronomically intimidated." They brought an end to such ancient evils as infanticide and gladiatorial contest.

Things are different now. The contemporary church is often a weak, ineffectual voice with an uncertain sound. It is so often the arch supporter of the status quo. Far from being disturbed by the presence of the church, the power structure of the average community is consoled by the church's silent and often vocal sanction of things as they are.

But the judgment of God is upon the church as never before. If the church of today does not recapture the sacrificial spirit of the early church, it will lose its authentic ring, forfeit the loyalty of millions, and be dismissed as an irrelevant social club with no meaning for the twentieth century. I am meeting young people every day whose disappointment with the church has risen to outright disgust.

Maybe again, I have been too optimistic. Is organized religion too inextricably bound to status-quo to save our nation and the world? Maybe I must turn my faith to the inner spiritual church, the church within the church, as the true *ecclesia* and the hope of the world. But again I am thankful to God that some noble souls from the ranks of organized religion have broken loose from the paralyzing chains of conformity and joined us as active partners in the struggle for freedom. They have left their secure congregations and walked the streets of Albany, Georgia, with us. They have gone through the highways of the South on tortuous rides for freedom. Yes, they have gone to jail with us. Some have been kicked out of their churches, and lost support of their bishops and fellow ministers. But they have gone with the faith that right defeated is stronger than evil triumphant. These men have been the leaven in the lump of the race. Their witness has been the spiritual salt that has preserved the true meaning of the Gospel in these troubled times. They have carved a tunnel of hope though the dark mountain of disappointment.

I hope the church as a whole will meet the challenge of this decisive hour. But even if the church does not come to the aid of justice, I have no despair about the future. I have no fear about the outcome of our struggle in Birmingham, even if our motives are presently misunderstood. We will reach the goal of freedom in Birmingham and all over the nation, because the goal of America is freedom. Abused and scorned though we may be, our destiny is tied up with the destiny of America. Before the pilgrims landed at Plymouth we were here. Before the pen of Jefferson etched across the pages of history the majestic words of the Declaration of Independence, we were here. For more than two centuries our fore-parents labored in this country without wages; they made cotton king; and they built the homes of their masters in the midst of brutal injustice and shameful humiliation—and yet out of a bottomless vitality they continued to thrive and develop. If the inexpressible cruelties of slavery could not stop us, the opposition we now face will surely fail. We will win our freedom because the sacred heritage of our nation and the eternal will of God are embodied in our echoing demands.

I must close now. But before closing I am impelled to mention one other point in your statement that troubled me profoundly. You warmly commended the Birmingham police force for keeping "order" and "preventing violence." I don't believe you would have so warmly commended the police force if you had seen its angry violent dogs literally biting six unarmed, nonviolent Negroes. I don't believe you would so quickly commend the policemen if you would observe their ugly and inhuman treatment of Negroes here in the city jail; if you would watch them push and curse old Negro women and young Negro girls; if you would see them slap and kick old Negro men and young boys; if you will observe them, as they did on two occasions, refuse to give us food because we wanted to sing our grace together. I'm sorry that I can't join you in your praise for the police department.

It is true that they have been rather disciplined in their public handling of the demonstrators. In this sense they have been rather publicly "nonviolent." But for what purpose? To preserve the evil system of segregation. Over the last few years I have consistently preached that nonviolence demands that the means we use must be as pure as the ends we seek. So I have tried to make it clear that it is wrong to use immoral means to attain moral ends. But now I must affirm that it is just as wrong, or even more so, to use moral means to preserve immoral ends. Maybe Mr. Connor and his policemen have been rather publicly nonviolent, as Chief [Laurie] Pritchett was in Albany, Georgia, but they have used the moral means of nonviolence to maintain the immoral end of flagrant racial injustice. T.S. Eliot has said that there is no greater treason than to do the right deed for the wrong reason.

I wish you had commended the Negro sit-inners and demonstrators of Birmingham for their sublime courage, their willingness to suffer and their amazing discipline in the midst of the most inhuman provocation. One day the South will recognize its real heroes. They will be the James Merediths, courageously and with a majestic sense of purpose, facing jeering and hostile mobs and with the agonizing loneliness that characterizes the life of the pioneer. They will be old oppressed, battered Negro women, symbolized in a seventy-two year old woman of Montgomery, Alabama, who rose up with a sense of dignity and with her people decided not to ride the segregated buses, and responded to one who inquired about her tiredness with ungrammatical profundity; "my feet is tired, but my soul is rested." They will be the young high school and college students, young ministers of the gospel and a host of their elders courageously and nonviolently sitting-in at lunch counters and willingly going to jail for conscience's sake. One day the South will know that when these disinherited children of God sat down at lunch counters they were in reality standing up for the best in the American dream and the most sacred values in our Judaeo-Christian heritage, and thusly, carrying our whole nation back to those great wells of democracy which were dug deep by the founding fathers in the formulation of the Constitution and the Declaration of Independence.

Never before have I written a letter this long, (or should I say a book?). I'm afraid it is much too long to take your precious time. I can assure you that it would have been much shorter if I had been writing from a comfortable desk, but what else is there to do when you are alone for days in the dull monotony of a narrow jail cell other than write long letters, think strange thoughts, and pray long prayers?

If I have said anything in this letter that is an overstatement of the truth and is indicative of an unreasonable impatience, I beg you to forgive me. If I have said anything in this letter that is an understatement of the truth and is indicative of

my having a patience that makes me patient with anything less than brotherhood, I beg God to forgive me.

I hope this letter finds you strong in the faith. I also hope that circumstances will soon make it possible for me to meet each of you, not as an integrationist or a civil rights leader, but as a fellow clergyman and a Christian brother. Let us all hope that the dark clouds of racial prejudice will soon pass away and the deep fog of misunderstanding will be lifted from our fear-drenched communities and in some not too distant tomorrow the radiant stars of love and brotherhood will shine over our great nation with all their scintillating beauty.

Yours for the cause of Peace and Brotherhood, Martin Luther King, Jr.

Indians of All Nations, The Alcatraz Proclamation to the Great White Father and His People (1969)

At the Native American takeover of Alcatraz Island in San Francisco Harbor on November 14, 1969, insurgents from the American Indian Movement raised their blue flag, featuring a red tepee and severed peace pipe as symbols of militancy and broken trust in government promises. With this proclamation, leaders mocked the depravity of white culture by proposing an Indian cultural center.

Fellow citizens, we are asking you to join with us in our attempt to better the lives of all Indian people.

We are on Alcatraz Island to make known to the world that we have a right to use our land for our own benefit.

In a proclamation of November 20, 1969, we told the government of the United States that we are here "to create a meaningful use for our Great Spirit's Land."

We, the native Americans, reclaim the land known as Alcatraz Island in the name of all American Indians by right of discovery.

We wish to be fair and honorable in our dealings with the Caucasian inhabitants of this land, and hereby offer the following treaty:

We will purchase said Alcatraz Island for twenty-four dollars in glass beads and red cloth, a precedent set by the white man's purchase of a similar island about 300 years ago. We know that $24 in trade goods for these 16 acres is more than was paid when Manhattan Island was sold, but we know that land values have risen over the years. Our offer of $1.24 per acre is greater than the $0.47 per acre the white men are now paying the California Indians for their lands.

We will give to the inhabitants of this island a portion of the land for their own to be held in trust . . . by the Bureau of Caucasian Affairs . . . in perpetuity—for as long as the sun shall rise and the rivers go down to the sea. We will further guide the inhabitants in the proper way of living. We will offer them our religion, our education, our life-ways in order to help them achieve our level of civilization and thus raise them and all their white brothers up from their savage and unhappy state. We offer this treaty in good faith and wish to be fair and honorable in our dealings with all white men.

We feel that this so-called Alcatraz Island is more than suitable for an Indian reservation, as determined by the white man's own standards. By this, we mean that this place resembles most Indian reservations in that:

1. It is isolated from modern facilities, and without adequate means of transportation.
2. It has no fresh running water.
3. It has inadequate sanitation facilities.
4. There are no oil or mineral rights.
5. There is no industry and so unemployment is very great.
6. There are no health-care facilities.
7. The soil is rocky and non-productive, and the land does not support game.
8. There are no educational facilities.
9. The population has always exceeded the land base.
10. The population has always been held as prisoners and kept dependent upon others.

Further, it would be fitting and symbolic that ships from all over the world, entering the Golden Gate, would first see Indian land, and thus be reminded of the true history of this nation. This tiny island would be a symbol of the great lands once ruled by free and noble Indians.

What use will we make of this land?

Since the San Francisco Indian Center burned down, there is no place for Indians to assemble and carry on tribal life here in the white man's city. Therefore, we plan to develop on this island several Indian institutions:

1. A Center for Native American Studies will be developed which will educate them to the skills and knowledge relevant to improve the lives and spirits of all Indian peoples. Attached to this center will be travelling universities, managed by Indians, which will go to the Indian Reservations, learning those necessary and relevant materials now about.

2. An American Indian Spiritual Center, which will practice our ancient tribal religious and sacred healing ceremonies. Our cultural arts will be featured and our young people trained in music, dance, and healing rituals.

3. An Indian Center of Ecology, which will train and support our young people in scientific research and practice to restore our lands and waters to their pure and natural state. We will work to de-pollute the air and waters of the Bay Area. We will seek to restore fish and animal life to the area and to revitalize sea-life which has been threatened by the white man's way. We will set up facilities to desalt sea water for human benefit.

4. A Great Indian Training School will be developed to teach our people how to make a living in the world, improve our standard of living, and to end hunger and unemployment among all our people. This training school will include a center for Indian arts and crafts, and an Indian restaurant serving native foods, which will restore Indian culinary arts. This center will display Indian arts and offer Indian foods to the public, so that all may know of the beauty and spirit of the traditional Indian ways.

Some of the present buildings will be taken over to develop an American Indian Museum which will depict our native food and other cultural contributions we have given to the world. Another part of the museum will present some of the things the white man has given to the Indians in return for the land and life he took:

disease, alcohol, poverty, and cultural decimation (as symbolized by old tin cans, barbed wire, rubber tires, plastic containers, etc.). Part of the museum will remain a dungeon to symbolize both those Indian captives who were incarcerated for challenging white authority and those who were imprisoned on reservations. The museum will show the noble and tragic events of Indian history, including the broken treaties, the documentary of the Trail of Tears, the Massacre of Wounded Knee, as well as the victory over Yellow-Hair Custer and his army.

In the name of all Indians, therefore, we reclaim this island for our Indian nations, for all these reasons. We feel this claim is just and proper, and that this land should rightfully be granted to us for as long as the rivers run and the sun shall shine.

We hold the rock!

Texas v. Johnson (1989)

In a controversial 1989 ruling, the U.S. Supreme Court held, 5–4, that the conviction of a Texas man for burning an American flag at a political demonstration was an abridgment of his right to free speech under the First Amendment to the Constitution. The court's decision invalidated the antidesecration law in Texas and 47 other states, setting off a wave of protest and legal activity. Congress passed the Flag Protection Act in 1989, but the high court struck it down on similar grounds.

Argued March 21, 1989
Decided June 21, 1989

JUSTICE BRENNAN delivered the opinion of the Court.

After publicly burning an American flag as a means of political protest, Gregory Lee Johnson was convicted of desecrating a flag in violation of Texas law. This case presents the question whether his conviction is consistent with the First Amendment. We hold that it is not.

I

While the Republican National Convention was taking place in Dallas in 1984, respondent Johnson participated in a political demonstration dubbed the "Republican War Chest Tour." As explained in literature distributed by the demonstrators and in speeches made by them, the purpose of this event was to protest the policies of the Reagan administration and of certain Dallas-based corporations. The demonstrators marched through the Dallas streets, chanting political slogans and stopping at several corporate locations to stage "die-ins" intended to dramatize the consequences of nuclear war. On several occasions they spray-painted the walls of buildings and overturned potted plants, but Johnson himself took no part in such activities. He did, however, accept an American flag handed to him by a fellow protestor who had taken it from a flagpole outside one of the targeted buildings.

The demonstration ended in front of Dallas City Hall, where Johnson unfurled the American flag, doused it with kerosene, and set it on fire. While the flag burned, the protestors chanted, "America, the red, white, and blue, we spit on you." After the demonstrators dispersed, a witness to the flag burning collected the flag's remains and buried them in his backyard. No one was physically injured or threatened with injury, though several witnesses testified that they had been seriously offended by the flag burning.

Of the approximately 100 demonstrators, Johnson alone was charged with a crime. The only criminal offense with which he was charged was the desecration of a venerated object in violation of Tex. Penal Code Ann. § 42.09(a)(3) (1989). After a trial, he was convicted, sentenced to one year in prison, and fined $2,000. The Court of Appeals for the Fifth District of Texas at Dallas affirmed Johnson's conviction . . . , but the Texas Court of Criminal Appeals reversed (1988), holding that the State could not, consistent with the First Amendment, punish Johnson for burning the flag in these circumstances. . . .

II

Johnson was convicted of flag desecration for burning the flag, rather than for uttering insulting words. This fact somewhat complicates our consideration of his conviction under the First Amendment. We must first determine whether Johnson's burning of the flag constituted expressive conduct, permitting him to invoke the First

Amendment in challenging his conviction. If his conduct was expressive, we next decide whether the State's regulation is related to the suppression of free expression. If the State's regulation is not related to expression, then the less stringent standard we announced in *United States v. O'Brien* (1968) for regulations of noncommunicative conduct controls. If it is, then we are outside of O'Brien's test, and we must ask whether this interest justifies Johnson's conviction under a more demanding standard. A third possibility is that the State's asserted interest is simply not implicated on these facts, and, in that event, the interest drops out of the picture.

The First Amendment literally forbids the abridgment only of "speech," but we have long recognized that its protection does not end at the spoken or written word. While we have rejected "the view that an apparently limitless variety of conduct can be labeled 'speech' whenever the person engaging in the conduct intends thereby to express an idea," *O'Brien,* we have acknowledged that conduct may be "sufficiently imbued with elements of communication to fall within the scope of the First and Fourteenth Amendments," *Spence v. Washington* (1974).

In deciding whether particular conduct possesses sufficient communicative elements to bring the First Amendment into play, we have asked whether "[a]n intent to convey a particularized message was present, and [whether] the likelihood was great that the message would be understood by those who viewed it."

Hence, we have recognized the expressive nature of students' wearing of black armbands to protest American military involvement in Vietnam, *Tinker v. Des Moines Independent Community School Dist.* (1969); of a sit-in by blacks in a "whites only" area to protest segregation, *Brown v. Louisiana* (1966); of the wearing of American military uniforms in a dramatic presentation criticizing American involvement in Vietnam, *Schacht v. United States* (1970); and of picketing about a wide variety of causes, see, e.g., *Food Employees v. Logan Valley Plaza, Inc.* (1968); *United States v. Grace* (1983).

Especially pertinent to this case are our decisions recognizing the communicative nature of conduct relating to flags. Attaching a peace sign to the flag, *Spence;* refusing to salute the flag, *West Virginia Board of Education v. Barnette* (1943);

and displaying a red flag, *Stromberg v. California* (1931), we have held, all may find shelter under the First Amendment. See also *Smith v. Goguen* (1974) (White, J., concurring in judgment) (treating flag "contemptuously" by wearing pants with small flag sewn into their seat is expressive conduct). That we have had little difficulty identifying an expressive element in conduct relating to flags should not be surprising. The very purpose of a national flag is to serve as a symbol of our country; it is, one might say, "the one visible manifestation of two hundred years of nationhood" (Rehnquist, J., dissenting).

Thus, we have observed: "[T]he flag salute is a form of utterance. Symbolism is a primitive but effective way of communicating ideas. The use of an emblem or flag to symbolize some system, idea, institution, or personality, is a shortcut from mind to mind. Causes and nations, political parties, lodges and ecclesiastical groups seek to knit the loyalty of their followings to a flag or banner, a color or design," *Barnette.* Pregnant with expressive content, the flag as readily signifies this Nation as does the combination of letters found in "America."

We have not automatically concluded, however, that any action taken with respect to our flag is expressive. Instead, in characterizing such action for First Amendment purposes, we have considered the context in which it occurred. In *Spence,* for example, we emphasized that Spence's taping of a peace sign to his flag was "roughly simultaneous with and concededly triggered by the Cambodian incursion and the Kent State tragedy." The State of Washington had conceded, in fact, that Spence's conduct was a form of communication, and we stated that "the State's concession is inevitable on this record."

The State of Texas conceded for purposes of its oral argument in this case that Johnson's conduct was expressive conduct, and this concession seems to us as prudent as was Washington's in *Spence.* Johnson burned an American flag as part—indeed, as the culmination—of a political demonstration that coincided with the convening of the Republican Party and its renomination of Ronald Reagan for President. The expressive, overtly political nature of this conduct was both intentional and overwhelmingly apparent. At his trial, Johnson explained his reasons for burning the flag as follows: "The American Flag was burned as Ronald Reagan was being renominated as President. And a more powerful statement of symbolic speech, whether you agree with it or not, couldn't have been made at that time. It's quite a just position. We had new patriotism and no patriotism."

In these circumstances, Johnson's burning of the flag was conduct "sufficiently imbued with elements of communication," *Spence,* to implicate the First Amendment.

III

The government generally has a freer hand in restricting expressive conduct than it has in restricting the written or spoken word. See *O'Brien; Clark v. Community for Creative Non-Violence* (1984); *Dallas v. Stanglin* (1989). It may not, however, proscribe particular conduct *because* it has expressive elements.

"[W]hat might be termed the more generalized guarantee of freedom of expression makes the communicative nature of conduct an inadequate basis for singling out that conduct for proscription. A law *directed* at the communicative nature of conduct must, like a law directed at speech itself, be justified by the substantial showing of need that the First Amendment requires," *Community for Creative Non-Violence v. Watt* (1983) (Scalia, J., dissenting).

It is, in short, not simply the verbal or nonverbal nature of the expression, but the governmental interest at stake, that helps to determine whether a restriction on that expression is valid. Thus, although we have recognized that, where "'speech' and 'nonspeech' elements are combined in the same course of conduct, a sufficiently important governmental interest in regulating the nonspeech element can justify incidental limitations on First Amendment freedoms," *O'Brien,* we have limited the applicability of *O'Brien's* relatively lenient standard to those cases in which "the governmental interest is unrelated to the suppression of free expression." In stating, moreover, that *O'Brien's* test "in the last analysis is little, if any, different from the standard applied to time, place, or manner restrictions," *Clark,* we have highlighted the requirement that the governmental interest in question be unconnected to expression in order to come under *O'Brien's* less demanding rule.

In order to decide whether *O'Brien's* test applies here, therefore, we must decide whether Texas has asserted an interest in support of Johnson's conviction that is unrelated to the suppression of expression. If we find that an interest asserted by the State is simply not implicated on the facts before us, we need not ask whether *O'Brien's* test applies. The State offers two separate interests to justify this conviction: preventing breaches of the peace and preserving the flag as a symbol of nationhood and national unity. We hold that the first interest is not implicated on this record, and that the second is related to the suppression of expression.

A

Texas claims that its interest in preventing breaches of the peace justifies Johnson's conviction for flag desecration. However, no disturbance of the peace actually occurred or threatened to occur because of Johnson's burning of the flag. Although the State stresses the disruptive behavior of the protestors during their march toward City Hall, it admits that "no actual breach of the peace occurred at the time of the flagburning or in response to the flagburning." The State's emphasis on the protestors' disorderly actions prior to arriving at City Hall is not only somewhat surprising, given that no charges were brought on the basis of this conduct, but it also fails to show that a disturbance of the peace was a likely reaction to Johnson's conduct. The only evidence offered by the State at trial to show the reaction to Johnson's actions was the testimony of several persons who had been seriously offended by the flag burning.

The State's position, therefore, amounts to a claim that an audience that takes serious offense at particular expression is necessarily likely to disturb the peace, and that the expression may be prohibited on this basis. Our precedents do not countenance such a presumption. On the contrary, they recognize that a principal "function of free speech under our system of government is to invite dispute. It may indeed best serve its high purpose when it induces a condition of unrest, creates dissatisfaction with conditions as they are, or even stirs people to anger," *Terminiello v. Chicago* (1949). See also *Cox v. Louisiana* (1965); *Tinker v. Des Moines Independent Community School Dist.; Coates v.*

Cincinnati (1971); *Hustler Magazine, Inc. v. Falwell* (1988). It would be odd indeed to conclude *both* that "if it is the speaker's opinion that gives offense, that consequence is a reason for according it constitutional protection," *FCC v. Pacifica Foundation* (1978), *and* that the Government may ban the expression of certain disagreeable ideas on the unsupported presumption that their very disagreeableness will provoke violence.

Thus, we have not permitted the government to assume that every expression of a provocative idea will incite a riot, but have instead required careful consideration of the actual circumstances surrounding such expression, asking whether the expression "is directed to inciting or producing imminent lawless action and is likely to incite or produce such action," *Brandenburg v. Ohio* (1969). To accept Texas' arguments that it need only demonstrate "the potential for a breach of the peace," and that every flag burning necessarily possesses that potential, would be to eviscerate our holding in *Brandenburg*. This we decline to do.

Nor does Johnson's expressive conduct fall within that small class of "fighting words" that are "likely to provoke the average person to retaliation, and thereby cause a breach of the peace," *Chaplinsky v. New Hampshire* (1942). No reasonable onlooker would have regarded Johnson's generalized expression of dissatisfaction with the policies of the Federal Government as a direct personal insult or an invitation to exchange fisticuffs.

We thus conclude that the State's interest in maintaining order is not implicated on these facts. The State need not worry that our holding will disable it from preserving the peace. We do not suggest that the First Amendment forbids a State to prevent "imminent lawless action." And, in fact, Texas already has a statute specifically prohibiting breaches of the peace, Tex. Penal Code Ann. § 42.01 (1989), which tends to confirm that Texas need not punish this flag desecration in order to keep the peace. See *Boos v. Barry*.

B

The State also asserts an interest in preserving the flag as a symbol of nationhood and national unity. In *Spence*, we acknowledged that the government's interest in preserving the flag's special

symbolic value "is directly related to expression in the context of activity" such as affixing a peace symbol to a flag. We are equally persuaded that this interest is related to expression in the case of Johnson's burning of the flag. The State, apparently, is concerned that such conduct will lead people to believe either that the flag does not stand for nationhood and national unity, but instead reflects other, less positive concepts, or that the concepts reflected in the flag do not in fact exist, that is, that we do not enjoy unity as a Nation. These concerns blossom only when a person's treatment of the flag communicates some message, and thus are related "to the suppression of free expression" within the meaning of *O'Brien*. We are thus outside of *O'Brien*'s test altogether.

IV

It remains to consider whether the State's interest in preserving the flag as a symbol of nationhood and national unity justifies Johnson's conviction.

As in *Spence*, "[w]e are confronted with a case of prosecution for the expression of an idea through activity," and "[a]ccordingly, we must examine with particular care the interests advanced by [petitioner] to support its prosecution." Johnson was not, we add, prosecuted for the expression of just any idea; he was prosecuted for his expression of dissatisfaction with the policies of this country, expression situated at the core of our First Amendment values.

Moreover, Johnson was prosecuted because he knew that his politically charged expression would cause "serious offense." If he had burned the flag as a means of disposing of it because it was dirty or torn, he would not have been convicted of flag desecration under this Texas law: federal law designates burning as the preferred means of disposing of a flag "when it is in such condition that it is no longer a fitting emblem for display," 36 U.S.C. § 176(k), and Texas has no quarrel with this means of disposal. The Texas law is thus not aimed at protecting the physical integrity of the flag in all circumstances, but is designed instead to protect it only against impairments that would cause serious offense to others. Texas concedes as much. . . .

Whether Johnson's treatment of the flag violated Texas law thus depended on the likely communicative impact of his expressive conduct. Our decision in *Boos v. Barry* tells us that this restriction on Johnson's expression is content-based. In *Boos*, we considered the constitutionality of a law prohibiting "the display of any sign within 500 feet of a foreign embassy if that sign tends to bring that foreign government into 'public odium' or 'public disrepute.'" Rejecting the argument that the law was content-neutral because it was justified by "our international law obligation to shield diplomats from speech that offends their dignity," we held that "[t]he emotive impact of speech on its audience is not a secondary effect" unrelated to the content of the expression itself.

According to the principles announced in *Boos,* Johnson's political expression was restricted because of the content of the message he conveyed. We must therefore subject the State's asserted interest in preserving the special symbolic character of the flag to "the most exacting scrutiny."

Texas argues that its interest in preserving the flag as a symbol of nationhood and national unity survives this close analysis. Quoting extensively from the writings of this Court chronicling the flag's historic and symbolic role in our society, the State emphasizes the "special place," quoting *Smith v. Goguen* (Rehnquist, J., dissenting). The State's argument is not that it has an interest simply in maintaining the flag as a symbol of something, no matter what it symbolizes; indeed, if that were the State's position, it would be difficult to see how that interest is endangered by highly symbolic conduct such as Johnson's. Rather, the State's claim is that it has an interest in preserving the flag as a symbol of nationhood and national unity, a symbol with a determinate range of meanings. According to Texas, if one physically treats the flag in a way that would tend to cast doubt on either the idea that nationhood and national unity are the flag's referents or that national unity actually exists, the message conveyed thereby is a harmful one, and therefore may be prohibited.

If there is a bedrock principle underlying the First Amendment, it is that the government may not prohibit the expression of an idea simply because society finds the idea itself offensive or disagreeable. See, e.g., *Hustler Magazine v. Falwell; City Council of Los Angeles v. Taxpayers for Vincent* (1984); *Bolger v. Youngs Drug Products Corp* (1983);

Carey v. Brown (1980); *FCC v. Pacifica Foundation; Young v. American Mini Theatres, Inc.* (1976); *Buckley v. Valeo* (1976); *Grayned v. Rockford* (1972); *Police Dept. of Chicago v. Mosley* (1972); *Bachellar v. Maryland* (1970); *United States v. O'Brien; Brown v. Louisiana; Stromberg v. California.*

We have not recognized an exception to this principle even where our flag has been involved. In *Street v. New York* (1969), we held that a State may not criminally punish a person for uttering words critical of the flag. Rejecting the argument that the conviction could be sustained on the ground that Street had "failed to show the respect for our national symbol which may properly be demanded of every citizen," we concluded that "the constitutionally guaranteed 'freedom to be intellectually . . . diverse or even contrary,' and the 'right to differ as to things that touch the heart of the existing order,' encompass the freedom to express publicly one's opinions about our flag, including those opinions which are defiant or contemptuous."

Nor may the government, we have held, compel conduct that would evince respect for the flag. "To sustain the compulsory flag salute, we are required to say that a Bill of Rights which guards the individual's right to speak his own mind left it open to public authorities to compel him to utter what is not in his mind."

In holding in *Barnette* that the Constitution did not leave this course open to the government, Justice Jackson described one of our society's defining principles in words deserving of their frequent repetition: "If there is any fixed star in our constitutional constellation, it is that no official, high or petty, can prescribe what shall be orthodox in politics, nationalism, religion, or other matters of opinion or force citizens to confess by word or act their faith therein."

In *Spence*, we held that the same interest asserted by Texas here was insufficient to support a criminal conviction under a flag-misuse statute for the taping of a peace sign to an American flag. "Given the protected character of [*Spence's*] expression and in light of the fact that no interest the State may have in preserving the physical integrity of a privately owned flag was significantly impaired on these facts," we held, "the conviction must be invalidated. See also *Goguen* (White, J., concurring in judgment) (to convict person who had sewn a flag onto the seat of his pants for "contemptuous" treatment of the flag would be "[t]o convict not to protect the physical integrity or to protect against acts interfering with the proper use of the flag, but to punish for communicating ideas unacceptable to the controlling majority in the legislature").

In short, nothing in our precedents suggests that a State may foster its own view of the flag by prohibiting expressive conduct relating to it. To bring its argument outside our precedents, Texas attempts to convince us that, even if its interest in preserving the flag's symbolic role does not allow it to prohibit words or some expressive conduct critical of the flag, it does permit it to forbid the outright destruction of the flag. The State's argument cannot depend here on the distinction between written or spoken words and nonverbal conduct. That distinction, we have shown, is of no moment where the nonverbal conduct is expressive, as it is here, and where the regulation of that conduct is related to expression, as it is here. In addition, both *Barnette* and *Spence* involved expressive conduct, not only verbal communication, and both found that conduct protected.

Texas' focus on the precise nature of Johnson's expression, moreover, misses the point of our prior decisions: their enduring lesson, that the government may not prohibit expression simply because it disagrees with its message, is not dependent on the particular mode in which one chooses to express an idea. If we were to hold that a State may forbid flag burning wherever it is likely to endanger the flag's symbolic role, but allow it wherever burning a flag promotes that role—as where, for example, a person ceremoniously burns a dirty flag—we would be saying that when it comes to impairing the flag's physical integrity, the flag itself may be used as a symbol—as a substitute for the written or spoken word or a "short cut from mind to mind"—only in one direction. We would be permitting a State to "prescribe what shall be orthodox" by saying that one may burn the flag to convey one's attitude toward it and its referents only if one does not endanger the flag's representation of nationhood and national unity.

We never before have held that the Government may ensure that a symbol be used to express only one view of that symbol or its referents. Indeed, in *Schacht v. United States,* we invalidated a federal statute permitting an actor portraying a member of one of our armed forces to "wear the uniform of that armed force if the portrayal does not tend to discredit that armed force." This proviso, we held, "which leaves Americans free to praise the war in Vietnam but can send persons like Schacht to prison for opposing it, cannot survive in a country which has the First Amendment."

We perceive no basis on which to hold that the principle underlying our decision in *Schacht* does not apply to this case. To conclude that the government may permit designated symbols to be used to communicate only a limited set of messages would be to enter territory having no discernible or defensible boundaries. Could the government, on this theory, prohibit the burning of state flags? Of copies of the Presidential seal? Of the Constitution? In evaluating these choices under the First Amendment, how would we decide which symbols were sufficiently special to warrant this unique status? To do so, we would be forced to consult our own political preferences, and impose them on the citizenry, in the very way that the First Amendment forbids us to do.

There is, moreover, no indication—either in the text of the Constitution or in our cases interpreting it—that a separate juridical category exists for the American flag alone. Indeed, we would not be surprised to learn that the persons who framed our Constitution and wrote the Amendment that we now construe were not known for their reverence for the Union Jack. The First Amendment does not guarantee that other concepts virtually sacred to our Nation as a whole—such as the principle that discrimination on the basis of race is odious and destructive—will go unquestioned in the marketplace of ideas. See *Brandenburg v. Ohio* (1969). We decline, therefore, to create for the flag an exception to the joust of principles protected by the First Amendment.

It is not the State's ends, but its means, to which we object. It cannot be gainsaid that there is a special place reserved for the flag in this Nation, and thus we do not doubt that the government has a legitimate interest in making efforts to "preserv[e] the national flag as an unalloyed symbol of our country," *Spence.* We reject the suggestion, urged at oral argument by counsel for Johnson, that the government lacks "any state interest whatsoever" in regulating the manner in which the flag may be displayed. Congress has, for example, enacted precatory regulations describing the proper treatment of the flag, and we cast no doubt on the legitimacy of its interest in making such recommendations. To say that the government has an interest in encouraging proper treatment of the flag, however, is not to say that it may criminally punish a person for burning a flag as a means of political protest.

"National unity as an end which officials may foster by persuasion and example is not in question. The problem is whether, under our Constitution, compulsion as here employed is a permissible means for its achievement," *Barnette.*

We are fortified in today's conclusion by our conviction that forbidding criminal punishment for conduct such as Johnson's will not endanger the special role played by our flag or the feelings it inspires. To paraphrase Justice Holmes, we submit that nobody can suppose that this one gesture of an unknown man will change our Nation's attitude towards its flag. See *Abrams v. United States* (1919) (Holmes, J., dissenting). Indeed, Texas' argument that the burning of an American flag "is an act having a high likelihood to cause a breach of the peace'" and its statute's implicit assumption that physical mistreatment of the flag will lead to "serious offense," tend to confirm that the flag's special role is not in danger; if it were, no one would riot or take offense because a flag had been burned.

We are tempted to say, in fact, that the flag's deservedly cherished place in our community will be strengthened, not weakened, by our holding today. Our decision is a reaffirmation of the principles of freedom and inclusiveness that the flag best reflects, and of the conviction that our toleration of criticism such as Johnson's is a sign and source of our strength. Indeed, one of the proudest images of our flag, the one immortalized in our own national anthem, is of the bombardment it survived at Fort McHenry. It is the Nation's resilience, not its rigidity, that Texas sees reflected in the flag—and it is that resilience that we reassert today.

The way to preserve the flag's special role is not to punish those who feel differently about these matters. It is to persuade them that they are wrong. "To courageous, self-reliant men, with confidence in the power of free and fearless reasoning applied through the processes of popular government, no danger flowing from speech can be deemed clear and present unless the incidence of the evil apprehended is so imminent that it may befall before there is opportunity for full discussion. If there be time to expose through discussion the falsehood and fallacies, to avert the evil by the processes of education, the remedy to be applied is more speech, not enforced silence," *Whitney v. California* (1927) (Brandeis, J., concurring).

And, precisely because it is our flag that is involved, one's response to the flag-burner may exploit the uniquely persuasive power of the flag itself. We can imagine no more appropriate response to burning a flag than waving one's own, no better way to counter a flag burner's message than by saluting the flag that burns, no surer means of preserving the dignity even of the flag that burned than by—as one witness here did—according its remains a respectful burial. We do not consecrate the flag by punishing its desecration, for in doing so we dilute the freedom that this cherished emblem represents.

V

Johnson was convicted for engaging in expressive conduct. The State's interest in preventing breaches of the peace does not support his conviction, because Johnson's conduct did not threaten to disturb the peace. Nor does the State's interest in preserving the flag as a symbol of nationhood and national unity justify his criminal conviction for engaging in political expression. The judgment of the Texas Court of Criminal Appeals is therefore

Affirmed.

Source: *Texas v. Johnson,* 491 U.S. 397.

ACT-UP Civil Disobedience Training

ACT-UP—the AIDS Coalition to Unleash Power—is a direct-action organization founded in New York City in the late 1980s to draw public attention to the AIDS/HIV crisis and to help end the spread of the disease. To advance its cause, ACT-UP has actively engaged in and promoted acts of civil disobedience across the United States. The text that follows is excerpted from organization training materials.

Nonviolent Response to Personal Violence

Nonviolence focuses on communication:

1. Your objectives must be reasonable. You must believe you are fair and you must be able to communicate this to your opponent.

2. Maintain as much eye contact as possible.

3. Make no abrupt gestures. Move slowly. When practical, tell your opponent what you are going to do before you do it. Don't say anything threatening, critical, or hostile.

4. Don't be afraid of stating the obvious; say simply, "You're shouting at me," or "You're hurting my arm."

5. Someone in the process of committing an act of violence has strong expectations as to how his/her victim will behave. If you manage to behave differently—in a nonthreatening manner you can interrupt the flow of events that would have culminated in an act of violence. You must create a scenario new to your opponent.

6. Seek to befriend your opponent's better nature; even the most brutal and brutalized among us have some spark of decency which the nonviolent defender can reach.

7. Don't shut down in response to physical violence; you have to play it by ear. The best rule is to resist as firmly as you can without escalating the anger or the violence. Try varying approaches and keep trying to alter your opponent's picture of the situation.

8. Get your opponent talking and listen to what s/he says. Encourage him/her to talk about what s/he believes, wishes, fears. Don't argue but at the same time don't give the impression you agree with assertions that are cruel or immoral. The listening is more important than what you say—keep the talk going and keep it calm.

—Adapted from an article by Markley Morris

Practicing Nonviolence

"Without a direct action expression of it, nonviolence, to my mind, is meaningless."

—M.K. Gandhi

Practice is a key word in understanding nonviolence. A nonviolent approach assumes that people take active roles, making choices and commitments and building on their experience. It also presents a constant challenge: to weave together the diversity of individual experiences into an ever-changing vision. There is no fixed, static "definition" of nonviolence.

Nonviolence is active. Although to some the word nonviolence implies passivity, nonviolence is actually an active form of resistance. It analyzes the sources of institutional violence and intervenes on a philosophical and political level through direct and persistent actions.

Gandhi's vision of nonviolence is translated as "clinging to truth" or sometimes "truth force," which includes both determination to speak out even when one's truth is unpopular, and willingness to hear the truth of other people's experience. He also defined two other components of nonviolence: the refusal to harm others and willingness to suffer for one's beliefs. Many activists who adopt nonviolent tactics are reluctant to accept these aspects philosophically, or to prescribe them to others. For example, Third World people in the U.S. and other countries are often pressed to use violent action to defend their lives. Some feminists point out that since our society pressures women to be self-sacrificing, the decision to accept suffering is often reinforcement of women's oppression rather than a free choice.

Jo Vellacott, in her essay "Women, Peace and Power," speaks of violence as "resourcelessness"—seeing few options, feeling like one's self or small group is alone against a hostile or at best indifferent universe. Many societal institutions and conventions, despite their original intention to benefit at least some people, perpetuate this violence by depriving people of their lives, health, self-respect or hope. Nonviolence then becomes resourcefulness—seeing the possibilities for change in oneself and in others, and having the power to act on those possibilities. Much of the task of becoming effectively nonviolent lies in removing the preconceptions that keep us from seeing those resources. Undoing the violence within us involves challenging myths that we are not good enough, not smart enough or not skilled enough to act. The best way to do this is to try it, working with friends or in small groups at first, and starting with roleplays or less intimidating activities like leafletting. As confidence in our own resourcefulness grows, we become more able to support each other in maintaining our nonviolent actions.

Anger and Emotional Violence

Getting rid of the patterns of violence that societal conditioning has placed in us is not always a polite process; it involves releasing despair, anger, and other emotions that haven't been allowed to surface before. The myth that emotions are destructive and unreliable prevents us from trusting our own experience and forces us to rely on rigid formulas and people we perceive as authorities for guidance. Most of us have been taught that expressing anger especially provokes disapproval, invalidation and physical attack, or else will hurt others and make us suffer guilt. This conditioning serves to make us both repress our own anger and also respond repressively to each other's anger.

Anger is a sign of life. It arises with recognition that injustice exists and contains the hope that things can be different. It is often hard to see this clearly because, as Barbara Deming says,

". . . our anger is in great part hidden—from others and even from ourselves—and when it is finally allowed to emerge into the open—this pride—it is shaking, unsure of itself, and so quick to be violent. For now it believes and yet it doesn't quite dare to believe that it can claim its rights at last."

To make room for a healthy expression of and response to this anger, it helps to create a general attitude of respect and support. Verbal violence—snide or vicious tones, interrupting, shouting down or misrepresenting what people say—is the antithesis of respect and communication. When people sense this happening, they should pause and consider their feelings and objectives. Clearing the air is especially important when people are feeling defensive or threatened; developing a sense of safety and acceptance of our anger with each other helps us concentrate all our emotional energies towards constructive, effective action.

"Non-violence is the constant awareness of the dignity and humanity of oneself and others; it seeks truth and justice; it renounces violence both in method and in attitude; it is a coura-

geous acceptance of active love and goodwill as the instrument with which to overcome evil and transform both oneself and others. It is the willingness to undergo suffering rather than inflict it. It excludes retaliation and flight."

—Wally Nelson, conscientious objector, civil rights activist, and tax resister

Nonviolence Training

Historically, nonviolence training was used extensively during the civil rights movement, in Gandhi's campaigns in India against the British, and in recent years in the struggles against nuclear technology, against U.S. policy in Central America and Southern Africa and for the rights of farm workers, women and people with AIDS, to name a few.

The purpose of training is for participants to form a common understanding of the use of nonviolence. It gives a forum to share ideas about nonviolence, oppression, fears and feelings. It allows people to meet and build solidarity with each other and provides an opportunity to form affinity groups. It is often used as preparation for action and gives people a chance to learn about an action, its tone, and legal ramifications. It helps people to decide whether or not they will participate in an action. Through role playing, people learn what to expect from police, officials, other people in the action and themselves.

Nonviolence training can range from several hours to several months. Most typical in the United States are sessions that run up to eight hours and have 10–25 people with two trainers leading the discussion and roleplays. Areas covered in a session include:

- History and philosophy of nonviolence, including role plays on the use of nonviolence and nonviolent responses to violence.
- Roleplays and exercises in consensus decision making, conflict resolution, and quick decision making.
- A presentation of legal ramification of civil disobedience and discussion on noncooperation and bail solidarity.
- Exercises and discussion of the role of oppression in our society and the progressive movement.

- What is an affinity group and what are the roles within the group.
- A sharing of fears and feelings related to nonviolence and nonviolent action.

Dr. Martin Luther King, Jr. wrote that the philosophy and practice of nonviolence has six basic elements.

First, nonviolence is resistance to evil and oppression. It is a human way to fight.

Second, it does not seek to defeat or humiliate the opponent, but to win his/her friendship and understanding.

Third, the nonviolent method is an attack on the forces of evil rather than against persons doing the evil. It seeks to defeat the evil and not the persons doing the evil and injustice.

Fourth, it is the willingness to accept suffering without retaliation.

Fifth, a nonviolent resister avoids both external physical and internal spiritual violence—not only refuses to shoot, but also to hate, an opponent. The ethic of real love is at the center of nonviolence.

Sixth, the believer in nonviolence has a deep faith in the future and the forces in the universe are seen to be on the side of justice.

Source: ACT-UP, AIDS Coalition to Unleash Power, http://www.actupny.org.

Glossary

abetting. Encouraging, urging, supporting, assisting, or participating in an illicit action or commission of a crime. For acts of civil disobedience, abettors bear legal culpability, as in the case of abolitionists offering food, a horse, or a canoe to help a slave slip away from an owner. Daniel Drayton created a major backlash against the Underground Railroad for his part in helping 77 slaves flee down the Chesapeake Bay aboard the schooner *Pearl* in 1848. *See also* complicity, sympathizing.

abolitionism. The drive to annul, cancel, or repeal a law or existing practice by halting or overturning, most notably the campaign to outlaw slavery before and during the U.S. Civil War. Abraham Lincoln's Emancipation Proclamation of January 1, 1863, was the official act that abolished slavery in many states; such notable figures as merchant Levi Coffin and orator Frederick Douglass supported the measure.

act of conscience. A deliberate choice, stand, or behavior exemplifying an individual's ethics or morals. Famous examples of such civil disobedience include the pacifism of the Winchester exiles of 1777, opposition to the execution of immigrants Nicola Sacco and Bartolomeo Vanzetti in the 1920s, defiance of federal intrusion on farmers' rights during the Whiskey Rebellion of 1794, and the obstruction of abortion clinics by right-to-life advocates in the late twentieth century.

activism. The zeal to support a cause, to bring about change, to confront wrongdoing, or to take vigorous countermeasures against a faulty practice or law, such as obscenity laws that muzzled comedian Lenny Bruce and poet Allen Ginsberg. Activism like that of Joan Baez and the Reverend William Sloane Coffin, Jr., during the Vietnam War and that of the Veterans Against the Iraq War opposed combat involving U.S. forces and emphasized the halting of international conflict. *See also* advocacy; agitation.

ad hoc. (*Latin*, lit. "for this") Situational, limited, and sometimes spur-of-the-moment, as in an ad hoc group formed for a specific occasion or purpose, such as the onetime formation of the colonial boarding party that burned the British brig *Gaspee* in June 1772 and Roy Wilkins's organization of a picket at the office of U.S. Attorney General Homer S. Cummings in November 1934 for conducting a national crime conference that omitted discussion of lynching. *See also* wildcat strike.

advocacy. Verbal promotion, argument, or pleading of an issue, such as pressure tactics or lobbying on behalf of animal welfare by members of People for the Ethical Treatment of Animals (PETA) or for the rights of illegal immigrants by the Sanctuary Movement. *See also* activism, propaganda.

agitation. A protest, demonstration, or stirring of public ferment or concern about a political or social issue. Socialists and members of the Industrial Workers of the World, for example, created unrest in mining communities on behalf of higher wages and safer working conditions in the early twentieth century. Similarly, Rosa Parks and the National Association for the Advancement of Colored People began a yearlong boycott in Montgomery, Alabama, in 1955–1956 to halt the segregation of travelers on public transportation.

allegation. An unproved assertion, broad accusation, or baseless charge against a person or group, exemplified by claims that members of the Bonus Army in 1932, Hollywood film stars in the 1940s, or perpetrators of the Pullman Strike of 1894 were Communists.

alternate service. The use of draftee energies and skills in situations other than service in battle, a compromise alleviating the problem of male members of pacifist faiths who refused to wear military uniforms, drill, or practice riflery. Some absolutist conscientious objectors abstained from alternate service because it validated military authority over the individual conscience.

anarchy. A chaotic, lawless, unprincipled, or disorganized situation lacking control or authority or violating a government system, exemplified by the confusion during the "Jerry Rescue" of October 1851 and the turmoil furthered by ACT-UP to call attention to the AIDS crisis in the 1980s and 1990s. *See also* insurrection, jayhawking, radicalism.

antimilitarism. Opposition to the glorification of military virtues and ideals or to the predominance of an aggressive armed force in the administration of a state, exemplified by members of the Catholic Worker movement, who denounced the administration of President John F. Kennedy for the 1961

Bay of Pigs invasion of Cuba. Unlike pacifism, antimilitarism strikes at the core of terrorism and war. *See also* pacifism. *Compare* chauvinism, jingoism, militarism.

apartheid. A rigidly structured policy of racial segregation that a government grounds on the legal, political, and educational inferiority of a single group. Americans risked arrest for civil disobedience on behalf of ending apartheid in South Africa through U.S. trade sanctions.

arraignment. An accusation or summons before a court to answer a charge of lawlessness or to offer information essential to a formal court trial; a legal preliminary undergone by youths involved in lunch counter sit-ins and voter registration programs of the 1960s and in civil confrontations that freedom fighter Gloria Richardson organized in Cambridge, Maryland.

asceticism. The abandonment or renunciation of physical luxuries and the restraint of normal pleasures in order to enhance spiritual purity through self-denial and austere living. Quaker zealot Benjamin Lay avoided luxury and idleness, lived in voluntary exile in a cave, and fasted to the point of death as a personal statement against the evils of slavery. *See also* boycott.

bigotry. A stubborn intolerance, racism, or blatant prejudice that disrespects the opinions, behaviors, ethnicity, religion, or beliefs of others; a description of the attitude of law officers who denied the legal rights of students picketing ROTC enlistment centers during the Vietnam War and of crowds who confronted children bused to inner-city Boston during the 1970s. *See also* intolerance. *Compare* pluralism.

Black Codes. State and local laws that standardized the restraint and discipline of slaves to ensure white supremacy. Educators of black children in covert classrooms violated Black Code laws against teaching literacy to the black underclass.

blacklisting. Boycotting, penalizing, or marginalizing the free choices and employment of an individual for suspicious or illicit behaviors, opinions, and beliefs. Such practice was carried out by the House Committee on Un-American Activities (commonly referred to as the House Un-American Activities Committee) during the 1940s and 1950s in its effort to rid Hollywood of alleged Communists and Communist sympathizers and by industrialists who refused to hire pro-union laborers. *See also* libel.

blasphemy. A profane, contemptuous, irreverent, defamatory, or sacrilegious attitude, utterance, or writing about God or religious ritual, a charge lev- eled at members of the Rogerene sect of Quakers for refusing to adhere to Puritan blue laws requiring Sunday church attendance and work stoppage on the Sabbath.

boycott. To engage in a concerted abstinence from purchasing, using, or patronizing products and services as a protest of company policy. A boycott relies on economic coercion to change or overturn faulty reasoning, the intent of the 1955–1956 Montgomery, Alabama, bus boycott against segregated seating.

burn in effigy. To hang or burn a mannequin, likeness, or picture of a person—typically a figure of authority—as a demonstration of public outrage or dislike, a dramatic but nonviolent method adopted by the Sons of Liberty in colonial America to terrify collectors of the British tea tax and stamp tax into abandoning their jobs and leaving the country.

capitulation. A surrender, fall from power, yielding of control, or submission of individuals or of captured territory to a superior force, as occurred at the conclusion of the American Indian Movement's occupations of Alcatraz Island and Mount Rushmore in 1971.

caste system. A rigid social or class structure based on birth or heredity that limits access to residence, employment, education, and/or citizenship. Such a system existed in the United States following the abolition of slavery and the limited absorption of free blacks into government and the social order. *See also* Jim Crow.

cell. A chapter, coven, or group organized around shared beliefs and concerns, such as the secret brotherhoods or units of the Ku Klux Klan, the neo-Nazis, or the Minutemen who patrol Arizona's border with Mexico for illegal immigrants. *See also* conspiracy, infiltration, paramilitary.

censure. Harsh blame, fault finding, reprimand, or condemnation—for instance, the official disapproval of the Catholic Church hierarchy of the Berrigan brothers' acts of civil disobedience against the Vietnam War draft and the vilification of Harriet Tubman for her rescue of slaves.

chattel. Movable personal property, livestock, or slaves. Abolitionists used state antislavery laws to release from bondage slaves who accompanied their owners on business trips or vacations into free territory.

chauvinism. Jingoism or fanatical glorification of a homeland or zealous patriotism based on the purported superiority of a person's race, culture, or gender. Such beliefs irritated suffragists who picketed the White House during World War I on behalf of full citizenship for women. *See also* jingoism, militarism. *Compare* patriotism.

civil disobedience. The resistance or criminal defiance of a law in the service of higher ideals, morals, or ethics, conceptualized by the eighteenth-century essayist Henry David Thoreau. Overt civil disobedience is the purpose of sit-ins on nuclear test sites, for example, or the collective breaching of military security to demand an end to arms development and deployment.

civil suit. A legal action or proceeding in which an individual seeks redress of a grievance by a legal remedy or intervention; this was the method chosen by members of Greenpeace to halt the despoliation of old-growth forests and by antivivisectionists to disrupt experiments on animals on college campuses.

class-action suit. A civil suit brought by a group of individuals against a company, government, or other party in the name of all victims of wrongdoing, a strategy of environmental agencies attempting to alleviate chemical pollution of air, groundwater, and soil and of private citizens seeking to eliminate obligatory flag saluting in public school classrooms.

coalition. A temporary or ad hoc union, alliance, or merger of individuals, political parties, factions, or pressure groups, such as the combined efforts of the Congress of Racial Equality, National Association for the Advancement of Colored People, Southern Christian Leadership Conference, and Student Nonviolent Coordinating Committee to achieve voting rights for black Southerners. *See also* ad hoc.

coercion. Domination, compulsion, or restraint by force, intimidation, or threat, as in the nonviolent approach to labor negotiations by use of sit-down strikes, walk-outs, informational pickets, and boycotts. *See also* intimidation.

coexistence. Survival at the same time or place in peace and cooperation through the application of policy or negotiated terms; coexistence was the goal of President Harry Truman's 1948 desegregation of the U.S. military and of the Sanctuary Movement in the 1980s.

company town. A community that is dependent on schools, merchandizing, medical care, and housing supplied by a principal employer, such as the mining towns where Mary "Mother" Jones and her disciple, Kate Richards O'Hare, harangued workers to demand fair wages and safe working environments. *See also* garnishee.

compliance. Conformity, submission, or deference to a regimen, demand, expectation, law, or statute, exemplified by the sale of homes in a restricted neighborhood to a specified race, religion, economic group, or caste. *See also* capitulation.

complicity. Participation in or direct involvement with a crime, as in supplying illegal aliens with clothing or cash to further a flight arranged by the Sanctuary Movement, or offering shelter to Standing Bear and the Ponca after their trek from an Oklahoma reservation to their Nebraska homeland in 1879. *See also* abetting, sympathizing.

conscientious objector. An individual who declines conscription into combat or refuses to join or abet an armed militia or force on the grounds of moral or religious pacifism, the choice of Mennonite and Quaker draftees during World War I, for example.

conservatism. An ideological preference for traditional, cautious, or restrained views and values; the promotion of moderation and the existing order rather than unwarranted change or alteration of conventional standards and established institutions. The predominance of male conservatism during the suffrage movement, for example, required leverage from women in each state to secure full citizenship through a vote of the U.S. Congress. *Compare* liberalism.

conspiracy. A plot or scheme of confederates or a secret cell to achieve a common goal or to commit an illegal, harmful, or subversive act, such as the spray painting of fur coats by members of People for the Ethical Treatment of Animals or the creation of anarchy by initiating the 1886 Haymarket Riot in Chicago. *See also* cell.

corruption. Ethical or moral contamination, graft, venality, racketeering, or dishonesty among officials, such as the collusion of railroad management with police and National Guardsmen during the Pullman Strike of 1894.

cult. A religious sect or splinter group that promotes extremism, false dogma, or unconventional standards, exemplified by the Mormon minority that perpetuates polygamous marriages and the coercion of young girls into wedlock with relatives or older men.

defiance. Revolt, rebellion, intractability, challenge, or insubordination to a government, employer, or military or religious order, as demonstrated by Dorothy Day's rallying of immigrant stoop laborers in the 1930s and the antimilitary blogs of soldiers fighting in the Iraq War. *See also* insurrection.

demagogue. A leader or rabble-rouser whose power over followers derives from emotional or prejudicial appeal through speeches and public harangue, the method of organizers of secret militias intent on violating gun control laws. *See also* diatribe.

diatribe. An emotional, bitter, or abusive harangue, denunciation, or verbal or written criticism intended to manipulate thought and enlist public sympathy. Labor leaders employed this method to persuade factory and dock workers to join unions, as did resisters of the U.S. Selective Service during the Cleburne County Draft War of 1918. *See also* demagogue, propaganda.

disputation. A debate, controversy, or contention emerging from polemical arguments over a belief, opinion, or dogma—the source of civil disobedience at penitentiaries preceding an execution and of demonstrations at the United Nations complex on behalf of the rights of political refugees seeking asylum. *See also* forum.

dissent. An objection, disagreement, protest, strike, uprising, or resistance to a majority opinion; a common occurrence at women's health clinics and at offices of Planned Parenthood by pro-life advocates.

dissident. A dissenter, objector, contestant, or protester who chooses to break with tradition, dogma, or convention; a description of gay patrons at the Stonewall Inn, site of a standoff between homosexuals and New York City police in summer 1969.

doctrinaire. Intractably opinionated or dogmatic on grounds of theory or principle without regard for changes of opinion, practicality, or the suitability of arguments to a specific case. *See also* bigotry, intolerance.

dogma. An unwavering doctrine, creed, tenet, philosophy, or article of faith, such as that espoused by opponents of anti–Vietnam War protestors: "My Country, Right or Wrong." *See also* intolerance, propaganda.

due process. The constitutional right to an established series of judicial proceedings designed to safeguard individual justice and equal treatment under the law. The arrest of members of Coxey's Army in 1894 displayed no respect for their grievances concerning government apathy toward hunger, homelessness, and unemployment.

ecofeminism. A woman-centered attachment to and reverence for nature premised on female nurturance of life and the protection of conditions affecting future generations. The term applies to women involved in Earth First!, Greenpeace, People for the Ethical Treatment of Animals, and other ecological protest movements.

egalitarianism. The furtherance, promotion, and affirmation of equality in civil rights, a standard of socialist efforts like those of the Industrial Workers of the World, which fought for fairness for job seekers of both genders and for all cultural, racial, and religious minorities, particularly non-English-speaking laborers.

ethics. Scruples, codes of behavior, or principles of fairness and right conduct governing professions

and social and governmental bodies, such as the standards that inspired the use of Erie Canal boats and rail lines to transport runaway slaves to Canada via the Underground Railroad. *Compare* morals.

exhibitionism. A compulsive, ego-driven public behavior that enables a grandstander or poser to draw an audience, as exemplified by the diminutive hunchback Benjamin Lay, who dressed in exotic costumes and performed eye-catching antics to advocate the abolition of slavery. In the late twentieth and early twenty-first centuries, the press accused members of Code Pink: Women for Peace and ACTUP of seeking attention by dressing in garish getups and brandishing banners featuring lurid or risqué slogans.

extortion. The levying, demanding, or exacting of illicit fees, dues, tribute, protection money, or payments through blackmail; such as the wresting of goods or protection money by Tories from patriots before the American Revolution. *See also* intimidation.

extralegal. Unsanctioned, unregulated, or outside the law, like the predations of Jayhawkers among Louisiana Cajuns during the U.S. Civil War and the suppression of slavery in Kansas Territory by John Brown and his marauders. *See also* paramilitary.

faction. A cohesive pressure group or minority that is out of harmony with a larger group, exemplified by the feminist followers of individualist Anne Hutchinson in the Massachusetts Bay Colony and by the "fighting Quakers," who banished pacifist members from Philadelphia to exile in Winchester, Virginia, at the beginning of the American Revolution.

Fifth Amendment rights. Guarantees in the Bill of Rights to freedom from self-incrimination and to rights of due process and eminent domain. In the 1940s and 1950s, for example, witnesses before the House Committee on Un-American Activities risked prison time for "taking the Fifth" and refusing to divulge personal knowledge of the Communist Party and its membership.

First Amendment rights. Guarantees in the Bill of Rights to freedom of religion, speech, the press, petition, and assembly; these were the most prominent justifications of civil disobedience among flag burners and among the Vietnam War protesters known as the Chicago Seven.

forum. A public assembly or judicial hearing that encourages the discussion of controversial issues, such as the pollution of a neighborhood by an industry or the forcing of uniforms on students in a school system. *See also* disputation.

Gandhian pacifism. Opposition to violence through resistance or nonaggressive protest or demonstration in the style of attorney Mohandas Gandhi, who challenged the British Raj and its control of native India. The Reverend Martin Luther King, Jr., traveled to India to study pacifist protest under Gandhi's tutelage as a means of advancing the American civil rights movement without bloodshed. *See also* mediation.

garnishee. To seize wages or to confiscate or repossess property from a worker who owes a debt to a third party. Mining firms demoralized employees by deducting funds from wages to requite personal bills to the company store. *See also* company town.

genocide. The deliberate and systematic extermination of a racial, ethnic, or religious group through murder, pogroms, or starvation. Chief Standing Bear protested the genocide of the Ponca in 1879 by returning from a barren Oklahoma reservation to better living conditions in his traditional homeland in Nebraska. *See also* pogrom.

gradualism. The promotion of incremental change to a policy or governmental situation. In contrast to editor William Lloyd Garrison's extreme demands for immediate and complete abolition of slavery, orator Frederick Douglass supported a step-by-step freeing of slaves to prevent mass hunger and wandering by homeless, unemployed people.

grassroots protest. Objection arising from anecdotal evidence of and popular disenchantment with a social, economic, or governmental situation. Examples include antiwar movements, the Bonus March of 1932, and support for Margaret Sanger's publication of birth control information.

guerrilla. A partisan or member of an irregular or underground force dedicated to harassment, sabotage, or overthrow of a governing power—for example, maroons who lived on the outskirts of slavery and resisted efforts to return them to bondage. *See also* insurgent, maroon, paramilitary.

habeas corpus. (*Latin,* lit. "let you have the body") A legal writ demanding that a magistrate or court release a prisoner from unlawful restraint or confinement; a demand following the Haymarket Riot of 1886 to dismiss from custody people jailed solely for their immigrant background, swarthy skin, or imperfect command of English.

harassment. Abrupt irritation or ongoing badgering, annoyance, torments, attacks, or raids. Carry Nation and members of the Woman's Christian Temperance Union employed such methods against the tipplers and saloon keepers of Kansas at the turn of the twentieth century. *See also* coercion, intimidation.

humanitarianism. The promotion of human welfare and commitment to the improvement of social conditions through benevolence, philanthropy, advocacy, and activism. This is the creed of such secular and religious groups as the American Friends Service Committee, the Mennonites, and the Sanctuary Movement. *See also* philanthropy.

hypocrisy. The pretense or feigned appearance of virtue, patriotism, or sanctity; the condemnation of another person for breaching a law or ethic that the critic flouts. Temperance workers lodged such charges against mayors and city councilmen who invested in gin mills and saloons yet claimed to uphold the quality of community life. *Compare* bigotry.

indictment. A formal charge of a legal offense, for example, the accusation of trespass on military property against native occupiers of Alcatraz Island in San Francisco Bay; Kaho'Olawe, Hawaii; Mount Rushmore in South Dakota; and Vieques, Puerto Rico.

infiltration. Penetration of a secret cell or incursion on a territory for the purpose of spying or surveillance; the practice employed by Federal Bureau of Investigation agents gathering evidence against the Ku Klux Klan, terrorists, or citizen militias, for example. *See also* cell.

insurgent. A guerrilla, freedom fighter, rebel, or insurrectionist, such as John Brown, leader of the attack on the federal arsenal at Harpers Ferry, Virginia (now West Virginia), in 1859 for the purpose of launching a race war to end slavery. *See also* guerrilla, insurrection, paramilitary.

insurrection. An open rebellion, uprising, mutiny, sedition, or revolt against civil authority; a description of prison strikes against the racial segregation of conscientious objectors and of grassroots tax resistance to dry up funds for the Pentagon. *See also* anarchy, sedition.

intimidation. Coercion, terrorism, inhibition, or bullying by threat; a method by which mill owners in Lawrence, Massachusetts, forced young girls to labor long hours in dangerous and unhygienic work conditions during the early twentieth century, and by which right-to-life groups forced abortion providers to quit their jobs late in the century. *See also* coercion. *Compare* persecution.

intolerance. Bigotry, narrow-mindedness, zealotry, or fanaticism, like the attitude of the Puritan hierarchy toward Quaker missionaries and Baptist ministers who refused to baptize infants. *See also* bigotry. *Compare* pluralism.

jayhawking. Varying degrees of rebellion, gangsterism, vigilantism, slave rescue, and defiance of government and the military, such as the rejection of enslavement by abolitionist marauders along the Missouri border with Kansas Territory before the U.S. Civil War; named for a fierce mythical bird, a cross between a blue jay and sparrow hawk.

Jim Crow. The systematic segregation, marginalization, mistreatment, or dehumanization of black people, named for an antebellum minstrel show character. This ideology encouraged the lynching of blacks in the Deep South and prevented black citizens from registering to vote. *See also* bigotry, intimidation, intolerance.

jingoism. Chauvinism, supernationalism, or fanatical exaltation of a homeland or zealous patriotism based on a belligerent foreign policy or militarism, like the attitude of the Federal Bureau of Investigation toward the antiwar speeches of anarchist orator Emma Goldman and the civil rights sermons of the Reverend Martin Luther King, Jr. *See also* chauvinism, militarism. *Compare* antimilitarism, patriotism.

libel. Defamation, calumny, aspersion, slander, or false or damaging writing, publications, or signs harming a person's reputation; a method by which moralist Anthony Comstock violated the free speech rights of birth control advocates beginning in the 1870s and by which Massachusetts police perpetrated injustice against immigrant strikers at Lawrence textile mills in 1912 and against Italian immigrants Nicola Sacco and Bartolomeo Vanzetti in the 1920s.

liberalism. A political philosophy based on the desire for change and progress, the protection of individual rights and freedoms, generous social programs, and a strong role for the federal government; the promotion of advancement and inclusiveness in the social order rather than dogmatic preservation of standard forms. The American Indian Religious Freedom Act of 1978, for example, illustrates liberalism toward the use of peyote as a form of religious ritual and spirituality. *See also* coexistence, pluralism. *Compare* bigotry, conservatism.

liberation. The emancipation, extrication, or release of a person or property, such as the abandoned military property that American Indians turned into Deganawidah-Quetzalcoatl University, a pan-Indian educational center for Chicanos and Native Americans founded in 1971 in Davis, California.

libertarianism. Advocacy of free will, thought, and action and respect for the freedoms of others, particularly the sexual behaviors and drug and alcohol use of consenting adults. Libertarians tend to support the use of marijuana as a treatment for illness and accept the lifestyle of homosexuals.

litigation. The initiation or prosecution of a lawsuit. Practitioners of civil disobedience, as well as the interests they oppose, have succeeded in mounting prolonged, vexatious legal battles. Litigation has succeeded in depriving the American Indian Movement, the woman suffrage movement, and the Industrial Workers of the World, for example, of leadership and resources. *See also* civil suit, class-action suit.

manumission. The emancipation or freeing of slaves, a choice of plantation owners who rid themselves of useless, handicapped, or elderly workers or who experienced a change of heart toward human bondage.

maroon. A black or mixed-race member of a free society (typically a runaway African slave) living in a remote area and fomenting guerrilla warfare against enslavers. Maroons contributed to the Underground Railroad by concealing runaways in thickets and backwaters of the Great Dismal Swamp of Virginia and North Carolina. *See also* guerrilla, insurgent.

mediation. Intervention, conciliation, or arbitration between disputants or warring parties to negotiate a compromise or peaceful settlement, exemplified by the intentions of Gandhian intercessors between the Hanoi government and the U.S. military during the Vietnam War. *See also* Gandhian pacifism, negotiation.

militarism. The glorification of military virtues and ideals or of the predominance of an aggressive armed force in the administration of the state—the spirit of the School of Americas, a U.S. training facility for Latin American assassins, infiltrators, and spies. *See also* warmongering. *Compare* antimilitarism, militia.

militia. A grassroots force or army of ordinary citizens who protect communities from insurgents or emergency situations. Before the U.S. Civil War, black militias provided policing and neighborhood patrols to protect free blacks from kidnap. *See also* maroon, mobilization.

mob action. A spontaneous outburst of disorderly conduct that triumphs by outnumbering, surprising, or overwhelming police or security forces—the method by which abolitionists freed runaway slave John Price from custody during the Oberlin-Wellington Rescue of 1858 and homeopath John Doy from a Missouri jail the following year.

mobilization. Mustering, assembly, equipping, or marshaling forces for a coordinated operation, as occurred during the Christiana Riot of 1851, which summoned freed slaves, Quakers, and abolitionists to the aid of a household threatened by a posse of slave hunters. *See also* militia.

morals. Codes of behavior or rules of virtue or sexual conduct governing individuals, such as the standards that Mormons violated by introducing polygamy to American society. *Compare* ethics.

negotiation. A dialogue, discussion, or mutual bargaining by which adversaries attain a peaceful settlement or compromise. César Chávez employed negotiation in the organization of the United Farm Workers against exploitation by California produce growers in the early 1960s. *See also* disputation, mediation.

neutralism. A preference for neutrality, nonalignment, or noninvolvement in conflicting parties, like the stance of conscientious objectors and antiwar advocates of the peace movement. *See also* disputation, mediation, negotiation.

noncombatants. Civilians who are not engaged in combat, particularly women, children, the elderly, and the handicapped or infirm. Pacifists and conscientious objectors participate in combat only as aides to noncombatants, who suffer hunger, disease, displacement, orphaning, or endangerment through no fault of their own.

nonviolent protest. Passive resistance. *See* Gandhian pacifism.

nullification. The cancellation, overriding, or counteraction of rights—for example, the action of individual states to vitiate the Fugitive Slave Law of 1850 by withholding the use of local jail cells and police forces to help enslavers recover their human chattel.

pacifism. Opposition to the use of violence or combat to settle international disputes. The U.S. government punished pacifists during World War I by imprisoning and tormenting men who refused to comply with the Selective Service draft.

paramilitary. An extralegal or quasi-legal regiment, patrol, or army that targets a particular threat to communities, such as the Liberty Men of post–Revolutionary War Maine, a cadre of farmers who fought for property rights against wealthy Boston speculators. *See also* maroon, militia.

passive resistance. Nonviolence, nonviolent protest. *See* Gandhian pacifism.

patriotism. Nationalism, loyalty, or devotion to a homeland—the spirit and underlying cause of mob action at the Boston Tea Party and copycat versions of tea tax resistance throughout the American colonies. *Compare* bigotry, chauvinism.

persecution. Abuse, torment, oppression, or subjugation, such as the mistreatment of displaced Native Americans forced to live in poverty on reservations and the exile of pacifist Quakers from Philadelphia to Winchester, Virginia, during the American Revolution. *See also* coercion. *Compare* intimidation.

philanthropy. A form of humanitarianism or promotion of human welfare through monetary donation or charitable aid—the choice of many abolitionists who were unable or unwilling to participate directly in the Underground Railroad. *See also* humanitarianism.

pillorying. Ridiculing, abusing, scorning, or punishing offenders; specifically, a method of punishing and suppressing dissent in colonial New England by locking the offender in a wooden frame with holes for the head and each arm.

pluralism. Tolerance of different cultural, ethnic, or religious groups within a society—the goal of integrationists, gay rights and women's rights advocates, and proponents of relaxed immigration laws. *Compare* bigotry, intolerance.

plutocracy. Control or government by a privileged, moneyed, or propertied class; a charge lodged by black draftees during the Vietnam War, which deployed a disproportionate number of poor, nonwhite soldiers to combat zones.

pogrom. A massacre, havoc, or organized assault against minorities; the reason for the emigration of European Jews before World War II.

politicize. To relate to or involve in government or state control, such as the worsening conflict over the teaching of evolution, the issue at stake in the Scopes trial of 1925, and earlier efforts by the U.S. Post Office to control public morality by suppressing the dissemination of birth control information.

pressure group. A lobby or special interest consortium that influences public policy and the legislation of events, priorities, or concerns, such as officials who prompted President Abraham Lincoln's advocacy of the Quaker right to pacifism and Grandmothers for Peace, a consortium, founded in 1982, of elderly female picketers of military enlistment at draft boards.

pro bono. (*Latin,* lit. "for good") Performed without fee or compensation, such as the unpaid work of civil rights attorneys to negotiate bail and probation for volunteers on the Freedom Rides of 1961 and the free medical service provided to illegal aliens sheltered by the Sanctuary Movement in the 1980s.

profiteering. Amassing unreasonable profits or raising prices on goods in short supply during a state of emergency, particularly wartime, a charge that householders lodged against merchants during food riots of the U.S. Civil War and World War I eras.

propaganda. Persuasive, one-sided literature, ideas, data, allegations, or rumors in support of a cause or to the detriment of a person, policy, or institution. Proslavery factions horsewhipped, jailed, and tormented disseminators of propaganda published by the abolitionist press, especially the ideas propagated by William Lloyd Garrison's weekly newspaper *The Liberator. Compare* libel.

protest. An act, demonstration, or gesture of disapproval, dissent, objection, or refusal of an idea or behavior, such as the saluting of the American flag, a violation of Jehovah's Witnesses' religious beliefs.

quasi-legal. Resembling or similar to lawful; a description of citizen militias that violate civil rights or that override statutes on behalf of a private agenda, such as those who violate the Fugitive Slave Law of 1850, brutalize illegal aliens, or stalk patients who enter women's health clinics.

radicalism. Advocacy of anarchy or revolutionary change of conditions or the overturning of laws, such as the demand for an end to chain gangs, slave auctions, abortion, the death penalty, or the U.S. Selective Service. *See also* anarchy, insurrection.

repression. The subjection, subduing, crushing, or subjugation of others, for example, the intimidation or terrorism of patients at women's health clinics by right-to-life advocates or the chaining of seamstresses within sweatshops of the Triangle Shirtwaist Company in the early twentieth century. *See also* intimidation, pogrom. *Compare* suppression.

retaliation. Vengeance, retribution, payback, or reprisal, such as the extralegal attacks of North and South Carolina Regulators in the 1760s and early 1770s against audacious brigands and pilferers and the branding of slave stealers with an S.

Sabbatarianism. Strict observation of or respect for the Sabbath, a contentious issue between Puritans and Quakers of the Massachusetts Bay Colony in the seventeenth century.

sabotage. Treachery, devastation, the obstruction of operations, hindrance of endeavors, or destruction of equipment or property—the method by which rescuers carried out the jailbreak of Fredric "Shadrach" Minkins in 1851 and by which Earth First! halted the cutting of old-growth forests in the 1980s and 1990s.

Second Amendment rights. The guarantee said to be contained in the Bill of Rights that private citizens have the right to own and bear arms and to raise a well-regulated militia. Disputed by some and curtailed by judicial rulings, the right to bear arms is actively promoted by the National Rifle Association and other groups.

sect. A distinct religious society or body of worshipers sharing common goals and beliefs or promulgating extreme divergence from a larger denomination—a description of the Rogerenes, for example, a Quaker offshoot formed by one family of colonial activists in Connecticut during the 1670s.

secularism. A system of beliefs that is not derived from religion or belief in god, such as the ideology of antivivisectionism, euthanasia, socialism, suffragism, or unionism.

sedition. Rebellion against, disruption of, or resistance to law, a charge lodged against individuals advocating the overthrow of the United States and, inappropriately, against Ammon Hennacy, a Christian anarchist with the Catholic Worker movement, for distributing socialist leaflets. *Compare* treason.

self-immolation. Deliberate burning or sacrifice of oneself, an act of extreme protest that marked civil disobedience during the Vietnam War and Iraq War.

shock troops. An advance or assault force of specially trained and equipped attackers; a term applied to individual cells of the colonial Sons of Liberty for their bold initiation of civil disobedience against British agents enforcing colonial taxation along the Atlantic seaboard.

sit-in. A staged occupation or trespass employed as a form of nonviolent disobedience; a successful desegregation tool of black college students used at lunch counters in Greensboro, North Carolina, in 1960, and a tactic of feminist advocates who occupied the editorial office of *Ladies' Home Journal* magazine in 1970 to demand the hiring of more women.

suppression. The restraint or curtailment of rights or behaviors, such as the police brutality against riders during the Journey of Reconciliation in 1947 and the New York police crackdown on Harlemites that radicalized activist Adam Clayton Powell, Jr., the previous decade. *Compare* repression.

sympathizing. Supporting, comforting, admiring, or championing an activist, a cause, or a belief, exemplified by families and friends who supported Jack Kevorkian in the euthanasia of severely crippled or dying patients and by feminists who visited the cell of Hester Vaughan, a poor immigrant woman wrongly accused of infanticide. Similarly, anti–Iraq War sympathizers Jane Fonda and Martin Sheen backed "Peace Mom" Cindy Sheehan by visiting her camp across from the ranch of President George W. Bush in Crawford, Texas. *See also* abetting, complicity.

tar and feathering. A barbaric, life-threatening punishment preferred by rowdies for the ludicrous results of coating a victim in hot tar and poultry feathers. British stamp agents incurred infection, skinning, hemorrhage, shock, and death from the coatings heaped on by Sons of Liberty. The Ku Klux Klan applied similar torture to free blacks following the U.S. Civil War. *See also* vigilantism.

terrorism. Extreme threat or use of force calculated to coerce or intimidate a person, group, or government, a charge that feminists have lobbed against abortion clinic bombers and that pacifists have lodged against the U.S. military for operating an offshore prison at Guantánamo, Cuba. *See also* tar and feathering, vigilantism. *Compare* coercion, intimidation.

theocracy. A church-state or political entity controlled or governed by godly or divinely inspired officials, exemplified by the Mormon enclave in Salt Lake City, Utah, where members valued religious law over state law as it applied to polygamy.

treason. Disloyalty to, betrayal of, or violation of allegiance to a homeland, a charge that federal agents lodged against Reies López Tijerina during the Alianza Movement of the 1960s and against immigrant factory workers who supported the 1920 mining strike at Matewan, West Virginia. *Compare* sedition.

unionism. Advocacy or furtherance of the unity of aim and action among wage earners of a particular trade or industry, the tenet of labor theoretician Mary Ritter Beard of the National Women's Trade Union and of organizers A. Philip Randolph, Mary "Mother" Jones, and Kate Richards O'Hare, among many others.

utopianism. Belief in the perfectability of human society through idealistic regimentation or communal living, such as the ideology of Shakers and of transcendentalist philosopher and abolitionist, Amos Bronson Alcott, of Concord, Massachusetts.

vigilantism. Advocacy of extralegal enforcement of an arbitrary standard of conduct, such as the scapegoating and ousting of Chinese laborers from San Francisco by unemployed whites in the 1880s; the six-year Booth War, beginning in 1854; and the tar and feathering of abolitionist spies by Southern enslavers. *See also* tar and feathering.

vivisection. The cutting, maiming, or savaging of living animals by laboratory scientists, pharmaceutical experimenters, and fur ranchers, targets of the Animal Liberation Front and People for the Ethical Treatment of Animals.

warmongering. Belligerence, militarism, or hawkish advocacy of combat, preemptive strikes, or aggressive politics, a charge that pacifists lobbed at the administration of President Ronald Reagan for investing in the Strategic Defense Initiative and surveillance satellite systems. *See also* militarism. *Compare* antimilitarism.

white flight. A demographic trend in which white residents abandon neighborhoods when nonwhites move in. During the civil rights movement, white homeowners charged black buyers with lowering property values and with initiating urban decay in formerly all-white communities and housing developments.

wildcat strike. A spontaneous uprising of workers who initiate a strike without union planning; a response to increasing work dangers and low pay among coal miners in Pennsylvania and West Virginia and among Pullman railcar workers in Chicago, Illinois.

xenophobia. Undue fear, criticism, hatred, prejudice, or contempt of foreigners or people from alien cultures and religions. This source of persecution led President Franklin D. Roosevelt to incarcerate Japanese Americans in concentration camps during World War II. *See also* coercion.

Bibliography

Primary Sources

Primary sources include works that provide eyewitness accounts of acts of conscience and civil disobedience.

Abbott, John Stevens Cabot. *South and North: or, Impressions Received During a Trip to Cuba and the South.* New York: Abbey & Abbott, 1860.

"Against the Traffic of Mens-Body." *Pennsylvania Magazine of History and Biography* 4 (1880): 28–30.

Aluli, Noa Emmett, and Davianna Pomaika'i McGregor. "*Maike Kaimaike Ola,* From the Ocean Comes Life." *Hawaiian Journal of History* 26 (1992): 231–54.

Anderson, John. *The Story of the Life of John Anderson, the Fugitive Slave.* London: W. Tweedie, 1863.

Baez, Joan. *Inside Santa Rita: The Prison Memoir of a War Protester.* Santa Barbara, CA: John Daniel, 1994.

Bassett, P.C. "A Visit to the Slave Mother Who Killed Her Child." *National Anti-Slavery Standard,* March 15, 1856, 1.

Bearse, Austin. *Reminiscences of Fugitive-Slave Law Days in Boston.* Boston: W. Richardson, 1880.

Bigelow, Albert. *The Voyage of the Golden Rule: An Experiment with Truth.* Garden City, NY: Doubleday, 1959.

Boardman, Elizabeth Jelinek. *The Phoenix Trip: Notes on a Quaker Mission to Haiphong.* Burnsville, NC: Celo, 1985.

Bradford, Sarah H. *Harriet, The Moses of Her People.* New York: George R. Lockwood, 1886.

———. *Scenes in the Life of Harriet Tubman.* Auburn, NY: W.J. Moses, 1869.

Brown, John. *Slave Life in Georgia: A Narrative of the Life, Sufferings, and Escape of John Brown, a Fugitive Slave, Now in England.* London: W.M. Watts, 1855.

Brown, Thomas. *Three Years in Kentucky Prisons.* Indianapolis, IN: Courier, 1857.

Burt, Elizabeth V., ed. *The Progressive Era: Primary Documents on Events from 1890 to 1914.* Westport, CT: Greenwood, 2004.

"Capital's House Delegate Held in Embassy Sit-In." *New York Times,* November 22, 1984.

Cary, Stephen G., et al. *Speak Truth to Power: A Quaker Search for an Alternative to Violence.* Philadelphia: American Friends Service Committee, 1955.

Cockrum, Colonel William. *History of the Underground Railroad as It Was Conducted by the Anti-Slavery League.* Oakland City, IN: J.W. Cockrum, 1915.

Coffin, Addison. *Life and Travels of Addison Coffin.* Cleveland, OH: W.G. Hubbard, 1897.

Coffin, Levi. *Reminiscences of Levi Coffin, the Reputed President of the Underground Railroad.* Cincinnati, OH: Western Tract Society, 1876.

Conway, Moncure Daniel. *Autobiography: Memories and Experiences of Moncure Daniel Conway.* Boston: Houghton Mifflin, 1904.

"Coxey in Washington." *Harper's Weekly,* May 12, 1894.

Craft, William. *Running a Thousand Miles for Freedom.* London: W. Tweedie, 1860.

Davidson, John Nelson. *Negro Slavery in Wisconsin and the Underground Railroad.* Milwaukee, WI: Parkman Club, 1897.

Davis, Angela Yvonne. *Angela Davis: An Autobiography.* New York: Random House, 1974.

Dawson, Henry B. *The Sons of Liberty in New York.* New York: privately published, 1859.

Day, Dorothy. *The Long Loneliness: The Autobiography of Dorothy Day.* San Francisco: Harper & Row, 1981.

Dellinger, Dave. *America's Lost Plantation.* Glen Gardner, NJ: Libertarian Press, 1961.

———. *Revolutionary Nonviolence.* Indianapolis, IN: Bobbs-Merrill, 1970.

Doy, John. *The Narrative of John Doy of Lawrence, Kansas: A Plain Unvarnished Tale.* New York: T. Holman, 1860.

Drayton, Daniel. *Personal Memoir of Daniel Drayton, for Four Years and Four Months a Prisoner (For Charity's Sake) in Washington Jail.* New York: American and Foreign Anti-Slavery Society, 1854.

El Saadawi, Nawal. "The Rite and the Right." *Feminist Voices* 9:6 (September 30, 1996): 1.

Elmer, Jerry. *Felon for Peace: The Memoir of a Vietnam-Era Draft Resister.* Nashville, TN: Vanderbilt University Press, 2006.

Fairbank, Calvin. *Rev. Calvin Fairbank During Slavery Times: How He "Fought the Good Fight" to Prepare "the Way."* Chicago: R.R. McCabe, 1890.

Farmer, James. *Lay Bare the Heart: An Autobiography of the Civil Rights Movement.* New York: Plume, 1985.

Fee, John Gregg. *Autobiography of John G. Fee: Berea, Kentucky.* Chicago: National Christian Association, 1891.

Finney, Charles G. *Memoirs of Rev. Charles G. Finney Written by Himself.* New York: A.S. Barnes, 1876.

Flynn, Elizabeth Gurley. *I Speak My Own Piece: Autobiography of "The Rebel Girl."* New York: Masses & Mainstream, 1955.

Foster, HI Nelson. *Kaho'olawe: Na Leo o Kanaloa.* Honolulu, HI Pohaku Press, 1995.

Fried, Albert, ed. *Communism in America: A History in Documents.* New York: Columbia University Press, 1997.

"The Fugitive Slave Case." *Cincinnati Gazette,* February 11, 1856, 3.

Gara, Larry, and Lenna Mae Gara, eds. *A Few Small Candles: War Resisters of World War II Tell Their Stories.* Kent, OH: Kent State University Press, 1999.

Gardner, Theodore. "The Last Battle of the Border War, a Tragic Incident in the Early History of Douglas County." *Collections of the Kansas State Historical Society 1919–1922* 15 (1923): 548–52.

Garrison, William Lloyd. "The Arrest—The Rescue—The Flight." *The Liberator,* February 21, 1851, 30.

———. "To the Public." *The Liberator,* January 1, 1831, 1.

Gilpin, Thomas. *Exiles in Virginia; with Observations on the Conduct of the Society of Friends During the Revolutionary War.* Philadelphia: C. Sherman, 1848.

Goldman, Emma. *Anarchism and Other Essays.* New York: Dover, 1969.

———. *Emma Goldman: A Documentary History of the American Years.* Ed. Candace Falk. Berkeley: University of California Press, 2005.

Gordon, Ann D., ed. *The Selected Papers of Elizabeth Cady Stanton and Susan B. Anthony.* 4 vols. New Brunswick, NJ: Rutgers University Press, 1997–2006.

Halberstam, David. *The Children.* New York: Fawcett, 1998.

"The Hanging of the Chicago Anarchists." *Harper's Weekly,* November 19, 1887.

Harper, Ida Husted. *The Life and Work of Susan B. Anthony.* New York: Hollenbeck, 1899.

Haviland, Laura S. *A Woman's Life-Work: Labors and Experiences of Laura S. Haviland.* Cincinnati, OH: Walden & Stowe, 1882.

"Helped Save Glover." *Milwaukee Sentinel,* June 10, 1900.

Higginson, Thomas Wentworth. *A Sermon Preached in Worcester, on Sunday, June 4, 1854.* Boston: James Monroe & Co., 1854.

Hildreth, Richard. *Atrocious Judges.* New York: Miller, Orton & Mulligan, 1856.

Hinton, Richard Josiah. *John Brown and His Men; with Some Account of the Roads They Travelled to Reach Harper's Ferry.* New York: Funk & Wagnalls, ca. 1894.

Houston, Jeanne Wakatsuki, and James Houston. *Farewell to Manzanar: A True Story of Japanese Americans During and After the World War II Internment.* Boston: Houghton Mifflin, 1973.

Hume, John F. *The Abolitionists, Together with Personal Memories of the Struggle for Human Rights, 1830–1864.* New York: G.P. Putnam's Sons, 1905.

"The 'Industrial Army.'" *Harper's Weekly,* May 12, 1894.

James, Henry Field. *Abolitionism Unveiled; or, Its Origin, Progress, and Pernicious Tendency.* Cincinnati, OH: E. Morgan & Sons, 1856.

Johnson, Oliver. *William Lloyd Garrison and His Times; or, Sketches of the Anti-Slavery Movement in America, and of the Man Who Was Its Founder and Moral Leader.* Boston: Houghton, Mifflin, 1881.

Jones, Mary Harris. *Autobiography of Mother Jones.* Ed. Mary Field Parton. Mineola, NY: Dover, 2004.

Kemble, Fanny. *Journal of a Residence on a Georgian Plantation in 1838–1839.* Ed. John A. Scott. Athens: University of Georgia Press, 1984.

Keys, Ancel, et al. *The Biology of Human Starvation.* Minneapolis: University of Minnesota Press, 1950.

Lee, J. Edward, and Ron Chepesiuk, eds. *South Carolina in the Civil War: The Confederate Experience in Letters and Diaries.* Jefferson, NC: McFarland, 2000.

Legler, Henry E. *Leading Events of Wisconsin History.* Milwaukee, WI: *Milwaukee Sentinel,* 1898.

"Letters on the Glover Incident." *Abbotsford Clarion* (Wisconsin), December 13, 1896.

Lewis, John, with Michael D'Orso. *Walking with the Wind: A Memoir of the Movement.* New York: Simon & Schuster, 1998.

Lockwood, Mary S. "A Timely Comparison." *American Monthly* 9 (July–December 1896): 447–536.

Lowance, Mason. *Against Slavery: An Abolitionist Reader.* New York: Penguin, 2000.

Lynd, Staughton, ed. *Nonviolence in America: A Documentary History.* Indianapolis, IN: Bobbs-Merrill, 1966.

Mann, Horace. *Slavery: Letters and Speeches.* Philadelphia: B.B. Mussey, 1853.

Marcus, Maeva, ed. *The Documentary History of the Supreme Court of the United States, 1789–1800.* New York: Columbia University Press, 1998.

Matthiessen, Peter. *In the Spirit of Crazy Horse.* New York: Viking, 1983.

Mattison, Hiram. *The Impending Crisis of 1860.* New York: Mason Brothers, 1859.

Means, Russell. *Where White Men Fear to Tread: The Autobiography of Russell Means.* New York: St. Martin's, 1997.

Melendez, Miguel. *We Took the Streets: Fighting for Latino Rights with the Young Lords.* New York: St. Martin's, 2003.

Monsivais, Pablo Martinez. "5 Lawmakers Arrested in Darfur Protest." *USA Today,* April 28, 2006.

Mulvaney, Patrick. "Thousands Protest SOA." *The Nation,* November 23, 2004.

Mumford, Thomas James, ed. *Memoir of Samuel Joseph May*. Boston: Roberts Brothers, 1873.

Nation, Carry A. *The Use and Need of the Life of Carry A. Nation*. Topeka, KS: F.M. Steves & Sons, 1905.

National Civil Liberties Bureau. *War-Time Prosecutions and Mob Violence: Involving the Rights of Free Speech, Free Press and Peaceful Assemblage*. Amsterdam, Netherlands: Fredonia, 1919.

"Now It Is Blood!" *Inter-Ocean* (Chicago), May 5, 1886.

O'Connor, Ellen. *Myrtilla Miner: A Memoir*. Boston: Houghton Mifflin, 1885.

Oliphant, Thomas P. "Surprise Airlift Drops Supplies to Wounded Knee Holdouts." *Boston Globe*, April 18, 1973.

Peck, Jim. *Freedom Ride*. New York: Simon & Schuster, 1962.

Pennington, James W.C. *The Fugitive Blacksmith: or, Events in the History of James W.C. Pennington*. London: Charles Gilpin, 1850.

Pickard, Kate. *The Kidnapped and the Ransomed: The Narrative of Peter and Vina Still After Forty Years of Slavery*. Syracuse, NY: William T. Hamilton, 1856.

Powell, Adam Clayton, Jr. *Adam by Adam: The Autobiography of Adam Clayton Powell, Jr.* New York: Kensington, 2002.

Pringle, Cyrus. *The Record of a Quaker Conscience*. New York: Macmillan, 1918.

Quinlan, Julia Duane. *My Joy, My Sorrow: Karen Ann's Mother Remembers*. Cincinnati, OH: St. Anthony Messenger Press, 2005.

Redpath, James. *Echoes of Harper's Ferry*. Boston: Thayer & Eldridge, 1860.

"The Riot at Lattimer, Pennsylvania." *Harper's Weekly*, September 25, 1897.

Ripley, C. Peter, ed. *The Black Abolitionist Papers*. 5 vols. Chapel Hill, NC: University of North Carolina Press, 1985–1992.

Robinson, William H. *From Log Cabin to the Pulpit; or, Fifteen Years in Slavery*. Eau Claire, WI: James H. Tifft, 1913.

Romo, David Dorado. *Ringside Seat to a Revolution: An Underground Cultural History of El Paso and Juárez: 1893–1923*. El Paso, TX: Cinco Puntos, 2005.

Roosevelt, Eleanor. *The Autobiography of Eleanor Roosevelt*. New York: Harper & Brothers, 1961.

———. *Courage in a Dangerous World: The Political Writings of Eleanor Roosevelt*. Ed. Allida M. Black. New York: Columbia University Press, 1999.

Sanger, Margaret. *The Selected Papers of Margaret Sanger*. Ed. Esther Katz, Cathy Moran Hajo, and Peter Engelman. Urbana: University of Illinois Press, 2002.

Seabury, Samuel. *American Slavery Distinguished from the Slavery of English Theorists, and Justified by the Law of Nature*. New York: Mason Brothers, 1861.

Severance, Frank H. *Old Trails on the Niagara Frontier*. Buffalo: unknown, 1899.

Seward, William Henry. *Autobiography of William H. Seward from 1801 to 1834*. New York: Derby & Miller, 1891.

Sharpton, Al, with Karen Hunter. *Al on America*. New York: Kensington, 2002.

Sheehan, Cindy. *Not One More Mother's Child*. New York: Koa, 2005.

———. *Peace Mom: A Mother's Journey Through Heartache to Activism*. New York: Atria, 2006.

Smedley, Robert C. *History of the Underground Railroad in Chester and the Neighboring Counties of Pennsylvania*. Mechanicsburg, PA: Stackpole, 2005.

Steinem, Gloria. *Outrageous Acts and Everyday Rebellions*. New York: Owl, 1995.

Sterling, Dorothy, ed. *Speak Out in Thunder Tones: Letters and Other Writings by Black Northerners, 1787–1865*. Garden City, NY: Doubleday, 1973.

Stevens, Doris. *Jailed for Freedom*. New York: Livewright, 1920.

Swerdlow, Amy. *Women Strike for Peace: Traditional Motherhood and Radical Politics in the 1960s*. Chicago: University of Chicago Press, 1993.

Swisshelm, Jane Grey. *Half a Century*. Chicago: Jansen, McClurg, & Co., 1880.

Tempest, Rone. "Active-Duty Soldiers Join Iraq War Protests." *Charlotte Observer*, May 1, 2006.

Theroux, Paul. *Sunrise with Seamonsters: Travels and Discoveries, 1964–1984*. New York: Houghton Mifflin, 1985.

Thomas, John. "Judge Conkling's Decision in the Case of the Rescue of Jerry." *The North Star*, October 30, 1851.

Thoreau, Henry David. *Civil Disobedience and Other Essays*. Mineola, NY: Dover, 1993.

"Underground Railroad." *Brooklyn Eagle*, May 14, 1882.

Ward, Samuel R. *Autobiography of a Fugitive Negro: His Anti-Slavery Labours in the United States, Canada, and England*. London: John Snow, 1855.

Warren, Mercy Otis. *History of the Rise, Progress, and Termination of the American Revolution*. Indianapolis, IN: Liberty Fund, 1988.

———. *Plays and Poems of Mercy Otis Warren*. Delmar, NY: Scholars' Facsimiles & Reprint, 1980.

Weiss, John. *Life and Correspondence of Theodore Parker*. New York: D. Appleton, 1864.

Wilkerson, Isabel. "Inventor of Suicide Machine Arrested on Murder Charge." *New York Times*, December 4, 1990.

Wilkins, Roy. *Standing Fast: The Autobiography of Roy Wilkins*. New York: Viking, 1982.

Williams, Carol J. "Guantánamo Stirs Protests." *Los Angeles Times*, February 16, 2007.

Woolman, John. *The Journal with Other Writings of John Woolman*. New York: E.P. Dutton, 1910.

Young, Brigham. "Shall the Mormon Question Be Revived?" *Harper's Weekly*, December 16, 1899.

Zonana, Victor F. "AIDS Underground Drug Tester: Hero or Just a Renegade?" *Los Angeles Times*, July 6, 1989.

Secondary Sources

Adams, Maurianne, and John H. Bracey, eds. *Strangers and Neighbors: Relations Between Blacks and Jews in the United States*. Amherst: University of Massachusetts Press, 1999.

Addelson, Kathryn Pyne. *Moral Passages: Toward a Collectivist Moral Theory*. New York: Routledge, 1994.

Adelson, Betty M. *The Lives of Dwarfs: Their Journey from Public Curiosity Toward Social Liberation*. New Brunswick, NJ: Rutgers University Press, 2005.

Anderson, Terry H. *The Movement and the Sixties*. New York: Oxford University Press, 1995.

Aptheker, Bettina. *The Morning Breaks: The Trial of Angela Davis*. 2nd ed. Ithaca, NY: Cornell University Press, 1999.

Arsenault, Raymond. *Freedom Riders: 1961 and the Struggle for Racial Justice*. New York: Oxford University Press, 2006.

Bacon, Margaret Hope. *I Speak for My Slave Sister: The Life of Abby Kelley Foster*. New York: Crowell, 1974.

———. *Rebellion at Christiana*. New York: Crown, 1975.

Baltzell, E. Digby. *Puritan Boston and Quaker Philadelphia*. New York: Free Press, 1979.

Barber, Lucy G. *Marching on Washington: The Forging of an American Political Tradition*. Berkeley: University of California Press, 2002.

Baym, Nina. "Between Enlightenment and Victorian: Toward a Narrative of American Women Writers Writing History." *Critical Inquiry* 18:1 (Autumn 1991): 22–41.

Beisel, Nicola Kay. *Imperiled Innocents: Anthony Comstock and Family Reproduction*. Princeton, NJ: Princeton University Press, 1998.

Bell, Daniel. *Marxian Socialism in the United States*. Ithaca, NY: Cornell University Press, 1996.

Biondo, Brenda. "Turning a Bombing Range into a Spiritual Homeland." *Christian Science Monitor*, December 31, 1998, 4.

Borenstein, Audrey. *Chimes of Change and Hours: Views of Older Women in Twentieth-Century America*. Cranbury, NJ: Associated University Presses, 1983.

Boyd, Herb. *We Shall Overcome*. Naperville, IL: Sourcebooks, 2004.

Bradshaw, Jim. "Some Thought Jayhawker Carrière Was Really a Hero." *Daily Advertiser* (Lafayette, LA), August 26, 1997.

Brasseaux, Carl A., Keith P. Fontenot, and Claude F. Oubre. *Creoles of Color in the Bayou Country*. Jackson: University Press of Mississippi, 1994.

Breen, T.H. *The Marketplace of Revolution: How Consumer Politics Shaped American Independence*. New York: Oxford University Press, 2004.

Brock, Peter. *Pacifism in the United States from the Colonial Era to the First World War*. Princeton, NJ: Princeton University Press, 1968.

———. *The Quaker Peace Testimony, 1660 to 1914*. York, UK: Sessions Book Trust, 1990.

Brodie, Janet Farrell. *Contraception and Abortion in Nineteenth-Century America*. Ithaca, NY: Cornell University Press, 1994.

Brown, Marshall, ed. *The Uses of Literary History*. Durham, NC: Duke University Press, 1995.

Bruns, Roger. *César Chávez: A Biography*. Westport, CT: Greenwood, 2005.

Buhle, Paul, and Nicole Schulman, eds. *Wobblies! A Graphic History of the Industrial Workers of the World*. New York: Verso, 2005.

Bumstead, John M., and Charles E. Clark. "New England's Tom Paine: John Allen and the Spirit of Liberty." *William and Mary Quarterly* 21:4 (October 1964): 561–70.

Bushnell, O.A. *The Gifts of Civilization: Germs and Genocide in Hawai'i*. Honolulu: University of Hawai'i Press, 1993.

Bynum, Victoria E. *Unruly Women: The Politics of Social and Sexual Control in the Old South*. Chapel Hill: University of North Carolina Press, 1992.

Cain, William E., ed. *A Historical Guide to Henry David Thoreau*. Oxford, UK: Oxford University Press, 2000.

Carnes, Mark Christopher. *Past Imperfect: History According to the Movies*. New York: Henry Holt, 1996.

Carson, Clayborne. *In Struggle: SNCC and the Black Awakening of the 1960s*. Cambridge, MA: Harvard University Press, 1995.

Chacón, Justin Akers, and Mike Davis. *No One Is Illegal: Fighting Violence and State Repression on the U.S.–Mexico Border*. Chicago: Haymarket, 2006.

Chatfield, Charles. *For Peace and Justice: Pacifism in America, 1914–1941*. Knoxville: University of Tennessee Press, 1971.

———, ed. *Peace Movements in America*. New York: Schocken, 1973.

"Cheerful Yesterdays V. The Fugitive Slave Period." *Atlantic Monthly* 79 (1897): 345–46.

Christenson, Ron. *Political Trials in History: From Antiquity to the Present*. Somerset, NJ: Transaction, 1991.

Churchill, Ward. *Perversions of Justice: Indigenous Peoples and Angloamerican Law*. San Francisco: City Lights, 2003.

Churchill, Ward, and Jim Vander Wall. *Agents of Repression: The FBI's Secret Wars Against the Black*

Panther Party and the American Indian Movement. Cambridge, MA: South End, 2002.

Clark, James I. *Wisconsin Defies the Fugitive Slave Law.* Madison: State Historical Society of Wisconsin, 1955.

Clinton, Catherine. *Fanny Kemble's Civil Wars.* Oxford, UK: Oxford University Press, 2001.

Clotfelter, Charles T. *After "Brown": The Rise and Retreat of School Desegregation.* Princeton, NJ: Princeton University Press, 2004.

Coffman, Elesha. "Maniac or Martyr?" *Christian History,* May 5, 2000.

Coffman, Tom. *The Island Edge of America: A Political History of Hawaii, 1900–1986.* Honolulu: University of Hawai'i Press, 1986.

Collison, Gary. *Shadrach Minkins: From Fugitive Slave to Citizen.* Cambridge, MA: Harvard University Press, 1997.

Coltelli, Laura. *Winged Words: American Indian Writers Speak.* Lincoln: University of Nebraska Press, 1992.

Cooney, Robert, and Helen Michalowski, eds. *The Power of the People: Active Nonviolence in the United States.* Culver City, CA: Peace Press, 1977.

Cornell, Julien. *Conscience and the State.* New York: Garland, 1973.

———. *The Conscientious Objector and the Law.* New York: John Day, 1943.

Cott, Nancy F. *No Small Courage: A History of Women in the United States.* New York: Oxford University Press, 2000.

Curran, Thomas F. *Soldiers of Peace: Civil War Pacifism and the Postwar Radical Peace Movement.* New York: Fordham University Press, 2003.

Curti, Merle. *Peace or War: The American Struggle, 1636–1936.* Boston: J.S. Canner, 1959.

Danchev, Alex, and John MacMillan. *The Iraq War and Democratic Politics.* New York: Routledge, 2005.

Danky, James P., ed. *African-American Newspapers and Periodicals: A National Bibliography.* Cambridge, MA: Harvard University Press, 1998.

Davidson, Miriam. *Convictions of the Heart: Jim Corbett and the Sanctuary Movement.* Tucson: University of Arizona Press, 1988.

De Leon, David. *Leaders from the 1960s.* Westport, CT: Greenwood, 1994.

Delfattore, Joan. *What Johnny Shouldn't Read: Textbook Censorship in America.* New Haven, CT: Yale University Press, 1994.

Dickson, Paul, and Thomas B. Allen. *The Bonus Army: An American Epic.* New York: Walker, 2005.

Dove, Rita. "Rosa Parks." *Time,* June 14, 1999.

Dreese, Michael A. *The Hospital on Seminary Ridge at the Battle of Gettysburg.* Jefferson, NC: McFarland, 2002.

Driscoll, James, et al. *Angels of Deliverance: The Underground Railroad in Queens, Long Island, and Beyond.* Flushing, NY: Queens Historical Society, 1999.

Du Bois, W.E.B. *The Gift of Black Folk: The Negroes in the Making of America.* Boston: Stratford, 1924.

Dunbar, Anthony P. *Against the Grain: Southern Radicals and Prophets, 1929–1959.* Charlottesville: University Press of Virginia, 1981.

Eastland, Terry, ed. *Freedom of Expression in the Supreme Court: The Defining Cases.* Lanham, MD: Rowman & Littlefield, 2000.

Edmonds, David C. *Yankee Autumn in Acadiana: A Narrative of the Great Texas Overland Expedition Through Southwestern Louisiana October–December 1863.* Lafayette, LA: Acadiana Press, 2005.

Edmunds, R. David. *The New Warriors: Native American Leaders Since 1900.* Lincoln: University of Nebraska Press, 2004.

Elbaum, Max. *Revolution in the Air: From Malcolm and Martin to Lenin, Mao and Che.* New York: Verso, 2002.

Ellis, Mark. *Race, War, and Surveillance: African Americans and the United States Government During World War I.* Bloomington: Indiana University Press, 2001.

Endean, Steve. *Bringing Lesbian and Gay Rights into the Mainstream: Twenty Years of Progress.* Ed. Vicki L. Eaklor. New York: Huntington Park Press, 2006.

Fischer, David Hackett. *Paul Revere's Ride.* New York: Oxford University Press, 1994.

Fisher, Miles Mark. "Friends of Humanity: A Quaker Anti-Slavery Influence." *Church History* 4:3 (September 1935): 187–202.

Forbes, Esther. *Paul Revere and the World He Lived In.* Boston: Houghton Mifflin, 1942.

Fosl, Catherine. *Subversive Southerner: Anne Braden and the Struggle for Racial Justice in the Cold War South.* New York: Palgrave Macmillan, 2002.

Franklin, V.P., and Bettye Collier Thomas. *Sisters in the Struggle: African-American Women in the Civil Rights–Black Power Movement.* New York: New York University Press, 2001.

Freedman, David. "African-American Schooling in the South Prior to 1861." *Journal of Negro History* 84:1 (Winter 1999): 1–47.

Frisken, Amanda. *Victoria Woodhull's Sexual Revolution.* Philadelphia: University of Pennsylvania Press, 2004.

Furniss, Norman F. *The Mormon Conflict, 1850–1859.* New Haven, CT: Yale University Press, 2005.

Galli, Mark. "Harriet Tubman." *Christian History* 37:6 (November/December 1999): 14.

Gallman, J. Matthew. *Mastering Wartime: A Social History of Philadelphia During the Civil War.* Philadelphia: University of Pennsylvania Press, 2000.

Gardner, Richard. *Grito! Reis Tijerina and the New Mexico Land Grant War of 1967.* Indianapolis, IN: Bobbs-Merrill, 1970.

Garrett, Clarke. *Spirit Possession and Popular Religion: From the Camisards to the Shakers.* Baltimore: Johns Hopkins University Press, 1987.

Gatewood, Willard B. *Aristocrats of Color: The Black Elite, 1880–1920.* Fayetteville: University of Arkansas Press, 2000.

Gill, Lesley. *The School of the Americas: Military Training and Political Violence in the Americas.* Durham, NC: Duke University Press, 2004.

Gillette, Howard. *Between Justice and Beauty: Race, Planning, and the Failure of Urban Policy in Washington, D.C.* Philadelphia: University of Pennsylvania Press, 2006.

Goossen, Rachel Waltner. *Women Against the Good War: Conscientious Objection and Gender on the American Home Front, 1941–1947.* Chapel Hill: University of North Carolina Press, 1997.

Gorney, Cynthia. *Articles of Faith: A Frontline History of the Abortion Wars.* New York: Simon & Schuster, 1998.

Grinde, Donald A., and Bruce E. Johansen. *Ecocide of Native America: Environmental Destruction of Indian Lands and Peoples.* Santa Fe, NM: Clear Light, 1995.

Grover, Kathryn. *The Fugitive's Gibraltar: Escaping Slaves and Abolitionism in New Bedford, Massachusetts.* Amherst: University of Massachusetts Press, 2001.

Guillermo, Kathy Snow. *Monkey Business: The Disturbing Case That Launched the Animal Rights Movement.* New York: National Press, 1993.

Hamm, Richard F. *Shaping the Eighteenth Amendment: Temperance Reform, Legal Culture, and the Polity, 1880–1920.* Chapel Hill: University of North Carolina Press, 1995.

Hamm, Thomas D., April Beckman, Marissa Florio, Kirsti Giles, and Marie Hopper. "A Great and Good People: Midwestern Quakers and the Struggle Against Slavery." *Indiana Magazine of History* 100:1 (March 2004): 3–25.

Hanson, Peter. *Dalton Trumbo, Hollywood Rebel: A Critical Survey and Filmography.* Jefferson, NC: McFarland, 2001.

Harvey, Robert. *A Few Bloody Noses: The Realities and Mythologies of the American Revolution.* Woodstock, NY: Overloook, 2002.

Hellerstein, Erna O. *Victorian Women: A Documentary Account of Women's Lives in Nineteenth-Century England, France and the United States.* Stanford, CA: Stanford University Press, 1981.

Hensel, W.U. *The Christiana Riot and the Treason Trials of 1851.* Lancaster, PA: New Era, 1911.

"A History of Protests at the Clinic." *Virginian-Pilot* (Hampton, VA), January 1, 1995.

Ho, Fred, ed., with Carolyn Antonio, Diane Fujino, and Steve Yip. *Legacy to Liberation: Politics and Culture of Revolutionary Asian Pacific America.* San Francisco: AK Press, 2000.

Hogeland, William. *The Whiskey Rebellion: George Washington, Alexander Hamilton, and the Frontier Rebels Who Challenged America's Newfound Sovereignty.* New York: Scribner's, 2006.

Holding, Reynolds. "Speaking Up for Themselves." *Time,* May 21, 2007, 65–67.

Horowitz, Helen Lefkowitz. "Victoria Woodhull, Anthony Comstock, and Conflict over Sex in the United States in the 1870s." *Journal of American History* 87:2 (September 2000): 403–34.

Horton, James Oliver, and Lois E. Horton. *Black Bostonians: Family Life and Community Struggle in the Antebellum North.* New York: Holmes and Meier, 1979.

Hoxie, Frederick E. *Parading Through History: The Making of the Crow Nation in America, 1805–1935.* New York: Cambridge University Press, 1995.

Hrebenar, Ronald J. *Interest Group Politics in America.* Armonk, NY: M.E. Sharpe, 1997.

Hunt, Andrew E. *David Dellinger: The Life and Times of a Nonviolent Revolutionary.* New York: New York University Press, 2006.

Hutton, James V., Jr. "The Quakers Exile in Winchester & Frederick County, Virginia, 1777–1788." *Winchester-Frederick County Historical Society Journal* 17 (2005): 63–82.

Hymowitz, Carol, and Michaele Weissman. *A History of Women in America.* New York: Bantam, 1978.

Inada, Lawson Fusao, ed. *Only What We Could Carry: The Japanese Internment Experience.* Berkeley, CA: Heyday, 2000.

Jensen, Joan M. "Not Only Ours but Others: The Quaker Teaching Daughters of the Mid-Atlantic, 1790–1850." *History of Education Quarterly* 24:1 (Spring 1984): 3–19.

Johnson, Troy R. *The Occupation of Alcatraz Island: Indian Self-Determination and the Rise of Indian Activism.* Urbana: University of Illinois Press, 1996.

Johnston, Robert D., ed. *The Politics of Healing: Histories of Alternative Medicine in Twentieth-Century North America.* New York: Routledge, 2004.

Kafer, Peter. *Charles Brockden Brown's Revolution and the Birth of American Gothic.* Philadelphia: University of Pennsylvania Press, 2004.

Kann, Mark E. *Punishment, Prisons, and Patriarchy: Liberty and Power in the Early American Republic.* New York: New York University Press, 2005.

Kars, Marjoleine. *Breaking Loose Together: The Regulator Rebellion in Pre-Revolutionary North Carolina.* Chapel Hill: University of North Carolina Press, 2002.

Kennedy, Kathleen. *Disloyal Mothers and Scurrilous Citizens: Women and Subversion During World War I.* Bloomington: University of Indiana Press, 1999.

Kerr-Ritchie, Jeffrey R. "Rehearsal for War; Black Militias in the Atlantic World." *Slavery and Abolition* 26:1 (April 2005): 1–34.

Ketchum, Richard M. *Divided Loyalties: How the American Revolution Came to New York.* New York: Henry Holt, 2002.

Klein, Rachel N. "Ordering the Backcountry: The South Carolina Regulation." *William and Mary Quarterly* 38:4 (October 1981): 661–80.

Klejment, Anne, and Nancy L. Roberts, eds. *American Catholic Pacifism: The Influence of Dorothy Day and the Catholic Worker Movement.* Westport, CT: Praeger, 1996.

Kohn, Stephen M. *American Political Prisoners: Prosecutions Under the Espionage and Sedition Acts.* Westport, CT: Greenwood, 1994.

————. *Jailed for Peace: The History of American Draft Law Violators, 1658–1985.* Westport, CT: Greenwood, 1986.

Kwitny, Jonathan. *Acceptable Risks.* New York: Poseidon, 1992.

Lande, R. Gregory. *Madness, Malingering, and Malfeasance: The Transformation of Psychiatry and the Law in the Civil War.* New York: Brassey's, 2003.

Langston, Donna Hightower. "American Indian Women's Activism in the 1960s and 1970s." *Hypatia* 18:2 (Spring 2003): 114–32.

Lapsansky, Emma Jones, and Anne A. Verplancke. *Quaker Aesthetics: Reflections on a Quaker Ethic in American Design and Consumption.* Philadelphia: University of Pennsylvania Press, 2003.

Leaming, Hugo Prosper. *Hidden Americans: Maroons of Virginia and the Carolinas.* New York: Garland, 1995.

Lehman, Daniel Wayne. *John Reed and the Writing of Revolution.* Athens: Ohio University Press, 2002.

Lehrer, Susan. *Origins of Protective Labor Legislation for Women, 1905–1925.* Albany: State University of New York Press, 1987.

Lens, Sidney. *Radicalism in America.* New York: Crowell, 1969.

Levine, Daniel H. *Bayard Rustin and the Civil Rights Movement.* New Brunswick, NJ: Rutgers University Press, 1999.

Levy, Leonard W. *Blasphemy: Verbal Offense Against the Sacred, from Moses to Salman Rushdie.* Chapel Hill: University of North Carolina Press, 1995.

Levy, Peter B. *Civil War on Race Street: The Civil Rights Movement in Cambridge, Maryland.* Gainesville: University Press of Florida, 2003.

Lovell, R.A., Jr. *Sandwich, a Cape Cod Town.* Sandwich, MA: Sandwich Archives and Historical Center, 1984.

Lumsden, Linda J. *Inez: The Life and Times of Inez Milholland.* Bloomington: Indiana University Press, 2004.

MacLean, Nancy K. *Behind the Mask of Chivalry: The Making of the Second Ku Klux Klan.* New York: Oxford University Press, 1994.

Martin, James J. *Men Against the State: The Expositors of Individualist Anarchism in America, 1827–1908.* New York: Libertarian Book Club, 1957.

Marty, Martin E. *Modern American Religion.* Chicago: University of Chicago Press, 1996.

Mathes, Valerie Sherer, and Richard Lowitt. *The Standing Bear Controversy: Prelude to Indian Reform.* Urbana: University of Illinois Press, 2003.

Mathre, Lynn. *Cannabis in Medical Practice: A Legal, Historical, and Pharmacological Overview of the Therapeutic Use of Marijuana.* Jefferson, NC: McFarland, 1997.

Mazur, Eric Michael. *The Americanization of Religious Minorities: Confronting the Constitutional Order.* Baltimore: Johns Hopkins University Press, 2004.

McAllister, J. Gilbert. *Archaeology of Kahoolawe.* New York: Kraus Reprint, 1973.

McAndrew, Mike. "Bold Raid Freed a Man." *Syracuse Post-Standard,* February 14, 2005.

McCaffrey, Katherine T. *Military Power and Popular Protest: The U.S. Navy in Vieques, Puerto Rico.* New Brunswick, NJ: Rutgers University Press, 2002.

McGregor, Deborah Kuhn, " 'Childbirth-Travells' and 'Spiritual Estates': Anne Hutchinson and Colonial Boston, 1634–1638." *Caduceus* 5:4 (Winter 1989): 1–33.

McLoughlin, William G. "Massive Civil Disobedience as a Baptist Tactic in 1773." *American Quarterly* 21:4 (Winter 1969): 710–27.

Middlekauff, Robert. *The Glorious Cause: The American Revolution, 1763–1789.* New York: Oxford University Press, 1982.

Mihesuah, Devon A. *Repatriation Reader: Who Owns American Indian Remains?* Lincoln: University of Nebraska Press, 2000.

Miller, John C. *Origins of the American Revolution.* Stanford, CA: Stanford University Press, 1959.

Miller, Mark Edwin. *Forgotten Tribes: Unrecognized Indians and the Federal Acknowledgment Process.* Lincoln: University of Nebraska Press, 2005.

Miller, Richard Brian. *Interpretations of Conflict.* Chicago: University of Chicago Press, 1991.

Miller, Sally M. *From Prairie to Prison: Life of Social Activist Kate Richards O'Hare.* Columbia: University of Missouri Press, 1993.

Mollin, Marian. *Radical Pacifism in Modern America: Egalitarianism and Protest.* Philadelphia: University of Pennsylvania Press, 2006.

Neiberg, Michael S. *Making Citizen-Soldiers: ROTC and the Ideology of American Military Service.* Cambridge, MA: Harvard University Press, 2000.

Nesper, Larry. *The Walleye War: The Struggle for Ojibwe Spearfishing and Treaty Rights.* Lincoln: University of Nebraska Press, 2002.

Ness, Immanuel, ed. *Encyclopedia of American Social Movements.* Armonk, NY: M.E. Sharpe, 2004.

Neville, John F. *Twentieth-Century Cause Célèbre: Sacco, Vanzetti, and the Press, 1920–1927.* Westport, CT: Praeger, 2004.

Newkirk, Ingrid. *Free the Animals: The Story of the Animal Liberation Front.* New York: Lantern, 2000.

Newman, Richard S. *The Transformation of American Abolitionism: Fighting Slavery in the Early Republic.* Chapel Hill: University of North Carolina Press, 2002.

Nichols, Jeffrey D. *Prostitution, Polygamy, and Power: Salt Lake City, 1847–1918.* Urbana: University of Illinois Press, 2002.

Oshinsky, David M. *"Worse Than Slavery": Parchman Farm and the Ordeal of Jim Crow Justice.* New York: Free Press, 1997.

Ostopowich, Melanie. *Greenpeace.* Mankato, MN: Weigl, 2002.

Parker, Alison M. *Purifying America: Women, Cultural Reform, and Pro-Censorship Activism, 1873–1933.* Urbana: University of Illinois Press, 1997.

Pestana, Carla Gardina. *Quakers and Baptists in Colonial Massachusetts.* Cambridge, UK: Cambridge University Press, 1991.

Peters, Pamela R. *The Underground Railroad in Floyd County, Indiana.* Jefferson, NC: McFarland, 2001.

Plum, Jay, "Blues, History, and the Dramaturgy of August Wilson." *African American Review* 27:4 (Winter 1993): 561–67.

Polner, Murray, and Jim O'Grady. *Disarmed and Dangerous: The Radical Lives and Times of Daniel and Philip Berrigan.* Boulder, CO: Westview, 1997.

Quarles, Benjamin. *Black Abolitionists.* New York: Oxford University Press, 1969.

Radune, Richard A. *Pequot Plantation: The Story of an Early Colonial Settlement.* New York: Research in Time, 2005.

Raskin, Jonah. *American Scream: Allen Ginsberg's "Howl" and the Making of the Beat Generation.* Berkeley: University of California Press, 2004.

Rice, Grantland S. *The Transformation of Authorship in America.* Chicago: University of Chicago Press, 1997.

Richards, Leonard L. *Shays's Rebellion: The American Revolution's Final Battle.* Philadelphia: University of Pennsylvania Press, 2002.

Ricks, Mary Kay. *Escape on the Pearl: The Heroic Bid for Freedom on the Underground Railroad.* New York: William Morrow, 2007.

Roeper, Richard. "Act by 'Martyr' to Protest War in Iraq a Futile Gesture." *Chicago Sun-Times,* November 9, 2006.

Rosten, June. "Inside-Out and Upside-Down." *Peacework,* April 2006.

Rourke, Mary. "Obituaries: William Sloan Coffin, Jr." *Los Angeles Times,* April 13, 2006.

Roussopoulos, Dimitrios I. *Our Generation Against Nuclear War.* Montreal, Quebec: Black Rose, 1983.

Runyon, Randolph Paul. *Delia Webster and the Underground Railroad.* Lexington: University Press of Kentucky, 1996.

Salvatore, Nick. *We All Got History: The Memory Books of Amos Webber.* New York: Random House, 1996.

Sanger, Alexander. *Beyond Choice: Reproductive Freedom in the 21st Century.* New York: Public Affairs, 2005.

Schudel, Matt, and Adam Bernstein. "William Sloan Coffin, Jr.: Chaplain Was Lifelong 'Disturber of the Peace.'" *Washington Post,* April 13, 2006.

Sharpless, Isaac. *Political Leaders of Provincial Pennsylvania.* Freeport, NY: Books for Libraries, 1919.

Shea, George William. *Spoiled Silk: The Red Mayor and the Great Paterson Textile Strike.* New York: Fordham University Press, 2001.

Shepard, Benjamin Heim, and Ronald Hayduk. *From ACT-UP to the WTO: Urban Protest and Community Building in the Era of Globalization.* New York: Verso, 2002.

Shrage, Laurie J. *Abortion and Social Responsibility: Depolarizing the Debate.* New York: Oxford University Press, 2003.

Sibley, Mulford Q., and Philip E. Jacob. *Conscription of Conscience: The American State and the Conscientious Objector, 1940–1947.* Ithaca, NY: Cornell University Press, 1952.

Sibley, Mulford Q., and Ada Wardlaw. *Conscientious Objectors in Prison, 1940–1945.* Philadelphia: Pacifist Research Bureau, 1945.

Simmons, Donald C. *Confederate Settlements in British Honduras.* Jefferson, NC: McFarland, 2001.

Singer, Gerald. *Vieques: A Photographically Illustrated Guide to the Island, Its History, and Its Culture.* San Juan, PR: Sombrero, 2004.

Smith, Christian. *Resisting Reagan: The U.S. Central American Peace Movement.* Chicago: University of Chicago Press, 1996.

Smith, John Howard. "'Sober Dissent' and 'Spirited Conduct': The Sandemanians and the American Revolution, 1765–1781." *Historical Journal of Massachusetts* 28:2 (Summer 2000): 142–66.

Smith, Margaret Supplee, and Emily Herring Wilson. *North Carolina Women: Making History.* Chapel Hill: University of North Carolina Press, 1999.

Sox, David. *John Woolman: Quintessential Quaker, 1720–1772.* Richmond, IN: Friends United Press, 1999.

Steel, Edward M., Jr., ed. *The Court-Martial of Mother Jones.* Lexington: University Press of Kentucky, 1995.

Steelwater, Eliza. *The Hangman's Knot: Lynching, Legal Execution, and America's Struggle with the Death Penalty.* Boulder, CO: Westview, 2003.

Stone, Geoffrey R. *Perilous Times: Free Speech in Wartime from the Sedition Act of 1798 to the War on Terrorism.* New York: W.W. Norton, 2004.

Strangis, Joel. *Lewis Hayden and the War Against Slavery.* North Haven, CT: Linnet, 1999.

Swift, David E. *Black Prophets of Justice: Activist Clergy Before the Civil War.* Baton Rouge: Louisiana State University Press, 1989.

Taylor, Alan. *Liberty Men and Great Proprietors: The Revolutionary Settlement on the Maine Frontier, 1760–1820.* Chapel Hill: University of North Carolina Press, 1990.

Taylor, William Banks. *Down on Parchman Farm: The Great Prison in the Mississippi Delta.* Columbus: Ohio State University Press, 1999.

Thomas, Marlo. *The Right Words at the Right Time.* New York: Simon & Schuster, 2002.

Thompson, Priscilla. "Harriet Tubman, Thomas Garrett, and the Underground Railroad." *Delaware History* 22:1 (1986): 1–21.

Tobin, Jacqueline L., and Raymond G. Dobard. *Hidden in Plain View: A Secret Story of Quilts and the Underground Railroad.* New York: Doubleday, 1999.

Tucker, Todd. *The Great Starvation Experiment: The Heroic Men Who Starved So That Millions Could Live.* New York: Free Press, 2006.

Upton, L.F.S. "Proceedings of Ye Body Respecting the Tea." *William and Mary Quarterly* 22:2 (April 1965): 287–300.

Uschan, Michael V. *The Scopes "Monkey" Trial.* New York: Gareth Stevens, 2005.

Utley, Robert Marshall. *Lone Star Justice: The First Century of the Texas Rangers.* New York: Oxford University Press, 2002.

Walmsley, Andrew S. *Thomas Hutchinson and the Origins of the American Revolution.* New York: New York University Press, 1999.

Walsh, James. *Liberty in Troubled Times: A Libertarian Guide to Laws, Society, Freedom and Rights in a Terrorized World.* Aberdeen, WA: Silver Lake, 2003.

Walsh, Richard. *Charleston's Sons of Liberty: A Study of the Artisans, 1763–1789.* Columbia: University of South Carolina Press, 1959.

Ware, Vron, and Les Back. *Out of Whiteness: Color, Politics, and Culture.* Chicago: University of Chicago Press, 2002.

Weisenburger, Steven. *Modern Medea: A Family Story of Slavery and Child-Murder from the Old South.* Boston: Hill and Wang, 1998.

Welch, Michael R. *Flag Burning: Moral Panic and the Criminalization of Protest.* Edison, NJ: Aldine de Gruyter, 2000.

Whitesell, Edward A. *Defending Wild Washington: A Citizen's Action Guide.* Seattle, WA: Mountaineers, 2004.

Williams, George W. *History of the Negro Race in America from 1619 to 1880: Negroes as Slaves, as Soldiers, and as Citizens.* New York: G.P. Putnam's Sons, 1882.

Williams, Heather Andrea. *Self-Taught: African American Education in Slavery and Freedom.* Chapel Hill: University of North Carolina Press, 2005.

Willis, Clyde E. *Student's Guide to Landmark Congressional Laws on the First Amendment.* Westport, CT: Greenwood, 2002.

Willis, James F. "The Cleburne County Draft War." *Arkansas Historical Quarterly* 26 (Winter 1967): 24–39.

Willison, George F. *Patrick Henry and His World.* Garden City, NY: Doubleday, 1969.

Winks, Robin W. *The Blacks in Canada.* Montreal, Canada: McGill-Queen's University Press, 2005.

Wright, Edward Needles. *Conscientious Objectors in the Civil War.* Philadelphia: University of Pennsylvania Press, 1931.

Wright, Jonathan A. *Shapers of the Great Debate on the Freedom of Religion: A Biographical Dictionary.* Westport, CT: Greenwood, 2005.

Wyman, Lillie B. Chace. "Harriet Tubman." *New England Magazine* 20:1 (March 1896): 110–18.

Yardley, Jonathan, "In the Fields of Despair." *Washington Post,* March 31, 1996.

Young, Wilmer J. *Visible Witness: A Testimony for Radical Peace.* Pendle Hill, PA: Pendle Hill Pamphlets, 1961.

Zeinert, Karen. *Valiant Women of the Vietnam War.* New York: Twenty-First Century Books, 2000.

Zinn, Howard. *Passionate Declarations: Essays on War and Justice.* New York: Perennial, 2003.

———. *SNCC: The New Abolitionists.* Cambridge, MA: South End, 2002.

Zinn, Howard, and Anthony Amove. *Voices of a People's History of the United States.* New York: Seven Stories, 2004.

Index

Maryland *(continued)*
  Mother Jones, **1:**173
  nuclear protest, **1:**32, 242; **2:**361, 370, 424, 425, 426, 427, 515, 517
  Regulators, **1:**247
  tax resistance, **1:**232, 295; **2:**464, 468, 513
  travel restrictions, **1:**244; **2:**372, 466, 517
  Vietnam War, **1:**30, 125; **2:**365, 468, 469, 470, 471, 516
  "Watermelon Army," **1:**326
  woman suffrage, **1:**333, 335, 336
  See also Baltimore, Maryland; Richardson, Gloria
Maryland v. Bachellar (1970), **2:**642
M*A*S*H* (1970), **1:**156
Mashburn, Linda, **2:**442, 500
Mass, Elmer, **2:**426, 577
Massachusetts
  abolitionism
    Fugitive Slave Act of 1850, **1:**133, 199; **2:**407, 408, 530
    slave rescue/recapture, **1:**98, 99, 137, 198, 199, 234, 235, 236, 239, 296, 300, 303, 305; **2:**345, 346, 348, 446, 447, 448, 449, 450, 451, 458, 459, 522, 527, 528, 529, 530, 531
    slavery, **1:**55, 56, 135, 136, 137, 206, 300, 302, 339; **2:**463, 528, 529, 531
    street patrols, **1:**39, 54–55, 56; **2:**448, 450, 452, 453, 529, 531
  abortion, **1:**9
  alien refugee abuse, **1:**257
  animal rights, **1:**22
  campaign finance corruption, **1:**244
  Civil War, **1:**76, 77, 239, 240; **2:**381, 382, 531
  colonial militia, **1:**75, 114, 194, 231–32; **2:**344, 424, 521
  colonial taxation, **1:**278, 279, 280, 288; **2:**384, 385, 393, 522, 523
  Comstock Act, **1:**34, 37, 207; **2:**394, 532
  death penalty, **1:**158, 230; **2:**395
  debt, **1:**264–65; **2:**395, 396
  draft, **1:**76, 84–85, 240; **2:**397, 399, 531
  First Amendment rights, **1:**188; **2:**405, 532
  Indian displacement, **1:**16; **2:**366
  Indian genocide, **1:**194
  Indian wars, **1:**232; **2:**344, 415, 521
  labor exploitation, **1:**159–60, *187*, 188; **2:**355, 418, 532
  Liberty Men, **1:**192
  religious dissent
    heresy, **1:**25, 228, 229, 230, 231, 248; **2:**343, 410, 411, 412, 517, 518, 519, 520, 521
    illegal assembly, **1:**158, 228, 230; **2:**343, 414, 437, 518

Massachusetts
  religious dissent *(continued)*
    religious persecution, **1:**25, 26, 27, 28, 158, 228, 229–30; **2:**343, 436, 437, 438, 439, 517, 518, 519, 520, 521–22
  Revolutionary War, **1:**75, 232, 234; **2:**527
  ROTC, **1:**252; **2:**361, 365, 441, 532
  Sacco and Vanzetti case, **1:**255–56; **2:**357, 441, 532
  tax resistance
    abolitionism, **1:**296, 300; **2:**349
    Baptists, **1:**26, 27–28, 295
    Quakers, **1:**231, 244, 295, 296, 297
    Shays's Rebellion, **1:**191, 264–65, 325
    table of acts of conscience, **2:**464, 465, 466, 522, 523, 527–28, 529, 532, 533
  Vietnam War, **1:**30, 61, 321, 322; **2:**470, 532
  War of 1812, **1:**234, 263; **2:**473, 528
  Winchester exiles, **2:**421
  witch trials, **1:**114, 156, 194, 195; **2:**344
  woman suffrage, **1:**37, 206, 296, 332, 337
  World War I, **1:**79, 241; **2:**477, 532
  World War II, **1:**83, 84–85; **2:**480, 532
  See also Boston, Massachusetts; Emerson, Ralph Waldo; Foster, Abigail "Abby" Kelley; Maule, Thomas; Thoreau, Henry David
Massachusetts Black Militia, **1:**39
Massar, Ivan, **2:**470, 586
Massasoit Guards, **1:**38–39, 55, 198; **2:**350, 351
Massasoit Volunteer Infantry, **1:**270
Masses, The, **1:**93, 172, 188
Masterman, Thomas, **1:**232; **2:**440, 569
Matear, Robert, **1:**286; **2:**466, 560
Matheny, David P., **1:**30
Mather, Cotton, **1:**195
Mather, Increase, **1:**26
Mathew, David, **1:**48
Matlack, Timothy, **1:**329, 331
Matthews, Carl Wesley, **1:**274; **2:**361, 444, 561
Matthews, John, **2:**389, 581
Matthews, Samuel, **1:**232; **2:**424, 545
Maudlin, Wright, **1:**235–36; **2:**349, 445, 510
Maui, Hawaii, **1:**177, 178, 179
Maule, Thomas, **1:**xvii, 194–95
  refusal to support the militia, **1:**114, 194, 231; **2:**424, 521
  religious persecution, **1:**114, 194, 231; **2:**343, 438, 521
  tax resistance, **1:**231, 295; **2:**465, 521
  witch trials, protest of, **1:**114, 194, 195; **2:**344
  writings, **1:**114, 194, 195; **2:**438, 521
Maurin, Peter, **1:**93

Mawney, John, **1:**138, 139; **2:**389, 580
Maxson, Delilah Bowland, **1:**55; **2:**506
Maxson, William, **1:**55; **2:**455, 506
Maxwell, Charles Kauluwehi, **1:**177, 179; **2:**367, 417, 501, 502
Maxwell, Thomas, **1:**50; **2:**389, 525
May, John, **1:**50; **2:**389, 525
May, Samuel Joseph
  American Anti-Slavery Society, **1:**5, 167
  Fugitive Slave Act of 1850, **1:**132; **2:**408, 551
  slave rescue/recapture, **1:**136, 137, 167, 168; **2:**408, 455, 549
Mayer, Julius M., **1:**145
Mayflower II, **1:**16; **2:**366
Mazyck, Isaac, **1:**282; **2:**389, 581
McAndrew, Helen Walker, **2:**462, 533
McAndrew, William, **2:**462, 533
McBride, Jesse, **1:**115, 307; **2:**404, 438, 455, 560, 564
McCabe, Irene, **1:**57
McCain, Franklin, **1:**273–74; **2:**444, 561
McCain, John, **1:**163, 266; **2:**374
McCarthy, Joseph, **1:**154
McCarty, Francis D., **1:**44
McClain, James, **1:**92
McClaughlin, Bert, **1:**120
McClelland, Samuel Swan, **1:**263–64; **2:**473, 562
McClellan's, **2:**625
McCloud, Donald, **1:**122; **2:**403, 591
McCloud, Edith, **1:**122; **2:**403, 591
McCloud, Janet Renecker, **1:**121, 122; **2:**403, 591
McCloud, Jeffrey, **1:**122; **2:**403, 591
McClunn, Thomas, **1:**232, 234, 296; **2:**348, 465, 587
McClure, Gathie, **1:**124
McClure, Lucy Barnett, **1:**124–25
McClure, Marie, **1:**124
McCord, Frank Owen, **1:**183; **2:**380, 483
McCormick Harvester, **1:**152
McCown, Ira, **1:**223
McCoy, Joseph, **1:**121; **2:**403, 590
McCoy, Winston, **1:**9
McCrackin, Maurice, **1:**297; **2:**465, 566
McCrory's Variety Store, **1:**223, 274
McCullagh, Robert, **1:**146; **2:**481, 539
McCulloch, William, **1:**328
McDaniel, Thomas, **1:**324; **2:**472, 498
McDew, Charles "Chuck," **1:**323; **2:**472, 541
McDougall, Alexander, **1:**289, 290; **2:**389, 430, 547, 548
McDougall, Hannah Roe Bostwick, **1:**289; **2:**345, 389, 430, 547, 548
McDowell, Mary Stone, **1:**241; **2:**422, 554
McEvers, James, **1:**281, 287, 288
McFarlane, James, **1:**191; **2:**396, 465, 571
McGill, Ralph, **2:**633

O

P

T

Y

Z